"How Much Can I Make?"

Actual Sales, Expenses, and/or Profits on 84 Franchise Opportunities

2014 (14th) Edition

Robert E. Bond
Publisher

Annie Barbarika
Senior Editor

Alison Mackey
Editor

Christopher Buenaventura
Graphic Design

Source Book Publications
Serving the Franchising Industry

1814 Franklin St., Suite 603
Oakland, CA 94612
(888) 612-9908

ISBN-10: 1-887137-91-2
ISBN-13: 978-1-887137-91-1

Preface

As a prospective franchisee, the single most important task ahead of you is to get an accurate and reliable sense of a business's potential sales, expenses, and profits. Without this analysis, you will have only a faint idea of how much you are going to earn as a result of your investment and considerable efforts.

Keep in mind that in acquiring a franchise, or any business for that matter, you are making an investment that has long-term responsibilities and consequences that are potentially far-reaching. If you find out 12 months after starting your business that you did not properly project the negative cash flows that would occur during the start-up phase, or didn't appreciate the magnitude of advertising/promotion costs, or assumed that revenues would be 30% higher than they actually are, then you have no one to blame but yourself. At that point, you can't re-negotiate your franchise contract. If you can't make the business work financially, the fact that you really enjoy being your own boss, really like the franchisor's management team and its vision, and really believe in the product/service is of secondary importance. If, six months after starting the business, you find yourself financially strapped, your options are severely limited. You can continue to limp along operating the business, working even harder, and most likely not enjoying what you are doing. You can borrow more money in the hopes of generating increased revenues. Or you can sell the business, most likely for substantially less than you invested.

Do yourself a favor. Take whatever time is necessary to do your homework. You will no doubt be under an inordinate amount of pressure from the franchisor to start your new business as soon as possible. Resist the temptation to do so until you are completely conversant with all facets of the particular business in which you are investing, as well as the dynamics of the industry itself. Spend the extra time and money to ensure that no stones are left unturned. In addition to the required research, make sure you fully understand what cash flow statements are about, the distinction between fixed and variable costs, and what industry operating standards are. Know where to go to get industry data. Call as many existing (and former) franchisees as are required to corroborate your projections. They will be able to tell you if your assumptions are either too optimistic or too pessimistic. Keep in mind that the existing franchisee base represents your best source of information on the business. You will only get one chance to perform your due diligence.

Given these alarmist warnings, it is incumbent on you to thoroughly research all aspects of the industry you are considering prior to making an irreversible investment. The risks are high. Your failure could well result in the loss of your investment (as well as any other property you may have pledged), your marriage (to the extent that your spouse was not equally committed to franchising and the inherent risks involved), and, possibly most important, your self-esteem. Contrary to much of the hype surrounding the industry, there are no guarantees. To think that you can simply pay a franchise fee and automatically step into a guaranteed money machine is naive at best, and financially fatal at worst. There is absolutely no substitute for extensive investigation. The burden is on you to do your homework and ensure that the choice is fully researched. Only you can maximize the likelihood of success and minimize the chances of failure or unfulfilled expectations.

"How Much Can I Make?" contains 84 financial performance representations in their entirety. The roster of franchisors runs from large, well-established operations like 7-Eleven and McDonald's to newer, smaller franchises with only a handful of operating units. Keep in mind that the financial data presented below is based on actual, verifiable operating results that the franchisors must be able to document. Understanding these financial statements is only one step in a long and tedious process. They nevertheless provide an invaluable source of critical background information that you will not find in any other source.

One of the most important exercises you can do is to rigorously determine what the net earnings from your investment

3

will be. Realize that you have an "opportunity cost" associated with your investment in the business. If you invest $100,000 of equity, that money could probably earn a minimum of 5% if deployed elsewhere and with considerably less risk. Accordingly, the first $5,000 earned is not really a profit, but a return on your investment. Does the remaining "adjusted net cash flow" adequately reward you for the stress and strain of running your own business, including putting in long, hard hours at work, wearing 10 hats at a time, living with financial uncertainty, and giving up much of your discretionary time? On the other side of the ledger are the advantages of owning your own business: the pride and independence of running your own show, the chance to start something from scratch and sell it 5–10 years later at a multiple of your original investment, and the opportunity to take full advantage of your management, sales, and people skills. Clearly there is a balance, but make sure that you have a strong sense of how realistic your expectations are and if they have a solid chance of being achieved.

Although the level of detail and applicability to your own investment may differ substantially among the various financial performance representations, you can still learn a great deal by reviewing the data presented. Just because a financial performance representation is not in the same industry you are considering, do not assume that you should not read it. Reviewing a wide range of actual operating results provides an invaluable chance to become acquainted with basic accounting practices—how to get from gross sales to net income, how to differentiate between fixed expenses (such as rent, equipment rental, and utilities) and variable expenses (direct labor, shipping, and percentage rent), and how to determine a break-even point. Consider how various aspects of a totally different type of business might apply to your own. This is a great chance to avoid saying six months from now, "Why wasn't I aware of that expense?" Devoting even a minimal amount of time and energy will provide invaluable insights.

Presuming that you are committed to maximizing your chances for success, you have a great deal of work ahead of you. Because it is tedious, many people will opt for the easy way out and do only a modest amount of homework. Many of these will ultimately regret their lack of research and, accordingly, their investment decision. Others may be happy with the decision to enter franchising, but may wish they had joined another franchise system. Still others will go out of business. I strongly recommend that you commit the next several months to learning everything you can about the franchising industry in general, the specific industry you are considering in particular, all of the franchise opportunities within that industry, and, most importantly, the individual franchise you ultimately select.

You have a great deal at risk, and you don't get a second chance. Your cheapest form of insurance is the time you put into investigating a business before you invest. Take full advantage of the tools available to you. Do your homework.

Good luck, and Godspeed.

Table of Contents

30-Minute Overview | 1

There are three stages in the franchise selection process: investigation, evaluation, and negotiation. This book is intended to assist the reader in the first two stages by providing a framework for developing reasonable financial guidelines upon which to make a well-researched and properly-documented investment decision.

Understand at the outset that the entire franchise selection process should take many months, and can involve a great deal of frustration. I suggest that you set up a realistic timeline for signing a franchise agreement, and that you stick to that schedule. There will be a lot of pressure on you to prematurely complete the selection and negotiation phases. Resist the temptation. The penalties are too severe for a seat-of-the-pants attitude. A decision of this magnitude clearly deserves careful consideration.

Before starting the selection process, briefly review the areas covered below.

FRANCHISE INDUSTRY STRUCTURE

The franchising industry is made up of two distinct types of franchises. The first, and by far the larger, includes product and trade name franchising. Included in this group are automotive and truck dealers, soft drink bottlers, and gasoline service stations. For the most part, these are essentially distributorships.

The second group encompasses business format franchisors. This book only includes information on this latter category.

LAYMAN'S DEFINITION OF FRANCHISING

Business format franchising is a method of market expansion by which one business entity expands the distribution of its products and/or services through independent, third-party operators. Franchising occurs when the operator of a concept or system (the franchisor) grants an independent businessperson (the franchisee) the right to duplicate its entire business format at a particular location and for a specified period, under terms and conditions set forth in the contract (franchise agreement). The franchisee has full access to all of the trademarks, logos, marketing techniques, controls, and systems that have made the franchisor successful. In effect, the franchisee acts as a surrogate for a company-owned store in the distribution of the franchisor's goods and/or services. It is important to keep in mind that the franchisor and the franchisee are separate legal entities.

Classic Business Format Model

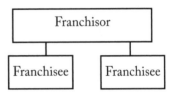

In return for a front-end franchise fee—which usually ranges from $15,000 – $35,000—the franchisor is obligated to "set up" the franchisee in business. This generally includes assistance in selecting a location, negotiating a lease, obtaining financing, building and equipping a site, and providing the necessary training, operating manuals, and start-up assistance. Once the training is completed and the store is open, the new franchisee should have a carbon copy of other units in the system and enjoy the same benefits they do, whether they are company-owned or not.

Business format franchising is unique because it is a long-term relationship characterized by an ongoing, mutually-beneficial partnership. Ongoing services include research and development, marketing strategies, advertising campaigns, group buying, periodic field visits, training updates, and whatever else is required to make the franchisee competitive and profitable. In effect, the franchisor acts as the franchisee's "back office" support organization. To reimburse the franchisor for this support, the franchisee pays the franchisor an ongoing royalty fee, generally 4 – 8% of gross sales. In many cases, franchisees also contribute an advertising fee to reimburse the franchisor for expenses incurred in maintaining a national or regional advertising campaign.

To work to maximum advantage, both the franchisor and the franchisees should share common objectives and goals. Both parties must accept the premise that their fortunes are mutually intertwined and that they are each better off working in a cooperative effort rather than toward self-serving goals. Unlike the parent/child relationship that has dominated franchising over the past 30 years, franchising is now becoming a true relationship of partners.

THE PLAYERS

1. The Franchisors

Source Book Publications routinely tracks approximately 3,200+ U.S. and Canadian franchisors. We believe this represents the number of legitimate, active franchisors in North America at any point in time. Profiles of many these franchisors can be found on our website www.WorldFranchising.com. Additionally, you can "rent" our full database of 3,200+ active North American franchisors, with over 25 fields of information, including primary contacts. Please visit www.FranchisorDatabase.com for details.

While you may already have your sights on a particular franchise opportunity, it would be short-sighted not to find out as much as you can about both the direct and indirect competition. You might discover that other franchises have similar products or services, but offer superior training and support, a reduced royalty fee, or vastly superior financing options. I strongly encourage you to read one of the available franchise directories to or research online to fully explore the options open to you.

2. The Regulatory Agencies

The offer and sale of franchises are regulated at both the federal and state levels. Federal requirements cover all 50 states. In addition, certain states have adopted their own requirements.

In 1979, after many years of debate, the Federal Trade Commission (FTC) implemented Rule 436. This rule required that franchisors provide prospective franchisees with a disclosure statement (called an offering circular) containing specific information about a company's franchise offering. The rule had two objectives: to ensure that potential franchisees have sufficient background information to make an educated investment decision and to provide them with adequate time to do so.

The Franchise Rule was substantially updated (and improved) on July 1, 2008 as the FTC tried to make the disclosure document more consistent with various state regulations. Among other things, the Uniform Franchise Offering Circular (UFOC) became the Franchise Disclosure Document (FDD), and Item 19 of the new FDD morphed from an Earnings Claims Statement to a Financial Performance Representation. Overall, the revisions were positive and resulted in considerably more and better information being available to the prospective franchisee. Unfortunately, the revisions did not require all franchisors to provide a Financial Performance Representation from which potential franchisees could better determine the overall profitability of their potential investments.

Certain "registration states" require additional safeguards to protect potential franchisees. Their requirements are generally more stringent than the FTC's requirements. These states include California, Florida, Hawaii, Illinois, Indiana, Maryland, Michigan, Minnesota, New York, North Dakota, Oregon, Rhode Island, South Dakota, Virginia, Washington, and Wisconsin. Separate registration is also required in the province of Alberta.

The regulations require that the franchisor provide a prospective franchisee with the required information at their first face-to-face meeting or at least 14 days prior to the signing of the franchise agreement, whichever is earlier. Required information includes:

[1] The franchisor and any predecessors.

[2] Identity and business experience of persons affiliated with the franchisor.

[3] Litigation.

[4] Bankruptcy.

[5] Franchisee's initial fee or other initial payments.

[6] Other fees.

[7] Franchisee's initial investment.

[8] Obligations of franchisee to purchase or lease from designated sources.

[9] Obligations of franchisee to purchase or lease in accordance with specifications or from approved suppliers.

[10] Financing arrangements.

[11] Obligations of the franchisor; other supervision, assistance or services.

[12] Exclusive area or territory.

[13] Trademarks, service marks, trade names, logotypes, and commercial symbols.

[14] Patents and copyrights.

[15] Obligations of the participant in the actual operation of the franchise business.

[16] Restrictions on goods and services offered by franchisee.

[17] Renewal, termination, repurchase, modification, and assignment of the franchise agreement and related information.

[18] Arrangements with public figures.

[19] Actual, average, projected, or forecasted financial performance representations.

[20] Information regarding franchises of the franchisor.

[21] Financial statements.

[22] Contracts.

[23] Acknowledgment of receipt by respective franchisee.

If you live in a registration state, make sure that the franchisor you are evaluating is, in fact, registered to sell franchises there. If not, and the franchisor has no near-term plans to register in your state, you should consider other options.

Keep in mind that neither the FTC nor any of the states has reviewed the disclosure document to determine whether the information submitted is true and accurate. They merely require that the franchisor make representations based upon a prescribed format. If the information provided is false, franchisors are subject to civil penalties. You should also be aware of the reality that neither the FTC nor the individual states have the staff or budget necessary to pursue a lengthy battle over possible misrepresentations. If you run into problems, your only real option is to retain an attorney and battle a franchisor, who may have an in-house legal staff and a bottomless war chest. While you might win the battle, you would most likely lose the war.

It is up to you to read and thoroughly understand all elements of the disclosure document and to take full advantage of the documentation that is available to you. Know exactly what you can expect from the franchisor and what your own obligations are. Under what circumstances can the relationship be unilaterally terminated by the franchisor? What is your protected territory? What are the terms of a renewal? Can you expand within your territory? While there is no question that the FDD is tedious reading, it nevertheless provides invaluable information. The penalties for not doing your homework are severe. You will have no one to blame but yourself. Hedge your bets by having a professional also review the FDD.

3. The Trade Associations

The International Franchise Association (IFA) was established in 1960 as a non-profit trade association to promote franchising as a responsible method of doing business. The IFA currently represents over 1,000 franchisors in the U.S. and around the world. It is recognized as the leading spokesperson for the industry. For most of its 40+ years, the IFA has represented the interests of franchisors only. In recent years, however, it has initiated an aggressive campaign to recruit franchisees into its membership and to represent their interests as well. The IFA's offices are located at 1501 K St., Suite 350, Washington, DC 20005. (202) 628-8000; Fax (202) 628-0812; www.franchise.org.

The Canadian Franchise Association (CFA), which has some 250+ members, is the Canadian equivalent of the IFA. Information on the CFA can be obtained by writing the group at 5399 Eglinton Ave. West, # 116, Toronto, ON M9C 5K6, Canada. (800) 665-4232 or (416) 695-2896; Fax (416) 695-1950; www.cfa.ca.

WHAT MAKES A WINNING FRANCHISE

Virtually every writer on the subject of franchising has his or her own idea of what determines a winning franchise. I believe there are five primary factors.

1. A product or service with clear advantages over the competition. These advantages may include brand recognition, a unique, proprietary product or service, or 30 years of proven experience.

2. A standardized franchise system that has been time-tested. A company that has operated numerous units, both company-owned and franchised, has usually worked out most of the bugs in the system. By the time a system has 30 or more operating units, it should be thoroughly tested.

3. Exceptional franchisor support. This includes not only the initial training program, but the ongoing support (research and development, refresher training, [800] help-lines, field representatives who provide on-site training, annual meetings, advertising and promotion, central purchasing, etc.).

4. The financial wherewithal and management experience to carry out any announced growth plans without short-changing its franchisees. Sufficient depth of management is often lacking in younger, high-growth franchises.

5. A strong mutuality of interest between franchisor and franchisees. Unless both parties realize that their relationship is one of long-term partners, the system will probably never achieve its full potential. A few telephone calls to existing and former franchisees can easily determine whether the necessary rapport between franchisor and franchisees exists.

THE NEGOTIATION PROCESS

Once you have narrowed your options down to your two or three top choices, you now have to negotiate the best deal you can with the franchisor. In most cases, the franchisor will tell you that the franchise agreement cannot be changed. Think twice before you accept the statement that the contract is non-negotiable. Notwithstanding the legal requirement that all of a franchisor's agreements be substantially the same at any point in time, there are usually a number of variables that are flexible. If the franchisor truly wants you as a franchisee, it may be willing to make concessions not available to the next applicant.

Will the franchisor take a short-term note for all or part of the franchise fee? Can you expand from your initial unit after you have proven yourself? If so, can the franchise fee on a second unit be eliminated or reduced? Can you get a right of first refusal on adjacent territories? Can the term of the agreement be extended from 10 to 15 years? Can you include a franchise cancellation right if the training and/or initial support do not meet your expectations or the franchisor's promises? The list goes on ad infinitum.

To successfully negotiate, you must have a thorough knowledge of the industry, the franchise agreement you are negotiating (and agreements of competitive franchise opportunities), and access to experienced professional advice. This can be a lawyer, an accountant, or a franchise consultant. Above all else, he or she should have proven experience in negotiating franchise agreements. Franchising is a unique method of doing business. Do not pay someone $100+ per hour to learn the industry. Make him or her demonstrate that he or she has been through the process several times before.

Negotiating a long-term agreement of this type is extremely tricky and fraught with pitfalls. The risks are extremely high. Do not think that you can handle the negotiations yourself, or that you can not afford outside counsel. In point of fact, you cannot afford *not* to employ an experienced professional advisor.

THE 4 R'S OF FRANCHISING

At a young age, we are taught that the three R's of reading, 'riting, and 'rithmetic are critical to our scholastic success. Success in franchising depends on four R's: realism, research, reserves, and resolve.

1. **Realism**

At the outset of your investigation, be realistic about your strengths, weaknesses, goals, and capabilities. I strongly recommend you take the time necessary to do a personal audit—possibly with the help of outside professionals—before investing your life's savings in a franchise.

Franchising is not a money machine. It involves hard work, dedication, setbacks, and long hours. Be realistic about the nature of the business you are buying. What traits will ultimately determine your success? Do you have them? If it is a service-oriented business, will you be able to keep smiling when you know the client is a fool? If it is a fast-food business, will you be able to properly manage a minimum-wage staff? How well will you handle the uncertainties that will invariably arise? Can you make day-to-day decisions based on imperfect information? Can you count on the support of your partner after you have gone through all of your working capital reserves and the future looks increasingly cloudy?

Be equally realistic about your franchise selection process. Have you thoroughly evaluated all of the alternatives? Have you talked with everyone you can, leaving no stone unturned? Have you carefully and realistically assessed the advantages and disadvantages of the system offered, the unique demographics of your territory, the near-term market trends, and the financial projections? The selection process is tiring. It is easy to convince yourself that the franchise opportunity in your hand is really the best one for you before you have done all your homework. The penalties for such laziness, however, are extreme.

2. Research

There is no substitute for exhaustive research!

There are a number of franchise directories out there, both in print and online, that cover the industry to varying degrees of thoroughness and accuracy. Spend the time required now to come up with an optimal selection. At a minimum, you will probably be in the business for five years. More likely, you will be in it for 10 years or more. Given the long-term commitment, allow yourself the necessary time to ensure you will not regret your decision. Research is a tedious, boring process, but doing it carefully and thoroughly can greatly reduce your risk and exposure. The benefits of this research will be immeasurable.

First, determine which industry groups hold your interest. Do not arbitrarily limit yourself to a particular industry in which you have first-hand experience. Next, request information from all of the companies that participate in those industries. The incremental cost of mailing (or calling) an additional 15

or 20 companies for information is insignificant in the big picture. Based on personal experience, you may feel you already know the best franchise. Step back. Assume there is a competing franchise out there with a comparable product or service, comparable management, etc., but which charges a royalty fee of sales that is 2% lower than your intuitive choice. Over a 10-year period, that could add up to a great deal of money. It certainly justifies your requesting initial information.

A thorough analysis of the literature you receive should allow you to reduce the list of prime candidates to six or eight companies. Aggressively evaluate each firm. Talking with current and former franchisees is the single best source of information you can get. Where possible, visit franchise sites. My experience is that franchisees tend to be candid in their level of satisfaction with the franchisor. However, since they do not know you, they may be less candid about their sales, expenses, and income. *"How Much Can I Make?"* should be of some assistance in filling this void. Go on the Internet or to the library and get studies that forecast industry growth, market saturation, industry problems, technical break-throughs, etc. Prevent finding out a year after becoming a franchisee of a coffee company that readily available reports suggested that the coffee market was over-saturated or that coffee was linked to some obscure form of colon cancer in rats.

3. Reserves

Like any new business, franchising is replete with uncertainty, uneven cash flows, and unforeseen problems. It is an imperfect world that might not bear any relation to the clean pro formas you prepared to justify getting into the business. Any one of these unforeseen contingencies could cause a severe drain on your cash reserves. At the same time, you will have fixed and/or contractual payments that must be met on a regular basis regardless of sales, such as rent, employee salaries, insurance, etc.

Adequate back-up reserves may be in the form of savings, commitments from relatives, bank loans, etc. Just make certain that the funds are available when and if you need them. To be absolutely safe, I suggest that you double the level of reserves recommended by the franchisor.

Keep in mind that the most common cause of business failure

is inadequate working capital. Plan properly so you do not become a statistic.

4. Resolve

Let's assume for the time being that you have demonstrated exceptional levels of realism, thoroughly researched your options, and lined up ample capital reserves. You have picked an optimal franchise that takes full advantage of your strengths. You are in business and bringing in enough money to achieve a positive cash flow. The future looks bright. Now the fourth R—resolve—comes into play. Remember why you chose franchising in the first place: to take full advantage of a system that has been time-tested in the marketplace. Remember also what makes franchising work so well: that the franchisor and franchisees maximize their respective success by working within the system for the common good. Invariably, two obstacles arise.

The first is the physical pain associated with writing that monthly royalty check. Annual sales of $500,000 and a 6% royalty fee result in a royalty check of $2,500 that must be sent to the franchisor every month. As a franchisee, you may look for any justification to reduce this sizable monthly outflow. Resist the temptation. Accept the fact that royalty fees are simply another cost of doing business. They are also a legal obligation that you willingly agreed to pay when you signed the franchise agreement. In effect, they are the dues you agreed to pay to belong to the club.

Although there may be an incentive, do not look for loopholes in the contract that might allow you to sue the franchisor or get out of the relationship. Do not report lower sales than actual in an effort to reduce royalties. If you have received the support that you were promised, continue to play by the rules. Honor your commitment. Let the franchisor enjoy the rewards it has earned from your success.

The second obstacle is the desire to change the system. You need to honor your commitment to be a "franchisee" and to live within the franchise system. What makes franchising successful as far as your customers are concerned is uniformity and consistency of appearance, product/service quality, and corporate image. The most damaging thing an individual franchisee can do is to suddenly and unilaterally introduce changes into a proven system. While these modifications may

work in one market, they only serve to diminish the value of the system as a whole. Imagine what would happen to the national perception of your franchise if every franchisee had the latitude to make unilateral changes in his or her operations. Accordingly, any ideas you have on improving the system should be submitted directly to the franchisor for its evaluation. Accept the franchisor's decision on whether or not to pursue an idea.

If you suspect that you have a penchant for being an entrepreneur, or for unrestrained experimenting and tinkering, you are probably not cut out to be a good franchisee. Seriously consider this question before you get into a relationship, instead of waiting until you are locked into an untenable situation.

SUMMARY

I hope that I have been clear in suggesting that the selection of an optimal franchise is both time- and energy-consuming. Done properly, the process may take six to nine months and involve the expenditure of several thousand dollars. The difference between a hasty, gut-feel investigation and an exhaustive, well-thought-out investigation may mean the difference between finding a poorly-conceived or even fraudulent franchise and an exceptional one.

There is a strong correlation between the efforts put into the investigative process and the ultimate degree of success you enjoy as a franchisee. The process is to investigate, evaluate, and negotiate. Do not try to bypass any one of these elements.

Financial Performance Representations

The harsh reality is that you cannot tell—much less guarantee—how much you might make from a specific investment. Even the most successful business model, whether a franchise or not, simply cannot be replicated by someone who is not prepared to run the business the way it should be run. Area demographics, such as population, disposable per capita income, and education, are critical. For a retail business, a heavily trafficked location is critical. Adequate capital is critical. Management and decision-making skills are critical. Hard work is critical. The list goes on. It is up to you to ensure that all of these factors are optimized. If any one of these critical factors is missing or marginal, chances are the business will not meet your expectations.

This compendium of financial performance representations is meant to provide prospective franchisees with a better sense of what they might earn from their efforts. Without a sure understanding of potential sales, expenses, and profits, an investor is inviting disappointment at best and failure at worst. I strongly encourage you to take whatever time is required to carefully review the following financial performance representations. Some are easy reading, others tedious and detail-oriented. But the better versed you are on the actual historical operating results of these 84 companies, however, the better positioned you will be to make an optimal franchise selection. You will be able to ask franchisors intelligent, penetrating questions when evaluating them. You will be better prepared to compare franchises within similar industries. You will have more credibility seeking the insights of existing franchisees. If you take the time to develop your own financial projections, you will not have to rely as heavily on expensive outside accountants and financial advisers. Most importantly, you will have a real understanding of the business before you commit your financial resources and your life. If your objective is to maximize your bottom line, taking full advantage of the financial performance representations in this book is an important start.

THE AVERAGE FRANCHISEE

The only in-depth study of actual franchisee earnings and satisfaction was conducted in 1997 by *Franchise Times* magazine. Based on answers from more than 1,000 franchisees, the Second Annual Franchisee Survey found that the average franchisee owned 3.5 units, had been in franchising for 8.9 years, and enjoyed net pre-tax earnings of $171,000, or roughly $50,000 per unit. Total annual household income before taxes averaged $118,000 for all franchisees. The median income, however, was $81,000. The initial start-up cost was $151,000 and the average loan size was $196,000, with a median of $88,000. Three-quarters of those surveyed answered that they were either "very" or "somewhat" satisfied with franchising. Just over 15% were "not too" satisfied, while only 9.8% were "not at all" satisfied. If you think that franchising is an automatic pot of gold, you should temper your enthusiasm with the facts of life brought out in the survey.

Whether these averages satisfy or alarm you, most prospective franchisees will probably be surprised to learn that even after 8+ years in the business, the average franchisee in the survey had pre-tax earnings of less than $50,000 per unit. Keep in mind, however, that the above statistics are only that—statistics. How well your earnings compare with those of the average franchisee is what counts. Yet if you hope to make $100,000 per year with your initial unit, you will have to be markedly more successful than the average franchisee. Picking up the right franchise in the right market is the first step.

THE MARKET VOID

The single most important factor in buying any business is calculating a realistic and verifiable projection of sales, expenses, and profits. Specifically, how much can you expect to earn after working 65 hours a week for 52 weeks a year? A prospective franchisee clearly does not have the experience to sit down and determine what his or her sales and profits will be over the next five years, especially if he or she has no applied experience in that particular business. The only source in a position to supply accurate information about a franchise opportunity is the franchisor itself.

It is unfortunate that not all franchisors are required to supply prospective franchisees with operating results. At a minimum, franchisors have information regarding net sales by all of their franchised units and certainly they have complete accounting information from any company-owned units. Similarly, if they have any sophistication, they must have developed computer models for outlets in various geographic and retail environments.

The sad reality, however, is that franchisors are not required to share this information, and roughly only 67% do. The likelihood that any such requirement will be implemented within the next couple of years is slim, leaving the franchisee to his or her own devices.

"How Much Can I Make?" has located and published 84 of these Item 19 documents for your review. Nowhere else can a potential franchisee find such a wealth of financial information on the industry. Any serious prospective investor would be short-sighted not to fully exploit this extraordinary resource.

GENERAL DISCLOSURE BACKGROUND

In 1979, the Federal Trade Commission adopted the "FTC Rule," which regulates the franchising industry. Titled "Disclosure Requirements and Prohibitions Concerning Franchising and Business Opportunities Ventures," the rule requires all franchisors to prepare and distribute a disclosure document according to a format prescribed by the FTC. The document must be delivered to a prospective franchisee at either the first personal meeting or at least 14 days prior to the signing of any contract or the payment of any consideration, whichever is earlier. In addition, 15 states have adopted their own disclosure laws, which are generally more demanding than the FTC's requirements. Chapter 1 provides more information about the requirements of both the FTC and the 15 "registration states."

FINANCIAL PERFORMANCE REPRESENTATIONS DEFINED

Financial performance representations are covered under Item 19 of both the FTC and the state Franchise Disclosure Document (FDD) requirements. As defined by the FTC Rule, a financial performance representation is "any oral, written, or visual representation to a prospective franchisee, including a representation disseminated in the general media and Internet, that states or suggests a specific level or range of potential or actual sales, income, gross profits, or net profits. A chart, table, or mathematical calculation that demonstrates possible results based upon a combination of variables is a financial performance representation."

In the broadest sense, financial performance representations are defined as estimates or historical figures detailing the level of sales, expenses, and/or income a prospective franchisee might realize as the owner of a particular franchise.

However, it is important to remember that neither the FTC nor the state regulatory agencies check financial performance representations for accuracy or completeness. The document is voluntary and unverified, and the information's format and level of detail are left completely to each company's discretion.

The only requirement for any Item 19 is that the franchisor has a "reasonable basis" for the financial performance representation at the time the statement is prepared. The franchisor is merely required to deliver the document to the franchisee before the franchise can be sold. Although federal and state agencies suggest that you should let them know if something is amiss, they often do not have the manpower or budget to pursue any but the most flagrant and obvious violations. For the most part, you are on your own. In the next chapter, we will show you how to put financial performance representations and other related resources to good use.

SETTING REALISTIC EXPECTATIONS

You can learn a great deal by reviewing financial performance representations. Identifying the sales and costs that would be relevant to your own business, as well as to your skills and your experience, is invaluable. Do not be swayed by the profit margin alone, as you should also consider the cost of sales, payrolls, operating expenses, and rent and occupancy. Furthermore, you should also note that the historical data used as the basis for the claims do not apply to every geographic region, individual location, or franchisee, whose experience and business acumen may vary.

There is no universal way to measure and report on those variables. If you are evaluating how variations in revenue and expenses could affect your bottom line, then you are putting financial performance representations to good use. At best, these documents help you set realistic expectations. But, in reality, the actual earnings of any franchise will vary from individual to individual. Does the actual net cash flow adequately reward you for the stress and strain of running your own business, putting in long hours, wearing 10 hats at a time, living with financial uncertainty, and giving up much of your discretionary time?

On the other side of the ledger are the advantages of business ownership: the pride and independence of running the show, the chance to start something from scratch and sell it 5–10 years later for a multiple of your original investment, and the opportunity to take full advantage of your management, sales, and people skills. Clearly there is a balance, but make sure that you have a strong sense of how realistic your expectations are and if they have a solid chance of being achieved.

Presuming that you are committed to maximizing your chances for success, you have a great deal of work ahead of you. It is important to review a wide range of financial performance representations, including ones outside the industry you are considering. A sampling of financial performance representations will acquaint you with basic accounting practices—how to calculate net income from gross sales, how to differentiate between fixed expenses (rent, equipment rental and utilities) and variable expenses (direct labor, shipping and percentage rent), and how to determine a break-even point. Devoting even a minimal amount of time and energy to this research will provide invaluable insights and serve you well when making an investment decision.

HOW CAN I RESEARCH A FRANCHISE?

In addition to the financial performance representations in this book, there are a number of sources for information on franchisors and franchise offerings.

1. Franchise Disclosure Documents (FDDs)

Although FDDs are public documents, many companies consider the information contained within them proprietary; thus, they do not make them readily accessible to the public. If you contact franchisors directly to request copies of FDDs, chances are they will not respond to your request, or they may wait weeks before granting it. Alternatively, you may try to purchase FDDs from the state (if the company has registered in that state).

What Items Are in an FDD? Every FDD contains the following 23 items:

Item 1	The Franchisor, and any Parents, Predecessors, and Affiliates
Item 2	Business Experience
Item 3	Litigation
Item 4	Bankruptcy
Item 5	Initial Fees
Item 6	Other Fees
Item 7	Estimated Initial Investment
Item 8	Restrictions on Sources of Products and Services
Item 9	Franchisee's Obligations
Item 10	Financing
Item 11	Franchisor's Assistance, Advertising, Computer Systems, and Training
Item 12	Territory
Item 13	Trademarks
Item 14	Patents, Copyrights, and Proprietary Information
Item 15	Obligation to Participate in the Actual Operation of the Franchise Business
Item 16	Restrictions on What the Franchisee May Sell
Item 17	Renewal, Termination, Transfer and Dispute Resolution
Item 18	Public Figures
Item 19	Financial Performance Representations
Item 20	Outlets and Franchisee Information
Item 21	Financial Statements
Item 22	Contracts
Item 23	Receipts

The easiest and quickest way to obtain FDDs and historical UFOCs is to purchase them directly from third-party companies that sell them. Among the various websites that sell FDDs directly online, one of the most popular is www.Franchise-Disclosures.com. Offering over 25,000 FDDs and UFOCs for roughly 3,000 North American franchisors, www.Franchise-Disclosures.com is the most comprehensive and up-to-date database of current FDD filings, as well as historical UFOCs dating back to 1997. In addition, every effort is made to provide all available financial performance representations (Item 19s), in their entirety, to the public. As a result, over 1,000 financial performance representations are available on www.Item19s.com, either as pre-selected packages or as individual statements.

All FDDs and historical UFOCs as well as individual Item 19s and Item 19 packages are available in PDF format and are delivered via email. Current-year FDD orders are typically processed in less than two hours. Prior year or unique orders may take longer.

Price: Entire FDD/UFOC – $220 per statement; Item 19 – $40 per statement; Food-Service Industry Package (114 earnings claims) – $250; Lodging Industry Package (34 earnings claims) – $150; Retail Industry Package (33 earnings claims) – $150; Service-Based Industry Package (266 earnings claims) – $450; All Four Industry Packages (446 earnings claims) – $700. Website: www.FranchiseDisclosures.com or www.Item19s.com.

2. Current and Former Franchisees

Without doubt, the most meaningful information that you can obtain on a particular franchise comes from existing franchisees, who tend to be very candid about their level of satisfaction with the franchisor, but less candid about their sales, expenses, and income. Depending on how well you have done your homework and your ability to ask meaningful questions that show a solid understanding of the basic business and its underlying economics, other franchisees should be willing to respond to your questions about: the major cost elements of the cash flow statement, the biggest surprises they encountered when they started their business, whether to buy supplies from the franchisor or from a third-party supplier, potential lenders, negotiable points in the franchise agreement, and more. In reviewing finances, pay particular attention to the major expense items and see if there are any expense categories that you may have left out. Spend some time at a franchised unit to get a feel for the day-to-day operations of the business.

The FDD should include a list of current franchisees, as well as franchisees who left the system within the last year. Past FDDs list franchisees that may no longer be in the system. Do not call only the franchisees specifically recommended by the franchisor. Contact as many as you can until you feel comfortable that you are hearing a consensus. You should also talk with as many former franchisees as you can. It is up to you to separate the truth from the fiction as to why they left the system. Too many disenchanted former franchisees should be a strong warning to be exceedingly cautious in your investigation and analysis.

3. State Franchise Regulators

If you are in a state with franchise registration requirements (see the section on Regulatory Agencies in Chapter 1), the state franchise regulators can tell you whether a franchisor is in good standing. They may also be able to tell you whether there are any pending complaints against a franchisor. The North American Securities Administrators Association, Inc. website (www.nasaa.org) contains a directory of each state's franchise regulators.

You can contact state franchise regulators to request a copy of the financial performance representation from any franchisor registered to do business in the state. Unfortunately, most of these state agencies cannot accommodate your request unless you are physically at their offices. The best bet is to call to learn your options. Some states are more helpful than others in providing access to their library of disclosure documents.

4. SEC

If a franchise is a publicly traded company, it is required to file certain information with the U.S. Securities and Exchange Commission. These filings are available online at www.edgar.gov.

5. www.WorldFranchising.com

www.WorldFranchising.com provides detailed profiles of approximately 700 North American franchisors resulting from an exhaustive 45-point questionnaire. The website also provides links to detailed profiles on leading franchise attorneys, consultants, and service providers. The data represents the most up-to-date, comprehensive and reliable information about the franchising industry.

The franchisor profiles are divided into 29 distinct industry categories and include the following information:

• Background—number of operating units, geographic distribution, and detailed description of the business.

• Capital requirements—initial cash investment and total investment, ongoing royalty and advertising fees, staffing levels, space needs, etc.

• Initial training and start-up assistance provided, as well as ongoing services.

• Franchisee evaluation criteria.

• Specific areas of geographic expansion: U.S., Canada and International.

• And much more…

6. Business and Industry Publications

The next best source of information is provided by various publications that compile general operating statistics on industries broken down by Standard Industrial Classification (SIC) codes. Three of the best-known annual industry surveys are 1) the *RMA Annual Statement Studies*, published by Robert Morris Associates of Philadelphia, PA, 2) *Almanac of Business and Industrial Financial Ratios*, edited by Leo Troy and published by Prentice Hall and 3) *Industry Norms and Key Business Rations*, published by Dun & Bradstreet Information Services. Although none of these publications provide detailed expense data, each is extremely helpful in determining industry averages/norms and key financial ratios. Based on actual tax returns for the entire spectrum of business categories (manufacturing, wholesaling, agriculture, service, and retailing), the composite financial data reflect actual operating results for major SIC code industries.

7. Franchise Attorneys

Franchising is a highly specialized field, and you should hire legal experts with experience representing franchisees or franchisors. www.FranchisingAttorney.com has a searchable directory that provides 25 fields of information about each attorney listed. Visit www.FindLegalHelp.org, a site sponsored by the American Bar Association, to learn about referral services and issues you should address when consulting with a lawyer. Another source for examining an attorney's credentials is www.MartinDale.com. The franchise associations below may also provide referrals to experienced franchise attorneys.

8. Franchise Consultants and Service Providers

If you are using a franchise consultant or service provider, they can likely assist you with your franchisor research. www.FranchisingSuppliers.com includes listings of firms that provide goods and services to the franchising community. These goods and services are designed to help franchisors and franchisees alike, and include advertising, consulting, translation, and Internet services.

9. Your Local Library

Industry trade associations publish composite financial statistics, usually on an annual basis. Consult the Directory of Trade Associations at your local business library for the address of the relevant trade association(s). Be prepared to pay reasonable fees to obtain as much industry-specific information as possible. Keep in mind that these statistics are made up solely of like-minded businesses that have similar expenses and competitive pressures.

Most industries are covered by one or more research houses that sell studies pertaining to the future of that industry. These cover new technology, industry trends, competitive trends, financial projections for various sales levels, and more. Even if these studies are somewhat outdated, it may be worthwhile to gather as much data as possible about an industry rather than risk your life savings based on incomplete information.

YOUR OWN CASH FLOW PROJECTIONS

Armed with financial performance representations, industry

operating statistics and the information gathered from conversations with existing and former franchisees, as well as input from trusted colleagues and consultants, you can now prepare your own financial projections. This exercise is the most critical step in the process of evaluating and selecting a franchise. Without a solid understanding of the financial aspects of the business, you may be throwing your time and money away. Investors who do not do their homework because they say they do not understand an income statement or they are not a "numbers person" may soon regret their lack of motivation.

A number of well-written books about preparing financial projections are available. Most are written for the layman who has little or no formal understanding of the process. (Some are even written by laymen with little or no formal understanding of the process themselves.) Purchase a few of these books and become proficient in the rudiments of accounting and finance. Remember, you are playing with your own money and livelihood. Do not put yourself in a position where you have to pay your accountant $100+ per hour every time you have a question. Learn the distinction between income statements and cash flow statements. Realize that you have an "opportunity cost" associated with your investment, and that you must receive an annual return on this investment, as well as the return of the investment itself, before a true net profit can be determined. Put a value on the psychic income earned by being your own boss. This is especially important when comparing your near-term hourly income with what you might earn working for someone else. Ask yourself if you would invest in the business if you were an investor rather than an owner/operator. Alternatively, would you loan money to the business if you were a banker?

If you do not know how to develop a pro forma cash flow model on a computer, have someone help you. Perform "what if" calculations to see what would happen under best- and worst-case scenarios. This represents the cheapest insurance you can buy to fully understand the dynamics of your new business. You will probably be sorely handicapped in the operation of your business unless you are "computerized." Learn the basics of operating a computer before you have made your investment. Your discretionary time is likely to be minimal during the start-up phase of your new business.

Although the process of generating realistic cash flow

statements may seem daunting without any prior business management experience, it is easier than you think. With a little common sense, you can learn it quickly.

To provide a starting point for your own financial projections, plug some numbers into the following tables. These tables are by no means complete and do not attempt to represent all possible scenarios. Each industry will have its own unique investment requirements and related operating expenses.

Table 1 lists Total Investment Requirements. In the second column, you should place the appropriate expenses listed by the franchisor in Item 7 of the disclosure document. In the third column, you should place your own well-researched estimate of what that expense or service will cost in your market. The sum of these various expenses represents the non-recurring expenses you will incur when starting the business. Some of the expenses, such as land and improvements, may not be appropriate if you can lease your space at an acceptable market rate over the term of your investment. Consult your financial advisor about the appropriate figures to include if you lease rather than purchase various expense items.

Table 2 is a Pro Forma Cash Flow Statement. The objective of a pro forma is to project monthly and annual sales over the next five years and deduct the corresponding operating expenses. The result is the pre-tax operating cash flow. From this number, deduct the non-cash items—depreciation and amortization—to determine pre-tax income. Further additions and subtractions determine net cash flow before taxes. It is worthwhile to construct a computer model that includes all of the items that will impact your business.

Hopefully, when the time comes, you can negotiate an agreement with a franchisor that allows you to extend the contract for successive 5 – 15 year periods, presuming you have performed satisfactorily. Over the next 7 – 15 years, you may attempt to build your business to its maximum potential. At some point, you may want to retire or try something else. The market value of your business will be a function of how much cash flow the business generates. Based on the current earnings potential, the prospective buyer will most likely use one of two valuation models. The first, and more simplistic, involves multiplying the current cash flow by some multiple (say three to five times) to arrive at a purchase price. The more sophisticated buyer will develop a 5 – 10 year cash flow statement, put in his or her own liquidation value and discount the annual cash flows at a rate that properly reflects the inherent risk of achieving those cash flows. As an example, if your business generates a legitimate cash flow of $150,000 after 10 years, you should be able to sell the business for $450,000 – $750,000. If you have done well selecting and managing the franchise, the real payoff will most likely come when you sell the business.

RECOMMENDATIONS REGARDING MANDATORY FINANCIAL PERFORMANCE REPRESENTATIONS

Virtually everyone agrees that the information included in a financial performance representation can be exceedingly helpful to a potential franchisee. Unfortunately, there are many reasons why franchisors do not willingly make their actual results available to the public. Many franchisors feel that prospective investors will be turned off if they have access to actual operating results and prefer to let them draw their own conclusions.

Other franchisors are understandably afraid of being sued for "misrepresentation." When publishing financial performance representations, franchisors face a considerable risk that it will be interpreted as a "guarantee" of sales or income for new units. Given today's highly litigious society and the propensity of courts to award large settlements to the little guy, it is not surprising that few franchisors provide such information.

Notwithstanding the potential problems, franchisors should be required to provide prospective franchisees with some form of earnings projection. To the extent that they are able to substantiate their claims, franchisors should be protected from frivolous and potentially devastating lawsuits filed by failed franchisees. Everyone should realize that the historical data used as the basis for the claims do not apply to every geographic region, individual location, or franchisee. Clearly, there is no universal methodology that covers all the variables. All parties involved—the franchisors, the franchisees, the regulatory agencies and the legal system—should rely on common business sense.

As it now stands, a franchisor is liable if it misrepresents its financial performance representation or any other items in the disclosure document. Normally, one would interpret this to mean that someone goes to jail if it is proven that he or she intentionally misled the prospective investor. Unfortunately, neither the FTC nor any registration state has the budget, manpower, or technical expertise to enforce such a punishment. Unless a violation is particularly flagrant, there is little chance that a franchisor will be severely penalized. Accordingly, you should not assume that anyone is going to protect or support you if you decide that you have been misled.

However, if there are mandatory requirements, there must be some corresponding penalties for fraudulent financial performance representations. Specifically, franchisees must have a "right of action" that would give regulatory bodies the budget and staff to aggressively police fraud and deception. And this funding should come from the registration fees paid by the franchisors themselves. Alternatively, a portion of the initial franchise fee paid by franchisees could also supplement the super agency's budget.

At some point, registration states and the FTC (or its successor) will find common ground upon which to merge their efforts and require the filing of a single disclosure document acceptable to all parties. This will go a long way toward reducing the expense, effort, and frustration built into the now largely redundant registration process. At that time, mandatory financial performance representations should be instituted along with general, common sense guidelines for their preparation, substantiation, and presentation. Equally important is a standard set of rules for documenting and penalizing fraud and deception.

TABLE 1		
FRONT-END INVESTMENT REQUIREMENTS		
	Franchisor's Item VII	Actual in Your Area
Initial Franchise Fee	$	$
Land & Improvements		
Leasehold Improvements		
Architectural/Engineering Fees		
Furniture & Fixtures		
Vehicles Purchased		
Initial Inventory		
Initial Signage		
Initial Advertising Commitment		
Initial Training Fees		
Travel/Lodging/Etc. for Initial Training		
Rent Deposits		
Utility Deposits		
Telephone Deposits		
Initial Insurance		
In-Store Graphics		
Yellow Page Advertising		
Initial Office Supplies		
Prepaid Sales Taxes		
Initial Business Permits/Fees		
Office Equipment:		
Computer Hardware		
Computer Software		
Computer Installation		
Computer Training		
Point-of-Sales Computer		
Answering Machine		
Fax Machine		
Postage Meter		
Telephone System (Including Installation)		
Copier		
Security System		
Initial Loan Fees		
Due Diligence Expenses		
Attorney Fees		
Accounting Fees		
Consultant Fees		
Book Purchases/Courses/Etc.		
Travel Expenses		
Telephone/Mailing Expenses		
Total Non-Recurring Expenses	$	$
Working Capital Requirements		
FRONT-END INVESTMENT REQUIREMENTS	$	$

	Month 1	Month 2	Month 3	Month 4	Month ...	Month 12
TABLE 2						
PRO FORMA CASH FLOW STATEMENT						
Gross Sales	$	$	$	$	$	$
Less Returns and Allowances						
Net Sales						
Less Cost of Goods Sold						
Gross Profit						
Gross Profits As A % Of Sales	%	%	%	%	%	%
Operating Expenses:						
Payroll:						
Direct Labor						
Indirect Labor						
Employee Benefits						
Payroll Taxes						
Owner Salary & Benefits						
Rent & Common Area Maintenance						
Equipment Rental/Lease Payments						
Advertising Fund Payments To Franchisor						
Yellow Page & Local Advertising						
Insurance						
Utilities:						
Telephone/Fax						
Gas & Electric						
Water						
Janitorial Expense						
Trash Removal						
Security						
Travel & Lodging						
Meals & Entertainment						
Delivery Charges						
Printing Expense						
Postage						
Operating Supplies						
Office Supplies						
Vehicle Expense						
Equipment Maintenance						
Uniforms & Laundry						
Professional Fees:						
Accounting						
Legal						
Consulting						
Repairs & Maintenance						
Business Licenses/Fees/Permits						
Dues & Subscriptions						

Property Taxes						
Business Taxes						
Bad Debt/Theft						
Bank Charges & Credit Card Fees						
Royalties to Franchisor						
Interest Expense						
Total Operating Expenses						
Pre-Tax Operating Cash Flow	$	$	$	$	$	$
Operating Cash Flow As A & Of Sales	%	%	%	%	%	%

ADJUSTMENT TO PRE-TAX NET CASH FLOW						
Pre-Tax Operating Cash Flow	$	$	$	$	$	$
Less Depreciation/Amortization						
Pre-Tax Income						
Plus Depreciation/Amortization						
Less Principal Payments						
Less Capital Expenditures						
Pre-Tax Net Cash Flow	$	$	$	$	$	$

ADJUSTMENT TO "REAL" CASH FLOW						
Pre-Tax Net Cash Flow						
Less Return On Invested Capital @ x%						
Pre-Tax "Real" Cash Flow						

Required Item 19 Preamble

The Federal Trade Commission requires that Financial Performance Representations begin with the following paragraph. This paragraph has been removed from all individual statements in this book in order to avoid redundancy.

The FTC's Franchise Rule permits a franchisor to provide information about the actual or potential financial performance of its franchised and/or franchisor-operated outlets, if there is a reasonable basis for the information, and if the information is included in the disclosure document. Financial performance information that differs from that included in this Item 19 may be given only if: (1) a franchisor provides the actual records of an existing outlet you are considering buying; or (2) a franchisor supplements the information provided in this Item 19, for example, by providing information about possible performance at a particular location or under particular circumstances.

How to Use the Data | 3

This book contains 84 financial performance representations that are categorized into food-service, retail, and service-based industries. The information at the beginning of each company's earnings data is the result of a 45-point questionnaire sent out annually to the franchising community. It is intended as a brief overview of the company; the text that follows provides a more in-depth analysis of the company's requirements and advantages.

In some cases, an answer has been abbreviated to conserve room and to facilitate the comparison of different companies. When no answer was provided to an item within the profile, "N/A" is used to signify "Not Available."

Please take a few minutes to acquaint yourself with the composition of the questionnaire data. Supplementary comments have been added where some interpretation of the franchisor's response is required.

FASTSIGNS

2542 Highlander Way
Carrollton, TX 75006
Tel: (800) 827-7446; (214) 346-5679
Fax: (866) 422-4927
Email: mark.jameson@fastsigns.com
Website: www.fastsigns.com
Mark L. Jameson, EVP Franchise Support & Development

Signage has never been more important. Right now, businesses are looking for new and better ways to compete. Industries are revamping to meet compliance standards and advertisers are expanding their reach into new media, like digital signage, QR codes and mobile websites. Join the franchise that's leading the next generation of business communication. Now more than ever, businesses look to FASTSIGNS® for innovative ways to connect with customers in a highly competitive marketplace. Our high standards for quality and customer service have made FASTSIGNS the most recognized brand in the industry, driving significantly more traffic to the Web than any other sign company.

BACKGROUND

IFA Member:	Yes
Established & First Franchised:	1985; 1986
Franchised Units:	550
Company-Owned Units:	0
Total Units:	550
Dist.:	US – 486; CAN – 26; O'seas – 38
North America:	50 States, 8 Provinces
Density:	58 in TX, 45 in CA, 36 in FL
Projected New Units (12 Months):	45
Qualifications:	5, 5, 1, 3, 4, 5

FINANCIAL/TERMS

Cash Investment:	$80K
Total Investment:	$178.2 – $289.5K
Minimum Net Worth:	$250K
Fees (Franchise):	$37.5K
Fees (Royalty):	6%
Fees (Advertising):	2%
Term of Contract (Years):	20/20
Avg. # of Employees:	2 – 3 FT, 0 PT
Passive Ownership:	Discouraged
Encourage Conversions:	Yes
Area Develop. Agreements:	Yes
Sub-Franchising Contracts:	No

Expand in Territory:	Yes	On-going Support:	C, D, E, G, H, I
Space Needs:	1,200 – 1,500 SF	Training:	1 Week Local Center;
			2 Weeks Dallas, TX; 1 Week On-Site
SUPPORT & TRAINING			
Financial Assistance Provided:	Yes (I)	SPECIFIC EXPANSION PLANS	
Site Selection Assistance:	Yes	US:	All United States
Lease Negotiation Assistance:	Yes	Canada:	All Canada except Quebec as Master/Area
Co-operative Advertising:	No		Developer Only
Franchisee Assoc./Member:	Yes/Member	Overseas:	UK, South America, Africa, Europe, Asia,
Size of Corporate Staff:	110		New Zealand, Mexico

ADDRESS/CONTACT

1. Company name, address, telephone and fax numbers

Comment: All of the data published in the book was current at the time the completed questionnaire was received or upon subsequent verification by phone. Over the 12-month period between annual publications, 10 – 15% of the addresses and/or telephone numbers become obsolete for various reasons. If you are unable to contact a franchisor at the address/telephone number listed, please call Source Book Publications at (510) 839-5471 or fax us at (510) 839-2104 and we will provide you with the current address and telephone number.

2. (800) 827-7446; (214) 346-5679. In many cases, you may find that you cannot access the (800) number from your area. Do not conclude that the company has gone out of business. Simply call the local number.

Comment: An (800) number serves two important functions. The first is to provide an efficient, no-cost way for potential franchisees to contact the franchisor. Making the prospective franchisee foot the bill artificially limits the number of people who might otherwise make the initial contact. The second function is to demonstrate to existing franchisees that the franchisor is doing everything it can to efficiently respond to problems in the field as they occur. Many companies have a restricted (800) line for their franchisees that the general public cannot access. Since you will undoubtedly be talking with the franchisor's staff on a periodic basis, determine whether an (800) line is available to franchisees.

3. Contact. You should honor the wishes of the franchisor and address all initial correspondence to the contact listed. It would be counter-productive to try to reach the president directly if the designated contact is the director of franchising.

Comment: The president is the designated contact several of the company profiles in this book. The reason for this varies among franchisors. The president is the best spokesperson for his or her operation, and no doubt it flatters the franchisee to talk directly with the president, or perhaps there is no one else around. Regardless of the justification, it is important to determine if the operation is a one-man show in which the president does everything or if the president merely feels that having an open line to potential franchisees is the best way for him or her to sense the "pulse" of the company and the market. Convinced that the president can only do so many things well, I would want assurances that, by taking all incoming calls, he or she is not neglecting the day-to-day responsibilities of managing the business.

4. Description of Business. The questionnaire provides franchisors with adequate room to describe their franchise and to differentiate it from the competition. In a few cases, some editing by the authors was required.

Comment: In instances where franchisors show no initiative or imagination in describing their operations, you must decide whether this is symptomatic of the company or simply a reflection on the individual who responded to the questionnaire.

BACKGROUND

1. **IFA.** There are two primary affinity groups associated with the franchising industry—the International Franchise Association (IFA) and the Canadian Franchise Association (CFA). Both the IFA and the CFA are described in Chapter One.

2. **Established: 1985.** FASTSIGNS was founded in 1985, and, accordingly, has 29 years of experience in its primary business. It should be intuitively obvious that a firm that has been in existence for over 29 years has a greater likelihood of being around five years from now than a firm that was founded only last year.

3. **1st Franchised: 1986.** 1986 was the year that FASTSIGNS's first franchised unit(s) were established.

Comment: Over ten years of continuous operation, both as an operator and as a franchisor, is compelling evidence that a firm has staying power. The number of years a franchisor has been in business is one of the key variables to consider in choosing a franchise. This is not to say that a new franchise should not receive your full attention. Every company has to start from scratch. Ultimately, a prospective franchisee has to be convinced that 1) the franchise has been in operation long enough, and 2) its key management personnel have adequate industry experience to have worked out the bugs normally associated with a new business. In most cases, this experience can only be gained through on-the-job training. Do not be the guinea pig that provides the franchisor with the experience it needs to develop a smoothly running operation.

4. **Franchised Units: 550.** As of 8/1/14, FASTSIGNS had 550 franchisee-owned and operated units.

5. **Company-Owned Units: 0.** As of 8/1/14, FASTSIGNS had no company-owned or operated units.

Comment: A younger franchise should prove that its concept has worked successfully in several company-owned units before it markets its "system" to an inexperienced franchisee. Without company-owned prototype stores, the new franchisee may well end up being the "testing kitchen" for the franchise concept itself.

If a franchise concept is truly exceptional, why does the franchisor not commit some of its resources to taking advantage of the investment opportunity? Clearly, a financial decision on the part of the franchisor, the absence of company-owned units should not be a negative in and of itself. This is especially true of proven franchises, which may have previously sold their company-owned operations to franchisees.

Try to determine if there is a noticeable trend in the percentage of company-owned units. If the franchisor is buying back units from franchisees, it may be doing so to preclude litigation. Some firms also "churn" their operating units with some regularity. If the sales pitch is compelling, but the follow-through is not competitive, a franchisor may sell a unit to a new franchisee, wait for him or her to fail, buy it back for $0.60 cents on the dollar, and then sell that same unit to the next unsuspecting franchisee. Each time the unit is resold, the franchisor collects a franchise fee, plus the negotiated discount from the previous franchisee.

Alternatively, an increasing or high percentage of company-owned units may well mean the company is convinced of the long-term profitability of such an approach. The key is to determine whether a franchisor is building new units from scratch or buying them from failing and/or unhappy franchisees.

6. **Total Units: 550.** As of 8/1/14, FASTSIGNS had a total of 550 operating units.

Comment: Like a franchisor's longevity, its experience in operating multiple units offers considerable comfort. Those franchisors with over 15 – 25 operating units have proven that their system works and have probably encountered and overcome most of the problems that plague a new operation. Alternatively, the management of franchises with less than 15 operating units may have gained considerable industry experience before joining the current franchise. It is up to the franchisor to convince you that it is providing you with as risk-free an operation as possible. You do not want to be providing a company with its basic experience in the business.

7. **Distribution: US – 486; CAN – 26; Overseas – 38.** As of 8/1/14, FASTSIGNS had 486 operating units in the U.S., 26 in Canada, and 38 Overseas.

8. **Distribution: North America: 50 States, 8 Provinces.** As of 8/1/14, FASTSIGNS had operations in 50 states and 8 Canadian provinces.

Comment: It should go without saying that the wider the geographic distribution, the greater the franchisor's level of success. For the most part, such distribution can only come from a large number of operating units. If, however, the franchisor has operations in 15 states, but only 18 total operating units, it is unlikely that it can efficiently service these accounts because of geographic constraints. Other things being equal, a prospective franchisee would vastly prefer a franchisor with 15 units in New York to one with 15 units scattered throughout the U.S., Canada, and overseas.

9. **Distribution: Density: TX, CA, FL.** The franchisor was asked "what three states/provinces have the largest number of operating units." As of 8/1/14, FASTSIGNS had the largest number of units in Texas, California, and Florida.

Comment: For smaller, regional franchises, geographic distribution could be a key variable in deciding whether to buy. If the franchisor has a concentration of units in your immediate geographic area, it is likely you will be well-served.

For those far removed geographically from the franchisor's current areas of operation, however, there can be problems. It is both time consuming and expensive to support a franchisee 2,000 miles away from company headquarters. To the extent that a franchisor can visit four franchisees in one area on one trip, there is no problem. If, however, your operation is the only one west of the Mississippi, you may not receive the on-site assistance you would like. Do not be a missionary who has to rely on his or her own devices to survive. Do not accept a franchisor's idle promises of support. If on-site assistance is important to your ultimate success, get assurances in writing that the necessary support will be forthcoming. Remember, you are buying into a system, and the availability of day-to-day support is one of the key ingredients of any successful franchise system.

10. **Projected New Units (12 Months): 45.** FASTSIGNS plans to establish 45 new units over the course of the next 12 months.

Comment: In business, growth has become a highly visible symbol of success. Rapid growth is generally perceived as preferable to slower, more controlled growth. I maintain, however, that the opposite is frequently the case. For a company of FASTSIGNS's size, adding 45 new units over a 12-month period is both reasonable and achievable. It is highly unlikely, however, that a new franchise with only five operating units can successfully attract, screen, train, and bring multiple new units on-stream in a 12-month period. If it suggests that it can, or even wants to, be properly wary. You must be confident a company has the financial and management resources necessary to pull off such a Herculean feat. If management is already thin, concentrating on attracting new units will clearly diminish the time it can and should spend supporting you. It takes many months, if not years, to develop and train a second level of management. You do not want to depend on new hires teaching you systems and procedures they themselves know little or nothing about.

11. **Qualifications: 5, 5, 1, 3, 4, 5.** This question was posed to determine which specific evaluation criteria were important to the franchisor. The franchisor was asked the following: "In qualifying a potential franchisee, please rank the following criteria from Unimportant (1) to Very Important (5)." The responses should be self-explanatory:

Financial Net Worth (Rank from 1–5)
General Business Experience (Rank from 1–5)
Specific Industry Experience (Rank from 1–5)
Formal Education (Rank from 1–5)
Psychological Profile (Rank from 1–5)
Personal Interview(s) (Rank from 1–5)

FINANCIAL/TERMS

12. **Cash Investment: $80K.** On average, a FASTSIGNS franchisee will have made a cash investment of $80,000 by the time he or she finally opens the initial operating unit.

Comment: It is important that you be realistic about the amount of cash you can comfortably invest in a business. Stretching beyond your means can have grave and far-reaching consequences. Assume that you will encounter periodic set-backs and that you will have to draw on your reserves. The demands of starting a new business are harsh enough without adding the uncertainties associated with inadequate working capital. Trust the franchisor's recommendations regarding the suggested minimum cash investment. If anything, there is an incentive for setting the recommended level of investment too low, rather than too high. The franchisor will want to qualify you to the extent that you have adequate financing. No legitimate franchisor wants you to invest if there is a chance that you might fail because of a shortage of funds.

Keep in mind that you will probably not achieve a positive cash flow until you've been in business for at least six months. In your discussions with the franchisor, be absolutely certain that the calculations include an adequate working capital reserve.

13. **Total Investment: $178.2 – $289.5K.** On average, FAST-SIGNS franchisees will invest a total of $178,200 – $289,500, including both cash and debt, by the time the franchise opens its doors.

Comment: The total investment should be the cash investment noted above plus any debt that you will incur in starting up the new business. Debt could be a note to the franchisor for all or part of the franchise fee, an equipment lease, building and facilities leases, etc. Make sure that the total includes all of the obligations that you assume, especially any long-term lease obligations.

Be conservative in assessing what your real exposure is. If you are leasing highly specialized equipment or a single-purpose building, it is naive to think that you will recoup your investment if you have to sell or sub-lease those assets in a buyer's market. If there is any specialized equipment that may have been manufactured to the franchisor's specifications, determine if the franchisor has any form of buy-back provision.

14. **Minimum Net Worth: $250K.** In this case, FASTSIGNS feels that a potential franchisee should have a minimum net worth of $250,000. Although net worth can be defined in vastly different ways, the franchisor's response should suggest a minimum level of equity that the prospective franchisee should possess. Net worth is the combination of both liquid and illiquid assets. Again, do not think that franchisor-determined guidelines somehow do not apply to you.

15. **Fees (Franchise): $37.5K.** FASTSIGNS requires a front-end, one-time-only payment of $37,500 to grant a franchise for a single location. As noted in Chapter 1, the franchise fee is a payment to reimburse the franchisor for the incurred costs of setting the franchisee up in business—from recruiting through training and manuals. The fee usually ranges from $15,000 – $30,000. It is a function of competitive franchise fees and the actual out-of-pocket costs incurred by the franchisor.

Depending on the franchisee's particular circumstances and how well the franchisor thinks he or she might fit into the system, the franchisor may finance all or part of the franchise fee. (See Section 32 below to see if a franchisor provides any direct or indirect financial assistance.)

The franchise fee is one area in which the franchisor frequently provides either direct or indirect financial support.

Comment: Ideally, the franchisor should do no more than recover its costs on the initial franchise fee. Profits come later in the form of royalty fees, which are a function of the franchisee's sales. Whether the franchise fee is $5,000 or $35,000, the total should be carefully evaluated. What are competitive fees and are they financed? How much training will you actually receive? Are the fees reflective of the franchisor's expenses? If the fees appear to be non-competitive, address your concerns with the franchisor.

Realize that a $5,000 differential in the one-time franchise fee is a secondary consideration in the overall scheme of things. You are in the relationship for the long-term.

By the same token, do not get suckered in by an extremely low fee if there is any doubt about the franchisor's ability to follow through. Franchisors need to collect reasonable fees to cover their actual costs. If they do not recoup these costs, they cannot recruit and train new franchisees on whom your own future success partially depends.

16. **Fees (Royalty): 6%.** Here, six percent of gross sales (or other measure, as defined in the franchise agreement) must be periodically paid directly to the franchisor in the form of royalties. This ongoing expense is your cost for being part of the larger franchise system and for all of the "back-office" support you receive. In a few cases, the amount of the royalty fee is fixed rather than variable. In others, the fee decreases as the volume of sales (or other measure) increases (i.e., 8% on the first $200,000 of sales, 7% on the next $100,000 and so on). In others, the fee is held at artificially low levels during the start-up phase of the franchisee's business, then increases

once the franchisee is better able to afford it.

Comment: Royalty fees represent the mechanism by which the franchisor finally recoups the costs it has incurred in developing its business. It may take many years and many operating units before the franchisor is able to make a true operating profit.

Consider a typical franchisor who has been in business for three years. With a staff of five, assume it has annual operating costs of $300,000 (including rent, travel, operating expenses, and reasonable owner's salaries). Assume also that there are 25 franchised units with average annual sales of $250,000. Each franchise is required to pay a 6% royalty fee. Total annual royalties under this scenario would total only $375,000. The franchisor is making a $75,000 profit. Then consider the personal risk the franchisor took in developing a new business and the initial years of negative cash flows. Alternatively, evaluate what it would cost you, as a sole proprietor, to provide the myriad services included in the royalty payment.

In assessing various alternative investments, the amount of the royalty percentage is a major ongoing expense. Assuming average annual sales of $250,000 per annum over a 15 year period, the total royalties at 5% would be $187,500. At 6%, the cumulative fees would be $225,000. You have to be fully convinced that the $37,500 differential is justified. While this is clearly a meaningful number, what you are really evaluating is the quality of management and the competitive advantages of the goods and/or services offered by the franchisor.

17. **Fees (Advertising): 2%.** Most national or regional franchisors require their franchisees to contribute a certain percentage of their sales (or other measure, as determined in the franchise agreement) into a corporate advertising fund. These individual advertising fees are pooled to develop a corporate advertising/ marketing effort that produces great economies of scale. The end result is a national or regional advertising program that promotes the franchisor's products and services. Depending on the nature of the business, this percentage usually ranges from 2 – 6% and is in addition to the royalty fee.

Comment: One of the greatest advantages of a franchised system is its ability to promote, on a national or regional basis, its products and services. The promotions may be through television, radio, print medias, or direct mail. The objective its name recognition and, over time, the assumption that the product and/or service has been "time-tested." An individual business owner could never justify the expense of mounting a major advertising program at the local level. For a smaller franchise that may not yet have an advertising program or fee, it is important to know when an advertising program will start, how it will be monitored, and its expected cost.

18. **Term of Contract (Years): 20/20.** FASTSIGNS's initial franchise period runs for twenty years. The first renewal period runs for an additional twenty years. Assuming that the franchisee operates within the terms of the franchise agreement, he or she has forty years within which to develop and, ultimately, sell the business.

Comment: The potential (discounted) value of any business (or investment) is the sum of the operating income that is generated each year plus its value upon liquidation. Given this truth, the length of the franchise agreement and any renewals are extremely important to the franchisee. It is essential that he or she has adequate time to develop the business to its full potential. At that time, he or she will have maximized the value of the business as an ongoing concern. The value of the business to a potential buyer, however, is largely a function of how long the franchise agreement runs. If there are only two years remaining before the agreement expires, or if the terms of the extension(s) are vague, the business will be worth only a fraction of the value assigned to a business with 15 years to go. For the most part, the longer the agreement and the subsequent extension, the better. (The same logic applies to a lease. If your sales are largely a function of your location and traffic count, then it is important that you have options to extend the lease under known terms. Your lease should never be longer than the remaining term of your franchise agreement, however.)

Assuming the length of the agreement is acceptable, be clear under what circumstances renewals might not be granted. Similarly, know the circumstances under which a franchise agreement might be prematurely and unilaterally canceled by the franchisor. I strongly recommend you have an experienced lawyer review this section of the franchise agreement. It would be devastating if, after spending years developing your business, there were a loophole in the contract that allowed the franchisor to arbitrarily cancel the relationship.

19. **Average Number of Employees: 2 – 3 FT.** The questionnaire asked, "Including the owner/operator, how many employees are recommended to properly staff the average franchised unit?" In FASTSIGNS's case, two to three full-time employees are required.

Comment: Most entrepreneurs start a new business based on their intuitive feel that it will be "fun" and that their talents and experience will be put to good use. They think that they will be doing what they enjoy and what they are good at. Times change. Your business prospers. The number of employees increases. You are spending an increasing percentage of your time taking care of personnel problems and less and less on the fun parts of the business. In Chapter 1, the importance of conducting a realistic self-appraisal was stressed. If you found that you really are not good at managing people, or you do not have the patience to manage a large minimum wage staff, cut your losses before you are locked into doing just that.

20. **Passive Ownership: Discouraged.** Depending on the nature of the business, many franchisors are indifferent as to whether you manage the business directly or hire a full-time manager. Others are insistent that, at least for the initial franchise, the franchisee be a full-time owner/operator. FASTSIGNS allows franchisees to hire full-time managers to run their outlets, but discourages it.

Comment: Unless you have a great deal of experience in the business you have chosen or in managing similar businesses, I feel strongly that you should initially commit your personal time and energies to make the system work. After you have developed a full understanding of the business and have competent, trusted staff members who can assume day-to-day operations, consider delegating these responsibilities. Running the business through a manager can be fraught with peril unless you have mastered all aspects of the business and there are strong economic incentives and sufficient safeguards to ensure the manager will perform as desired.

21. **Conversions Encouraged: Yes.** This section pertains primarily to sole proprietorships or "mom and pop" operations. To the extent that there truly are centralized operating savings associated with the franchise, the most logical people to join a franchise system are sole practitioners who are working hard but only eking out a living. The implementation of proven systems and marketing clout could significantly reduce operating costs and increase profits.

Comment: The franchisor has the option of 1) actively encouraging such independent operators to become members of the franchise team, 2) seeking out franchisees with limited or no applied experience, or 3) going after both groups. Concerned that it may be very difficult to break independent operators of the bad habits they have picked up over the years, many franchisors choose the second option, thinking, "They will continue to do things their way. They won't, or can't, accept corporate direction." Other franchisors are simply selective in the conversions they allow. In many cases, the franchise fee is reduced or eliminated for conversions.

22. **Area Development Agreements: Yes.** This means that FASTSIGNS offers an area development agreement, in this case, for two years. Area development agreements are more fully described in Chapter 1. Essentially, area development agreements allow an investor or investment group to develop an entire area or region. The schedule for development is clearly spelled out in the area development agreement.

Comment: Area development agreements represent an opportunity for the franchisor to choose a single franchisee or investment group to develop an entire area. The franchisee's qualifications should be strong and include proven business experience and the financial depth to pull it off. An area development agreement represents a great opportunity for an investor to tie up a large geographical area and develop a concept that may not have proven itself on a national basis. Keep in mind that this is a quantum leap from making an investment in a single franchise and is relevant only to those with development experience and deep pockets.

23. **Sub-Franchising Contracts: No.** FASTSIGNS does not grant sub-franchising agreements. (See Chapter One for a more thorough explanation.) Like area development agreements, sub-franchising allows an investor or investment group to develop an entire area or region. The difference is that the sub-franchisor becomes a self-contained business, responsible for all relations with franchisees within its area, from initial training to ongoing support. Franchisees pay their royalties to the sub-franchisor, who in turn pays a portion to the master franchisor.

Comment: Sub-franchising is used primarily by smaller franchisors who have a relatively easy concept and who are prepared to sell a portion of the future growth of their business to someone for some front-end cash and a percentage of the future royalties they receive from their franchisees.

24. **Expand in Territory: Yes.** Under conditions spelled out in the franchise agreement, FASTSIGNS will allow its franchisees to expand within their exclusive territory.

Comment: Some franchisors define the franchisee's exclusive territory so tightly that there would never be room to open additional outlets within an area. Others provide a larger area in the hopes that the franchisee will do well and have the incentive to open additional units. There are clearly economic benefits to both parties from having franchisees with multiple units. There is no question that it is in your best interest to have the option to expand once you have proven to both yourself and the franchisor that you can manage the business successfully. Many would concur that the real profits in franchising come from managing multiple units rather than being locked into a single franchise in a single location. Additional fees may or may not be required with these additional units.

25. **Space Needs: 1,200 – 1,500 SF.** The average FASTSIGNS retail outlet will require 1,200 – 1,500 square feet. Types of leased space might be a Storefront (SF), Strip Center (SC), a Free-Standing (FS) building, Convenience Store (C-store) location, Executive Suite (ES), Home-Based (HB), Industrial Park (IP), Kiosk (KI), Office Building (OB), Power Center (PC), Regional Mall (RM), or Warehouse (WH).

Comment: Armed with the rough space requirements, you can better project your annual occupancy costs. It should be relatively easy to get comparable rental rates for the type of space required. As annual rent and related expenses can be as high as 15% of your annual sales, be as accurate as possible in your projections.

SUPPORT & TRAINING

26. **Financial Assistance Provided: Yes (I)** indicates that FASTSIGNS provides indirect financial assistance. Indirect (I) assistance might include making introductions to the franchisor's financial contacts, providing financial templates for preparing a business plan or actually assisting in the loan application process. In some cases, the franchisor becomes a co-signer on a financial obligation (such as equipment or space lease). Other franchisors are directly (D) involved in the process. In this case, the assistance may include a lease or loan made directly by the franchisor. Any loan would generally be secured by some form of collateral. A very common form of assistance is a note for all or part of the initial franchise fee. The level of assistance will generally depend on the relative strengths of the franchisee.

Comment: The best of all possible worlds is one in which the franchisor has enough confidence in the business and in you to co-sign notes on the building and equipment leases and allow you to pay off the franchise fee over a specified period of time. Depending on your qualifications, this could happen. Most likely, however, the franchisor will only give you some assistance in raising the necessary capital to start the business. Increasingly, franchisors are testing a franchisee's business acumen by letting him or her assume an increasing level of personal responsibility in securing financing. The objective is to find out early in the process how competent a franchisee really is.

27. **Site Selection Assistance: Yes.** This means that FASTSIGNS will assist the franchisee in selecting a site location. While the phrase "location, location, location" may be hackneyed, its importance should not be discounted, especially when a business depends on retail traffic counts and accessibility. If a business is home- or warehouse-based, assistance in this area is of negligible or minor importance.

Comment: Since you will be locked into a lease for a minimum of three, though probably five, years, optimal site selection is absolutely essential. Even if you were somehow able to sub-lease and extricate yourself from a bad lease or bad location, the franchise agreement may not allow you to move to another location. Accordingly, it is imperative that you get it right the first time.

If a franchisor is truly interested in your success, it should treat your choice of a site with the same care it would use in choosing a company-owned site. Keep in mind that many firms provide excellent demographic data on existing locations at a very reasonable cost.

28.**Lease Negotiations Assistance: Yes.** Once a site is selected, FASTSIGNS will be actively involved in negotiating the terms of the lease.

Comment: Given the complexity of negotiating a lease, an increasing number of franchisors are taking an active role in lease negotiations. There are far too many trade-offs that must be considered—terms, percentage rents, tenant improvements, pass-throughs, kick-out clauses, etc. This responsibility is best left to the professionals. If the franchisor doesn't have the capacity to support you directly, enlist the help of a well-recommended broker. The penalties for signing a bad long-term lease are very severe.

29.**Co-operative Advertising: No.** This refers to the existence of a joint advertising program in which the franchisor and franchisees each contribute to promote the company's products and/or services (usually within the franchisee's specific territory).

Comment: Co-op advertising is a common and mutually-beneficial effort. By agreeing to split part of the advertising costs, whether for television, radio, or direct mail, the franchisor is not only supporting the franchisee, but guaranteeing itself royalties from the incremental sales. A franchisor that is not intimately involved with the advertising campaign—particularly when it is an important part of the business—may not be fully committed to your overall success.

30.**Franchisee Association/Member: Yes, Member.** This response notes that the FASTSIGNS system includes an active association made up of FASTSIGNS franchisees and that, consequently, the franchisor is a member of such franchisee association.

Comment: The empowerment of franchisees has become a major rallying cry within the industry over the past five years. Various states have recently passed laws favoring franchisee rights, and the subject has been widely discussed in congressional staff hearings. There are even political groups that represent franchisee rights on a national basis. Similarly, the IFA is now actively courting franchisees to become active members. Whether they are equal members remains to be seen.

Franchisees have also significantly increased their clout with respect to the franchisor. If a franchise is to grow and be successful in the long term, it is critical that the franchisor and its franchisees mutually agree they are partners rather than adversaries.

31.**Size of Corporate Staff: 110.** FASTSIGNS has 110 full-time employees on its staff to support its 550 operating units.

Comment: There are no magic ratios that tell you whether the franchisor has enough staff to provide the proper level of support. It would appear, however, that FASTSIGNS' staff of 110 is adequate to support 550 operating units. Less clear is whether a staff of three, including the company president and his wife, can adequately support 15 fledgling franchisees in the field.

Many younger franchises may be managed by a skeleton staff, assisted by outside consultants who perform various management functions during the start-up phase. From the perspective of the franchisee, it is essential that the franchisor have actual in-house franchising experience, and that the franchisee not be forced to rely on outside consultants to make the system work. Whereas a full-time, salaried employee will probably have the franchisee's objectives in mind, an outside consultant may not have the same priorities. Franchising is a unique form of business that requires specific skills and experience—skills and experience that are markedly different from those required to manage a non-franchised business. If you are thinking about establishing a long-term relationship with a firm that is just starting out in franchising, you should insist that the franchisor prove it has an experienced, professional team on board and in place to provide the necessary levels of support to all concerned.

32.**Ongoing Support:** C, D, E, G, H, I. Like initial training, the ongoing support services provided by the franchisor are of paramount importance. Having a solid and responsive team behind you can certainly make your life much easier and allow you to concentrate your energies on other areas. As is noted below, the franchisors were asked to indicate their support for nine separate ongoing services:

Service Provided	Included in Fees	At Add'l. Cost	N/A
Central Data Processing	A	a	N/A
Central Purchasing	B	b	N/A
Field Operation Evaluation	C	c	N/A
Field Training	D	d	N/A
Initial Store Opening	E	e	N/A
Inventory Control	F	f	N/A
Franchisee Newsletter	G	g	N/A
Regional or National Meetings	H	h	N/A
800 Telephone Hotline	I	i	N/A

If the franchisor provides the service at no additional cost to the franchisee (as indicated by letters A–I), a capital letter was used to indicate this. If the service is provided, but only at an additional cost, a lower case letter was used. If the franchisor responded with a N/A, or failed to note an answer for a particular service, the corresponding letter was omitted from the data sheet.

33. Training: 1 Week Local Center; 2 Weeks Dallas, TX; 1 Week On-Site.

Comment: Assuming that the underlying business concept is sound and competitive, adequate training and ongoing support are among the most important determinants of your success as a franchisee. The initial training should be as lengthy and as "hands-on" as necessary to allow the franchisee to operate alone and with confidence. Obviously, every potential situation cannot be covered in any training program. But the franchisee should come away with a basic understanding of how the business operates and where to go to resolve problems when they come up. Depending on the business, there should be operating manuals, procedural manuals, company policies, training videos, (800) help-lines, etc. It may be helpful at the outset to establish how satisfied recent franchisees are with a company's training. It is also good to have a clear understanding about how often the company updates its manuals and training programs, the cost of sending additional employees through training, etc.

Remember, you are part of an organization that you are paying (in the form of a franchise fee and ongoing royalties) to support you. Training is the first step. Ongoing support is the second step.

SPECIFIC EXPANSION PLANS

34.**U.S.: All United States.** FASTSIGNS is currently focusing its growth on the entire United States. Alternatively, the franchisor could have listed particular states or regions into which it wished to expand.

35.**Canada: All Canada Except Quebec as Master/Area Developer Only.** FASTSIGNS is currently seeking additional franchisees in all Canadian provinces except for Quebec, in which it is only seeking Master Franchisees and Area Developers. Specific markets or provinces could have also been indicated.

36.**Overseas:** UK, **South America, Africa, Europe, Asia, New Zealand, Mexico.** FASTSIGNS is currently expanding overseas with a focus on the United Kingdom, South America, Africa, Europe, Asia, New Zealand, and Mexico.

Comment: You will note that many smaller companies with less than 15 operating units suggest that they will concurrently expand throughout the U.S., Canada, and internationally. In many cases, these are the same companies that foresee a 50%+ growth rate in operating units over the next 12 months. The chances of this happening are negligible. As a prospective franchisee, you should be wary of any company that thinks it can expand throughout the world without a solid base of experience, staff, and financial resources. Even if adequate financing is available, the demands on existing management will be extreme. New management cannot adequately fill the void until they are able to fully understand the system and absorb the corporate culture. If management's end objective is expansion for its own sake rather than by design, the existing franchisees will suffer.

Note: The statistics noted in the profiles preceding each company's analysis are the result of data provided by the franchisors themselves by way of a detailed questionnaire. Similarly, the data in the summary comparisons in the Introduction Chapter were taken from the company profile data. The figures used throughout each company's analysis, however, were generally taken from the FDDs. In many cases, the FDDs, which are only printed annually, contain information that is somewhat out of date. This is especially true with regard to the number of operating units and the current level of investment. A visit to our website at www.WorldFranchising.com should provide current data.

If you have not already done so, please invest some modest time to read Chapter 1: 30-Minute Overview.

The Franchise Bookstore
Order Form

Call (888) 612-9908 or (510) 839-5471; Fax (510) 839-2104; or email info@worldfranchising.com

Item #	Title	Price	Qty.	Total

Basic postage (1 Book)	$8.50
Each additional book add $4.00	
California tax (if CA resident)	
Total due in U.S. dollars	
Deduct 15% if total due is over $100.00	
Net amount due in U.S. dollars	

Please include credit card number and expiration date for all charge card orders. Checks should be made payable to Source Book Publications. All prices are in U.S. dollars.

Mailing Information: All books are shipped by USPS Priority Mail (2nd Day Air). Please print clearly and include your phone number in case we need to contact you. Postage and handling rates are for shipping within the U.S. Please call for international rates.

Name: _____

Company: _____

Address: _____

City: _____

☐ Check enclosed
☐ Charge my American Express
☐ Charge my MasterCard
☐ Charge my VISA

Card #: _____

Expiration Date: _____

Signature: _____

Security Code: _____

Title: _____

Telephone No.: (   ) _____

State/Prov.: _____

Zip: _____

Special Offer — Save 15%

If your total order exceeds $100.00, deduct 15% from your bill.

Please send order to:
Source Book Publications
1814 Franklin St., Ste. 603, Oakland, CA 94612
Satisfaction Guaranteed. If not fully satisfied, return for a prompt, 100% refund.

Food-Service Franchises | 4

AuntieAnne's

PRETZEL PERFECT

AUNTIE ANNE'S

48-50 W. Chestnut St., # 200
Lancaster, PA 17603
Tel: (717) 435-1479
Fax: (717) 442-1471
Email: lengels@auntieannesinc.com
Website: www.auntieannes.com
Linda Engels, Franchise Development Specialist

Auntie Anne's, Inc. is a franchise organization with a commitment to exceeding our customers' expectations. We've built our company on the quality of our products and strong support for our franchisees, nurturing relationships for the long-term growth of the franchise system. That approach continues to drive our growth. We provide our customers with pretzels, dips, and drinks which are mixed, twisted, and baked to a golden brown in full view of our customers. Each and every one of our pretzels comes with the Pretzel Perfect Guarantee —we guarantee you'll love your pretzel or we'll replace it with one that you do.

BACKGROUND
IFA Member:	Yes
Established & First Franchised:	1988; 1991
Franchised Units:	1,146
Company-Owned Units:	17
Total Units:	1,163

Distribution:	US – 1,163; CAN – 0; O'seas – 471
North America:	48 States, 0 Provinces
Density:	117 in PA, 74 in NY, 68 in CA
Projected New Units (12 Months):	125
Qualifications:	4, 2, 2, 2, 3, 5

FINANCIAL/TERMS
Cash Investment:	Varies
Total Investment:	$194.9 – 367.6K
Minimum Net Worth:	$400K
Fees (Franchise):	$30K
Fees (Royalty):	7%
Fees (Advertising):	1%
Term of Contract (Years):	20/Variable
Average Number of Employees:	4 FT, 4 PT
Passive Ownership:	Allowed
Encourage Conversions:	N/A
Area Development Agreements:	No
Sub-Franchising Contracts:	No
Expand in Territory:	Yes
Space Needs:	400 – 600 SF

SUPPORT & TRAINING
Financial Assistance Provided:	Yes (I)
Site Selection Assistance:	Yes
Lease Negotiation Assistance:	Yes
Co-operative Advertising:	Yes
Franchisee Association/Member:	Yes/Member
Size of Corporate Staff:	150
On-going Support:	C, D, E, G, H, I
Training:	3 Weeks Lancaster, PA

SPECIFIC EXPANSION PLANS
US:	All United States
Canada:	Yes
Overseas:	All Countries

Other than this Item 19, we do not make any financial performance representations. We also do not authorize our employees or representatives to make any such representations either orally or in writing. If you are purchasing an existing outlet, however, we may provide you with the actual records of that outlet. If you receive any other financial performance information or projections of your future income, you should report it immediately to the franchisor's management by contacting the Legal Department, Auntie Anne's, Inc. 48-50 W. Chestnut Street, Suite 200, Lancaster, PA 17603, 717-435-1435, the Federal Trade Commission and the appropriate state regulatory agencies.

A new franchisee's individual financial results are likely to differ from the results stated in the financial performance representation.

Your sales will be affected by your own operational ability, which may include your experience with managing a business, your capital and financing (including working capital), continual training of you and your staff, customer service orientation, product quality, your business plan, and the use of experts, e.g., an accountant, to assist you with your business plans.

Your sales may be affected by franchise location and site criteria, including traffic count, local household income, residential and/or daytime populations, ease of ingress and egress, parking, visibility of your sign, physical condition of premises, number and type of other businesses around your location, competition, inflation, economic conditions, seasonal conditions (particularly in colder climates), inclement weather (e.g., hurricanes), changes in the Homeland Security threat level, etc.

Written substantiation for the financial performance representation will be made available to the prospective franchisee upon reasonable request.

We encourage you to consult with your own accounting, business, and legal advisors to assist you to prepare your budgets and projections, and to assess the likely or potential financial performance of your franchise. We also encourage you to contact existing franchisees to discuss their experiences with the system and their franchise business. Notwithstanding the information set forth in this financial performance representation, existing franchisees of our are your best source of information about franchise operations.

Tables 1 through 8 present net sales or average net sales, average expenses and average net operating income figures for the year ended December 31, 2012 for a majority of Auntie Anne's franchises that operated under the same ownership for the entire year, obtained from the unaudited profit and loss statements submitted by Auntie Anne's franchisees. All of the

Auntie Anne's franchisees report financial information based upon a uniform reporting system. The Notes which follow each table apply to that table and should be read in conjunction with the information contained in the table. The information presented on Tables 1 through 8 excludes sales information from Subway Co-branded Locations. Net sales or average net sales, average expenses and average net operating income vary widely for these types of locations. Franchisees of Subway Co-Brand Locations may not find this information useful.

As used throughout the following Tables 1- 8, the following definitions apply:

- Net Sales – Net Sales includes, without limitation, monies, gift card redemptions or credit received from the sale of food, beverages, and merchandise, from tangible property of every kind and nature, promotional or otherwise, and for services performed from or at the Shop, including without limitation off-premises services such as catering and delivery. Net Sales will not include the initial sales or reloading of gift cards, coupon discounts, the sale of food or merchandise for which refunds have been made in good faith to customers, the discounted portion of employee meals, the sale of equipment used in the operation of the Franchised Business, nor will it include sales, meals, use or excise tax imposed by a governmental authority directly on sales and collected from customers; provided that the amount for the tax is added to the selling price or absorbed therein, and is actually paid by you to a governmental authority.
- Cost of Goods Sold – Cost of Goods Sold (sometimes referred to as COGS) is a figure which reflects the cost of materials used to produce the products you sell to your customers. It includes the cost of food ingredients (pretzel mix, butter, beverages, etc.), paper products (cups, napkins, bags, straws, etc.) and retail items (Auntie Anne's At Home® pretzel kits, etc.).
- Gross Profit – Gross profit is Net Sales minus Cost of Goods Sold.
- Operating Expenses – Operating expenses are the day-to-day costs incurred in conducting normal business operations.
- Labor – Labor includes wages paid to your employees and payroll taxes paid for your employees. Labor does not include actual wages and related expenses you pay to yourself.
- Rent – Rent includes the base rent for your lease including extra charges, such as common area maintenance (CAM) charges, real estate taxes, percentage rents, etc.
- Other Expenses – Other expenses include such things as utilities (electric, telephone), royalties, ad fund fees, advertising, insurance (Workers' Comp, property, casualty, liability, health, etc.), licenses, permits, repairs, uniforms, store supplies, etc.

- Total Expenses – The total of Labor, Rent and Other Expenses
- Net Operating Income – Gross Profit minus Total Expenses

We include the following Regions, and their respective states, in the information presented in Tables 1 - 9:

a. Mid-Atlantic Region: (i) West Virginia; (ii) District of Columbia; (iii) Virginia; (iv) Maryland; (v) Pennsylvania; and (vi) Delaware.

b. Northeast Region: (i) New York; (ii) Connecticut; (iii) New Hampshire; (iv) Massachusetts; (v) New Jersey; (vi) Vermont; and (vii) Rhode Island.

c. Southeast Region: (i) North Carolina; (ii) Georgia; (iii) Alabama; (iv) Arkansas; (v) Tennessee; (vi) Florida; (vii) South Carolina; (viii) Louisiana; and (ix) Mississippi.

d. Midwest Region: (i) Kansas; (ii) North Dakota; (iii) Iowa; (iv) Kentucky; (v) Michigan; (vi) Illinois; (vii) Indiana; (viii) Missouri; (ix) Missouri; (x) Nebraska; (xi) Ohio; (xii) Minnesota; (xiii) Wisconsin; and (xiv) South Dakota

e. Western Region: (i) Nevada; (ii) Oregon; (iii) Texas; (iv) Oklahoma; (v) California; (vi) Washington; (vii) New Mexico; (viii) Colorado; and (ix) Arizona.

Table 1
Net Sales Range 2012 Fiscal Year—Various Venues
ALL REGIONS

2012	Enclosed Malls	Airports	Outlet Centers	Walmarts	Alternative Locations	Train Stations
Sample Size	505	27	36	20	18	6
High Sales	$2,917,579	$2,018,780	$1,374,434	$406,571	$721,519	$1,162,249
Low Sales	$143,325	$343,557	$149,839	$63,346	$130,455	$308,322
Average Sales	$545,354.26	$892,927.19	$577,545.44	$269,779.95	$356,057.50	$851,708.83
% of Stores at or Above Average	40.00%	40.74%	30.56%	55.00%	38.89%	66.67%
# of Stores at or Above Average	202	11	11	11	7	4
Median Sales	$486,022	$784,047	$514,773.50	$301,559	$322,346	$967,797.50
# of Stores at or Above Median	253	14	18	10	9	3
Total Number	565	32	38	22	24	6
Percent Included in Sample	89.38%	84.38%	94.74%	90.91%	75.00%	100.00%

Approximately 70% of Auntie Anne's franchises are located in enclosed malls. THE FOLLOWING TABLES RELATE ONLY TO AUNTIE ANNE'S FRANCHISES OPERATED IN ENCLOSED MALLS and do not include franchises operated in airports, outlet centers, Walmarts, alternative locations, train stations, casinos, concession trailers/trucks, farmer's markets, seasonal locations, strip malls and colleges and universities.

Table 2
Net Sales of Franchises In Operation For All 12 Months Of 2012
By Sales Range – Systemwide – Enclosed Malls
ALL REGIONS

Sales Range	Low	High	Number of Franchises
1	$700,000	and up	107
2	$550,000	$699,999	94

3	$400,000	$549,999	153
4	$250,000	$399,999	114
5	up to	$249,999	37

Average Net Sales: $545,354.26 (202 franchises, or 40.00%, were at or above this figure)
Median Net Sales: $486,022.00 (253 franchises were at or above this figure)

Notes to Table 2:

1. As of December 31, 2012, there were 625 enclosed mall Auntie Anne's locations. Of those 625, 565 Auntie Anne's locations within enclosed malls were open for business and under the same ownership from January 1, 2012 through December 31, 2012. This table does not include 60 enclosed mall locations which were neither under the same ownership nor open for the entire 2012 fiscal year. Of those 565 locations, 505 (representing 89.38% of the 565) are included within the information contained in Table 2.

2. We have not included financial information in Table 2 for an enclosed mall location if: (i) the franchise was not in operation for the entire 2012 fiscal year; (ii) the ownership of the franchised location changed during the 2012 fiscal year; or (iii) the franchisee submitted late, incomplete, or illegible financial information or submitted such information in an unacceptable format.

Table 3
Average Net Sales and Net Operating Income as a percentage of Average Net Sales
for 2012 Fiscal Year – Systemwide – Enclosed Malls

ALL REGIONS

ALL REGIONS	Average	% of Net Sales	% of Stores at or Above Average	# of Stores at or Above Average
Net Sales	$545,354.26	100.00%	40.00%	202
Cost of Goods Sold	$105,307.91	19.31%	38.61%	195
Gross Profit	$416,046.35	80.69%	39.80%	201
Operating Expenses				
Labor	$144.028.06	26.41%	38.42%	194
Rent	$82,948.38	15.21%	40.20%	203
Other Expenses	$88,620.07	16.25%	39.21%	198
Total Expenses	$315,596.51	57.87%	40.20%	203
Net Operating Income	$124,449.84	22.82%	42.57%	215

Average Net Sales: $545,354.26 (202 franchises, or 40.00%, were at or above this figure)
Median Net Sales: $486,022.00 (253 franchises were at or above this figure)

Notes to Table 3:

1. As of December 31, 2012, there were a total of 625 Auntie Anne's locations operating within enclosed malls. Of those 625 locations, 565 operated under the same ownership from January 1, 2012 through December 31, 2012. This table does not include 60 enclosed mall locations which were neither under the same ownership nor open for the entire 2012 fiscal year. Of those 565 locations, 505 (representing 89.38% of the 565) are included within the information contained in Table 3.

2. We have not included financial information in Table 3 for an enclosed mall location if: (i) the franchise was not in operation for the entire 2012 fiscal year; (ii) the ownership of the franchised location changed during the 2012 fiscal year; or (iii) the franchisee submitted late, incomplete, or illegible financial information or submitted such information in an unacceptable format.

Table 4

MID-ATLANTIC REGION

Average Net Sales and Net Operating Income as a percentage of Average Net Sales for 2012 Fiscal Year - Enclosed Malls

MID ATLANTIC REGION	Average	% of Net Sales	% ofStores at or Above Average	# of Stores at or Above Average
Net Sales	$589,212.11	100.00%	43.37%	36
Cost of Goods Sold	$115,073.13	19.53%	42.17%	35
Gross Profit	$474,138.98	80.47%	40.96%	34
Operating Expenses				
Labor	$146,890.58	24.93%	44.58%	37
Rent	$82,607.54	14.02%	44.58%	37
Other Expenses	$92,565.22	15.71%	39.76%	33
Total Expenses	$322,063.34	54.66%	43.37%	36
Net Operating Income	$152,075.65	25.81%	34.94%	29

Average Net Sales: $589,212.11 (36 franchises, or 43.37%, were at or above this figure)
Median Net Sales: $526,718 (42 franchises were at or above this figure)

Notes to Table 4:

1. As of December 31, 2012, there were a total of 116 Auntie Anne's locations operating within enclosed malls in the Mid-Atlantic Region. Of those 116 locations, 97 operated under the same ownership from January 1, 2012 through December 31, 2012. This table does not include 19 enclosed mall locations which were neither under the same ownership nor open for the entire 2012 fiscal year. Of those 97 locations, 83 (representing 85.57% of the 97) are included within the information contained in Table 4.

2. We have not included financial information in Table 4 for an enclosed mall location if: (i) the franchise was not in operation for the entire 2012 fiscal year; (ii) the ownership of the franchised location changed during the 2012 fiscal year; or (iii) the franchisee submitted late, incomplete, or illegible financial information or submitted such information in an unacceptable format.

Table 5

NORTHEAST REGION

Average Net Sales and Net Operating Income as a percentage of Average Net Sales
for 2012 Fiscal Year – Enclosed Malls

NORTHEAST REGION	Average	% of Net Sales	% of Stores at or Above Average	# of Stores at or Above Average
Net Sales	$696,508.45	100.00%	35.82%	24
Cost of Goods Sold	$135,261.94	19.42%	32.84%	22
Gross Profit	$561,246.51	80.58%	32.84%	22
Operating Expenses				
Labor	$183,738.93	26.38%	34.33%	23
Rent	$108,237.41	15.54%	37.31%	25
Other Expenses	$111,650.30	16.03%	31.34%	21
Total Expenses	$403,626.65	57.95%	32.84%	22
Net Operating Income	$157,619.86	22.63%	38.81%	26

Average Net Sales: $696,508.45 (24 franchises, or 35.82%, were at or above this figure)
Median Net Sales: $565,069 (34 franchises were at or above this figure)

Notes to Table 5:

1. As of December 31, 2012, there were a total of 94 Auntie Anne's locations operating within enclosed malls in the Northeast Region. Of those 94 locations, 84 operated under the same ownership from January 1, 2012 through December 31, 2012. This table does not include 10 enclosed mall locations which were neither under the same ownership nor open for the entire 2012 fiscal year. Of those 84 locations, 67 (representing 79.76% of the 84) are included within the information contained in Table 5.

2. We have not included financial information in Table 5 for an enclosed mall location if: (i) the franchise was not in operation for the entire 2012 fiscal year; (ii) the ownership of the franchised location changed during the 2012 fiscal year; or (iii) the franchisee submitted late, incomplete, or illegible financial information or submitted such information in an unacceptable format.

Table 6

SOUTHEAST REGION

Average Net Sales and Net Operating Income as a percentage of Average Net Sales
for 2012 Fiscal Year – Enclosed Malls

SOUTHEAST REGION	Average	% of Net Sales	% of Stores at or Above Average	# of Stores at or Above Average
Net Sales	$515,220.95	100.00%	38.83%	40
Cost of Goods Sold	$97,788.94	18.98%	38.83%	40
Gross Profit	$417,432.01	81.02%	39.81%	41
Operating Expenses				
Labor	$139,367.27	27.05%	36.89%	38
Rent	$78,210.54	15.18%	40.78%	42
Other Expenses	$84,187.10	16.34%	37.86%	39
Total Expenses	$301,764.91	58.57%	37.86%	39
Net Operating Income	$115,667.10	22.45%	45.63%	47

Average Net Sales: $515,220.95 (40 franchises, or 38.83%, were at or above this figure)
Median Net Sales: $476,677 (52 franchises were at or above this figure)

Notes to Table 6:

1. As of December 31, 2012, there were a total of 119 Auntie Anne's locations operating within enclosed malls in the Southeast Region. Of those 119 locations, 109 operated under the same ownership from January 1, 2012 through December 31, 2012. This table does not include 10 enclosed mall locations which were neither under the same ownership nor open for the entire 2012 fiscal year. Of those 109 locations, 103 (representing 94.50% of the 109) are included within the information contained in Table 6.

2. We have not included financial information in Table 6 for an enclosed mall location if: (i) the franchise was not in operation for the entire 2012 fiscal year; (ii) the ownership of the franchised location changed during the 2012 fiscal year; or (iii) the franchisee submitted late, incomplete, or illegible financial information or submitted such information in an unacceptable format.

Table 7

MIDWEST REGION

Average Net Sales and Net Operating Income as a percentage of Average Net Sales
for 2012 Fiscal Year – Enclosed Malls

MIDWEST REGION	Average	% of Net Sales	% of Stores at or Above Average	# of Stores at or Above Average
Net Sales	$509,140.44	100.00%	41.22%	54
Cost of Goods Sold	$95,260.18	18.71%	43.51%	57

Gross Profit	$413,880.26	81.29%	41.98%	55
Operating Expenses				
Labor	$132,732.91	26.07%	51.15%	67
Rent	$77,694.83	15.26%	41.98%	55
Other Expenses	$82,175.27	16.14%	45.80%	60
Total Expenses	$292,603.01	57.47%	42.75%	56
Net Operating Income	$121,277.25	23.82%	42.75%	56

Average Net Sales: $509,140.44 (54 franchises, or 41.22%, were at or above this figure)
Median Net Sales: $475,240 (66 franchises were at or above this figure)

Notes to Table 7:

1. As of December 31, 2012, there were a total of 151 Auntie Anne's locations operating within enclosed malls in the Midwest Region. Of those 151 locations, 139 operated under the same ownership from January 1, 2012 through December 31, 2012. This table does not include 12 enclosed mall locations which were neither under the same ownership nor open for the entire 2012 fiscal year. Of those 139 locations, 131 (representing 94.24% of the 139) are included within the information contained in Table 7.

2. We have not included financial information in Table 7 for an enclosed mall location if: (i) the franchise was not in operation for the entire 2012 fiscal year; (ii) the ownership of the franchised location changed during the 2012 fiscal year; or (iii) the franchisee submitted late, incomplete, or illegible financial information or submitted such information in an unacceptable format.

Table 8

WESTERN REGION

Average Net Sales and Net Operating Income as a percentage of Average Net Sales for 2012 Fiscal Year – Enclosed Malls

WESTERN REGION	Average	% of Net Sales	% of Stores at or Above Average	# of Stores at or Above Average
Net Sales	$496,430.36	100.00%	46.28%	56
Cost of Goods Sold	$99,186.79	19.98%	41.32%	50
Gross Profit	$397,243.57	80.02%	46.28%	56
Operating Expenses				
Labor	$136,419.06	27.48%	47.11%	57
Rent	$79,081.36	15.93%	44.63%	54
Other Expenses	$84,045.66	16.93%	48.76%	59
Total Expenses	$299,546.08	60.34%	50.41%	61
Net Operating Income	$97,697.49	19.68%	46.28%	56

Average Net Sales: $496,430.36 (56 franchises, or 46.28%, were at or above this figure)
Median Net Sales: $473,918 (61 franchises)

Notes to Table 8:

1. As of December 31, 2012, there were a total of 145 Auntie Anne's locations operating within enclosed malls in the Western Region. Of those 145 locations, 136 operated under the same ownership from January 1, 2012 through December 31, 2012. This table does not include 9 enclosed mall locations which were neither under the same ownership nor open for the entire 2012 fiscal year. Of those 136 locations, 121 (representing 88.97% of the 136) are included within the information contained in Table 8.

2. We have not included financial information in Table 8 for an enclosed mall location if: (i) the franchise was not in operation for the entire 2012 fiscal year; (ii) the ownership of the franchised location changed during the 2012 fiscal year; or (iii) the franchisee submitted late, incomplete, or illegible financial information or submitted such information in an unacceptable format.

Table 9

ALL REGIONS

Average Net Sales Per Transaction (NSPT) For 2013 for Enclosed Malls (EM)

Region	Average EM NSPT	Number of EM's open for all of 2013 used to calculate NSPT	Number of EM's open for all of 2013	% EM's used to calculate NSPT is to EM's open for all of 2013	Median EM NSPT	#/% of EM's that Met or Exceeded Average NSPT
Mid Atlantic	$5.22	124	130	95.38%	$5.21	60/48.4%
Northeast	$5.40	101	115	87.83%	$5.30	47/43.6%
Southeast	$5.34	121	127	95.28%	$5.33	60/46.5%
Midwest	$5.55	144	147	97.96%	$5.46	63/43.8%
Western	$5.57	134	148	90.54%	$5.45	62/46.3%
Total All Regions	$5.43	624	667	93.55%	$5.36	292/46.8%

Notes to Table 9:

1. The above table shows Net Sales Per Transaction ("NSPT") averages experienced by Auntie Anne's enclosed mall locations which were open and reported sales for the entire fiscal year ended December 29, 2013. The NSPT averages are based on data received from 624 of 667 Auntie Anne's franchised locations that operated in enclosed malls and reported sales for all 52 weeks of 2013. Data from company-owned stores is not included in Table 9. These 624 locations represent 93.55% of the 667 total enclosed mall locations that were open for the entire fiscal year ended December 29 2013. The NSPT average is obtained from the valid transaction count data as reported to us by Auntie Anne's franchisees based upon a uniform reporting system. The NSPT average is derived by dividing total Net Sales by the total number of cash register sales transactions as reported to us by Auntie Anne's franchisees for the fiscal year ended December 29, 2013. An average NSPT is determined for each Region and for the total of all the Regions.

2. We have not included Net Sales or cash register sales transactions in Table 9 for an enclosed mall location if there was not a full 52 weeks' worth of data. Some reasons why there is not a full 52 weeks' worth of data include: (i) technical problems with cash application software, (ii) equipment problems such as cash register malfunctions, phone line failures, modem malfunction, power outages, and (iii) data validation problems such as receiving data that is incomplete or in an unacceptable format.

BASKIN-ROBBINS

130 Royall St.
Canton, MA 02021
Tel: (800) 777-9983, (781) 737-5136

Fax: (818) 996-5163
Email: erin.venuti@dunkinbrands.com
Website: www.baskinrobbins.com
Erin Venuti, Director of Franchising

BASKIN-ROBBINS develops, operates and franchises retail stores that sell ice cream, frozen yogurt and other approved services. In some markets, BASKIN-ROBBINS, together with TOGO's and/or DUNKIN' DONUTS, offers multiple brand combinations of the three brands. TOGO's, BASKIN-ROBBINS and DUNKIN' DONUTS are all subsidiaries of Dunkin' Brands, Inc.

BACKGROUND			
IFA Member:	Yes	Encourage Conversions:	No
Established & First Franchised:	1950; 1950	Area Development Agreements:	Yes
Franchised Units:	6,000	Sub-Franchising Contracts:	No
Company-Owned Units:	1	Expand in Territory:	Yes
Total Units:	6,001	Space Needs:	N/A

Distribution: US – 3,358; CAN – 620; O'seas – 2,022

North America:	41 States, 9 Provinces
Density:	554 in CA, 195 in IL, 181 in NY
Projected New Units (12 Months):	27
Qualifications:	N/A

SUPPORT & TRAINING

Financial Assistance Provided:	Yes (D)
Site Selection Assistance:	N/A
Lease Negotiation Assistance:	Yes
Co-operative Advertising:	No
Franchisee Association/Member:	Yes/Member
Size of Corporate Staff:	N/A
On-going Support:	B,C,D,G,H,I
Training:	51 Days Randolph, MA; 3.5 Days Another Location

FINANCIAL/TERMS

Cash Investment:	$100K
Total Investment:	$250K
Minimum Net Worth:	$300K
Fees (Franchise):	$40K
Fees (Royalty):	5-5.9%
Fees (Advertising):	5%
Term of Contract (Years):	20
Average Number of Employees:	N/A
Passive Ownership:	Discouraged

SPECIFIC EXPANSION PLANS

US:	All United States
Canada:	All Canada
Overseas:	All Countries

Before you start to review the information in this Item 19, we want to call your attention to these important points:

1. A new franchisee's individual financial results may differ from the results stated in the financial performance representations in this Item 19.

2. We will make written substantiation for the financial performance representations in this Item 19 available to prospective franchisees upon reasonable request.

3. If you are thinking of entering into an agreement to operate an alternative point of distribution ("APOD") or a Baskin-Robbins Express (either as a Restaurant or a DD/BR Combo Restaurant), please note that the information in this Item 19 does not apply to either APOD or Baskin-Robbins Express Restaurants. We do not make financial performance representations about APOD or Baskin-Robbins Express Restaurants. We do not offer Territorial Franchise Agreements.

4. If you are thinking of entering into an agreement to operate a Restaurant or DD/BR Combo Restaurant in Alaska or Hawaii, please note that the information in this Item 19 does not apply to Restaurants or DD/BR Combo Restaurants in those states. We do not make financial performance representations about Restaurants or DD/BR Combo Restaurants in Alaska or Hawaii.

5. There are five tables that follow in this Item 19. You should read them together with all of the notes and explanatory information that follows in this Item 19.

BASKIN-ROBBINS RESTAURANTS: The following tables and notes provide financial performance representations that are historical, and that are based on information from existing Baskin-Robbins Restaurants (exclusive of DD/BR Combo Restaurants, APOD Restaurants, Baskin-Robbins Express and Restaurants operating under Territorial Franchise Agreements) that have been open for business to the public for at least one year during a one year measuring period from OCTOBER 28, 2012 TO OCTOBER 26, 2013. Restaurants sold under Territorial Franchise Agreements ("TFAs") may not follow the standard prototype for a Restaurant. Restaurants operating under a TFA include some, but not all Restaurants located in the States of Arkansas, Georgia, Idaho, Kansas, Missouri, Mississippi, Montana, Nebraska, Oklahoma, Oregon, Tennessee and Washington. For more information regarding the "Regions", please refer to Appendix V at the end of this FDD. The Region descriptions are approximations. Some Restaurant locations included in this data may not precisely follow the descriptions contained in Appendix V. (For example, some Restaurants near the boundary of another Region may be included in that other Region's data.)

Table 1:

CONTINENTAL U.S. BASKIN-ROBBINS SINGLE BRAND RESTAURANTS

AVERAGE RESTAURANT SALES FOR THE PERIOD OCTOBER 28, 2012 TO OCTOBER 26, 2013

Regions	Total Number of Restaurants in Sample	Average Sales	% Restaurants at or Above Average
East	201	$298,430	47.76%
Central	183	$326,753	52.46%
West	468	$352,891	44.44%
Total Continental United States	852	$332,925	46.36%

Total Number of Restaurants in Sample includes locations that reported more than 40 weeks of reported sales within specified time period.

"% Restaurants at or Above Average" means the percentage of Restaurants included in the data whose reported average sales are at or above the stated average, meaning that these Restaurants performed better than the stated average.

Table 2:

CONTINENTAL U.S. BASKIN-ROBBINS SINGLE BRAND RESTAURANTS

AVERAGE COST OF GOODS SOLD AND AVERAGE LABOR COST

FOR THE PERIOD NOVERMBER 1, 2012 THROUGH OCTOBER 31, 2013

Regions	Total Number of Restaurants in Sample	Cost of Goods Sold Average	% of Restaurants with Cost of Goods Sold at or Below the Average Shown	Labor Cost Average	% of Restaurants with Labor at or Below the Average Shown
East	181	31.4%	53.6%	24.6%	48.6%
Central	175	29.3%	48.0%	24.2%	51.4%
West	436	31.0%	56.7%	22.7%	55.0%
Total Continental United States	792	30.7%	55.2%	23.5%	53.8%

"% Restaurants with Cost of Goods Sold at or below the Average shown" and "% Restaurants with Labor at or below the Average shown" means the percentage of Restaurants included in the data who performed as well as or better than the averages shown (meaning these units have cost ratios that are as good as, or better than, the average shown).

DUNKIN' DONUTS/BASKIN-ROBBINS COMBO RESTAURANTS:

The following tables and notes provide financial performance representations that are historical, and that are based on information from existing DD/BR Combo Restaurants that have been open for business to the public for at least one year during a one year measuring period from OCTOBER 28, 2012 TO OCTOBER 26, 2013. For more information regarding the "Regions", please refer to Appendix V at the end of this FDD. The Region descriptions are approximations. Some DD/BR Combo Restaurant locations included in this data may not precisely follow the descriptions contained in Appendix V. (For example, some DD/BR Combo Restaurants near the boundary of another Region may be included in that other Region's data.)

Table 3:

CONTINENTAL U.S. DUNKIN' DONUTS/BASKIN-ROBBINS COMBO RESTAURANTS

AVERAGE DD/BR COMBO RESTAURANT SALES FOR THE PERIOD OCTOBER 28, 2012 TO OCTOBER 26, 2013

FREE STADING SITE TYPE

Regions	Drive-Thru Restaurants			Non Drive-Thru Restaurants		
	Total Number of Restaurants in Sample	Aveage Sales	% Restaurants at or Above Average	Total Number of Restaurants in Sample	Average Sales	% Restaurants at or Above Average
Mid-Atlantic	60	$1,242,125	50%	16	$1,049,956	47%
Mid West	161	$1,251,017	45%	24	$934,508	46%
Northeast	64	$1,645,115	48%	78	$1,239,148	51%
South Atlantic	118	$1,226,482	42%	N/A	N/A	N/A
South Central/ West	N/A	N/A	N/A	N/A	N/A	N/A
Total Continental United States	403	$1,305,096	45%	117	$1,152,402	44%

"% Restaurants at or Above Average" means the percentage of Restaurants included in the data whose reported average sales are at or above the stated average, meaning that these Restaurants performed better than the stated average.

N/A means that we have not included information for this site type in this region due to sample sizes of less than 10 Restaurants.

Table 4:

CONTINENTAL U.S. DUNKIN' DONUTS/BASKIN-ROBBINS COMBO RESTAURANTS

AVERAGE DD/BR COMBO RESTAURANT SALES FOR THE PERIOD OCTOBER 28, 2012 TO OCTOBER 26, 2013

SHOPPING CENTER/STOREFRONT SITE TYPE

Regions	Drive-Thru Restaurants			Non Drive-Thru Restaurants		
	Total Number of Restaurants in Sample	Average Sales	% Restaurants at or Above Average	Total Number of Restaurants in Sample	Average Sales	% Restaurants at or Above Average
Mid Atlantic	19	$1,264,545	42%	29	$834,395	52%
Mid West	50	$1,045,219	46%	52	$904,612	46%
Northeast	15	$1,275,675	33%	257	$1,071,866	44%
South Atlantic	30	$1,119,807	43%	29	$865,889	52%
South Central/ West	N/A	N/A	N/A	N/A	N/A	N/A
Total Continental United States	114	$1,131,725	46%	367	$1,013,127	47%

"% Combo Restaurants at or Above Average" means the percentage of Combo Restaurants included in the data whose reported average sales are at or above the stated average, meaning that these Restaurants performed better than the stated average.

N/A means that we have not included information for this site type in this region due to sample sizes of less than 10 Restaurants.

Table 5:

CONTINENTAL U.S. DUNKIN' DONUTS/BASKIN-ROBBINS COMBO RESTAURANTS

AVERAGE COST OF GOODS SOLD & AVERAGE LABOR COST STATED AS A PERCENT OF TOTAL SALES

FOR THE PERIOD NOVEMBER 1, 2012 TO OCTOBER 31, 2013

Regions	Total Number of Combo Restaurants in Sample	Average Cost of Goods Sold	% Combo Restaurants with Cost of Goods Sold at or Below the Average Shown	Average Labor Cost	% Combo Restaurants with Labor at or Below the Average Shown
Mid Atlantic	123	30.8%	52.8%	24.5%	53.7%
Mid West	285	31.2%	59.3%	24.6%	56.1%
Northeast	411	28.6%	56.7%	24.7%	55.5%
South Atlantic	176	31.6%	49.4%	26.2%	55.1%
South Central/ West	14	35.2%*	42.9%	27.4%	35.7%
Total Continental United States	1,009	30.2%	53.6%	24.9%	55.6%

"% Combo Restaurants with Cost of Goods Sold at or Below the Average Shown" and "% DD/BR Combo Restaurants with Labor at or Below the Average Shown" means the percentage of DD/BR Combo Restaurants included in the data who performed as well as or better than the averages shown (meaning these units have cost ratios that are as good as, or better than, the average shown).

* The Cost of Goods Sold published for this Region are lower than your Cost of Goods Sold will be because we currently subsidize up to 2% of the Cost of Goods Sold to certain Combo Restaurants in this Region. You will not be eligible to receive this subsidy (even if you will open a new Combo Restaurant in this Region).

NOTES REGARDING SALES DATA (Tables 1, 3 & 4 above):

(1) The sales figures are compiled by using historical sales that are reported to us by franchisees. We have not audited or verified the reports.

(2) We provide you sales data that includes average sales and the percentage of Restaurants reporting who have actually attained or surpassed the stated average. This sales data does not include sales tax. The vast majority of the Restaurants that comprise this data are franchised, although our affiliate, DBI Stores LLC, may own and operate a small number of Restaurants at any given time (see Item 20).

(3) Sales in states or regions with a higher concentration of Restaurants that have been in operation for a substantial period of time tend to have higher sales than states or regions with a lower concentration of Restaurants that have been in operation for a lesser time period. These higher concentration states or regions significantly increase the overall average due to both their higher sales and their larger numbers. Therefore, the sales performance of Restaurants outside of these higher concentration areas may not be commensurate with the overall average sales. (See Item 20 for the number of Restaurants per state).

(4) Many of the Restaurants included in this data have been open and operating for several years. These franchisees have achieved their level of sales after spending many years building customer goodwill at a particular location.

(5) Your sales will be affected by your own operational ability, which may include your experience with managing a business, your capital and financing (including working capital), continual training of you and your staff, customer service orientation, product quality, your business plan, and the use of experts (for example, an accountant) to assist in your business plan.

(6) Your sales may be affected by Restaurant location and site criteria, including traffic count and which side of the street your Restaurant is located on (for example, whether your Restaurant is on the morning drive side or afternoon drive side of traffic), local household income, residential and/or daytime populations, ease of ingress and egress, seating, parking, the physical condition of your Restaurant, the size of your site, and the visibility of your exterior sign(s). Additionally, many of the Restaurants included in the sales figures are freestanding Restaurants or located at the end of a strip center, and if your Restaurant is not, your sales could be substantially lower than the figures in the chart. Your sales may also be negatively affected if you do not adhere to our standards and system, including proper equipment layout, design and construction criteria, customer queuing and flow, and local Restaurant marketing.

(7) Individual locations may have layouts and seating capacities that vary from the typical location.

(8) Other factors that could have an effect upon your sales may include consumer preferences, competition (national and local), inflation, local construction and its impact on traffic patterns, and reports on the health effects of consuming food similar to that served in the Restaurants, as well as the impact of federal, state and local government regulations.

(9) Your sales may be affected by consumer preferences for certain menu items over others, changes in the menu and regional differences in products or product demand, including whether there are products not available to you or your region but sold in other regions. Menus are continually being revised, both adding and discontinuing products and product line extensions. Not all Restaurants may have these new products. New products may not be successful for all Restaurants. Marketing activity associated with new products may be at higher than normal levels and, therefore, sales increases may not be maintained after this temporary marketing activity is completed.

(10) Sales may be affected by fluctuations due to seasonality (particularly in colder climates), weather and periodic marketing and advertising programs. Inclement weather may cause temporary Restaurant closings in some areas.

(11) The above data reflects historical sales. There is no assurance that future sales will correspond to historical sales.

(12) There are numerous factors that may affect sales at your Restaurant. The factors listed above and below are not an all-inclusive list of those factors.
(13) The Restaurant with the highest sales for the applicable Region may have characteristics that are not available to you.

(14) Many Baskin-Robbins franchisees actively pursue cake sales opportunities. If you do not, your sales may be negatively affected. Additionally, seasonality and weather may significantly affect sales of ice cream and related products.

(15) Restaurants with a drive-thru window tend to have higher sales than Restaurants without a drive-thru window. Many of the Restaurants included in the statistics above have a drive-thru window. Some individual Restaurants' sales may include wholesale accounts and other distribution outlets, which may not be available to you. Not all of these opportunities have been successful for all participating franchisees. These opportunities may have been added, expanded, reduced or eliminated from individual reporting Restaurants at varying times during the reporting period. The contracts for such opportunities may have been terminated or expired without renewal in the reported or future periods. Additionally, some products that are sold in the Restaurants included in the statistics above may not be available for sale in your state or region.

NOTES REGARDING COGS AND LABOR DATA (Tables 2 & 5 above):

"COGS" means the cost of goods sold including food, beverages and items served or associated with the food or beverage, such as cups, napkins, straws, bags, plastic utensils and wrapping paper.

"Labor" means crew and management payroll and training costs. It does not include payroll tax and workers' compensation. (Table 2 above)

"Labor" means crew, management, training, payroll tax and workers' compensation. (Table 5 above)

(1) COGS and Labor are stated as a percentage of gross sales (excluding sales tax and discounts). The vast majority of Restaurants that comprise this data are franchised, although our affiliate, DBI Stores LLC, may own and operate a small number of Restaurants at any given time (see Item 20).

(2) The cost figures from franchised Restaurants are compiled from individual Restaurants by using cost data that are reported to us by franchisees. We have not audited or verified the reports, nor have franchisees confirmed that the reports are prepared in accordance with generally accepted accounting principles or in accordance with our definition of COGS and Labor.

(3) Your costs will be affected by your own operational ability, which may include your experience with managing quick service restaurant operations, your experience building and managing an organization, continual training of you and your staff, your business plan, and using experts (e.g., an accountant) to assist in your business plan. Your costs may be negatively affected by not adhering to our standards and system.

(4) Many of the Restaurants included in this data have been open and operating for several years. Those franchisees may have lower cost percentages due to years of experience managing costs. For new franchisees, COGS and Labor cost percentages may initially exceed those of experienced operators.

(5) There is no assurance that future costs will correspond to historical costs because of factors such as inflation, changes in menu and other variables.

(6) Factors affecting your COGS include, but are not limited to, the price of raw materials; your ability to manage and implement proper controls of waste, ruin, loss, theft and the portion sizes served to the public; regional differences; temporary shortages; seasonal and weather fluctuations; and fluctuations due to periodic marketing and advertising programs. Addi

tionally, freight charges may be higher in some areas. If the cost of gasoline increases in the U.S., the cost of freight will rise as well.

(7) The COGS data above reflects average Restaurant's aggregate cost. Different food and beverage items have different cost percentages. Customer demand for products varies among Restaurants and regions and if your Restaurant sells a high percentage of high cost items, your food cost percentage will be higher than if you have a lower percentage of higher cost items. Your costs may be affected by changes in the menu and regional differences in products including whether there are products not available to you or your region but sold in other regions. Menus are continually being revised, both adding and discontinuing products and product line extensions. New products are not successful in all Restaurants where they are introduced.

(8) Factors affecting your Labor include, among other things, the local labor market and any applicable federal or state minimum wage law; pending healthcare legislation, employee turnover and your operational abilities, including your ability to train and retain employees; your compensation that may be included in labor, which varies among franchisees; menu, product mix, Restaurant layout, your salary and benefits programs, and scheduling. Restaurants must be staffed in accordance with our standards.

(9) Some franchisees purchase finished products manufactured at another location. The cost of this finished product will vary depending upon the number of Restaurants being serviced by the manufacturing location and other factors. These franchisees may pay more for food costs but may pay less for other items such as labor, equipment, distribution and rent.

(10) COGS may be particularly affected by the fluctuations in the price of coffee and other items and ingredients.

(11) Restaurants with lower sales may have higher COGS and Labor cost percentages because of less efficiencies and economies of scale, and more waste.

(12) The retail sales price that you establish will also affect the COGS and Labor percentages.

(13) If you are in a geographic area with fewer Restaurants, you may have higher COGS as a percentage of sales due to less distribution efficiencies.

ADDITIONAL NOTES REGARDING SALES, COGS AND LABOR DATA (All Tables above):

You should conduct an independent investigation of the sales, costs and expenses you will incur in operating your franchised business. Franchisees or former franchisees, listed in this disclosure document, may be one source of this information.

The "Total Number of Restaurants/DD/BR Combo Restaurants in Sample" in Tables 2 & 5 is a subset of the "Total Number of Restaurants/Combo Restaurants in Sample" in Tables 1, 3 & 4, because not all Restaurants or DD/BR Combo Restaurants in Tables 2 & 5 reported COGS and Labor data for the twelve month reporting period.

All of the Restaurants or DD/BR Combo Restaurants in Tables 2 & 5 reported at least one month of COGS and Labor data for the twelve month reporting period.

Our nation's current economic conditions are unusually volatile both in terms of consumer spending as well as the costs of doing business, such as for example, energy, commodities, credit, etc. As a result, historical performance results may not be as useful in your financial planning as they may have been in less volatile times (in terms of anticipated sales or anticipated costs). If you choose to use the historical financial information appearing in this franchise disclosure document, you must carefully consider the potential impact of the current economic volatility, price spikes in the cost of commodities, and in your potential sales volume.

There are numerous factors that may affect COGS and Labor at your Restaurant. The factors listed in this Item 19 are not an all-inclusive list of those factors.

Other than the preceding financial performance representation, we do not make any financial performance representations. We do not make any representations about a franchisee's future financial performance. We also do not authorize our employees or representatives to make any such representations either orally or in writing. If you are purchasing an existing outlet, however, we may provide you with the actual records of that outlet. If you receive any other financial performance information or projections of your future income, you should report it to the franchisor's management by contacting Richard Emmett, Senior Vice President, Chief Legal and Human Resources Officer, Legal Dept. 3 East A, 130 Royall Street, Canton, MA 02021, 781-737-3000, the Federal Trade Commission, and the appropriate state regulatory agencies.

APOD, BASKIN-ROBBINS EXPRESS, TERRITORIAL FRAN-CHISES, ALASKA AND HAWAII, GAS & CONVENIENCE DD/BR COMBO RESTAURANTS AND REGIONS WITH INSUFFICIENT DATA:

We do not make financial performance representations for the following Restaurants or DD/BR Combo Restaurants: APOD, Baskin-Robbins Express, restaurants under Territorial

Franchise Agreements, Restaurants in Alaska & Hawaii, Gas & Convenience DD/BR Combo Restaurants or Site Types in Regions with a sample size of less than ten Restaurants. The FTC's Franchise Rule permits a franchisor to provide information about the actual or potential financial performance of its franchise and/or franchisor-owned outlets, if there is a reasonable basis for the information, and if the information is included in the disclosure document. Financial performance information that differs from that included in Item 19 may be given only if: (1) a franchisor provides the actual records of an existing outlet you are considering buying; or (2) a franchisor supplements the information provided in this Item 19, for example, by providing information about possible performance at a particular location or under particular circumstances.

We do not make any representations about a franchisee's future financial performance or the past financial performance of company-owned or franchised outlets. We also do not authorize our employees or representatives to make any such representations either orally or in writing. If you are purchasing an existing outlet, however, we may provide you with the actual records of that outlet. If you receive any other financial performance information or projections of your future income, you should report it to the franchisor's management by contacting Richard Emmett, Senior Vice President, Chief Legal and Human Resources Officer, Legal Dept. 3 East A, 130 Royall Street, Canton, MA 02021, 781-737-3000, the Federal Trade Commission, and the appropriate state regulatory agencies.

IF APPLICABLE, HISTORICAL SALES AND PROFIT DATA FOR EXISTING RESTAURANT TO BE SOLD BY US:

If the subject Restaurant is an existing Restaurant being sold by us, we may provide to you unaudited historical sales and profit data for the Restaurant. Statements prepared by us are prepared in accordance with generally accepted accounting principles. Statements prepared by past franchisee(s) of the Restaurant, if any, were submitted to us by franchisee(s) that we require to prepare statements in accordance with generally accepted accounting principles. We cannot assure you that in all cases they were so prepared.

Historical costs do not correspond to future costs because of such factors as inflation, changes in minimum wage laws, the local labor market, financing, real estate related costs and other variables. For example, actual costs such as rent, taxes, depreciation, amortization interest, insurance, payroll, and utilities may vary from historical costs. Historical sales may also not correspond to future sales because of such factors as the duration, if any, that the Restaurant was closed, changes in Restaurant management and employees, remodel or refurbishment, if any, over or under reporting of sales, changes in competition and other variables.

Your accountant should develop your own data for these accounts based on your particular financing and other costs. All information should be evaluated in light of current market conditions including such cost and price information as may then be available.

BURGER KING CORPORATION

5505 Blue Lagoon Dr.
Miami, FL 33126
Tel: (866) 546-4252, (305) 378-7579
Fax: (305) 378-7721
Email: jchristina@whopper.com
Website: www.bk.com
Joseph Christina, Senior Vice President of Franchise Operations U.S. West

The BURGER KING system operates more than 12,000 restaurants in all 50 states and in 73 countries and U.S. territories worldwide. Approximately 90 percent of BURGER KING restaurants are owned and operated by independent franchisees, many of them family-owned operations that have been in business for decades. In 2008, Fortune magazine ranked Burger King Corp. (BKC) among America's 1,000 largest corporations and in 2010, Standard & Poor's included shares of Burger King Holdings, Inc. to the S&P MidCap 400 index. BKC was recently recognized by Interbrand on its top 100 "Best Global Brands" list and Ad Week has named it one of the top three industry-changing advertisers within the last three decades. To learn more about Burger King Corp., please visit the company's Web site at www.bk.com.

BACKGROUND
IFA Member:	Yes
Established & First Franchised:	1954; 1961

Franchised Units:	10,144	Area Development Agreements:	No
Company-Owned Units:	1,079	Sub-Franchising Contracts:	No
Total Units:	11,223	Expand in Territory:	Yes
Distribution:	US – 7,250; CAN – 295; O'seas – 4,533	Space Needs:	3,600 SF
North America:	50 States, 10 Provinces		
Density:	N/A	SUPPORT & TRAINING	
Projected New Units (12 Months):	N/A	Financial Assistance Provided:	No
Qualifications:	N/A	Site Selection Assistance:	Yes
		Lease Negotiation Assistance:	Yes
		Co-operative Advertising:	No
FINANCIAL/TERMS		Franchisee Association/Member:	Yes/Member
Cash Investment:	Varies	Size of Corporate Staff:	928
Total Investment:	$294K – 2.8MM	On-going Support:	C, D, E, F, H
Minimum Net Worth:	$1.5MMK	Training:	240 Hours Classroom; 440 Hours Restaurant
Fees (Franchise):	$50K		
Fees (Royalty):	4.5%		
Fees (Advertising):	4%		
Term of Contract (Years):	20/20	SPECIFIC EXPANSION PLANS	
Average Number of Employees:	15 FT, 35 PT	US:	All United States
Passive Ownership:	Discouraged	Canada:	All Canada
Encourage Conversions:	Yes	Overseas:	All Countries

Editor's Note: Information relating to "Fuel Co-Branded Restaurants" has been removed from this Item 19 for this publication. If you would like to see the full Burger King Item 19, you can purchase it at www.Item19s.com.

This Item includes certain infonnation about (a) gross sales of franchised and BKC-operated BURGER KING Restaurants during the 12-month period ended December 31, 2013 ("Sales Distributions"), and (b) selected cost factors for certain BKC-operated BURGER KING Restaurants during that period ("Cost Factors"). Sales Distributions are provided separately for "Traditional Restaurants," "Non-Traditional Restaurants," and four types of "Fuel Co-Branded Restaurants," as those tenns are used for purposes of this Item. Cost Factors are provided only for BKC-owned "Traditional Restaurants." For purposes of this Item, "Non-Traditional Restaurants" include the following types of BURGER KING Restaurants:

(1) Limited menu in-line facilities;
(2) Restaurants or food courts at institutional locations (such as airports, military facilities, colleges, schools, office buildings, retail stores, tourist locations, and turnpikes; see Item I);
(3) Conversion Restaurant facilities;
(4) Double drive-thru facilities;
(5) Mall location facilities; and
(6) Mobile restaurant units (buses/trailers).
(7) Big Box Retail

For purposes of this Item, "Traditional Restaurants" are all

Restaurants other than those included as "Non-Traditional Restaurants". There were 6,999 Burger King franchised restaurants and 51 BKC-owned Burger King Restaurants open during the entire 12-month period ended December 31, 2013.

The Sales Distributions and Cost Factors presented here do not reflect the sales distributions or cost factors of all the varying facility types or sizes or facility locations.

The Sales Distributions and Cost Factors should be read together with all of the related infonnation about the factual bases and material assumptions underlying them. BKC will make available to you, on reasonable request, data used in preparing the Sales Distributions and Cost Factors, in a fonn that does not identify any individual franchised Restaurant.

Your individual financial results are likely to differ from the results shown in the Sales Distributions and Cost Factors. In providing the Sales Distributions and Cost Factors, BKC is not making a representation or guarantee that you will or may achieve any level of sales shown in the Sales Distributions or experience costs comparable to those shown in the Cost Factors. BKC does not make any representation or guarantee of future sales, costs, income or profits.

Other than the Sales Distributions and Cost Factors presented in this Item, or as described below in connection with the sale by BKC of a Restaurant, BKC does not furnish, or authorize the furnishing, to prospective Franchisees of any oral or written infonnation of actual, potential, average or projected sales, costs, income or profits of BURGER KING restaurants. If you obtain this infonnation, do not rely on it because it is intended for internal use only by BKC as a basis for BKC's own investment decisions.

You should construct your own pro fonna cash flow statement and make your own projections concerning potential sales, operating costs, total capital investment requirements, cash injection, debt, overall potential cash flow, and other financial aspects of operating a BURGER KING Restaurant. You should not rely solely on infonnation provided by BKC, but should conduct your own independent investigation of costs and sales potential for your proposed Restaurant. You should consult an accountant, attorney and existing BURGER KING Franchisees.

The data used in preparing the Sales Distributions and Cost Factors have been prepared on a basis consistent with generally accepted accounting principles to the extent applicable; BKC has not independently confirmed gross sales reported by Franchisees for Franchisee-owned Restaurants, but has relied on gross sales as reported by Franchisees.

THE REVENUE FIGURES IN THIS ITEM 19 DO NOT RE-FLECT THE COSTS OF SALES, OPERATING EXPENSES, OR OTHER COSTS OR EXPENSES THAT MUST BE DEDUCTED FROM THE GROSS REVENUE OR GROSS SALES FIGURES TO OBTAIN YOUR NET INCOME OR PROFIT. YOU SHOULD CON-DUCT AN INDEPENDENT INVESTIGATION OF THE COSTS AND EXPENSES YOU WILL INCUR IN OPERATING YOUR BURGER KING® RESTAURANT. FRANCHISEES OR FORMER FRANCHISEES, LISTED IN THIS DISCLOSURE DOCUMENT, MAY BE ONE SOURCE OF THIS INFORMATION.

Sale of Restaurants Operated by BKC

From time to time BKC may offer certain of its company op-erated Restaurants for sale. In connection with the sale of a BURGER KING Restaurant operated by BKC, BKC gives the prospective purchaser certain historical financial information for the specific Restaurant(s) being sold. This historical financial information is given only to the potential purchaser of that Restaurant. BKC also provides the prospective purchaser with the name and last known address of each owner of the Restaurant during the 5 years preceding the sale.

The following historical financial information is provided on the offered Restaurant(s): (1) 24 months of gross sales of the specific Restaurant (in some cases, the Restaurant may have been operated by a franchisee for part of the 24- month period); and (2) if available, an unaudited operating statement of actual sales and expenses of BKC's own operation of the Restaurant for 13 months or a shorter period. The operating statement is prepared on a basis consistent with generally accepted accounting principles, except for the following:

It excludes depreciation.

It is prepared on a pre-tax basis, except for the labor line, which includes any targeted job tax credits.

Since BKC is primarily a self-insured company, the casualty line may not reflect the fully allocated insurance cost.

ACTUAL SALES ARE OF SPECIFIC COMPANY-OWNED AND OPERATED RESTAURANTS AND FRANCHISED RESTAU-RANTS AND DO NOT INDICATE THE ACTUAL OR PROB-ABLE SALES, THAT YOU MAY OR WILL REALIZE. ACTUAL EXPENSES ARE OF SPECIFIC COMPANY-OWNED AND OP-ERATED RESTAURANTS AND DO NOT REPRESENT THE ACTUAL OR PROBABLE EXPENSES THAT YOU MAY OR WILL INCUR. BKC DOES NOT REPRESENT THAT YOU CAN EXPECT TO GAIN ANY LEVEL OF SALES, EXPENSE, INCOME, OR GROSS OR NET PROFITS.

Exhibit 19-1
SALES DISTRIBUTION "TRADITIONAL" AND "NON-TRADITIONAL" RESTAURANTS
JANUARY 1, 2013 – DECEMBER 31, 2013
PERCENTAGE OF RESTAURANTS AT SALES LEVEL (3)

Annual Sales Level - Range	Traditional[1]			Non-Traditional[2]		
	Consolidated	Company	Franchise	Consolidated	Company	Franchise
Above $1.5M	27%	23%	27%	36%	0%	36%
$1.3M – $1.5M	19%	28%	19%	10%	0%	10%
$1.1M – $1.3M	22%	22%	22%	10%	0%	10%

$0.9M – $1.1M	19%	23%	19%	17%	0%	17%
$0.7M – $0.9M	10%	4%	10%	12%	0%	12%
Below $0.7M	3%	0%	3%	16%	0%	16%
Total Restaurant Sample	6,545	51	6,494	505	0	505
Mean Average Sales	1,191,704.94	1,303,199.25	1,190,829.33	1,051,041.46		1,051,041.46
Median Average Sales	1,145,651.34	1,271,730.28	1,145,255.38	904,424.43		904,424.43
High Annual Sales		2,684,437.08	4,817,256.90			4,817,256.90
Low Annual Sales		792,158.45	361,675.81			232,861.43

The sales levels, sales ranges and median sales shown above reflect the experience of certain franchised and BKC-operated Restaurants and should not be considered as the actual or potential sales that you will realize. BKC does not represent that you can expect to attain any particular sales level.

Notes:

(1) The information provided in this Sales Distribution is sales information for a total of 6,545 Restaurants treated as "Traditional" Restaurants for purposes of this Item. Of those Restaurants, 6,494 were Franchisee-owned and 51 were BKC-owned as of December 31,2013. Only those Restaurants with 12 months of actual sales as of December 31, 2013 are reported in this chart.

(2) The information provided in this Sales Distribution is sales information for a total of 505 Restaurants treated as "Non-Traditional" Restaurants for purposes of this Item. Of those Restaurants, 505 were operated by Franchisees and 0 were operated by BKC as of December 31,2013. Only those Restaurants with 12 months of actual sales as of December 31, 2013 are reported in this chart.

(3) Due to rounding percentages may not equal 100%.

(4) Figures do not include "Temporarily Closed" restaurants.

Remodels: Comparison

Our 20/20 Image was widely implemented in 2011. A total of 535 BURGER KING Restaurants, with an estimated CAPEX remodel expenditure of $250,000 or more, were remodeled in the United States to the 20/20 Image Standards between January 2011 and June 30, 2013 (the "20/20 Remodel Restaurants"). We reviewed the sales of these 20/20 Remodel Restaurants for a period of no less than 6 months and no more than 12 months after the 20/20 remodel was completed (the "Post-Period") and the same period of 6-12 months immediately before the completion of the 20/20 remodel (the "Pre-Period"). We then compared the actual sales of each of these 20/20 Remodel Restaurants against a specific group of Burger King restaurants in the same region of the country. This "control group" was made up of 40-60 other Burger King restaurants in the region that had similar seasonality and sales trends as the 20/20 Remodel Restaurant (the "Control Restaurants"). The 20/20 Remodel Restaurants with a low cost remodel* experienced an average sales increase from the Pre-Period to the Post-Period of 9.5% above the average increase or decrease in sales for the Control Restaurants during these periods. 237 of the 20/20 Remodel Restaurants were low cost remodels, of which 104 had a sales increase that was 9.5% or more than the results of the Control Restaurants. The 20/20 Remodel Restaurants with the 20/20 standard remodel experienced an average sales increase from the Pre-Period to the Post-Period of 10.6% above the average increase or decrease in sales for the Control Restaurants. 126 of these 20/20 Remodel Restaurants were standard remodels, of which 49 had a sales increase of 10.6% or more than the results of the Control Restaurants. The 20/20 Remodel Restaurants with the 20/20 enhanced remodel experienced an average sales increase from the Pre-Period to the Post-Period of 14.0% above the average increase or decrease in sales for the Control Restaurants. 172 of these 20/20 Remodel Restaurants were enhanced remodels, of which 81 had a sales increase of 14.0% or more than the results of the Control Restaurants.

* We look at remodels in terms of scope, not necessarily CAPEX expenditure, due to large variables across the US. As such, we identifY remodels as low cost, meaning lower in scope, standard, meaning average in scope, and enhanced, meaning greater in scope.

Exhibit 19-3

CERTAIN REPRESENTATIVE COST FACTORS FOR BKC-OPERATED TRADITIONAL RESTAURANTS

JANUARY 1, 2013 – DECEMBER 31, 2013

Type of Expense/Cost[1]	Avg Cost	Variable Cost as % of Gross Sales
Food Cost	$468,937	31.9%
Labor Including Fringe Benefits[2]	$422,012	28.7%
Repair & Maintenance (Building & Equipment)[3]	$25,302	1.7%
Utilities[4]	$72,134	4.9%
Other Expenses[5]	$59,218	4.0%
Insurance	$6,782	0.5%
Property Taxes	$34,462	2.3%
Royalty	N/A	N/A
Advertising	$65,206	4.4%

BASIS OF PRESENTATION

The financial information provided in this Cost Factor table is based upon an analysis of certain actual operating costs for the 12-month period beginning January 1, 2013 and ending December 31, 2013, experienced by 51 "Traditional Restaurants" that were open and operated by BKC for those 12 months. Restaurants sold or acquired by BKC during that time period and Restaurants that were closed for any time during that period are not included in the sample on which the analysis was performed.

Dollar amounts are given in the "Avg Cost" column for and variable costs are shown as a representative percentage of gross sales. Certain expense items for which information is provided have both an average cost and variable cost component as reflected by the analysis.

THESE COST FACTORS ARE BASED UPON THE EXPERIENCE OF BKC-OPERATED TRADITIONAL RESTAURANTS AND SHOULD NOT BE CONSIDERED AS THE ACTUAL OR POTENTIAL COSTS THAT YOU OR ANY FRANCHISEE WILL INCUR FOR THESE TYPES OF EXPENSES.

EXPLANATORY NOTES

1. These are not the only costs or expenses of operating a BURGER KING Restaurant. Other types of expenses that you will incur include, rent or other occupancy expense (including property taxes); insurance expense; legal and accounting expense; miscellaneous expenses such as operating supplies, uniforms, cleaning expense, laundry and linens, cash shortages, non-capital parts and supplies; non-cash expenses including depreciation and amortization; income taxes; advertising expense; and royalties. As discussed in Item 6 of this Disclosure Document, a Franchisee must pay BKC an advertising contribution based on gross sales, and may incur other advertising expenses, including investment spending contributions. Additional advertising expenditures typically range from 0.5% to 2.0% of gross sales in addition to the required advertising fund contribution. Item 6 of this Disclosure Document also discusses the royalty payable to BKC by Franchisees. In developing your projections, you should make appropriate allowances for these and other expenses.

2. Labor and Fringe Benefits: This item includes wages and fringe benefits for salaried Restaurant managers and hourly workers. Labor expense is affected by staffing levels and the level of fringe benefits provided to employees, and by labor market conditions in the areas of the Restaurants and by mandated minimum wage levels. It does not include wages and fringe benefits for non-restaurant personnel. Franchisees who elect to provide more limited fringe benefits to employees and who are more conservative in staffing levels may experience lower costs. Franchisees operating in areas with tighter labor markets may experience higher costs.

3. Repair & Maintenance: The cost of repairs and maintenance of the Restaurant building and equipment can vary with the age and condition of the building. This does not include costs of improvements or remodeling that may be required from time to time.

4. Utilities: This includes telephone, broadband services, water, gas, electricity and hauling of waste. These costs vary depending upon the region, area and/or government jurisdictions in which the Restaurant is located.

5. Other Expenses: This includes controllables, taxes and licensing fees, as well as pas related items. These costs vary depending upon the region, area and/or government jurisdictions in which the Restaurant is located.

Checkers BURGERS • FRIES • COLAS

CHECKERS DRIVE-IN RESTAURANT

4300 W. Cypress St., # 600
Tampa, FL 33607
Tel: (888) 913-9135, (813) 283-7069
Fax: (813) 936-6201
Email: mercksont@checkers.com
Website: www.checkersfranchise.com
Tena Merckson, Franchise Administration Manager

Quick-service, fast-food restaurant (double drive-thru). Total below reflect ownership of both CHECKERS and RALLY's brands.

BACKGROUND
IFA Member:	Yes
Established & First Franchised:	1986; 1991
Franchised Units:	455
Company-Owned Units:	322
Total Units:	777
Distribution:	US – 776; CAN – 0; O'seas – 1
North America:	40 States, 0 Provinces
Density:	85 in GA, 191 in FL, 32 in AL
Projected New Units (12 Months):	35

Qualifications:	5, 4, 5, 4, 4, 4

FINANCIAL/TERMS
Cash Investment:	N/A
Total Investment:	$453 – 627K
Minimum Net Worth:	$750K
Fees (Franchise):	$30K
Fees (Royalty):	4%
Fees (Advertising):	3 – 5%
Term of Contract (Years):	20/Agrmt.
Average Number of Employees:	4 FT, 20 PT
Passive Ownership:	Discouraged
Encourage Conversions:	Yes
Area Development Agreements:	Yes
Sub-Franchising Contracts:	No
Expand in Territory:	Yes
Space Needs:	15,000 – 25,000 SF

SUPPORT & TRAINING
Financial Assistance Provided:	No
Site Selection Assistance:	Yes
Lease Negotiation Assistance:	N/A
Co-operative Advertising:	Yes
Franchisee Association/Member:	Yes/Member
Size of Corporate Staff:	N/A
On-going Support:	A, B, C, D, E, F, G, H, I
Training:	5 Weeks FL

SPECIFIC EXPANSION PLANS
US:	All United States
Canada:	All Canada
Overseas:	All Countries

Statements of Average Net Sales of Checkers Restaurants

TABLE A

ALL RESTAURANTS

Category of Restaurant	Average Net Sales 2013 Fiscal Year	Number of Restaurants	% Attaining or Exceeding Average
Company-Owned	$1,007,834	171	69 or 40%
Franchised	$963,197	282	133 or 47%
Company-Owned and Franchised	$975,776	453	202 or 45%

TABLE B

TOP 25% OF RESTAURANTS

Category of Restaurant	Average Net Sales 2013 Fiscal Year	Number of Restaurants	% Attaining of Exceeding Average

Company-Owned	$1,322,825	43	16 or 37%
Franchised	$1,383,840	79	28 or 35%
Company-Owned and Franchised	$1,356,315	122	44 or 36%

TABLE C

FIRST YEAR OF OPERATIONS FOR NEW RESTAURANTS

Category of Restaurant	Average Net Sales 2013 Fiscal Year	Number of Restaurants	% Attaining or Exceeding Average
Company-Owned	$1,124,621	1	1 or 100%
Franchised	$1,021,578	31	14 or 45%
Company-Owned and Franchised	$1,024,798	32	15 or 47%

Not all Checkers Restaurants have sold these amounts. Your individual results may differ. There is no assurance that you will do as well. A new franchisee's financial results are likely to differ from the results stated in the financial performance representation.

Table A comprises Average Net Sales information for the 171 company-owned Checkers Restaurants, the 282 franchised Checkers Restaurants and the 453 Checkers Restaurants (company-owned and franchised combined) that were open and operating during the entire 52-week period ending December 30, 2013 (the "2013 Fiscal Year"). Table A does not include the Average Net Sales for the 5 company-owned Checkers Restaurants and the 51 franchised Checkers Restaurants that were not open and operating during the entire 2013 Fiscal Year.

Table B comprises Average Net Sales information for the 43 company-owned Checkers Restaurants comprising the top 25% of the 171 company-owned Checkers Restaurants, the 79 franchised Checkers Restaurants comprising the top 25% of the 282 franchised Checkers Restaurants and the 122 Checkers Restaurants comprising the top 25% of the 453 Checkers Restaurants (company-owned and franchised combined) that were open and operating during the entire 2013 Fiscal Year.

Table C comprises Average Net Sales information during the first 52-week period of operations for the 1 company-owned Checkers Restaurant, the 31 franchised Checkers Restaurants and the 32 Checkers Restaurants (company-owned and franchised combined) that opened on or after January 1, 2011. Table C does not include the Average Net Sales for the 4 company-owned Checkers Restaurants and the 22 franchised Checkers Restaurants that were open and operating during the 2013 Fiscal Year, but opened after March 1, 2013.

For purposes of this Item 19, "Average Net Sales" means the mean average of reported Net Sales. The Net Sales figures for franchised Checkers Restaurants were derived from unaudited financial reports submitted by franchisees for the purpose of computing royalties. We compiled the Net Sales figures for company-owned Checkers Restaurants on the basis of generally accepted accounting principles, consistently applied.

Statement of Operating Margin Before Occupancy Cost (Company-Owned)

	Company-Owned Restaurants	% of Net Sales	Top 25% of Company-Owned Restaurants	% of Net Sales	New Free-standing Restaurant (Mobile, AL Location 6287)	% of Net Sales
Net Sales	$1,007,834	100.0%	$1,322,825	100.0%	$1,173,103	100.0%
Food & Paper Costs (1)	$328,120	32.6%	$426,708	32.3%	$414,522	35.3%
Labor and Benefit Costs (2)	$312,766	31.0%	$360,684	27.3%	$325,966	27.8%
Gross Margin	$366,948	36.4%	$535,433	40.5%	$432,615	36.9%

Total Operating Costs (3)	$170,952	17.0%	$190,779	14.4%	$152,073	13.0%
Operating Margin Before Occupancy and Royalty Costs (4)	$195,996	19.4%	$344,654	26.1%	$280,542	23.9%
Royalty Costs (5)	$40,313	4.0%	$52,913	4.0%	$46,924	4.0%
Operating Margin Before Occupancy Costs (4) (6)	$155,682	15.4%	$291,741	22.1%	$233,618	19.9%

(1) Food, paper, and packaging costs, less supplier rebates

(2) Wages, bonuses, payroll taxes, workers compensation, medical insurance, and other benefits

(3) Operating costs include marketing expenditures (NPF contributions, regional cooperative contributions, and restaurant-specific promotions), utility costs (electricity, gas, water, and sewer), and other routine expenses (maintenance and repairs, supplies, bank charges, uniforms, and other services)

(4) Operating margin excludes multi-unit supervision costs typically charged against restaurant costs for company-owned Checkers Restaurants

(5) Royalty costs are not incurred by company-owned Checkers Restaurants, but are included to present theoretical franchise costs

(6) Occupancy costs are excluded because of the significant variations due to local market factors.

Not all Checkers Restaurants have achieved these amounts. Your individual results may differ. There is no assurance that you will do as well. A new franchisee's financial results are likely to differ from the results stated in the financial performance representation.

The Statement of Operating Margin Before Occupancy Costs for the average Checkers Restaurant consists of the Average Net Sales and various categories of costs of the 171 company-owned Checkers Restaurants that were open and operating during the entire 2013 Fiscal Year. (It excludes the results of 5 company-owned Checkers Restaurants that were not open and operating during the entire 2013 Fiscal Year). Of the 171 companyowned Checkers Restaurants used for calculating the Operating Margin Before Occupancy and Royalty Costs, 70 or 41% attained or surpassed the stated amount of $195,996.

The Statement of Operating Margin Before Occupancy Costs for the Top 25% Checkers Restaurants consists of the Average Net Sales and various categories of costs of the 43 company-owned Checkers Restaurants comprising the top 25% of the 171 companyowned Checkers Restaurants that were open and operating during the entire 2013 Fiscal Year. (It excludes the results of 5 company-owned Checkers Restaurants that were not open and operating during the entire 2013 Fiscal Year). Of the 43 company-owned Checkers Restaurants used for calculating the Operating Margin Before Occupancy and Royalty Costs for the Top 25%, 16 or 37% attained or surpassed the stated amount of $344,654.

The Statement of Operating Margin Before Occupancy Costs for the New Freestanding Design Checkers Restaurant consists of the reported Net Sales and various categories of costs for Checkers Restaurant Number 6287 located in Mobile, Alabama. Checkers Restaurant Number 6287 is the only New Freestanding Design Checkers Restaurant that was open and operating during the entire 2013 Fiscal Year. 33 or 19% of the 171 company-owned Checkers Restaurants that were open and operating during the entire 2013 Fiscal Year attained or surpassed the stated amount of $280,542 for the Operating Margin Before Occupancy and Royalty Costs for Checkers Restaurant Number 6287.

Average Return on Investment of Checkers Company-Owned Restaurant

The following table comprises the average return on investment for the 1 company-owned Checkers Restaurant (identified in Table C) that opened after January 1, 2011. Average return on investment is a measure of the restaurant's operating margin before occupancy costs (see notes (4) and (6) in the table immediately above) during the first 52-week period of operations, including an assumed royalty rate divided by total investment not including real estate or site development costs. The below table does not include the average return on investment for the 4 company-owned Checkers Restaurants that were open and operating during the 2013 Fiscal Year, but opened after March 1, 2013.

Category of Restaurant	Average Net Sales During First 52-week Period of Operations	Average Total Cost	Average Return on Investment	% Attaining or Exceeding Average
Company-Owned	$1,124,621	$474,500	52.4%	1 or 100%

Checkers Restaurants Average Sales to Invetment Ratio

The following table comprises the average sales to investment ratio for the Checkers Restaurants (company-owned and franchised combined) that were open and operating during the entire 2013 Fiscal Year. Sales to investment ratio is a measure of the Average Net Sales information divided by the Average Total Cost information. The Average Net Sales information is for the first 52-week period of operations for the 32 Checkers Restaurants (company-owned and franchised combined) that opened on or after January 1, 2011. The Total Cost information is derived from a combination of the 55 Checkers Restaurants and Rally's Restaurants that opened after January 1, 2011, but before December 31, 2013. The below table does not include the average sales to investment ratio for the 4 company-owned Checkers Restaurants and the 22 franchised Checkers Restaurants that were open and operating during the 2013 Fiscal Year, but opened after March 1, 2013.

Category of Restaurant	Average Net Sales During First 52-week Period of Operations	Average Total Cost	Average Sales to Investment Ratio	% Attaining or Exceeding Average
Company-Owned and Franchised	$1,024,798	$409,611	2.5x	33 or 60%

Checkers Restaurants Same Store Sales

The following charts disclose company-owned, franchised and network-wide samestore-sales information for our fiscal years ending January 2, 2012 for 2011, December 31, 2012 for 2012 and December 30, 2013 for 2013. The same-store-sales information is derived from Checkers Restaurants that were open at least 18 fiscal periods prior to the beginning of the first fiscal year of the comparison and that operated continuously during all 3 fiscal years. We exclude from the calculations any sales comparison for days when a restaurant was temporarily closed during any of the fiscal years of the comparison. Same-store-sales is a measure of percentage increase (or decrease) of the revenues reported over one fiscal year to the previous fiscal year.

Category	FY 2011	# of Restaurants	FY 2012	# of Restaurants	FY 2013	# of Restaurants
Company-Owned	5.9%	179	5.5%	173	3.4%	172
Franchised	-.02%	301	3.7%	299	0.8%	302
System	2.2%	480	4.4%	472	1.8%	474

Not all Checkers Restaurants have achieved these amounts. Your individual results may differ. There is no assurance that you will do as well. A new franchisee's financial results are likely to differ from the results stated in the financial performance representation.

GENERAL

These results are based on the performance of specific Checkers Restaurants and should not be considered as the actual or probable results that you will realize. We do not represent that you can expect to attain these financial results. Your own financial results are likely to differ from these results. If you are purchasing the assets of existing companyowned restaurants, you should not rely on these results, but should instead review the actual financial results of the restaurants being purchased.

Written substantiation for the above financial performance representations will be made available to the prospective franchisee upon reasonable request. However, we will not disclose the identity or sales data of any particular Checkers Restaurant without the consent of that owner, except to any applicable state registration authorities or except in connection with the sale of a particular existing Checkers Restaurants that we own.

Other than the preceding financial performance representations, we do not make any financial performance representations. We also do not authorize our employees or representatives to make any such representations either orally or in writing. If you are purchasing an existing outlet, however, we may provide you with the actual records of that outlet. If you receive any other financial performance information or projections of your future income, you should report it to the franchisor's management by contacting Vincent C. Brockman at 4300 West Cypress Street, Suite 600, Tampa, Florida 33607 or at (813) 283-7000, the Federal Trade Commission, and the appropriate state regulatory agencies.

CHURCH'S CHICKEN

980 Hammond Dr., Bldg. # 2, # 1100
Atlanta, GA 30328
Tel: (800) 639-3495, (770) 350-3876
Fax: (770) 512-3924
Email: jfraser@churchs.com
Website: www.churchsfranchise.com
Jodi Fraser, Franchise Sales Manager

Founded in San Antonio, Texas, in 1952, Church's Chicken is a highly recognized brand name in the Quick Service Restaurant sector and is one of the largest quick service chicken concepts in the world. Church's serves up a rich tradition of gracious Southern hospitality and freshly prepared, high quality, authentic Southern-style fare, to help people provide affordable, complete meals for their families. Church's menu includes flavorful chicken both Original and Spicy, Tender Strips™ and chicken sandwiches with classic sides and handmade from scratch honey butter biscuits. The Church's system consists of more than 1,675 locations in 24 countries. For more information on Church's Chicken, visit www.churchs.com.

BACKGROUND

IFA Member:	Yes
Established & First Franchised:	1952; 1967
Franchised Units:	1,417
Company-Owned Units:	258
Total Units:	1,675

Distribution:	US – 1,321; CAN – 16; O'seas – 338
North America:	29 States, 2 Provinces
Density:	490 in TX, 86 in GA, 75 in CA
Projected New Units (12 Months):	120
Qualifications:	5, 5, 5, 3, 4, 5

FINANCIAL/TERMS

Cash Investment:	$650K
Total Investment:	$424.3 – 1,251.6K
Minimum Net Worth:	$1.5M
Fees (Franchise):	$25K
Fees (Royalty):	5%
Fees (Advertising):	5%
Term of Contract (Years):	20/10
Average Number of Employees:	15 FT, 6 PT
Passive Ownership:	Not Allowed
Encourage Conversions:	Yes
Area Development Agreements:	Yes
Sub-Franchising Contracts:	No
Expand in Territory:	Yes
Space Needs:	850 – 2,200 SF

SUPPORT & TRAINING

Financial Assistance Provided:	No
Site Selection Assistance:	Yes
Lease Negotiation Assistance:	No
Co-operative Advertising:	Yes
Franchisee Association/Member:	Yes/Member
Size of Corporate Staff:	163
On-going Support:	C, D, E, G, H, I
Training:	5 Weeks Regional

SPECIFIC EXPANSION PLANS

US:	All United States
Canada:	Selected provinces
Overseas:	ME, Mex, Brazil, Ecuador, Peru, Colombia, Panama, Carib., N. Africa, China, Thailand, E. Europe, AUS

The first six tables that follow present information about the actual sales of domestic Church's restaurants in our 2013 fiscal year.

Table 1: 2013 Sales by Asset Type (Franchised Restaurants)

Below are average franchised restaurant sales for fiscal year 2013 by type of Church's Restaurant. Thirteen (13) franchised Church's Restaurants that were not in operation for at least 26 weeks during fiscal year 2013 were excluded. We included thirteen (13) franchised Church's Restaurants that were not in operation the full year but were open more than 26 weeks, and we annualized their sales numbers. Seven (7) franchised Church's Restaurants that have closed in 2014 are also excluded. The table includes only franchised restaurants in the continental United States, and does not include 117 franchised restaurants located in Puerto Rico. This sales data was compiled from the information submitted to us by our franchisees for purposes of royalty reporting. We believe the information submitted by our franchisees to be accurate, but we have not audited or otherwise verified that information.

2013 Annual Sales	Free Standing With Drive Thru Tower Image	Free Standing With Drive Thru All Other Images	Free Standing Without Drive Thru	In-Line	C-Store	Co-branded	Other
Franchised Restaurant Average	$787,720	$730,979	$700,418	$537,726	$579,327	$231,317	$527,684
Franchised Restaurant Count	37	589	81	46	135	21	16
No. of Franchised Restaurants at or Above Franchised Restaurant Average	18	270	35	20	52	10	7
% of Franchised Restaurants at or above Franchised Restaurant Average	48.6%	45.8%	43.2%	43.5%	38.5%	47.6%	43.8%
Franchised Restaurant Average – Top Quartile	$966,720	$851,101	$809,150	$663,281	$686,800	$279,128	$621,773
Franchised Restaurant Count – Top Quartile	9	147	20	12	24	5	4
No. of Franchised Restaurants at or above Franchised Restaurant Average – Top Quartile	3	55	7	4	12	2	2
% of Franchised Restaurants at or above Franchised Restaurant Average – Top Quartile	8.1%	9.3%	8.6%	8.7%	8.9%	9.5%	12.5%

Notes To Table 1: 2013 Sales By Asset Type (Franchised Restaurants)

1. "Free-Standing" and "In-Line" restaurants are described in Item 7. "C-Store" means a restaurant attached to or part of a convenience store or travel plaza. "Co-branded" means a restaurant which shares operating space with another branded restaurant or business.

2. The Tower image reflects our 1,850 square foot model is characterized by the use of a flat panel extending above the fascia mounted behind the building signs combined with the Tower color scheme.

Table 2: 2013 Sales by Asset Type (Company Restaurants)

Below are average company-owned restaurant sales for fiscal year 2013 by type of Church's Restaurant. We included six (6) company-owned restaurants that were not in operation the full year but were open more than 26 weeks, and we annualized their sales numbers. One (1) company-owned restaurant that closed in 2014 is excluded. All company-owned Church's Restaurants in Table 2 are currently operated by our wholly-owned subsidiary, Cajun Restaurants. This sales data was com-piled from Cajun Operating's unaudited income statement for fiscal year 2013, which is the data underlying our audited financial statements.

2013 Annual Sales	Free Standing With Drive Thru Tower Image	Free Standing with Drive Thru All Other Images	Free Standing Without Drive Thru	In-Line	C-Store	Other
Company Owned Restaurant Average	$978,885	$853,293	$697,096	$588,524	$676,257	$410,943
Company Owned Restaurant Count	29	193	29	3	2	1
No. of Company Owned Restaurants at or above Company Owned Restaurant Average	14	87	13	N/A	N/A	
% of Company Owned Restaurnts at or above Company Owned Restaurant Average	48.3%	45.1%	44.8%	N/A		
Company-Owned Restaurant Average – Top Quartile	$1,095,460	$1,005,453	$770,730	$588,534	$770,433	$410,943
Company Owned Restaurant Count – Top Quartile	7	48	7	1	1	1
No. of Company Owned Restaurants at or above Company Owned Restaurant Average – Top Quartile	3	17	3	1	1	1
% of Company Owned Restaurants at or above Company Owned Restaurant Average – Top Quartile	10.3%	8.8%	10.3%	33.3%	50.0%	100.0%

Table 3: 2013 System-wide Sales by Asset Type (Company and Franchised Restaurants)

Below are system-wide average restaurant sales for fiscal year 2013 by type of Church's Restaurant. This table combines the information from Table 1 and Table 2. Please see those Tables for information on excluded stores.

2013 Annual Sales	Free Standing With Drive Thru Tower Image	Free Standing with Drive Thru All Other Images	Free Standing Without Drive Thru	In-Line	C-Store	Co-branded	Other
System-wide Restaurant Average	$871,717	$761,166	$699,542	$540,836	$580,742	$231,317	$520,817
System-wide Restaurant Count	66	782	110	49	137	22	16
No. of System-wide Restaurants at or above System-wide Restaurant Average	31	346	48	21	52	10	7

% of System-wide Restaurants at or above System-wide Restaurant Average	47.0%	44.2%	43.6%	42.9%	38.0%	45.5%	43.8%
System-wide Restaurant Average – Top Quartile	$1,023,583	$886,710	$796,112	$666,444	$686,808	$279,128	$616,010
System-wide Restaurant Count – Top Quartile	17	196	28	12	34	5	4
No. of System-wide Restaurants at or above System-wide Restaurant Average – Top Quartile	5	70	10	5	12	2	2
% of System-wide Restaurants at or above System-wide Restaurant Average – Top Quartile	7.6%	9.0%	9.1%	10.2%	8.8%	9.1%	12.5%

Table 4: 2013 Income Statement Summary (Franchised Restaurants Only)

Below is a summary based on reports submitted by our franchisees for fiscal year 2013 for 34 free-standing "Tower" model franchised restaurants. Table 3 excludes data related to 3 free-standing "Tower" model franchised restaurants for which we did not receive sufficient profit and loss information from the franchisee. The following income statement data was compiled from the unaudited profit and loss statements submitted to us quarterly by franchisees, as required by Section 4.B of the Franchise Agreement. We have not audited or verified this information and therefore cannot attest to its accuracy.

	Tower Image
Sales	100.0%
Food Cost	34.9%
Labor	26.8%
Gross Profit Margin	38.3%
Controllables	10.0%
Marketing	5.0%
Royalty	5.0%
Controllable Profit Margin	18.3%
Non-Controllables	2.2%
Restaurant Operating Profit, pre-tax (EBITDAR)	16.1%
Unit Count	34

Table 5: 2013 Income Statement Summary (Company Restaurants Only)

Below is a summary based on Cajun Operating's unaudited income statement for fiscal year 2013 for 28 company-owned free-standing "Tower" model restaurants. The operating costs information reflected in the following table is based on company financial statements (see Notes below).

	Tower Image
Sales	100.0%
Food Cost	34.0%
Labor – Management	5.8%
Labor – Shift Management	3.6%
Labor – Crew	12.0%
Labor – Other	3.5%
Labor – Total	24.8%
Gross Profit Margin	41.1%
Controllables	11.1%
Marketing	5.0%
Royalty	5.0%
Controllable Profit Margin	20.1%
Non-Controllables	2.0%
Restaurant Operating Profit, pre-tax (EBITDAR)	18.1%
Unit Count	29

Table 6: 2013 System-wide Income Statement Summary (Company and Franchised Restaurants)

Below is a system-wide summary that combines the information from Tables 4 and 5. Please see those Tables for the bases of this information.

	Tower Image
Sales	100.0%

Food Cost	34.4%
Labor	25.7%
Gross Profit Margin	39.9%
Controllables	10.6%
Marketing	5.0%
Royalty	5.0%
Controllable Profit Margin	19.3%
Non-Controllables	2.1%
Restaurant Operating Profit, pre-tax (EBITDAR)	17.2%
Unit Count	63

Notes To Table 4, Table 5 and Table 6: 2013 Income Statement Summary

1. Food costs include the delivered cost of food, beverages, paper and promotional items (i.e., limited-time offerings) to the restaurants. Delivered costs include distribution and freight costs. The calculation of food costs is primarily a function of the mix of products sold and the cost of commodities which compromise the products.

2. Labor costs include unit hourly labor, which is comprised of the average hourly rate and the number of hours worked (a direct correlation to sales volume). The cost of labor will vary from location to location and will be dependent upon factors beyond our control, including, without limitation, local minimum wage laws and local labor market conditions. Labor costs also include the salaries of general and assistant managers. Most company-owned restaurants employ one salaried general manager and one salaried assistant manager. The other components of labor expense are: payroll taxes, health insurance, vacation, wages, sick pay, bonuses and workers' compensation insurance. We make no warranties, representations, predictions, promises or guaranties with respect to the actual labor expenses likely to be experienced by individual franchisees. Also, with respect to labor costs, because a certain number of employees will be necessary to open and operate a restaurant irrespective of its Gross Sales, units that have lower than average Gross Sales probably will experience higher than average labor costs.

We do not provide detailed labor costs in Table 5 for franchised restaurants because our franchisees do not use a standard chart of accounts to prepare financial reports that are submitted to us and labor may be booked under different categories in the franchisees' reports.

3. The Marketing fee is described as 5.0% because franchisees are required to pay up to 5% of gross income to the Advertising Fund. [See Item 6 and Item 11.] The percentage of income from company-owned restaurants which is spent on marketing may be higher or lower than 5.0%.

4. The Royalty fee is described as 5.0% because franchisees are required to pay 5% of gross income to Cajun. [See Item 6.] Company-owned restaurants do not pay a royalty fee.

5. Tables 4, 5 and 6 exclude occupancy costs, i.e. rent or mortgage payments.

6. Tables 4, 5 and 6 exclude certain overhead and other expenses which are not classified as "store-level" for internal accounting purposes.

7. "Controllables" refers to miscellaneous store-level costs which are affected by or decided by management, such as the cost of maintenance and repair. "Non-controllables" refers to miscellaneous store-level costs where the owner has no decision-making ability regarding the expenditure, such as the cost of local operating permits.

8. "EBITDAR" is earnings before Interest, Taxes, Depreciation, Amortization and Real Estate.

9. Franchisees will incur other costs in connection with the operation of Church's Restaurants including, without limitation, occupancy costs (such as rent or mortgage payments), utilities, office expenses, legal and accounting expenses, insurance expenses, and various other general administrative expenses. Expenses in the operation of Restaurants will vary from franchisee to franchisee and from location to location, and are dependent upon seasonal, local and other factors beyond our control, such as the franchisee's efficiency in the utilization of products, the costs of transportation and the fluctuation in market prices for food and other products.

Table 7: Sales from Newly Built Star Image Restaurants

Below are the annualized sales at three company restaurants that were built in the new "Star Image" building design. Annualized sales were derived by taking the average sales per week for the first four weeks after the opening date and multiplying by 75% to obtain "stabilized weekly sales" (the average weekly sales we believe sales will stabilize at) and multiply that number by 52 weeks.

Restaurant Address and Restaurant #	Date of Opening	Annualized Sales
731 W Ocean Blvd, Los Fresnos, Texas # 2107	1/20/14	$1,351,012
140 98th Street, Albuquerque, MN # 2109	1/8/14	$1,678,976
6001 Miller Road, Columbus, GA # 2108	2/28/14	$1,748,552

Table 8: Sales Impact at Newly Remodeled Company Restaurants

Below are existing company-operated restaurants taht were recently scraped and rebuilt in the new "Star Image" and the sales impact after the remodel was completed. On average the sales impact was 17.2%[1].

Restaurant Address and #	Remodel Date[2]	Sales Impact[9]
1308 N Texas St, Weslaco, TX # 3060	9/17/2012	+25.7%[3]
205 W Business 83, Weslaco, TX # 197	12/16/2013	+23.9%[4]
921 W. Tyler, Harlingen, TX # 557	5/29/2013	+ 16.2%[5]
1045 W US 83 Frontage Rd, Alamo, TX # 1319	8/17/2013	+8.3%[6]
1104 Ruben M Torres Blvd, Brownsville, TX # 1442	12/17/2012	-3.3%[7]
5407 Central Ave NW, Albuquerque, NM # 695	3/12/2014	+31.4%

Notes to Table 8:

1. That average was determined by calculating the average weekly sales volume for these restaurants for the weeks after the reopening after remodel and comparing them to the same number of weeks prior to the restaurants being closed to complete the remodel. We then removed the highest and lowest sales experienced (restaurant #s 1421 and 695) and averaged the remaining restaurants.

2. Date on which restaurant reopened for business after closing down for remodel.

3. As of April 1, 2014, Restaurant #3060 has been open over one year since undergoing a scrape and rebuild. When comparing the sales in the 52 weeks prior to closure of Restaurant #3060 for the scrape and rebuild to the 52 weeks after it opened after completion of the scrape and rebuild, Restaurant #3060 experienced a sale increase of 25.7%.

4. As of April 1, 2014, Restaurant #197 has only been open 15 weeks since undergoing a scrape and rebuild. When comparing the sales in the 15 weeks prior to closure of Restaurant #197 for the scrape and rebuild to the 15 weeks since it opened after completion of the scrape and rebuild, Restaurant #197 experienced a sale increase of 23.9%.

5. As of April 1, 2014, Restaurant #557 has only been open 43 weeks since undergoing a scrape and rebuild. When com-paring the sales in the 43 weeks prior to closure of Restaurant #557 for the scrape and rebuild to the 43 weeks since it opened after completion of the scrape and rebuild, Restaurant #557 experienced a sale increase of 16.2%.

6. As of April 1, 2014, Restaurant #1319 has only been open 32 weeks since undergoing a scrape and rebuild. When comparing the sales in the 32 weeks prior to closure of Restaurant #1319 for the scrape and rebuild to the 32 weeks since it opened after completion of the scrape and rebuild, Restaurant #1319 experienced a sale increase of 8.3%.

7. As of April 1, 2014, Restaurant #1442 has been open more than a year since undergoing a scrape and rebuild. When comparing the sales in the 52 weeks prior to closure of Restaurant #1442 for the scrape and rebuild to the 52 weeks since it opened after completion of the scrape and rebuild, Restaurant #1442 experienced a sale decrease of 3.3%.

8. As of April 1, 2014, Restaurant #695 has only been open 2 weeks since undergoing a scrape and rebuild. When comparing the sales in the 2 weeks prior to closure of Restaurant #695 for the scrape and rebuild to the 2 weeks since it opened after completion of the scrape and rebuild, Restaurant #695 experienced a sale increase of 31.4%.

9. The table includes all company operated restaurants that have undergone a scrape and rebuild to the new Star Image in the last 24 months. We make no representations that if you

scrape and rebuild any existing restaurant, you will experience the same sales increases.

Written substantiation for these financial performance representations will be made available to prospective franchisees upon reasonable request.

Other than the preceding financial performance representation, we do not make any financial performance representations. We also do not authorize our employees or representatives to make any such representations either orally or in writing. If you are purchasing an existing Restaurant, however, we may provide you with the actual records of that Restaurant.

If you receive any other financial performance information or projections of your future income, you should report it to our management by contacting Craig Prusher, Cajun Global's General Counsel, at 980 Hammond Drive, Suite 1100, Atlanta, GA 30328, or 770-350-3800, the Federal Trade Commission and the appropriate state regulatory agencies.

Your individual financial results are likely to differ from results described in this Item 19. You should conduct an independent investigation of the costs and expenses you will incur in operating your Restaurant. Franchisees or former franchisees identified in this Franchise Disclosure Document may be one source of information.

CICI'S PIZZA

1080 W. Bethel Rd.
Coppell, TX 75019
Tel: (972) 745-9318
Fax: (469) 675-6405
Email: tmccord@cicispizza.com
Website: www.cicispizza.com
Tom McCord, Vice President of Real Estate & Franchise Development

Declared America's Favorite Pizza Chain*, CiCi's Pizza is the nation's largest pizza buffet concept with more than 500 restaurants in 34 states. The leading brand is now baking fresh franchise opportunities in the Southeast and across the country. With no significant direct competitors in the pizza buffet segment, now is the time to invest in CiCi's Pizza. Franchisees benefit from 27 years of brand heritage, a 2-to-1 sales-to-investment ratio and four distinct revenue streams: the custom buffet, catering, to-go orders and a game room. Learn more about CiCi's Pizza financing and incentive programs at cicispizza.com/franchising. (*CiCi's Pizza ranked No. 1 in 2012 Market Force consumer study.)

BACKGROUND

IFA Member:	Yes
Established & First Franchised:	1985; 1988
Franchised Units:	512

Company-Owned Units:	10
Total Units:	522
Distribution:	US – 522; CAN – 0; O'seas – 0
North America:	34 States, 0 Provinces
Projected New Units (12 Months):	50
Qualifications:	5, 4, 1, 1, 3, 5

FINANCIAL/TERMS

Cash Investment:	$250K
Total Investment:	$446 – 715K
Minimum Net Worth:	$750K
Fees (Franchise):	$30K
Fees (Royalty):	4% with Ranges
Fees (Advertising):	3%/$2.3K/Mo.
Term of Contract (Years):	10/1-10
Average Number of Employees:	8 FT, 15 PT
Passive Ownership:	Allowed
Encourage Conversions:	No
Area Development Agreements:	Yes
Sub-Franchising Contracts:	No
Expand in Territory:	Yes
Space Needs:	3,600 – 4,000 SF

SUPPORT & TRAINING

Financial Assistance Provided:	Yes (D)
Site Selection Assistance:	Yes
Lease Negotiation Assistance:	Yes
Co-operative Advertising:	No
Franchisee Association/Member:	No
Size of Corporate Staff:	40
On-going Support:	C, D, E, F, G, H
Training:	8-12 Weeks Dallas, TX

SPECIFIC EXPANSION PLANS

US:	South, Southeast, N. Central, Midwest, S. West
Canada:	Yes
Overseas:	No

CICI'S PIZZA RESTAURANTS

I. ANALYSIS OF AVERAGE SALES AND CERTAIN AVERAGE COSTS AND EXPENSES FOR COMPANY-OWNED CICI'S PIZZA RESTAURANTS

Part I of this Financial Performance Representation analyzes average sales and certain average costs and expenses for company-owned CiCi's Pizza Restaurants. To Go Units are not included.

BASES AND ASSUMPTIONS

The analysis was based on the operating results of the 9 company-owned CiCi's Pizza Restaurants in the Dallas/Ft. Worth, Texas ("DFW") market that were open and operating for at least 18 months before December 29, 2013, and that we operated during the entire period of our fiscal year ended December 29, 2013 ("Sample Restaurants")[1].

These Restaurants offer substantially the same products and services that your Restaurant will offer. Each of the Sample Restaurants used a uniform accounting system, and the data was prepared on a basis consistent with generally accepted accounting principles during the applicable period. The Sample Restaurants averaged 14.9 years in operation. The information has not been audited.

[1] There are a total of 12 company-owned restaurants, 11 in Texas and 1 in Florida. The Florida Restaurant is located outside the DFW market and we intend to sell it. Accordingly, it is excluded from the sample restaurant information in the Financial Performance Representation. For 2013 that Restaurant had sales of $797,363. Also excluded are 2 Restaurants that we acquired from franchisees in 2013.

TABLE 1
Average sales for Sample Restaurants
Fiscal Year 2013 (unaudited)

NO. OF RESTAURANTS	9
RANGE (IN SALES):	
HIGH	$1,452,629
LOW	$758,603
AVERAGE*	$1,076,674

*4 Restaurants (44%) attained or exceeded average sales.

TABLE 2
Average sales, costs, and expenses for the Sample Restaurants
Fiscal Year 2013 (unaudited)[1]

Number of Restaurants	9
AVERAGE SALES* [2]	$1,076,674
AVERAGE COSTS AND EXPENSES	
FOOD AND PAPER	$339,460
GROSS MARGIN[3]	$737,214
Team Labor[4]	$203,448
Management[5]	$92,634
Taxes and Benefits[6]	$43,445
Operating Expenses[7]	$105,691
Advertising[8]	$29,709
Videos/Other Income[9]	($19,969)
CONTROLLABLE PROFIT[10]	$282,256
Occupancy[11]	$95,625

RESTAURANT EBITDA* [12]	$186,631

* 4 Restaurants (44.4%) attained or exceeded average sales, and
4 Restaurants (44.4%) attained or exceeded average Restaurant EBITDA.

Notes to Table 2

(1) Methodology. The arithmetic mean average of gross sales was calculated along with the mean average costs and expenses. Our fiscal year is based on 52 or 53 weeks, rather than the full calendar year, and ends on the last Sunday of the calendar year. The year 2013 ended on December 29, 2013 and was a 52-week year.

(2) Average Sales. The sales figures set forth above represent all food and beverage sales for on-premises and carry-out consumption.

(3) Gross Margin. Gross margin is average sales less the cost of sales, which includes beverage cost, food cost, and cost of paper products. We or JMC negotiate contracts for quantity and price for both beverages and certain food products to take advantage of volume discounts. We purchase a substantial portion of our food products from JMC. This supplier is generally available to franchisees. However, certain items must be purchased locally, like fresh produce. The price of the products you purchase from JMC or other suppliers may vary according to the location of the Restaurant, delivery costs, the amount of mark-up imposed, and other factors, all of which may differ from our historical experience.

(4) Team Labor. Hourly wages (including vacation) for food preparation and service employees. The amount of hourly labor necessary to operate a CiCi's Pizza Restaurant will vary from Restaurant to Restaurant, but should vary consistently with the sales volume of the Restaurant. Hourly wages may vary significantly by geographic location, the supply of and demand on the local labor pool, state and federally mandated minimum wage laws.

(5) Management. Management costs include payroll expenses for 2 to 3 restaurant managers and quarterly bonuses for meeting performance objectives. The number of managers will vary based on sales volume and your requirements may differ from those of a Company-owned Restaurant. We typically require a franchisee (or its Operator) with a single franchised Restaurant to initially operate the Restaurant as General Manager with 1 or 2 Assistant Managers.

(6) Taxes and Benefits. Unemployment taxes, FICA, employee injury insurance or workers compensation where required, and the paid portion of group health benefits and retirement benefits for managers are included in this category. Through economies of scale we may be able to obtain and/or provide those benefits at a cost less than that available to you. Further, benefit costs may vary substantially depending on the geographic location of the Restaurant and the level of benefits (i.e., medical insurance, retirement plans, vacation and non-management bonuses) provided by you.

(7) Operating Expenses. Operating expenses include the cost of utilities, repair, maintenance, smallwares (including dishware, utensils, pans and glasses), laundry and cleaning services and dishwasher supplies. Utilities include electricity, gas, water and telephone costs for the operation of the Restaurant. The pro rata share of common area utility costs are included under rent and lease payments. These costs are subject to local market conditions and may vary depending on the geographic location of the Restaurant.

(8) Advertising. The advertising includes cost of marketing the CiCi's brand and System.

(9) Videos/Other Income. This figure represents the company's portion of the revenue earned from video games, rack machines ($0.50 for stickers, toys, etc.) and other amusement equipment. We do not own any of this equipment and provide space in return for a percentage of the income.

(10) Controllable Profit. This is the net profit that is controlled by restaurant management.

(11) Occupancy. Occupancy costs include rent and lease costs, common area maintenance expenses, tax and insurance paid to the landlord, our property and casualty insurance and property taxes. Rent and lease costs include the base rent and percentage rent. Common area maintenance costs typically include franchisee's pro rata charges for parking lot maintenance, lighting, real estate taxes, tenant improvement allowance credits, taxes on the common areas and costs of maintaining the common areas. Rental costs will vary as a result of space requirements and local market conditions. Other occupancy costs include personal property taxes, other real estate taxes not included in rent and lease and other operating licenses required by state and local agencies. You should investigate occupancy costs in the area in which you plan to locate a CiCi's Pizza Restaurant.

(12) Restaurant EBITDA. Restaurant EBITDA is earnings before interest, taxes, depreciation and amortization.

Sales realized and costs and expenses incurred will vary from Restaurant to Restaurant. The sales, costs and expenses of your Restaurant will be directly affected by many factors, such as the Restaurant's size; geographic location; and competition in the marketplace; the presence of other CiCi's Pizza Restaurants; the quality of management and service at the Restaurant; contractual relationships with lessors and vendors; the extent to which you finance the construction and operation of the Restaurant; your legal, accounting, real estate and other professional fees; federal, state and local income, or other taxes; discretionary expenditures; accounting methods used and certain benefits and economies of scale that we may derive as a result of operating Restaurants on a consolidated basis.

Part I of this Financial Performance Representation does not include any estimates of the federal income tax that would be payable on the net income from a Restaurant or state or local net income or gross profits taxes that may be applicable to the particular jurisdiction in which a Restaurant is located. Each franchisee should consult with its tax adviser regarding the impact that federal, state and local taxes will have on the amounts shown.

Certain fees which you must pay to us under the Franchise Agreement (see Items 5 and 6), and other differences between the expenses of a franchised Restaurant and a company-owned Restaurant are not reflected in the table. These include initial franchise fees, ongoing royalties and any interest expense you would incur if you finance any of the initial investment for the Restaurant. Therefore, you should use this information only as a reference to conduct your own analysis.

Governmental regulations, such as national menu labeling standards under the Patient Protection and Affordable Care Act, imposed or removed as a result of the current economic environment, may have an effect on costs associated with opening a CiCi's Pizza Restaurant or CiCi's To Go Unit. Each franchisee should do their best to familiarize themselves with governmental action(s) that could affect them.

This analysis is based on certain historical data of the Sample Restaurants and should not be considered to be a projection of the actual or potential sales, costs, income or profits that you will realize. The individual financial results of any franchised Restaurant are likely to differ from the information described above, and your success will depend largely on your ability.

II. SYSTEMWIDE GROSS SALES

Part II of this Financial Performance Representation analyzes average system-wide Restaurant sales. To Go Units are not included.

BASES AND ASSUMPTIONS

The sales numbers reported below are based on the reported sales of the 454 company-owned and franchised CiCi's Pizza Restaurants open and operating for at least 18 months before December 29, 2013 and in operation during the entire period of our fiscal year ended December 29, 2013. Of the 454 Restaurants, 442 are franchised and 12 are Company-owned at fiscal year-end.

We compiled these figures from the individual Restaurants' actual reported gross sales. We have not audited or otherwise verified the information. The franchised Restaurants are substantially similar to the company-owned Restaurants. Our 2013 fiscal year was a 52-week year.

The average gross sales of the 454 CiCi's Pizza Restaurants for the fiscal year ended December 29, 2013 was $913,150. The highest sales level of any of the 454 Restaurants was $2,101,981, and the lowest was $417,590.

The 454 Restaurants were divided into 3 categories. The High category represents annual gross sales in excess of $1,000,000; the Medium category represents annual gross sales ranging between $700,000 and $1,000,000; and the Low category represents annual gross sales below $700,000. The ranges of sales and averages within the High, Medium, and Low categories are listed below:

VOLUME	HIGH	MEDIUM	LOW	OVERALL AVG.
NO. OF UNITS	143 (31.5%)	221 (48.7%)	90 (19.8%)	454 (100%)
RANGE (IN SALES)				
HIGH	$2,101,981	$999,809	$699,611	-
LOW	$1,001,912	$700,148	$417,590	-
AVERAGE*	$1,211,462	$842,754	$612,026	$913,150

* 59 (41.3%) of the Restaurants in the High category attained or exceeded High category average sales; 118 (53.4%) of the Restaurants in the Medium category attained or exceeded Medium category average sales; 60 (66.7%) of the Restaurants in the Low category attained or exceeded Low category average sales; 194 (42.7%) of total Restaurants included attained or exceeded overall average sales.

Data from these Restaurants should not be considered as predictive of the average or probable sales that should or would be realized by you. We do not represent that you can expect to attain similar results.

Sales of your Restaurant will be directly affected by a number of factors, like the brand recognition of CiCi's Pizza Restaurants in the market, competition in the market, the quality of management and service at the Restaurant, your pricing decisions and other factors.

Some Restaurants have sold this amount. Your individual results may differ. There is no assurance that you'll sell as much.

We have written substantiation in our possession to support the information appearing in this Item 19 and such substan-

tiation will be made available to you on reasonable request.

Other than the preceding Financial Performance Representation, CiCi Enterprises, LP does not make any financial performance representations. We also do not authorize our employees or representatives to make any such representations either orally or in writing. If you are purchasing an existing outlet, however, we may provide you with the actual records of that outlet. If you receive any other financial performance information or projections of your future income, you should report it to the franchisor's management by contacting Rebecca Minor, 1080 W. Bethel Road, Coppell, Texas 75019, (972) 745-4200, the Federal Trade Commission, and the appropriate state regulatory agencies.

DENNY'S

203 E. Main St.
Spartanburg, SC 29319
Tel: (800) 304-0222, (770) 777-0796
Fax: (864) 597-7708
Email: dwong@dennys.com
Website: www.dennysfranchising.com
Doug Wong, Senior Director of Franchise Recruiting

For over 60 years, Denny's has been the trusted leader in family dining. Today, Denny's is a true icon, with brand awareness of almost 100%. Having grown to almost 1,700 restaurants and system-wide sales of over $2.5 billion, Denny's is one of the largest and most recognized full-service family restaurant chains in the United States. We rank in the top 100 Chains in Food Service Sales in Nation's Restaurant News, Bond's Top 100 Franchises and are ranked #1 in category by Entrepreneur Magazine's Franchise 500. If you are an experienced restaurateur or businessman, we invite you to contact us and learn more about growth opportunities within our great brand.

BACKGROUND

IFA Member:	Yes
Established & First Franchised:	1953; 1963
Franchised Units:	1,532
Company-Owned Units:	160
Total Units:	1,692
Distribution:	US – 1,589; CAN – 65; O'seas – 38

North America:	50 States, 5 Provinces
Density:	345 in CA, 174 in TX, 127 in FL
Projected New Units (12 Months):	40
Qualifications:	5, 5, 5, 3, 1, 5

FINANCIAL/TERMS

Cash Investment:	$350 – 400K
Total Investment:	$1.178 – 2.621MM
Minimum Net Worth:	$1M
Fees (Franchise):	$40K
Fees (Royalty):	4.5%
Fees (Advertising):	3%
Term of Contract (Years):	20/10 or 20
Average Number of Employees:	50 FT, 25 PT
Passive Ownership:	Discouraged
Encourage Conversions:	Yes
Area Development Agreements:	Yes
Sub-Franchising Contracts:	No
Expand in Territory:	Yes
Space Needs:	4,550 SF

SUPPORT & TRAINING

Financial Assistance Provided:	Yes (I)
Site Selection Assistance:	Yes
Lease Negotiation Assistance:	Yes
Co-operative Advertising:	Yes
Franchisee Association/Member:	Yes/Member
Size of Corporate Staff:	250
On-going Support:	C, D, e, G, H, I
Training:	10 – 13 weeks at the nearest certified training restaurant

SPECIFIC EXPANSION PLANS

US:	All United States
Canada:	All Canada
Overseas:	India, China, UK, Carib, C. Amer, Indo

The following financial schedule contains information relating to the performance of Denny's restaurants. The information is provided for the purpose of helping you evaluate the potential earnings capability of the Restaurant. The information presented does not represent the actual performance of any single resaurant. The notes following the schedule attempt to explain the information and provide the underlying assumptions.

THE NET SALES, GROSS PROFITS, AND EBITDA ARE A COMPILATION OF THE RESULTS OF INDIVIDUAL DENNY'S RESATURANTS, AND SHOULD NOT BE CONSIDERED AS THE ACTUAL OR PROBABLE NET SALES, GROSS PROFITS, OR EBITDA THAT YOU WILL REALIZE. WE DO NOT REPRESENT THAT YOU CAN EXPECT TO ATTAIN ANY OF THE RESULTS REFLECTED IN THE SCHEDULE. ACTUAL RESULTS WILL VARY FROM RESTAURANT TO RESTAURANT AND WE CANNOT ESTIMATE OR GUARANTY THE RESULTS OF ANY SPECIFIC RESTAURANT.

IN 2007, DI, OUR AFFILIATE, BEGAN SELLING RESTAU-RANTS OWNED AND OPERATED BY DI IN A STRATEGIC PROGRAM TO FOCUS ON HIGHER VOLUME RESTAURANTS IN A SMALLER NUMBER OF MARKETS. THE OPERATING RESULTS FOR RESTAURANTS SOLD BY DI DO NOT APPEAR IN THE FOLLOWING TABLE. THE OPERATING PERFORMANCE OF DI'S REMAINING COMPANY RESTAURANTS WHICH WE PRESENT, AND IN PARTICULAR AVERAGE UNIT VOLUMES AND MAJOR EXPENSE CATEGORIES, IS UNLIKE RESULTS IN FRANCHISE OPERATED UNITS.

ACTUAL SALES AND EARNINGS OF THE RESTAURANT ARE AFFECTED BY MANY FACTORS, INCLUDING YOUR OWN EFFORTS, ABILITY, AND CONTROL OF THE RESTAURANT, AS WELL AS FACTORS OVER WHICH YOU DO NOT HAVE ANY CONTROL.

WE DO NOT REPRESENT THAT THE RESTAURANT WILL BE PROFITABLE.

I. DI Restaurant Operating Performance

Denny's Company Restaurant Operating Performance

	Top Third		Middle Third		Bottom Third	
	$	%	$	%	$	%
Net Sales	2,724	100%	1,819	100%	1,466	100%
Food	627	23%	444	24%	371	25%
Crew Labor	581	21%	400	22%	316	22%
Management Labor	191	7%	152	8%	145	10%
Gross Profit	1,325	49%	824	45%	633	43%
Taxes/Fringe Benefits	225	8%	158	9%	135	9%
Utilities	97	4%	74	4%	66	4%
Repair & Maintenance	39	1%	35	2%	28	2%
Other Expense	152	6%	114	6%	193	7%
EBITDA before Royalties, Advertising Occupancy Cost, and Management Fees	$812	30%	$443	24%	$302	21%

EBITDA defined as Earnings Before Interest, Taxes, Depreciation, and Amortization without considering major capital expenditures. Above numbers reflect a total of 151 stores that were open the entire year - 54 units in the Top and Middle thirds and 53 units in the Bottom Third. All dollar figures in thousands.

NOTES TO FINANCIAL SCHEDULE

A. The schedule presents the actual operating results with respect to sales and selected costs of 161 Denny's restaurants owned and operated by DI in the United States during the twelve month period beginning December 26, 2012, and ending December 26, 2013, excluding only those restaurants which were open for only part of such period. The three tiers are comprised of 54 Denny's restaurants in the top and middle tiers and 53 Denny's restaurants in the bottom tier. The schedule is based upon data received from DI's employees at each restaurant who, in the normal course of business, collect such data.

B. "Net Sales" reflected on the schedule represent all revenue derived from the restaurants, including all sales of food, goods, wares, merchandise, and all services made in, upon, or from the restaurants, including catering services, whether for cash, check, credit, or otherwise, without reserve or deduction for inability to collect same. Net Sales do not include rebates or refunds to customers or the amount of any sales taxes or other similar taxes that restaurants may be required to collect from customers to be paid to any federal, state, or local taxing authority.

C. We are not able to provide similar information relating to Denny's restaurants operated by our franchisees because we do not have reliable information relating to costs incurred by franchise operators. However, during the same period (a twelve month period beginning December 26, 2012, and ending December 26, 2013) the average Net Sales of all Denny's restaurants (including both franchised restaurants and restaurants owned and operated by DI) were $1,472,000. This figure excludes former company restaurants bought in 2013 and any restaurant that was open for only part of such period. See sales information below.

D. There are no material differences between the operations of the restaurants being franchised by us and the restaurants owned and operated by DI. Both groups of restaurants will operate under the same System, and with similar operating requirements.

E. The restaurants included in the schedule have been open for periods as short as one year and as long as 55 years. No restaurant has been open for less than twelve months.

F. The final line of the schedule reflects the restaurant profit before deducting expenses which differ among individual restaurants. These additional expenses, which are likely to be significant, will vary widely among restaurants, and may include, but not necessarily be limited to, the following:

- Royalty fees and Brand Building contributions

- Occupancy cost
- Management fees
- Interest or financing charges not included in lease payments
- Taxes
- Depreciation on property and equipment
- Any preopening or amortization of organization costs
- Accounting, legal fees, and general administrative expenses

We strongly encourage you to consult with your financial advisors in reviewing the schedule and, in particular, in estimating the categories and amount of additional expenses which you will incur in establishing and operating the Restaurant. The schedule contains only some of the categories in which you may incur expenses.

G. The schedule was prepared from the internal operating records of DI which, in turn, were prepared in accordance with generally accepted accounting principles. The schedule is unaudited. We will substantiate the data set forth in the schedule to all prospective franchisees upon reasonable request.

H. Except for the schedule set forth in this Item, and profit and loss statements which we may provide to you where we sell you a company Restaurant (see the section titled, "Company Restaurant P&L's," below), we do not make information available to prospective franchisees in this state concerning actual, average, projected, or forecasted sales, costs, income, or profits. You should be aware that the financial performance of any particular restaurant may be affected by a number of factors, including, but not limited to the following:

1. The schedule does not reflect debt service costs. You will incur such costs to the extent you finance the initial franchise fee and the development and construction cost of the Restaurant and the furniture, fixtures, and equipment, or to the extent you borrow funds to acquire the property and build the Restaurant.

2. The Restaurant may face competition from restaurants and food service outlets offering many different types of cuisine. The intensity of this competition will vary depending upon the location of the Restaurant. Further, the tastes of a community or community segment may not be accustomed to the type of products offered by the Restaurant. As such, appreciation for and acceptance of the products offered by the Restaurant may have to be developed to varying degrees depending upon the particular community.

3. You may not have comparable restaurant and food service experience and expertise as found in the Denny's restaurants owned and operated by DI. While we will provide

certain assistance to you (see Item 11), you and the staff of the Restaurant will be primarily responsible for the daily operations of the Restaurant in accordance with the terms of the Franchise Agreement.

4. The quality and effectiveness of your managerial skills will affect, positively or negatively, the sales results of the Restaurant. Decisions with respect to location, additional advertising programs, employees, cost controls, and other factors may impact the results of the Restaurant.

5. Geographic and socio-economic variations from locality to locality may affect the results of the Restaurant, as well as factors bearing upon business cycles and performance of the national and world economy.

We recommend that you make your own independent investigation to determine whether or not the franchise may be profitable, and consult with an attorney and other advisors prior to executing any agreement.

We require all prospects who have never been Denny's franchisees, as a condition of being approved, to consult with an independent financial advisor and to review with that person operating statements for the restaurants to be acquired or developed and all other terms of the transaction. This review should include current and pro forma P&L's, as applicable. A prospective franchisee with financial expertise, or who has a person with such expertise on its staff, would be excused. Otherwise, the financial advisor would need to be a third party, and not affiliated with any other party to the transaction, including sellers, brokers, lenders or developers.

I. Except for the schedule set forth in this Item, and profit and loss statements which we may provide to you in circumstances in which we sell you a former company Restaurant (see the section titled, "Company Restaurant P&L's," below), we do not furnish, or authorize our salespersons to furnish, any oral or written information concerning the actual, average, projected, or forecasted sales, costs, income, or profits of a Denny's restaurant. Actual results vary from unit to unit, and we cannot estimate the results of any particular restaurant.

II. Sales of Denny's Restaurants

For 2013, 1533 Denny's restaurants in the US and Canada were open the entire year. We operated 161 restaurants and 1,372 were franchised. Restaurants open less than one full year have been omitted, of which there were 2 Company-owned and 52 franchised, as well as 2 former company restaurants. These totals also exclude 10 Denny's Fresh Express (nontraditional). The average sales of the franchised and Company-owned restaurants combined was $1,472,000. Franchised restaurants included in the analysis had average sales of $1,409,000. Company-owned restaurants included in the analysis had average sales of $2,006,000.

Franchised Restaurants:

Sales Range	Number of Franchised Restaurants	Percentage of Franchised Restaurants
Over $2,000,000	94	7%
$1,400,000 to $2,000,000	526	38%
$1,000,000 to $1,400,000	601	44%
Under $1,000,000	151	11%
TOTAL	1372	100%

Company-Owned Restaurants:

Sales Range	Number of Company-Owned Restaurants	Percentage of Company-Owned Restaurants
Over $2,000,000	56	35%
$1,400,000 to $2,000,000	88	55%
$1,000,000 to $1,400,000	17	11%
Under $1,000,000	0	0%
TOTAL	161	100%

NOTES AND ASSUMPTIONS

A. The size of the restaurants may vary significantly. Over the past few years we had several restaurant plans available, ranging from "Diner" concepts with 101 to 113 seats to classic buildings with 98 to 150 seats. Our "D Series" prototype has an average of 144 seats.

B. We compiled the figures provided above from our financial statements and from sales reports submitted to us by our franchise operators on a 52 week basis. The sales information provided by our franchise operators has not been audited and has not necessarily been prepared on a basis consistent with generally accepted accounting principles.

C. The 2 former company restaurants, both were open all of 2012, had an average volume in YE 2012 of $2,410,000.

III. Company Restaurant P&L's

If we sell to you a company restaurant, we will share with you information relating to the historical performance of the restaurant. Typically, this information consists of the profit and loss statement (the "P&L") for the restaurant, which is prepared in the normal course of business by DI, the seller. The P&L is prepared in accordance with generally accepted accounting principles, but it is not audited. The P&L does not include royalty payments that you will be required to pay under your Franchise Agreement with us. P&L information will be shared with you only after we have come to some preliminary understandings regarding your purchase of the company restaurant, but before you make any binding commitment to purchase the company restaurant under the terms of a Purchase Agreement. The information will be subject to a confidentiality agreement. (See Exhibit H.)

In providing P&L's, we neither represent nor warrant that the level of sales achieved by DI will be the same as the sales which you may achieve. Moreover, various expenses incurred by DI in the operation of the company restaurant will likely differ from the expenses you incur. For example, to the extent you borrow funds to acquire the company restaurant, the P&L figures will not reflect debt service costs which you will be required to pay. As a consequence, the results of your operation of the former company restaurant will not be the same as the results of operation by DI. Therefore, we strongly encourage you to consult with your financial advisors in reviewing P&L's for the company restaurant, in particular, in estimating the categories and amount of additional expenses which you will incur in establishing and operating the restaurant.

IV. New and Emerging Markets Incentive Program

The savings estimate of up to $1 million is based on the potential savings of developing, opening, and operating five Denny's restaurants under the New and Emerging Market Incentive Program, in comparison to developing, opening, and operating five Denny's restaurants without the incentive program. See Item 12 of this Disclosure Document for details of this program. The components of estimates regarding potential savings under the New and Emerging Market Program are as follows:

Initial Franchise Fee Potential Savings:

First Restaurant — pay $30,000	= savings of $10,000
Second Restaurant — pay $30,000	= savings of $10,000
Third Restaurant — pay $10,000	= savings of $30,000
Fourth Restaurant — pay $10,000	= savings of $30,000
Fifth Restaurant — pay $10,000	= savings of $30,000
	Total = $110,000

Royalty Payment Potential Savings (based on $1,409,000 average franchise restaurant sales volume):

1st year — pay 2% = 2.5% savings	= $35,225
2nd year — pay 2% = 2.5% savings	= $35,225
3rd year — pay 3% = 1.5% savings	= $21,135
4th year — pay 3% = 1.5% savings	= $21,135
5th year — pay 3% = 1.5% savings	= $21,135
Total	= $133,855
$133,855 x 5 restaurants	= $669,275

Brand Building Payment Potential Savings (based on $1,409,000 average franchise restaurant sales volume):

Pay 2.5% brand building = 0.5% savings for 5 years = $35,225 x 5 restaurants = $176,125

NRO Training (up to $10,000 x 5) — up to $50,000
Total Potential Savings = $1,005,400

We reserve the right to select the vendors, specifications, terms and conditions for these services.

DOC POPCORN

3200 Carbon Pl., # 103
Boulder, CO 80301
Tel: (866) 559-9744, (720) 389-0649
Fax: (720) 961-0551
Email: hannah@docpopcorn.com
Website: www.docpopcornfranchising.com
Hannah MacKay, Development Coordinator

Doc Popcorn (DP) is the largest franchised retailer of fresh-popped kettle-cooked popcorn offering a fun, simple and affordable business opportunity. With several different models from which to choose, we offer flexible options from which to grow.

BACKGROUND

IFA Member:	Yes
Established & First Franchised:	2003; 2009
Franchised Units:	87
Company-Owned Units:	1
Total Units:	88
Distribution:	US – 88; CAN – 0; O'seas – 0
North America:	26 States, 0 Provinces
Density:	N/A

Projected New Units (12 Months):	30
Qualifications:	4, 2, 1, 3, 4, 5

FINANCIAL/TERMS

Cash Investment:	$72K
Total Investment:	$72 – 378K
Minimum Net Worth:	$250K
Fees (Franchise):	$37.5K
Fees (Royalty):	6%
Fees (Advertising):	0%
Term of Contract (Years):	10/10
Average Number of Employees:	0 FT, 2 – 3 PT
Passive Ownership:	Discouraged
Encourage Conversions:	Yes
Area Development Agreements:	Yes
Sub-Franchising Contracts:	Yes
Expand in Territory:	Yes
Space Needs:	120 SF

SUPPORT & TRAINING

Financial Assistance Provided:	No
Site Selection Assistance:	Yes
Lease Negotiation Assistance:	Yes
Co-operative Advertising:	Yes
Franchisee Association/Member:	No
Size of Corporate Staff:	10
On-going Support:	A, B, C, D, E, H, I
Training:	5 Days Boulder, CO; 2 Days On-Site

SPECIFIC EXPANSION PLANS

US:	Yes
Canada:	Yes
Overseas:	Yes

Table One

As of December 31, 2013 we had 43 PopKiosk Doc Popcorn Businesses in operation. The information in Table One below is a historical financial performance representation for the 32 PopKiosk Doc Popcorn Businesses that were in operation for at least 52 weeks at the end of the 2013 ("Table One Reporting Group"). The representation in Table One is an historic financial performance representation about a subset of the franchise system's existing outlets. Table One shows the average 2013 yearly gross revenue for the Table One Reporting Group and the average 2013 yearly gross revenue achieved by the top 1/3 of the Table One Reporting Group.

Reporting Group	Average 2013 Gross Revenue of Top 1/3	Average 2013 Gross Revenue
32 Doc Popcorn Businesses (PopKiosks)	$264,006.02	$180,759.45
Number of Reporting Group that achieved or surpassed the average	5*	14*
Percentage of Reporting Group that achieved or surpassed the average	15.6%	43.8%

*This group includes a PopKiosk operated by our affiliate. Franchised outlets will share some of the same characteristics as our affiliate, including degree of competition, services or goods sold, and services supplied by us. Except for the fact that this affiliate does not pay royalties, it shares all other characteristics as franchised outlets, including purchasing products at the same prices as franchisees.

Table Two

As of December 31, 2013 we had two PopShop Doc Popcorn Businesses in operation. The information in Table Two below is a historical financial performance representation these two PopShop Doc Popcorn Businesses in operation ("Table Two Reporting Group"). Table Two shows the average 2013 yearly gross revenue for the Table Two Reporting Group. The representation in Table Two is an historic financial performance representation about a subset of the franchise system's existing outlets.

Average 2013 Yearly Revenue for Table Two Reporting Group the Reporting Period	$288,416.88
Number of PopShop Doc Popcorn Businesses at or above the Average Yearly Revenue	1
Percentage of PopShop Doc Popcorn Businesses at or above the Average Yearly Revenue	50%

Explanatory Notes for Table One and Table Two

1. We have not audited these amounts but have no reason to doubt the accuracy of the information provided to us by our franchisees.

2. Your revenues or expenses may be higher or lower in your first year of business.

3. The figures presented above do not reflect the operating expenses or other costs or expenses that must be deducted from the gross revenue figures to obtain your net income or profit. You should conduct an independent investigation of the costs and expenses you will incur in operating your Franchise. Franchisees or former franchisees listed in this Franchise Disclosure Document may be one source of this information.

Other than the information provided in this Item 19, we do not make any representations about a franchisee's future financial performance or the past financial performance of company-owned or franchised outlets. We also do not authorize our employees or representatives to make any such representations either orally or in writing. If you are purchasing an existing outlet, however, we may provide you with the actual records of that outlet. Written substantiation of all data illustrated above will be made available to you on reasonable request. If you receive any other financial performance information or projections of your future income, you should report it to the 'Doc Popcorn Development, Inc.'s management by contacting Garth Moore at 3200 Carbon Place, Unit 103, Boulder, Colorado 80301 and (720) 389-6049, the Federal Trade Commission, and the appropriate state regulatory agencies.

DUNKIN' DONUTS

130 Royall St.
Canton, MA 02021
Tel: (800) 777-9983, (781) 737-5136
Fax: (818) 996-5163

Email: erin.venuti@dunkinbrands.com
Website: www.dunkinfranchising.com
Erin Venuti, Franchisee Recruitment

Founded in 1950, today Dunkin' Donuts is the number one retailer of coffee-by-the-cup in America, selling 2.7 million cups a day, nearly one billion cups a year. Dunkin' Donuts is also the largest coffee and baked goods chain in the world and sells more donuts, coffee and bagels than any other quick service restaurant in America. Dunkin' Donuts has more than 6,500 shops in 29 countries worldwide. Based in Canton, Massachusetts, Dunkin' Donuts is a subsidiary of Dunkin' Brands, Inc. For more information, visit www.DunkinDonuts.com.

BACKGROUND
IFA Member:	Yes
Established & First Franchised:	1950; 1955
Franchised Units:	9,000
Company-Owned Units:	15
Total Units:	9,015
Distribution:	US – 7,263; CAN – 78; O'seas – 1,856
North America:	39 States, 5 Provinces
Density:	490 in MA, 359 in NY, 237 in IL
Projected New Units (12 Months):	350
Qualifications:	5, 4, 2, 2, 5, 4

FINANCIAL/TERMS
Cash Investment:	$750K
Total Investment:	$240 – 1,670K
Minimum Net Worth:	$1.5M
Fees (Franchise):	$40 – 80K
Fees (Royalty):	5.9%
Fees (Advertising):	5%
Term of Contract (Years):	20
Average Number of Employees:	N/A
Passive Ownership:	Discouraged

Encourage Conversions:	Yes
Area Development Agreements:	Yes
Sub-Franchising Contracts:	No
Expand in Territory:	Yes
Space Needs:	N/A

SUPPORT & TRAINING
Financial Assistance Provided:	Yes (D)
Site Selection Assistance:	N/A
Lease Negotiation Assistance:	Yes
Co-operative Advertising:	No
Franchisee Association/Member:	Yes/Member
Size of Corporate Staff:	N/A
On-going Support:	C,E,G,H,I
Training:	51 Days Randolph, MA; 3.5 Days Another Location

SPECIFIC EXPANSION PLANS
US:	All United States
Canada:	PQ, ON
Overseas:	All Countries

Before you start to review the information in this Item 19, we want to call your attention to these important points:

1. A new franchisee's individual financial results may differ from the results stated in the financial performance representations in this Item 19.

2. We will make written substantiation for the financial performance representations in this Item 19 available to prospective franchisees upon reasonable request.

3. If you are thinking of entering into an agreement to operate an alternative point of distribution ("APOD") Restaurant (whether Dunkin' Donuts or DD/BR Combo Restaurant) please note that the information in this Item 19 does not apply to APOD Restaurants. We do not make financial performance representations about APOD Restaurants.

4. If you are thinking of entering into an agreement to operate a Restaurant or DD/BR Combo Restaurant in Alaska or Hawaii, please note that the information in this Item 19 does not apply to Restaurants or DD/BR Combo Restaurants in those states. We do not make financial performance representations about Restaurants or DD/BR Combo Restaurants in Alaska or Hawaii.

5. There are seven tables that follow in this Item 19. You should read them together with all of the notes and explanatory information that follows in this Item 19.

DUNKIN' DONUTS RESTAURANTS: The following tables and notes provide financial performance representations that are historical, and that are based on information from existing Dunkin' Donuts Restaurants (exclusive of DD/BR Combo and APOD Restaurants) that have been open for business to the public for at least one year during a one-year measuring period from OCTOBER 28, 2012 TO OCTOBER 26, 2013.

The site types listed in the following tables are defined as follows:

Freestanding: A Restaurant, either newly constructed or an existing structure (to be retrofit), that does not share any common walls with any third party.

Shopping Center/Storefront: A Restaurant that shares a common wall (or walls) with third parties. The Restaurant could be an anchor (endcap) or inline tenant space in a strip center, or it could be a location in a high density, multiple level construction (typically urban/downtown office building setting), sharing common wall and ceiling/floor construction with any third party.

Gas/Convenience Restaurants: A Restaurant that is a sub-or shared tenancy within a Gas/Convenience host environment.

For more information regarding the "Regions", please refer to Appendix V-B at the end of this FDD. The Region descriptions are approximations. Some Restaurant locations included in this data may not precisely follow the descriptions contained in Appendix V-B. (For example, some Restaurants near the boundary of another Region may be included in that other Region's data.)

Table 1:

CONTINENTAL U.S. DUNKIN' DONUTS SINGLE BRANDED RESTAURANTS

AVERAGE RESTAURANT SALES FOR THE PERIOD OCTOBER 28, 2012 TO OCTOBER 26, 2013

FREE STANDING SITE TYPE

Drive-Thru Restaurants				Non Drive-Thru Restaurants		
Regions	Total Number of Restaurants in Sample	Average Sales	% Restaurants at or Above Average	Total Number of Restaurants in Sample	Average Sales	% Restaurants at or Above Average
Mid-Atlantic	252	$1,251,269	42%	85	$946,266	42%
Mid West	83	$1,120,513	43%	18	$839,518	50%
Northeast	1,079	$1,345,719	46%	382	$1,058,224	46%
South Atlantic	157	$1,132,556	50%	31	$1,046,142	52%
South Central/ West	32	$984,281	44%	12	$894,670	58%
Total Continental United States	1,603	$1,291,117	46%	528	$1,028,318	44%

"% Restaurants at or Above Average" means the percentage of Restaurants included in the data whose reported average sales are at or above the stated average, meaning that these Restaurants performed better than the stated average.

Table 2:

CONTINENTAL U.S. DUNKIN' DONUTS SINGLE BRANDED RESTAURANTS

AVERAGE RESTAURANT SALES FOR THE PERIOD OCTOBER 28, 2012 TO OCTOBER 26, 2013

SHOPPING CENTER/STOREFRONT SITE TYPE

Drive-Thru Restaurants				Non Drive-Thru Restaurants		
Regions	Total Number of Restaurants in Sample	Average Sales	% of Restaurants at or Above Average	Total Number of Restaurants in Sample	Average Sales	% of Restaurants at or Above Average
Mid Atlantic	74	$1,078,036	49%	190	$779,815	46%
Mid West	66	$888,841	48%	94	$688,663	45%
Northeast	245	$1,194,725	41%	799	$861,825	45%
South Atlantic	91	$973,379	41%	88	$854,117	49%
South Central/ West	57	$858,640	53%	15	$731,471	33%
Total Continental United States	533	$1,066,915	45%	1,186	$832,742	45%

"% Restaurants at or Above Average" means the percentage of Restaurants included in the data whose reported average sales are at or above the stated average, meaning that these Restaurants performed better than the stated average.

Table 3:

CONTINENTAL U.S. DUNKIN' DONUTS SINGLE BRANDED RESTAURANTS

AVERAGE RESTAURANT SALES FOR THE PERIOD OCTOBER 28, 2012 TO OCTOBER 26, 2013

GAS & CONVENIENCE SITE TYPE

Regions	Drive-Thru Restaurants			Non Drive-Thru Restaurants		
	Total Number of Restaurants in Sample	Aveage Sales	% Restaurants at or Above Average	Total Number of Restaurants in Sample	Average Sales	% Restaurants at or Above Average
Mid-Atlantic	28	$741,903	43%	45	$582,534	42%
Mid West	44	$691,625	39%	36	$505,478	42%
Northeast	324	$918,495	46%	37	$609,668	44%
South Atlantic	45	$732,082	49%	37	$474,295	51%
South Central/ West	N/A	N/A	N/A	N/A	N/A	N/A
Total Continental United States	441	$865,626	46%	431	$586,511	44%

"% Restaurants at or Above Average" means the percentage of Restaurants included in the data whose reported average sales are at or above the stated average, meaning that these Restaurants performed better than the stated average.

N/A means that we have not included information for this site type in this region due to sample sizes of less than 10 Restaurants.

Table 4:

CONTINENTAL U.S. DUNKIN' DONUTS SINGLE BRANDED RESTAURANTS

AVERAGE COST OF GOODS SOLD & AVERAGE LABOR COST STATED AS A PERCENTAGE OF TOTAL SALES

FOR THE PERIOD NOVEMBER 1, 2012 TO OCTOBER 31, 2013

Regions	Total Number of Restaurants in Sample	Average Cost of Goods Sold	% Restaurants With Cost of Goods Sold at or Below the Average Shown	Average Labor Cost	% of Restaurants with Labor at or Below the Average Shown
Mid Atlantic	658	28.8%	52.3%	24.5%	58.7%
Mid West	338	31.1%	55.3%	24.8%	54.7%
Northeast	3,125	27.5%	53.8%	25.0%	54.0%
South Atlantic	437	31.7%	57.7%	25.1%	52.2%
South Central/ West	126	33.4%*	53.2%	26.4%	45.2%
Total Continental United States	4,684	28.5%	55.5%	25.0%	54.3%

"% Restaurants with Cost of Goods Sold at or Below the Average Shown" and "% Restaurants with Labor at or Below the Average Shown" means the percentage of Restaurants included in the data who performed as well as or better than the averages shown (meaning these units have cost ratios that are as good as, or better than, the average shown).

* The Cost of Goods Sold published for this Region are lower than your Cost of Goods Sold will be because we currently subsidize up to 2% of the Cost of Goods Sold to certain single branded Restaurants in this Region. You will not be eligible to receive this subsidy (even if you will open a new single branded Restaurant in this Region).

DUNKIN' DONUTS/BASKIN-ROBBINS COMBO RESTAURANTS: The following tables and notes provide financial performance representations that are historical, and that are based on information from existing DD/BR Combo Restaurants that have been open for business to the public for at least one year during a one-year measuring period from OCTOBER 28,

2012 TO OCTOBER 26, 2013. For more information regarding the "Regions", please refer to Appendix V-B at the end of this FDD. The Region descriptions are approximations. Some DD/BR Combo Restaurant locations included in this data may not precisely follow the descriptions contained in Appendix V-B. (For example, some DD/BR Combo Restaurants near the boundary of another Region may be included in that other Region's data.)

Table 5:

CONTINENTAL U.S. DUNKIN' DONUTS/BASKIN-ROBBINS COMBO RESTAURANTS

AVERAGE DD/BR COMBO RESTAURANT SALES FOR THE PERIOD OCTOBER 28, 2012 TO OCTOBER 26, 2013

FREE STANDING TYPE

Regions	Drive-Thru Restaurants			Non Drive-Thru Restaurants		
	Total Number of Restaurants in Sample	Average Sales	% Restaurants at or Above Average	Total Number of Restaurants in Sample	Average Sales	% Restaurants at or Above Average
Mid Atlantic	69	$1,242,125	50%	16	$1,049,956	47%
Mid West	161	$1,251,017	45%	24	$934,508	46%
Northeast	64	$1,645,115	48%	78	$1,239,148	51%
South Atlantic	118	$1,226,482	42%	N/A	N/A	N/A
South Central/West	N/A	N/A	N/A	N/A	N/A	N/A
Total Continental United States	403	$1,305,096	45%	117	$1,152,402	44%

"% Restaurants at or Above Average" means the percentage of Restaurants included in the data whose reported average sales are at or above the stated average, meaning that these Restaurants performed better than the stated average.

N/A means that we have not included information for this site type in this region due to sample sizes of less than 10 Restaurants.

Table 6:

CONTINENTAL U.S. DUNKIN' DONUTS/BASKIN-ROBBINS COMBO RESTAURANTS

AVERAGE DD/BR COMBO RESTAURANT SALES FOR THE PERIOD OCTOBER 28, 2012 TO OCTOBER 26, 2013

Shopping Center/Storefront Site Type

Regions	Drive-Thru Restaurants			Non Drive-Thru Restaurants		
	Total Number of Restaurants in Sample	Average Sales	% Restaurants at or Above Average	Total Number of Restaurants in Sample	Average Sales	% Restaurants at or Above Average
Mid Atlantic	19	$1,264,545	42%	29	$834,395	52%
Mid West	50	$1,045,219	46%	52	$904,612	46%
Northeast	15	$1,275,675	33%	257	$1,071,866	44%
South Atlantic	30	$1,119,807	43%	29	$865,889	52%
South Central/West	N/A	N/A	N/A	N/A	N/A	N/A
Total Continental United States	114	$1,131,725	46%	367	$1,013,127	47%

"% DD/BR Combo Restaurants at or Above Average" means the percentage of DD/BR Combo Restaurants included in the data whose reported average sales are at or above the stated average, meaning that these Restaurants performed better than the stated average.

N/A means that we have not included information for this site type in this region due to sample sizes of less than 10 Restaurants.

Table 7:

CONTINENTAL U.S. DUNKIN' DONUTS/BASKIN-ROBBINS COMBO RESTAURANTS

AVERAGE COST OF GOODS SOLD & AVERAGE LABOR COST STATED AS A PERCENTAGE OF TOTAL SALES

FOR THE PERIOD NOVEMBER 1, 2012 TO OCTOBER 31, 2013

Regions	Total Number of Combo Restaurants in Sample	Average Cost of Goods Sold	% Combo Restaurants with Cost of Goods Sold at or Below the Average Shown	Average Labor Cost	% Combo Restaurants with Labor at or Below the Average Shown
Mid Atlantic	123	30.8%	52.8%	24.5%	53.7%
Mid West	285	31.2%	59.3%	24.6%	56.1%
Northeast	411	28.6%	56.7%	24.7%	55.5%
South Atlantic	176	31.6%	49.4%	26.2%	55.1%
South Central/ West	14	35.2%*	42.9%	27.4%	35.7%
Total Continental United States	1,009	30.2%	53.6%	24.9%	55.6%

"% DD/BR Combo Restaurants with Cost of Goods Sold at or Below the Average Shown" and "% DD/BR Combo Restaurants with Labor at or Below the Average Shown" means the percentage of DD/BR Combo Restaurants included in the data who performed as well as or better than the averages shown (meaning these units have cost ratios that are as good as, or better than, the average shown).

* The Cost of Goods Sold published for this Region are lower than your Cost of Goods Sold will be because we currently subsidize up to 2% of the Cost of Goods Sold to certain DD/BR Combo Restaurants in this Region. You will not be eligible to receive this subsidy (even if you will open a new DD/BR Combo Restaurant in this Region).

NOTES REGARDING SALES DATA (Tables 1, 2, 3, 5 & 6 above)

(1) The sales figures are compiled by using historical sales that are reported to us by franchisees. We have not audited or verified the reports.

(2) We provide you sales data that includes average sales and the percentage of Restaurants reporting who have actually attained or surpassed the stated average. This sales data does not include sales tax. The vast majority of the Restaurants that comprise this data are franchised, although our affiliates, DBI Stores LLC and Star Dunkin', LP, may own and operate a small number of Restaurants at any given time (see Item 20).

(3) Sales in states or regions with a higher concentration of Restaurants that have been in operation for a substantial period of time tend to have higher sales than states or regions with a lower concentration of Restaurants that have been in operation for a lesser time period. These higher concentration states or regions significantly increase the overall average due to both their higher sales and their larger numbers. Therefore, the sales performance of Restaurants outside of these higher concentration areas may not be commensurate with the overall average sales. (See Item 20 for the number of Restaurants per state).

(4) Many of the Restaurants included in this data have been open and operating for several years. These franchisees have achieved their level of sales after spending many years building customer goodwill at a particular location.

(5) Your sales will be affected by your own operational ability, which may include your experience with managing a business, your capital and financing (including working capital), continual training of you and your staff, customer service orientation, product quality, your business plan, and the use of experts (for example, an accountant) to assist in your business plan.

(6) Your sales may be affected by Restaurant location and site criteria, including traffic count and which side of the street your Restaurant is located on (for example, whether your Restaurant is on the morning drive side or afternoon drive side of traffic), local household income, residential and/or daytime populations, ease of ingress and egress, seating, parking, the physical condition of your Restaurant, the size of your site, and the visibility of your exterior sign(s). Additionally, many of the Restaurants included in the sales figures are freestanding Restaurants or located at the end of a strip center, and if your Restaurant is not, your sales could be substantially lower than the figures in the chart. Your sales may also be negatively affected if you do not adhere to our standards and system, including proper equipment layout, design and construction criteria, customer queuing and flow, and local Restaurant marketing.

(7) Individual locations may have layouts and seating capacities that vary from the typical location.

(8) Other factors that could have an effect upon your sales may include consumer preferences, competition (national and local), inflation, local construction and its impact on traffic patterns, and reports on the health effects of consuming food similar to that served in the Restaurants, as well as the impact of federal, state and local government regulations.

(9) Your sales may be affected by consumer preferences for certain menu items over others, changes in the menu and regional differences in products or product demand, including whether there are products not available to you or your region but sold in other regions. Menus are continually being revised, both adding and discontinuing products and product line extensions. Not all Restaurants may have these new products. New products may not be successful for all Restaurants. Marketing activity associated with new products may be at higher than normal levels and, therefore, sales increases may not be maintained after this temporary marketing activity is completed.

(10) Sales may be affected by fluctuations due to seasonality (particularly in colder climates), weather and periodic marketing and advertising programs. Inclement weather may cause temporary Restaurant closings in some areas.

(11) The above data reflects historical sales. There is no assurance that future sales will correspond to historical sales.

(12) There are numerous factors that may affect sales at your Restaurant. The factors listed above and below are not an all-inclusive list of those factors.

(13) The Restaurant with the highest sales for the applicable Region may have characteristics that are not available to you.

(14) If you own a Combo Restaurant, the following may be applicable to you: many Baskin-Robbins franchisees actively pursue cake sales opportunities. If you do not, your sales may be negatively affected. Additionally, seasonality and weather may significantly affect sales of ice cream and related products.

(15) Some individual Restaurants' sales may include wholesale accounts and other distribution outlets, which may not be available to you. Not all of these opportunities have been successful for all participating franchisees. These opportunities may have been added, expanded, reduced or eliminated from individual reporting Restaurants at varying times during the reporting period. The contracts for such opportunities may have been terminated or expired without renewal in the reported or future periods. Additionally, some products that are sold in the Restaurants included in the statistics above may not be available for sale in your state or region.

NOTES REGARDING COGS AND LABOR DATA (Tables 4 & 7 above)

"COGS" means the cost of goods sold including food, beverages and items served or associated with the food or beverage, such as cups, napkins, straws, bags, plastic utensils and wrapping paper.

"Labor" means crew, management, training, payroll tax and workers' compensation.

(1) COGS and Labor are stated as a percentage of gross sales (excluding sales tax and discounts). The vast majority of Restaurants that comprise this data are franchised, although our affiliates, DBI Stores LLC and Star Dunkin', LP, may own and operate a small number of Restaurants at any given time (see Item 20).

(2) The cost figures from franchised Restaurants are compiled from individual Restaurants by using cost data that are reported to us by franchisees. We have not audited or verified the reports, nor have franchisees confirmed that the reports are prepared in accordance with generally accepted accounting principles or in accordance with our definition of COGS and Labor.

(3) Your costs will be affected by your own operational ability, which may include your experience with managing quick service restaurant operations, your experience building and managing an organization, continual training of you and your staff, your business plan, and using experts (e.g., an accountant) to assist in your business plan. Your costs may be negatively affected by not adhering to our standards and system.

(4) Many of the Restaurants included in this data have been open and operating for several years. Those franchisees may have lower cost percentages due to years of experience managing costs. For new franchisees, COGS and Labor cost percentages may initially exceed those of experienced operators.

(5) There is no assurance that future costs will correspond to historical costs because of factors such as inflation, changes in menu and other variables.

(6) Factors affecting your COGS include, but are not limited to, the price of raw materials; your ability to manage and implement proper controls of waste, ruin, loss, theft and the portion sizes served to the public; regional differences; temporary shortages; seasonal and weather fluctuations; and fluctuations due to periodic marketing and advertising programs. Additionally, freight charges may be higher in some areas. If the

cost of gasoline increases in the U.S., the cost of freight will rise as well.

(7) The COGS data above reflects average Restaurant's aggregate cost. Different food and beverage items have different cost percentages. Customer demand for products varies among Restaurants and regions and if your Restaurant sells a high percentage of high cost items, your food cost percentage will be higher than if you have a lower percentage of higher cost items. Your costs may be affected by changes in the menu and regional differences in products including whether there are products not available to you or your region but sold in other regions. Menus are continually being revised, both adding and discontinuing products and product line extensions. New products are not successful in all Restaurants where they are introduced.

(8) Factors affecting your Labor include, among other things, the local labor market and any applicable federal or state minimum wage law; pending healthcare legislation, employee turnover and your operational abilities, including your ability to train and retain employees; your compensation that may be included in labor, which varies among franchisees; menu, product mix, Restaurant layout, your salary and benefits programs, and scheduling. Restaurants must be staffed in accordance with our standards.

(9) Some franchisees purchase finished products manufactured at another location. The cost of this finished product will vary depending upon the number of Restaurants being serviced by the manufacturing location and other factors. These franchisees may pay more for food costs but may pay less for other items such as labor, equipment, distribution and rent.

(10) COGS may be particularly affected by the fluctuations in the price of coffee and other items and ingredients.

(11) Restaurants with lower sales may have higher COGS and Labor cost percentages because of less efficiencies and economies of scale, and more waste.

(12) The retail sales price that you establish will also affect the COGS and Labor percentages.

(13) If you are in a geographic area with fewer Restaurants, you may have higher COGS as a percentage of sales due to less distribution efficiencies.

ADDITIONAL NOTES REGARDING SALES, COGS AND LABOR DATA (All Tables above)

You should conduct an independent investigation of the sales, costs and expenses you will incur in operating your franchised business. Franchisees or former franchisees, listed in this disclosure document, may be one source of this information.

The "Total Number of Restaurants/Combo Restaurants in Sample" in Tables 4 & 7 is a subset of the "Total Number of Restaurants/Combo Restaurants in Sample" in Tables 1, 2, 3, 5 & 6, because not all Restaurants or Combo Restaurants in Tables 4 & 7 reported COGS and Labor data for the twelve month reporting period.

All of the Restaurants or Combo Restaurants in Tables 4 & 7 reported at least one month of COGS and Labor data for the twelve month reporting period.

Our nation's current economic conditions are unusually volatile both in terms of consumer spending as well as the costs of doing business, such as for example, energy, commodities, credit, etc. As a result, historical performance results may not be as useful in your financial planning as they may have been in less volatile times (in terms of anticipated sales or anticipated costs). If you choose to use the historical financial information appearing in this franchise disclosure document, you must carefully consider the potential impact of the current economic volatility, price spikes in the cost of commodities, and in your potential sales volume.

There are numerous factors that may affect COGS and Labor at your Restaurant. The factors listed in this Item 19 are not an all-inclusive list of those factors.

Other than the preceding financial performance representations, we do not make any financial performance representations. We do not make any representations about a franchisee's future financial performance. We also do not authorize our employees or representatives to make any such representations either orally or in writing. If you are purchasing an existing outlet, however, we may provide you with the actual records of that outlet. If you receive any other financial performance information or projections of your future income, you should report it to the franchisor's management by contacting Richard Emmett, Senior Vice President, Chief Legal and Human Resources Officer, Legal Dept. 3 East A, 130 Royall Street, Canton, MA 02021, 781-737-3000, the Federal Trade Commission, and the appropriate state regulatory agencies.

DUNKIN' DONUTS ALTERNATIVE POINTS OF DISTRIBUTION, ALASKA & HAWAII, GAS & CONVENIENCE COMBO RESTAURANTS AND REGIONS WITH INSUFFICIENT DATA

We do not make financial performance representations about Dunkin' Donuts restaurants in these categories: alternative points of distribution; Restaurants or Combo Restaurants in Alaska and Hawaii; Gas & Convenience Combo Restaurants;

or Site Types in Regions with a sample size of less than ten Restaurants. The FTC's Franchise Rule permits a franchisor to provide information about the actual or potential financial performance of its franchise and/or franchisor-owned outlets, if there is a reasonable basis for the information, and if the information is included in the disclosure document. Financial performance information that differs from that included in Item 19 may be given only if: (1) a franchisor provides the actual records of an existing outlet you are considering buying; or (2) a franchisor supplements the information provided in this Item 19, for example, by providing information about possible performance at a particular location or under particular circumstances.

We do not make any representations about a franchisee's future financial performance or the past financial performance of company-owned or franchised outlets in these categories. We also do not authorize our employees or representatives to make any such representations either orally or in writing. If you are purchasing an existing outlet, however, we may provide you with the actual records of that outlet. If you receive any other financial performance information or projections of your future income, you should report it to the franchisor's management by contacting Richard Emmett, Senior. Vice President, Chief Legal and Human Resources Officer, Legal Dept. 3 East A, 130 Royall Street, Canton, MA 02021, 781-737-3000, the Federal Trade Commission, and the appropriate state regulatory agencies.

IF APPLICABLE, HISTORICAL SALES AND PROFIT DATA FOR EXISTING RESTAURANT TO BE SOLD BY US

If the subject Restaurant is an existing Restaurant being sold by us, we may provide to you unaudited historical sales and profit data for the Restaurant. Statements prepared by us are prepared in accordance with generally accepted accounting principles. Statements prepared by past franchisee(s) of the Restaurant, if any, were submitted to us by franchisee(s) that we require to prepare statements in accordance with generally accepted accounting principles. We cannot assure you that in all cases they were so prepared.

Historical costs do not correspond to future costs because of such factors as inflation, changes in minimum wage laws, the local labor market, financing, real estate related costs and other variables. For example, actual costs such as rent, taxes, depreciation, amortization interest, insurance, payroll, and utilities may vary from historical costs. Historical sales may also not correspond to future sales because of such factors as the duration, if any, that the Restaurant was closed, changes in Restaurant management and employees, remodel or refurbishment, if any, over or under reporting of sales, changes in competition and other variables.

Your accountant should develop your own data for these accounts based on your particular financing and other costs. All information should be evaluated in light of current market conditions including such cost and price information as may then be available.

GENERAL NUTRITION CENTERS

300 Sixth Ave., Fl. 4
Pittsburgh, PA 15222
Tel: (800) 766-7099, (412) 338-2503
Fax: (412) 402-7105
Email: bpollock@gncfranchising.com
Website: www.gncfranchising.com
Bruce Pollock, Senior Director of Franchise Development

RESULTS OF OPERATIONS OF FRANCHISED STORES

BASIS OF DATA

Below is certain historical financial information regarding GNC Stores operated by franchisees that operated within the United States from January 1, 2013 through December 31, 2013. Your individual financial results may differ from the results stated in this Item.

The historical financial information below is based upon information regarding the actual gross sales of GNC franchised Stores open and operated continuously by our franchisees during our 2013 fiscal year (January 1, 2013 through December 31, 2013). Of the 1,012 franchise-operated Stores that were open and operating in the United States as of December 31, 2013, 929 or 91.8%, of those had been in business continuously throughout the fiscal year 2013. No data has been presented for the franchisees who were terminated, reacquired, not renewed or left our system for other reasons during our last fiscal year. (See Item 20 for more information.) None of the information presented in this Item includes data from GNC Stores operated by us or GNC/Rite Aid or from GNC Stores located on military bases.

AVERAGE GROSS RETAIL SALES

The average gross retail sales of the 929 Stores described above during the fiscal year 2013 was $535,901.31. 41.3% of the 929 Stores (384 Stores) actually attained or surpassed the average gross retail sales of $535,901.31 for the fiscal year 2013. (See Note below.) Gross sales is the amount of sales of all products sold in a Store, whether for cash or on a charge, credit or time basis, without reserve or deduction for inability or failure to collect, and includes income of every kind related to the franchised business. Gross sales do not include excise or sales taxes paid to the government. To compute gross sales, you should deduct the amount of over-rings, refunds, allowances or discounts to customers. (See Attachment E of the Franchise Agreement for our definition of Gross Sales).

OPERATING COSTS AND EXPENSES

The average gross retail sales described in this Item do not include average costs and expenses necessary to operate the GNC Store as experienced by GNC franchisees in certain categories, including but not limited to the following: (1) Fixed Expenses - Occupancy, Local Advertising, National Advertising, Royalties, and POS Maintenance; (2) Variable Expenses - Cost of Sales, Wages, and Benefits, Debt Service, Income Taxes, Depreciation, Supply Expenses, Janitorial Services, Telephone Expenses, Credit Card Expenses, Travel/ Entertainment and Discretionary Expenses; and (3) Initial Startup Expenses - initial franchise fee, Initial Promotional Materials, Construction Handling Fees, Security Deposits, Additional Site Selection Assistance, Initial Training Costs, and Miscellaneous Opening Costs. (See Items 7 and 8 of this Disclosure Document for further explanation.)

Actual gross sales and earnings capability will vary depending upon the expenses noted above, as well as a variety of internal and external factors which we cannot estimate, such as: general population of the market, general economic conditions in the market, recognition and brand patronage, the products offered in your Store, competition and price of competitive products and services in the market, your ability to generate repeat customers and create customer loyalty, acquisitions and strategic alliances, competition, e-commerce, new regulations of the supplement industry, taxes, differences in management skills and experience levels, the availability of financing, general economic climate, demographics, Store location, Store size, discounts, and changing consumer preferences. In addition, promotions and discounts we may institute to maintain market share in the increasingly competitive nutritional supplement environment may potentially reduce your earnings capability.

We cannot estimate or project the results of operations of a particular franchise, and make no guarantee or assertion that you will attain the results set forth in this Item. We strongly recommend that you make your own independent investigation of whether or not the franchise may be "profitable," and confer with your attorney, accountant, or other business advisor before executing any agreement with us.

We will provide you with substantiation for the data set forth in this Item upon reasonable request.

Other than the preceding financial performance representation, we do not make any financial performance representations. We also do not authorize our employees or representatives to make any such representations either orally or in writing. If you are purchasing an existing outlet, however, we may provide you with the actual records of that outlet. If you receive any other financial performance information or projections of your future income, you should report it to the franchisor's management by contacting Greg Johnston, General Nutrition Corporation, 300 Sixth Avenue, Pittsburgh, Pennsylvania 15222, (412) 288-4600, the Federal Trade Commission, and the appropriate state regulatory agencies.

NOTE:

1. The figures contained in this Item were compiled by us based upon the reports generated from the POS Cash Registers of our franchisees operating throughout the period represented (See Item 11). We have assumed that the franchisees' information is accurate, complete, and contains no material misrepresentations or omissions. We have not audited or verified this information. This information has not been separately audited or verified by an independent certified public accountant, and it may not have been prepared on a basis consistent with generally accepted accounting principles.

JACK IN THE BOX

9330 Balboa Ave.
San Diego, CA 92123
Tel: (858) 571-4044
Fax: (858) 694-1501
Email: grant.kreutzer@jackinthebox.com
Website: www.jackinthebox.com/franchise
Grant Kreutzer, Director, Franchise Business Development

Jack in the Box Inc. (NASDAQ: JACK), based in San Diego, is a restaurant company that operates and franchises Jack in the Box® restaurants, one of the nation's largest hamburger chains, with over 2,200 restaurants in 21 states. Additionally, through a wholly owned subsidiary, the company operates and franchises Qdoba Mexican Grill, a leader in fast-casual dining, with over 600 restaurants in 46 states, the District of Columbia, and Canada. Jack in the Box is known for its premium QSR menu items—offering a broad selection of distinctive, innovative products targeting fast-food lovers who want delicious, craveable and affordable food that is served quickly by our friendly employees. The "breakfast all day" proposition is a major differentiator for the brand, and our breakfast menu is quite extensive.

BACKGROUND

IFA Member:	No
Established & First Franchised:	1951; 1982
Franchised Units:	1,592

Company-Owned Units:	642
Total Units:	2,234
Distribution:	US – 2,234; CAN – 0; O'seas – 0
North America:	21 States, 0 Provinces
Density:	927 in CA, 615 in TX, 174 in AZ
Projected New Units (12 Months):	N/A
Qualifications:	N/A

FINANCIAL/TERMS

Cash Investment:	$750K
Total Investment:	$1.2 – 2.5MM
Minimum Net Worth:	$1.5MM
Fees (Franchise):	$50K
Fees (Royalty):	5%
Fees (Advertising):	5%
Term of Contract (Years):	N/A
Average Number of Employees:	10 FT, 10 PT
Passive Ownership:	Allowed
Encourage Conversions:	N/A
Area Development Agreements:	No
Sub-Franchising Contracts:	No
Expand in Territory:	No
Space Needs:	N/A

SUPPORT & TRAINING

Financial Assistance Provided:	No
Site Selection Assistance:	N/A
Lease Negotiation Assistance:	N/A
Co-operative Advertising:	No
Franchisee Association/Member:	No
Size of Corporate Staff:	0
On-going Support:	A, B, C, D, E, F, G, H, I
Training:	N/A

SPECIFIC EXPANSION PLANS

US:	No
Canada:	No
Overseas:	No

The table below represents the sales and operating figures of franchise-operated Jack in the Box restaurants in the continental United States (i.e., excluding Hawaii) that were in operation for more than 360 days within the twelve-month period ended September 30, 2013, and were operated by the same franchisee(s) for that entire period. The figures for fifty-four (54) of those restaurants were excluded because the franchisee did not submit complete financial information for that period. One thousand five hundred ninety-one (1,591) restaurants are represented in the table, comprising approximately 71% of all Jack in the Box restaurants, and 89% of franchised Jack in the Box restaurants as of September 30, 2013.

The information in the table was prepared using financial information provided to us by franchisees. The franchisees' financial information is not audited and may not have been prepared in accordance with generally accepted accounting practices. The footnotes to the table describe the primary types of items that we ask franchisees to include in each financial category, but we cannot guarantee that all franchisees used these categories in the manner we have requested. The data used in preparing this Item 19 will be made available to prospective franchisees upon reasonable request.

Various categories of costs have been excluded from the financial calculations in the table below. The excluded categories are: occupancy costs, depreciation and amortization, interest, income taxes, general and administrative expenses, officer compensation and other income and expenses. Because any development fees paid to us under a development agreement and the initial franchise fee and royalties paid to us under a franchise agreement would normally appear in the excluded categories, those fees are not represented in the table.

You should consider that this information gives no weight to regional sales and cost variations. Sales and costs may differ widely from one geographic region to another. You must make your own investigation into the likely costs in your geographic area.

You should also consider that sales and expenses vary from restaurant to restaurant. Your restaurant's sales, costs and expenses will be directly affected by many factors, including but not limited to the restaurant's size and geographic location; competition from other restaurants in the market; the presence of other Jack in the Box restaurants in the market; the quality of management and service at your restaurant; operating hours; contractual terms you have negotiated with vendors and lessors; the extent to which you finance the construction and operation of your restaurant; legal, accounting, real estate and other professional fees; federal, state and local income tax rates; and discretionary expenditures. Please also note that

recessionary economic conditions, including higher levels of unemployment, lower levels of consumer confidence, and decreased consumer spending can reduce restaurant traffic and sales and impose practical limits on pricing.

Written substantiation for the financial performance representation will be made available to you upon reasonable request.

THIS INFORMATION SHOULD NOT BE CONSIDERED AS THE ACTUAL OR POTENTIAL SALES, COSTS, OR OPERATING PROFITS THAT YOU WILL REALIZE. A FRANCHISEE'S INDIVIDUAL FINANCIAL RESULTS MAY DIFFER FROM THE RESULTS SHOWN IN THIS ITEM 19. THE COSTS IN THIS STATEMENT DO NOT REPRESENT ALL COSTS YOU WILL INCUR. WE DO NOT REPRESENT THAT ANY OPERATOR CAN EXPECT TO ATTAIN ANY PARTICULAR COSTS OR OPERATING PROFITS PRESENTED. WE DO NOT REPRESENT THAT YOU WILL DERIVE INCOME FROM YOUR RESTAURANT THAT EXCEEDS YOUR INVESTMENT IN YOUR RESTAURANT. IF YOU CHOOSE TO PURCHASE A FRANCHISE FROM US, YOU ACCEPT THE RISK THAT YOUR ACTUAL RESULTS MAY VARY GREATLY FROM THE RESULTS SHOWN HERE. WE URGE YOU TO CONSULT WITH APPROPRIATE FINANCIAL, BUSINESS AND LEGAL ADVISERS TO CONDUCT YOUR OWN ANALYSIS.

In the table on the following page, we have divided the restaurants into five ranges based on sales volume. We have calculated the average sales and certain expenses of restaurants in each of the five ranges.

Jack in the Box Inc. Average Sales and Costs of Franchise-owned Restaurants in 5 Sales Ranges In the Continental U.S. (i.e., excluding Hawaii) for the 12-Month Period Ended September 30, 2013						
	Below $1,000,000	$1,000,000 to $1,250,000	$1,250,000 to $1,500,000	$1,500,000 to $1,750,000	$1,750,000 and above	Total/ Average
Number of Restaurants	330	447	374	261	179	1,591
	21%	28%	24%	16%	11%	100%
% by State						
CA	23%	34%	43%	54%	61%	40%
AZ	12%	11%	10%	9%	5%	10%
TX	43%	31%	24%	20%	20%	29%
Other	22%	25%	23%	18%	13%	21%
Sales (1)	851,451	1,130,938	1,369,665	1,615,596	1,968,771	1,302,856
	100.0%	100.0%	100.0%	100.0%	100.0%	100.0%
Cost of Sales (2)	266,782	349,365	421,419	496,768	605,024	402,119
	31.3%	30.9%	30.8%	30.7%	30.7%	30.9%
Labor						

Production Labor (3)	189,509	230,444	262,962	297,496	353,465	254,438
	22.3%	20.4%	19.2%	18.4%	18.0%	19.5%
Management Comp. (4)	39,548	42,194	48,223	54,226	58,204	46,837
Payroll Taxes/Ins. (5)	33,654	41,605	48,242	55,855	66,483	46,652
Total labor	262,710	314,243	359,426	407,577	478,152	347,928
	30.9%	27.8%	26.2%	25.2%	24.3%	26.7%
Gross profit	321,958	467,330	588,820	711,251	885,594	552,809
	37.8%	41.3%	43.0%	44.0%	45.0%	42.4%
Operating Costs						
Advertising (6)	43,687	57,697	70,214	82,725	101,080	66,720
Utilities (7)	42,776	45,302	49,052	52,413	54,741	47,888
Other (8)	63,398	68,458	74,269	78,992	91,777	73,126
Total Operating Costs	149,862	171,456	193,535	214,130	247,598	187,734
	17.6%	15.2%	14.1%	13.3%	12.6%	14.4%
Operating Margin Before Occupancy Costs, Royalties, and Other Costs Described in this Item 19***	172,097	295,874	395,285	497,121	637,996	365,075
	20.2%	26.2%	28.9%	30.8%	32.4%	28.0%

***(Our Standard Royalty is 5% of Gross Sales.) (This table excludes nontraditional locations.)

(1) Product sales and promotional sales

(2) Food and packaging costs, less supplier rebates

(3) Wages of hourly employees and team leaders, including overtime

(4) Wages and bonuses paid to restaurant and assistant restaurant managers

(5) Payroll taxes, paid time-off, workers' compensation and medical insurance

(6) Marketing Fee, as described in the franchise agreement, and restaurant specific promotional programs

(7) Electricity, gas, water and sewer

(8) Maintenance and repairs, menu panels, uniforms, supplies, bank charges, and other services

Except for the information that the FTC Rule permits franchisors to provide, as outlined in the first paragraph of this Item 19, we do not furnish information about the actual or potential sales, costs, income or profits of Jack in the Box restaurants. We specifically instruct our employees and other agents that, other than by providing the written representations permitted by the FTC Rule, they are not authorized to make claims, estimates or other statements about the earnings, sales, profits, or prospects of success of Jack in the Box restaurants. If you receive any such unauthorized representations, whether oral or written, you should immediately notify us by contacting our General Counsel, Phillip H. Rudolph, 9330 Balboa Avenue, San Diego, California 92123 (858) 571-2435.

KENTUCKY FRIED CHICKEN

1900 Colonel Sanders Ln.
Louisville, KY 40213
Tel: (866) 2YUM-YUM, (502) 874-8201
Fax: (502) 874-8224
Email: susan.burton@yum.com
Website: www.kfcfranchise.com
Susan Burton, Franchising Contact

Of the approximately 3,192 domestic, single-brand KFC locations open at least a year as of December 31, 2013, 161 were owned and operated by KFCC or its subsidiaries and, 3,031 were owned or operated by KFC franchisees.

2013 Average Performance (Single-Brand KFC Locations)

Single-Brand KFCs Open for at Least One Year as of December 31, 2013

Ownership	Count*	Average Net Sales	Average Cost of Product	Product as % of Net Sales	Average Cost of Labor	Labor as % of Net Sales
Company	161	$1,080,000	$352,000	32.6%	$318,000	29.5%
Franchise	3,031	$1,004,000				
Total	3,192	$1,010,000				

NOTES:

1. This financial performance representation reflects the averages for a sub-set of all single-brand KFC locations in the continental United States and Alaska during the calendar year 2013. The sub-set consists of KFCC Restaurants as of December 31, 2013, and all single-brand KFC outlets which were owned or operated by franchisees of KFC as of December 31, 2013. The financial performance representation does not include non-traditional, Express, multi-brand, seasonal or any type of KFC location other than single-brand KFC locations. All KFC locations included had been open a minimum of one year as of December 31, 2013.

2. Of the 161 single-brand, KFCC Restaurants which are included in this financial performance representation and which were open for at least one year as of December 31, 2013; 65, or 40.4%, attained or exceeded the stated average result; and, 96, or 59.6%, did not attain the results stated above. Of the 3,031 single-brand, KFC outlets owned and operated by franchisees of KFC which are included in this financial performance representation and which were open for at least one year as of December 31, 2013; 1,337, or 44.1%, attained or exceeded the stated average result; and, 1,694, or 55.9%, did not attain the results stated above.

3. Characteristics of the included locations may differ materially from the characteristics of the outlet(s) that you may develop or acquire depending on your experience; competition in your trade area; the physical condition of the included locations as compared to your outlet(s); employment and labor conditions in your trade area; and the length of time that the included locations have operated as compared to your outlet(s). Your individual financial results may differ substantially from the results stated in this financial performance representation. Written substantiation for this financial performance representation is available upon reasonable request.

4. "Average Net Sales" is the mathematical average of the total annual cash or other payments received after discounts and promotions for the sale or use of any products, goods or services that were sold from the KFCC Restaurants included within the group.

5. "Average Cost of Sales" is the mathematical average of the total annual delivered cost of food, beverages, paper and promotional items to the KFCC Restaurants included within the group, expressed as a percentage of Average Net Sales. This does not include any financial results from KFC outlets that were owned and operated by franchisees of KFC.

6. "Average Cost of Labor" is the mathematical average of the total annual hourly labor costs; the salaries and related costs of management; payroll taxes; health insurance; vacation; sick

pay; bonuses; and workers' compensation insurance for all employees at the KFCC Restaurants included within the group, expressed as a percentage of Average Net Sales. This does not include any financial results from KFC outlets that were owned and operated by franchisees of KFC.

The operations of KFCC Restaurants are similar to those of the franchised KFC outlets offered by this FDD, except that KFCC Restaurants do not have certain expenses that franchised outlets have, such as payment of royalties. KFCC-owned Restaurants also benefit from economies of scale that are not available to outlets that are owned singly or in small groups by a franchisee.

Your individual financial results may materially differ from the results stated in these financial performance representations. Written substantiation for this financial performance representation is available upon reasonable request. You are urged to consult with appropriate financial and legal advisors in connection with the information set forth in these statements.

MCDONALD'S

Campus Office Building, 2915 Jorie Blvd.
Oak Brook, IL 60523
Tel: (888) 800-7257, (630) 623-6196
Fax: (630) 623-5658
Email: bob.villa@us.mcd.com
Website: www.aboutmcdonalds.com
Bob Villa, National Franchise Manager

Quick-service restaurant.

BACKGROUND
IFA Member:	Yes
Established & First Franchised:	1955; 1955
Franchised Units:	28,691
Company-Owned Units:	6,738
Total Units:	35,429
Distribution:	US – 14,278; CAN – 1,427; O'seas – 19,724
North America:	50 States, 6 Provinces
Density:	877 in FL, 1,216 in TX, 1,349 in CA
Projected New Units (12 Months):	N/A
Qualifications:	3, 5, 3, 3, 4, 4

FINANCIAL/TERMS
Cash Investment:	$750K
Total Investment:	$1.1 – 2.3MM
Minimum Net Worth:	N/A
Fees (Franchise):	$45K
Fees (Royalty):	12.5%
Fees (Advertising):	4%
Term of Contract (Years):	20/20
Average Number of Employees:	50 PT
Passive Ownership:	Allowed
Encourage Conversions:	N/A
Area Development Agreements:	Yes
Sub-Franchising Contracts:	No
Expand in Territory:	Yes
Space Needs:	2,000 SF

SUPPORT & TRAINING
Financial Assistance Provided:	No
Site Selection Assistance:	N/A
Lease Negotiation Assistance:	N/A
Co-operative Advertising:	Yes
Franchisee Association/Member:	Yes/Member
Size of Corporate Staff:	N/A
On-going Support:	C, D, E, G, H, I
Training:	N/A

SPECIFIC EXPANSION PLANS
US:	All United States
Canada:	All Canada
Overseas:	All Countries

Of the approximately 12,113 domestic traditional McDonald's restaurants opened at least 1 year as of December 31, 2013, approximately 72% had annual sales volumes in excess of $2,200,000; approximately 62% had annual sales volumes in excess of $2,400,000; and approximately 51% had annual sales volumes in excess of $2,600,000. The average annual sales volume of domestic traditional McDonald's restaurants open at least 1 year as of December 31, 2013, was $2,658,000 during 2013. The highest and lowest annual sales volume in 2013 for these domestic traditional McDonald's restaurants was $10,316,000 and $228,000, respectively.

The pro forma statements included below show annual sales volumes of $2,200,000, $2,400,000, and $2,600,000. These pro forma statements have been derived from independent franchisee traditional restaurant financial statements to provide information relevant to a prospective franchisee (see Note 1). Specific assumptions used in the presentation of these pro forma statements are indicated above and below each statement.

The pro forma statements are based upon a total of 10,139 independent franchisee traditional restaurants open and operated by a franchisee for at least 1 year. A FRANCHISEE'S INDIVIDUAL FINANCIAL RESULTS MAY DIFFER FROM THE RESULTS STATED IN THE PRO FORMA STATEMENTS FOR THE REASONS DESCRIBED IN THIS ITEM OR FOR OTHER REASONS. Substantiation of the data used in preparing the earnings claims, including computations of all actual or average profit or earnings, will be made available to prospective franchisees upon reasonable request.

It is anticipated that the information reported in these pro forma statements reflects the operating results before occupancy costs for independent franchisee restaurants open for at least 1 year. However, the operating income before occupancy cost figures appearing below should not be construed as the financial results or "profit" before occupancy costs which might be experienced by a franchisee with a similar sales volume or an indication that any particular sales volume will be obtained. An individual franchisee is likely to experience operating expense variations including, but not limited to, general insurance, legal and accounting fees, labor costs, and store management benefits (life and health insurance, etc.). Additionally, market conditions, operational and management methods employed by a franchisee, different geographic areas of the country, and menu price variations may significantly affect operating results. The nature of these variables makes it difficult to estimate the financial results for any particular franchisee or location.

PRODUCT SALES (see Note 2)	$2,200,000	100.0%	$2,400,000	100.0%	$2,600,000	100.0%
TOTAL COST OF SALES	692,000	31.5%	752,000	31.3%	812,000	31.2%
GROSS PROFIT	1,508,000	68.5%	1,648,000	68.7%	1,788,000	68.8%
OTHER OPERATING EXPENSES (excluding rent, service fees, depreciation and amortization (D&A), interest, and income taxes)*	961,000	43.7%	1,029,000	42.9%	1,097,000	42.2%
OPERATING INCOME BEFORE OCCUPANCY COSTS (excluding rent, service fees, D&A, interest, and income taxes) (see Note 3)**	548,000	24.9%	619,000	25.8%	691,000	26.6%

Of the 10,139 independent franchisee traditional restaurants included in the pro forma statements above, approximately 44% had operating income before occupancy costs greater than $548,000; approximately 33% had operating income before occupancy costs greater than $619,000; and approximately 23% had operating income before occupancy costs greater than $691,000.

* OTHER OPERATING EXPENSES — Includes, but is not limited to, the following costs: labor, franchisee's salary as manager, payroll taxes, advertising fee (as described in Item 6), promotion, outside services, linen, operating supplies, small equipment, maintenance and repair, utilities, office supplies, legal and accounting fees, insurance, real estate and personal property taxes, business operating licenses, and non-product income or expense. This is a combination of the Total Controllable Expenses and Other Operating Expenses excluding rent, service fees, D&A, and interest included in our typical store financial statements.

** OPERATING INCOME BEFORE OCCUPANCY COSTS — Represents Operating Income excluding rent, service fees, D&A, interest, and income taxes. The rent paid to McDonald's will vary based upon sales and McDonald's investment in land, site improvements, and building costs. Refer to Item 6 for information regarding franchise fees (including rent and service fees paid to McDonald's). D&A and interest will vary based upon the purchase price and required reinvestment of the specific restaurant acquired. Refer to Item 7 for a description of investment costs.

Additionally, organization overhead costs such as salaries and benefits of non-restaurant personnel (if any), cost of an automobile used in the business (if any), and other discretionary expenditures may significantly affect profits realized in any given operation. The nature of these variables makes it difficult to estimate the performance for any particular restaurant with sales of any given volume.

THESE SALES, PROFITS, OR EARNINGS ARE AVERAGES OF SPECIFIC RESTAURANTS AND SHOULD NOT BE CONSIDERED AS THE ACTUAL OR POTENTIAL SALES, PROFITS, OR EARNINGS THAT WILL BE REALIZED BY ANY OTHER FRANCHISEE. MCDONALD'S DOES NOT REPRESENT THAT ANY FRANCHISEE CAN EXPECT TO ATTAIN THESE SALES, PROFITS, OR EARNINGS.

Note 1 — Data for McOpCo company restaurants is not included in the pro forma statements because of certain expenses that are typically incurred by a McOpCo-operated restaurant that are not incurred by restaurants franchised to individuals. If data for McOpCo-operated restaurants open for at least 1 year were included along with franchised restaurants, the percent of total restaurants in each category would not be statistically different and the range of Operating Income Before Occupancy Costs would be $568,000 to $713,000.

Note 2 — The description of this line, "Product Sales," is to clarify that only product sales are included. Non-product sales and associated costs are included in Other Operating Expenses.

Note 3 — We are not presenting average occupancy costs in the above calculation because a wide variety of rent charts and ownership options exist. In addition, the effective rent paid by a franchisee may be more in any particular month than the stated percent rent indicated in the franchisee's lease because a portion of the rent may be fixed regardless of the sales level for a given month. The range of effective rent percentages in 2013 for franchised restaurants was 0% to 37.6%. Refer to Item 6 for a description of rents.

MOE'S SOUTHWEST GRILL

200 Glenridge Pt. Pkwy., #200
Atlanta, GA 30342
Tel: (800) 227-8353, (404) 255-3250
Fax: (404) 257-7073
Email: scorp@moes.com
Website: www.moes.com
Peter Ortiz, Senior Director of Franchise Sales

BACKGROUND

IFA Member:	Yes
Established & First Franchised:	2000; 2001
Franchised Units:	425

Company-Owned Units:	4
Total Units:	429
Distribution:	US – 838; CAN – 27; O'seas – 33
North America:	48 States, 4 Provinces
Density:	71 in FL, 49 in PA, 68 in TX
Projected New Units (12 Months):	40
Qualifications:	4, 4, 1, 2, 3, 3

FINANCIAL/TERMS

Cash Investment:	$60 – 100K
Total Investment:	$450.6 – 768.8K
Minimum Net Worth:	$50 – 182K
Fees (Franchise):	$30K
Fees (Royalty):	7.50%
Fees (Advertising):	Varies, $150/month for national
Term of Contract (Years):	15/15
Average Number of Employees:	4 FT, 0 PT
Passive Ownership:	Not Allowed
Encourage Conversions:	Yes
Area Development Agreements:	Yes
Sub-Franchising Contracts:	No
Expand in Territory:	No
Space Needs:	1,212 SF

SUPPORT & TRAINING

Financial Assistance Provided:	Yes (I)
Site Selection Assistance:	Yes
Lease Negotiation Assistance:	Yes
Co-operative Advertising:	Yes
Franchisee Association/Member:	Yes/Not a Member
Size of Corporate Staff:	120
On-going Support:	C, D, E, f, G, h, I

Training:	On-Going Regional, Annual, On-Line; 5 Weeks On-Site; 3 Weeks Horsham, PA

SPECIFIC EXPANSION PLANS

US:	All United States
Canada:	All Canada
Overseas:	All Countries

Other than in this Item 19, we do not make any additional representations about a franchisee's future financial performance or the past financial performance of company-owned or franchised outlets. We also do not authorize our employees or representatives to make any additional representations either orally or in writing. If you receive any additional financial performance information or projections of your future income, you should report it to the franchisor's management by contacting the Legal Department, Moe's Franchisor LLC, 200 Glenridge Point Parkway, Suite 200, Atlanta, GA 30342, 404-255-3250, the Federal Trade Commission, and the appropriate state regulatory agencies.

Below is a profit and loss statement ("P&L Statement") for the calendar year 2013 (the "Period") for Restaurants that have been open continuously for 3 or more years ("Three-Year Group") and that provided us with complete financial information for the full Period.

PROFIT AND LOSS STATEMENT FOR THREE-YEAR GROUP OF RESTAURANTS		
During Period	Average	Percentage of Total Gross Sales during the Period
Total Gross Sales	$1,242,729	
Cost of Goods (i.e. food, beverages, paper)	$369,863	29.8%
Personnel Expenses (i.e. salaries and payroll, medical insurance, unemployment taxes)	$273,497	22.0%
Advertising (i.e. NAMF, co-op, local marketing, coupons, discounts)	$138,042	11.1%
Operating Expenses (i.e. royalties, maintenance, utilities, pest control, security, other controllable expenses)	$155,700	12.5%
Occupancy Expenses (i.e. rent, cam payments, equipment lease expense)	$95,862	7.7%
General and Administrative Expenses (i.e. credit card fees, bank service charges, general liability insurance, legal/accounting fees, business license & fees)	$21,189	1.7%
Earnings Before Interest, Taxes, Depreciation and Amortization (EBITDA)	$188,577	15.2%

Bases

"Gross Sales" means Net Sales plus the amount of any discounts from redemptions of coupons and other reductions made to calculate Net Sales. "Net Sales" has the same meaning shown in Item 6 that is used for purposes of calculating royalties due under the Franchise Agreement. There were 387 Restaurants that were in operation continuously for 3 years before the end of the Period. Of these 387 Restaurants, we received financial information for the full period from 150 Restaurants.

Of the 150 franchised Restaurants represented in the Three-Year Group, 64 Restaurants (or 42.7% of the Three-Year Group) attained or exceeded the Average Total Gross Sales in the table above. Of the 150 Restaurants represented in the Three-Year group, 69 Restaurants (or 46% of the Three-Year Group) attained or exceeded the Earnings Before Interest, Taxes, Depreciation and Amortization (EBITDA) in the table above.

Three of the Restaurants reflected in the table above had a Carvel Express Shoppe that operated in them for the Period.

The Restaurants whose results are reflected in the table above were in operation continuously for the three-year period before the end of the Period. The table does not include results for Restaurants that (i) did not submit full and complete financial information for the entire Period or (ii) opened or closed during the Period or during the three-year period before the end of the Period. Two of the Restaurants reflected in the table above had a Carvel Express Shoppe that operated in it for the full three-year period, and one of the Restaurants reflected in the table above had a Carvel Express Shoppe that operated in them for part of the three-year period (one Carvel Express Shoppe closed in November 2013). The information in the P&L Statement includes the information for the operations of the three Carvel Express Shoppes discussed in the previous sentence.

The above data for the Three-Year Group has been taken from financial reports submitted by franchisees. We have not audited or verified these financial reports nor have we asked questions of the submitting franchisees to determine whether they are in fact accurate and complete, although we have no information or other reason to believe that they are unreliable. We did not use any reports that were incomplete or for which the information was presented in a manner that prohibited us from applying the information to one of the categories in the P&L Statements.

The data is for specific franchised Restaurants and should not be considered as the actual or potential sales, costs or profits that will be achieved by any other franchised Restaurant. Actual results vary from Restaurant to Restaurant and we cannot estimate the results of any specific Restaurant. A new franchisee's sales results are likely to be lower than the results shown above and expenses are likely to be higher than the results shown above. There may be other expenses in operating a Restaurant that are not identified in the P&L Statements. You should conduct an independent investigation of the expenses in operating a Restaurant, and franchisees and former franchisees listed in Exhibits D and E to this Disclosure Document may be one source for obtaining additional information on expenses in operating a Restaurant.

Assumptions

The data shown above is for Restaurants throughout the System, which includes various types of real estate locations (traditional and non-traditional venues) and formats. Sales, costs and profits for each format can vary widely. We suggest that you speak with franchisees of the same format type you intend to operate to better understand factors that may affect your potential sales, costs and profits.

Sales, costs and profits also can vary considerably due to a variety of other factors, such as demographics of the Restaurant's trade area; competition from other restaurants in the trade area; traffic flow, accessibility and visibility; economic conditions in the Restaurant's trade area; advertising and promotional activities; and the business abilities and efforts of the management of the Restaurant.

Increases in oil prices may increase food costs which could significantly increase the cost of goods.

Written substantiation for the financial performance representation will be made available to you on reasonable request.

PAPA JOHN'S INTERNATIONAL

2002 Papa John's Blvd.
Louisville, KY 40299
Tel: (888) 255-7272

Fax: (502) 261-4799
Email: regan_clauson@papajohns.com
Website: www.papajohns.com
Regan Clauson, Franchise Qualification Specialist

Papa John's International, headquartered in Louisville, KY., is the world's third-largest pizza company, owning and franchising over 3,400 restaurants in all 50 states and 35 countries. For 13 out of the last 15 years, consumers have rated Papa John's #1 in customer satisfaction among all national pizza chains in the highly regarded American Customer Satisfaction Index (ACSI).

BACKGROUND

IFA Member:	Yes
Established & First Franchised:	1985; 1986
Franchised Units:	3,891
Company-Owned Units:	598
Total Units:	4,489
Distribution:	US – 3,201; CAN – 85; O'seas – 1,201
North America:	50 States, 7 Provinces
Density:	247 in FL, 211 in TX, 207 in CA
Projected New Units (12 Months):	120
Qualifications:	5, 5, 4, 3, 4, 5

FINANCIAL/TERMS

Cash Investment:	Varies
Total Investment:	$129.9 – 644.2K
Minimum Net Worth:	$250K – 2MM
Fees (Franchise):	$25K/Unit
Fees (Royalty):	5%
Fees (Advertising):	7%
Term of Contract (Years):	10/10
Average Number of Employees:	8 FT, 18 PT
Passive Ownership:	Discouraged

Encourage Conversions:	N/A
Area Development Agreements:	Yes
Sub-Franchising Contracts:	No
Expand in Territory:	Yes
Space Needs:	1,200 – 1,500 SF

SUPPORT & TRAINING

Financial Assistance Provided:	No
Site Selection Assistance:	Yes
Lease Negotiation Assistance:	No
Co-operative Advertising:	Yes
Franchisee Association/Member:	Yes/Not a Member
Size of Corporate Staff:	13,990
On-going Support:	A, B, C, D, E, F, G, H, I
Training:	1 Week Papa John's University, Louisville, KY; Mentoring: Varied Location (Varies); 5 Weeks Mgmt. Training: Varied Locations

SPECIFIC EXPANSION PLANS

US:	All United States
Canada:	Yes
Overseas:	Yes

Presented below are average restaurant-level sales revenues of our domestic franchised and company-owned Papa John's restaurants for our fiscal year ended December 29, 2013, along with average restaurant-level cash expenses for company-owned Papa John's restaurants only. The following revenue and cash flow data is drawn from our financial books and records, which are kept on a basis consistent with Generally Accepted Accounting Principles ("GAAP") in the United States. All information is based on actual historical costs and results. Thus, there are no material assumptions associated with the data, other than the principles of GAAP. A number of factors may affect the comparability of the expense (or cash outflow) data, which is drawn solely from company-operated restaurants, to franchised restaurants and the data's effectiveness as a guide or template for potential operating results of a franchised restaurant. The most significant of these factors are discussed in the notes following the data. You should carefully consider these factors when reviewing, analyzing considering the data presented below.

Restaurant Revenues:

Average Sales – Company-owned restaurants $984,857

289 Company-owned restaurants, 45.2% of the total included in the data, achieved sales revenues of $984,857 or greater in 2013.

Average Sales – Franchised restaurants $782,816

1,015 Franchised restaurants, 43.7% of the total included in the data, achieved sales revenues of $782,810 or greater in 2013.

Average Cash Flows (Company-owned restaurants only):		Percent of Sales
Food Costs	$307,579	31.2%
Labor Costs and Taxes	$199,957	20.3%
Manager's Labor and Taxes	$43,010	4.4%
Mileage	$45,068	4.6%
Advertising	$92,020	9.3%
Controllables*	$63,183	6.4%

Rent and Common Area Maintenance	$34,619	3.5%
Other Non-Controllables**	$44,112	4.5%
Training Costs	$3,705	0.4%
Store Bonuses	$18,840	1.9%
Pre-Tax Cash Flows	$127,994	13.7%

298 Company-owned restaurants, 46.6% of the total included in the data, achieved $127,994 or greater annual pre-tax cash flows in 2013.

*Controllables includes: cash over and short, smallwares, repairs and maintenance, commissions, telephone expenses, utilities, cleaning supplies, computer supplies, office supplies, laundry service, uniforms, equipment rental, postage, donations, dues and subscriptions, meals and entertainment, travel and lodging, employee incentives, professional fees, and special events.

**Other Non-Controllables includes: property taxes, management health insurance, general insurance, credit card charges, bank charges, business licenses, and worker's compensation insurance.

Notes and Comments

Historical Performance Data

The foregoing information is drawn from actual historical data from our domestic restaurants. Historical information may not be a reliable predictor of future results or experience. Future performance may be affected by many factors at variance from the conditions that yielded past results and experience, including without limitation: volatility of commodity costs (such as cheese); inflation or rising costs in general, especially for labor and energy; general economic upturn or downturn; changing consumer tastes, perferences or sensibilities; and effectiveness of advertising or promotional campaigns. We do not make any guarantee of future sales, costs or profits.

Expense Data: Company-Owned Restaurants Only

Because we do not maintain or audit the accounting records of our franchsiees, we would be unable to make any representation with respect to the reliability of the expense data of franchised restaurants. We are unable to determine, for example, whether franchisees' accounting and financial records are kept in a manner that would permit reporting of cost data in accordance with GAAP or whether the franchisees' bookkeeping and accounting systems, practices and controls are sufficiently robust to ensure that the data is reliable. As a result, we present only Company-owned restaurant data with respect to expense or cash outflow) items. We have also excluded restaurants that were acquired from franchisees or divested to franchisees during the year from the Company-owned restaurants because we cannot verify or make any representations as to their expense data for the part of the year during which the restaurants were franchised rather than Company-owned. See "Full Year Only" note below for the number of Company-owned restaurants included in the average cash flow data.

Full Year Only

At the close of our fiscal year, there were 3,202 total domestic (United States) Papa John's restaurants, 665 of which were company-owned, including restaurants owned by franchisees in which we have a majority interest (a total of 191 restaurants). However, the foregoing data is drawn only from standard (or "traditional") restaurants that were open the entire year of 2013 because including results from Non-Traditional Restaurants and restaurants that were open only part of the year would skew the annual revenue and expense data. Therefore, the total number of restaurants included in the foregoing data in 2,961, comprising 2,322 franchised restaurants and 639 Company-owned restaurants.

Averages

The sales revenue data presented in based on averages for our domestic restaurants. Many restaurants have lower sales performance than the average for all restaurants. With a data base consisting of more than 3,000 restaurants, the lowest performing restaurants may have performance data that vary significantly from the average. Some restaurants have sold or earned as much as shown in the foregoing data. Your individual results may differ. We make no assurance that you will sell or earn as much. Similarly, the cash expense data for our Company-owned restaurants represents averages across a population of more than 600 restaurants. Thus, many Company-owned restaurants have costs that are higher than the system-wide average. Performance of a particular restaurant, in terms of both revenues and expenses, may be afffected by many factors, including without limitaion: location (whether the restaurant is in a free-standing building, in-line in a strip center or an end-cap in a strip center; whether the restaurant is in a high-visibility, high-traffic location); population density in the restaurant's trade area; business acumen and managerial skills of restaurant management personnel; prevailing wage rates and quality of the available labor pool; availability and cost of commercial rental property; the presence and aggressiveness of the competition; and utility costs.

Core Business Revenues

The revenue figures for both franchised and Company-owned restaurants include only sales of food and beverages arising in the ordinary course of retail operations. Non-recurring items, such as proceeds from the sale of used furniture or equipment, are not included.

Non-Cash Items

The cash flow data does not include depreciation expense or any other non-cash items. Over time, worn-out or obsolete restaurant equipment will have to be replaced and leasehold improvements, signage, computer systems and restaurant furnishings may have to be refurbished, remodeled, upgraded or replaced. The foregoing cash flow data does not include any reserves for funding any of these types of improvements or upgrades.

Royalty

Company-owned restaurants do not pay a royalty. The expenses incurred by a franchised restaurant will include our standard royalty.

Economies of Scale

Because we operate more than 600 company-owned restaurants, we are able to achieve certain economies of scale and operational efficiencies that may not be available to a franchisee operating one restaurant or a limited number of restaurants, as is the case for the typical franchisee. For example, we have a multi-tiered management hierarchy. At the higher levels of management, we are able to rely on the expertise of management executives with a wealth of experience in the restaurant and food service industries. You may not be able to achieve the same level of management expertise. You will be relying principally on your own business acumen and managerial skills and perhaps that of your Principal Operator. However, the income from our company-owned restaurants ultimately must bear the costs of our management team and other corporate office overheat. These costs are not reflected in the foregoing cash flow data, which reflect operational cash flows at the restaurant level, excluding the burden of corporate overhead.

Because of the size of our Company-owned operations, we are able to support a marketing department, with personnel dedicated to marketing functions, as well as dedicated cash management, payroll and other administrative functions. You and your Principal Operator will perform most of these functions, although some administrative functions may be out-sourced. Unless you are dedicated to specific functions, such as marketing.

We are a publicly-traded company and have raised significant capital through our stock offerings. We typically do not require bank financing for construction or equipping of our restaurants or for capital improvements or for updating or replacement of worn-out or obsolete equipment in our restaurants. However, to the extent that we do require financing, we are able to draw on a significant line of credit from our primary bank. It is unlikely that these types of financing efficiencies will be available to you.

We are able to obtain economies of scale in other areas, such as insurance, that may not be available to franchisees. Because of the size of our operations, insurance risks are spread over a greater number of restaurants, which enables us to bargain for lower group-rate insurance costs. We are also able to use the size of our operations to achieve volume discounts and other cost savings based on our purchasing power. These cost savings, in areas including telephone services and advertising, may not be available to franchisees operating on a smaller scale.

Restaurant and Market Maturity

Sales of a particular restaurant may be affected by how long the restaurant has been in operation and how successfully the surrounding market has been penetrated. Typically, sales "ramp up" as the restaurant and market develop. New restaurants (open for less than one year) typically do not operate as efficiently or a profitably as more mature restaurants. In particular, sales at restaurants open less than one year are typically lower than more mature restaurants, as it takes some time to establish consumer recognition and build a customer base in a new trade area. Greater penetration (the greater the number and concentration of restaurants) in a market also may affect performance. Clusters of restaurants may be able to pool resources to purchase advertising on local television or radio, which would be prohibitively expensive for a single restaurant, or even a small cluster of restaurants in a large media market. The foregoing Company-owned restaurant data represents averages for all of our domestic restaurants, some of which are long-established in their location and some of which are relatively new. Most of our Company-owned restaurants are in highly developed and highly penetrated markets.

Market Location

Our company-owned restaurants are typically in and around major metropolitan areas, such as Atlanta, St. Louis and Nashville. Many franchised restaurants are operated in less densely populated areas, with more limited access to advertising media.

Traditional Restaurants Only

The foregoing data refers only to standard (or "traditional") Papa John's restaurants. Performance data for Non-Traditional Restaurants varies widely, depending upon the nature of the non-traditional location, number of events or sales dates and other widely varying factors. Thus, this Item 19 is applicable to traditional Papa John's restaurants only. We do not furnish or authorize our sales persons to furnish any oral or written information concerning the actual or potential sales, costs, income or profits of a Papa John's Non-Traditional Restaurant.

Other Data

Except as described below, we do not furnish or authorize the furnishing to prospective franchisees of any oral or written information other than the data provided above. We may provide to you the actual performance data of a particular restaurant that you are considering purchasing. Also, we may, but we have no obligation to, provide to you supplemental data consisting of a segmentation or subset of the above data. For example, we may provide data for a particular region or individual state. If we do so, that supplemental data will be in writing and will be limited to the types of information set forth in the above data. We do not furnish and do not authorize anyone to furnish supplemental data that is outside the scope of the data provided above. If you obtain any other financial information concerning Papa John's restaurants, do not rely on it as a representation of Papa John's.

Your Own Due Diligence

You should construct your own pro forma cash flow statement and make your own projections concerning potential sales, operating costs, total capital investment requirements, operating cash requirements, debt, cash flow, and other financial aspects of operating a Papa John's restaurant. You should not rely solely on the information provided by us. You should conduct your own investigation of revenue and expense potential for your proposed Papa John's restaurant, including consultation with your own attorney, accountant or other advisor and other Papa John's franchisees.

CAUTION

AS A CONSEQUENCE OF THE FACTORS DISCUSSED ABOVE, AND OTHER VARIABLES THAT WE CANNOT ACCURATELY PREDICT, A NEW FRANCHISEE'S INDIVIDUAL FINANCIAL RESULTS ARE LIKELY TO DIFFER FROM THE RESULTS SHOWN IN THE DATA INCLUDED IN THIS ITEM 19.

Substantiation of Data

Substantiation of the data used in preparing the data set forth in this Item 19 will be available to prospective franchisees upon reasonable request.

PAPA MURHPY'S

8000 N.E. Parkway Dr., # 350
Vancouver, WA 98662
Tel: (800) 257-7272, (360) 260-7272
Fax: (360) 260-0500
Email: rhonda.mcgrew@papamurphys.com
Website: www.papamurphys.com
Rhonda McGrew, Manager Business Development

Papa Murphy's is the largest take-and-bake pizza company in the world with over 1,400 locations in the U.S. and Canada. The entire concept is built around the idea of take 'n' bake menu options. By baking Papa Murphy's pizzas at home, customers get to experience the home-baked aroma of a convenient, delicious meal that the brand is known for. To franchise owners, Papa Murphy's offers an opportunity that is attractive with a simplistic business model at a great investment price.

BACKGROUND

IFA Member:	Yes
Established & First Franchised:	1981; 1982
Franchised Units:	1,362
Company-Owned Units:	68
Total Units:	1,430
Distribution:	US – 1,407; CAN – 19; O'seas – 4
North America:	38 States, 3 Provinces
Density:	180 in CA, 145 in WA, 98 in OR
Projected New Units (12 Months):	100
Qualifications:	4, 3, 2, 3, 2, 5

FINANCIAL/TERMS	
Cash Investment:	$80K
Total Investment:	$226 – $414.3K
Minimum Net Worth:	$270K
Fees (Franchise):	$25K
Fees (Royalty):	5%
Fees (Advertising):	2%
Term of Contract (Years):	10/5
Average Number of Employees:	2 FT, 8 – 10 PT
Passive Ownership:	Allowed
Encourage Conversions:	Yes
Area Development Agreements:	Yes
Sub-Franchising Contracts:	No
Expand in Territory:	Yes
Space Needs:	1,200 – 1,400 SF

SUPPORT & TRAINING	
Financial Assistance Provided:	Yes (I)
Site Selection Assistance:	Yes
Lease Negotiation Assistance:	Yes
Co-operative Advertising:	Yes
Franchisee Association/Member:	Yes/Member
Size of Corporate Staff:	150
On-going Support:	C, D, E, G, H, I
Training:	2 Days POS Training; 5 Days Owners Class at Corp; 23 Days Certified Training Store

SPECIFIC EXPANSION PLANS	
US:	Midwest, Central, South
Canada:	Yes
Overseas:	No

Under the three sections below, we have provided an unaudited statement of system store performance, benchmark costs, average annual Net Sale percentage increase, and new store performance. Information for franchise-owned stores has been taken from their respective selfreported weekly sales and profit and loss statement. We have not audited or verified these figures or reports nor have we asked questions of the submitting franchisees to determine whether they are in fact accurate and complete, although we have no information or other reason to believe that they are unreliable. We do not know whether the information was prepared consistent with generally accepted accounting principles.

The amount of sales realized and costs and expenses incurred will vary from store to store. The sales, costs and expenses of your Franchised Store will be directly affected by many factors, such as the Franchised Store's size, geographic location, menu mix, and competition in the marketplace; the presence of other Papa Murphy's stores; the quality of management and service at the Franchised Store; contractual relationships with lessors and vendors; the extent to which you finance the construction and operation of the Franchised Store; your legal, accounting, real estate and other professional fees; federal, state and local income, gross profits or other taxes; discretionary expenditures; and accounting methods used. You should, therefore, use this analysis only as a reference.

You are urged to consult with appropriate financial, business and legal advisors to conduct your own analysis of the information contained in this section.

System Store Performance

All stores included in this System Store Performance section are traditional stores, in that the stores are not located within another retailer's space, such as a grocery or department store. As of December 30, 2013 (the end of our 2013 fiscal year) there were 1,396 stores open. Of the 1,396 stores open, 1,286 traditional Papa Murphy's Take 'N' Bake Pizza stores were open and operating during the entire period of our fiscal year, and 110 stores were either non-traditional or were not open for the full fiscal year. The following statements are based on information reported by the 1,286 traditional Papa Murphy's Take 'N' Bake Pizza stores, both franchise-owned and company-owned, in operation as of December 30, 2013. These stores represent 64 companyowned stores and 1,222 franchise-owned stores (collectively referred to herein as "System Stores"). The System Stores were divided into three groups with the same number of stores in each group, except for one less store in the Medium Group based on Net Sales results: top third ("High"), middle third ("Medium"), and lower third ("Low").

The average annual Net Sales of the System Stores was $586,229 ("System Store Average") per store. Of the 1,286 stores, 521 met or exceeded this average. These System Stores offer substantially the same menu and product mix that your Franchised Store will offer.

The High Group's average Net Sales are $870,188; the Medium Group's average Net Sales are $534,541; and the Low Group's average Net Sales are $353,837. The ranges of Net Sales and averages within the High, Medium and Low categories are listed below:

VOLUME	HIGH	MEDIUM	LOW
Number of Stores	429	428	429
Net Sales:			
Highest	$1,881,257	$637,055	$448,093
Lowest	$637,407	$449,122	$138,317
Average Net Sales by Category	$870,188	$534,541	$353,837
Number of Stores Exceeding Average Net Sales by Category	164	200	235
Total System Store Average Net Sales	$586,229		

Benchmark Costs

This section is based on the sales and operating costs of 638 stores that were open and operating for all of the trailing 52 weeks ending on September 30, 2013, our fiscal third quarter of 2013, and submitted profit and loss statements in the appropriate format for this period ("Benchmark Stores"). Note: As franchised stores have 90 days to submit year-end financial statements, fiscal year 2013 sales and operating costs are not currently available.

The average Net Sales for the Benchmark Stores over the 52 weeks was $640,993. The range of Net Sales was between $198,234 and $1,805,368. These results have not been audited and though the numbers appear to accurately reflect the level of results expected, there is no guarantee that they are in whole or part correct.

VOLUME CATEGORY		HIGH	MEDIUM	LOW
Number of Stores		213	212	213
By Category:	Notes			
Average Gross Sales	1	$1,065,290	$703,304	$475,979
Average Discounts (on Gross Sales)	2	14.0%	14.4%	14.8%
Average Net Sales	3	$915,668	$601,701	$405,426
Number of Stores Exceeding Average Net Sales		88	101	115
Below are represented as a % of Net Sales				
Average COGS	4	36.5%	37.1%	38.2%
Average Employee Labor	5	14.8%	15.3%	17.2%
Average Management	6	4.4%	4.9%	5.9%
Average Payroll Taxes	7	2.2%	2.2%	2.5%
Average Advertising	8	7.5%	8.7%	9.5%
Average Rent and CAM	9	4.1%	5.9%	8.0%
Average Other Store Expenses	10	7.9%	9.2%	11.2%
Average Royalties	11	5.0%	5.0%	5.0%
Average Store Contribution	12	17.6%	11.7%	2.5%

The notes to the above table are an integral part of the bases and assumptions of this analysis. You should particularly note the following:

The table of Benchmark Stores' sales and average food and labor costs is based upon the self-reported profit and loss statements submitted by a portion of the System Stores. The average sales and average costs reflected in the analysis are of certain stores and should not be considered as the actual or potential sales, costs, income or profits that you will realize. We do not represent that any franchisee can expect to attain the sales, costs, income or profits described in this section, or any particular level of sales, costs, income or profits. In addition, we do not represent that any franchisee will derive income that exceeds the initial payment for or investment in the Franchised Store. The individual financial results of any

Franchised Store are likely to differ from the information described in this section, and your success will depend largely on your ability. Substantiation of the data used in preparing this analysis will be made available on reasonable request.

The analysis does not include any estimates of the federal income tax that would be payable on the net income from a store or state or local net income or gross profits taxes that may be applicable to the particular jurisdiction in which a store is located. Each franchisee is strongly urged to consult with its tax advisor regarding the impact that federal, state and local taxes will have on the amounts shown in the analysis.

Notes:

(1) Average Gross Sales. The gross sales figures set forth above represent all food and beverage sales before any coupons or other discounts are taken. It does not include sales taxes collected.

(2) Discount Percentages. The percentages included above include coupons and discounts offered on promotional items or offers. This percentage may also include any discount offered to employees. The percentage is calculated on gross sales.

(3) Average Net Sales. The sales figures set forth above represent all food and beverage sales, net of discounts. This is the amount on which you will calculate your royalty payments.

(4) Cost of Goods ("COGS"). Average COGS includes all food inventory and packaging delivered to the store and used in creating the product for sale, but excludes cleaning supplies and similar items. We negotiate contracts for quantity and price for both beverages and certain food products to take advantage of volume discounts. (See ITEM 8.)

(5) Employee Labor. Hourly wages, both regular and overtime (including crew, assistant managers, shift leaders), for food preparation and service. No corporate management personnel are included in labor costs. The amount of hourly labor necessary to operate a Franchised Store will vary from unit to unit, but should incrementally increase or decrease with the sales volume of the Franchised Store. Hourly wages may vary significantly by geographic location, the supply of and demand on the local labor pool, and state and federally mandated minimum wage laws. Labor includes wages only and does not include payroll taxes, medical or workers compensation insurance or 401(k) plan contributions.

(6) Management. Management costs include payroll expenses (salaries, bonuses for meeting performance objectives, and vacation) for the Franchised Store manager. The number of managers may vary based on sales volume and your requirements may differ from those of a Benchmark Store. In some cases, a franchise owner serves as the store manager and draws little or no salary.

(7) Payroll Taxes. Unemployment taxes (both federal and state), FICA, employee injury insurance or workers compensation where required.

(8) Advertising. This category is comprised of four types of expenditures: (a) local store marketing and merchandising, (b) contribution to the Advertising and Development Fund, (c) contribution to the Sales Building Print Plan, and (d) your Franchised Store's designated percentage contribution to your local advertising cooperative, which can be different for each designated marketing area.

(9) Rent and Common Area Maintenance ("CAM"). Rent and CAM includes rent and lease costs, common area maintenance expenses and tax and insurance due the landlord. Rent and lease costs include the base rent and any percentage rent. Common area maintenance costs typically include franchisee's pro rata charges for parking lot maintenance, lighting, real estate taxes, taxes on the common areas and costs of maintaining the common areas. Rental costs will vary as a result of space requirements and local market conditions.

(10) Other Store Expenses. Other store expenses include the cost of direct supervision, bank fees, accounting and payroll services, utilities, repairs and maintenance, telephone, employee benefits, insurance, janitorial, smallwares, taxes and licenses, broadband/Internet, point-of-sale system costs, credit card processing charges, uniforms, and laundry and supplies. Utilities include electricity, gas, water and telephone costs for the operation of the Franchised Store. The pro rata share of common area utility costs is included under rent and lease payments. (See Note 9.) These costs are subject to local market conditions and may vary depending on the geographic location of the Franchised Store. The Other category also includes personal property taxes, other real estate taxes not included in rent and lease and other operating licenses required by state and local agencies. You should investigate property taxes in the area in which you plan to locate your Franchised Store.

(11) Royalties. Royalties include a royalty and services fee equal to 5 percent of your Franchised Store Net Sales.

(12) Store Contribution. The store contribution represents revenue less expenses described herein, and this figure does not reflect other costs which you may incur as a franchisee, which may include general and administrative costs, depreciation (consult with your tax advisor regarding depreciation and amortization schedules and the period over which the assets may be amortized or depreciated as well as the effect, if any, of recent and proposed tax legislation), and financing costs, if any. In addition, you will also be subject to local state and federal

income taxes which are not reflected in the preceding table.

Statement of Average Annual Net Sale Percentage Increase

This statement includes the average Net Sales percentage increase for Papa Murphy's Take 'N' Bake Pizza stores based on a comparison of Net Sales: (i) in 2007 and 2006 for stores that were in operation for the entire 12-month period ended December 31, 2007; (ii) in 2008 and 2007 for stores that were in operation for the entire 12-month period ended December 29, 2008; (iii) in 2009 and 2008 for stores that were in operation for the entire 12-month period ended December 28, 2009; (iv) in 2010 and 2009 for stores that were in operation for the entire 12-month period ended January 3, 2011; (v) in 2011 and 2010 for stores that were in operation for the entire 12-month period ended January 2, 2012; (vi) in 2012 and 2011 for stores that were in operation for the entire 12-month period ended December 31, 2012; and (vii) in 2013 and 2012 for stores that were in operation for the entire 12-month period ended December 30, 2013. Only stores that were open all weeks in both years are compared.

Average Same Store Net Sales Percentage Increase			
Comparison Year	Stores	Percentage Increase	Number and Percentage of Stores Above Average
2006 v 2005	765	2.4%	408 (53%)
2007 v 2006	828	6.0%	398 (48%)
2008 v 2007	899	9.2%	461 (51%)
2009 v 2008	987	2.7%	489 (50%)
2010 v 2009	1,059	-2.9%	540 (51%)
2011 v 2010	1,113	5.8%	567 (51%)
2012 v 2011	1,179	3.1%	589 (50%)
2013 v 2012	1,215	3.0%	590 (49%)

Papa Murphy's had positive year-over-year comparable store sales performance for seven out of the last eight years.

New Store Performance

Since 2007, new stores have achieved average weekly Net Sales in excess of $8,000, on average, within their first fiscal year. The actual annual average Net Sales achieved may vary due to seasonality, location characteristics, owner involvement, marketing plans and competition, as well as other factors disclosed in this Disclosure Document.

Other than the preceding financial performance representation, we do not make any financial performance representations. We also do not authorize our employees or representatives to make any such representations either orally or in writing. If you are purchasing an existing outlet, however, we may provide you with the actual records of that outlet. If you receive any other financial performance information or projections of your future revenue and/or income, you should report it to the franchisor's management by contacting Victoria Blackwell, Papa Murphy's International LLC, at 8000 NE Parkway Drive, Suite 350, Vancouver, Washington 98662, (360) 449-4122, the Federal Trade Commission, and the appropriate state regulatory agencies.

RITA'S ITALIAN ICE

1210 NorthBrook Dr., # 310

Trevose, PA 19053

Tel: (800) 677-7482, (215) 876-9300

Fax: (866) 449-0974

Email: e.taylor@ritascorp.com

Website: www.ritasice.com

Eric Taylor, Senior Vice President and Chief Development Officer

Rita's is the largest Italian Ice chain in the nation. With a 30 year proven business model, Rita's offers a variety of frozen treats including its famous Italian Ice, Old Fashioned Frozen Custard, and layered Gelati as well as its signature Misto and Blendini creations.

BACKGROUND

IFA Member:	Yes
Established & First Franchised:	1984; 1989
Franchised Units:	555
Company-Owned Units:	0
Total Units:	555
Distribution:	US – 555; CAN – 0; O'seas – 0
North America:	22 States, 0 Provinces
Density:	196 in PA, 120 in NJ, 82 in MD

Projected New Units (12 Months):	66
Qualifications:	3, 3, 3, 3, 3, 5

FINANCIAL/TERMS

Cash Investment:	$100K
Total Investment:	$140.2 – 413.9K
Minimum Net Worth:	$300K
Fees (Franchise):	$30K
Fees (Royalty):	6.5%
Fees (Advertising):	3%
Term of Contract (Years):	10/10
Average Number of Employees:	2 FT, 15 PT
Passive Ownership:	Discouraged
Encourage Conversions:	No
Area Development Agreements:	Yes
Sub-Franchising Contracts:	No
Expand in Territory:	Yes
Space Needs:	800 – 1,200 SF

SUPPORT & TRAINING

Financial Assistance Provided:	Yes (I)
Site Selection Assistance:	Yes
Lease Negotiation Assistance:	Yes
Co-operative Advertising:	Yes
Franchisee Association/Member:	No
Size of Corporate Staff:	60
On-going Support:	C, D, E, F, G, H, I
Training:	4 Days On-Site; 5 Days Corporate Office

SPECIFIC EXPANSION PLANS

US:	All United States
Canada:	Yes
Overseas:	Yes

Included in this Item 19 are Rita's estimates of (1) 2013 average sales of Proprietary Products at franchised Shops ("Average Sales"), described in Section I, below, and (2) 2013 average food costs for ingredients for the Proprietary Products at franchised Shops ("Costs of Goods Sold"), described in Section II, below. No Financial Performance Representations are being made on the Fixed Satellite Unit or the Express Unit.

I. 2013 AVERAGE SALES OF PROPRIETARY PRODUCTS AT FRANCHISED SHOPS

The following chart represents our estimates of the Average Sales of franchised Shops for Italian ice, gelati, frozen custard, Misto shakes, and Blendini in 2013:

*	Top Third	Middle Third	Bottom Third
Number of Shops	163	163	163
Range of Sales:			
High	$672,556	$271,181	$196,313
Low	$273,191	$196,939	$65,403
Average	$340,341	$232,933	$152,546

* If a Franchisee also has a Mobile Unit the sales of the Mobile Unit are included with the sales of the Standard Shop.

Although Rita's obtained reports from Franchisees as to Gross Sales at franchised Shops for the 2013 season for marketing and research purposes, Rita's is not able to independently verify reported sales. In preparing the Average Sales figure for this Item 19, Rita's estimated Average Sales from franchised Shops. Reported sales were typically lower than estimated Average Sales. As stated in Item 6 of this disclosure document, Royalty Fees and Advertising Fees on Proprietary Products are based on estimated sales. Rita's describes below how Rita's estimated the Average Sales contained in this Item 19.

The sales estimates described in this Item 19 represent only the sales by Franchisees of Proprietary Products containing the proprietary Rita's Mixes. These Proprietary Products were Italian ice, gelati, frozen custard, Misto shakes, and Blendini. Not included in the sales calculations described in this Item 19 are any other products sold by Franchisees, such as pretzels and promotional items.

The information in the Chart above is based on Shops that have been open for at least 1 full season. Shops opened less than 1 full season are not included in the calculations. A full season is defined as 1 entire selling season for which Rita's requires operation and the Shop must be opened at least 5 days before spring. Florida franchised Shops may have been open for as many as 10 to 12 months. Where a Shop was open for a period longer than the selling season, all sales for such Shop were included in Rita's determination of Average Sales.

The Chart divides franchisees into three categories (Top Third, Middle Third, and Bottom Third), based on their sales as compared with the sales for the 489 total Shops considered in arriving at these figures. 59 franchisees (36% of the Shops in the Top Third) attained or surpassed the average sales for the Top Third; 75 franchisees (46% of the Shops in the Middle Third) attained or surpassed the average sales for the Middle Third; and 88 franchisees (54% of the Shops in the Bottom Third) attained or surpassed the average sales for the Bottom Third. The average sales represent the average sales for franchisees within each category. High sales and Low sales represent the Franchisee within each category that attained the highest and lowest sales.

As noted in Item 6 of this disclosure document, each Franchisee must pay to Rita's a Royalty Fee in the amount of 6 ½% of the projected sales to be made by a Franchisee based on a Franchisee's purchase of Rita's proprietary Rita's Mixes. In calculating the Royalty Fee, Rita's estimates the projected sales that can be expected to be made from a Franchisee's purchase of Rita's Mixes, based on the amount of Rita's Mixes required for use in Rita's recipes for each product.

In calculating the Average Sales, Rita's estimated Franchisees' Average Sales based on the amount of Rita's Mixes purchased, Franchisees' prices, and the percentage of each type of Proprietary Product sold by Franchisees relative to all Proprietary Products sold (the "Product Percentages"). The historical data from which Rita's calculated the Product Percentages was provided to Rita's by each franchisee via weekly reporting of retail sales figures for each product during the 2013 season. Rita's knows the prices charged by each Franchisee because each Franchisee must notify Rita's of its prices so that Rita's may calculate the Royalty Fee to be paid by such Franchisee. The numbers in the chart above have been rounded to the nearest thousand.

Franchisee's Sales are generally lower during the first several years of operation for franchised Shops. Therefore, franchised Shops open for the first two to three years may be more likely than other franchised Shops to be in the Bottom Third in sales.

The Product Percentages for the 2013 season, as determined from Franchisees' franchised Shop register tapes (described in I, above) are described below. The Product Percentages vary based upon a Franchisee's location.

Proprietary Product	Percentage of All Proprietary Products Reported for Sale
ITALIAN ICE	32.7%
GELATI	27.2%
CUSTARD	22.3%
MISTO SHAKE	4.8%
BLENDINI	5.5%
MISCELLANEOUS	7.5%
TOTAL	100.00%

In calculating the Royalty Fee and Average Sales above Rita's assumed certain "usage" and "wastage" figures for franchisees. Rita's measures Franchisees' "usage" figures by comparing (1) the expected yield for Rita's Mixes that Rita's calculates and (2) the amount of Proprietary Products sold using such mixes. Rita's defines "wastage" as the Rita's Mix that will not be used in Proprietary Products that are sold (e.g., product that will be thrown away or given away in connection with promotions). Usage estimates vary among the franchisees' location. Such usage figures vary widely for some franchisees, and are much higher for some franchisees. Rita's believes that the reason for the variation is due to a variety of factors including certain Franchisees' reporting, give-away programs, over-portioning, internal theft, changes in product mix, the timing of the purchases, inexperience, and wastage. In calculating the Royalty Fee and Average Sales, Rita's assumed that some "wastage" would occur, as there is a certain amount of "wastage" that occurs in all sales of Proprietary Products that use the Rita's Mix. The Royalty Fee calculation for the 2013 season provided for 7% wastage. Accordingly, for purposes of the calculations above, when Rita's estimated projected sales on which a Franchisee owed Rita's a Royalty Fee, Rita's reduced its projections of sales expected to be made from a given amount of Rita's Mixes by 7%.

II. 2013 COSTS OF GOODS SOLD FOR PROPRIETARY PRODUCTS AT FRANCHISED SHOPS

Rita's estimates that Rita's Franchisees' Costs of Goods Sold represent 19% of Franchisees' revenue from sales of the products. Rita's has calculated the estimated Costs of Goods Sold of 19% based on (1) portions for ingredients reported in Rita's proprietary recipes, (2) 2013 prices for such ingredients, (3) the System-wide average selling price in 2013 for each Proprietary Product sold, (4) a weighted average of Proprietary Products sold as determined by Franchisee reports of Product Percentages in 201 (as defined in Section I, above), and (5) average cost of paper and packaging in 2013. Rita's calculation of Costs of Goods Sold assumes that proper recipes are followed, Franchisees adhere to proper serving sizes for Proprietary Products, and Franchisees maintain product wastage levels of 7%.

Rita's does not obtain reports from Franchisees as to Costs of Goods Sold at franchised Shops. Accordingly, to prepare the Costs of Goods Sold figures in this Item 19 it was necessary for Rita's to estimate the Costs of Goods Sold figures from franchised Shops. Rita's does not know what percentage of Franchisees incurred actual Costs of Goods Sold higher or lower than the estimated Costs of Goods Sold of 19%. Rita's describes below how it estimated the Costs of Goods Sold contained in this Item 19.

The calculation of Costs of Goods Sold contained in this Item 19 represents Costs of Goods Sold only for the products that Rita's requires each Franchisee to sell (i.e., kids, regular, large and quart Italian ice; regular and large gelati; kids, regular and large custard; regular and large Misto shakes; and Blendinis). As described in Section I, above, each franchisee provided its historical data to Rita's via weekly reporting of retail sales figures for each product during the 2013 season. Rita's used this data to estimate the Costs of Goods Sold in the 2013 season. Rita's can estimate the total cost of the ingredients for each Proprietary Product because the recipes for each Proprietary Product are prescribed by Rita's, Franchisees were required in 2013 to purchase the Rita's Mixes from Rita's, and Franchisees may also purchase the remaining ingredients from Rita's. Rita's has used the prices it charged in 2013 to Franchisees for ingredients. Rita's has determined the average selling price (not including sales tax) for each Proprietary Product during the 2013 season based on the prices submitted by Franchisees. In order to approximate the food costs resulting from wastage, in calculating Costs of Goods Sold for this Item 19, Rita's reduced the average selling price for each Proprietary Product by 7%. To determine the total pretax sales represented by the register tapes, as adjusted to reflect wastage, Rita's multiplied the adjusted average selling price by the number of units of each Proprietary Product sold (as reflected on the register tapes). Rita's also estimated the total cost of ingredients necessary to produce the total sales represented by the register tapes by multiplying the total number of each Proprietary Product sold by the estimated total costs for the ingredients for each item. Rita's determined estimated total costs for all sales represented by the register tapes by adding the estimated total costs for each Proprietary Product. Rita's determined Costs of Goods Sold by dividing the estimated total costs by the pre-tax adjusted sales. From this calculation, Rita's determined Costs of Goods Sold to be 19% of Franchisees' sales of all Proprietary Products.

As described in Item 6, above, each Franchisee must pay to Rita's a Royalty Fee based upon the amount of Rita's Mixes purchased by the Franchisee. This Royalty Fee has not been included in the calculations to determine Costs of Goods Sold in this Item 19. As a Franchisee, payment of the Royalty Fee would be an additional cost.

The calculations in this Item 19 used in determining Costs of Goods Sold are made under the assumption that Franchisees adhere to Rita's proprietary recipes and serving sizes. Although Rita's has provided each Franchisee with training and support to assist each Franchisee in adhering to these recipes and serving sizes, Rita's Franchisees have indicated to Rita's that an indeterminate number of Franchisees may serve portions to guests larger than those Rita's specifies. However, Rita's strongly encourages Franchisees to adhere to Rita's standards, specifications and portion controls for purposes of System consistency.

Costs of Goods Sold vary depending on store location, menu, Product Percentages, seasonal variances in raw material prices, and Franchisees' ability to effectively control costs. The average new Franchisee generally finds the first year of operation of each franchised Shop to be the most challenging. During the first year of operation a new Franchisee typically experiences higher wastage levels due to sampling, couponing and other promotional programs designed to build brand and product acceptance and due to higher amounts of "throw-aways" resulting from inexperience in planning. Historical costs do not correspond to future costs because of factors such as inflation, changes in menu and market driven changes in raw material costs.

Rita's obtained reports from Franchisees as to Gross Sales at franchised Shops for the 2013 season for marketing and research purposes, but we have not relied on these reports in this Item 19 because we cannot independently verify reported sales. (Reported sales are typically less than estimated Average Sales.) Actual sales and food costs vary from franchise to franchise, and Rita's cannot estimate the sales or food costs for a particular franchise. As stated in Item 6 of this disclosure document, Royalty Fees and Advertising Fees are based on estimated sales. Rita's recommends that you make your own independent investigation to determine whether or not the franchise may be profitable, and consult with an attorney and other advisors before signing the Development Agreement or the Franchise Agreement.

Rita's will make available to you for inspection and review before your purchase of a franchise the data used in formulating the information contained in this Item 19 upon your reasonable request.

Some outlets have sold this amount. Your individual results may differ. There is no assurance that you'll sell as much.

Other than the preceding financial performance representation, Rita's does not make any financial performance representations. We also do not authorize our employees or representatives to make any such representations either orally or in writing. If you are purchasing an existing outlet, however, we may provide you with the actual records of that outlet. If you receive any other financial performance information or projections of your future income, you should report it to the franchisor's management by contacting Rita's Franchise Company, Franchise Department at 1210 Northbrook Drive, Suite 310, Trevose, PA 19053 and (800) 677-7482, the Federal Trade Commission, and the appropriate state regulatory agencies.

TROPICAL SMOOTHIE CAFE, LLC

1117 Perimeter Center W., # W200
Atlanta, GA 30338
Tel: (770) 821-1900
Fax: (770) 821-1895
Email: cwatson@tropicalsmoothie.com
Website: www.tropicalsmoothiefranchise.com
Charles Watson, Vice President of Franchise Development

Tropical Smoothie Café's business model is unique, as we offer both real fruit smoothies and a variety of fresh, flavorful food. We are two franchises in one! Our initial store development costs are lower because we do not utilize deep fryers, grills, or hooding systems (healthier too!) and our balanced business model of 50% Food Sales and 50% Smoothie sales allow us to drive higher gross sales and service all dayparts: breakfast, lunch, dinner, snack times, and dessert. In fact, for full year 2012, the top 50% of our Cafés had average gross sales over $669,000*! Get the franchisee solutions, strength, and support you need at Tropical Smoothie Café.
*Based on Calendar year 2013, 61 of 283 or 21.6% of the Ca-

fes gained or surpassed this sales level. Your results may differ. There is no assurance you will do as well. Offer made by prospectus only.

BACKGROUND

IFA Member:	Yes
Established & First Franchised:	1997; 1998
Franchised Units:	399
Company-Owned Units:	1
Total Units:	400
Distribution:	US – 400; CAN – 0; O'seas – 0
North America:	36 States, 0 Provinces
Density:	110 in FL, 75 in VA, 20 in NV
Projected New Units (12 Months):	100
Qualifications:	3, 5, 4, 2, 1, 5

FINANCIAL/TERMS

Cash Investment:	$100 – 125K
Total Investment:	$165 – 424K
Minimum Net Worth:	$300K
Fees (Franchise):	$25K
Fees (Royalty):	6%
Fees (Advertising):	4%
Term of Contract (Years):	15/10
Average Number of Employees:	1 FT, 10 – 12 PT
Passive Ownership:	Not Allowed
Encourage Conversions:	Yes
Area Development Agreements:	No
Sub-Franchising Contracts:	No
Expand in Territory:	Yes
Space Needs:	1,200 – 1,600 SF

SUPPORT & TRAINING		Training:	1 Week Corporate Office; 2 Weeks Local stores; 1 Week Store Opening
Financial Assistance Provided:	Yes (D)		
Site Selection Assistance:	Yes		
Lease Negotiation Assistance:	Yes	SPECIFIC EXPANSION PLANS	
Co-operative Advertising:	Yes	US:	All United States
Franchisee Association/Member:	No	Canada:	No
Size of Corporate Staff:	25	Overseas:	No
On-going Support:	A, B, C, D, E, F, G, H, I		

FINANCIAL PERFORMANCE REPRESENTATIONS: INDIVIDUAL UNIT TROPICAL SMOOTHIE CAFE FRANCHISES

The following tables provide historical sales information for Tropical Smoothi Cafe® franchised stores ("Stores") that were open at least one full year as of (a) the calendar year 2011 for 245 Stores (b) the calendar year 2010 for 262 Stores; and (c) the calendar year 2009 for 233 Stores. The tables do not include any financial performance information for any other types of franchises, such as non-traditional locations (i.e. college campus or other captive locations) or seasonal locations, and do not include any franchises of any type that had not been open for at least one year on December 31, 2011, December 31 2010 and December 31,2009, respectively. The information presented is not a forecast of future potential performance. The gross revenue figures are based on the same computation for computing royalties as required under the Franchise Agreement.

The tables provide the average gross revenues for the following categories of Stores in 2011, 2010, and 2009 on a category and cumulative basis: (a) our top 10% revenue producing Stores (meaning the average gross revenue for the number of Stores that were in the top 10% of gross revenues for that year); (b) our top 25% revenue producing Stores (which includes the Stores that are in the top 10%); (c) our top 50% revenue producing Stores (which includes the Stores that are in the top 10% and the top 25%); and (d) our top 75% revenue producing Stores. We present the average gross sales for the year in that category as well as the number and percentage achieving or surpassing the average gross sales in that category alone and cumulative for all Stores. For example, 24 of the 62 Stores in the top 25% for 2010 (or 39%), and 113 of the 250 total Stores for 2010 (or 45%) achieved or surpassed that average.

Average Gross Revenues in 2013

	Top 10%	Top 25%	Top 50%	Top 75%	Total
No. of Stores	28	71	142	212	283
Avg. Gross Revenues	$907,812	$775,639	$669,054	$597,406	$526,403
No. that Attained or Surpassed Stated Result in Category (Cumulative)	9	24	61	83	134
Percent that Attained or Surpassed Stated Result in Category (Cumulative)	32%	34%	43%	39%	47%

As of December 29, 2013, there were 359 franchised Stores and 1 company-owned Store. Of the 359 franchised Stores, 309 were franchised Stores that had been open for at least 12 months as of December 29, 2013. Of the 309 Stores, 26 Stores were excluded since they were non-traditional locations. Of the 283 Stores referenced in the above table, all reported sufficient financial performance information to be included in this financial performance representation.

Average Gross Revenues in 2012

	Top 10%	Top 25%	Top 50%	Top 75%	Total
No. of Stores	26	66	130	195	261

Avg. Gross Revenues	$882,011	$743,762	$640,600	$569,739	$500,050
No. that Attained or Surpassed Stated Result in Category (Cumulative)	11	24	49	76	117
Percent that Attained or Surpassed Stated Result in Category (Cumulative)	42%	36%	38%	39%	45%

As of December 30, 2012, there were 329 franchised Stores and 0 company-owned Stores. Of the 329 franchised Stores, 261 were franchised Stores that had been open for at least 12 months as of December 30, 2012. Of the 329 Stores, 3 Stores were excluded since they were non-traditional locations. Of the 261 Stores referenced in the above table, all reported sufficient financial performance information to be included in this financial performance representation.

Average Gross Revenues in 2011

	Top 10%	Top 25%	Top 50%	Top 75%	Total
No. of Stores	25	61	122	184	245
Avg. Gross Revenues	$829,297	$710,319	$608,796	$540,516	$477,463
No. that Attained or Surpassed Stated Result in Category (Cumulative)	10	22	47	75	106
Percent that Attained or Surpassed Stated Result in Category (Cumulative)	40%	37%	39%	41%	43%

As of December 31, 2011, there were 301 franchised Stores and 4 company-owned Stores. Of the 301 franchised Stores, 261 were franchised Stores that had been open for at least 12 months as of December 31, 2011. Of the 261 Stores, 16 Stores were excluded since they were non-traditional locations. Of the 245 Stores referenced in the above table, all reported sufficient financial performance information to be included in this financial performance representation.

As stated, the sales for each of the Stores presented are limited to the sales results for Stores that had been open for a full 12 months of operations as of December 29, 2013, December 30, 2012 and December 31, 2011, respectively. Sales during the first year of operations are likely to be significantly less than for those that have been open for a year or more.

All Tropical Smoothie Café® Stores offer substantially the same products and services to the public. None of the franchised Tropical Smoothie Café® Stores received any services not generally available to other franchisees and substantially the same services will be offered to new franchisees.

We obtained these historical financial results from the information submitted by our franchisees. Neither we nor an independent certified public accountant has independently audited or verified the information. Some Stores have sold the

amounts shown in the tables. Your individual results may differ. There is no assurance you will sell as much.

YOUR INDIVIDUAL FINANCIAL RESULTS MAY DIFFER SUBSTANTIALLY FROM THE RESULTS DISCLOSED IN THIS ITEM 19.

The foregoing data relates to revenues only; we are not presenting any information on the costs and expenses of operating a Store. Operating a Store incurs a wide variety of expenses that will reduce the Store's income from the revenue levels shown. Examples of the types of these expenses include, without limitation, rent and occupancy expenses; food and beverage product and supply costs; salaries, wages and other personnel-related expenses; federal, state and local taxes and fees; utilities; financing costs (including on loans and leases); royalties and other amounts due us.

CHARACTERISTICS OF THE INCLUDED FRANCHISED STORES MAY DIFFER SUBSTANTIALLY FROM YOUR STORE DEPENDING ON YOUR PREVIOUS BUSINESS AND MANAGEMENT EXPERIENCE, COMPETITION IN YOUR AREA, LENGTH OF TIME THAT THE INCLUDED STORES HAVE OPERATED COMPARED TO YOUR STORE, AND THE SERVICES OR GOODS SOLD AT YOUR STORE COMPARED TO

THE INCLUDED STORES. THE SALES, PROFITS AND EARNINGS OF AN INDIVIDUAL FRANCHISEE MAY VARY GREATLY DEPENDING ON THESE AND A WIDE VARIETY OF OTHER FACTORS, INCLUDING THE LOCATION OF THE STORE, POPULATION AND DEMOGRAPHICS IN YOUR MARKET AREA, ECONOMIC AND MARKET CONDITIONS, LABOR AND PRODUCT COSTS, ETC.

WE HAVE WRITTEN SUBSTANTIATION IN OUR POSSESSION TO SUPPORT THE INFORMATION APPEARING IN THIS FINANCIAL PERFORMANCE REPRESENTATION. WRITTEN SUBSTANTIATION WILL BE MADE AVAILABLE TO YOU ON REASONABLE REQUEST.

We recommend that you make your own independent investigation to determine whether or not the franchise may be prof-itable, and consult with an attorney and other advisors prior to executing the franchise agreement.

Other than the preceding financial performance representation, we do not make any financial performance representations about a franchisee's future financial performance or the past financial performance of company-owned or franchised outlets. We also do not authorize our employees or representatives to make any such representations either orally or in writing. If you are purchasing an existing outlet, however, we may provide you with the actual records of that outlet. If you receive any other financial performance information or projections of your future income, you should report it to our management by contacting Mike Rotondo, our CEO at 1117 Perimeter Center West, Suite W200, Atlanta, Georgia 30338 and 770-821-1900, the Federal Trade Commission, and the appropriate state regulatory agencies.

WINGSTOP

5501 LBJ Freeway, 5th Fl.
Dallas, TX 75240
Tel: (972) 686-6500
Fax: (972) 686-6502
Email: dvernon@wingstop.com
Website: www.wingstopfranchise.com
David Vernon, Chief Development Officer

This financial performance representation contains actual 2013 average annual net sales information for (1) all Wingstop Restaurants (both franchised and owned by us), (2) separately for all franchised Wingstop Restaurants, and (3) separately for all company-owned Wingstop Restaurants, in operation in the United States during the entire 2013 fiscal year.

The actual 2013 average annual net sales (defined below) for all Wingstop Restaurants in the system in the United States that were open for operation during the entire period from December 30, 2012 through December 28, 2013 (the "2013 Fiscal Year"), including both franchised and our own Restaurants, were $974,025.[1] We define net sales as gross receipts net of (that is, after deducting amounts for) sales tax, coupons/promotions, and voids. The average includes all Restaurants that were open during the entire 2013 Fiscal Year, even if their ownership changed during that time period.[2]

The total number of Restaurants included in this average was 526 (23 we owned and 503 franchised). The number of franchised Restaurants open for operation during the entire 2013 Fiscal Year whose actual 2013 net sales exceeded the $974,025 average totaled 225 (43%). The number of our own 23 Restaurants open for operation during the entire 2013 Fiscal Year whose actual 2013 net sales exceeded the $974,025 average totaled 16 (70%).

We obtained the net sales information for franchised Restaurants from weekly royalty reports submitted by franchisees and information polled from POS systems in the Restaurants. We have not independently audited that information. The franchised Restaurants that were open for operation during the entire 2013 Fiscal Year and whose average net sales are reported above are substantially similar to the Restaurant franchises we currently offer. The actual 2013 average annual net sales for the 503 franchised Wingstop Restaurants open for operation during the entire 2013 Fiscal Year were $958,313. The number of franchised Restaurants open for operation during the entire 2013 Fiscal Year whose actual 2013 net sales exceeded this $958,313 franchised Restaurant average totaled 211 (42%).

The actual 2013 average annual net sales for our 23 company-owned Wingstop Restaurants open for operation during the entire 2013 Fiscal Year were $1,206,332. The number of our company-owned Restaurants open for operation during the entire 2013 Fiscal Year whose actual 2013 net sales exceeded this $1,206,332 company-owned Restaurant average totaled 10 (43%).

The actual average annual net sales numbers reported above do not reflect the costs of sales, operating expenses, or other costs or expenses that must be deducted from the net sales figures to obtain your net income or profit. You should conduct an independent investigation of the costs and expenses you will incur in operating your Wingstop Restaurant. Franchisees or former franchisees, listed in the Franchise Disclosure Document, may be one source of this information.

The actual net sales volumes of Wingstop Restaurants vary widely. Our experience indicates that there are numerous factors affecting the sales of a particular Wingstop Restaurant, including: traffic count; accessibility and visibility of a site; the local marketplace and competition; general economic conditions; the franchisee's management skill, experience, business acumen, and ability to promote and market Wingstop Restaurants effectively in the local market; and the degree of adherence to our methods and procedures in operating the Restaurant.

Chicken wings and other chicken products are the principal food items sold by Wingstop Restaurants. The availability of these products from independent suppliers throughout the United States and their wholesale cost are determined by market factors (including the supply needs of competitive businesses) over which we have little control. These supply chain issues will impact your operating costs and results during the franchise term.

Some Wingstop Restaurants have sold this amount. Your individual results may differ. There is no assurance that you'll sell as much. Written substantiation of all financial performance information presented in this financial performance representation will be made available to you upon reasonable request.

This financial performance representation was prepared without an audit. Prospective franchisees or sellers of franchises should be advised that no certified public accountant has audited these figures or expressed his/her opinion with regard to their contents or form.

Other than the preceding financial performance representation, we do not make any financial performance representations. We also do not authorize our employees or representatives to make any such representations either orally or in writing. If you are purchasing an existing outlet, however, we may provide you with the actual records of that outlet. If you receive any other financial performance information or projections of your future income, you should report it to the franchisor's management by contacting Charles Morrison, Wingstop Restaurants Inc., 5501 LBJ Freeway, 5th Floor, Dallas, Texas 75240, (972) 686-6500, the Federal Trade Commission, and the appropriate state regulatory agencies.

1. Average annual net sales are calculated by dividing total sales during the 2013 Fiscal Year for all Restaurants in the system that were open for operation during the entire 2013 Fiscal Year by the number of Restaurants that were open for operation during the entire 2013 Fiscal Year.

2. We are using the December 30, 2012 through December 28, 2013 time period because December 28, 2013 is the date on which we ended our 2013 fiscal year. Our 2013 fiscal year contained 52 weeks.

WING ZONE

900 Circle 75 Pkwy., # 930
Atlanta, GA 30339
Tel: (877) 333-9464 x16, (404) 875-5045 x16

Fax: (404) 875-6631
Email: clint@wingzone.com
Website: www.wingzone.com
Clint Lee, Director of Franchise Development

Delivery & Take-out of 15 taste-tempting flavors of fresh, cooked-to-order Buffalo wings. We also feature chicken fingers, grilled or fried chicken sandwiches, half-pound burgers, salads, sides, appetizers and desserts—all delivered hot and fresh to your door. A great opportunity in urban and suburban markets, near apartments, campuses, military bases, hospitals and offices.

BACKGROUND		Passive Ownership:	Allowed
IFA Member:	Yes	Encourage Conversions:	No
Established & First Franchised:	1991; 1999	Area Development Agreements:	Yes
Franchised Units:	96	Sub-Franchising Contracts:	No
Company-Owned Units:	4	Expand in Territory:	Yes
Total Units:	100	Space Needs:	1,200 SF
Distribution:	US – 95; CAN – 0; O'seas – 5		
North America:	24 States, 0 Provinces	SUPPORT & TRAINING	
Density:	18 in FL, 10 in NC, 10 in VA	Financial Assistance Provided:	Yes (I)
Projected New Units (12 Months):	24	Site Selection Assistance:	Yes
Qualifications:	5, 5, 3, 4, 3, 5	Lease Negotiation Assistance:	Yes
		Co-operative Advertising:	No
FINANCIAL/TERMS		Franchisee Association/Member:	Yes/Member
Cash Investment:	$100K	Size of Corporate Staff:	15
Total Investment:	$225 – 295K	On-going Support:	A, B, C, D, E, F, G, H, I
Minimum Net Worth:	$250K	Training:	21 Days Atlanta, GA
Fees (Franchise):	$25K		
Fees (Royalty):	5%	SPECIFIC EXPANSION PLANS	
Fees (Advertising):	2%	US:	SE, NE, MW, SW
Term of Contract (Years):	10/10	Canada:	Near Border
Average Number of Employees:	5 FT, 10 PT	Overseas:	Yes

Background

This Item includes certain historical revenue information for certain franchisee-operated Businesses, and certain cost information (which franchisees must report to us via the required POS System) for franchisee-operated Businesses for the period December 3, 2012 through December 1, 2013. The success of your franchise will depend largely upon your individual abilities and your market, and the financial results of your franchise are likely to differ, perhaps materially, from the results summarized in this Item.

Substantiation of the data used in preparing this financial performance representation will be made available for your review upon reasonable request.

Historical Operations Statements

"Chart A," below, shows the overall actual average Business results of 42 Franchisee Businesses that have been open at least one full Accounting Period and have been operating under the same ownership for at least 15 consecutive months as of March 12, 2014.

The expenses detailed in Chart A for Franchisee Businesses are based on information we derived directly from the information reported by each franchisee in the required POS System. This information is not audited. The Franchisee Businesses included in Chart A have been operating under the same ownership for at least 15 consecutive months as of March 12, 2014. We excluded one resale that changed ownership during the Accounting Period.

CHART A:
Average Actual Historical Operations for the 42 Franchisee Businesses
Operating Under the Same Ownership At Least 15 Months as of March 12, 2014

	Gross Revenues (Note 1)	Labor (Note 2)	COGS (Note 3)
Franchisee Businesses (AVG)	$583,886	22.9%	34.8%

Of the 42 Franchisee Businesses included in Chart A, 15 (or 35.7%) met or exceeded the average Franchisee Business Gross Revenues of $583,886; 21 (or 50%) met or exceeded the average Franchisee Business Labor of 22.9%; and 21 (or 50%) met or exceeded the average Franchisee Business COGS of 34.8%.

Notes to Chart A:

(1) As noted above, Gross Revenues includes the total revenue from the sale of products, net of any refunds to customers, determined on a cash basis.

(2) The 42 Franchisee Restaurants are managed in a variety of ways, including solely by the Franchisee's owner or principal, solely by an employee-manager, or by a combination of both the Franchisee's owner/principal and employee-manager. Labor costs do not include bonuses on profits to Business managers or the cost of area and regional personnel who may be needed if you operate more than one Business.

(3) Cost of Goods Sold includes expenses for food, beverage and paper. Cost of Goods Sold also includes the cost of frying oil which averages 1.4% of Sales.

Notes:

Some outlets have sold this amount. Your individual results may differ. There is no assurance that you'll sell as much.

The above charts do not reflect the performance of any particular location. Rather, they represent the average of the 42 Franchisee Businesses that have been open the full Accounting Period and have been operating under the same ownership for at least 15 consecutive months as of March 12, 2014.

Actual results vary from Business to Business, and we cannot estimate the result of a particular Business. Revenues and expenses vary depending on whether the Business is company operated or franchisee operated, whether the Business is located in a metropolitan market or a non-metropolitan market, and type or kind of restaurant (for example, Traditional or Full-Service). In particular, the revenues and expenses of a franchisee-owned Business will be directly affected by many factors, such as: (a) geographic location; (b) competition from other firms in the market; (c) population density of the market; (d) proximity to other Businesses; (e) advertising effectiveness based on market saturation; (f) whether the franchisee assumes the position as or hires a manager; (g) the payment of royalties, national advertising production and promotional fees; (h) the franchisee's product and service pricing; (i) vendor prices on merchandise; (j) salaries and benefits to non-Business personnel; (k) Business personnel benefits (life and health insurance, etc.); (l) employment conditions in the market; and (m) whether the Business is a Traditional Restaurant, or Full-Service Restaurant. Also, a fixed expense as a percentage of revenue will vary, generally inversely, to the revenue of a Business.

We recommend that you make your own independent investigation to determine whether or not the franchise may be profitable to you. You should use the above information only as a reference in conducting your analysis and preparing your own projected income statements and cash flow statements. We suggest strongly that you consult your financial advisor or personal accountant concerning financial projections and federal, state and local income taxes and any other applicable taxes that you may incur in operating a Business.

Written substantiation for the financial performance representation will be made available to the prospective franchisee upon reasonable request.

Other than the preceding financial performance representation, we do not make any financial performance representations. We also do not authorize our employees or representatives to make any such representations either orally or in writing. If you are purchasing an existing outlet, however, we may provide you with the actual records of that outlet. If you receive any other financial performance information or projections of your future income, you should report it to the franchisor's management by contacting Adam Scott, our Chief Financial Officer and Director, at 900 Circle 75 Parkway, Suite 930, Atlanta, Georgia 30339 and (404) 875-5045, the Federal Trade Commission, and the appropriate state regulatory agencies.

Retail Franchises | 5

7-ELEVEN franchisease℠

7-ELEVEN

1722 Routh St., # 1000
Dallas, TX 75227
Tel: (800) 782-0711, (972) 828-7011
Fax: (972) 828-8997
Email: dorian.cunion@7-11.com
Website: www.franchise.7-11.com
Dorian Cunion, Franchise Marketing & Recruiting Manager

7-ELEVEN stores were born from the simple concept of giving people "what they want, when and where they want it." This idea gave rise to the entire convenience store industry. While this formula still works today, customers' needs are changing at an accelerating pace. We are meeting this challenge with an infrastructure of daily distribution of fresh foods, pasties and time-sensitive products, and an information system that greatly improves ordering and merchandising decisions.

BACKGROUND

IFA Member:	Yes
Established & First Franchised:	1927; 1964
Franchised Units:	6,220
Company-Owned Units:	1,000
Total Units:	7,220
Distribution:	US – 8,160; CAN – 489; O'seas – 44,400
North America:	32 States, 5 Provinces
Density:	727 in VA, 855 in FL, 1,587 in CA
Projected New Units (12 Months):	N/A
Qualifications:	4, 4, 4, 3, 5, 5

FINANCIAL/TERMS

Cash Investment:	Varies by Store
Total Investment:	Varies
Minimum Net Worth:	$50K
Fees (Franchise):	Varies by Store
Fees (Royalty):	Gross Profit Split
Fees (Advertising):	N/A
Term of Contract (Years):	10/10
Average Number of Employees:	8 FT, 5 PT
Passive Ownership:	Discouraged
Encourage Conversions:	Yes
Area Development Agreements:	No
Sub-Franchising Contracts:	No
Expand in Territory:	Yes
Space Needs:	2,400 SF

SUPPORT & TRAINING

Financial Assistance Provided:	Yes (D)
Site Selection Assistance:	N/A
Lease Negotiation Assistance:	N/A
Co-operative Advertising:	No
Franchisee Association/Member:	Yes/Member
Size of Corporate Staff:	1,000
On-going Support:	A, B, C, D, E, F, G, H, I
Training:	1 Week Dallas, TX; 5 – 8 Weeks Various Training Stores throughout US

SPECIFIC EXPANSION PLANS

US:	NW, SW, MW, NE, Great Lakes, Southeast
Canada:	Western Canada
Overseas:	Select Countries

We provide unaudited financial statements that show the most recently available annual averages of the actual sales, earnings and other financial performance (before applicable franchisee income taxes, if any) of franchised 7-Eleven stores in each Market Area in this state (excluding stores that the same franchisee did not operate for the full calendar year). The Unaudited Statements of Average Franchisee Sales and Earnings are attached as Exhibit H to this disclosure document.

THE FINANCIAL STATEMENTS ATTACHED AS EXHIBIT H CONTAIN HISTORICAL AVERAGES OF SPECIFIC FRANCHISES. YOU SHOULD NOT CONSIDER ANY OF THE NUMBERS TO BE THE ACTUAL OR POTENTIAL SALES, EARNINGS OR OTHER FINANCIAL PERFORMANCE THAT YOU WILL ATTAIN. WE DO NOT REPRESENT THAT ANY FRANCHISEE CAN EXPECT TO ATTAIN THESE SALES, EARNINGS OR OTHER FINANCIAL PERFORMANCE, AND YOUR INDIVIDUAL FINANCIAL RESULTS MAY DIFFER FROM THE RESULTS CONTAINED IN THE FINANCIAL PERFORMANCE REPRESENTATIONS.

As described in Item 11, we prepare bookkeeping records for our franchisees based on financial information they submit to us. We prepared the financial statements attached as Exhibit H using information from these bookkeeping records. The financial statements are only as accurate as the information submitted to us by our current franchisees. The financial statements are unaudited. The form and classification of the financial statements are consistent with the accounting provisions and definitions in the franchise agreement. We use the retail method of accounting to account for the stores' operations, in accordance with generally accepted accounting principles and the franchise agreement.

If a store you want to franchise has operated for at least the last 12 months, we will also give you a supplemental disclosure for that store. The supplemental disclosure, called "Here Are The Facts," shows the actual operating results of the store for the last 12 months. We will prepare the supplemental disclosure in the same manner, and using the same information, as the financial statements attached as Exhibit H. You should not use the supplemental disclosure to predict any results at a particular store you franchise.

Many factors will affect the actual sales and earnings of a store you franchise, including your own efforts, ability and control of the store, as well as factors over which you have no control. Therefore, you should not predict any future results of a store based on historical operating summaries for any particular store or averages for a group of stores that we may provide. Actual results vary from store to store, and we cannot estimate the results of any particular store. We will make available to you, upon reasonable request, substantiation of the data used to prepare the material in this Item 19.

EXHIBIT H: UNAUDITED STATEMENTS OF AVERAGE FRANCHISEE SALES AND EARNINGS FOR THE CALENDAR YEAR 2013

Editor's Note: 7-Eleven produces an exceptionally informative Exhibit H that is 120 pages in its entirety. What follows is an introductory section, as well as a sample of earnings data for two specific markets. If you would like to see the full 7-Eleven Exhibit H, you may purchase the enitre Item 19 document (Exhibit H included) at www.item19s.com.

See Item 19 for a complete explanation of this section.

NOTE: The average franchisee sales and earnings that follow are for the 2013 calendar year and are before applicable franchisee income taxes, if any.

The average franchisee sales and earnings that follow may include payments to franchisees under the Store Development Program, or other various programs we have offered in the past. These programs were based on various factors, including store location, franchisee performance, etc. Actual franchisee earnings were affected by the franchisee's eligibility for one or more of these programs. Some of these programs may not be available in your area.

The average franchisee sales and earnings that follow may include sales of Consigned Gasoline, although not all 7-Eleven Stores sell Consigned Gasoline. If a 7-Eleven Store does sell Consigned Gasoline, we may decide to discontinue the gasoline sales and remove the gasoline equipment from such store. The discontinuation of gasoline sales would affect actual franchisee earnings.

The average franchisee sales and earnings that follow may include a lower 7-Eleven Charge than you will be required to pay (see Item 6).

If there are less than 100 franchise outlets in the state where this Disclosure Document is presented, this Exhibit will also contain an additional list of franchise outlets (without financial information) from contiguous states until at least 100 franchise outlets are listed.

Letter codes in front of store numbers in the store lists refer to the following:

A: Included in the Top Third
B: Included in the Middle Third
C: Included in the Bottom Third
D: Strip center location

E: Freestanding location
F: Payroll operating expense includes a salary paid to one or more Franchisees

UNAUDITED STATEMENT OF AVERAGE FRANCHISEE SALES AND EARNINGS

FOR THE CALENDAR YEAR 2013

TRADITIONAL STORES

MARKET: 2111 - NORTH COUNTY MARKET

TOTAL SALES RANGE	BOTTOM THIRD	MIDDLE THIRD	TOP THIRD
NUMBER OF STORES IN AVERAGE	24	25	25
PERCENT OF FRANCHISED STORES IN THE 7-ELEVEN SYSTEM (OPERATED BY THE SAME FRANCHISEE FOR THE YEAR 2013) WHICH ACHIEVED OR EXCEEDED MEDIAN SALES AVERAGE WITHIN EACH RANGE	77.2%	39.7%	16.4%
TOTAL SALES (AVERAGE WITHIN EACH RANGE)	$1,297,322	$1,734,507	$2,153,498
GROSS PROFIT	508,026	683,062	831,360
PERCENT OF SALES	39.1%	39.3%	38.6%
LESS 7-ELEVEN CHARGE	255,209	342,113	418,886
*GAS COMMISSION	1,760	3,315	5,332
OTHER INCOME	91	143	170
FRANCHISEE'S GROSS INCOME	$254,667	$343,408	$417,977
SELLING EXPENSES			
CASUAL & TEMPORARY LABOR	$141	$0	$0
PAYROLL (NOT INCL FRAN. DRAW)	117,705	156,189	184,433
STORE MANAGER PAYROLL	0	0	0
STORE MANAGER BONUS	0	0	0
STORE MANAGER BONUS TAXES	0	0	0
PAYROLL TAXES	12,349	15,811	18,699
PAPER BAGS	927	1,322	1,565
INVENTORY VARIATION	4,539	4,627	5,510
MONEY ORDER REPORTING VARIATION	0	0	0
COUPON VARIATION	0	0	0
LOTTERY TICKET INVENTORY VARIATION	603	232	380
LOTTO/LOTTERY REPORTING VARIATION	54	447	159
LOTTO SALES REPORTING VARIATION	6-	29	39
SUPPLIES	3,097	3,289	3,844
TELEPHONE	1,563	1,890	2,511
CONTRACT MAINTENANCE EQUIPMENT	10,902	11,054	11,238
OTHER MAINTENANCE EQUIPMENT	928	787	462
BUILDING MAINTENANCE	523	691	747
OUTSIDE PREMISES MAINTENANCE	3,110	2,354	2,251

TAXES AND LICENSE	1,693	1,137	1,248
CASH VARIATION	1,553	1,466	2,551
RETURNED CHECKS	29	2	28
RUBBISH REMOVAL	1,638	2,437	3,276
JANITORIAL & LAUNDRY	1,498	1,525	2,063
BAD MERCHANDISE	0	0	0
SECURITY EXPENSE	371	427	934
MISCELLANEOUS EXPENSE	1,672	2,060	1,578
ADVERTISING FEES	7,539	10,245	12,470
ADVERTISING	38	82	133
MONEY ORDER LOSSES	0	0	0
WORKERS COMPENSATION	7,032	8,526	10,173
CRIME & CASUALTY LOSSES	203	27	1
EMPLOYEE GROUP INSURANCE	1,787	2,683	3,128
PRE-EMPLOYMENT EXPENSES	11	5	36
MISCELLANEOUS EMPLOYEE EXPENSES	774	1,333	701
CHECK CASHING EXPENSES	42	12	0
CREDIT CARD EXPENSES	8,072	10,455	13,244
INTEREST EXPENSE	1,288	1,227	1,405
TOTAL SELLING EXPENSES	$191,732	$242,396	$284,823
MERCHANDISE SALES FOR STORES USED IN THESE AVERAGE			
WERE A HIGH OF ...	1,584,548	1,879,855	2,560,625
AND A LOW OF ...	747,387	1,585,969	1,889,755
THERE MAY ALSO BE GENERAL & ADMINISTRATIVE EXPENSE RELATING TO THE OPERATION OF A 7-ELEVEN STORE. YOU MAY OR MAY NOT HAVE THESE EXPENSES. RANGE OF G&A EXPENSES, MINUS THE INTEREST EXPENSE:			
WERE A HIGH OF ...	95,490	70,584	70,461
AND A LOW OF ...	1,250	680	1,136

(EXAMPLES OF G&A EXPENSES ARE: OFFICER SALARY/BONUS, EMPLOYEE BONUS, PAYROLL TAXES, EQUIPMENT RENTAL, TRAVEL/ENTERTAINMENT, OUTSIDE INSURANCE COVERAGE, PROFESSIONAL SERVICE, MEMBER DUES, FINES/PENALTIES, MISC. G&A EXPENSES).

THE PAYROLL AND PAYROLL TAX NUMBERS MAY INCLUDE PAYROLL PAID TO AN INCORPORATED FRANCHISEE, OR PAYROLL PAID TO A SPOUSE OR OTHER FAMILY MEMBER OF THE FRANCHISEE. THE USE OF FAMILY MEMBERS AS EMPLOYEES, OR THE USE OF A CORPORATION AS THE FRANCHISEE, MAY IMPACT THE PAYROLL EXPENSES AT A PARTICULAR STORE.

*GAS COMMISSION INCLUDES COMMISSION AMOUNTS PAID TO FRANCHISEES FOR THE SALE OF CONSIGNED GASOLINE UNDER A NON-CONTRACTUAL POLICY FOR CALCULATING COMMISSIONS. WE HAVE MADE VARIOUS CHANGES TO THIS POLICY AND ADDITIONAL CHANGES MAY BE MADE IN THE FUTURE WHICH COULD AFFECT THE ACTUAL FRANCHISEE EARNINGS AND THE AMOUNT OF GAS COMMISSION RECEIVED BY FRANCHISEES.

THE ABOVE UNAUDITED STATEMENT WAS PREPARED IN ACCORDANCE WITH THE ACCOUNTING PROVISIONS AND DEFINITIONS SPECIFIED IN THE FRANCHISE AGREEMENT AND IS CONSISTENT WITH GENERALLY ACCEPTED ACCOUNTING PRINCIPLES. THE INFORMATION INDICATES

THE AVERAGE OF THOSE FRANCHISED 7-ELEVEN STORES IN THE ABOVE MARKET AREA WHICH WERE OPERATED THROUGHOUT THE CALENDAR YEAR BY THE SAME FRANCHISEE. THE OPERATING EXPENSES LINE SHOWN AS OTHER INCOME INCLUDES MISCELLANEOUS INCOME TO THE FRANCHISEE FROM COMMISSIONS (FOR THOSE STORES NOT INCLUDED IN TOTAL SALES) AND INCENTIVE AWARDS. THE AVERAGES SHOWN ARE NOT IN EXCESS OF THE AVERAGE OF SALES AND EARNINGS ACTUALLY ACHIEVED BY EXISTING FRANCHISEES. THE FRANCHISE OPERATIONS FROM WHICH THESE AVERAGES ARE TAKEN ARE SUBSTANTIALLY SIMILAR TO THE FRANCHISE OFFERED AND DID NOT RECEIVE ANY SERVICES NOT GENERALLY AVAILABLE TO OTHER FRANCHISEES.

THESE SALES OR EARNINGS ARE AVERAGES OF SPECIFIC FRANCHISES AND SHOULD NOT BE CONSIDERED AS THE ACTUAL OR POTENTIAL SALES OR EARNINGS THAT WILL BE REALIZED BY ANY OTHER FRANCHISEE. THE FRANCHISOR DOES NOT REPRESENT THAT ANY FRANCHISEE CAN EXPECT TO ATTAIN THESE SALES OR EARNINGS.

UNAUDITED STATEMENT OF AVERAGE FRANCHISEE SALES AND EARNINGS
FOR THE CALENDAR YEAR 2013
TRADITIONAL STORES
MARKET: 2112 - DESERT COAST MARKET

TOTAL SALES RANGE	BOTTOM THIRD	MIDDLE THIRD	TOP THIRD
NUMBER OF STORES IN AVERAGE	25	25	26
PERCENT OF FRANCHISED STORES IN THE 7-ELEVEN SYSTEM (OPERATED BY THE SAME FRANCHISEE FOR THE YEAR 2013) WHICH ACHIEVED OR EXCEEDED MEDIAN SALES AVERAGE WITHIN EACH RANGE	87.2%	58.8%	20.8%
TOTAL SALES (AVERAGE WITHIN EACH RANGE)	$1,143,022	$1,512,642	$2,042,666
GROSS PROFIT	440,344	574,400	773,250
PERCENT OF SALES	38.5%	37.9%	37.8%
LESS 7-ELEVEN CHARGE	220,760	291,418	391,943
*GAS COMMISSION	4,739	7,116	8,793
OTHER INCOME	1,081	137	129
FRANCHISEE'S GROSS INCOME	$225,404	$290,236	$390,229
SELLING EXPENSES			
CASUAL & TEMPORARY LABOR	$355	$136	$230
PAYROLL (NOT INCL FRAN. DRAW)	98,821	119,168	167,389
STORE MANAGER PAYROLL	0	0	0
STORE MANAGER BONUS	0	0	0
STORE MANAGER BONUS TAXES	0	0	0
PAYROLL TAXES	10,559	12,319	17,216
PAPER BAGS	774	956	1,568
INVENTORY VARIATION	2,841	2,976	4,422
MONEY ORDER REPORTING VARIATION	0	0	0
COUPON VARIATION	0	0	0
LOTTERY TICKET INVENTORY VARIATION	488	763	613
LOTTO/LOTTERY REPORTING VARIATION	41-	7-	113
LOTTO SALES REPORTING VARIATION	46	18	13

SUPPLIES	2,498	3,847	3,903
TELEPHONE	1,490	2,363	2,256
CONTRACT MAINTENANCE EQUIPMENT	11,394	11,790	11,268
OTHER MAINTENANCE EQUIPMENT	684	428	572
BUILDING MAINTENANCE	747	1,029	812
OUTSIDE PREMISES MAINTENANCE	2,586	4,766	3,916
TAXES AND LICENSE	1,188	2,1,21	2,089
CASH VARIATION	1,785	3,369	3,008
RETURNED CHECKS	18	14	9
RUBBISH REMOVAL	2,395	2,468	3,473
JANITORIAL & LAUNDRY	1,641	1,733	3,418
BAD MERCHANDISE	0	0	0
SECURITY EXPENSE	219	770	543
MISCELLANEOUS EXPENSE	1,694	1,733	3,418
ADVERTISING FEES	6,278	8,616	11,598
ADVERTISING	26	93	111
MONEY ORDER LOSSES	17	0	0
WORKERS COMPENSATION	5,691	7,236	8,641
CRIME & CASUALTY LOSSES	29	42	94
EMPLOYEE GROUP INSURANCE	44	1,528	4,111
PRE-EMPLOYMENT EXPENSES	15	10	760
MISCELLANEOUS EMPLOYEE EXPENSES	1,426	3,057	1,487
CHECK CASHING EXPENSES	0	2	3
CREDIT CARD EXPENSES	6,040	8,463	10,346
INTEREST EXPENSE	1,252	1,503	1,740
TOTAL SELLING EXPENSES	$163,011	$204,478	$268,767
MERCHANDISE SALES FOR STORES USED IN THESE AVERAGE			
WERE A HIGH OF ...	1,334,783	1,64,172	2,691,166
AND A LOW OF ...	600,518	1,343,245	1,664,242
THERE MAY ALSO BE GENERAL & ADMINISTRATIVE EXPENSE RELATING TO THE OPERATION OF A 7-ELEVEN STORE. YOU MAY OR MAY NOT HAVE THESE EXPENSES. RANGE OF G&A EXPENSES, MINUS THE INTEREST EXPENSE:			
WERE A HIGH OF ...	38,089	119,181	89,927
AND A LOW OF ...	323	1,315	1,514

(EXAMPLES OF G&A EXPENSES ARE: OFFICER SALARY/ BONUS, EMPLOYEE BONUS, PAYROLL TAXES, EQUIPMENT RENTAL, TRAVEL/ENTERTAINMENT, OUTSIDE INSURANCE COVERAGE, PROFESSIONAL SERVICE, MEMBER DUES, FINES/PENALTIES, MISC. G&A EXPENSES).

THE PAYROLL AND PAYROLL TAX NUMBERS MAY INCLUDE PAYROLL PAID TO AN INCORPORATED FRANCHISEE, OR PAYROLL PAID TO A SPOUSE OR OTHER FAMILY MEMBER OF THE FRANCHISEE. THE USE OF FAMILY MEMBERS AS EMPLOYEES, OR THE USE OF A CORPORATION AS THE FRANCHISEE, MAY IMPACT THE PAYROLL EXPENSES AT A PARTICULAR STORE.

*GAS COMMISSION INCLUDES COMMISSION AMOUNTS PAID TO FRANCHISEES FOR THE SALE OF CONSIGNED GASOLINE UNDER A NON-CONTRACTUAL POLICY FOR CALCULATING COMMISSIONS. WE HAVE MADE VARIOUS CHANGES TO THIS POLICY AND ADDITIONAL CHANGES MAY BE MADE IN THE FUTURE WHICH COULD AFFECT THE ACTUAL FRANCHISEE EARNINGS AND THE AMOUNT OF GAS COMMISSION RECEIVED BY FRANCHISEES.

THE ABOVE UNAUDITED STATEMENT WAS PREPARED IN ACCORDANCE WITH THE ACCOUNTING PROVISIONS AND DEFINITIONS SPECIFIED IN THE FRANCHISE AGREEMENT AND IS CONSISTENT WITH GENERALLY ACCEPTED ACCOUNTING PRINCIPLES. THE INFORMATION INDICATES THE AVERAGE OF THOSE FRANCHISED 7-ELEVEN STORES IN THE ABOVE MARKET AREA WHICH WERE OPERATED THROUGHOUT THE CALENDAR YEAR BY THE SAME FRANCHISEE. THE OPERATING EXPENSES LINE SHOWN AS OTHER INCOME INCLUDES MISCELLANEOUS INCOME TO THE FRANCHISEE FROM COMMISSIONS (FOR THOSE STORES NOT INCLUDED IN TOTAL SALES) AND INCENTIVE AWARDS. THE AVERAGES SHOWN ARE NOT IN EXCESS OF THE AVERAGE OF SALES AND EARNINGS ACTUALLY ACHIEVED BY EXISTING FRANCHISEES. THE FRANCHISE OPERATIONS FROM WHICH THESE AVERAGES ARE TAKEN ARE SUBSTANTIALLY SIMILAR TO THE FRANCHISE OFFERED AND DID NOT RECEIVE ANY SERVICES NOT GENERALLY AVAILABLE TO OTHER FRANCHISEES.

THESE SALES OR EARNINGS ARE AVERAGES OF SPECIFIC FRANCHISES AND SHOULD NOT BE CONSIDERED AS THE ACTUAL OR POTENTIAL SALES OR EARNINGS THAT WILL BE REALIZED BY ANY OTHER FRANCHISEE. THE FRANCHISOR DOES NOT REPRESENT THAT ANY FRANCHISEE CAN EXPECT TO ATTAIN THESE SALES OR EARNINGS.

FLOOR COVERINGS *international*

FLOOR COVERINGS INTERNATIONAL

5250 Triangle Pkwy., # 100
Norcross, GA 30092
Tel: (800) 955-4324, (770) 874-7600
Fax: (770) 874-7605
Email: djames@floorcoveringsinternational.com
Website: www.flooring-franchise.com
Denise James, Franchise Administrator

FLOOR COVERINGS INTERNATIONAL is the 'Flooring Store at your Door.' FCI is the first and leading mobile 'shop at home' flooring store. Customers can select from over 3,000 styles and colors of flooring right in their own home! All the right ingredients are there to simplify a buying decision. We offer all the brand names you and your customers will be familiar with. We carry all types of flooring, as well as window blinds.

BACKGROUND

IFA Member:	Yes
Established & First Franchised:	1988; 1989
Franchised Units:	92
Company-Owned Units:	0
Total Units:	92
Distribution:	US – 83; CAN – 9; O'seas – 0
North America:	43 States, 5 Provinces
Density:	7 in CA, 7 in NY, 6 in MN
Projected New Units (12 Months):	35
Qualifications:	5, 5, 4, 3, 4, 4

FINANCIAL/TERMS

Cash Investment:	$150K
Total Investment:	$133 – 305.5K
Minimum Net Worth:	$50K
Fees (Franchise):	$49.5K
Fees (Royalty):	5%
Fees (Advertising):	2%
Term of Contract (Years):	10/10
Average Number of Employees:	1 FT, 1 PT
Passive Ownership:	Discouraged
Encourage Conversions:	Yes
Area Development Agreements:	Yes
Sub-Franchising Contracts:	No
Expand in Territory:	Yes
Space Needs:	N/A

SUPPORT & TRAINING		On-going Support:	A, B, C, D, E, G, H, I
Financial Assistance Provided:	Yes (D)	Training:	1 Week Atlanta, GA
Site Selection Assistance:	Yes		
Lease Negotiation Assistance:	N/A	SPECIFIC EXPANSION PLANS	
Co-operative Advertising:	No	US:	All United States
Franchisee Association/Member:	Yes/Member	Canada:	All Canada
Size of Corporate Staff:	12	Overseas:	No

Background

This Item sets forth certain historical data submitted by our franchisees. Written substantiation of the data used in preparing this information will be made available upon reasonable request. We have not audited this information, nor independently verified this information. The information is for the period January 1, 2013 through December 31, 2013 (the "Measurement Period").

Importantly, the success of your franchise will depend largely upon your individual abilities and your market, and the financial results of your franchise are likely to differ, perhaps materially, from the results summarized in this item.

You should not use this information as an indication of how well your franchise will do. A number of factors will affect the success of your franchise. These factors include the current market conditions, the type of market in your franchise area, the location of your franchise area, the competition and your ability to operate the franchise.

Gross Sales

This Table presents the Gross Sales as reported to us by most of our 47 U.S. franchisees that were open and operating for more than 24 months as of December 31, 2013 and for whom we have complete sales data (the "Reporting Franchisees"). This table excludes franchises who had not been open and operating for a full 24 months as of December 31, 2013, those for whom we do not have complete sales data and those that do not operate the franchise as a full time venture. The following table presents the high, low, average and median Gross Sales for the 47 Reporting Franchisees during the Measurement Period.

Gross Sales
For Calendar Year 2013

Years in Operation	Number of Reporting Franchises	High	Low	Average	Median	Number of Reporting Franchisees Meeting or Exceeding the Average
Over 2 Years	47	$2,987,748	$117,621	$719,484	$498,690	14 (30%)

Notes:

1. Gross Sales is defined as a franchisee's total sales invoices or other items or services billed to the customer for all "Completed Sales", less any discounts, cancellations or returns by FCI. Sales of products and services are deemed to be Completed Sales for purposes of reporting to FCI when the franchisee completes the final installation of all products and/or services sold to the customer.

2. The Average Gross Sales is defined as the sum of the Gross Sales of the Reporting Franchisees divided by the number of Reporting Franchisees in each operating category.

3. The median means the amount that falls in the middle when all other amounts disclosed are arranged highest to lowest. In other words, half of the Reporting Franchisees exceeded the median value stated above and half did not in each operating category.

Average Job Size, Closing Rates and Slippage Rates

The following table presents the average job size, closing rate and slippage rates for 20 of our franchisees open less than 2 years and 48 of our franchisees open and operating for more than 2 years as of December 31, 2013, that reported data in these categories to us. We excluded franchisees that did not report the number of jobs, closing rates and slippage rates to us.

Average Job Size, Closing Rate and Slippage Rates
For Calendar Year 2013

Years in Operation	Number of Franchises	Average Job Size	Closing Rate	Slippage Rate	Number of Reporting Franchisees Meeting or Exceeding the Average
Less than 2 Years	20	$4,070	39%	44%	Job Size: 8 (40%)
					Closing Rate: 9 (45%)
					Slippage Rate: 8 (40%)
Over 2 Years	48	$4,702	53%	33%	Job Size: 5 (10%)
					Closing Rate: 20 (42%)
					Slippage Rate: 22 (46%)

Notes:

1. Average Job Size is defined as the total Gross Sales of all jobs in each operating category divided by the number of jobs performed by franchisees in each operating category.

2. Average Closing Rate is the average percentage of jobs landed over the number of first proposals.

3. Average Slippage Rate is the average percentage of first proposals over the number of leads.

Assumptions

1. Your results may vary upon the location of your business. This analysis does not contain information concerning operating costs or expenses. Operating costs and expenses may vary substantially from business to business.

2. Expenses and costs, as well as the actual accounting and operational methods employed by a franchisee, may significantly impact profits realized in any particular operation.

CAUTION

Some outlets have sold these amounts. Your individual results may differ. There is no assurance you'll sell as much. Actual results vary from business to business, and we cannot estimate the result of a particular business. Gross Sales, revenues, expenses and Gross Margin on Sales may vary. In particular, the revenues and expenses of your Franchised Business will be directly affected by many factors, such as: (a) geographic location; (b) competition from other similar businesses in your area; (c) advertising effectiveness based on market saturation; (d) your product and service pricing; (e) vendor prices on materials, supplies and inventory; (f) labor costs (g) ability to generate customers; (h) customer loyalty; and (i) employment conditions in the market.

Importantly, you should not consider the Gross Sales presented above to be the actual potential revenues that you will realize. We do not represent that you can or will attain these revenues or any particular level of revenues or percentage of costs or expenses. We do not represent that you will generate income, which exceeds the initial payment of, or investment in, the franchise.

Therefore, we recommend that you make your own independent investigation to determine whether or not the franchise may be profitable to you. You should use the above information only as a reference in conducting your analysis and preparing your own projected income statements and cash flow statements. We suggest strongly that you consult your financial advisor or personal accountant concerning financial projections and federal, state and local income taxes and any other applicable taxes that you may incur in operating a Franchised Business.

Other than the preceding financial performance representation, Floorcoverings International, Ltd. does not make any financial performance representations. We also do not authorize our employees or representatives to make any such either orally or in writing. If you are purchasing an existing outlet, however, we may provide you with the actual records of that outlet. If you receive any other financial performance information or projections of your future income, you should report it to the franchisor's management by contacting Thomas Wood, Floorcoverings International, Ltd., 5250 Triangle Parkway, Suite 100, Norcross, Georgia 30092 and 800-955-4324, the Federal Trade Commission, and the appropriate state regulatory agencies.

HONEYBAKED.

HONEYBAKED HAM CO. & CAFE

3875 Mansell Rd.
Alpharetta, GA 30022
Tel: (866) 968-7424, (678) 966-3224
Fax: (678) 966-3134
Email: mdemis@hbham.com
Website: www.honeybakedfranchising.com
Mar Demis, Franchise Development Department

The HONEYBAKED HAM CO. & CAFE is a truly exciting franchise opportunity with 50 years of experience building a strong brand. We are the original (and the world's largest) specialty retailer of high quality spiral-sliced glazed hams, turkeys and other special occasion center-of-the-table products complemented by a full service cafe.

BACKGROUND

IFA Member:	Yes
Established & First Franchised:	1957; 1998
Franchised Units:	186
Company-Owned Units:	234
Total Units:	420
Distribution:	US – 420; CAN – 0; O'seas – 0
North America:	39 States, 0 Provinces
Density:	41 in FL, 41 in GA, 37 in CA
Projected New Units (12 Months):	N/A
Qualifications:	4, 3, 4, 3, 2, 4

FINANCIAL/TERMS

Cash Investment:	$100 – 125K
Total Investment:	$281.8 – 431.9K
Minimum Net Worth:	$350K
Fees (Franchise):	$30K
Fees (Royalty):	5-6%
Fees (Advertising):	2%
Term of Contract (Years):	10/10
Average Number of Employees:	2 – 3 FT, 7 PT
Passive Ownership:	Not Allowed
Encourage Conversions:	Yes
Area Development Agreements:	Yes
Sub-Franchising Contracts:	No
Expand in Territory:	Yes
Space Needs:	2,000 SF

SUPPORT & TRAINING

Financial Assistance Provided:	No
Site Selection Assistance:	Yes
Lease Negotiation Assistance:	Yes
Co-operative Advertising:	No
Franchisee Association/Member:	No
Size of Corporate Staff:	110
On-going Support:	C, D, E, F, G, h, I
Training:	1 Week Franchise Location; 2 Weeks Atlanta, GA

SPECIFIC EXPANSION PLANS

US:	25 States
Canada:	No
Overseas:	No

Table No. 1
Net Sales of 176 Franchised Stores for 2013 Fiscal Year

	Top 10%	Top 25%	Top 50%	Top 75%	Franchised Store Average
Average Net Sales	$1,125,155	$947,329	$806,839	$712,738	$622,195
No. of Stores	17	44	87	132	176
No. of Stores at or Above Average	7	19	35	54	76
Percentage of Stores at or Above Average	41.2%	45.5%	40.2%	41.7%	43.2%

NOTES TO TABLE NO. I

1. Table No. 1 displays the average net sales (as defined in Item 6) of 176 franchised HoneyBaked Stores that were in operation during our last fiscal year, which included the period from October 1, 2012 to September 29, 2013. Eight franchise HoneyBaked Stores were excluded from this data because they were not open during the full fiscal year. The table includes data for 12 Franchised Stores which had additional sales from seasonal Pop-Up Retail locations.

2. The Franchised Store information in Table No. 1 is based on sales reports received from our Customer Management System or POS system. We have not audited or verified this information.

3. The Top 10% column includes the average net sales of 17 Franchised Stores that achieved the top 10% of net sales of all Franchised Stores that were open during the period. The Top 25% column includes the average net sales of 44 Franchised Stores that achieved the top 10% of net sales of all Franchised Stores that were open during the period. The Top 50% column includes the average net sales of 87 Franchised Stores that achieved the top 50% of net sales of all Franchised Stores that were open during the period. The Top 75% column includes the average net sales of 132 Franchised Stores that achieved the top 75% of net sales of all Franchised Stores that were open during the period. The Franchised Store Average column includes the average net sales of all 176 Franchised Stores included in the table.

Table No. 2
Historical Sales and Certain Expenses for 40 Franchised Stores
For Calendar Year 2012

Calendar Year 2012	40 Stores		7 Stores		18 Stores		15 Stores	
	Franchise Store Avg.		<$500K		$500K – $700K		>$700K	
Total Net Revenue	$653,917	100.0%	$388,844	100.0%	$593,360	100.0%	$850,287	100.0%
Total Cost of Goods	$264,017	40.4%	$157,772	40.6%	$238,650	6.2%	$344,039	40.5%
Gross Profit	$389,900	59.6%	$231,073	59.4%	$354,709	59.8%	$506,248	59.5%
Hourly Labor	$80,926	12.4%	$50,574	13.0%	$73,920	12.5%	$103,497	12.2%
Manager/Operator Salary	$35,500	5.4%	$26,429	6.8%	$25,663	4.3%	$51,539	6.1%
Fringe Benefits/Payroll Taxes	$14,581	2.2%	$11,989	3.1%	$11,060	1.9%	$20,015	2.4%
Total Labor/Wages	$131,007	20.0%	$88,992	22.9%	$110,642	18.6%	$175,051	20.6%
Profit after COGS and Labor	$258,893	39.6%	$142,081	36.5%	$244,067	41.1%	$331,197	39.0%
Misc./All Other Expenses/Royalties	$130,142	19.9%	$68,615	17.6%	$131,946	22.2%	$156,691	18.4%
Advertising - Local Spend	$19,062	2.9%	$16,769	4.3%	$21,211	3.6%	$17,553	2.1%
Profit After COGS, Labor and All Other Operating Costs	$109,689	16.8%	$56,697	14.6%	$90,910	15.3%	$156,953	18.5%
Rent (Base Rent, CAM Charges, Taxes, Insurance, Trailer/Storage Rental)	$55,326	8.5%	$36,933	9.5%	$45,691	7.7%	$75,471	8.9%
Income (EBITDA)	$54,363	8.3%	$19,764	5.1%	$45,218	7.6%	$81,483	9.6%

NOTES TO TABLE NO. 2

1. Table No. 2 presents net sales, costs and expense data for 40 Franchised Stores that were open during the entire period from January 1, 2012 to December 31, 2012 and that provided year-end profit and loss statements to us on our standardized form for this period. Table No. 2 does not include any data related to 145 Franchised Stores that were open in 2012 that did not provide profit and loss statements to us or whose statements were not provided to us in the correct format. We have not audited or verified this information.

2. Total Net Revenue includes the net sales of the Franchised Stores as defined in Item 6.

3. Costs of Goods include the total costs of food and beverage sales as well as paper and packaging supplies.

4. Gross Profit is calculated by subtracting Total Cost of Goods from Total Net Revenue.

5. Labor costs include hourly employee and managerial wages, payroll taxes, workers' compensation, vacation pay and benefits. The costs of providing group health insurance for employees and workers' compensation insurance will vary depending on many factors including the extent and amount of coverage provided, the loss experience of the group and which insurance provider is chosen. Therefore, you may encounter higher relative costs in obtaining comparable insurance coverage.

6. Miscellaneous/All Other Expenses/Royalties includes store operating expenses including supplies, menus, uniforms, credit card fees, bank charges, utilities, dues and licenses, maintenance contracts, trash removal, exterminators, royalty fees and contributions to the Advertising Fund.

7. Advertising includes the local advertising expenditures made by a franchisee outside of the contributions to the Advertising Fund.

8. Profit after COGS, Labor and All Other Operating Costs is calculated by subtracting Costs of Goods Sold, Labor Costs and Miscellaneous, All Other Operating Expenses, Royalties and Advertising from Net Revenues.

9. Rent includes base rent, common area maintenance charges, taxes, insurance, and trailer storage and rental expenses.

10. Income (EBITDA) is earning before interest, income, tax, depreciation and amortization.

11. The cost and expense data presented in Table No. 2 does not reflect all costs and expenses that must be deducted from the net sales figures to obtain your net income or profit. You should conduct an independent investigation of the costs and expenses you will incur in operating a franchised HoneyBaked Store. Franchisees or former franchisees listed in this disclosure document may be one source of this information.

The franchised HoneyBaked Stores reflected in this financial performance representation offer inventory and services for sale that are substantially similar to the inventory and services that you will offer for sale in your HoneyBaked Store. The data has not been audited. Written substantiation for the financial performance representation will be made available to you upon reasonable request. Some HoneyBaked Stores have achieved the net sales and expense results described in this financial performance representation. Your individual results may differ. There is no assurance you will achieve these results.

This financial performance representation is provided as a reference only and is not intended to be used as a statement or forecast of earnings, sales, profits, or the prospects or chances of success that may be achieved by any individual franchised HoneyBaked Store. The actual sales of your HoneyBaked Store depend on many factors; including its location, site criteria, local household income, residential and business population during the day and at night, ease of ingress and egress, seating, parking, the physical condition of your HoneyBaked Store and the size and visibility of the store. Your sales will be impacted by your own operational ability, your experience with managing a business, your capital and financing (including working capital), training, customer service at your HoneyBaked Store, product quality and your business plan. Your sales may also be impacted by the weather and by promotions you run and those run by yor competitors. We recommend that you make your own independent investigation to determine whether or not the franchise may be profitable, and consult with an attorney and other advisors before executing any agreement. We also recommend that you develop a business plan to assist you in your initial decision, planning and operation of the franchise.

Other than the preceding financial performance representation, we do not make any financial performance representations. We also do not authorize our employees or representatives to make any such representations either orally or in writing. If you are purchasing an existing outlet, however, we may provide you with the actual records of that outlet. If you receive any other financial performance information or projections of your future income, you should report it to our management by contacting Molly Kesmodel, Vice President, Franchise Operations & Development, The HBH Franchise Company, LLC, 3875 Mansell Road, Alpharetta, Georgia 30022-1532, (678) 966-3255, the Federal Trade Commission and the appropriate state regulatory agencies.

NYS COLLECTION EYEWEAR

230 Liberty St.
Metuchen, NJ 08840
Tel: (732) 429-1500
Email: brubin@nyscollection.com
Website: www.kf-franchising.com
Brian Rubin, Franchise Operations Manager

NYS Collection offers the latest in today's eyewear without the high price tag typically associated with premium sunglasses. Founded in 1996 by two young entrepreneurs, the company started with one retail location at the World Trade Center in New York City. Today, NYS Collection sunglasses are sold in more than 10,000 retail locations worldwide. In the last decade, the company has established itself as the leading eyewear provider for the specialty retail industry. NYS Collection Eyewear is currently offering franchise opportunities to entrepreneurs interested in being a part of a dynamic and rapidly growing organization.

BACKGROUND

IFA Member:	No
Established & First Franchised:	2000; 2011
Franchised Units:	47
Company-Owned Units:	0
Total Units:	47
Distribution:	US – 47; CAN – 0; O'seas – 0

North America:	12 States, 0 Provinces
Density:	10 in CO, 7 in NY, 6 in FL
Projected New Units (12 Months):	N/A
Qualifications:	N/A

FINANCIAL/TERMS

Cash Investment:	N/A
Total Investment:	$80.7 – 99.4K
Minimum Net Worth:	N/A
Fees (Franchise):	$15K
Fees (Royalty):	0%
Fees (Advertising):	$1,250/yr.
Term of Contract (Years):	N/A
Average Number of Employees:	N/A
Passive Ownership:	Allowed
Encourage Conversions:	Yes
Area Development Agreements:	No
Sub-Franchising Contracts:	No
Expand in Territory:	No
Space Needs:	N/A

SUPPORT & TRAINING

Financial Assistance Provided:	Yes (D)
Site Selection Assistance:	Yes
Lease Negotiation Assistance:	Yes
Co-operative Advertising:	No
Franchisee Association/Member:	Yes/Member
Size of Corporate Staff:	N/A
On-going Support:	A, B, C, D, E, F, G, H, I
Training:	N/A

SPECIFIC EXPANSION PLANS

US:	No
Canada:	No
Overseas:	No

As of December 31, 2013, we had 52 franchised locations in the United States. These franchised locations represent units that are similar to the opportunity being offered. Of the 52 franchised units in operations on December 31, 2013, 23 were year round operations which had been in continuous operation for a full year or more as of December 31, 2013. The remaining units were in continuous operation for less than one full year, or are seasonal, and are not considered to be representative examples.

We collect data and measure performance of franchised locations based on a point of sale computer reporting system.

During the 12 month period January 1, 2013 to December 31, 2013, the above referenced 23 year-round locations recorded the following sales:

Average Retail Sales: $243,203.66

IMPORTANT CAUTIONS AND NOTES:

1. The information presented in this Item 19 should not be considered to the the actual or probable revenues that you will experience. Actual results will vary from franchisee to franchisee. Factors such as length of time the kiosk has been

open, location, demographics, the franchisee's prior business experience, the franchisee's marketing efforts, the franchisee's cost controls and others will have an effect on your individual resutls.

2. You should not assume your business will reach the levels of revenues disclosed above within any particular timeframe based upon this information. It might take you longer to ramp up.

3. The information presented in this Item 19 reflects is based on retail sales recorded by our franchised locations. It does not include any of the expenses of operating the business, for example, rent, payroll, taxes, interest charges, or owner compensation. It also does not include royalty fees, advertising fees, or other amounts due under the Franchise Agreement. When preparing a profit projection for your store, you will have to estimate your retail sales and identify and plan for these additional expenses.

4. Although we believe the information provided in this Item 19 is reasonably accurate, it is not exact and may contain errors. The information presented in this Item 19 has not been audited or reviewed.

5. You should not regard the data from our affiliate as being statistically valid as a predictor of your sales, expenses or profits. Although it may be useful information, we do not believe it is a reliable indicator of your probable success or lack thereof in the business. You should conduct an independent evaluation of this franchise opportunity with your own advisors, using the information contained here as just one factor. You should not accord undue weight to any one factor.

THE INFORMATION CONTAINED IN THIS ITEM 19 SHOULD NOT BE CONSIDERED TO THE ACTUAL OR PROBABLE SALES THAT YOU WILL REALIZE. YOUR RESULTS WILL LIKELY DIFFER FROM THE RESULTS CONTAINED IN THIS ITEM. WE DO NOT REPRESENT THAT YOU WILL ATTAIN COMPARABLE SALES.

We will provide you with substantiation of the information contained in this Item 19 upon written request from you and subject to your signing an agreement to maintain the confidentiality of the information.

SNAP-ON TOOLS

2801 80th St., P.O. Box 1410
Kenosha, WI 53143
Tel: (800) 786-6600, (877) 476-2766
Fax: (262) 656-5635
Email: thomas.j.kasbohm@snapon.com
Website: www.snaponfranchise.com
Tom Kasbohm, Director of Franchising

The premier solutions provider to the vehicle service industry. Premium quality products, delivered and sold with premium service. We are proud of our heritage and are boldly addressing the future needs of our customers with improved efficiency, creating products and services from hand tools to data and management systems. Contact us today for discussion.

BACKGROUND

IFA Member:	Yes
Established & First Franchised:	1920; 1991
Franchised Units:	4,581
Company-Owned Units:	214
Total Units:	4,795
Distribution:	US – 3,458; CAN – 361; O'seas – 976
North America:	50 States, 12 Provinces
Density:	364 in CA, 244 in TX, 193 in NY
Projected New Units (12 Months):	N/A
Qualifications:	3, 4, 2, 2, 3, 5

FINANCIAL/TERMS

Cash Investment:	$30.2 – 80.3K
Total Investment:	$152.7 – 319K
Minimum Net Worth:	$30K
Fees (Franchise):	$7.5 – 15K
Fees (Royalty):	$110/month
Fees (Advertising):	0%
Term of Contract (Years):	10/5
Average Number of Employees:	1 FT, 0 PT
Passive Ownership:	Allowed
Encourage Conversions:	Yes
Area Development Agreements:	No
Sub-Franchising Contracts:	No
Expand in Territory:	Yes
Space Needs:	N/A

SUPPORT & TRAINING		Training:	6 Days National Training Facility;
Financial Assistance Provided:	Yes (D)		Minimum 3 Weeks On-The-Job
Site Selection Assistance:	N/A		
Lease Negotiation Assistance:	N/A	SPECIFIC EXPANSION PLANS	
Co-operative Advertising:	No	US:	All United States
Franchisee Association/Member:	No	Canada:	All Canada
Size of Corporate Staff:	0	Overseas:	Australia, Benelux, Germany, Japan, New
On-going Support:	A, B, C, D, E, F, G, h, I		Zealand, S. Africa, UK

reported by numerous franchisees in the Snap-on system for sales activity during the 2013 reporting period. Paid Sales are presented in $25,000 increments. This information reflects a number of assumptions and limitations noted after the State-

ment, and which you should read together with the Statement.

THE NOTES THAT FOLLOW THIS STATEMENT ARE AN IN-TEGRAL PART OF THE STATEMENT.

REPORTED PAID SALES FOR 2013	Number of Franchisees Reporting	%
Less than $50,000	4	0.1%
$50,000 to $74,999	5	0.2%
$75,000 to $99,999	4	0.1%
$100,000 to $124,999	3	0.1%
$125,000 to $149,999	8	0.3%
$150,000 to $174,999	15	0.5%
$175,000 to $199,999	19	0.7%
$200,000 to $224,999	36	1.3%
$225,000 to $249,999	37	1.3%
$250,000 to $274,999	63	2.2%
$275,000 to $299,999	83	2.9%
$300,000 to $324,999	94	3.3%
$325,000 to $349,999	129	4.5%
$350,000 to $374,999	135	4.8%
$375,000 to $399,999	169	5.9%
$400,000 to $424,999	189	6.7%
$425,000 to $449,999	181	6.4%
$450,000 to $474,999	199	7.0%
$475,000 to $499,999	206	7.2%
$500,000 to $524,999	199	7.0%
$525,000 to $549,999	152	5.3%
$550,000 to $574,999	138	4.9%
$575,000 to $599,999	116	4.1%
Over $600,000	658	23.2%
TOTAL	2,842	100.0%

THE PAID SALES FIGURES USED IN THIS STATEMENT ARE REPORTED BY SPECIFIC FRANCHISEES AND SHOULD NOT BE CONSIDERED THE ACTUAL OR PROBABLE PAID SALES THAT MAY BE REALIZED BY ANY FRANCHISEE. YOUR PAID SALES MAY BE AFFECTED BY A NUMBER OF COMMERCIAL VARIABLES AND COMPETITIVE MARKET CONDITIONS. SNAP-ON DOES NOT REPRESENT THAT YOU OR ANY FRANCHISEE CAN EXPECT TO ATTAIN ANY PARTICULAR LEVEL OF PAID SALES.

NOTES:

I. Franchisee Information Included in the Statement.

We compiled the Statement from information reported to us by our franchisees. We did not verify these reports.

The Statement includes only information received from franchisees who operated for all 12 months of the 2013 reporting period and for which we have received Paid Sales information for the full period. Accordingly, franchisees who began or ended operations during calendar year 2013 are not included in the Statement nor are franchisees who failed to submit all Paid Sales information for all of 2013. Some franchisees included in the Statement may have operated part of the year as a Gateway Franchisee and part of the year as a Standard Franchisee, but to be included, they must have operated during the entire calendar year as a Gateway Franchisee or a Standard Franchisee or a combination thereof. We have not attempted to verify the information received from franchisees and have no knowledge whether franchisees prepared the information submitted to us in accordance with generally accepted accounting principles.

If a franchisee operated an additional van under a Franchise Agreement, the Paid Sales of that additional van are not included in this Statement, either as sales under the franchise under which that additional van operates or as a separate franchise. If a franchisee operated an additional franchise, that additional franchise is reported as a separate "franchise" in the Statement.

The Statement does not include information on Paid Sales for Snap-on employees who sell tools and equipment to customers that are similar to a franchisee's customers or Paid Sales of Independents.

II. Definition of "Paid Sales".

Snap-on franchisees do not have to report their total revenue to us. A franchisee's Paid Sales (defined below) should approximate "total revenues," except that a franchisee's sales of tools and equipment purchased from a source other than

Snap-on and the value of tools and equipment accepted by a franchisee as a trade-in may not be included in the Paid Sales figure reported to us.

The Statement does not include information about franchisee expenses, or profits and losses; it sets forth Paid Sales only, and a prospective franchisee should discuss the significance of the numbers with an advisor of his choice.

A franchisee's Paid Sales means the sum of: (1) all of the franchisee's cash sales and revolving account collections; (2) all open accounts and credit sales assigned to Snap-on or Snap-on Credit by the franchisee; and (3) all leases assigned to Snap-on or Snap-on Credit by the franchisee. To the extent sales taxes are reported to Snap-on by franchisee, they are included in Paid Sales (each of these terms is defined below). All franchisees included in the Statement were requested to use the same definition of Paid Sales in the reports submitted to Snap-on.

Cash Sales – Those sales for which a franchisee receive a cash payment at the time of the sale, including any cash down payment received on an open account, credit sale or a lease.

Revolving Account Collections – As described in Item 7, Revolving Account sales are credit sales between a franchisee and a franchisee's customer where a franchisee extends personal credit, usually at no interest, to finance the customer's purchase of tools and equipment. Revolving account collections are the collections made by a franchisee on revolving account financing extended by the franchisee.

Open Account Sales – Open account sales are short term credit sales made by a franchisee to businesses which the franchisee assigns to Snap-on and for which Snap-on gives the franchisee immediate credit as if the franchisee's customer had paid in cash (See Item 10). Included in Paid Sales is the dollar amount of the credit (which excludes any down payment and trade-in allowance) given to a franchisee when Snap-on accepted assignment of an open account.

Credit Sales – For certain customer purchases a franchisee may assign to Snap-on Credit with Snap-on Credit's consent the credit sales contracts (including "Extended Credit Contracts") for customer purchases (See Item 10). Snap-on Credit credits a franchisee the net sales price (which excludes any down payment and trade-in allowance) for the tools or equipment being sold. This credit is included in Paid Sales.

Leases – For certain tools and equipment, Snap-on Credit has offered in the past and may in the future offer certain customers the opportunity to lease the Products. Such a lease with a customer of a franchisee may be assigned to Snap-on Credit. Once Snap-on Credit accepts the assignment, the franchisee receives a credit calculated in the same manner as for an Extended Credit Sales contract. This credit is included in Paid Sales.

Sales Tax – Most states require that a franchisee collect and pay sales tax on purchases made by franchisee's customers. To the extent sales taxes are reported to Snap-on by franchisee they are included in Paid Sales.

III. Other Notes and Assumptions.

Percentage totals may not equal 100% due to rounding.

Reported Paid Sales are based on franchisee reports submitted weekly and do not correspond exactly with the calendar year. Some weekly reports cover Paid Sales beginning a few days before the start of the calendar year; others end a few days after. In all cases Paid Sales figures in this Appendix reflect no more than one year's Paid Sales.

The Statement reflects the various levels of Paid Sales in all parts of the United States and the prospective franchisee should not assume that the level of sales shown will be reflected in his particular area or in his particular franchise.

Substantiation of the data used in preparing this Statement will be made available to a prospective franchisee upon reasonable request; however, no information that relates to any specific franchise will be made available.

Except for the financial performance representations above, we do not furnish or authorize our employees to furnish any oral or written information concerning the potential sales, costs, income or profits of a Snap-on franchise. You will be asked to sign the Claims Representation Form attached as Appendix N as confirmation that you have not received any financial performance representations other than as provided in this Item 19. Please carefully consider this, and accurately complete this form.

Results vary, and we cannot estimate the results of any particular franchisee.

WIRELESS ZONE

34 Industrial Park Pl.
Middletown, CT 06457
Tel: (866) 994-3577, (860) 798-4473
Fax: (860) 632-9343
Email: clayn@wirelesszone.com
Website: www.wirelesszone.com
Clay Neff, National Vice President of Franchise Growth

WIRELESS ZONE stores are primarily retail, with strong emphasis on local ownership, networking and community involvement. Franchise provides local field support staff, centralized advertising and purchasing, initial and on-going training and strong commissions and residual income from Verizon Wireless phones, service, accessories, wireless email, etc. Join a winning team!

BACKGROUND

IFA Member:	Yes
Established & First Franchised:	1988; 1989
Franchised Units:	452
Company-Owned Units:	23
Total Units:	475
Distribution:	US – 475; CAN – 0; O'seas – 0
North America:	13 States, 0 Provinces
Density:	46 in CT, 38 in PA, 23 in NY
Projected New Units (12 Months):	65
Qualifications:	2, 4, 3, 2, 1, 5

FINANCIAL/TERMS

Cash Investment:	$100 – 150K
Total Investment:	$65.3 – 228.5K
Minimum Net Worth:	N/A
Fees (Franchise):	$30K
Fees (Royalty):	10%
Fees (Advertising):	$800/Mo.
Term of Contract (Years):	7/7
Average Number of Employees:	2 FT, 1 PT
Passive Ownership:	Not Allowed
Encourage Conversions:	Yes
Area Development Agreements:	No
Sub-Franchising Contracts:	Yes
Expand in Territory:	Yes

Space Needs:	1,000 SF	On-going Support:	B, C, D, E, G, H
		Training:	2 Days 3rd party trainer new store; Up to 1 Week executive trainer
SUPPORT & TRAINING			
Financial Assistance Provided:	Yes (D)		
Site Selection Assistance:	Yes	SPECIFIC EXPANSION PLANS	
Lease Negotiation Assistance:	Yes	US:	FL and VA to ME
Co-operative Advertising:	No	Canada:	No
Franchisee Association/Member:	Yes/Member	Overseas:	No
Size of Corporate Staff:	64		

Below are tables containing financial performance representations based on Providers' postpay activations and upgrades data (unaudited) of all franchised Stores for the calendar year 2013, as provided to us by Providers. Providers report postpay activations and upgrades data to us using a reporting system applicable to all of the Stores. We have not audited these figures. The average number of postpay activation and upgrade transactions in the tables are net of any deactivations. We offered substantially the same services to all of the Stores whose data is reported in the tables below. The Stores offer substantially the same products and services to consumers.

Wireless Zone® Franchised Stores
January 1, 2013 – December 31, 2013
(unaudited)

All Franchised Stores Open At Any Time During 2013 (409 Stores)

		Number of Stores that Attained or Surpassed the Average
Average Gross Commission per Postpay Activation	$418	(219 of 409 Stores or 54%)
Average Number of Postpay Activations Per Store Per Month	39	(163 of 409 Stores or 40%)
Average Gross Commission per Upgrade	$483	(187 of 409 Stores or 46%)
Average Number of Upgrades Per Store Per Month	100	(150 of 409 Stores or 37%)
Average Gross Commission per Transaction (Postpay Activations & Upgrades Combined)	$465	(210 of 409 Stores or 51%)
Average Number of Combined Transactions Per Store Per Month (Postpay Activations & Upgrades Combined)	139	(153 of 409 Stores or 37%)
Average Gross Monthly One-Time Residual Per Store	$575	(152 of 409 Stores or 37%)

Franchised Stores Open 12 Full Months In 2013 (358 Stores)

		Number of Stores that Attained or Surpassed the Average
Average Gross Commission per Postpay Activation	$417	(188 of 358 Stores or 53%)
Average Number of Postpay Activations Per Store Per Month	40	(141 of 358 Stores or 39%)
Average Gross Commission per Upgrade	$483	(161 of 358 Stores or 45%)

Average Number of Upgrades Per Store Per Month	104	(137 of 358 Stores or 38%)
Average Gross Commission Per Transaction (Postpay Activations & Upgrades Combined)	$465	(182 of 358 Stores o5 51%)
Average Number of Combined Transactions Per Store Per Month (Postpay Activations & Upgrades Combined)	143	(136 of 358 Stores or 38%)
Average Gross Monthly One-Time Residual Per Store	$589	(140 of 358 Stores or 39%)

Top 10% of Franchised Stores Open 12 Full Months In 2013 (36 Stores)

		Number of Stores that Attained or Surpassed the Average
Average Gross Commission per Postpay Activation	$396	(13 of 36 Stores or 36%)
Average Number of Postpay Activations Per Store Per Month	79	(15 of 36 Stores or 42%)
Average Gross Commission per Upgrade	$485	(15 of 36 Stores or 42%)
Average Number of Upgrades Per Store Per Month	237	(14 of 36 Stores or 39%)
Average Gross Commission Per Transaction (Postpay Activations & Upgrades Combined)	$463	(18 of 36 Stores or 50%)
Average Number of Combined Transactions Per Store Per Month (Postpay Activations & Upgrades Combined)	316	(13 of 36 Stores or 36%)
Average Gross Monthly One-Time Residual Per Store	$1,178	(15 of 36 Stores or 42%)

Bottom 10% of Franchised Stores Open 12 Full Months In 2013 (36 Stores)

		Number of Stores that Attained or Surpassed the Average
Average Gross Commission per Postpay Activation	$447	(14 of 36 Stores or 39%)
Average Number of Postpay Activations Per Store Per Month	15	(13 of 36 Stores or 36%)
Average Gross Commission per Upgrade	$479	(18 of 36 Stores or 50%)
Average Number of Upgrades Per Store Per Month	36	(19 of 36 Stores or 53%)
Average Gross Commission per Transaction (Postpay Activations & Upgrades Combined)	$470	(19 of 36 Stores or 53%)
Average Number of Combined Transactions Per Store Per Month (Postpay Activations & Upgrades Combined)	51	(18 of 36 Stores or 50%)
Average Gross Monthly One-Time Residual Per Store	$212	(16 of 36 Stores or 44%)

New Franchised Stores Opened In 2013 (14 Stores)

		Number of Stores that Attained or Surpassed the Average
Average Gross Commission per Postpay Activation	$427	(7 of 14 Stores or 50%)

Average Number of Postpay Activations Per Store Per Month	50	(7 of 14 Stores or 50%)
Average Gross Commission per Upgrade	$489	(9 of 14 Stores or 64%)
Average Number of Upgrades Per Store Per Month	85	(6 of 14 Stores or 43%)
Average Gross Commission per Transaction (Post-pay Activations & Upgrades Combined)	$466	(6 of 14 Stores or 43%)
Average Number of Combined Transactions Per Store Per Month (Postpay Activations & Upgrades Combined)	136	(6 of 14 Stores or 43%)
Average Gross Monthly One-Time Residual Per Store	$852	(6 of 14 Stores or 43%)

The first table above reports data for all 409 Stores that were open at any time as a franchised Store for a full month during 2013. There were 397 franchised Stores open on January 1, 2013 and during the year, 15 franchised Stores opened, totaling 412 franchised Stores that were technically open at any time during 2013. One store was not open for a full month during 2012; 2 franchised Stores did not do any business in 2013 and were treated as closed on January 1, 2013 for purposes of the table.

The second table reports data for all 358 Stores that were open as franchised Stores during the entire calendar year 2013. A total of 370 franchised Stores open as of January 1, 2013 remained continuously open during the entire calendar year 2013, of which 12 were continuously open but were converted from franchised Stores to company-owned Stores during the year. These 12 company-owned Stores are excluded from the second table. The third table reports data for the top 10% of the 358 franchised Stores that were open during the entire calendar year 2013, and the fourth table reports data for the bottom 10% of these 358 franchised Stores. The rankings of the top 10% and bottom 10% of these 358 franchised Stores were based on the total number of transactions per Store per month, postpay activations and upgrades combined.

Finally, the last table above reports data for all franchised Stores that opened during 2013 and had at least one full month of data. A total of 15 franchised Stores opened in 2013, 1 which opened in December 2013. Because we omitted data for the month in which each of these 15 franchised Stores opened, since using only a partial month's data would understate the number of transactions occurring per month, there is no data to report for the 1 franchised Store that opened in December 2013. The data in the 5 tables above is unaudited.

Other than the preceding financial performance representation, Automotive Technologies, Inc. does not make any financial performance representations. We also do not authorize our employees or representatives to make any such representations

either orally or in writing. If you are purchasing an existing outlet, however, we may provide you with the actual records of that outlet. If you receive any other financial performance information or projections of your future income, you should report it to the franchisor's management by contacting Susan E. Suhr, 34 Industrial Park Place, Middletown, Connecticut 06457, telephone number 860/632-9494 extension 1800, the Federal Trade Commission, and the appropriate state regulatory agencies.

The financial performance representation figures do not reflect the costs of sales, operating expenses, royalties or other costs or expenses that must be deducted from the gross revenue or gross sales figures to obtain your net income or profit. You should conduct an independent investigation of the costs and expenses you will incur in operating your Wireless Zone® Store. Franchisees or former franchisees, listed in this Disclosure Document, may be one source of this information.

The data reported in the above tables are averages and could vary greatly by geographic region, the length of time the Store has been in business, the length of time Provider has been operating in the area, your particular Provider, the terms of our contract with Provider, the service plan selected by the Store customer and customer usage. Results also vary from Store to Store.

Actual results may vary from franchise to franchise, and we cannot estimate the results of any particular franchise.

Some Stores have realized the number of transactions listed in the charts. Your individual results may differ. There is no assurance that you will realize as many transactions or commission levels or residuals.

Written substantiation for the financial performance representation will be made available to the prospective franchisee upon reasonable request.

Service-Based Franchises | 6

1-800-GOT-JUNK?

THE WORLD'S LARGEST JUNK REMOVAL SERVICE

1-800-GOT-JUNK?

887 Great Northern Way, # 301
Vancouver, BC V5T 4T5
Tel: (866) 475-6842, (800) 468-5865
Fax: (514) 370-4625
Email: jason.isley@1800gotjunk.com
Website: www.1800gotjunk.com
Jason Isley, Franchise Developement Director

1-800-GOT-JUNK? has revolutionized customer service in junk removal for 25 years. By setting the mark for service standards and professionalism, an industry that once operated without set rates, price lists or receipts, now has top service standards. You will have the expert advice and support that is key to success. Our intensive training program will get you on track; our on-going support and continuing education will keep you there. Centralized call center allows you to focus on your business.

BACKGROUND
IFA Member:	Yes
Established & First Franchised:	1989; 1998
Franchised Units:	162
Company-Owned Units:	1
Total Units:	163
Distribution:	US – 136; CAN – 21; O'seas – 5
North America:	44 States, 9 Provinces

Density:	45 in CA, 20 in FL, 13 in NY
Projected New Units (12 Months):	1
Qualifications:	5, 5, 1, 2, 4, 5

FINANCIAL/TERMS
Cash Investment:	$70 – 100K
Total Investment:	$125 – 250K
Minimum Net Worth:	$250K
Fees (Franchise):	$12K
Fees (Royalty):	8%
Fees (Advertising):	1%
Term of Contract (Years):	5/15
Average Number of Employees:	2 FT, 2 PT
Passive Ownership:	Not Allowed
Encourage Conversions:	No
Area Development Agreements:	No
Sub-Franchising Contracts:	No
Expand in Territory:	Yes
Space Needs:	N/A

SUPPORT & TRAINING
Financial Assistance Provided:	Yes (D)
Site Selection Assistance:	N/A
Lease Negotiation Assistance:	N/A
Co-operative Advertising:	Yes
Franchisee Association/Member:	Yes/Member
Size of Corporate Staff:	68
On-going Support:	a, B, C, D, G, H, I
Training:	5 Days Vancouver, BC

SPECIFIC EXPANSION PLANS
US:	All United States
Canada:	Yes
Overseas:	No

The following table presents the average gross sales realized by certain 1-800-GOT-JUNK? franchisees as of December 31, 2013. We have provided you with this information to help you make a more informed decision about our franchises. You should not use this information as an indication of how well your specific Franchised Business will do. The actual numbers you experience will vary depending upon several factors, including competition, management and market demographics. You should conduct your own research to assist you in preparing projections for your own Franchised Business.

The information provided below was compiled from our 130 Franchised Businesses that were in existence during at least the entire 12 month period covered and none of the underlying data supplied to us has been audited. You should note that gross sales will be dependent, among other things, upon the size of the territory in which the Franchised Business operates and number of trucks operating in that territory.

Average Gross Sales of 1-800-GOT-JUNK? Franchisees
For the Twelve Months Ending December 31, 2013

US Franchsiees of 1-800-GOT-JUNK? LLC	Total Franchisees	Average Gross Sales (US$)	% of Franchisees at or above Average	Median Gross Sales (US$)	% of Franchisees at or above Median
Franchisees operating for more than 12 months, but less than 24 months	6	$261,518	67%	$301,146	50%
Franchisees operating for more than 24 months, but less than 36 months	5	$610,815	60%	$610,832	60%
Franchisees operating for more than 36 months, but less than 48 months	3	$686,886	33%	$510,681	67%
Franchisees operating for more than 48 months, but less than 60 months	7	$623,597	43%	$411,973	57%
Franchisees operating for more than 60 months, but less than 72 months	12	$343,462	33%	$292,168	50%
Franchisees operating for more than 72 months	97	$866,991	38%	$629,439	51%

Some franchisees have sold this amount. Your individual results may differ. There is no assurance you will sell as much.

There is no assurance that any other 1-800-GOT-JUNK? Franchised Business will perform as well as, or anywhere near, the 130 Franchised Businesses used in preparing the averages shown above.

The earnings claims figures do not reflect the costs of sales or operating expenses that must be deducted from the gross revenue or gross sales figures to obtain your net income or profit. The best source of cost and expense data may be from franchisees and former franchisees, some of whom may be listed in Exhibit A.

Substantiation of the data used in preparing this earnings claim will be made available to you upon reasonable request. Other than the preceding financial performance representation, 1-800-GOT-JUNK? does not make any financial performance representations. We also do not authorize our employees or representatives to make any such representations either orally or in writing. If you are purchasing an existing outlet, however, we may provide you with the actual records of that outlet. If you receive any other financial performance information or projections of your future income, you should report it to the franchisor's management by contacting our Franchise Development Manager at 887 Great Northern Way, Suite 301, Vancouver, B.C., Canada, V5T 4T5; or by phone at 1-800-GOT-JUNK; the Federal Trade Commission; and the appropriate state regulatory agencies.

AAMCO TRANSMISSIONS

201 Gibraltar Rd., # 150
Horsham, PA 19044
Tel: (800) 523-0402, (800) 292-8500
Fax: (215) 956-0340
Email: chapword@americandriveline.com
Website: www.aamcotransmissions.com
Curt Hapword, VP Franchise Sales & Development

AAMCO Transmissions is the world's largest chain of transmission specialists and one of the leaders in total car care services. AAMCO has approximately 900 automotive centers throughout the United States, Canada and Puerto Rico. Established in 1962, AAMCO is proud to have served more than 35 million drivers.

BACKGROUND
IFA Member:	Yes
Established & First Franchised:	1963; 1963
Franchised Units:	900
Company-Owned Units:	12
Total Units:	912
Distribution:	US – 838; CAN – 27; O'seas – 33
North America:	48 States, 4 Provinces
Density:	71 in FL, 49 in PA, 68 in TX

Projected New Units (12 Months):	40
Qualifications:	4, 4, 1, 2, 3, 3

FINANCIAL/TERMS
Cash Investment:	$60 – 100K
Total Investment:	$224 – 299K
Minimum Net Worth:	$50 – 182K
Fees (Franchise):	$39.5K
Fees (Royalty):	7.50%
Fees (Advertising):	Varies, $150/month for national
Term of Contract (Years):	15/15
Average Number of Employees:	4 FT, 0 PT
Passive Ownership:	Allowed
Encourage Conversions:	Yes
Area Development Agreements:	Yes
Sub-Franchising Contracts:	No
Expand in Territory:	No
Space Needs:	1,212 SF

SUPPORT & TRAINING
Financial Assistance Provided:	Yes (I)
Site Selection Assistance:	Yes
Lease Negotiation Assistance:	Yes
Co-operative Advertising:	Yes
Franchisee Association/Member:	Yes/Not a Member
Size of Corporate Staff:	120
On-going Support:	C, D, E, f, G, h, I
Training:	On-Going Regional, Annual, On-Line; 5 Weeks On-Site; 3 Weeks Horsham, PA

SPECIFIC EXPANSION PLANS
US:	All United States
Canada:	All Canada
Overseas:	All Countries

In this Item 19, we disclose: (i) the average gross sales in 2013 of franchised U.S. AAMCO Centers that were operated for two years or more as of December 28, 2013 segmented by qualities; and (ii) the average gross sales in 2013 of franchised U.S. AAMCO Centers that were operated for five years or more as of December 28, 2013, segmented by qualities.

Some AAMCO Centers have earned this amount. Your individual results may differ. There is no assurance that you will earn as much. Written substantiation of all financial performance information presented in this financial performance representation will be made available to you upon reasonable request.

This financial performance representation and the included data was prepared without an audit. We therefore cannot make representations or warranties as to the accuracy of this franchisee-reported information. Prospective franchisees or sellers of franchises should be advised that no certified public accountant has audited these figures or expressed his/her opinion with regard to their contents or form.

AAMCO urges you to consult with your own financial, business, and legal advisors to conduct you own analysis of the information contained in this section of Item 19 and in this entire franchise disclosure document. Gross sales results depend not only on the scope of services which a Center offers, but on, among other things, the quality of a Center's management team, the Center's operating hours, the energy and dedication of a Center's owner, and the quality of the services which the Center performs.

Please read carefully all of the information in this Item 19 (including the table below as well as the notes that follow the table) for explanation of how these results are determined.

Average Gross Sales of Franchised Centers – 2013

	Centers that are at least 2 Years Old				Centers that are at least 5 Years Old			
	# of Centers in Quartile	Average Gross Sales of Centers in Quartile	# of Centers in Quartile that met or exceeded Average	% of Centers that met or exceeded Average	# of Centers in Quartile	Average Gross Sales of Centers in Quartile	# of Centers in Quartile that met or exceeded Average	% of Centers that met or exceeded Average
Top Quartile	170	$962,408	71	41.8%	160	$972,922	64	40.0%
2nd Quartile	171	$657,963	82	48.0%	161	$665,569	76	47.2%
3rd Quartile	170	$509,568	90	52.9%	160	$518,378	82	51.3%
Bottom Quartile	171	$323,873	98	57.3%	161	$327,984	92	57.1%
Total	682	$614,030	302	44.3%	642	$620,826	284	44.2%

Notes:

1. The table presents the average gross sales for franchised U.S. AAMCO Centers that were open for at least 48 weeks during the 2013 fiscal year (December 30, 2012 through December 28, 2013). The information on the Centers included in the table are separated among (i) Centers that were operated for two years of more as of December 28, 2013 (682 Centers met this criterion); and (ii) Center that were operated for five years or more as of December 28, 2013 (642 Centers met this criterion). Centers that did not operate for at least 48 weeks during 2013, or that were not open for the requisite period of time, have not been included in the results. Among the results for the Centers open for at least two years, 21 Centers operating at year end were not included in the results because they were not open for at least two years. Among the results for the Centers open for at least five years, 61 Centers operating at year end were not included in the results because they were not open for at least five years.

2. The results in the table are separated into quartiles. Each quartile represents, as closely as possible, 25% of the Centers operating during 2013 that met the requisite criteria. As an example, the "Top Quartile" represents the quartile of Centers with the highest average gross sales during 2013, and the "Bottom Quartile" represents the quartile of Centers with the lowest average gross sales during 2013.

3. THE FIGURES IN THE CHART DO NOT REFLECT THE COSTS OF SALES, OPERATING EXPENSES OR OTHER COSTS OR EXPENSES THAT MUST BE DEDUCTED FROM THE GROSS SALES FIGURES TO OBTAIN YOUR NET INCOME OR PROFIT. YOU SHOULD CONDUCT AN INDEPENDENT INVES-TIGATION OF THE COSTS AND EXPENSES YOU WILL INCUR IN OPERATING YOUR CENTER. FRANCHISEES OR FORMER FRANCHISEES, LISTED IN THIS DISCLOSURE DOCUMENT, MAY BE ONE SOURCE OF THIS INFORMATOIN. The following is a non-exclusive list of the types of costs and expenses an AAMCO franchisee may incur: (1) costs of goods sold; (2) labor costs, including taxes and benefits; (3) rent, utilities, trash collection, material disposal, maintenance and other charges to occupy your premises; (4) advertising and marketing expenses; (5) administrative costs, such as maintenance, insurance, security, training, supplies, and professional fees; (6) Initial License Fee, Franchise Fees, and advertising costs; (7) debt service; and (8) taxes. You may incur other costs. The expenses you may incur vary from Center to Center, and in different market areas.

4. Actual results vary from franchisee to franchisee and we cannot estimate or predict the results that you will experience. Your individual financial results are likely to differ from the results shown in the charts. In addition to the points noted above, your results will be affected by factors such as prevailing economic or market area condition, demographics, geographic location, interest rates, your capitalization level, the amount and terms of any financing that you may secure, the property values and lease rates, your business and management skills, staff strengths and weaknesses, and the cost and effectiveness of your marketing activities.

5. We strongly advise you to conduct an independent investigation of this information and the opportunity to buy a franchise so that you can decide whether or not you think the franchise will meet your financial needs. Among other things, we recommend that you contact the current and former franchisees listed in this Disclosure Document and that you also consult

with a qualified attorney, accountant, and other professional advisors before entering into a Franchise Agreement. We suggest that you develop and review with your own professional advisors a pro forma cash flow statement, balance sheet and statement of operations, and that you make your own financial projections regarding sales, costs, customer base, and business development for your own Center.

6. Written substantiation of the data used in preparing the information in this Item 19 will be made available to you upon reasonable request.

7. Other than the preceding financial performance representation, we do not make any financial performance representa-tions. We also do not authorize our employees or represen-tatives to make any such representations either orally or in writing. If you are purchasing an existing outlet, however, we may provide you with the actual records of that outlet. If you receive any other financial performance information or pro-jections of your future income, you should report it to the franchisor's management by contacting Richard Kolman at 201 Gibralter Road, Horsham, PA 19044 (or 610-668-2900 ext. 212), the Federal Trade Commission, and the appropriate state regulatory agencies.

8. A NEW FRANCHISEE'S INDIVIDUAL RESULTS ARE LIKE-LY TO DIFFER FROM THE RESULTS STATED IN THE FI-NANCIAL PERFORMANCE REPRESENTATIONS ABOVE.

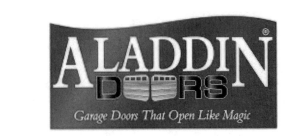

ALADDIN DOORS

2255 Lois Dr., # 6
Rolling Meadows, IL 60008
Tel: (888) 325-2334, (847) 310-3515
Fax: (847) 310-3518
Email: mike@aladdindoors.com
Website: www.aladdindoors.com
Mike Haneberg, Franchise Development Manager

Aladdin Doors has been the number one choice for all garage door needs in Chicago, IL, Minneapolis, MN and surround-ing areas with over 45 years of experience. Our family-owned company has a long-lasting reputation of excellence with re-gard to garage door installation, garage door repair, and any other garage door situation that needs to be addressed. Our vision is to be known as the worldwide leader in quick, high quality and comprehensive overhead garage door services, de-livering exceptional services and products to each customer. We'll continue to grow the Aladdin brand through people, innovation and technology, resulting in unsurpassed loyalty from our customers and a solid business model for our com-pany-owned locations. Our mission is to grant our custom-ers' wishes by providing a hassle-free experience for all their garage door needs while exceeding their expectations. As the owner of an Aladdin Doors franchise, you can expect to re-ceive first-rate support from our management team.

BACKGROUND
IFA Member:	Yes
Established & First Franchised:	2004; 2013
Franchised Units:	2
Company-Owned Units:	2
Total Units:	4
Distribution:	US – 4; CAN – 0; O'seas – 0
North America:	3 States, 0 Provinces
Density:	2 in IL, 1 in MN, 1 in NC
Projected New Units (12 Months):	6
Qualifications:	4, 3, 1, 4, 4, 5

FINANCIAL/TERMS
Cash Investment:	$30K
Total Investment:	$29.9 – 100K
Minimum Net Worth:	$100K
Fees (Franchise):	$10 – 35K
Fees (Royalty):	6.5%
Fees (Advertising):	3%
Term of Contract (Years):	10/10
Average Number of Employees:	1 FT, 1 PT
Passive Ownership:	Not Allowed
Encourage Conversions:	Yes
Area Development Agreements:	No
Sub-Franchising Contracts:	No
Expand in Territory:	No
Space Needs:	800 SF

SUPPORT & TRAINING

Financial Assistance Provided:	Yes (I)
Site Selection Assistance:	N/A
Lease Negotiation Assistance:	N/A
Co-operative Advertising:	Yes
Franchisee Association/Member:	No
Size of Corporate Staff:	15
On-going Support:	a, d, i

Training: 3 Days within First 60 Days of Operation Franchisee Location; 12 Days Rolling Meadows, IL

SPECIFIC EXPANSION PLANS

US:	IL, MN
Canada:	Yes, Ontario
Overseas:	No

The following statement is based on historical financial data of our affiliate, Action Doors, Inc. Action Doors, Inc. has been operating a garage door installation and repair service business since February 2004. While the services and products offered and sold by Action Doors, Inc. are substantially similar to those that will be offered and sold by Aladdin Doors franchise businesses, the company operations differ in that they have operated throughout the Chicago metropolitan area, an area much larger than any territory that will be granted to an Aladdin Doors franchisee. Action Doors, Inc. has operated in this large territory by maintaining a number of trained technicians who deliver the services to customers.

During the initial operation of the business, it is expected that the franchise owner will be acting as the technician for the Aladdin Doors business and performing all of the installation and repair services with the possibility of hiring one part-time helper during the initial period of operation.

The following statement is of the actual annual gross revenue, cost of goods sold and gross profit realized by Action Doors, Inc. as a result of the services conducted by three of its trained technicians during the calendar year 2013. The average of the figures for the 3 technicians is presented in the second table. During 2013, services to customers were performed by Action Doors, Inc. through a total of 8 technicians. The following statement is based on the services provided by a subset of 3 of the 8 technicians. These 3 technicians were the only techni-

cians of the total of 8 who worked on a full-time basis for Action Doors, Inc. and who worked with Action Doors, Inc. for the full period of January 1, 2013 through December 31, 2013. Technician A has been a technician of Action Doors, Inc. since April 2008, Technician B has been a technician of Action Doors, Inc. since January 2009, and Technician C has been a technician of Action Doors, Inc. since November 2007.

None of the technicians had previous experience in providing garage door installation and repair services and were trained by Action Doors, Inc. These technicians did not rely solely on their own marketing and sales skills in procuring customers. The securing of customers for the worked they performed was done predominantly by Action Doors, Inc.

The figures were below were compiled internally from sales receipts, supplier invoices and other internal recordkeeping of our Action Doors, Inc. The data has not been audited.

The following actual annual Gross Revenue, Cost of Goods Sold and Gross Profit reflects the experience of 3 technicians of our affiliate, and should not be considered as the actual or probable Gross Revenue or Gross Profit that will be realized by any given franchise. A new franchisee's individual financial results may differ from the results stated in the financial performance representation. The following data is from our affiliate which had been in business for almost 9 years as of January 1, 2013.

ACTUAL ANNUAL GROSS REVENUE, COST OF GOODS SOLD AND GROSS PROFIT
OF 3 TECHNICIANS OF AFFILIATE FOR 2013

	Technician A			Technician B			Technician C		
	Repairs	Doors	Total	Repairs	Doors	Total	Repairs	Doors	Total
Gross Revenue	$227,289	$2,450	$229,739	$165,676	$30,310	$195,986	$180,296	$38,475	$218,771
Cost of Goods Sold	$35,921	$1,232	$37,153	$26,779	$14,043	$40,822	$27,234	$17,622	$44,856
Gross Profit	$191,368	$1,218	$192,586	$138,897	$16,267	$155,164	$153,062	$20,853	$173,915

AVERAGE ACTUAL ANNUAL GROSS REVENUE, COST OF GOODS SOLD AND GROSS PROFIT
OF 3 TECHNICIANS OF AFFILIATE FOR 2013

	Repairs	Doors	Total
Gross Revenue	$191,087	$23,745	$214,832
Cost of Good Sold	$29,978	$10,966	$40,944
Gross Profit	$161,109	$12,779	$173,888

2 of the 3 technicians exceeded the average annual total Gross Revenue of $214,833.
2 of the 3 technicians exceeded the average annual Gross Profit of $173,888.

Notes to tables:

1. Gross Revenue is the total of all money received for the services rendered to a customer, whether for installation of garage doors and openers or for providing repair services.

2. Repair Revenue includes revenue received from garage door and opener repairs and replacements of springs, cable, garage door openers, sections, rollers, hinges, drums, brackets, bottom rubber, weather stripping, gears, sprockets, capacitors, remotes, keypads, tracks and other parts related to garage doors and garage door openers.

3. Doors Revenue include the installation of a new garage doors and the installation of a new garage door opener in connection with the installation of the new doors.

4. To the extent that any installation or repair services performed for a customer were performed by more than one technician, Action Doors, Inc. internally allocated a percentage of the revenue and cost of goods to each technician involved in performing the installation or the repair services and that share is included in the revenue figures provided.

5. Cost of Goods Sold means the total amount paid to suppliers for the garage doors, openers and replacement parts used in the installation or repair service, including shipping charges and applicable sales taxes.

6. Gross Profit means Gross Revenue minus Cost of Goods Sold.

EXPLANATORY NOTES AND ASSUMPTIONS:

The following should be considered in reviewing and determining whether to rely on these figures:

Your results may vary as a start-up business. Action Doors, Inc. has been in operation for over 8 years and has developed brand awareness within the geographic area where it operates.

Your results may vary with a newly trained technician providing the installation and repair services. The technicians included in the above statement had a minimum of 2 years of experience as a technician by the beginning of the period covered by the statement.

During the initial operation of the business, it is expected that the franchise owner will be acting as the technician and performing all of the installation and repair services with the possibility of hiring one part-time helper during the initial period of operation. During the initial period, it is expected that the new franchise owner will also be responsible for marketing, advertising and promoting the business.

This actual statement of total Gross Revenues and Gross Profit does not include information concerning net profits that may be realized in the operation of an Aladdin Doors business. Net profits in the operation of an Aladdin Doors business will vary from franchisee to franchisee and from location to location and are dependent upon the total gross revenues you achieve and upon your ability to minimize expenses as well as numerous other factors beyond your control. We make no representations in this Item 19 with respect to the net profits likely to be experienced by an Aladdin Doors business.

You will incur numerous costs and expenses in connection with the operation of an Aladdin Doors business in addition to the Cost of Goods Sold, including other labor costs; occupancy costs (such as office rent and utilities); cost of equipment, materials and supplies needed to perform services; transportation expenses, including gasoline and maintenance of the van; advertising and promotional expenses; royalties and advertising contributions paid to us; legal and accounting expenses; insurance expenses; taxes; various other general and administrative expenses and debt service. This is not an all-inclusive list of expenses.

Factors which may cause material differences in the gross revenue and gross profits of technicians for an Aladdin Doors franchise business from the gross revenue and gross profit of technicians of our affiliate include:

- Management and business experience and the amount of time the franchise owner spends working in the business
- Quality of customer service
- Prices charged to customers
- Marketing and promotional efforts and related skills of the franchise owner
- Demographic factors, including geographic size, number of non-multi-unit housing units, income levels and economic conditions in the franchise territory
- Local competition in the franchise territory
- Weather and climate of the franchise territory.

The above list is not an all-inclusive list of factors. You should carefully consider these and other factors in evaluating this information and in making any decision to purchase a franchise.

The information in this statement is provided for reference only. You should make your own independent investigation on the revenues and profit potential of the franchise business. You should seek the advice of legal, business and financial advisors before making a determination concerning the revenues and profit potential of the Aladdin Doors franchise business.

Written substantiation of the data used in preparing this statement will be made available to prospective franchisees on reasonable request.

Other than the above financial performance representations, we do not make any representations about a franchisee's future financial performance or the past financial performance of companyowned or franchised outlets. We also do not authorize our employees or representatives to make any such representations either orally or in writing. If you are purchasing an existing outlet, however, we may provide you with the actual records of that outlet. If you receive any other financial performance information or projections of your future income, you should report it to the franchisor's management by contacting Alaa Kareem Abdelaal, 2255 Lois Drive Unit 6, Rolling Meadows, Illinois 60008 (888) 325-2334, or the Federal Trade Commission, and the appropriate state regulatory agencies.

ALWAYS BEST CARE SENIOR SERVICES

1406 Blue Oaks Rd.
Roseville, CA 95747
Tel: (855) 430-2273, (916) 722-1822
Fax: (916) 722-8780
Email: jbrown@abc-seniors.com
Website: www.franchisewithalwaysbestcare.com
Jake Brown, Chief Operating Officer

Always Best Care Senior Services offers three distinct revenue streams: Assisted living finder and referral assistance, non-medical in-home care, and skilled home health care. We have been in business since 1996, and have contracts with companies representing more than 2,000 assisted living communities. We provide the following: An exclusive insurance program, 56 hours of classroom training plus 204 hours of on-the-job training, outsourced staffing services free for the first six months, national contracts, 24/7 call center so franchisees never miss a lead, award-winning national advertising support, and a virtual office (all-in-one web-based software system).

BACKGROUND

IFA Member	Yes
Established & First Franchised:	1996;2007
Franchised Units:	185
Company-Owned Units:	0
Total Units:	185
Dist.:	US-185; CAN-0; O'seas-0
North America:	30 States, 0 Provinces
Density:	44 in CA, 26 in NJ, 18 in NC
Projected New Units (12 Months):	50
Qualifications:	5, 5, 3, 2, 3, 4

FINANCIAL/TERMS

Cash Investment:	$60.2 – $109.4K
Total Investment	$60.2 – 109.4K
Minimum Net Worth:	$200K
Fees (Franchise):	$44.9K
Fees (Royalty):	6%

Fees (Advertising):	2%	Lease Negotiation Assistance:	N/A
Term of Contract (Years):	10/5	Co-operative Advertising:	Yes
Avg. # of Employees:	3 FT, 0 PT	Franchisee Assoc./Member:	Yes/Member
Passive Ownership:	Allowed	Size of Corporate Staff:	17
Encourage Conversions:	Yes	On-going Support:	C,D,G,H,I
Area Develop. Agreements:	Yes	Training:	Pre and post training modules about 90 days
Sub-Franchising Contracts:	No		one-on-one with sales trainer; 7 Days Corporate office;
Expand in Territory:	Yes		2 Weeks at franchise location
Space Needs:	N/A		

SUPPORT & TRAINING

		SPECIFIC EXPANSION PLANS	
		US:	All States
Financial Assistance Provided:	Yes (I)	Canada:	Yes
Site Selection Assistance:	N/A	Overseas:	Germany, UK, Australia

This Item 19 sets forth certain historical data regarding Always Best Care Franchised Business locations. Written substantiation of the data used in preparing this information will be made available to prospective franchisees upon request. The representations made in this Item 19 are based upon the period of time indicated below.

The success of your franchise will depend largely upon your personal abilities, your use of those abilities and your market. The financial results of your Franchise will likely differ, perhaps materially, from the results summarized in this Item.

SYSTEMWIDE GROWTH

In the table below, we have included annual revenue information for all Franchised Businesses that operated at any point during the calendar year listed, regardless of whether any were newly opened in that year of closed for business or otherwise left the brand in that year. The figures included in the table below do not include any information for company owned businesses.

2011 Annual Revenue	2012 Annual Revenue	Percent Increase 2012 over 2011	2013 Annual Revenue	Percent Increase 2013 over 2012
$20,778,883.77	$40,057,782.59	92.78%	$66,010,542.74	64.79%

MONTHLY AVERAGE NUMBER OF CLIENTS

The table below lists the monthly average number of Clients for Franchised Businesses broken down into 3 categories based upon their Annual Revenue during the calendar year ending December 31, 2013. In the table below, we have only included information relating to Franchised Businesses that were continuously open and operating for the entire 2013 calendar year and whose Annual Revenue was at least $500,000 for in 2013. There were 40 Always Best Care Senior Services

Franchised Businesses that were continuously open for business and operating during the entirety of the 2013 calendar year, with revenues of at least $500,000. All of these Franchised Businesses reported information to us for this financial performance representation. 53 Franchised Businesses were continuously open for business and operating during the entirety of the 2013 calendar year had revenues lower than $500,000 in 2013. The information for those 53 Franchised Businesses was not included in the table below.

2013 Annual Revenue	$503,356 to $964,634	$1,027,223 to $2,804,888	$10,650,409
Monthly Average Number of Clients	28	55	480
Number of Franchisees in Annual Revenue Category (out of 94)	22	17	1

Number (and Percentage) of Franchisees that Met or Exceeded Average Number of Clients (in Category)	9 (43%)	8 (47%)	1 (100%)

NOTE:

1. The "Monthly Average Number of Clients" was calculated by adding the number of unique Clients of the Franchised Business for each month during the year, calculating the total number of Clients for all months in 2013, and then dividing that number by 12 months.

ANNUAL REVENUE GROWTH

The table below contains certain information related to Annual Revenues realized by Franchised Businesses during calendar 2013, and compares it with Annual Revenues realized during 2012. The data is broken down into 5 categories based upon the Franchised Businesses' 2013 level of Annual Revenue. The table below also lists the number and percentage of franchisees that met or exceeded the category average. We have only included information relating to Franchised Businesses that were continuously open and operating for the entire 2012 and 2013 calendar years in this table. Any Franchised Businesses that were either newly opened in 2012 or 2013 or closed for business or otherwise left the brand in 2012 or 2013 were excluded. There were 20 new Franchised Business openings in 2012 and 14 new Franchised Business openings in 2013. 15 Franchised Businesses were terminated in 2012 and 17 were terminated in 2013. None of these Franchised Businesses were included in the table below.

2013 Annual Revenue	% of Franchisees	Average Percent Increase over 2012	Number of Franchisees in Annual Revenue Category	Number (and Percentage) of Franchisees that Met or Exceeded Average Percent Increase (in Category)
Over $2,000,000	5.1%	160%	4	1 (25%)
Over 1,000,000 but under $2,000,000	18.0%	22%	14	5 (36%)
Over $500,000 but under $1,000,000	26.9%	68%	21	12 (57%)
Over $250,000 but under $500,000	18.0%	41%	14	7 (50%)
Under $250,000	32.0%	66%	25	15 (60%)

NOTES:

1. The information in the "Annual Revenue" column in the Annual Revenue Growth chart is based upon the results of all Unit Franchisees which had billed Clients for services for at least 2 full calendar years as of December 31, 2013. The numbers are not related to when franchisees signed franchise agreements. The numbers do not include results from franchises which were terminateed in during the year listed.

2. "Annual Revenue" means the total of all revenues from the operation of each franchisee's business whether received in cash, in services in kind, from barter and/or exchange, on credit (whether or not payment is received therefore) or otherwise during the calendar year referenced. Annual Revenue does not include the amount of all sales tax receipts or similar tax receipts which, by law, are chargeable to Clients, if these taxes are separately stated when the Client is charged and if these taxes are paid to the appropriate taxing authority. In addition, Annual Revenue does not include the amount of any documented refunds, charge backs, credits and allowances given in good faith to Clients by a franchisee.

3. The information in this table is broken out by Franchised Business. A Franchised Business may contain between 1 to 8 Assigned Areas. Less than 10% of the Franchised Businesses have 3 or more Assigned Areas.

4. The % of Franchisees was calculated by dividing the total number of Franchised Businesses within each respective revenue category that were open for at least 2 years and comparing them against the total number for all Franchised Businesses for 2013 that were open for at least 2 years.

5. The "Average Percent Increase" was calculated by dividing the total Annual Revenue for 2012 for all Franchised Business within each respective revenue level and comparing them against the total Annual Revenue for all Franchised Businesses for 2013.

If you have become an ABCSP franchisee, your financial results may differ from the results presented in this Item 19. Some franchisees have achieved these results. There is no assurance that your business will achieve these results.

Written substantiation of the information set out in this Item 19 will be provided to prospective franchisees on reasonable request.

Other than the preceeding financial performance representation, ABCSP Inc. does not make any financial performance representations. We also do not authorize our employees or representatives to make any such representations either orally or in writing. If you are purchasing an existing outlet, however, we may provide you with the actual records of that outlet. If you receive any other financial performance information or projections of your future income, you should report it to the franchisor's management by contacting Michael Newman, 1406 Blue Oaks Blvd., Roseville, California 95747, 1-888-430-CARE, the Federal Trade commission, and the appropriate state regulatory authorities.

ANAGO CLEANING SYSTEMS

5203 NW 33rd. Ave.
Fort Lauderdale, FL 33309
Tel: (800) 213-5857, (954) 752-3111
Fax: (954) 752-1200
Email: judy@anagocleaning.com
Website: www.anagocleaning.com
Judy Walker, Vice President of Marketing

Anago is a franchised commercial cleaning company, with both Master and Unit Franchises available across the U.S. and internationally. The Master has the exclusive developmental rights to sell Unit Franchises in a defined territory, and simultaneously sells cleaning contracts, business to business within the territory, and assigns them to those who purchased a Unit Franchise. This is a huge industry, estimated at over $100 billion annually, with projected double-digit growth.

BACKGROUND
IFA Member:	Yes
Established & First Franchised:	1989; 1991
Franchised Units:	2,447
Company-Owned Units:	0
Total Units:	2,447
Distribution:	US – 2,438; CAN – 4; O'seas – 5
North America:	15 States, 1 Province
Density:	N/A

Projected New Units (12 Months):	200
Qualifications:	3, 3, 3, 2, 2, 2

FINANCIAL/TERMS
Cash Investment:	$1 – 24K
Total Investment:	$7 – 33K
Minimum Net Worth:	$1 – 24K
Fees (Franchise):	$4.5 – 32K
Fees (Royalty):	10%
Fees (Advertising):	Varies
Term of Contract (Years):	10/10
Average Number of Employees:	1-2 FT, Varies PT
Passive Ownership:	Not Allowed
Encourage Conversions:	N/A
Area Development Agreements:	No
Sub-Franchising Contracts:	No
Expand in Territory:	Yes
Space Needs:	N/A

SUPPORT & TRAINING
Financial Assistance Provided:	Yes (D)
Site Selection Assistance:	N/A
Lease Negotiation Assistance:	N/A
Co-operative Advertising:	Yes
Franchisee Association/Member:	No
Size of Corporate Staff:	25
On-going Support:	A,C,D,G,H,I
Training:	56-66 Hours Unit Franchise - Master Office

SPECIFIC EXPANSION PLANS
US:	All United Stated
Canada:	All Canada
Overseas:	All Countries

Set forth below is information showing the unaudited Annual Sales and Gross Margins as self-reported by certain Anago Master Franchise Owners' busiesses during our 2013 fiscal year.

	FY 2013
Average Annual Sales	$3,123,016
Average Annual Master Owner Gross Margin (AAGM)	$951,938
Percentage (%) AAGM	30.6%

NOTES:

"Average Annual Sales" means total collected billing for all janitorial work to include day porter services, special or un-scheduled services, and sales of supplies by the Master Owners as well as revenue collected by the Master Owners for the sale of Unit Franchises. These numbers do not include any federal, state, or local taxes collected behalf of Franchised outlets.

"Average Annual Gross Margin" means amounts attained after royalty has been paid to us and after payments are made to the Unit Franchisees for cleaning service contracts but does not include any prepayments for additional janitorial work, supplies, or equipment made by the Unit Franchisees, which can increase actual Gross Margin achieved. These numbers do not include any federal, state, or local taxes collected and paid on behalf of franchised outlets.

The information in this Item comes from current Owners of Anago Subfranchise Businesses ("Master Owners") as of December 31, 2013. All Master Owners included in this survey, have territories that have been opened as franchised outlets and not corporately held for at least one full year as of December 31, 2013. Some Anago Master Franchise Owners own multiple territories. The charts above reflect the Gross Margins of their combined territories. In 2013, two (20.0%) of the Master Franchise Owners included in the survey had multiple territories.

The figures reflect averages for ten (10) Master Owners representing 43.5% of Master Owners whose territories have been opened for at least one full year as of December 31, 2013. Of these ten Master Owners, six (60.0%) had higher Gross Margins. You will be opening a new territory and therefore may not experience similar results.

Gross Margin does not reflect your profits or net income,

because we will take deductions from Gross Margin before sending monies to you. Your portion of the Gross Margin is subject to further deductions and adjustments authorized by the Franchise Agreement. Please also refer to Item 6 for more details about additional deductions and adjustments.

In addition to deductions and adjustments made by us as described in Item 6 above, you will incur other expenses that will reduce your profits or net income, such as land, building and/or equipment rent, labor, debt service, depreciation and amortization, advertising, administrative expenses such as accounting or legal expenses, taxes, licenses, insurance, and others. These expenses vary from Master Owner to Master Owner.

The information set forth in the Charts reflect the actual results of existing Anago Master Franchise Owners' businesses, and should not be considered as the actual or probable results that will be realized by any Master Franchisee. A new Master Franchisee's individual financial results are likely to be lower.

Substantiation for the data set forth in these tables will be made available to you at our headquarters upon reasonable request.

Actual results vary from franchise to franchise and are dependent on a variety of internal and external factors, some of which we cannot estimate or forecast, such as competition, taxes, and the general economic climate. Accordingly, we cannot and do not estimate the results of a particular Subfranchise.

We recommend that you make your own independent investigation to determine whether or not the Subfranchise may be profitable, and consult with an attorney and other advisors before executing any agreement.

Other than the preceding financial performance representation, AFI does not make any financial performance representations. We also do not authorize our employees or representatives to make any such representations either orally or in writing. If you are purchasing an existing Anago Subfranchise Rights Business, however, we may provide you with the actual records of that Anago Subfranchise Rights Business. If you receive any other financial performance information or projections of your future income, you should report it to our management by contacting Terry Mollica, at Anago Franchising, Inc, 1100 Park Central Blvd., Suite 1200, Pompano Beach, FL 33064, phone number 800-213-5857, as well as the Federal Trade Commission and the appropriate state regulatory agencies.

ANYTIME FITNESS

12181 Margo Ave. S. # 100
Hastings, MN 55033
Tel: (800) 704-5004, (651) 438-5000
Fax: (651) 438-5099
Email: cathyw@anytimefitness.com
Website: www.anytimefitness.com
Cathy Wandmacher, Franchise Sales

Anytime Fitness is the #1 co-ed fitness club chain in the world. We've boiled our business model down to the core essentials which members expect. Our loyal family of preferred vendors supply our franchisees with quality products at the best available prices. Financial and real estate support available. More than half of our franchisees own multiple clubs. Enjoy the freedom of spending time with your friends and family - and the knowledge that you're making your community a better place to live.

BACKGROUND

IFA Member:	Yes
Established & First Franchised:	2002; 2002
Franchised Units:	2,015
Company-Owned Units:	25
Total Units:	2,040
Distribution:	US – 1,682; CAN – 59; O'seas – 274
North America:	49 States, 4 Provinces
Density:	156 in TX, 119 in MN, 112 in LA

Projected New Units (12 Months):	400
Qualifications:	3, 2, 2, 2, 3, 4

FINANCIAL/TERMS

Cash Investment:	$80K
Total Investment:	$78.6 – 345.5K
Minimum Net Worth:	$250K
Fees (Franchise):	$29.9K
Fees (Royalty):	$499/month
Fees (Advertising):	$300/month
Term of Contract (Years):	5/5
Average Number of Employees:	1 FT, 2 PT
Passive Ownership:	Discouraged
Encourage Conversions:	Yes
Area Development Agreements:	Yes
Sub-Franchising Contracts:	Yes
Expand in Territory:	Yes
Space Needs:	4,000 SF

SUPPORT & TRAINING

Financial Assistance Provided:	Yes (D)
Site Selection Assistance:	Yes
Lease Negotiation Assistance:	Yes
Co-operative Advertising:	Yes
Franchisee Association/Member:	Yes/Member
Size of Corporate Staff:	162
On-going Support:	A, B, C, D, E, F, G, H, I
Training:	1 week Hastings, MN

SPECIFIC EXPANSION PLANS

US:	All States
Canada:	All Provinces
Overseas:	Mexico, Aus., NZ, Eng., Scotland, Grand Cayman, The Netherlands, Poland, Spain, Qatar, Japan, India

AVERAGE MEMBER NUMBERS

We had 1,647 Anytime Fitness clubs open for at least 12 months as of February 28, 2014. The average number of members at these clubs as of that date was 811. 696 of the 1,647 clubs that were open for at least 12 months as of February 29, 2014 (42%) had 811 or more members, and 951 (58%) had less than 811 members. This is an increase from an average of 737 members as of February 28, 2011, 769 members as of February 29, 2012, and 806 members as of February 28, 2013.

We also had 43 Anytime Fitness Express clubs open for at least 12 months as of February 28, 2014. The average number of members at these clubs was 523. 14 of the 43 clubs that were open for at least 12 months as of February 28, 2014 (33%) had 523 or more members, and 29 (67%) had less than 523 members.

STATEMENT OF ANNUAL PROJECTED REVENUES AND EARNINGS FOR AN ANYTIME FITNESS CENTER

The following are statements of projected annual revenues and earnings for a franchised Anytime Fitness center. These projections are for a second year of operation. They assume that at the end of the first year you have a fixed number of memberships, and, even though most of our clubs continue to increase their memberships after the first year, that you remain at that level for the entire year, adding as many new members as the number of members that leave. (During the first year, it will take you time to build your member base.) We have listed below 3 projections, one based on a center having 500 members, one based on 811 members, and one based on 1,000 members. They are based on revenue information provided to us by our designated billing processor for our franchisees in the United States in 2013, and on the 28 Anytime Fitness centers that we or our affiliates operated in the United States during all or part of 2013.

The first example, for a 500-member club, is intended to give you an idea of the revenues, expenses and projected income of a club that performs well below our average, but is still profitable. Of the 1,647 Anytime Fitness clubs open for at least 12 months as of February 28, 2014, 1,383 (84%) had over 500 members as of February 28, 2014. The 811-member example will give you an idea of the revenues, expenses and income of

a club that is able to maintain throughout the year the same number of members as the average number of members we had in our clubs that were open for at least 12 months as of February 28, 2014 (a relatively strong time of year for club memberships). Of the 1,647 Anytime Fitness clubs open for at least 12 months as of February 28, 2014, 696 (42%) had over 811 members as of February 28, 2014. The 1,000-member example gives you an idea of the revenues, expenses and profitability of a high achieving club. Of the 1,647 Anytime Fitness clubs open for at least 12 months as of February 28, 2014, 381 (23%) had over 1,000 members as of February 28,2014.

The assumptions we made in compiling these projections are detailed following the projections. Any change in these assumptions would require material alterations to the projections.

Revenues[1]	500 Members	811 Members	1,000 Members
Enrollment Fee[2]	$11,000	$17,900	$22,100
Membership Fees[3,4]	202,000	327,600	403,900
Vending Revenues[5]	1,500	2,400	3,000
Personal Training[6]	45,000	73,900	91,000
Total Revenues[7]	$260,000	$421,800	$520,100
Operating Expenses[1]			
Rent[8]	83,300	83,300	83,300
Equipment Lease[9]	45,800	45,800	45,800
Personal Training Commissions	22,750	36,950	45,550
Royalties	6,600	6,600	6,600
Processing/Credit Card Fees[10]	10,900	17,800	21,900
Bad Debt[11]	7,300	11,800	14,500
Utilities[12]	19,100	19,100	19,100
Insurance	2,650	2,650	2,650
Proximity Cards[2,3]	1,300	2,100	2,600
Advertising Funds[13]	3,600	3,600	3,600
Local Advertising[14]	6,000	8,200	9,200
Anytime Health Fees[15]	2,700	2,700	2,700
Vending Products[5]	500	700	900
Maintenance	6,200	10,000	12,300
Software/Web Hosting[16]	2,400	2,400	2,400
Bodyworkz Fees[17]	1,900	1,900	1,900
Annual Conference Fee	399	399	399

Miscellaneous[18]	12,000	15,000	17,500
Total Operating Expenses	$236,599	$272,199	$294,099
	500 Members	811 Members	1,000 Members
Income Before Salaries, Depreciation, Interest, Taxes and Debt Expense[19]	$23,401	$149,601	$226,001
Manager Salary and Payroll Costs[19]		$35,000	$45,000
Income Before Depreciation, Interest, Taxes and Debt Expense[19]	$12,401	$114,611	$181,011

These figures are only estimates of what we think you can earn based on the assumptions described below. Your results will differ. There is no assurance that you will sell as many memberships or earn as much.

These figures were perpared without an audit. Prospective franchsiees or sellers of franchises should be advised that no certified public accountant has audited these figures or expressed his/her opinion with regard to the content or form.

NOTES AND ASSUMPTIONS

1. We rounded most revenues and expenses to the nearest $100.

2. In projecting enrollment fee revenues and the cost of proximity cards, we assumed that 45% of your members would be replaced through attrition, and that the average enrollment fee you charge is $49. The 45% attrition rate is an average in the industry.

3. In projecting membership revenues, we had to make certain assumptions regarding the types of memberships you will sell in your center and the prices you will charge for each type of membership. Based on reports we received from our designated billing processor, the average Anytime Fitness franchisee for whom they processed memberships fees in 2013 had 75% as many membership agreements in effect as members. In other words, if you have 500 members, on average, you could expect to have 375 memberships, with approximately 75% of those memberships being individual memberships, and 25% of those memberships being couples (or family or multiple) memberships. Some of these memberships will be for fitness only, while others will include tanning memberships. It is up to you to set your own prices for each type of membership you sell (subject to minimum and maximum amounts we may specify). Based on the report from our designated processor, the average monthly membership fees paid under each membership agreement to our Anytime Fitness franchisees for

whom they processed billings in 2013 was $33.66 per member. (Individual memberships would typically pay lower fees, couples memberships would pay fees higher than the average, and those with tanning would pay higher fees than those without tanning.) We used this average in compiling the membership fee projection. However, membership rates will vary significantly between clubs, depending upon what you elect to charge, how your rates are affected by competition, the number of members you have who add tanning memberships, the number of couples memberships you sell, the number of memberships you sell that receive corporate discounts, and we do not represent that any franchisee can expect to attain any particular level of sales.

4. Under the 2010 Affordable (Health) Care Act, you are required to collect sales taxes on tanning services, and remit those taxes to the Internal Revenue Service. We assumed that you will collect the tax and pay it to the taxing authorities, which has no effect on your bottom line, and that tanning sales will not be impacted by this new tax.)

5. It is up to you to determine whether you offer vending machines in your center, the products you place in those machines and the vending prices. The amounts we have projected for vending revenue reflect the per membership revenues we receive from vending. We also do not tell you the sources from which you can purchase vending products. We assumed you would purchase your vending products from a warehouse seller such as Sam's Club, and that you pick up these items. If you go to other sources, or have these products delivered, your expenses will likely be higher.

6. Most of our clubs hire personal trainers to provide personal training services to their members. Members pay the trainers, and our franchisees typically collect a percentage of what the trainers receive. (In some cases, franchisees charge trainers a monthly rental, and allow them to keep all or a greater share of the training revenues they receive.) We have projected training revenues equal to $91.08 per member per year. The training fees will vary by trainer, but the average training fee is $40

an hour. Thus, the training revenues assume you have between 3 and 4 members per day, 5 days per week, taking training. We believe that this is consistent with the average for all our franchisees, but many franchisees do not report their training revenues to us. We also projected that you pay one-half of these revenues to your trainer. If you perform all or a portion of the training services yourself, this would increase your income from operating your center.

7. There are other revenue sources we have not included. For example, we have recommended that our clubs charge members $1 a month for membership in Anytime Health ($2 for a couples or family membership). While we included in expenses the fees you pay us for each member (which we cap at $225 a month), since the majority of our clubs have elected not to separately charge their members for these memberships, we did not include them in revenues. Likewise, we recommend that our franchisees charge members a club enhancement fee of $20-$25 per year that can be used to purchase new equipment and upgrade their club. While more than a third of our clubs are charging these fees, and most of our newer clubs are charging them, we have not included these fees in revenues because we also did not include in your expenses the cost of purchasing new equipment or upgrading your facilities. Thus, if you are charging these fees, your cash flow would increase.

8. Your rent can vary significantly depending on the size and location of your center. However, in our experience, the number of members you have does not necessarily correlate to the size of your center. Our projections therefore assumed that the center had 4,600 square feet, and that the gross rent paid was $18.11 per square foot per year. If you have a larger center, or you pay more for rent, your rent expense could increase significantly.

9. This amount assumes you enter into a 3 year lease purchase agreement for your equipment, paying approximately 15% down, and financing the balance. It assumes that you utilize a router with 1 connection. For a center with 4,600 square feet, we estimated that the balance was $110,500. (Larger centers will typically have more equipment. See Item 7 for additional information about the range of initial investment for equipment and improvements.) Our projection assumes an interest rate of 10% per annum. We also assumed you are required to pay sales tax of 6 5/8% on these lease payments. These numbers will likely be different for each franchisee, as you may decide to make more of a down payment (which would lower your payments), you may decide to finance your equipment over a longer period of time (which will also lower your payments), you may have to pay a higher interest rate (which would increase your payments), and your sales tax may be higher or lower than 6 5/8%. In our company-owned centers, we typically purchase these assets without leasing.

10. Processing and credit card fees will vary depending on how many members prepay their membership fees, how many pay by credit card, and the credit card they use. In our experience, costs for these services generally average about 5% of your membership fees and 1.5% on enrollment fees and personal training fees.

11. We assumed you would have 3.6% bad debt on your membership fees. This is consistent with the bad debt experience for our franchisees in 2013 as reported to us by our designated billing processor.

12. This amount includes gas, electric, water, cable, Internet and telephone. It assumes utilities average $4.15 per square foot.

13. This amount is based on our current requirement that you contribute $300 per month to our General Advertising Fund.

14. We expect you to spend at least $6,000 per year for advertising. Our projection assumes your spending on local advertising increases more as you have more members.

15. As noted in footnote 7, you will be selling Anytime Health memberships for us, and you keep everything you charge for those memberships above $0.50 for individual members, and $1.00 for couples or family memberships. However, the maximum amount you must pay us each month for these memberships is $225 (and $675 if you own 3 or more centers).

16. In some states, you will also be required to pay sales tax on these fees. We have not included those sales taxes because they are payable in only a handful of states.

17. You are not required to use the Bodyworkz Training Program, but our revenue projection assumes that you do so. Thus, we have also assumed expenses of $160 per month for using this program. (If you have more than 2 centers, the fee is actually reduced to $135 per month for the second and any subsequent center.)

18. Miscellaneous includes janitorial services, legal and accounting fees, cell phone, supplies, licenses, and other similar items. Many of these costs can vary significantly depending on the location of your center and the time you spend looking for the best possible cost on these items. The projections are consistent with the experience of our company owned centers.

19. The low projection assumes you act as manager of your center and do not receive a separate salary. As your business grows, you may wish to hire a manager to oversee the club operations. We are assuming you would pay that manager $2,000 per month, plus commissions and limited benefits, so that with payroll costs, the total cost for a manager will be

$35,000 a year. This is consistent with what we understand to be the average compensation our franchisees pay their managers. In the 1,000 member projection, we assumed the manager would receive a salary closer to $2,500 per month, plus commissions and benefits. Except as noted in footnote 6, the projections assume you do not hire any other employees to help you. (Because our centers are designed to operate 24 hours a day, without the necessity of having staff on premises, you should not need any other employees. However, some states or municipalities may require you have an employee on premises whenever your center is open. If you are an absentee-owner, or you operate in a location that requires the center to be staffed at all times, your expenses will increase significantly because you will have to pay salaries and benefits to employees. In our company-owned centers, we do pay a manager, or a management fee, to somebody to oversee the centers for us. Thus, we had additional expenses for wages or management fees.)

20. Because each location is different, actual revenues, expenses and income will vary at each location. We do not represent that any franchisee can expect to attain the revenues or income shown in these statements. Also, because these statements are for a second year of operation, results for a new franchisee are likely to differ from the results shown in the projections.

21. We also recommend that you set aside at least $500 per month to defray the cost of remodeling and acquiring new equipment for your Anytime Fitness center as a condition to renewing your franchise. We have not deducted these amounts from the projected income because (i) these are still your monies and therefore it would not affect your profitability to set the amounts aside, and (ii) we recommend that you charge your members a club enhancement that will generate these amounts and we did not include the club enhancement fees in the projected revenues.

We gave you information above about the number of all our centers that were open for at least 12 months as of February 28, 2014. We or our affiliates operated 17 of those centers for the entire 12 months months ended February 28, 2014. 16 of those 17 centers (94%) exceeded the membership numbers, revenue and income projections in the first (500 members) column, and 9 (53%) exceeded the membership numbers, revenues and income projections in the second (811 members) column, and 6 (35%) exceeded the membership numbers, revenues and income projections in the third (1,000 members) column. Because our franchisees are not required to give us this level of detail as to their revenues and expenses, we cannot tell you how many of our franchisees exceeded the projected revenues or projected profits.

STATEMENT OF ANNUAL PROJECTED REVENUES AND EARNINGS FOR AN ANYTIME FITNESS EXPRESS® CENTER

The following are statements of projected annual revenues and earnings for a franchised Anytime Fitness Express® center. These projections are for a second year of operation. They assume that at the end of the first year you have a fixed number of memberships, and, even though most of our clubs continue to increase their memberships after the first year, that you remain at that level for the entire year, adding as many new members as the number of members that leave. (During the first year, it will take you time to build your member base.) We have listed below 3 projections, one based on a center having 350 members, one based on 523 members, and one based on 700 members. They are based on revenue information provided to us by our designated billing processor for our 43 Anytime Fitness Express franchisees that operated during all of the 12 months ended February 28, 2014, and our expense experience operating Anytime Fitness centers.

The first example, for a 350-member club, is intended to give you an idea of the revenues, expenses and projected income of a club that performs well below our average, but is still profitable. Of the 43 Anytime Fitness Express clubs open for at least 12 months as of ended February 28, 2014, 32 (74%) had over 350 members as of February 28, 2014. The 523-member example will give you an idea of the revenues, expenses and income of a club that is an above average club, and is able to maintain throughout the year the same number of members as the average number of members at those of our clubs that were open for at least 12 months as of February 28 2014. Of the 43 Anytime Fitness Express clubs that were open for at least 12 months of February 28, 2014, 14 (33%) had 523 or more members as of February 28, 2014. The third example gives you an idea of the revenues, expenses and profitability of a high-achieving club with 650 members. Of the 43 Anytime Fitness Express clubs that were open for at least 12 months as of February 28, 2014, 14 (33%) had 650 or more members as of February 28, 2014.

Revenues[1]	350 Members	523 Members	650 Members
Enrollment Fee[2]	$7,700	$11,500	$14,300
Membership Fees [3,4]	138,900	207,600	258,000
Vending Revenues[5]	1,100	1,600	2,000
Total Revenues[6]	$147,700	$220,700	$274,300

Operating Expenses[1]			
Rent[7]	34,400	34,400	34,400
Equipment Lease[8]	35,100	35,100	35,100
Royalties	5,400	5,400	5,400
Processing/Credit Card Fees[9]	7,300	11,000	13,600
Bad Debt[10]	5,000	7,500	9,300
Utilities[11]	10,400	10,400	10,400
Insurance	2,000	2,000	2,000
Proxomity Cards [2,3]	900	1,300	1,700
Advertising Fund[12]	3,600	3,600	3,600
Local Advertising[13]	4,000	5,300	6,000
Anytime Health Fees[14]	2,700	2,700	2,700
Vending Products[5]	500	700	900
Maintenance	4,300	6,400	8,000
Software/Web Hosting[15]	2,400	2,400	2,400
Annual Conference Fee	399	399	399
Miscellaneous[16]	10,000	12,000	14,000
Total Operating Expenses	$128,409	$140,609	$151,839
Income Before Salaries, Depreciation, Interest, Taxes, and Debt Expenses[17]	$19,291	$80,291	$124,391

These figures are only estimates of what we think you can earn based on the assumptions described below. Your results may differ. There is no assurance that you will sell as many memberships or earn as much.

These figures were prepared without an Audit. Prospective franchisees or sellers of franchises should be advised that no certified public accountant has audited these figures or expressed his/her opinion with regard to the content or form.

NOTES AND ASSUMPTIONS

1. We rounded most revenues and expenses to the nearest $100.

2. In projecting enrollment fee revenues and the cost of proximity cards, we assumed that 45% of your members would be replaced through attrition, and that the average enrollment fee you charge is $49. The 45% attrition rate is an average in the industry.

3. In projecting membership revenues, we had to make certain assumptions regarding the types of memberships you will sell in your center and the prices you will charge for each type of membership. Based on reports we received from our designat-ed billing processor, the average Anytime Fitness franchisee for whom they processed memberships fees in 2013 had 75% as many membership agreements in effect as members. In other words, if you have 350 members, on average, you could expect to have 262 memberships, with approximately 75% of those memberships being individual memberships, and 25% of those memberships being couples (or family or multiple) memberships. Some of these memberships will be for fitness only, while others will include tanning memberships. It is up to you to set your own prices for each type of membership you sell (subject to minimum and maximum amounts we may specify). Based on the report from our designated processor, the average monthly membership fees paid under each membership agreement to our Anytime Fitness Express franchisees for whom they processed billings in 2013 was $33.08 per member. (Individual memberships would typically pay lower fees, couples memberships would pay fees higher than the average, and those with tanning would pay higher fees than those without tanning.) We used this average in compiling the membership fee projection. However, membership rates will vary significantly between clubs, depending upon what you elect to charge, how your rates are affected by competition, the number of members you have who add tanning memberships, the number of couples memberships you sell, and the number of memberships you sell that receive corporate discounts, and

we do not represent that any franchisee can expect to attain any particular level of sales.

4. Under the 2010 Affordable (Health) Care Act, you are required to collect sales taxes on tanning services, and remit those taxes to the Internal Revenue Service. We assumed that you will collect the tax and pay it to the taxing authorities, which has no effect on your bottom line, and that tanning sales will not be impacted by this new tax.)

5. It is up to you to determine whether you offer vending machines in your center, the products you place in those machines and the vending prices. The amounts we have projected for vending revenue reflect the per membership revenues we receive from vending. We also do not tell you the sources from which you can purchase vending products. We assumed you would purchase your vending products from a warehouse seller such as Sam's Club, and that you pick up these items. If you go to other sources, or have these products delivered, your expenses will likely be higher.

6. There are other revenue sources we have not included. For example, we have recommended that our clubs charge members $1 a month for membership in Anytime Health ($2 for a couples or family membership). While we included in expenses the fees you pay us for each member (which we cap at $225 a month), since the majority of our clubs have elected not to separately charge their members for these memberships, we did not include them in revenues. Likewise, we recommend that our franchisees charge members a club enhancement fee of $20-25 per year that can be used to purchase new equipment and upgrade their club. While more than a third of our clubs are charging these fees, and most of our newer clubs are charging them, we have not included these fees in revenues because we also did not include in your expenses the cost of purchasing new equipment or upgrading your facilities. Thus, if you are charging these fees, your cash flow would increase.

7. Your rent can vary significantly depending on the size and location of your center. However, in our experience, the number of members you have does not necessarily correlate to the size of your center. Our projections therefore assumed that the center had 2,500 square feet, and that the gross rent paid was $13.76 per square foot per year. If you have a larger center, or you pay more for rent, your rent expense could increase significantly.

8. This amount assumes you enter into a 3 year lease purchase agreement for your equipment, paying approximately 15% down, and financing the balance. It assumes that you do not lease a router. For a center with 2,500 square feet, we estimated that the balance was $85,000. (Larger centers will typically have more equipment. See Item 7 for additional information about the range of initial investment for equipment and im-

provements.) Our projection assumes an interest rate of 10% per annum. We also assumed you are required to pay sales tax of 6 5/8% on these lease payments. These numbers will likely be different for each franchisee, as you may decide to make more of a down payment (which would lower your payments), you may decide to finance your equipment over a longer period of time (which will also lower your payments), you may have to pay a higher interest rate (which would increase your payments), and your sales tax may be higher or lower than 6 5/8%. In our company-owned centers, we typically purchase these assets without leasing.

9. Processing and credit card fees will vary depending on how many members prepay their membership fees, how many pay by credit card, and the credit card they use. In our experience, costs for these services generally average about 5% of your membership fees and 1.5% on enrollment fees and personal training fees.

10. We assumed you would have 3.6% bad debt on your membership fees. This is consistent with the bad debt experience for our franchisees in 2013 as reported to us by our designated billing processor.

11. This amount includes gas, electric, water, cable, Internet and telephone. It assumes utilities average $4.17 per square foot.

12. This amount is based on our current requirement that you contribute $300 per month to our General Advertising Fund.

13. We expect you to spend at least $4,000 per year for advertising. Our projection assumes your spending on local advertising increases as you have more members.

14. As noted in footnote 7, you will be selling Anytime Health memberships for us, and you keep everything you charge for those memberships above $0.50 for individual members, and $1.00 for couples or family memberships. However, the maximum amount you must pay us each month for these memberships is $225 (or $675 if you own 3 or more centers).

15. In some states, you will also be required to pay sales tax on these fees. We have not included those sales taxes because they are payable in only a handful of states.

16. Miscellaneous includes janitorial services, legal and accounting fees, cell phone, supplies, licenses, and other similar items. Many of these costs can vary significantly depending on the location of your center and the time you spend looking for the best possible cost on these items. The projections are consistent with the experience of our company owned centers.

17. The projection assumes you act as manager of your center

and do not receive a separate salary. We therefore have not included any additional expense for salary. The projections assume you do not hire any other employees to help you. Because our centers are designed to operate 24 hours a day, without the necessity of having staff on premises, you should not need any other employees. However, some states or municipalities may require you have an employee on premises whenever your center is open. If you are an absentee-owner, or you operate in a location that requires the center to be staffed at all times, your expenses will increase significantly because you will have to pay salaries and benefits to employees. In our company-owned centers, we do pay a manager, or a management fee, to somebody to oversee the centers for us. Thus, we had additional expenses for wages or management fees.

18. Because each location is different, actual revenues, expenses and income will vary at each location. We do not represent that any franchisee can expect to attain the revenues or income shown in these statements. Also, because these statements are for a second year of operation, results for a new franchisee are likely to differ from the results shown in the projections.

ADDITIONAL ASSUMPTIONS APPLICABLE TO BOTH ANYTIME FITNESS CENTERS AND ANYTIME FITNESS EXPRESS CENTERS:

A. We did not provide any allowance for corporate or personal income taxes.

B. While we did include expenses for a lease/purchase of your equipment, we did not include any other expenses for depreciation, amortization, interest, or the repayment of debt. We anticipate every franchisee will fund its initial investment differently, and we therefore cannot project how you would account for these items.

C. The projections are based on economic conditions that existed in March 2014, with no consideration in any category for inflation related adjustments or further weaknesses in general economic conditions.

D. The projections assume you follow our guidelines in terms of the products and services you offer and the way you operate your business. If you do not, your results will likely vary

dramatically from the results we have projected.

Written substantiation for the financial performance representations made in this Item 19 will be made available to you upon reasonable request.

We recommend you use QuickBooks Pro, the desktop version, as your accounting system. Most of the centers we used in compiling these projections used the accounting system we and our affiliates use in centers we operate. That system is consistent with generally accepted accounting principles.

We provided substantially the same services to those centers as we will offer to you. All of these centers offered substantially the same products and services as you are expected to offer.

RESULTS OF REINVENTIONS AND RELOCATIONS

This Disclosure Document is being given both to existing Anytime Fitness franchisees who will be signing a new franchsie agreement as a condition to renewing their existing franchise, and to prospective new franchisees. If you are an existing franchisee who is nearing the expiration of your Franchise Agreement, you must upgrade, or "reinvent" your anytime Fitness Center.

Between July 17, 2011, and August 2013, we had 184 Anytime Fitness centers that completed their reinventions, and 74 that relocated their business, all as part of the renewal of their franchise. We compared their average results for the months after their reinvention or relocation, through February 2014, to their average results for the 6-12 months before their reinvention or relocation. While individual clubs varied significantly from the averages, some having very high improvements, and some showing negative results, on average, these centers showed increases in average monthly revenues and new memberships, and decreases in average monthly attrition, following their reinvention or relocation.

If you renew your franchise, and complete your reinvention or relocation, your results will likely differ from the averages. In fact, there is no assurance that you will increase your Gross Revenues or memberships, or decrease attrition following your reinvention or relocation. However, the results for these centers were as follows:

REINVENTIONS (184 IN TOTAL)

	Average Percentage	Number and Percentage Achieving Better Than Average Results	Number and Percentage Showing Less Than Average Results
Increase in average monthly gross revenues	17.8%	30 (40.5%)	44 (59.5%)

Increase in average monthly memberships	17.1%	31 (41.9%)	43 (58.1%)
Decrease in average monthly attrition	5.7%	46 (62.1%)	28 (37.8%)

RELOCATIONS (74 IN TOTAL)

	Average Percentage	Number and Percentage Achieving Better Than Average Results	Number and Percentage Showing Less Than Average Results
Increase in average monthly revenues	17.8%	30 (40.5%)	44 (59.5%)
Increase in average monthly memberships	17.1%	31 (41.9%)	43 (58.1%)
Decrease in average monthly attrition	5.7%	46 (62.2%)	28 (37.8%)

The figures above are based upon reports from our franchisees, and from their billing processor, and have not been audited.

We do not furnish or authorize our salespersons to furnish any other oral or written information concerning the actual, average or potential sales, costs, income or profits of an Anytime Fitness or Anytime Fitness Express business. If you receive any other oral or written information concerning the actual, average or potential sales, income or profits of an Anytime Fitness or Anytime Fitness Express center from any of our representatives, or from a person claiming to act on our behalf, you should immediately report that incident to us, as we have not authorized that information. You should not rely on any oral or written estimate or projection of sales, income or profits, or statement of actual, average, estimated or potential sales, income or profits of an existing or future Anytime Fitness or Anytime Fitness Express center, because reliance on that in-

formation would not be reasonable in light of the fact that we have not authorized that information to be provided to you or to any other prospective franchisee.

Other than the preceding financial performance representations, Anytime Fitness does not make any financial performance representations. We also do not authorize our employees or representatives to make any such representations either orally or in writing. If you are purchasing an existing outlet, however, we may provide you with the actual records of that outlet. If you receive any other financial performance information or projections of your future income, you should report it to the franchisor's management by contacting Meredith Mergens at 12181 Margo Avenue South, Suite 100, Hastings, Minnesota 55033, telephone: (651) 438-5000, the Federal Trade Commission, and the appropriate state regulatory agencies.

archadeck®
outdoor living

ARCHADECK

2924 Emerywood Pkwy., # 101
Richmond, VA 23794
Tel: (800) 722-4668, (804) 353-6999 x102

Fax: (804) 358-1878
Email: spucel@outdoorlivingbrands.com
Website: www.archadeck.com
Shemar Pucel, President and Chief Executive Officer

ARCHADECK, founded in 1980, started the nation's first network specializing in custom-designed and built decks, porches, and other outdoor products. Because construction experience is not required, our franchisees come from a variety of professional backgrounds.

BACKGROUND

IFA Member:	No
Established & First Franchised:	1980; 1984
Franchised Units:	56
Company-Owned Units:	0
Total Units:	56
Distribution:	US – 55; CAN – 1; O'seas – 0
North America:	20 States, 1 Province
Density:	6 in NC, 5 in TX
Projected New Units (12 Months):	25
Qualifications:	5, 5, 1, 3, 4, 5

FINANCIAL/TERMS

Cash Investment:	$80 – 100K
Total Investment:	$80 – 100K
Minimum Net Worth:	$250K
Fees (Franchise):	$49.5K
Fees (Royalty):	2.5 – 5.5%
Fees (Advertising):	1%
Term of Contract (Years):	8/8
Average Number of Employees:	1 FT, 1 PT
Passive Ownership:	Not Allowed

Encourage Conversions:	Yes
Area Development Agreements:	Yes
Sub-Franchising Contracts:	No
Expand in Territory:	Yes
Space Needs:	N/A

SUPPORT & TRAINING

Financial Assistance Provided:	Yes (D)
Site Selection Assistance:	N/A
Lease Negotiation Assistance:	N/A
Co-operative Advertising:	No
Franchisee Association/Member:	Yes/Member
Size of Corporate Staff:	35
On-going Support:	C, D, G, H, I
Training:	20 Business Days Richmond, VA; 9 Days On-Site

SPECIFIC EXPANSION PLANS

US:	All United States
Canada:	All Canada
Overseas:	Europe

Actual results will vary from franchise to franchise, territory to territory and market to market, and we cannot estimate the results for any particular franchise. Except as provided by applicable law, we will not be bound by allegations of any unauthorized representation as to sales, income, profits, or prospects or chances for success, and you will be required to acknowledge that you have not relied on any such representation in purchasing your franchise.

Written substantiation of the data used in preparing the financial performance representations included in this Item 19 will be made available to you upon reasonable request.

A. Average Gross Sales for ARCHADECK Franchisees for the 12 Months Ending December 31, 2013

The following table presents the average annual gross sales realized by certain ARCHADECK franchisees in 2013. We have provided this information to help you to make a more informed decision regarding the ARCHADECK franchise system. You should not use this information as an indication of how your specific franchise business may perform. The success of your franchise will depend largely on your individual abilities and your market. The actual numbers you experience will be influenced by a wide variety of factors including your management, market size and demographics and competition. You should conduct your own independent research and due diligence to assist you in preparing your own projections.

The information provided in the table below was compiled from 51 ARCHADECK franchisees that were operational for the entire 12 month period ending December 31, 2013. The data excludes franchisees that either began operations, ceased active operations, or temporality ceased operations during this period.

Sales Volume	# of Franchisees	Sales in Dollars			% of Franchisees Above Avg. (and %)	Years in Business			% of Franchisees
		Minimum	Average	Maximum		Minimum	Average	Maximum	
Greater than $600K	16	685,475	1,476,345	7,517,680	1 (6.25%)	4.2	13.5	25.9	31.4%
Between $300K-$600K	19	306,336	409,098	547,949	7 (36.8%)	1.0	7.4	13.2	37.3%
Less than $300K	16	36,300	167,727	272,559	7 (43.7%)	1.0	9.7	25.6	31.4%
Franchisees	51		668,196				10.0		100%

The Gross Sales figures presented above represent the total dollar value of customer contracts sold by the 51 franchises listed above in the reported period. ARCHADECK contracts are for design and construction services and can be long term in nature. Gross Sales should not be construed as a measure of revenue or cash collections, which can vary substantially from Gross Sales dependent on several factors, including franchisees' backlog of projects, size of projects or contract terms. The financial performance representations above do not reflect the costs of sales, royalties or operating expenses that must be deducted from the gross sales figures to obtain a net income or owner's profit number. The best source of cost and expense data may be from current or former franchisees as listed in this disclosure document.

B. Average 2013 Contract Price and Residential Contract Price by Project Type for ARCHADECK Franchisees

The following table presents data regarding the average project size for the entire ARCHADECK franchise system for the 12 months ending December 31, 2013. The information provided was compiled from every ARCHADECK franchisee that sold at least one project during that period. We have provided this information to help you to make a more informed decision regarding our franchise system. You should not use this information as an indication of how your specific franchise business may perform. The success of your franchise will depend largely on your individual abilities and your market. The actual numbers you experience will be influenced by a wide variety of factors including your management, market size and demographics and competition. You should conduct your own independent research and due diligence to assist you in preparing your own projections.

Residential Project Types	Contract Sales Price	# of Projects	# of Projects at or Above Average (and %)
Average Residential Project	22,184	1,496	523 (35.0%)
Average Builder Projects	3,502	397	114 (28.7%)
Average Overall Project	18,266	1,893	676 (35.7%)

Some ARCHADECK franchisees have achieved the averages shown in the table above. Your individual results may differ. There is no assurance that you will achieve the averages shown in the table above.

The following data presents additional breakdown of the average contract value of the 1,496 Residential Projects by project type completed by the entire ARCHADECK franchise system for the 12 months ending December 31, 2013. The information provided was compiled from every ARCHADECK franchisee that sold one of these project types during that period. The nine Residential Project Types presented below represent the most commonly sold project types sold by ARCHADECK franchisees.

Residential Project Types	Average Sales Price	# of Projects	# of Projects at or Above Average	% of Projects at or Above Average
Decks	17,770	736	276	37.5%
Screened Porches	29,267	175	65	37.1%
Open Porches	11,053	106	58	54.7%
Deck/Porch Combination	36,502	156	65	41.7%
Sunroom	24,540	68	26	38.2%
Deck/Sunroom Combination	36,017	30	11	36.7%
Pergola	10,335	78	28	35.9%
Hardscape Patio	11,839	96	32	33.3%
Hardscape Patio with Other Design Elements	15,416	51	20	39.2%

The Residential Project types listed above are defined as follows:

1. "Deck" Residential Projects include structures built on or above the ground and covered by wood or composite decking material.
2. "Screen Porches" Residential Projects include structures built on or above the ground with roof coverings and enclosed with screens.
3. "Open Porches" Residential Projects include structures built on or above the ground with roof covering and no material, neither windows nor screen, enclosing the structure.
4. "Deck/Porch Combination" Residential Projects include projects involving both a deck and a porch structure.
5. "Pergola" Residential Projects include structures built on or above the ground covered with open roof that provides partial shade.
6. "Hardscape Patio" Residential Projects include concrete, natural stone or paver patio coverings built at ground elevation.
7. "Hardscape Patios with Other Design Elements" Residential Projects include projects with hardscape patios built at ground elevation that include and additional hardscape feature built above the ground such as sitting walls, retaining walls, fireplaces, fire pits, outdoor kitchens or other hardscape decorative design features.

The financial performance representations above do not reflect the costs of sales, royalties or operating expenses that must be deducted from revenues to obtain a net income or owner's profit. The best source of cost and expense data may be from current or former franchisees as listed in this disclosure document.

C. Gross Margin Benchmarking Study for ARCHADECK Franchisees for the 12 Months Ending December 31, 2012

We do not provide prospective franchisees with projections of income, profits or earnings. There is no guarantee that you, as a new ARCHADECK franchisee, will attain the same level of sales or profits that have been attained by our existing franchisees. The success of your franchise will depend largely on your individual abilities and your market. However, we do provide prospective franchisees with information from a financial benchmarking study (the "Benchmarking Study") conducted for the ARCHADECK franchise system by Profit Planning Group ("PPG"), an independent third party financial benchmarking organization serving trade associations and franchise networks across the country.

In 2013, PPG conducted an independent financial Benchmarking Study for ARCHADECK franchisees. The Benchmarking Study was conducted solely on a voluntary basis. Interested franchisees were required to submit their income statements for the year ending December 31, 2012, to PPG. PPG then calculated certain financial metrics to allow participants to compare their financial performance against their peer group of ARCHADECK franchisees. 43 out of 54 (79.6%) ARCHADECK franchisees participated in the Benchmarking Study. We have reviewed the composition of franchise participants and believe it contains a random, representative sampling of ARCHADECK franchisees based on level of sales, years in the business and geography.

As defined in the Benchmarking Study, Gross Profit Margin measures profitability after material, construction labor and other direct construction costs are subtracted from gross revenue. It is calculated by dividing gross profit dollars by gross revenues. While Gross Profit Margin measures profitability after material, construction labor and other direct costs are subtracted from gross revenue, it excludes royalties, any commissions and other operating expenses.

The Gross Profit Margin figure provided by the Benchmarking Study is the median. The median for any variable is the middle number of all values reported arrayed from lowest to highest. Unlike the mean (or average), the median is not influenced by any extremely high or low variables reported. Therefore, the Benchmarking Study reports the median as the preferred statistic for its analysis.

As reported in the Benchmarking Study, the median Gross Profit Margin of the participating ARCHADECK franchisee is 32.1%. The table below provides a further breakdown of Gross Profit Margins among the ARCHADECK franchisees participating in the Benchmarking Study.

	Participating ARCHADECK Franchise	Sales Under $450,000	Sales Over $450,000	Less than 11 Years in Business	More than 11 Years in Business
Number and % of Participating Franchisees Reporting	43/100%	21/48.8%	22/51.2%	23/53.5%	20/46.5%
Gross Profit Margin (Median)	32.1%	31.4%	32.7%	29.1%	33.8%

The above results taken from the Benchmarking Study are provided to prospective franchisees in evaluating the experience of existing ARCHADECK franchisees who participated in the study and not as a projection or forecast of what a new ARCHADECK franchisee may experience. A new franchisee's financial results are likely to differ from the results provided above.

This financial information utilized in the benchmarking study was based entirely upon information voluntarily reported by the 43 ARCHADECK franchisees, none of which information was audited or otherwise reviewed or investigated by us or by any independent accountant or auditing firm, and no one has audited, reviewed or otherwise evaluated this information for accuracy or expressed his/her opinion with regard to its content or form.

In preparing any pro forma financial projections, you and other prospective franchisees must keep in mind that each individual franchisee's experience is unique and results may vary, depending on a number of factors. These factors include general economic conditions of the franchise territory, demographics, competition, effectiveness of the franchisee in the management of the franchise business and the use of the ARCHADECK operating systems, scope of investment and the overall efficiency of the franchise operation.

Notes That Apply To Subsections A, B and C Above:

A. You are likely to achieve results that are different, possibly significantly and adversely, from the results shown above. Many factors, including those described in the preceding paragraph, are unique to each ARCHADECK franchise and may significantly impact the financial performance of your ARCHADECK franchise.

B. The actual results included above relate to results for the reporting ARCHADECK franchises and should not be considered as the actual or probable performance results that you should expect through the operation of your ARCHADECK franchise. There is no assurance that you or any other ARCHADECK franchisee will do as well. If you rely on these figures in preparing your own pro forma financial statements or otherwise, you must accept the risk of not doing as well. We do not make any promises or representations of any kind that you will achieve any particular results or level of sales or profitability or even achieve break-even results in any particular year of operation.

C. As with other businesses, we anticipate that a new ARCHADECK franchise will not achieve sales volumes or maintain expenses similar to an ARCHADECK franchise that has been operating for a number of years.

D. You are responsible for developing your own business plan for your ARCHADECK franchise, including capital budgets, financial statements, projections, pro forma financial statements and other elements appropriate to your particular circumstances. In preparing your business plan, we encourage you to consult with your own accounting, business and legal advisors to assist you to identify the expenses you likely will incur in connection with your ARCHADECK franchise, to prepare your budgets, and to assess the likely or potential financial performance of your ARCHADECK franchise.

E. In developing the business plan for your ARCHADECK franchise, you are cautioned to make necessary allowance for changes in financial results to income, expenses or both that may result from operation of your ARCHADECK franchise during periods of, or in geographic areas suffering from, economic downturns, inflation, unemployment, or other negative economic influences.

F. Some ARCHADECK franchisees have achieved the results shown in the tables above. Your individual results may differ. There is no assurance that you will perform as well.

Other than the preceding financial performance representations, we do not make any financial performance representations. We also do not authorize our employees or representatives to make any such representations either orally or in writing. If you are purchasing an existing outlet, however, we may provide you with the actual records of that outlet. If you receive any other financial performance information or projections of your future income, you should report it to the franchisor's management by contacting Chris Grandpre, Archadeck Franchising Corporation, 2924 Emerywood Parkway, Suite 101, Richmond, Virginia 23294, (804) 353-6999, the Federal Trade Commission, and the appropriate state regulatory agencies.

BRIGHTSTAR CARE

1125 Tri-State Pkwy., # 700
Gurnee, IL 60031
Tel: (877) 689-6898, (847) 693-2029
Fax: (866) 360-0393
Email: franchise@brightstarcare.com
Website: www.brightstarfranchise.com
Son Kim, Franchise Director

Are you ready to build a business you can feel great about? At BrightStar, we are in the business of providing the full continuum of homecare, childcare, staffing and support services for individuals, families and healthcare facilities. We help keep parents and grandparents out of nursing facilities and in the comfort of their own homes, as well as assisting parents with their childcare needs. BrightStar also provides healthcare staffing solutions to businesses. We have received several awards recognizing our rapid growth, advanced systems technology and senior leadership.

BACKGROUND

IFA Member:	Yes
Established & First Franchised:	2002; 2005
Franchised Units:	282
Company-Owned Units:	2
Total Units:	284
Distribution:	US – 277; CAN – 0; O'seas – 0
North America:	38 States, 0 Provinces
Density:	31 in CA, 24 in TX, 26 in FL
Projected New Units (12 Months):	60
Qualifications:	4, 4, 2, 4, 4, 5

FINANCIAL/TERMS

Cash Investment:	$100K
Total Investment:	$93 – 172K
Minimum Net Worth:	$500K
Fees (Franchise):	$48K
Fees (Royalty):	5%
Fees (Advertising):	1%, capped at 3%
Term of Contract (Years):	10/10
Average Number of Employees:	3 FT, 2 PT
Passive Ownership:	Not Allowed
Encourage Conversions:	Yes
Area Development Agreements:	No
Sub-Franchising Contracts:	No
Expand in Territory:	No
Space Needs:	400 – 800 SF

SUPPORT & TRAINING

Financial Assistance Provided:	Yes (I)
Site Selection Assistance:	Yes
Lease Negotiation Assistance:	Yes
Co-operative Advertising:	Yes
Franchisee Association/Member:	Yes/Member
Size of Corporate Staff:	70
On-going Support:	a, C, D, E, G, h, I
Training:	5 Days Gurnee, IL; 5 Days Gurnee, IL

SPECIFIC EXPANSION PLANS

US:	All United States
Canada:	BC, AB, SK, MB
Overseas:	UK, Autralia

FACTUAL BACKGROUND:

The financial performance representation information in this Item 19 includes certain financial performance information relating to our franchisees' operation of their respective BrightStar agencies as of December 31, 2013. The Revenue dollars are calculated based upon the date the franchisee's minimum Revenue performance requirements begin (the "Start Date") which is the date a franchisee has the ability to perform 50% or more of the BrightStar business model, regardless of whether the franchisee has obtained personal care licensure.

In some instances, franchisees operate more than one Bright-Star agency. Except as stated below, the information contained in Item 19 includes information for all BrightStar agencies operated by our franchisees as of December 31, 2013. If a franchisee operates more than one BrightStar agency, the information in Sections A-C and Sections E-F include financial information for the franchisee's first agency only. Information for first locations only is presented in certain sections of this Item 19 because during the economic downturn of 2008 through 2012 many franchisees were unable to secure the capital needed to follow the full business model in their additional locations. Delays were allowed in securing office location and personnel to follow the business model in these additional locations (where appropriate as noted in Item 20 we worked with franchisees to downsize to one location if they lacked the access to capital required to develop their additional units).

Item 19 also includes financial information for our franchise agency resale transactions – i.e., transferred locations. The information disclosed for the resale transactions depends on the amount of the agency's weekly Revenue as of the date of transfer. Specifically, if the agency's weekly Revenue immediately prior to the transfer was less than $10,000 per week, any Revenue earned by the franchisee prior to the transfer was not included in the information contained in this Item 19. In such situations, the Revenue reflected in this Item 19 includes Revenue earned by the new franchisee since the date of transfer. If, however, at the time of transfer the agency's weekly Revenue exceeded $10,000, the Revenue included in this Item 19 reflects all Revenue earned by the agency since the agency's Start Date (as defined below).

This Item 19 does not contain any information for our terminated franchised agencies as of December 31, 2013 or agencies with a Start Date after December 31, 2012.

FRANCHISEE RESULTS:

We used our Athena Business System to gather the information for this Item 19 relating to our franchisee's Revenue, gross margin, mix of business, and National Account information. As described in more detail in Section E, we also received certified survey information from our franchisees to assist with the break-even information contained in Section E. Revenue in this section includes revenue derived from outside the defined franchisee territories.

Our franchisees' experience has shown that the success of a BrightStar franchised agency has a strong correlation to the amount of time and energy a franchisee spends on recruiting, advertising and marketing, inbound sales call conversion, making sales calls, customer satisfaction (measured by Net Promoter Score) and employee retention. As noted in Item 1, it is not necessary that you have experience in the healthcare industry prior to acquiring your Agency franchise. As an example, of the 138 franchisees that are included in Table A under the heading "2013 Revenue for Franchisees open 12 months or longer," 114 of these 138 franchisees (83%) had no prior healthcare experience prior to becoming a BrightStar franchisee and there is little, if any correlation between performance and healthcare experience.

A. Franchisee Revenue (First Location Only)

Table A illustrates the average Revenue, displayed by quartile, earned by our franchisees for their first location only during: (i) the 2013 calendar year for franchisees open 12 months or longer; (ii) the 2013 calendar year for franchisees open 24 months or longer; (iii) their first 12 months of operation commencing on their Start Date; (iv) their second year (months 13 through 24) of operation commencing on their Start Date; (v) their third year (months 25 through 36) of operation commencing on their Start Date; (vi) their fourth year (months 37 through 48) of operation commencing on their Start Date; (vii) their fifth year (months 49 through 60) of operation commencing on their Start Date; and (viii) their sixth year (months 61 through 72) of operation commencing on their Start Date.

For purposes of this financial performance representation, "Quartile" refers to the relative performance of the BrightStar Agencies. Specifically, "Quartile 1" refers to the top 25% of performing Agencies, "Quartile 2" refers to the next highest 25% of performing Agencies, "Quartile 3" refers to the next highest 25% of performing Agencies, and "Quartile 4" refers to the bottom 25% of performing Agencies.

Table A (First Locations Only)

Full-Time First Location Agencies	Average Revenue	Median Revenue	High Amount	Low Amount	Number of Agencies	Number & Percentage of Agencies that Attained or Exceeded the Average Revenue Amount	Number & Percentage of Agencies that Attained or Exceeded the Median Revenue Amount
2013 Revenue for Franchises open 12 months or longer[1]	1,350,329	1,113,920	6,005,081	46,415	138	56 (40.6%)	69 (50%)
Quartile 1	2,545,141	2,164,212	6,005,081	1,739,885	35	12 (30%)	17 (50%)
Quartile 2	1,416,920	1,452,546	1,704,861	1,117,980	34	19 (60%)	17 (50%)
Quartile 3	936,252	926,082	1,109,859	760,071	34	17 (50%)	17 (50%)
Quartile 4	493,076	521,815	754,976	46,415	35	22 (60%)	17 (50%)
2013 Revenue for Franchisees open 24 months or longer[2]	1,419,694	1,156,848	6,005,081	46,415	124	53 (40%)	62 (50%)
Quartile 1	2,616,509	2,292,611	6,005,081	1,766,955	31	8 (30%)	15 (50%)
Quartile 2	1,505,766	1,556,648	1,764,042	1,181,411	31	16 (50%)	15 (50%)
Quartile 3	996,964	1,030,124	1,132,284	828,001	31	17 (50%)	15 (50%)
Quartile 4	559,537	576,045	797,275	46,415	31	16 (50%)	15 (50%)
First Year Performance[3]	385,529	322,492	1,598,714	21,780	138	53 (40%)	69 (50%)
Second Year Performance[4]	898,177	753,345	3,661,793	42,355	124	47 (40%)	62 (50%)
Third Year Performance[5]	1,211,993	1,075,782	3,176,752	119,300	96	36 (40%)	48 (50%)
Fourth Year Performance[6]	1,485,549	1,287,939	4,275,808	316,077	71	30 (40%)	35 (50%)
Fifth Year Performance[7]	1,668,663	1,532,806	5,058,024	557,871	40	15 (40%)	20 (50%)
Sixth Year Performance[8]	2,009,645	1,728,974	5,273,437	748,038	15	4 (30%)	7 (50%)
Seventh Year Performance[9]	2,342,301	1,709,078	5,929,763	638,979	6	2 (30%)	3 (50%)

NOTES:

1. The 2013 Revenue information includes Revenues earned by franchisees for their first BrightStar agency from the time period of January 1, 2013 through December 31, 2013 if the franchisee had operated its BrightStar agency at least 12 months prior to December 31, 2013.

Of the 138 agencies opened by franchisees as their first loca-

tion that were in operation for a period of at least 12 months as of December 31, 2013, 105 of these agencies were awarded a territory with a population of less than 400,000 people. The average 2013 Total Revenue for these 105 franchise agencies open at least 12 months as of December 31, 2013 is $1,169,336 of which 36 members (34%) attained or exceeded this stated average.

2. The 2013 Revenue information includes Revenues earned

by franchisees for their first BrightStar agency from the time period of January 1, 2013 through December 31, 2013 if the franchisee had operated its BrightStar agency at least 24 months prior to December 31, 2013.

Of the 124 agencies opened by franchisees as their first location that were in operation for a period of at least 24 months as of December 31, 2013, 91 of these agencies were awarded a territory with a population of less than 400,000 people. The average 2013 Total Revenue for these 91 franchise agencies open at least 24 months as of December 31, 2013 is $1,261,206, of which 32 members (35%) attained or exceeded this stated average.

3. First year performance includes a snapshot of the average Revenues earned by new franchisees after operating their first BrightStar agency for a period of 12 months following the franchisee's Start Date. As noted above, if a franchisee operates more than one BrightStar agency, the information in the table above only includes Revenue for the franchisee's first BrightStar agency. Accordingly, of the 255 franchised BrightStar agencies that were in operation as of December 31, 2013, 138 of these agencies represent a franchisee's first BrightStar agency and were in operation for a period of at least 12 months as of December 31, 2013. Because the Start Date for each franchisee differs, the first year performance Revenue information includes Revenues earned by franchisees during 12 month time periods in 2006, 2007, 2008, 2009, 2010, 2011, 2012, and 2013.

Of the 138 agencies opened by franchisees as their first location that were in operation for a period of at least 12 months as of December 31, 2013, 105 of these agencies were awarded a territory with a population of less than 400,000 people. The average first year performance Revenue for these 105 franchise agencies is $348,124, of which 41 members (39%) attained or exceeded this stated average.

4. Second year performance includes a snapshot of the average Revenues earned by new franchisees during their 13th through 24th months of operation following their Start Date. As noted above, if a franchisee operates more than one BrightStar agency, the information in the table above only includes Revenue for the franchisee's first BrightStar agency. Accordingly, of the 255 franchised BrightStar agencies in operation as of December 31, 2013, 124 of these agencies represent a franchisee's first BrightStar agency and were in operation for a period of at least 24 months as of December 31, 2013. Because the Start Date for each franchisee differs, the second year performance Revenue information includes Revenues earned by franchisees during 12 month time periods in 2007, 2008, 2009, 2010, 2011, 2012, and 2013.

Of the 124 agencies opened by franchisees as their first loca-

tion that were in operation for a period of at least 24 months as of December 31, 2013, 93 of these agencies were awarded a territory with a population of less than 400,000 people. The average second year performance Revenue for these 93 franchise agencies is $826,798 of which 36 members (38.7%) attained or exceeded this stated average.

5. Third year performance includes a snapshot of the average Revenues earned by new franchisees during their 25th through 36th months of operation following their Start Date. As noted above, if a franchisee operates more than one BrightStar agency, the information in the table above only includes Revenue for the franchisee's first BrightStar agency. Accordingly, of the 255 franchised BrightStar agencies in operation as of December 31, 2013, 96 of these agencies represent a franchisee's first BrightStar agency and were in operation for a period of at least 36 months as of December 31, 2013. Because the Start Date for each franchisee differs, the third year performance Revenue information includes Revenues earned by franchisees during 12 month time periods in 2008, 2009, 2010, 2011, 2012 and 2013.

Of the 96 agencies opened by franchisees as their first location that were in operation for a period of at least 36 months as of December 31, 2013, 66 of these agencies were awarded a territory with a population of less than 400,000 people. The average third year performance Revenue for these 66 franchise agencies is $1,111,428, of which 23 members (34.8%) attained or exceeded this stated average.

6. Fourth year performance includes a snapshot of the average Revenues earned by new franchisees during their 37th through 48th months of operation following their Start Date. As noted above, if a franchisee operates more than one BrightStar agency, the information in the table above only includes Revenue for the franchisee's first BrightStar agency. Accordingly, of the 255 franchised BrightStar agencies in operation as of December 31, 2013, 71 of these agencies represent a franchisee's first BrightStar agency and were in operation for a period of at least 48 months as of December 31, 2013. Because the Start Date for each franchisee differs, the fourth year performance Revenue information includes Revenues earned by franchisees during 12 month time periods in 2009, 2010, 2011,2012 and 2013.

Of the 71 agencies opened by franchisees as their first location that were in operation for a period of at least 48 months as of December 31, 2013, 43 of these agencies were awarded a territory with a population of less than 400,000 people. The average fourth year performance Revenue for these 43 franchise agencies is $1,368,250, of which 15 members (34.9%) attained or exceeded this stated average.

7. Fifth year performance includes a snapshot of the aver-

age Revenues earned by new franchisees during their 49th through 60th months of operation following their Start Date. As noted above, if a franchisee operates more than one Bright-Star agency, the information in the table above only includes Revenue for the franchisee's first BrightStar agency. Accordingly, of the 255 franchised BrightStar agencies in operation as of December 31, 2013, 40 of these agencies represent a franchisee's first BrightStar agency and were in operation for a period of at least 60 months as of December 31, 2013. Because the Start Date for each franchisee differs, the fourth year performance Revenue information includes Revenues earned by franchisees during 12 month time periods in 2010, 2011, 2012, and 2013.

Of the 40 agencies opened by franchisees as their first location that were in operation for a period of at least 60 months as of December 31, 2013, 18 of these agencies were awarded a territory with a population of less than 400,000 people. The average fifth year performance Revenue for these 18 franchise agencies is $1,571,481, of which 7 members (38.9%) attained or exceeded this stated average.

8. Sixth year performance includes a snapshot of the average Revenues earned by new franchisees during their 61st through 72nd months of operation following their Start Date. As noted above, if a franchisee operates more than one BrightStar agency, the information in the table above only includes Revenue for the franchisee's first BrightStar agency. Accordingly, of the 255 franchised BrightStar agencies in operation as of December 31, 2013, 15 of these agencies represent a franchisee's first BrightStar agency and were in operation for a period of at least 72 months as of December 31, 2013. Because the Start Date for each franchisee differs, the sixth year performance Revenue information includes Revenues earned by franchisees during 12 month time periods in 2010, 2011, 2012 and 2013.

Of the 15 agencies opened by franchisees as their first location that were in operation for a period of at least 72 months as of December 31, 2013, 9 of these agencies were awarded a territory with a population of less than 400,000 people. The average sixth year performance Revenue for these 9 franchise agencies is $1,722,371, of which 5 members (55.6%) attained or exceeded this stated average.

9. Seventh year performance includes a snapshot of the average Revenues earned by new franchisees during their 62nd through 84th months of operation following their Start Date. As noted above, if a franchisee operates more than one BrightStar agency, the information in the table above only includes Revenue for the franchisee's first BrightStar agency.

Accordingly, of the franchised BrightStar agencies in operation as of December 31, 2013, 6 of these agencies represent a franchisee's first BrightStar agency and were in operation for a period of at least 84 months as of December 31, 2013. Because the Start Date for each franchisee differs, the sixth year performance Revenue information includes Revenues earned by franchisees during 12 month time periods in 2010, 2011, 2012 and 2013.

Of the 6 agencies opened by franchisees as their first location that were in operation for a period of at least 72 months as of December 31, 2013, 4 of these agencies were awarded a territory with a population of less than 400,000 people. The average seventh year performance Revenue for these 4 franchise agencies is $1,632,308, of which 2 members (33%) attained or exceeded this stated average.

B. Franchisee Margins (First Locations Only)

The following table identifies our franchisees' Gross Margin percentage. Gross Margin percentage is defined as Gross Margin divided by Revenues. Gross Margin is defined as Revenues less Cost of Goods Sold. Cost of Goods sold includes all direct and indirect costs related to field employees including payroll, payroll taxes, benefits, screening costs, workers' comp insurance, crime bond costs, professional and general liability insurance. We use a 20% average load onto known payroll costs to estimate COGS. The 20% is based on the franchise system average estimates. The two items with the largest variability due to state, local and county statutory differences in addition to unemployment insurance claims experience include: payroll taxes, that has a range of 6.9% - 15.2%, per payroll dollar (or approximately 3.0% - 8.4% of sales) and workers' comp insurance, that has a range of .5% - 16.3% per payroll dollar (or approximately .3% - 8.8% of sales). Some states with higher workers' comp insurance rates include Texas, Pennsylvania, and California among others. The payroll taxes include Social Security, Medicare, and State. State taxes can range from a low of 1.68% in North Dakota to a high of 9.5% in Illinois.

The information contained in this table includes information for all agencies opened by franchisees as their first location (regardless of how long the agencies were in operation during the particular year), including all resale locations, for the full year as of December 31, 2013 Specifically, out of our 255 total franchised agencies in existence in 2013, 165 of these agencies were opened by franchisees as their first location. If a franchisee operates more than one BrightStar agency, the information contained in the table below only includes information for the franchisee's first BrightStar agency.

	Average Gross Margin Percentage	High Margin	Low Margin	Number of Agencies	Number and % of Agencies that attained or exceeded Average Amount
2013	38.9%	58.70	21.7	165	77 (46.7)

NOTES:

1. Cost of Goods sold includes the direct cost of Nurse visits associated with billable services

C. Data Analysis of Client and Employee Statistics (First Location Only)

Hours Billed per Client per Week

The information in the chart below reflects the average, high and low hours billed per client per week during calendar year 2013 for all franchisee first locations, including all resale locations, open and operating for at least 3 months, as of December 31, 2013. As of December 31, 2013 we had 165 franchised BrightStar agencies opened by franchisees as their first location.

Average Hours Billed per Week	High Per Week	Low Per Week	Number of Agencies	Number and Percentage of Agencies that Attained or Exceeded Average Amount
22.8	55.6	2.4	165	72 (44%)

NOTES:

1. Information related to visits and assessments are excluded from the above chart as it skews the information since the assessment is billed to one company and the services are billed to another so it artificially inflates the client and employee count to include this data.

2. Excluding skilled care the average hours per client per week are 25.2 (most franchisees will begin to perform skilled care in their second year).

Number of Clients and Employees Serviced Per Location

The information in the chart below reflects the average weekly hours works per employee, average, high and low number of employees worked per week and average, high and low number of clients per week during the four pay periods running from November 24, 2013 through December 15, 2013 (selected near year-end prior to year-end holiday fluctuations) based upon various Revenue levels per location to provide data on the volume of clients and employees that an individual office coordinates. The information below contains information for all franchisee first locations for all ongoing clients. Specifically, out of the 255 total franchised agencies in existence as of December 31, 2013, 165 of those agencies were opened as a franchisee's first location. We opened 17 new agencies in 2013 and most of these fall in the below $15,000 weekly Revenue level as of the end of the year that contributes to the large weighting of franchisees falling into the less than $5,000, $5,001-$10,000, and $10,001-$15,000 weekly Revenue categories.

Average Weekly Revenue	Avg Weekly Hrs Worked Per Employee	Avg # of Employees	High # of Employees	Low # of Employees	Avg # of Customers	High # of Customers	Low # of Customers	Agency Count
0-5,000	9.6	15.8	29	6	15	36	4	14
5,000-10,000	12.3	24	38	10	26	59	8	21
10,000-20,000	16.9	42	64	15	46	104	11	43
20,000-30,000	19.9	57	89	37	58	92	32	41
30,000-40,000	19.7	74	111	47	78	191	35	22
40,000-50,000	17.8	87	122	68	88	149	38	11
50,000-60,000	21.3	79	89	60	127	192	58	5
>60,000	19.3	138	258	76	176	348	62	8

D. Franchisee Mix of Business

The table below provides average information for the 2013 calendar year, by line of business. The table below includes all agencies in operation in 2013, regardless of whether: (i) the agency was the franchisee's first, second or subsequent Bright-Star agency, and (ii) the agency operated during the entire 12 month period.

2013 System Wide agenceies - 255 units	Revenue Mix
Medical Personal Care	46.9%
Medical Skilled Home Care	10.9%
Non-Medical Caregiver	15.8%
Subtotal	73.5%
Staffing	26.5%
Total	100.0%

NOTES:

1. Staffing business includes National Accounts

E. Break-Even – Franchisees (First Location Only)

The table below provides detail on the number of franchisees achieving break-even in a particular month. At the end of each calendar year we send surveys to all franchisees that have been operating for a period of at least 12 months, commencing on their Start Date. As of December 31, 2013, we had 138 franchisees that had operated their first agency for a period of at least 12 months. While we have utilized current year surveys and historical surveys in order to prepare a more comprehensive schedule, the table excludes those franchisees who responded to the survey but had not yet achieved break-even as of the survey date. The information in the table below was taken from the surveys we received and includes cumulative data from only those franchisees that responded to the survey.

	Average Months to Achieve Breakeven[1]	Median Months to Achieve Breakeven	Low	High	Total Number of Franchisees	Number and % of Franchisees that attained or exceeded Average Amount	Numner and % of Franchisees that attained or exceeded Median Amount
Agencies open at least 12 months as of December 31, 2013[2]	11.2	11.0	3	27	99	56 (56.6%)	50 (51%)

NOTES:

1. Franchisee's agency break-even information includes all first locations open at least 12 months as of December 31, 2013. For these agencies break-even occurred between months 3 and 27 with an average of month 11.2, 56 (56.6%) of franchisees were at or less than the average break-even month, 50 (51%) were more than the average break-even month.

2. Because the Start Date for each franchisee differs, the franchisee's break-even point for the franchisees included in the table above occurred in years 2006, 2007, 2008, 2009, 2010, 2011, 2012, and 2013.

F. National Accounts

Beginning in August 2007, we made a concentrated effort to seek out and establish contracts that were national in scope to supplement the Revenues of our franchisees ("National Account Contracts"). National Account Contracts are approved by the local franchisee with the exception of national pricing for nurse assessment services (up to 2 hours per assessment). The following table illustrates the total national account Revenues contributed to the system by the national account program for all locations from January 1, 2013 through December 31, 2013. The table also illustrates the average dollar amount of National Account Contract Revenue received by our franchisees as of December 31, 2013, as well as the margins, and dollars per franchisee contributed.

Total System Wide National Accounts Revenue	Average $ per location (first locations open 12 months)	High Revenue per location	Low Revenue per location	Number and Percentage of Franchisee First Location Agencies that Attained or Exceeded Average	Average Margin of National Accounts	Number of All Agencies open for 12 months in 2013
$25,968,612	$123,031	$919,966	$780	50 (34.7%)	46.7%	238

NOTES:

1. Total National Account Revenues includes Revenue from all agencies in operation as of December 31, 2013.

2. The high and low numbers in the chart above represent the high and low Revenue for calendar year 2013 received by a franchisee's first location as of December 31, 2013.

G. Payer Sources

The table below provides average information for the 2013 calendar year, by payer source. The table below includes all agencies in operation in 2013, regardless of whether: (i) the agency was the franchisee's first, second or subsequent Bright-Star agency, and (ii) the agency operated during the entire 12 month period.

Self Pay – Private Individual	55.0%
National Account	10.6%
State Medicaid Waiver Programs	8.4%
Local Contract Account	6.2%
LTC Insurance	5.0%
Other	14.8%
Total	100.0%

ADDITIONAL NOTES:

Some outlets have achieved these results. Your individual financial results may differ from the results stated in this Item 19. There is no assurance you will achieve these results.

You are likely to achieve results that are different, possibly significantly and adversely, from the results shown above. Many factors, including location of your Agency, clients located within your territory, management capabilities, local market conditions, and other factors, are unique to each BrightStar agency and may significantly impact the financial performance of your business.

The Item 19 figures do not reflect all of the operating expenses or other costs or expenses that must be deducted from the average total sales price or gross Revenue to obtain net income or profit. In particular, the costs and expenses contained in this Item 19 do not include the expenses which are payable according to the terms of the franchise agreement. There may be other costs and expenses not identified, and the costs and expenses of company owned locations may differ from franchisee owned locations. The figures in this Item 19 will vary depending on many factors, such as: (a) geographic location; (b) competition from other providers in your area; (c) advertising effectiveness; (d) whether you operate the franchised business personally or hire a general manager; (e) your pricing; (f) vendor prices on supplies; (g) employee salaries and benefits (life and health insurance, etc.); (h) insurance costs; (i) weather conditions; (j) ability to generate clients; (k) client loyalty; (l) employment conditions in the market and (m) licensure status and/or availability to perform skilled care. You should conduct an independent investigation of the costs and expenses you will incur in operating your business.

We believe that the information in this Item 19 has been compiled using generally accepted accounting principles, but the data is unaudited and no assurance can be offered that the data does not contain inaccuracies that an audit might disclose. Actual results will vary from business to business, and we cannot estimate the results of any particular BrightStar agency. Written substantiation for the financial performance representation will be made available to the prospective franchisee upon reasonable request.

BRIGHTWAY INSURANCE

3733 W. University Blvd.
Jacksonville, FL 32217
Tel: (888) 254-5014, (904) 764-9554
Fax: (904) 482-0739
Email: matt.flagler@brightway.com
Website: www.brightway.com
Matt Flagler, Director of Franchise Development

Brightway Insurance is a Property & Casualty Insurance franchise that offers the look and feel of a direct writer agency with the selection, service and pricing options of a leading independent agency. Our business model enables our offices to consistently produce a substantially higher volume of new business than a traditional captive or independent agency, as well as achieve higher overall quality and retention. We achieve this by handling all of the policy servicing functions in our centralized customer service center, thus allowing our agencies to focus on new business development.

BACKGROUND

IFA Member:	Yes
Established & First Franchised:	2003; 2007
Franchised Units:	111
Company-Owned Units:	2
Total Units:	113
Distribution:	US – 113; CAN – 0; O'seas – 0
North America:	7 States, 0 Provinces
Density:	102 in FL, 4 in GA, 3 in TX
Projected New Units (12 Months):	30
Qualifications:	5, 5, 2, 2, 5, 5

FINANCIAL/TERMS

Cash Investment:	$150 – 175K
Total Investment:	$150 – 175K
Minimum Net Worth:	$250K

Fees (Franchise):	$60K
Fees (Royalty):	15 – 45%
Fees (Advertising):	N/A
Term of Contract (Years):	5/5
Average Number of Employees:	3-5 FT, 0 PT
Passive Ownership:	Discouraged
Encourage Conversions:	Yes
Area Development Agreements:	No
Sub-Franchising Contracts:	No
Expand in Territory:	Yes
Space Needs:	1,000 SF

SUPPORT & TRAINING

Financial Assistance Provided:	Yes (I)
Site Selection Assistance:	Yes
Lease Negotiation Assistance:	No
Co-operative Advertising:	No
Franchisee Association/Member:	No
Size of Corporate Staff:	130
On-going Support:	A, C, D, E, G, H, I
Training:	3 Weeks Jacksonville, FL

SPECIFIC EXPANSION PLANS

US:	SE
Canada:	No
Overseas:	No

PART I:

Part I of this Item sets forth certain historical information for the franchised Associate Agencies operating for at least one full calendar year. This Item 19 contains information for Representative Associate Agencies that were open at least one full calendar year as of December 31, 2013. Excluded from this Part I are the following: (i) AAOs who have not been receiving commissions for a full calendar year as of December 31, 2013; (ii) our company-owned Agency; (iii) AAOs who were not "fully staffed", which means AAOs that did not have three producers earning commissions throughout 2013, which we currently require of new AAOs. The AAO's included in Part I of this Item shall be referred to as the "Representative Associate Agencies."

We have segregated the data by (i) the population of the county in which the Representative Associate Agency is located (as determined by 2012 U.S. Census data), and (ii) the number of years for which a Representative Associate Agency has received commissions for every month in a complete twelve-

month period ("Tenure"). We have further broken this information into four sets of tables.

In Table 1-A, we provide the average Gross Revenues of the Representative Associate Agencies that are located in a county with a population that below 500,000 people, for the twelve-month period beginning January 1, 2013, and ending December 31, 2013. In Table 1-B, we provide the Gross Revenue of the Representative Associate Agencies that are located in a county with a population that exceeds 500,000 people, for the twelvemonth period beginning January 1, 2013, and ending December 31, 2013. When examining these figures, please note that Gross Revenue already incorporates the percentage of commissions that are retained by us as a royalty, comprising 15% of the Brightway Sales Commissions owed to us for New Accounts and 45% of the Brightway Sales Commissions owed to us for Renewal Accounts (as described more fully in Item 6). In other words, the royalty owed to us has already been deducted before arriving at the Gross Revenue figures set forth in Tables 1- A and 1-B. Additionally, please note that some of the AAOs below brought books of business with them when they opened their Agency, which increased their initial revenue figures. The Gross Revenue information presented in this Item is derived from our own records of the weekly gross commissions earned by Associate Agencies. Substantiation of the data used in preparing this information will be made available upon reasonable request.

In Table 2-A, we provide the average number of producers and employees of Representative Associate Agencies that are located in a county with a population below 500,000 people. In Table 2-B, we provide the average number of producers and employees of Representative Associate Agencies that are located in a county with a population that exceeds 500,000 people. The number of producers per Agency is calculated based on the number of people that received commissions in 2013 at a particular Agency. The number of employees per Agency is calculated based on the number of employees reported in OneApp (our insurance license tracker) as of February 21, 2014.

In Table 3-A, we provide the average number of policies that qualify as "New Business" that were written during the 2013 calendar year by the Representative Associate Agencies that are located in a county with a population below 500,000 people. In Table 3-B, we provide the average number of policies that qualify as "New Business" that were written during the 2013 calendar year by the Representative Associate Agencies that are located in a county with a population that exceeds 500,000 people. See Item 6 for a description of the difference between New Business and Renewal Business.

In Table 4-A, we provide the average revenue of the "New Business" policies that were written during the 2013 calendar year by the Representative Associate Agencies that are located in a county with a population below 500,000 people. In Table 4-B, we provide the average revenue of the "New Business" policies that were written during the 2013 calendar year by the Representative Associate Agencies that are located in a county with a population that exceeds 500,000 people.

Importantly, the success of your Associate Agency will depend largely upon your individual abilities and your market, and the financial results of your franchise are likely to differ, perhaps materially, from the results summarized in this Item. We believe that the following financial data has been compiled using generally accepted accounting principles, but we have not audited the data and no assurance can be offered that the data does not contain inaccuracies that an audit might disclose. Additionally, the data below does not contain expense and operating cost information, including AAO Shared Expenses and other expenses that you will incur as an AAO (as described more fully in Item 6).

TABLE I-A

GROSS REVENUE OF REPRESENTATIVE ASSOCIATE AGENCIES FOR AGENCIES

WITH COUNTY POPULATION BELOW 500,000 PEOPLE[1]

Tenure[2]	Offices	Average[3]	Low	High	Top 25% Average
4+	12	$282,590[4]	$141,114	$690,317	$459,821[4]
3	2	$210,710[5]	$124,114	$297,306	$297,306[5]
2	5	$104,435[6]	$45,908	$197,089	$197,089[6]
1	4	$59,788[7]	$42,125	$77,074	$77,074[7]
Total	23	$198,862[8]	$42,125	$690,317	$278,704[8]

TABLE I-B

GROSS REVENUE OF REPRESENTATIVE ASSOCIATE AGENCIES FOR AGENCIES

WITH COUNTY POPULATION OVER 500,000 PEOPLE[1]

Tenure[2]	Offices	Average[3]	Low	High	Top 25% Average
4+	25	$356,084[4]	$88,247	$1,021,537	$666,643[4]
3	10	$309,728[5]	$124,287	$801,307	$599,765[5]
2	7	$200,464[6]	$106,301	$291,624	$279,174[6]
1	9	$70,736[7]	$30,494	$115,261	$114,967[7]
Total	51	$275,279[8]	$30,494	$1,021,537	$483,730[8]

Notes to Tables 1-A and 1-B

1. In Table 1-A, the term "Gross Revenue" means the Brightway Sales Commissions (commissions paid by the Contracted Companies to us or assigned by you to us for the sale, renewal, service or delivery of a specific policy through you) earned by our Representative Associate Agencies located in counties with a population below 500,000 people during the 2013 calendar year, less the 15% royalty owed to us for New Business and the 45% royalty owed to us for Renewal Business. "Gross Revenue" is exclusive of: (a) "AAO Shared Expenses" (as described more fully in Note 3 to Item 6); and (b) all other costs and expenses you incur in the operation of your Agency, including all other fees payable to us or our affiliates.

In Table 1-B, the term "Gross Revenue" means the Brightway Sales Commissions (commissions paid by the Contracted Companies to us or assigned by you to us for the sale, renewal, service or delivery of a specific policy through you) earned by our Representative Associate Agencies located in counties with a population over 500,000 people during the 2013 calendar year, less the 15% royalty owed to us for New Business and the 45% royalty owed to us for Renewal Business. "Gross Revenue" is exclusive of: (a) "AAO Shared Expenses" (as described more fully in Note 3 to Item 6); and (b) all other costs and expenses you incur in the operation of your Agency, including all other fees payable to us or our affiliates.

2. "Tenure" is defined as the number of years for which a Representative Associate Agency has received commissions in every month for a complete twelve-month period.

3. "Average Gross Revenue" was calculated by taking the sum of Gross Revenue achieved by each Associate Agency in each subset of Associate Agencies and dividing that sum by the total number of Associate Agencies in that subset of Associate Agencies.

4. Of the 12 Associate Agencies with Tenure of at least four years located in counties with less than 500,000 people, 5 Associate Agencies, or 42%, exceeded the Average Gross Revenue. Of the 3 Associate Agencies with the top 25% of Gross Revenue in this subset of Associate Agencies, 1 Associate Agencies, or 33%, exceeded the top 25% Average Gross Revenue.

Of the 25 Associate Agencies with Tenure of at least four years located in counties with greater than 500,000 people, 10 Associate Agencies, or 40%, exceeded the Average Gross Revenue. Of the 6 Associate Agencies with the top 25% of Gross Revenue in this subset of Associate Agencies, 2 Associate Agencies, or 33%, exceeded the top 25% Average Gross Revenue.

5. Of the 2 Associate Agencies with Tenure of at least three years but less than four years located in counties with less than 500,000 people, 1 Associate Agency, or 50%, exceeded the Average Gross Revenue. Of the 1 Associate Agencies with the top 25% of Gross Revenue in this subset of Associate Agencies, 0 Associate Agencies, or 0%, exceeded the top 25% Average Gross Revenue.

Of the 10 Associate Agencies with Tenure of at least three years but less than four years located in counties with greater than 500,000 people, 4 Associate Agencies, or 40%, exceeded the Average Gross Revenue. Of the 3 Associate Agencies with the top 25% of Gross Revenue in this subset of Associate Agencies, 1 Associate Agencies, or 33%, exceeded the top 25% Average Gross Revenue.

6. Of the 5 Associate Agencies with Tenure of at least two years but less than three years located in counties with less than 500,000 people, 2 Associate Agencies, or 40%, exceeded the Average Gross Revenue. Of the 1 Associate Agencies with the top 25% of Gross Revenue in this subset of Associate Agencies, 0 Associate Agencies, or 0%, exceeded the top 25% Average Gross Revenue.

Of the 7 Associate Agencies with Tenure of at least two years but less than three years located in counties with greater than 500,000 people, 4 Associate Agencies, or 57%, exceeded the Average Gross Revenue. Of the 2 Associate Agencies with the top 25% of Gross Revenue in this subset of Associate Agencies, 1 Associate Agencies, or 50%, exceeded the top 25% Average Gross Revenue.

7. Of the 4 Associate Agencies with Tenure of at least one year but less than two years located in counties with less than 500,000 people, 2 Associate Agencies, or 50%, exceeded the Average Gross Revenue. Of the 1 Associate Agencies with the top 25% of Gross Revenue in this subset of Associate Agencies, 0 Associate Agencies, or 0%, exceeded the top 25% Average Gross Revenue.

Of the 9 Associate Agencies with Tenure of at least one year but less than two years located in counties with greater than 500,000 people, 5 Associate Agencies, or 56%, exceeded the Average Gross Revenue. Of the 2 Associate Agencies with the top 25% of Gross Revenue in this subset of Associate Agencies, 1 Associate Agencies, or 50%, exceeded the top 25% Average Gross Revenue.

8. Of the 23 Associate Agencies whose Gross Revenues are presented in Table 1-A above (and are located in counties with less than 500,000 people), 9 Associate Agencies, or 39%, exceeded the overall Average Gross Revenue set forth in Table 1-A. Of the 6 Associate Agencies with the top 25% of Gross Revenue in this subset of Associate Agencies, 1 Associate

Agencies, or 17%, exceeded the top 25% Average Revenue.

Of the 51 Associate Agencies whose Gross Revenues are presented in Table 1-B above (and are located in counties with greater than 500,000 people), 19 Associate Agencies, or 37%,

exceeded the overall Average Gross Revenue set forth in Table 1-B. Of the 13 Associate Agencies with the top 25% of Gross Revenue in this subset of Associate Agencies, 5 Associate Agencies, or 38%, exceeded the top 25% Average Gross Revenue.

TABLE 2-A

PRODUCERS AND EMPLOYEES OF REPRESENTATIVE ASSOCIATE AGENCIES FOR AGENCIES WITH COUNTY POPULATION BELOW 500,000 PEOPLE[1]

Tenure[2]	Offices	Average Producers[3]	Average Employees[3]	Top 25% Prod. By Rev.	Top 25% Emp. by Rev.
4+	12	4.0[4]	5.2[4]	5.7[4]	6.0[4]
3	2	4.0[5]	5.5[5]	5.0[5]	7.0[5]
2	5	2.8[6]	3.8[6]	4.0[6]	5.0[6]
1	4	3.3[7]	3.5[7]	3.0[7]	3.0[7]
Total	23	3.6[8]	4.6[8]	5.8[8]	6.6[8]

TABLE 2-B

PRODUCERS AND EMPLOYEES OF REPRESENTATIVE ASSOCIATE AGENCIES FOR AGENCIES WITH COUNTY POPULATION ABOVE 500,000 PEOPLE[1]

Tenure[2]	Offices	Average Producers[3]	Average Employees[3]	Top 25% Prod. By Rev.	Top 25% Emp. By Rev.
4+	25	4.5[4]	5.4[4]	6.4[4]	8.0[4]
3	10	4.2[5]	5.1[5]	7.5[5]	10.0[5]
2	7	3.3[6]	4.0[6]	3.5[6]	4.0[6]
1	9	2.4[7]	3.2[7]	2.5[7]	3.0[7]
Total	51	3.9[8]	4.8[8]	5.4[8]	6.7[8]

Notes to Tables 2-A and 2-B

1. In Tables 2-A and 2-B, the number of producers per Associate Agency is calculated based on the number of people that received commissions in 2013 at a particular Associate Agency. The number of employees per Associate Agency is calculated based on the number of employees reported in OneApp (our insurance license tracker) as of February 21, 2014. Table 2-A includes the Representative Associate Agencies located in counties with a population below 500,000. Table 2-B includes the Representative Associate Agencies located in counties with a population above 500,000.

2. "Tenure" is defined as the number of years for which a Representative Associate Agency has received commissions in every month for a complete twelve-month period.

3. "Average Producers" was calculated by taking the sum of producers employed by each Associate Agency in each subset of Associate Agencies and dividing that sum by the total number of Associate Agencies in that subset of Associate

Agencies. "Average Employees" was calculated by taking the sum of employees of each Associate Agency in each subset of Associate Agencies and dividing that sum by the total number of Associate Agencies in that subset of Associate Agencies.

4. Of the 12 Associate Agencies with Tenure of at least four years located in counties with less than 500,000 people, 3 Associate Agencies, or 25%, had more than the number of Average Producers. Of the 3 Associate Agencies with the top 25% of Gross Revenue in this subset of Associate Agencies, 2 Associate Agencies, or 67%, exceeded the top 25% number of Average Producers. Of the 12 Associate Agencies with Tenure of at least four years located in counties with less than 500,000 people, 4 Associate Agencies, or 33%, had more than the number of Average Employees. Of the 3 Associate Agencies with the top 25% of Gross Revenue in this subset of Associate Agencies, 2 Associate Agencies, or 67%, exceeded the top 25% number of Average Employees.

Of the 25 Associate Agencies with Tenure of at least four years located in counties with greater than 500,000 people,

10 Associate Agencies, or 40%, had more than the number of Average Producers. Of the 6 Associate Agencies with the top 25% of Gross Revenue in this subset of Associate Agencies, 2 Associate Agencies, or 33%, exceeded the top 25% number of Average Producers. Of the 25 Associate Agencies with Tenure of at least four years located in counties with greater than 500,000 people, 10 Associate Agencies, or 40%, had more than the number of Average Employees. Of the 6 Associate Agencies with the top 25% of Gross Revenue in this subset of Associate Agencies, 2 Associate Agencies, or 33%, exceeded the top 25% number of Average Employees.

5. Of the 2 Associate Agencies with Tenure of at least three years but less than four years located in counties with less than 500,000 people, 1 Associate Agencies, or 50%, had more than the number of Average Producers. Of the 1 Associate Agencies with the top 25% of Gross Revenue in this subset of Associate Agencies, 0 Associate Agencies, or 0%, exceeded the top 25% number of Average Producers. Of the 2 Associate Agencies with Tenure of at least three years but less than four years located in counties with less than 500,000 people, 1 Associate Agencies, or 50%, had more than the number of Average Employees. Of the 1 Associate Agencies with the top 25% of Gross Revenue in this subset of Associate Agencies, 0 Associate Agencies, or 0%, exceeded the top 25% number of Average Employees.

Of the 10 Associate Agencies with Tenure of at least three years but less than four years located in counties with greater than 500,000 people, 2 Associate Agencies, or 20%, had more than the number of Average Producers. Of the 3 Associate Agencies with the top 25% of Gross Revenue in this subset of Associate Agencies, 1 Associate Agencies, or 33%, exceeded the top 25% number of Average Producers. Of the 10 Associate Agencies with Tenure of at least three years but less than four years located in counties with greater than 500,000 people, 3 Associate Agencies, or 30%, had more than the number of Average Employees. Of the 3 Associate Agencies with the top 25% of Gross Revenue in this subset of Associate Agencies, 1 Associate Agencies, of 33%, exceeded the top 25% number of Average Employees.

6. Of the 5 Associate Agencies with Tenure of at least two years but less than three years located in counties with less than 500,000 people, 3 Associate Agencies, or 60%, had more than the number of Average Producers. Of the 1 Associate Agencies with the top 25% of Gross Revenue in this subset of Associate Agencies, 0 Associate Agencies, or 0%, exceeded the top 25% number of Average Producers. Of the 5 Associate Agencies with Tenure of at least two years but less than three years located in counties with less than 500,000 people, 3 Associate Agencies, or 60%, had than the number of Average Employees. Of the 1 Associate Agencies with the top 25% of Gross Revenue in this subset of Associate Agencies, 0 Associate Agencies, or 0%, exceeded the top 25% number of Average Employees.

Of the 7 Associate Agencies with Tenure of at least two years but less than three years located in counties with greater than 500,000 people, 2 Associate Agencies, or 29%, had more than the number of Average Producers. Of the 2 Associate Agencies with the top 25% of Gross Revenue in this subset of Associate Agencies, 1 Associate Agencies, or 50%, exceeded the top 25% number of Average Producers. Of the 7 Associate Agencies with Tenure of at least two years but less than three years located in counties with greater than 500,000 people, 1 Associate Agencies, or 14%, had more than the number of Average Employees. Of the 2 Associate Agencies with the top 25% of Gross Revenue in this subset of Associate Agencies, 1 Associate Agencies, or 50%, exceeded the top 25% number of Average Employees.

7. Of the 4 Associate Agencies with Tenure of at least one year but less than two years located in counties with less than 500,000 people, 1 Associate Agencies, or 25%, had more than the number of Average Producers. Of the 1 Associate Agencies with the top 25% of Gross Revenue in this subset of Associate Agencies, 0 Associate Agencies, or 0%, exceeded the top 25% number of Average Producers. Of the 4 Associate Agencies with Tenure of at least one year but less than two years located in counties with less than 500,000 people, 2 Associate Agencies, or 50%, had more than the number of Average Employees. Of the 1 Associate Agencies with the top 25% of Gross Revenue in this subset of Associate Agencies, 0 Associate Agencies, or 0%, exceeded the top 25% number of Average Employees.

Of the 9 Associate Agencies with Tenure of at least one year but less than two years located in counties with greater than 500,000 people, 5 Associate Agencies, or 56%, had more than the number of Average Producers. Of the 2 Associate Agencies with the top 25% of Gross Revenue in this subset of Associate Agencies, 1 Associate Agencies, or 50%, exceeded the top 25% number of Average Producers. Of the 9 Associate Agencies with Tenure of at least one year but less than two years located in counties with greater than 500,000 people, 4 Associate Agencies, or 44%, had more than the number of Average Employees. Of the 2 Associate Agencies with the top 25% of Gross Revenue in this subset of Associate Agencies, 1 Associate Agencies, or 50%, exceeded the top 25% number of Average Employees.

8. Of the 23 Associate Agencies whose data are presented in Table 2-A above (and are located in counties with less than 500,000 people), 10 Associate Agencies, or 43%, had more than the number of Average Producers. Of the 6 Associate Agencies with the top 25% of Gross Revenue in this subset of Associate Agencies, 2 Associate Agencies, or 33%, exceeded

the top 25% number of Average Producers. Of the 23 Associate Agencies whose data are presented in Table 2-A above (and are located in counties with less than 500,000 people), 10 Associate Agencies, or 43%, had more than the number of Average Employees. Of the 6 Associate Agencies with the top 25% of Gross Revenue in this subset of Associate Agencies, 2 Associate Agencies, or 33%, exceeded the top 25% number of Average Employees.

Of the 51 Associate Agencies whose data are presented in Table 2-B above (and are located in counties with greater than 500,000 people), 25 Associate Agencies, or 49%, had more than the number of Average Producers. Of the 13 Associate Agencies with the top 25% of Gross Revenue in these 51 Associate Agencies, 2 Associate Agencies, or 15%, exceeded the top 25% number of Average Producers. Of the 51 Associate Agencies whose data are presented in Table 2-B above (and are located in counties with greater than 500,000 people), 21 Associate Agencies, or 41%, had more than the number of Average Employees. Of the 13 Associate Agencies with the top 25% of Gross Revenue in these 51 Associate Agencies, 5 Associate Agencies, or 38%, exceeded the top 25% number of Average Employees.

TABLE 3-A

"NEW BUSINESS" POLICIES OF REPRESENTATIVE ASSOCIATE AGENCIES FOR AGENCIES

WITH COUNTY POPULATION BELOW 500,000 PEOPLE[1]

Tenure[2]	Offices	Average[3]	Low	High	Top 25%
4+	12	1,261[4]	679	3,162	2,032[4]
3	2	1,149[5]	836	1,461	1,461[5]
2	5	643[6]	221	1,037	1,037[6]
1	4	453[7]	290	632	632[7]
Total	23	977[8]	221	3,162	1,506[8]

TABLE 3-B

"NEW BUSINESS" POLICIES OF REPRESENTATIVE ASSOCIATE AGENCIES FOR AGENCIES

WITH COUNTY POPULATION OVER 500,000 PEOPLE[1]

Tenure[2]	Offices	Average[3]	Low	High	Top 25%
4+	25	1,246[4]	393	3,136	2,251[4]
3	10	1,424[5]	636	3,480	2,636[5]
2	7	1,137[6]	523	1,881	1,756[6]
1	9	492[7]	267	812	680[7]
Total	51	1,132[8]	267	3,480	1,945[8]

Notes to Tables 3-A and 3-B

1. In Table 3-A, we present the average number of policies that qualify as "New Business" that were written during the 2013 calendar year by the Representative Associate Agencies located in a county with a population over 500,000. In Table 3-B, we present the average number of policies that qualify as "New Business" that were written during the 2013 calendar year by the Representative Associate Agencies located in a county with a population below 500,000.

2. "Tenure" is defined as the number of years for which a Representative Associate Agency has received commissions in every month for a complete twelve-month period.

3. The Average number of New Business policies was calculated by taking the sum of the New Business policies written by each Associate Agency in each subset of Associate Agencies and dividing that sum by the total number of Associate Agencies in that subset of Associate Agencies.

4. Of the 12 Associate Agencies with Tenure of at least four years located in counties with less than 500,000 people, 6 Associate Agencies, or 50%, exceeded the Average number of New Business policies. Of the 3 Associate Agencies with the top 25% of New Business policies in this subset of Associate Agencies, 1 Associate Agencies, or 33%, exceeded the top 25% Average number of New Business policies.

Of the 25 Associate Agencies with Tenure of at least four years located in counties with greater than 500,000 people, 9 Associate Agencies, or 36%, exceeded the Average number of New Business policies. Of the 6 Associate Agencies with the top 25% of New Business policies in this subset of Associate

Agencies, 2 Associate Agencies, or 33%, exceeded the top 25% Average number of New Business policies.

5. Of the 2 Associate Agencies with Tenure of at least three years but less than four years located in counties with less than 500,000 people, 1 Associate Agencies, or 50%, exceeded the Average number of New Business policies. Of the 1 Associate Agencies with the top 25% of New Business policies in this subset of Associate Agencies, 0 Associate Agencies, or 0%, exceeded the top 25% Average number of New Business policies.

Of the 10 Associate Agencies with Tenure of at least three years but less than four years located in counties with greater than 500,000 people, 4 Associate Agencies, or 40%, exceeded the Average number of New Business policies. Of the 3 Associate Agencies with the top 25% of New Business policies in this subset of Associate Agencies, 1 Associate Agencies, or 33%, exceeded the top 25% Average number of New Business policies.

6. Of the 5 Associate Agencies with Tenure of at least two years but less than three years located in counties with less than 500,000 people, 2 Associate Agencies, or 40%, exceeded the Average number of New Business policies. Of the 1 Associate Agencies with the top 25% of New Business policies in this subset of Associate Agencies, 0 Associate Agencies, or 0%, exceeded the top 25% Average number of New Business policies.

Of the 7 Associate Agencies with Tenure of at least two years but less than three years located in counties with greater than 500,000 people, 3 Associate Agencies, or 43%, exceeded the Average number of New Business policies. Of the 2 Associate Agencies with the top 25% of New Business policies in this subset of Associate Agencies, 1 Associate Agencies, or 50%, exceeded the top 25% Average number of New Business

policies.

7. Of the 4 Associate Agencies with Tenure of at least one year but less than two years located in counties with less than 500,000 people, 1 Associate Agencies, or 25%, exceeded the Average number of New Business policies. Of the 1 Associate Agencies with the top 25% of New Business policies in this subset of Associate Agencies, 0 Associate Agencies, or 0%, exceeded the top 25% Average number of New Business policies.

Of the 9 Associate Agencies with Tenure of at least one year but less than two years located in counties with greater than 500,000 people, 5 Associate Agencies, or 56%, exceeded the Average number of New Business policies. Of the 2 Associate Agencies with the top 25% of New Business policies in this subset of Associate Agencies, 1 Associate Agencies, or 50%, exceeded the top 25% Average number of New Business policies.

8. Of the 23 Associate Agencies whose data are presented in Table 3-A above (and are located in counties with less than 500,000 people), 8 Associate Agencies, or 35%, exceeded the overall Average number of New Business policies set forth in Table 3-A. Of the 6 Associate Agencies with the top 25% of New Business policies in this subset of Associate Agencies, 1 Associate Agencies, or 17%, exceeded the top 25% Average number of New Business policies.

Of the 51 Associate Agencies whose data are presented in Table 3-B above (and are located in counties with greater than 500,000 people), 19 Associate Agencies, or 37%, exceeded the overall Average number of New Business policies set forth in Table 3-B. Of the 13 Associate Agencies with the top 25% of New Business policies in this subset of Associate Agencies, 5 Associate Agencies, or 38%, exceeded the top 25% Average number of New Business policies.

TABLE 4-A

AVERAGE REVENUE PER "NEW BUSINESS" POLICY OF REPRESENTATIVE ASSOCIATE AGENCIES

IN COUNTIES WITH POPULATION BELOW 500,000 PEOPLE[1]

Tenure[2]	Offices	Averages[3]	Top 25%
4+	12	$99[4]	$115[4]
3	2	$118[5]	$139[5]
2	5	$97[6]	$130[6]
1	4	$117[7]	$157[7]
Total	23	$103[8]	$106[8]

TABLE 4-B

AVERAGE REVENUE PER "NEW BUSINESS" POLICY OF REPRESENTATIVE ASSOCIATE AGENCIES
IN COUNTIES WITH POPULATION ABOVE 500,000 PEOPLE[1]

Tenure[2]	Offices	Average[3]	Top 25%
4+	25	$126[4]	$153[4]
3	10	$137[5]	$148[5]
2	7	$130[6]	$127[6]
1	9	$137[7]	$155[7]
Total	51	$131[8]	$148[8]

Notes to Tables 4-A and 4-B

1. In Table 4-A, we present the average revenue of each policy that qualifies as "New Business" that was written during the 2013 calendar year by the Representative Associate Agencies located in a county with a population over 500,000. In Table 4-B, we present the average revenue of each policy that qualifies as "New Business" that was written during the 2013 calendar year by the Representative Associate Agencies located in a county with a population below 500,000.

2. "Tenure" is defined as the number of years for which a Representative Associate Agency has received commissions in every month for a complete twelve-month period.

3. The Average revenue per policy was calculated by taking the sum of the revenues of all the New Business policies written by each Associate Agency in each subset of Associate Agencies and dividing that sum by the total number of Associate Agencies in that subset of Associate Agencies.

4. Of the 12 Associate Agencies with Tenure of at least four years located in counties with less than 500,000 people, 6 Associate Agencies, or 50%, exceeded the Average revenue per policy. Of the 3 Associate Agencies with the top 25% Average revenue per policy, 2 Associate Agencies, or 67%, exceeded the top 25% Average revenue per policy.

Of the 25 Associate Agencies with Tenure of at least four years located in counties with greater than 500,000 people, 11 Associate Agencies, or 44%, exceeded the Average revenue per policy. Of the 6 Associate Agencies with the top 25% Average revenue per policy, 3 Associate Agencies, or 50%, exceeded the top 25% Average revenue per policy.

5. Of the 2 Associate Agencies with Tenure of at least three years but less than four years located in counties with less than 500,000 people, 1 Associate Agencies, or 50%, exceeded the Average revenue per policy. Of the 1 Associate Agencies with the top 25% Average revenue per policy, 0 Associate Agencies, or 0%, exceeded the top 25% Average revenue per policy.

Of the 10 Associate Agencies with Tenure of at least three years but less than four years located in counties with greater than 500,000 people, 5 Associate Agencies, or 50%, exceeded the Average revenue per policy. Of the 3 Associate Agencies with the top 25% Average revenue per policy, 1 Associate Agencies, or 33%, exceeded the top 25% Average revenue per policy.

6. Of the 5 Associate Agencies with Tenure of at least two years but less than three years located in counties with less than 500,000 people, 3 Associate Agencies, or 60%, exceeded the Average revenue per policy. Of the 1 Associate Agencies with the top 25% Average revenue per policy, 0 Associate Agencies, or 0%, exceeded the top 25% Average revenue per policy.

Of the 7 Associate Agencies with Tenure of at least two years but less than three years located in counties with greater than 500,000 people, 3 Associate Agencies, or 43%, exceeded the Average revenue per policy. Of the 2 Associate Agencies with the top 25% Average revenue per policy, 1 Associate Agencies, or 50%, exceeded the top 25% Average revenue per policy.

7. Of the 4 Associate Agencies with Tenure of at least one year but less than two years located in counties with less than 500,000 people, 2 Associate Agencies, or 50%, exceeded the Average revenue per policy. Of the 1 Associate Agencies with the top 25% Average revenue per policy, 0 Associate Agencies, or 0%, exceeded the top 25% Average revenue per policy.

Of the 9 Associate Agencies with Tenure of at least one year but less than two years located in counties with greater than 500,000 people, 4 Associate Agencies, or 44%, exceeded the Average revenue per policy. Of the 2 Associate Agencies with the top 25% Average revenue per policy, 1 Associate Agencies, or 50%, exceeded the top 25% Average revenue per policy.

8. Of the 23 Associate Agencies whose data are presented in Table 4-A above (and are located in counties with less than 500,000 people), 10 Associate Agencies, or 43%, exceeded the

overall Average revenue per policy set forth in Table 4-A. Of the 6 Associate Agencies with the top 25% Average revenue per policy in this subset of Associate Agencies, 2 Associate Agencies, or 33%, exceeded the top 25% Average revenue per policy.

Of the 51 Associate Agencies whose data are presented in Table 4-B above (and are located in counties with greater than 500,000 people), 21 Associate Agencies, or 41%, exceeded the overall Average revenue per policy set forth in Table 4-B. Of the 13 Associate Agencies with the top 25% Average revenue per policy in this subset of Associate Agencies, 6 Associate Agencies, or 46%, exceeded the top 25% Average revenue per policy.

PART II

Part II of this Item sets forth certain revenue and expense information for the franchised Associate Agencies operating for at least one full calendar year. This Part II of Item 19 contains information for Associate Agencies that were open at least one full calendar year as of December 31, 2013 and that reported their expenses to Brightway in response to a survey sent to all Associate Agencies. Excluded from this Part II are the following: (i) AAOs who have not been receiving commissions for a full calendar year as of December 31, 2013; (ii) our company-owned Agency; and (iii) AAOs whose survey results were incomplete or materially deficient. The AAOs included in Part II of this Item shall be referred to as the "Representative Associate Agencies". There are 69 Representative Associate Agencies contained in Part II.

In Table 5, we provide certain revenue and expense information for the Representative Associate Agencies. The primary purpose of Table 5 below is to disclose the average annual amount of various types of expenses incurred by Representative Associate Agencies as of the end of 2013. Table 5 is also intended to show how the different types of expenses change in relation to the amount of corresponding average revenues reported. The information set forth in Table 5 is the result of averaging reported annual expenses from Representative Associate Agencies that by the end of the 2013 calendar year were open anywhere from one full year to six or more years. See Part I of Item 19 for a breakout of average annual revenue based on number of years open (which we refer to as "Tenure").

When examining these figures, please note that Gross Revenue already incorporates the percentage of commissions that are retained by us as a royalty, comprising 15% of the Brightway Sales Commissions owed to us for New Accounts and 45% of the Brightway Sales Commissions owed to us for Renewal Accounts (as described more fully in Item 6). In other words, the royalty owed to us has already been deducted before arriving at the Gross Revenue figures set forth in Table 5. Additionally, please note that some of the AAO's below brought books of business with them when they opened their Agency, which increased their initial revenue figures. Substantiation of the data used in preparing this information will be made available upon reasonable request.

TABLE 5
AVERAGE REVENUE AND EXPENSE INFORMATION OF REPRESENTATIVE ASSOCIATE AGENCIES
FOR THE 2013 CALENDAR YEAR

	Average[1]	% of Rev.	Top 25% Average[1]	% of Rev. (Top 25%)
Revenue	256,554[2]		$434,532[2]	
Total Compensation	146,975[3]	57.3%	$216,688[3]	49.9%
Gross Profit	109,579[4]	42.7%	$217,844[4]	50.1%
Total Other Expenses	78,934[5]	30.8%	$88,002[5]	20.3%
Owner Benefit	30,645[6]	11.9%	$129,842[6]	29.9%
Owner Pre-Tax Earnings	$59,380[6]	23.1%	$196,412[6]	45.2%
Avg. No. of Producers (including owner)	3.57[7]		4.44[7]	
Avg. Revenue per Producer	$71,864[8]		$97,868[8]	
Avg. Total Compensation per Producer (including owner)	$41,169[9]		$48,804[9]	

Notes to Table 5

1. In this Table 5, we present average revenue and expense information for the Representative Associate Agencies contained in Part II of this Item. The averages were calculated by taking the sum of each line item for each of the Representative Associate Agencies and dividing that sum by the total number of Representative Associate Agencies in this Part II, which is 69. The "Top 25% Average" column in Table 5 represent the averages of the top 17 of the 69 Representative Associate Agencies (in terms of Owner Pre-Tax Earnings6) in this Part II of Item 19.

2. The term "Revenue" means the Brightway Sales Commissions (commissions paid by the Contracted Companies to us or assigned by you to us for the sale, renewal, service or delivery of a specific policy through you) earned by our Representative Associate Agencies, less the 15% royalty owed to us for New Business and the 45% royalty owed to us for Renewal Business. "Revenue" is exclusive of: (a) "AAO Shared Expenses" (as described more fully in Note 3 to Item 6); and (b) all other costs and expenses you incur in the operation of your Agency, including all other fees payable to us or our affiliates. Of the 69 Representative Associate Agencies, 27 Associate Agencies, or 39%, exceeded the average Revenue set forth in Table 5. Of the 17 Representative Associate Agencies with the top 25% of Owner Pre-Tax Earnings, 6 Associate Agencies, or 35%, exceeded the average top 25% Revenue set forth in Table 5.

3. The term "Total Compensation" means the total payroll, payroll taxes and pension, and insurance and benefits reported by the Representative Associate Agencies, including owner compensation. Of the $146,975 in average Total Compensation, there was an average of $133,933 in total payroll (including an average of $28,735 in payroll for the owner(s) of the Agency), $10,030 in payroll taxes and pension, and $3,012 in insurance and benefits. Of the 69 Representative Associate Agencies, 28 Associate Agencies, or 41%, exceeded the average Total Compensation set forth in Table 5. Of the 69 Representative Associate Agencies, 26 Associate Agencies, or 38%, exceeded the $28,735 average payroll for the owner(s) of the Agency. Of the $216,688 in average top 25% Total Compensation, there was an average of $195,556 in total payroll (including an average of $66,570 in payroll for the owner(s) of the Agency), $13,477 in payroll taxes and pension, and $7,654 in insurance and benefits. Of the 17 Representative Associate Agencies with the top 25% of Owner Pre-Tax Earnings, 3 Associate Agencies, or 18%, exceeded the average top 25% Total Compensation set forth in Table 5. Of the 17 Representative Associate Agencies with the top 25% of Owner Pre-Tax Earnings, 6 Associate Agencies, or 35%, exceeded the $66,570 top 25% average payroll for the owner(s) of the Agency.

4. The term "Gross Profit" means the Revenue subtracted by the Total Compensation, which includes owner compensation. Of the 69 Representative Associate Agencies, 24 Associate Agencies, or 35%, exceeded the average Gross Profit set forth in Table 5. Of the 17 Representative Associate Agencies with the top 25% of Owner Pre-Tax Earnings, 7 Associate Agencies, or 41%, exceeded the average top 25% Gross Profit set forth in Table 5.

5. The term "Total Other Expenses" means the total advertising expenses, selling expenses, dues and subscriptions, rent, utilities and upkeep, telephone, automation and service agreement expenses, accounting, legal, and finance related expenses, errors & omissions and other insurance expenses and other office expenses (continuing education, supplies, printing, postage and miscellaneous) reported by the Representative Associate Agencies. Of the $78,934 in average Total Other Expenses, there was an average of $8,670 in advertising expenses, $6,475 in selling expenses, $4,505 in dues and subscriptions, $25,126 in rent, utilities, and upkeep, $12,830 in telephone, automation and service agreement expenses, $6,408 in legal, accounting and finance related expenses, $6,104 in errors & omissions and other insurance expenses and $8,816 in other office expenses. Of the 69 Representative Associate Agencies, 22 Associate Agencies, or 32%, exceeded the average Total Other Expenses set forth in Table 5. Of the 17 Representative Associate Agencies with the top 25% of Owner Pre-Tax Earnings, 7 Associate Agencies, or 41%, exceeded the average top 25% Total Other Expenses set forth in Table 5.

6. The term "Owner Benefit" means Revenues less the sum of Total Compensation, including owner compensation, and Total Other Expenses. Of the 69 Representative Associate Agencies, 28, or 41%, exceeded the average Owner Benefit set forth in Table 5. Of the 17 Representative Associate Agencies with the top 25% of Revenue, 7 Associate Agencies, or 41%, exceeded the average top 25% Owner Benefit set forth in Table 5. Combining the average Owner Benefit set forth in Table 5 and the average payroll for the owner set forth in Note 3 of Table 5 results in a total of $59,380 in "Owner Pre-Tax Earnings". Of the 69 Representative Associate Agencies, 28, or 41%, exceeded the $59,380 average pre-tax earnings to the owner(s) of the Agency. Combining the average top 25% Owner Benefit set forth in Table 5 and the average payroll for the owner set forth in Note 3 of Table 5 results in a total of $196,412 in "Owner Pre-Tax Earnings" for the top 25% Agencies. Of the 17 top 25% Representative Associate Agencies, 7, or 41%, exceeded the $196,412 average pre-tax earnings to the owner(s) of the Agency.

7. The term "Average Number of Producers" means the average number of producers, including owners, reported by each of the Representative Associate Agencies who eligible to receive commissions as of 12/31/2013. Of the 69 Representative Associate Agencies, 34, or 49%, exceeded the Average Number of

Producers set forth in Table 5. Of the 17 Representative Associate Agencies with the top 25% of Owner Pre-Tax Earnings, 6 Associate Agencies, or 35%, exceeded the top 25% Average Number of Producers set forth in Table 5.

8. The term "Average Revenue per Producer" means the average Revenue set forth in Table 5 divided by the Average Number of Producers set forth in Table 5. Of the 69 Representative Associate Agencies, 31, or 45%, exceeded the Average Revenue per Producer set forth in Table 5. Of the 17 Representative Associate Agencies with the top 25% of Owner Pre-Tax Earnings, 6 Associate Agencies, or 35%, exceeded the top 25% Average Revenue per Producer set forth in Table 5.

9. The term "Average Total Compensation per Producer" means the average Total Compensation set forth in Table 5 divided by the Average Number of Producers set forth in Table 5. Of the 69 Representative Associate Agencies, 22, or 32%, exceeded the Average Total Compensation per Producer set forth in Table 5. Of the 17 Representative Associate Agencies with the top 25% of Owner Pre-Tax Earnings, 3 Associate Agencies, or 18%, exceeded the average top 25% Total Compensation per Producer set forth in Table 5.

PART III

Part III of this Item sets forth information regarding the average amount of "New Business" premiums sold by each producer working in the office of franchised Associate Agencies operating for between four and five years as of December 31, 2013. The AAOs included in Part III of this Item shall be referred to as the "Representative Associate Agencies." There are 15 Representative Associate Agencies contained in Part III. Part III also presents industry average data for independent agencies that have been operating between four and five years as of December 31, 2013, as reported in the IIABA 2013 Best Practices Study, which captured annual new business property and casualty insurance premium data from the top ~250 agencies in the country broken out by line of business to highlight how the best performing agencies in the country fare. These are among the best-performing agencies selling personal and commercial lines of property and casualty insurance throughout the U.S. The results of the comparative analysis presented are based upon a comparison of the personal lines new business premium data captured in the Study versus the New Business premiums (which is predominately personal lines premiums) generated by similarly tenured Representative Associate Agencies (who are predominately located in Florida).

BRIGHTWAY Average Dollar Value of "New Business" Premiums sold per Producer during the 2013 calendar year (tenure of 4-5 years): $598,020

INDUSTRY Average Dollar Value of "New Business" Premi-

ums per Producer during the 2013 calendar year (tenure of 4-5 years): $246,504

The Brightway Average Dollar Value of "New Business" Premiums sold per Producer during the 2013 calendar year was calculated by summing the total premiums of all "New Business" sold by Representative Associate Agencies during the 2013 calendar year, and dividing that number by the total number of producers of the Representative Associate Agencies. Of the 42 producers in the 15 Representative Associate Agencies, 12 producers, or 29%, exceeded the Brightway Average Dollar Value of "New Business" Premiums sold per Producer during the 2013 calendar year set forth above. The Industry Average Dollar Value of "New Business" Premiums sold per Producer during the 2013 calendar year is set forth in the IIABA 2013 Best Practices Study.

GENERAL NOTES TO ITEM 19

1. Some AAOs have earned the above amounts. There is no assurance that you will earn as much. You should not use the information set forth in the above charts as an indication of how well your franchise will do. Actual results vary from Associate Agency to Associate Agency, and we cannot estimate the performance of a particular Associate Agency. Revenues and expenses may vary. In particular, the revenues and expenses of your business will be directly affected by many factors, such as: (a) geographic location; (b) advertising effectiveness based on market saturation; (c) whether you operate the business personally or hire a manager; (d) employee salaries and benefits; (e) insurance costs; (f) ability to generate customers; (g) customer loyalty; and (h) employment conditions in the market.

2. No assurances can be given and we do not represent that any particular AAO will achieve financial results similar to the sales reported here. Your sales as a start-up enterprise may vary substantially as compared to the sales disclosed in the charts above. We are providing you with the preceding data with the understanding that you will do your own research to develop data with which to perform your analysis. Reviewing this limited amount of information cannot substitute for thorough research on your part and careful evaluation of this franchise opportunity with professional and legal advisors.

3. This analysis does not contain complete information concerning the operating costs and expenses that you will incur in operating your Associate Agency. Operating costs and expenses may vary substantially from business to business.

4. There is no assurance that you will do as well as the Associate Agencies discussed above. If you rely upon the above figures, you must accept the risk of not doing as well. Importantly, you should not consider the Gross Revenues presented in the tables above to be the actual potential gross revenues

that you will realize. We do not represent that you can or will attain these levels of sales or revenues, or any particular level of sales or revenues. We do not represent that you will generate income, which exceeds the initial payment of, or investment in, the franchise. Therefore, we recommend that you make your own independent investigation to determine whether or not the franchise may be profitable to you. You should use the above information only as a reference in conducting your analysis and preparing your own projected income statements and cash flow statements. We suggest strongly that you consult your financial advisor or personal accountant concerning the preparation of your financial projections, including any applicable taxes that you may incur in operating an Associate Agency.

5. Other than the preceding financial performance representation, we do not make any financial performance representations. We also do not authorize our employees or representatives to make any such representations either orally or in writing. If you are purchasing an existing Associate Agency, however, we may provide you with the actual records of that Associate Agency. If you receive any other financial performance information or projections of your future income, you should report it to our management by contacting David Miller from our corporate offices at Brightway Insurance, Inc., 3733 West University Boulevard, Suite 100, Jacksonville, Florida 32217, (904) 764-9554, the Federal Trade Commission, and the appropriate state regulatory agencies.

CMIT SOLUTIONS

500 N. Capital of TX HWY, Bldg. 6, # 200
Austin, TX 78746
Tel: (800) 710-2648, (512) 789-4512
Fax: (512) 692-3711
Email: svandermause@cmitsolutions.com
Website: www.cmitfranchise.com
Sheri Vandermause, Vice President of Franchise Development

CMIT Solutions offers IT-managed services and computer support to small businesses. Franchise can be home-based, as we service the clients remotely or at their place of business.

BACKGROUND

IFA Member:	Yes
Established & First Franchised:	1996; 1996
Franchised Units:	144
Company-Owned Units:	0
Total Units:	144
Distribution:	US – 143; CAN – 1; O'seas – 0
North America:	32 States, 1 Province
Projected New Units (12 Months):	20
Qualifications:	2, 3, 4, 2, 4, 4

FINANCIAL/TERMS

Cash Investment:	$50 – 70K
Total Investment:	$129.2 – 171.5K
Minimum Net Worth:	$350K
Fees (Franchise):	$49.5K
Fees (Royalty):	6 – 0%
Fees (Advertising):	2%
Term of Contract (Years):	10/10
Average Number of Employees:	1-2 FT, 1-2 PT
Passive Ownership:	Allowed
Encourage Conversions:	Yes
Area Development Agreements:	Yes
Sub-Franchising Contracts:	No
Expand in Territory:	No
Space Needs:	N/A

SUPPORT & TRAINING

Financial Assistance Provided:	No
Site Selection Assistance:	N/A
Lease Negotiation Assistance:	N/A
Co-operative Advertising:	No
Franchisee Association/Member:	No
Size of Corporate Staff:	17
On-going Support:	A, B, C, d, G, H, I
Training:	2 Weeks Austin, TX; 2 Weeks Jump Start

SPECIFIC EXPANSION PLANS

US:	All United States
Canada:	Yes
Overseas:	No

The following survey of CMIT franchisees was conducted during March 2014 (the "March 2014 Survey"). We have relied on the March 2014 Survey to show information regarding prices charged for specified services and information regarding the costs and billing rates of employed technicians. The March 2014 Survey report measures only a few aspects of the historic financial performance of those existing franchisees who responded to the survey.

At the time of the March 2014 Survey there were a total of 122 franchisees in the CMIT System operating 137 territories. A total of 64 franchisees voluntarily responded to the survey, which represents 52% of the operating franchisees in the system. The number of responses varied for each question asked, as not all CMIT Solutions franchisees surveyed offer all of the products or services referred to in the survey. We have not audited this information to confirm that it is correct, and have relied on the information provided directly by responding franchisees. There are no material differences between the businesses operated by the respondents to this survey and the franchise offering described in this franchise disclosure document.

"Cash Flow Break-Even" Calculation

For planning purposes, the achievement of $8,000 in monthly gross professional services revenue is an approximate cash flow break-even figure, based on our estimate of the expenses needed to run a CMIT Solutions business. The monthly cash flow break-even figure will be more for some franchisees and less for others, depending on the level of the franchisee's overhead expenses. This information is based on our experience and was not supplied directly by our franchisees. We cannot estimate the number or percentage of franchisees whose expenses met or exceeded these estimates.

The chart below shows expenses compiled directly from the estimates we provide in Items 6 and 7 and is intended for your general assistance in preparing your own cost estimates. For Technical Staffing, we used the lowest figure representing a typical monthly expense for a part-time Level 2 Technician while the business is starting. During the initial launch period of the franchise we have found that a new franchised business does not have enough client business to justify a full-time technician, and it usually either hires or contracts with a part-time technician or shares a full-time technician with a neighboring franchisee. Based on these estimated costs, we conclude that $8,000 in Gross Professional Services (GPS) revenues is a workable cash flow break-even figure. Your actual cash flow break-even may differ from this based on your individual decision to charge additional expenses to your business, or your individual decision to rent outside office space, etc.

Cash Flow Break-Even Calculation

Monthly Recurring Expenses - CMIT		Notes	In FDD
Marketing	$2,000.00		Item 7
Technical Staffing*	$3,000.00		Item 7
Royalty	$600.00		Item 6
MDF	$150.00		Item 6
Technology Fee	$ 75.00		Item 6
Virtual office	$100.00		Item 7
Autotask	$ 60.00		Item 6
Convention club	$ 50.00		Item 6
Technology Insurance	$125.00		Item 7
Cell phone, Internet	$200.00		Item 7**
Miscellaneous expenses	$200.00		Item 7**
Total Recurring Monthly Expenses (Fixed costs)	$6,560.00		Not applicable
Total Variable Network Operations Center Cost (Variable costs)	$1,248.00	Assumes 78 managed seats***	Not applicable
Total Monthly Recurring Expenses	$7,808.00		

*Calculation: The fixed expense for a part-time (20 hours/week) technician of $3,000 is calculated as follows: The average hourly cost of a Level 2 Technician is $28.62, as per our March 2014 Survey. Calculation: $28.62 x 20 hours a week x 52 weeks / 12 months = $2,480 per month. We round up this figure to $3,000/month for budgeting purposes.

**While not specifically broken out in Item 7, these figures are estimated averages based on management's 17 years' experience as a franchisor.

*** This assumes our Marathon Performance+ offering, and uses reported costs and the average prices charged by our Franchisees as provided in the March 2014 Survey.

Survey Response Regarding Prices Being Charged for Marathon Managed Services

"Managed Services" refers to long-term recurring revenue contracts for delivery of services such as remote monitoring and remediation, help desk support, back-up and disaster recovery services, data security and intrusion prevention, cloud computing solutions, and a host of other services. CMIT Solutions' managed services are offered under the brand name "MARATHON" and are in many cases delivered by a centralized service center. This efficiency allows CMIT Solutions to reduce the cost to the franchisee, and ultimately deliver higher levels of service at greatly reduced cost to the end-user. The terms "managed seat" or "managed employee" refers to the price for contract services charged to clients on a per/device or per/employee basis. Servers are more complex to monitor, proactively manage, and require different tools and skill sets to manage effectively. Our CMIT Solutions Marathon program has three service levels: "Marathon Performance," which represents the 24X7 monitoring maintenance and remediation only; "Marathon Performance Plus" which adds business hours or 24X7 help desk services to the monitoring; and Marathon Performance Ultra, which adds any necessary on-site work by a technician that may be required – all for a flat monthly fee.

Prices Charged for Marathon Managed Services

The table below shows the lowest monthly charges, the average monthly charges, and the highest monthly charges per "managed seat" and "per server" for our Marathon managed service offerings as reported to us in the March 2014 Survey. Most of our Franchisees offer two levels of Marathon service.

		Prices Charged to Clients under each of CMIT Solutions' Marathon Offerings (Prices shown on a "per-workstation" or "per server" basis)		
	Per Workstation Costs	Marathon Performance (Basic Workstation or Laptop Monitoring) $3.00 per workstation	Marathon Performance+ (Includes "Performance" plus End-User 8am-5pm Help-Desk) $16.00	Marathon Ultra (Includes "Performance+" and Unlimited On-Site Support)
	# of Franchisees Offering	56	25	55
Per workstation pricing to end user	Low	$15.00	$25.00	$30.00
	Average	$27.71	$54.59	$83.36
	High	$48.00	$85.00	$135.00
	Per Server Cost	Marathon Performance per Server $30 per server	Marathon Performance Plus per Server $30 per server	Marathon Ultra per Server
	# of Franchisees Offering	57	51	55
Per server pricing to end user	Low	$70.00	$125.00	$75.00
	Average	$121.91	$188.73	$286.18
	High	$210.00	$385.00	$500.00

Marathon Client Size and Number

For centralized Marathon services provided in February 2014, a centrally managed service for which we receive full operating data from our supplier, we have summarized the number of clients in our system for which Marathon services were provided. The data was generated for 117 franchisees, which is every franchisee in our system offering Marathon services in February 2014. This compilation of data from 117 franchisees constituted 96% of the total of 122 franchisees in operation at that time.

The data for February 2014 shows that the average size of a client receiving CMIT Solutions Marathon service was 9.7 desktops and 1.3 servers managed, per client.

The table below shows the low, average and high number of clients served by CMIT Solutions franchisees during the month of February of 2014.

The Number of Marathon Clients Served in February 2014

# of Franchisees Reporting	# of Clients: Low Figure	# of Clients: Average Figure	# of Clients: High Figure	# of Franchisees that Exceeded Average	% of Franchisees that Exceeded Average
117	1	17.9	132	43	37%

Survey of Labor Costs and Billing Rates

The table below shows the hourly pay rate and client hourly billing rate for Levels 1, 2 and 3 Technicians reported by our franchisees in the March 2014 Survey.

A "Level 1 Technician" is defined as an entry-level or junior technician with 2 years' experience, mostly on desktops.

A "Level 2 Technician" is defined as a senior technician with 2 – 5 years' experience, including network, server and workstations.

A "Level 3 Technician" is defined as a Network Engineer or a Sales Engineer.

Your labor costs will be determined by a number of factors, including the payment market where your franchise is located, the supply of qualified technicians, and the local economy.

Technician Labor Costs and Billing Rates

# Reporting in Survey		Technician – Hourly Labor Cost			# Exceeded Average	% Exceeded Average
		Low	Average	High		
34	Level 1 Technician	$10.00	$22.12	$50.00	16	47%
44	Level 2 Technician	$14.00	$28.62	$60.00	16	36%
31	Level 3 Technician	$20.00	$39.50	$90.00	14	45%

# Reporting in Survey		Technician – Hourly Billing Rate			# Exceeded Average	% Exceeded Average
		Low	Average	High		
44	Level 1 Technician	$95.00	$119.19	$165.00	24	55%
48	Level 2 Technician	$85.00	$120.93	$165.00	22	46%
41	Level 3 Technician	$85.00	$130.61	$180.00	20	49%

The difference between the amount charged for the specific services cited in the March 2014 Survey and the amount paid to employee technicians for the services illustrates a narrow measure of net revenue and does not reflect other expenses that may be directly or indirectly paid from that revenue, such as office and equipment overhead, taxes, franchise royalties, and employee wages and benefits.

The rates charged to clients and paid to employee technicians in your market will be affected by a number of factors, including the strength of the market in your area for computer services, employee payment rate levels, and the existence of competition for computer services and qualified computer technicians in your market.

Revenue Snap Shot

The following revenue table shows a breakdown of gross revenue figures to illustrate the sources of revenue in a single franchised CMIT Solutions business. These figures are not representative of what you may expect to make in your business, and are based on the 2013 revenue of a single franchise owner. This owner reported to us total Gross Annual Revenue of $1,021,892. In 2013, 10 franchisees reported achieving revenues of $1,000,000 or more, which puts this franchisee in the top 10% of the CMIT Solutions System. That means that 10 franchisees, or 10% of the entire CMIT Solutions System that had operated for the entire 12 months of 2013 met or exceeded this Gross Annual Revenue figure. The figures in this table are revenue figures only; they do not reflect the franchisee's fees paid to us or the overhead expenses carried by this franchised business, and they are based entirely on the information supplied by the franchisee; the figures have not been audited or otherwise independently confirmed.

	Revenue	Percentage of Gross Revenue
Managed Services	$417,556.50	41%
Professional Services	$358,449/78	35%
Hardware/Software	$241,750.85	24%
Other	$4,134.56	0.4%
Total	$1,021,891.69	100%

These figures do not reflect the costs of sales, operating expenses, or other costs or expenses that must be deducted from the gross revenue or gross sales figures to obtain your net income or profit. You should conduct an independent investigation of the costs and expenses you will incur in operating your CMIT Solutions business. Franchisees or former franchisees listed in this franchise disclosure document may be one source of this information. Some of our franchisees have earned and charged these amounts. Your individual results may differ. There is no assurance that you will earn or charge as much. We have written substantiation to support the representations presented in this Item 19. Written substantiation of the data used in preparing this statement will be made available to you on reasonable request.

Other than the preceding financial performance representation, CMIT Solutions does not make any financial performance representations. We also do not authorize our employees or representatives to make such representations either orally or in writing. If you are purchasing an existing outlet, however, we may provide you with the actual records of that outlet. If you receive any other financial performance information or projections of your future income, you should report it to our management by contacting Sheri Vandermause at 500 N. Capital of Texas Hwy., Bldg 6 Ste 200, Austin TX 78746, telephone number (800) 710-2648, the Federal Trade Commission, and the appropriate state regulatory agencies.

COLOR GLO INTERNATIONAL

7111-7115 Ohms Ln.
Minneapolis, MN 55439
Tel: (800) 333-8523, (952) 835-1338
Fax: (952) 835-1395
Email: scott@colorglo.com
Website: www.colorglo.com
Scott L. Smith, Vice President Franchise Sales

The leader in the leather and fabric restoration and repair industry. From automotive to marine to aircraft to all-leather furniture, COLOR-GLO leads the way with innovative products and protected application techniques. We serve all US and foreign car manufacturers. We were also recently awarded a Top 100 Franchise by Franchise Gator and a Top 50 Franchise by Franchise Business Review.

BACKGROUND

IFA Member:	Yes
Established & First Franchised:	1976; 1984
Franchised Units:	125
Company-Owned Units:	0
Total Units:	125
Distribution:	US – 90; CAN – 1; O'seas – 32

North America:	30 States, 1 Province	Expand in Territory:	Yes
Density:	12 in FL, 8 in WA, 7 in OR	Space Needs:	N/A
Projected New Units (12 Months):	12		
Qualifications:	4, 4, 3, 4, 3, 3	SUPPORT & TRAINING	
		Financial Assistance Provided:	Yes (D)
FINANCIAL/TERMS		Site Selection Assistance:	Yes
Cash Investment:	$44.9K	Lease Negotiation Assistance:	N/A
Total Investment:	$51 – 54.8K	Co-operative Advertising:	No
Minimum Net Worth:	$50K	Franchisee Association/Member:	Yes/Member
Fees (Franchise):	$30K	Size of Corporate Staff:	15
Fees (Royalty):	4% or $300 monthly	On-going Support:	B, C, D, G, H, I
Fees (Advertising):	0%	Training:	2 weeks Headquarters, MN;
Term of Contract (Years):	10/10		1 week Franchisee's territory
Average Number of Employees:	1 FT, 0 PT		
Passive Ownership:	Discouraged	SPECIFIC EXPANSION PLANS	
Encourage Conversions:	N/A	US:	All United States
Area Development Agreements:	Yes	Canada:	All Canada
Sub-Franchising Contracts:	Yes	Overseas:	All Countries

A new franchisee's financial results may differ from the results stated.

Written substantiation for the financial performance representation will be made available to the prospective franchisee upon request.

The following Calculation of Potential Gross Profit includes estimates of gross profit at seven different sales volumes. During the calendar year individual gross sales of existing Color Glo franchisees ranged from $20,000 to $30,000. The actual amount of total revenue may vary among franchisees as each franchisee has the right to charg more for each service or to discount as necessary. Market conditions and geographic differences may also cause a difference in the amount a franchisee may charge for services rendered.

The calculation does not include any estimate of a franchisee's overhead expenses, such as office space, vehicle costs, or insurance, or advertising, legal and accounting fees. Paying for office space is optional to each franchisee. The purchase of a cehicle varies based upon the age and quality of the vehicle.

Most franchisees earn the amounts disclosed in categories 3-5. Your individual results may differ. There is no assurance that you will earn this much.

Unaudited Calculation of Potential Annual Gross Profit

GROSS SALES	COST OF PRODUCT	MAINTENANCE FEE	GROSS PROFIT
$20,000	$2,500	$800	$16,700
$50,000	$2,500	$2,000	$45,500
$100,000	$2,500	$4,000	$93,500
$150,000	$2,500	$6,000	$141,500
$200,000	$2,500	$8,000	$184,500
$250,000	$2,500	$10,000	$237,500
$300,000	$2,500	$12,000	$285,500

The definition of the factors used to calculate the revenue and costs are as follows:

1) Gross Sales. During the calendar year, the individual gross sales of existing Color Glo franchisees ranged from $20,000.00 to $30,000.00. Gross sales are the results of the number of services performed times the price charged to the customer for the service. The existing franchisees of Color Glo will charge differently for the type of service performed. Following is an example of charges for repair and/or re-dye of leather seats. The pricing will range from $30.00 on the low side to $250.00 on the high side with $80.00 being on the medium side. Thus using the $30,000.00 figure for gross sales, the franchisee would need to repair and/or re-dye 375 leather seats per year at an average price of $80.00.

2) Cost of Product. Color Glo's existing franchisees cost of product ranges from 8% to 13% of gross sales. The variance depends primarily upon the efficiency in the use of products by the franchisee as well as the size of the services performed and the number of services performed. Experience usually re-sults in a more efficient use of the products. The $2,500.00 product cost is shown for the example using zero gross sales due to the minimum purchase requirement contained in the franchise agreement. The cost of product figures includes the proprietary Color Glo products.

3) Maintenance Fee. The Maintenance Fee is calculated at 4% of Gross Sales.

4) Gross Profit. Gross Profit is calculated by subtracting cost of product and royalty from Gross Sales. The estimated gross profit in the above examples ranges from 83% to 88% of gross sales.

5) Net Profit. To calculate Net Profit, expenses incurred for overhead expenses such as office space, vehicle expense, insurance, advertising, legal and accounting fees. Color Glo does not obtain these costs from franchisees. The above calculation includes the minimal estimate for vehicle expense, insurance and advertising expenses only.

Percentage of franchisees in operation for the last calendar year that achieved the above Gross Sales and Gross Profit levels:

2 (3.23%)	4 (6.45%)	9 (14.52%)	42 (35.48%)	14 (22.58%)	9 (14.52%)	1 (1.61%)

COMFORCARE SENIOR SERVICES

2520 Telegraph Rd., # 201
Bloomfield Hills, MI 48302
Tel: (800) 886-4044, (248) 745-9700
Fax: (248) 745-9763
Email: pleblanc@comforcare.com
Website: www.comforcarefranchise.com
Phil LeBlanc, Vice President of Franchise Development

ComForcare Senior Services franchise members provide non-medical home care (assistance with the activities of daily living via companion and personal care services) and skilled nursing services to all members of the community, but primarily to the exploding market of those over the age of 65. ComForcare franchise members provide the increasingly-needed services that support individuals' independence, dignity, and quality of life.

BACKGROUND

IFA Member:	Yes
Established & First Franchised:	1996; 2001
Franchised Units:	197
Company-Owned Units:	0
Total Units:	197
Distribution:	US – 193; CAN – 3; O'seas – 1
North America:	32 States, 1 Province
Density:	13 in MI, 19 in NJ, 29 in CA
Projected New Units (12 Months):	40
Qualifications:	5, 5, 2, 4, 3, 5

FINANCIAL/TERMS

Cash Investment:	$50 – 75K
Total Investment:	$77.8 – 141.8K
Minimum Net Worth:	$300K
Fees (Franchise):	$42K
Fees (Royalty):	5 – 3% (Decl.)
Fees (Advertising):	0%
Term of Contract (Years):	10/10
Average Number of Employees:	2 FT, Varies Based on Case Load PT
Passive Ownership:	Not Allowed
Encourage Conversions:	No
Area Development Agreements:	No
Sub-Franchising Contracts:	No
Expand in Territory:	Yes
Space Needs:	500 (avg) SF

SUPPORT & TRAINING

Financial Assistance Provided:	Yes (I)
Site Selection Assistance:	Yes
Lease Negotiation Assistance:	Yes
Co-operative Advertising:	No
Franchisee Association/Member:	No
Size of Corporate Staff:	30
On-going Support:	A, B, C, D, E, G, H, I
Training:	1 Week Home; 2 Weeks Bloomfield Hills, MI;1 Week Franchise Location

SPECIFIC EXPANSION PLANS

US:	All United States
Canada:	All Canada
Overseas:	Australia/New Zealand, Europe, Asia, South America

Other than the preceding financial performance representation, ComForcare does not make any financial performance representations. We also do not authorize our employees or representatives to make any such representations either orally or in writing. If you are purchasing an existing outlet, however, we may provide you with the actual records of that outlet. If you receive any other financial performance information or projections of your future income, you should report it to the franchisor's management by contacting Philip LeBlanc at ComForcare Health Care Holdings, Inc., 2520 S. Telegraph Road, Suite 201, Bloomfield Hills, MI 48302, 248-745-9700, the Federal Trade Commission and the appropriate state regulatory agencies.

This Item 19 contains historical financial performance data as provided by certain franchisees; and thus we have a reasonable basis and written substantiation for the representation set forth below. Written substantiation of the data used in preparing this information and for the financial performance representation made in this Item 19 will be made available to you upon reasonable request. The representations made in this Item 19 are based upon the franchise system's outlets existing for the period of time indicated below unless otherwise specifically excluded, as discussed below.

Importantly, the success of your franchise will depend largely upon your personal abilities, your use of those abilities and your market. Some franchisees have generated gross sales in the amounts shown in the table below. Your individual results may differ. There is no assurance you will achieve gross sales in these amounts.

The data in Table A below contains certain information re-

lated to gross sales realized only by our franchisees open for the period January 1, 2013 through December 31, 2013 and does not include any sales taxes. We consider an office to be open once they have completed their training, their assigned door opening tasks and are able to provide, at least, unlicensed homemaker/companionship services within their exclusive area.

The gross sales amounts presented in Table A below are based upon information reported to us by only ComForcare franchisees whose offices have been open for at least 24-months for the period ending December 31, 2013, and only for those offices that have reported a full 12 months of gross sales data in each of the last two years. We have found that first and second year performance is not indicative of the franchise system as a whole. The gross sales amounts presented in Table A below do not include: (1) data for territories purchased and not yet opened by franchise owners and (2) data for territories held by owners for resale that have been idled pending location of a buyer. In some instances ComForcare franchise owners have purchased more than one franchise territory and report franchise sales and royalty information as a single unit for all territories they own and/or operate multiple territories out of one central office. In all such instances, we have reported these as single office gross sales data in the table below which has resulted in higher average gross sales.

The information has been extracted from royalty reports reported to ComForcare. We have not audited this information, nor have we independently verified this information. These figures are only estimates of what we think your gross sales could be. Your individual results may differ. There is no assurance that you will achieve the same results.

In addition, in conjunction with the services provided to seniors, the population size, density of seniors and number of people over the age of 65 in the exclusive areas for the franchise owners represented in Table A below may not be similar to, or representative of, the exclusive area you may purchase.

TABLE A – GROSS SALES INFORMATION FOR FRANCHISEES OPERATING AT LEAST TWO FULL YEARS							
Franchisee Time in Business	Total Owners	Average Owner's Gross Sales	Number/ Percent Attained or Exceeded Average	Median Owner's Gross Sales	Number/ Percent Attained or Exceeded Median	Highest and Second Highest Owner's Gross Sales	Lowest and Second Lowest Owner's Gross Sales
Franchisees – 109 months and greater	23	$1,380,731	7 (30%)	$898,840	12 (52%)	$6,560,194 $4,461,943	$463,558 $180,391
Franchisees – 85-108 months	22	$1,061,329	10 (45%)	$990,986	11 (50%)	$2,337,692 $1,003,081	$301,346 $202,410
Franchisees – 61-84 months	14	$1,012,000	4 (29%)	$743,066	7 (50%)	$2,826,403 $1,764,040	$448,120 $322,930
Franchisees – 49-60 months	26	$849,454	8 (31%)	$686,039	13 (50%)	$3,345,692 $1,848,083	$192,842 $190,436
Franchisees – 37-48 months	17	$650,472	6 (35%)	$397,017	9 (53%)	$2,208,282 $1,826,376	$188,936 $119,929
Franchisees – 25-36 months	13	$500,307	6 (46%)	$442,533	7 (54%)	$1,044,455 $935,057	$243,287 $191,630
Total/Average	115	$947,174	35 (30%)	$727,009	58 (50%)	n/a	n/a

Table Notes

(a) The 23 franchisees operating for 109 months and greater as listed in this table includes gross sales of $4,461,943 for the 12 months ended December 31, 2013 for the first franchisee who originally began operations on May 1, 1996, which is a sister company to ComForcare and who is affiliated through a common owner.

(b) The 115 owner's data listed in the table and corresponding sales information includes the results of 17 additional franchise territories that were purchased by franchise owners who report sales and royalty information as a single unit for all territories owned and/or operate multiple territories out of one central office. For purposes of this data, 9 franchise owners have one additional territory operated out of a single office and 8 franchise owners have two additional territories operating out of a single office. We have included this data in the table as if they were single franchise owners, although this results in higher average reported gross sales results.

(c) This table includes offices opening in each year from 1996 through December 31, 2011 with the distribution of start dates as follows: 2011 – 13, 2010 – 17, 2009 – 26; 2008 – 8; 2007 – 6; 2006 – 12; 2005 – 10; 2004 – 8; 2003 - 10 ; 2002 – 4 and 1996 – 1. We consider an office to be open once they have completed their training, their assigned door opening tasks and are able to provide, at least, unlicensed homemaker/companionship services within their exclusive area.

Average Gross Margin % - Table B

The information contained in the tables below is historical, based on unaudited reporting by individual franchisees and may not be relied upon as a projection or forecast of what Gross Sales, Gross Margins or Marketing (Selling) Expenses a new franchisee may experience. The franchised offices that reported data for Table B below may not be the same as those reporting under Table A above. These are not the only metrics associated with the operations of your business. There is no assurance that your metrics will be comparable to our other franchisees. These Business Performance Metrics were generated from our internal 2013 Benchmarking Survey. Only offices that were open since January 1, 2013 were allowed to participate and all figures reported were only through the first six months of 2013 ending June 30, 2013. Not all offices that were open prior to January 1, 2013 participated in the 2013 Benchmarking Survey. Moreover, only offices that provided both information on their Gross Sales and Costs of Goods Sold (as defined below) were included in Table B. These figures were not independently audited.

TABLE B — 2013 AVERAGE GROSS MARGINS %			
Franchisee Annualized Gross Sales	Total Owners	Average Owner's Gross Margin %	Number/Percent Attained or Exceeded Average
Up to $300,000	14	30.47%	7 (50%)
$300,000 to $900,000	37	37.05%	18 (49%)
$900,000 and Over	22	34.25%	13 (59%)
Total/Average	73	35.07%	38 (52%)

Gross Margin means total revenue (gross sales) less the Cost of Goods Sold (COGS). COGS, for purposes of this disclosure, includes direct costs related to direct care staff including wages, state and federal related payroll taxes and workers' compensation insurance. Gross Margin % means the percentage derived by dividing Gross Margins by Gross Sales.

These disclosure figures do not reflect all other costs or expenses that must be deducted from the gross revenue or gross sales figures to obtain your net income or profit. You should conduct an independent investigation of costs and expenses you will incur in operating your franchise business. Current franchisees or former franchisees listed in the disclosure document may be one source of this information.

Based on all of the matters mentioned in this Item 19, we recommend that you make your own independent investigation to determine whether or not the franchise may be profitable to you and worth the risk. We suggest strongly that you consult your financial advisor or personal accountant concerning financial projections and federal, provincial and local income taxes and any other applicable taxes that you may incur in owning and operating a franchised business.

ComForcare will provide written substantiation for the financial performance representation to any prospective franchisee upon written, reasonable request.

COMFORT KEEPERS

6640 Poe Ave., # 200
Dayton, OH 45414
Tel: (888) 836-7488, (937) 665-1320
Fax: (937) 665-1360
Email: larryfrance@comfortkeepers.com
Website: www.comfortkeepersfranchise.com
Larry France, Manager, Franchise Development

COMFORT KEEPERS is the service leader with 95% client satisfaction. We provide in-home care, such as companionship, meal preparation, light housekeeping, grocery and clothing shopping, grooming and assistance with recreational activities for the elderly and others who need assistance in daily living.

BACKGROUND
IFA Member:	Yes
Established & First Franchised:	1998; 1999
Franchised Units:	666
Company-Owned Units:	17
Total Units:	683
Distribution:	US – 683; CAN – 57; O'seas – 40
North America:	47 States, 5 Provinces
Density:	45 in OH, 58 in FL, 88 in CA
Projected New Units (12 Months):	23
Qualifications:	5, 5, 2, 3, 3, 4

FINANCIAL/TERMS

Cash Investment:	$77.5K	SUPPORT & TRAINING	
Total Investment:	$77.5 – $109.6K	Financial Assistance Provided:	Yes (D)
Minimum Net Worth:	$300K	Site Selection Assistance:	No
Fees (Franchise):	$45K	Lease Negotiation Assistance:	No
Fees (Royalty):	5%	Co-operative Advertising:	Yes
Fees (Advertising):	2%	Franchisee Association/Member:	Yes/Member
Term of Contract (Years):	10/10	Size of Corporate Staff:	60
Average Number of Employees:	2 FT, 4 – 5 PT	On-going Support:	C, D, G, h, I
Passive Ownership:	Allowed	Training:	4 Weeks & Ongoing Dayton, OH
Encourage Conversions:	Yes		
Area Development Agreements:	No	SPECIFIC EXPANSION PLANS	
Sub-Franchising Contracts:	No	US:	All United States
Expand in Territory:	Yes	Canada:	Yes
Space Needs:	400 – 700 SF	Overseas:	Yes

Table A, Table B, and Tables PMG 1 through 3 are historical financial performance representations, based on revenue and, as applicable, expense experience reported by franchisees; we have not included in any of these tables the revenues or expense information for the Franchised Businesses we operate on behalf of our affiliate, SDX. For purposes of Table A, Table B, and Table PMG-1, "net revenue" means that revenue on which a franchisee pays royalty fees (but which is, in the Franchise Agreement, called "Gross Revenue"), that is, the total amount of money the franchisee and its owners receive for all goods sold and services rendered in connection with the Marks, and all other income of any kind derived directly or indirectly in connection with the operation of a Franchised Business, including Client deposits and payments for mileage charges but excluding sales tax and Client refunds. Tables PMG-2 and PMG-3 are based on billed revenue, rather than on revenue received.

Table A, on the next page, shows information relating to all Franchised Businesses operating at September 30, 2013 that had been operating for at least one year and reported revenue for every month during the period October 1, 2012 through September 30, 2013 (the "Reporting Period"). Table A shows net revenue achieved during the Reporting Period by Franchised Businesses that had been operating the specified number of months. The last line in the table shows information relating to net revenue for the Reporting Period for all of the Franchised Businesses included above in the table.

We used the Start Date for a Franchised Business as the date its operations began. Under a Startup Agreement, the Start Date is the end of the month after the franchisee completes initial training. Under an Expansion Agreement executed before January 1, 2007, the Start Date is the date of execution of the Expansion Agreement; under an Expansion Agreement executed January 1, 2007 or after, the Start Date is 60 days after the date of execution of the Expansion Agreement.

For purposes of the net revenue shown in Tables A and B below, we used the Gross Revenue figures from the royalty reports the franchisees filed with us; these revenues are reported on a cash basis.

While we have not audited this information or independently confirmed the royalty reports, we have no reason to believe that any franchisee would overstate its revenues to us.

TABLE A

Number of Months in Operation (1)	Total # of Franchised Businesses (2)	Average Net Revenue	Number and Percentage of Franchised Businesses Meeting or Exceeding Average	Median Net Revenue	Highest Franchised Business Net Revenue	Lowest Franchised Business Net Revenue
73 or more	441	$775,459	169/38%	$591,527	$4,910,843	$24,345
61 to 72	31	$518,645	10/32%	$435,797	$2,619,071	$37,381

49 to 60	24	$377,448	11/46%	$346,634	$1,090,656	$67,942
37 to 48	34	$339,419	15/44%	$323,857	$848,397	$21,591
25 to 36	23	$277,586	9/39%	$194,884	$877,997	$48,748
12 to 24	21	$237,809	7/33%	$183,555	$1,067,087	$9,592
All Franchised Businesses Open One Year or More Ending September 30, 2013	574	$679,500	211/37%	$505,849	$4,910,843	$9,592

Notes to Table A:

(1) Franchised Businesses operating 73 or more months had Start Dates between March 1, 1998 and September 30, 2007. Franchised Businesses operating 61 to 72 months had Start Dates between October 30, 2007 and September 30, 2008. Franchised Businesses in each subsequent descending tier of months shown in this table had Start Dates one year later than those in the preceding tier.

(2) The total number of Franchised Businesses that had been operating at least 12 months at September 30, 2013 is 574; we have excluded the Franchised Businesses we manage on behalf of SDX. The number in this column represents all Franchised Businesses that reported revenue for every month during the Reporting Period and that had been operating for at least 12 months at September 30, 2013. The table excludes 9 Franchised Businesses that closed during the Reporting Period and 59 Franchised Businesses that reported no revenue or did not file a royalty report for one or more months during the Reporting Period. Each of the Franchised Businesses included in the table provided the homemaker/companionship services and personal care services that you must provide under the Franchise Agreement and most provided Personal Technology Services and Equipment under the SafetyChoice® program. 72 Franchised Businesses participated in a pilot program for PDN Services during the Reporting Period.

Table B represents the same Franchised Businesses and the same revenues as in Table A, but in Table B the revenue is shown on a per "franchise entity" basis, rather than on a per "Franchised Business" basis. That is, if a franchise entity owns multiple Franchised Businesses, revenues from all of those Franchised Businesses are aggregated and reported for that franchise entity.

TABLE B

Number of Franchise Entities (1)	Total # of Franchsied Businesses (2)	Average Net Revenue per Entity	Number and Percentage of Franchised Entities Meeting or Exceeding Average	Median Net Revenue per Entity	Highest Franchise Entity Net Revenue	Lowest Franchise Entity Net Revenue
313	574	$1,246,112	38/12%	$579,910	$4,910,843	$54,075

Notes to Table B:

(1) Of the 313 franchise entities, 3 franchise entities had 8 Franchised Businesses each; 2 franchise entities had 6 Franchised Businesses each; 6 franchise entities had 5 Franchised Businesses each; 11 franchise entities had 4 Franchised Businesses each; 39 franchise entities had 3 Franchised Businesses each; 95 franchise entities had 2 Franchised Businesses; and 157 had 1 Franchised Business each. Each Franchised Business is operated under a separate Franchise Agreement with its own Territory.

(2) The total number of Franchised Businesses that had been operating at least 12 months at September 30, 2013 is 574; we have excluded the Franchised Businesses we manage on behalf of SDX. The number in this column represents all Franchised Businesses that reported revenue for every month during the Reporting Period and that had been operating for at least 12 months at September 30, 2013. The table excludes 9 Franchised Businesses that closed during the Reporting Period and 59 Franchised Businesses that reported no revenue or did not file a royalty report for one or more months during the Reporting Period. Each of the Franchised Businesses included in the table provided the homemaker/companionship services and personal care services that you must provide under the Franchise Agreement and most provided Personal Technology Services and Equipment under the SafetyChoice® program. 72 Franchised Businesses participated in a pilot program for PDN Services during the Reporting Period.

The following three tables are historical financial performance representations for the 12 months ended September 30, 2013, for a limited group of franchisees (the "PMG Group"). These tables do not include data from the Franchised Businesses we manage on behalf of SDX. The PMG Group consists of smaller groups of franchisees ("performance management groups") who have voluntarily come together to improve the performance of their Franchised Businesses. These franchisees meet periodically in person or by telephone to discuss their performance goals and their actual outcomes. In order to participate in the performance management groups, the franchisees must own one or more units that have been in operation for at least a year, they must agree to a uniform system of revenue and expense reporting, and they must provide CKFI with financial reports based on that uniform system of revenue and expense reporting. Although CKFI staff facilitate the PMG Group meetings, CKFI provides no additional instruction or business guidance to the PMG Group. PMG Group members pay a fee to CKFI to offset costs associated with the program. All 93 members of the PMG Group, representing 220 Franchised Businesses, provided data presented in Tables PMG 1 and 2. 29 of the Franchised Businesses are held by single unit franchisees; the remainder of the Franchised Businesses are held by 64 multi-unit franchisees. 30 franchisees held 2 Franchised Businesses each; 20 franchisees held 3 each; 7 franchisees held 4 each; 3 franchisees held 5 each; 2 franchisees held 6 each;

1 franchisee held 7; and 1 franchisee held 9. The Franchised Businesses in the PMG Group are located throughout the country, in 30 different states. All of the Franchised Businesses in the PMG Group had been operating at least one year as of September 30, 2013. The Franchised Businesses in the PMG Group offer the homemaker/companionship and personal care services that you must offer under the Franchise Agreement; all but one also offer Personal Technology Services and Equipment, which you must offer under the Franchise Agreement. In addition, 40 of the 220 Franchised Businesses participated in the PDN Services pilot during the Reporting Period.

Table PMG-1 represents the average net revenues of the Franchised Businesses in the PMG Group for the twelve months ending September 30, 2013, based on length of time in operation (using the Start Date as the commencement of operations). We used the Gross Revenue figures from the royalty reports that PMG Group members filed with us, which reflect revenues reported on a cash basis. While we have not audited this information or independently confirmed the royalty reports, we have no reason to believe that any franchisee would overstate its revenues to us.

TABLE PMG-I

Time in Operation (Years)	No. of Franchised Businesses	Average Net Revenue	# and % Meeting/ Exceeding Average	Median Net Revenue	Highest Net Revenue	Lowest Net Revenue
10 or more	102	$1,067,603	40 / 39%	$880,089	$4,910,843	$139,875
8 to 10	37	$916,785	14 / 37%	$720,702	$4,038,315	$3,955
5 to 8	44	$690,342	18 / 41%	$522,428	$2,619,071	$17,682
2 to 5	35	$276,323	15 / 43%	$224,597	$832,912	$2,313
More than 1 but less than 2	2	$37,858	1 / 50%	$37,858	$73,659	$2,057
Total	220	$828,516	87 / 40%	$579,449	$4,910,843	$2,057

Table PMG-2 is a statement of the average performance of the PMG Group as a whole, based on the costs listed and then measured against their Net Revenue for the twelve months ending September 30, 2013. As indicated above, the members of the PMG Group have agreed to a uniform methodology for reporting revenue and expenses and the revenue and expense information shown comes from the reports provided by the PMG Group members to CKFI. The information in Table PMG-2 reflects reporting of both revenues and expenses on an accrual basis by members of the PMG Group; accordingly, the average net revenue figure is different from that shown in Table PMG-1, which reflects net revenue reported, on a cash basis, on the franchisees' royalty reports to CKFI. While we have not audited this information or independently confirmed the expense information or the information on the sub-categories of revenue, because a franchisee's financial per-

formance does not affect its obligations to us and because of the specific commitment of PMG Members to accurate and uniform financial reporting, we have no reason to believe that any franchisee would misrepresent its revenue and expense information.

PMG Group members who own more than one Franchised Business report expenses on an aggregated basis for all of their Franchised Businesses; typically, due to the nature of the business (services-based, rather than a location-based retail operation), multi-unit franchisees operate and manage their Franchised Businesses as a whole. The averages shown in Table PMG-2 represent the billed revenues and accrued expenses reported (on a single unit or aggregated basis) divided by 220, the number of Franchised Businesses held by franchisees in the PMG Group. Thus, the average shown does not take into account that a multi-unit franchisee may have one or more of its Franchised Businesses that are performing well below the "average" shown. For the 29 single unit franchisees in the PMG Group, we have indicated in the applicable note to Table PMG-2 the number and percentage of their Franchised Businesses that met or exceeded the average shown for certain line items.

TABLE PMG-2

Revenue	AVERAGE for all PMG Group Members	As percent of Total Revenue Billed
In-home Care Service Revenue[1]	$820,097	98.4%
Personal Technology Services[2]	$4,487	0.5%
All Other Revenue[3]	$9,007	1.1%
Total Revenue[4]	$833,592	100.0%
Cost of Sales		
Caregiver (CG) Payroll[5]	$409,802	49.2%
CG Payroll Taxes and Benefits[6]	$47,510	5.7%
CG Workers' Compensation Insurance[7]	$21,213	2.5%
Cost of Personal Technology Equipment[8]	$2,805	0.3%
Direct Revenue Incentive Compensation[9]	$1,804	0.2%
Franchise Royalty[10]	$33,434	4.0%
Direct Costs for All Other Revenue[11]	$6,161	0.7%
Total Cost of Sales[12]	$522,731	62.7%
Gross Profit[13]	$310,860	37.3%

Notes to Table PMG-2:

(1) This represents revenue billed by the franchisees for providing homemaker/companionship and personal care services; in addition, 40 of the 220 Franchised Businesses participated in the PDN Services pilot during the Reporting Period. Each franchisee sets its own rates; typically, franchisees will charge different rates for different types of services and may charge more or less depending on the number of hours of service a Client needs and whether live-in care is required. Of the 29 single unit franchisees, 20, or 69%, met or exceeded the average shown.

(2) This represents revenue billed by the franchisees for the

sale or lease of Personal Technology Services and Equipment under the SafetyChoice® program. 1 franchisee, owning 3 Franchised Businesses, and 6 single-unit franchisees did not have revenue from the SafetyChoice® program. Of the 23 single unit franchisees that had such revenue, 18, or 78%, met or exceeded the average shown.

(3) This represents revenue billed for ancillary services that CKFI has approved but does not require, such as PDN Services (which was offered by a limited number of franchisees under a pilot program during the Reporting Period) and reimbursements for transportation services, grocery purchases, and similar items. Of the 29 single unit franchisees, 16, or 55%, met or exceeded the average shown.

(4) Of the 29 single unit franchisees, 21, or 72%, met or exceeded the average shown.

(5) This represents wage expense for caregivers. Hourly wages will vary depending on the economic conditions in a given area. Typically, where hourly wages are higher, rates for services are higher.

(6) This represents payroll taxes and benefits (for example, health and/or life insurance) associated with caregivers. Payroll taxes vary significantly by state, but typically where payroll taxes are higher, rates for services are higher.

(7) This represents workers compensation insurance coverage for caregivers. CKFI requires that you carry workers compensation with Part Two (employer's liability) policy limits at no less than state minimum. Workers compensation rates vary significantly by state.

(8) This represents the cost paid to CKFI for SafetyChoice® equipment and services that were then sold or leased to Clients.

(9) This represents the bonuses and other incentives that the franchisees paid to employees.

(10) This represents the royalty fees paid to CKFI. All Franchised Businesses in the PMG Group pay royalty fees under a tiered royalty structure , with franchisees under older franchise agreements generally paying royalty fees based on lower royalty tier breakpoints. (See note 5 to the Item 6 table in this disclosure document for more information on how the tiered royalty structure works.) The 4% rate represents a blend of the royalty fees calculated under the tiered royalty structure. You will pay royalty fees based on a flat 5% of Gross Revenues, as described in Item 6 of this disclosure document.

(11) This represents costs such as mileage reimbursement costs paid to caregivers and, for those franchisees participating

in a pilot program for private duty nursing, private duty nurse wages (and related payroll expenses).

(12) The expenses that are included in the Cost of Sales calculation do not include all of the expenses associated with operating a Franchised Business.

(13) Gross Margin means Total Revenue less Total Cost of

Sales. Of the 29 single unit franchisees, 18, or 62%, met or exceeded the average shown.

Table PMG-3 is a statement of the actual performance of the highest-performing single unit owner and the lowest-performing single unit owner in the PMG Group for the twelve months ending September 30, 2013. Revenue and expenses included in the table were reported on an accrual basis.

TABLE PMG-3

Revenue	Highest-Performing Single Unit		Lowest Performing Single Unit	
	Actual	As percent of Total Revenue	Actual	As percent of Total Revenue
In-home Care Service Revenue[1]	$5,086,285	99.6%	$380,491	96.5%
Personal Technology Services[2]	$6,754	0.1%	$4,595	1.2%
All Other Revenue[3]	$14,860	0.3%	$9.015	2.3%
Total Revenue	$5,107,899	100.00%	$394,101	100.00%
Cost of Sales				
Caregiver (CG) Payroll[4]	$2,623,353	51.4%	$162,421	41.2%
CG Payroll Taxes and Benefits[5]	$245,494	4.8%	$34,728	8.8%
CG Workers' Compensation Insurance[6]	$171,486	3.4%	$18,252	4.6%
Cost of Personal Technology Equipment[7]	$2,831	0.1%	$3,501	0.9%
Direct Revenue Incentive Compensation[8]	$0	0.0%	$0	0.0%
Franchise Royalty[9]	$188,274	3.7%	$18,913	4.8%
Direct Costs for All Other Revenue[10]	$13,453	0.3%	$5,440	1.4%
Total Cost of Sales[11]	$3,244,891	63.5%	$243,255	61.7%
Gross Profit[12]	$1,863,008	36.5%	$150,846	38.3%

Notes to Table PMG-3:

(1) This represents revenue billed by the franchisee for providing homemaker/companionship and personal care services; in addition 5 of the 29 single unit franchisees participated in the PDN Services pilot program during the Reporting Period. Each franchisee sets its own rates; typically, franchisees will charge different rates for different types of services and may charge more or less depending on the number of hours of service a Client needs and whether live-in care is required.

(2) This represents revenue billed by the franchisee for the sale or lease of Personal Technology Services and Equipment under the SafetyChoice® program.

(3) This represents revenue billed for ancillary services that CKFI has approved but does not require, such as PDN Services (which was offered by 5 of the 29 single-unit franchisees under a pilot program during the Reporting Period) and for reimbursements for transportation services, grocery purchases, and similar items.

(4) This represents wage expense for caregivers. Hourly wages will vary depending on the economic conditions in a given area. Typically, where hourly wages are higher, rates for services are higher.

(5) This represents payroll taxes and benefits (for example, health and/or life insurance) associated with caregivers. Payroll taxes vary significantly by state, but typically where payroll

taxes are higher, rates for services are higher.

(6) This represents workers compensation insurance coverage for caregivers. CKFI requires that you carry workers compensation with Part Two (employer's liability) policy limits at no less than state minimum. Workers compensation rates vary significantly by state.

(7) This represents the cost paid to CKFI for SafetyChoice® equipment and services that were then sold or leased to Clients.

(8) This represents the bonuses and other incentives that the franchisees paid to employees.

(9) All Franchised Businesses in the PMG Group pay royalty fees under a tiered royalty structure, with franchisees under older franchise agreements generally paying royalty fees based on lower royalty tier breakpoints. (See note 5 to the Item 6 table in this disclosure document for more information on how the tiered royalty structure works.) The two rates shown represents a blend of the royalty fees calculated under the tiered royalty structure. You will pay royalty fees based on a flat 5% of Gross Revenues, as described in Item 6 of this disclosure document.

(10) This represents costs associated with mileage reimbursements to caregivers.

(11) The expenses that are included in the Cost of Sales calculation do not include all of the expenses associated with operating a Franchised Business.

(12) Gross Margin means Total Revenue less Total Cost of Sales.

We will make available to you upon reasonable request written substantiation of the information contained in the tables above.

The financial performance representations in Tables A and B do not reflect the costs of sales, and none of the financial performance representations in any of the tables reflects all of the operating expenses, or other costs or expenses that must be deducted from the gross revenue or gross sales figures to obtain your net income or profit. The net revenue and net profit of your Franchised Business will depend on many factors, including the prices you charge for services and products, labor costs and general economic conditions in your area, your ability to network and generate Clients, and competition from other similar businesses in your area. There is no assurance that your Franchised Business will do as well as the Franchised Businesses in the tables above. You should conduct an independent investigation of the costs and expenses you will incur in operating your Franchised Business. Franchisees or former franchisees listed in the disclosure document may be one source of this information.

THE RESULTS GIVEN IN THESE TABLES ARE HISTORIC REPRESENTATIONS OF FINANCIAL RESULTS ACHIEVED BY CERTAIN COMFORT KEEPERS® FRANCHISED BUSINESSES. A NEW FRANCHISEE'S RESULTS ARE LIKELY TO DIFFER FROM THE RESULTS STATED IN THE TABLES. ACTUAL RESULTS VARY FROM FRANCHISED BUSINESS TO FRANCHISED BUSINESS, AND THE SUCCESS OF YOUR FRANCHISED BUSINESS WILL DEPEND IN LARGE PART UPON YOUR SKILLS AND ABILITIES, COMPETITION FROM OTHER BUSINESSES, AND OTHER ECONOMIC AND BUSINESS FACTORS. WE MAKE NO REPRESENTATION OR WARRANTY THAT YOU WILL, OR ARE LIKELY TO, ACHIEVE THE RESULTS SHOWN IN THE TABLES.

Other than the preceding financial performance representations, CKFI does not make any financial performance representations. We also do not authorize our employees or representatives to make any such representations either orally or in writing. If you are purchasing an existing outlet, however, we may provide you with the actual records of that outlet. If you receive any other financial performance information or projections of your future income, you should report it to the franchisor's management by contacting Jim Brown, Vice President of Franchise Development, 6640 Poe Avenue, Suite 200, Dayton, OH 45414, 937-665-1300, the Federal Trade Commission, and the appropriate state regulatory agencies.

COVERALL HEALTH-BASED CLEANING SYSTEM

350 SW 12th Ave.
Deerfield, FL 33442
Tel: (800) 537-3371, (561) 922-2500
Fax: (561) 922-2424
Email: diane.emo@coverall.com
Website: www.coverall.com
Diane Emo, Vice President of Marketing

As a COVERALL Franchised Business Owner, you will be fully trained and certified in the Health-Based Cleaning System Program, and prepared to help your customers improve the cleanliness, health and wellness of their facilities. COVERALL is recognized as a leading brand in the commercial cleaning industry. The COVERALL® Program removes the maximum amount of dirt as quickly as possible, kills germs that can cause illness, and improves air quality. For over 28 years we've helped thousands entrepreneurs build commercial cleaning franchised businesses by implementing our program. Are you ready to start your business today?

BACKGROUND

IFA Member:	Yes
Established & First Franchised:	1985; 1985
Franchised Units:	8,045
Company-Owned Units:	0
Total Units:	8,045
Distribution:	US – 7,652; CAN – 295; O'seas – 98

North America:	40 States, 3 Provinces
Density:	1,030 in FL, 531 in OH, 1,111 in CA
Projected New Units (12 Months):	1
Qualifications:	3, 3, 2, 2, 3, 5

FINANCIAL/TERMS

Cash Investment:	$3.9 – 21.9K
Total Investment:	$14.1 – 47.7K
Minimum Net Worth:	$12.2K
Fees (Franchise):	$11.3 – 37K
Fees (Royalty):	5%
Fees (Advertising):	0%
Term of Contract (Years):	20/20
Average Number of Employees:	1 – 2 FT, 2 – 3 PT
Passive Ownership:	Discouraged
Encourage Conversions:	Yes
Area Development Agreements:	No
Sub-Franchising Contracts:	Yes
Expand in Territory:	Yes
Space Needs:	N/A

SUPPORT & TRAINING

Financial Assistance Provided:	Yes (D)
Site Selection Assistance:	N/A
Lease Negotiation Assistance:	N/A
Co-operative Advertising:	No
Franchisee Association/Member:	No
Size of Corporate Staff:	62
On-going Support:	A, B, D, G, H, I
Training:	32 – 48 Hours Local Regional Support Center

SPECIFIC EXPANSION PLANS

US:	All United States
Canada:	No
Overseas:	No

We do not make any representations about a franchisee's future financial performance or the past financial performance of company-owned or franchised outlets. We also do not authorize our employees or representatives to make any such representations either orally or in writing. If you are purchasing an existing outlet, however, we may provide you with the actual records of that outlet. If you receive any other financial performance information or projections of your future income, you should report it to the franchisor's management by contacting the Compliance Director in the Legal Department at the Global Support Center located at 350 SW 12th Avenue, Deerfield Beach, Florida 33442 (561-922-2534); the Federal Trade Commission, and the appropriate state regulatory agencies.

We sell our franchises as packages. The Franchise Package is described as a specified amount of Initial Business, which we must offer to you within a certain amount of time. For convenience and to be consistent with business practices in the janitorial franchise industry, we describe these Franchise Packages in terms of monthly Gross Dollar Volume (i.e., a P-1500 Franchise Package means $1,500.00 in monthly Gross Dollar Volume). In addition, under the Franchise Agreement, we will guarantee your Initial Business for up to a maximum of 12 months, subject to the conditions described in Item 11 above. The Franchise Package purchased is not a guarantee that you will earn an equivalent amount of Gross Dollar Volume each month; neither does it mean that we are obligated at any time to replace lost customers to enable you to maintain that level of Gross Dollar Volume.

If we do not offer the Initial Business within the specified time, you may request a refund of a portion of the initial franchisee fee, as described in Item 5, above.

The monthly Gross Dollar Volume of the Initial Business that you purchase should not be considered as the actual or potential income or profit, you will realize. The total monthly Gross Dollar Volume you achieve are affected by many factors such as: the Initial Business may be offered in stages during the specified time period; you may decline a customer; you may lose a customer for poor service; the customer may cancel through no fault of your own and you did not perform the required inspections to earn the extended guarantee; and you may lose a customer through no fault of your own and there is a time lag before the replacement customer is offered.

Other factors affecting your Gross Dollar Volume are the quality and efficiency of your cleaning services; the degree to which you finance the purchase and operation of the franchise; and business expenses associated with operating your business, many of which expenses you control, such as wages to employees.

We make no disclosure as to when, or if, you will recover your investment in your franchised business. There are too many variables to permit a reliable estimate. Commercial cleaning customers can be lost for any number of reasons, including but not limited to, poor service, the customer chooses a lower priced provider, the customer goes out of business or files for bankruptcy protection, economic circumstances cause the customer to terminate outside vendors. In 2013, average customer attrition rate was 2.19% per month. You can expect to lose customers, and that is a risk of doing business. In 2013, the average life of a customer was forty-five (45) months, which is not an assurance that you will retain your customers for a similar period of time.

COVERALL'S FULFILLMENT OF FRANCHISE PACKAGES

We analyzed our compliance with the Franchise Agreement concerning the amount, timeliness, and refund requirements for Initial Business provided to our franchisees. We reviewed all franchise sales made during our fiscal year, and determined whether or not as of December 31, 2013 the Initial Business had been offered in compliance with the Franchise Agreement.

During our fiscal year January 1, 2013 to December 31, 2013, we sold 523 franchises. Of those sold, as of the close of the fiscal year: (a) franchisees either had their packages timely filled or have accepted our performance in 137 cases; or 26%; (b) we and the franchisee made a mutually acceptable adjustment to the franchise package, such as by our recalculation of the franchise fee or an extension of time to provide customers, in 58 cases; or 11%; (c) the time for us to provide initial customers under franchise packages had not expired in 328 cases, or 63%; and (d) it is undetermined whether the package has been filled in 0 cases, or 0%.

Therefore, we complied with the amount, timeliness, and recalculation requirements for Initial Business provided to our franchisees in 100% of the cases. Our compliance could not be determined in less than one percent of the sales. Substantiation of the data used in preparing these statistics will be made available upon request.

The basis for our claim about Initial Business is Paragraph 13 of the Franchise Agreement.

CRESTCOM INTERNATIONAL

6900 E. Belleview Ave., 3rd Fl.
Greenwood Village, CO 80111
Tel: (888) 273-7826, (303) 267-8200
Fax: (303) 267-8207
Email: charles.parsons@crestcom.com
Website: www.crestcom.com
Charles Parsons, Director of International Marketing

For more than 25 years, Crestcom International franchisees have trained business people across the globe in the areas of management and leadership. Today, Crestcom has grown to become one of the training industry's most successful and widely used management and leadership programs among Fortune magazine's Top 100 Companies. Each month, thousands of business professionals across six continents participate in the Crestcom Bullet Proof Manager training. Crestcom's proprietary training is improving the way businesses motivate, communicate, and help managers succeed. Businesses turn to Crestcom to help transform managers into leaders and generate real business results. Crestcom's training program accommodates organizations of all sizes, from small to mid-sized businesses, to global multi-national organizations. Crestcom currently has franchise owners in over 62 countries and the Bullet Proof Manager training Program is available in 25 languages.

BACKGROUND

IFA Member:	Yes
Established & First Franchised:	1987; 1992
Franchised Units:	192
Company-Owned Units:	0
Total Units:	192
Distribution:	US – 31; CAN – 14; O'seas – 147
North America:	25 States, 4 Provinces
Density:	N/A
Projected New Units (12 Months):	30
Qualifications:	3, 3, 4, 4, 5, 3

FINANCIAL/TERMS

Cash Investment:	$69.5K
Total Investment:	$85.3 – 104K
Minimum Net Worth:	N/A
Fees (Franchise):	$69.5K
Fees (Royalty):	35.5%
Fees (Advertising):	N/A
Term of Contract (Years):	7/7
Average Number of Employees:	0-2 FT, 0 PT
Passive Ownership:	Not Allowed
Encourage Conversions:	N/A
Area Development Agreements:	Yes
Sub-Franchising Contracts:	No
Expand in Territory:	Yes
Space Needs:	N/A

SUPPORT & TRAINING

Financial Assistance Provided:	Yes (D)
Site Selection Assistance:	N/A
Lease Negotiation Assistance:	N/A
Co-operative Advertising:	No
Franchisee Association/Member:	Yes/Member
Size of Corporate Staff:	15
On-going Support:	C, D, G, H
Training:	7 Days United States

SPECIFIC EXPANSION PLANS

US:	All United States
Canada:	All Canada
Overseas:	All Countries

Below is a chart showing our estimate of gross revenue margins before expenses related to the sale or marketing of Materials. This chart has not been prepared in accordance with the statement on Standards for Accountant's Services on Prospective Financial Information.

ESTIMATE OF GROSS REVENUE MARGINS BEFORE EXPENSES[1]-[9]

GROSS MARGIN PER PARTICIPANT ATTENDING THE BULLET PROOF® MANAGER PROGRAM						
Materials (per participant)	Recommended Retail Price[3]	Cost of Materials as % of Recommended Retail[5]	Fees as % of Recommended Retail[6]	Est. Shipping as % of Recommended Retail[7]	Total % of Recommended Retail	Gross Revenue Margin (%/$s) [2][4][8]
BPM Materials[1]	$4,320	2.13%	35.5%	.5%	38.13%	61.87% $2,672.78

THE ACCOMPANYING FOOTNOTES ARE AN INTEGRAL PART OF THIS CHART AND SHOULD BE READ IN THEIR ENTIRETY FOR A FULL UNDERSTANDING OF THE INFORMATION CONTAINED IN IT.

FOOTNOTES:

(1) The estimated gross revenue margins reflected in the chart above relate only to Franchisees' sales of Materials for and enrollments of participants in The BULLETPROOF® Manager programs (the "BPM Programs"), and exclude sales of other Materials or enrollments in other programs Franchisees can offer. We offer other programs and Materials that may have greater or lesser margins. We estimate that more than 95 percent of all sales revenues are derived from the BPM Programs.

(2) The term "Gross Revenue Margin" as used in the chart refers to the amount or percentage, as indicated, of the applicable total revenues that remain after deduction of only those costs specifically identified in the chart. A Franchisee will have other costs as well. See footnote 4 below.

(3) The recommended retail price for the 2013 calendar year was $4,320 per participant. This recommended retail price is stated in the Procedures Manual and is subject to change. In prior years, the recommended retail price may have been lower. Franchisees may charge a fee that is higher or lower than our recommended retail price. They sometimes will reduce the per participant fee they charge for clients who enroll multiple managers to attend the BPM Programs. Market conditions, such as competition, market recognition, quality of a Franchisee's training skills and location may affect a Franchisee's actual retail pricing.

(4) The costs shown in the chart are based on the costs in effect as of the date of this Disclosure Document and are subject to change. This chart shows certain costs incurred in marketing the Materials and conducting BPM Programs only. They do not include all of the expenses a Franchisee will incur during the term of its franchise agreement, including the initial investment in the franchise, start-up costs, overhead, and certain operating expenses. Operating expenses vary substantially and are based on particular factors relevant to each Franchisee. A Franchisee may incur operating expenses for a computer, DVD player, iPad, tablet computer, projector, or other equipment, automobile, telephone and voice mail system or service, marketing and advertising, direct mail, special incentive offers, Facilitator's or other instructional items or materials, amounts paid to Facilitators for those Franchisees who do not conduct their own Live Instruction programs, amounts paid to telemarketers for those Franchisees who elect to employ telemarketers, New Materials introductory surcharge (discussed below), and other isolated and/or recurring expenses. It also does not include amounts representing the Franchisee's (and its authorized representatives') time or effort, or account for interest expense, appreciation or depreciation of assets, capital expenses and carrying costs which will vary from Franchisee to Franchisee. Franchisees may operate from an office location, in which case there may be office lease and other related expenses, although most of our Franchisees operate out of their homes. Franchisees will also incur costs related to the attendance at our annual international convention and other Additional Meetings. You should refer to Items 5, 6 and 7 of this Disclosure Document for a discussion of other initial franchise fees, other fees and expenses, and initial investment considerations.

(5) The actual cost of the Materials for participants in the BPM Programs or other programs we offer varies. Depending on the number of participants a client enrolls, the mix of Materials the client receives is different. Further, many Franchisees purchase additional Materials to give to clients as a bonus for early payment. Some Franchisees also offer free or "scholarship" enrollments as a bonus for clients who enroll a specified number of their managers in the BPM Programs. The expenses shown in the chart assume these incentive Materials come from the Franchisee's own inventory and the costs of any free enrollments or bonus Materials are not reflected in the chart. Franchisees are not required to offer free enrollments or give bonus Materials. Based on our estimates, the average expense for required Materials for one participant in a BPM Program, including the payment of the Media Access Fee owed to us for any Materials that we grant you the right to access and market is approximately $92 or 2.13 percent of the current recommended retail price of $4,320. This recommended retail price is stated in the Procedures Manual and is subject to change.

(6) The aggregate fees paid to us when a Franchisee sells the Materials generally total 35.5 percent of a Franchisee's Gross Revenues. This is comprised of a Distribution Fee of 34 percent and a Royalty Fee of 1.5 percent. The gross revenue margins shown on the chart assume that the standard Distribution Fee of 34 percent is paid on all Gross Revenues. A lower Distribution Fee may be payable based on certain Gross Revenues under our PSR Program, as described in Item 6. The chart also does not consider the credits that may be granted to a Franchisee under our Merit Program, as described in Item 6. The fees due us are paid as a Franchisee receives the proceeds from BPM Programs, which may not always be at the time of the sale. We recommend that Franchisees require enrollment fees and other amounts paid by a client be paid on a cash basis or on a basis of 25 percent down, with the balance payable in 30, 60, and 90 days. You may agree to other terms. The gross revenue margins shown on the chart assume that all amounts owed by clients are collected at the time of the sale, and that all Distribution Fees, Royalty Fees, and any other fees or amounts

owed to us by Franchisees are paid at the time of the sale.

(7) We estimate shipping costs at 0.5 percent of the retail price of the Materials. This may be higher depending on the location of a Franchisee and other factors, particularly for shipments of small quantities of Materials.

(8) We periodically introduce New Materials or programs to our inventory of Materials available to franchises. There is a one-time introductory surcharge to offset our production costs of these Materials at the earlier of (i) the first order of any unit of the New Materials; or (ii) six months from the date the New Materials become available. The current introductory surcharge is $400 per new training program unit. Franchisees are required to acquire the rights to access and market any New Materials within six months of their availability. Since the introductory surcharge is a one-time charge, we have not included it in the chart as the percentage effect would constantly vary as rights to more of these New Materials are acquired over the life of a franchise.

(9) The data in the chart has been compiled based on the experience of our U.S. Franchisees only. Our system is comprised of Franchisees operating within the United States and Franchisees and distributors operating in other countries. Our foreign franchise/distributorship programs operate in a manner similar to our franchise system within the United States as it relates to the information contained in the chart, although retail prices for the Materials distributed internationally may differ from the recommended retail price presented in the chart and are often subject to customs and duty expenses as well as higher shipping costs. International prices are also subject to change with exchange rate fluctuations. The results of our foreign franchise/distributorship programs are not included in this data. Also, at different times we have promoted other franchise programs in addition to the CRESTCOM Business franchise program offered under this Disclosure Document. These programs generally had lower initial franchise fees and higher Distribution Fees and Royalty Fees. We currently do not offer any of these programs. We currently do not have any U.S. Franchisees participating in any of these programs.

CAUTION: YOUR ACTUAL FINANCIAL RESULTS ARE LIKELY TO DIFFER FROM THE FIGURES PRESENTED. WE DO NOT REPRESENT THAT THE GROSS REVENUE MARGINS CONTAINED IN THIS CHART REPRESENT YOUR NET INCOME. YOU WILL HAVE OTHER EXPENSES AS NOTED ABOVE.

YOUR ABILITY TO ACHIEVE ANY LEVEL OF GROSS REVENUES MARGINS AND INCOME WILL DEPEND UPON FACTORS NOT WITHIN OUR CONTROL, INCLUDING THE OCCURRENCE OF CERTAIN START UP AND OPERATING EXPENSES AND THE AMOUNT OF THOSE EXPENSES, AND YOUR LEVEL OF EXPERTISE. IF POSSIBLE, SHOW THESE FIGURES TO SOMEONE WHO CAN ADVISE YOU, LIKE A LAWYER OR ACCOUNTANT.

YOU SHOULD NOTE THAT THE INFORMATION CONTAINED IN THIS ITEM IS NOT INTENDED TO EXPRESS OR INFER AN ESTIMATE, PROJECTION OR FORECAST OF INCOME, SALES, PROFITS OR EARNINGS TO BE DERIVED IN CONNECTION WITH ANY PARTICULAR FRANCHISE. THE INFORMATION PRESENTED IN THE CHART IS LIMITED TO AN ESTIMATE OF GROSS REVENUE MARGINS BEFORE OPERATING EXPENSES THAT COULD BE DERIVED BY A FRANCHISEE FROM THE ENROLLMENT OF ONE BULLET PROOF MANAGER PARTICIPANT AT OUR CURRENT RECOMMENDED RETAIL PRICE. WE MAKE NO REPRESENTATION AS TO WHETHER YOU WILL EVER BE ABLE TO SELL ANY OF THE MATERIALS, HOW MANY PARTICIPANTS YOU MAY BE ABLE TO ENROLL, OR THE LENGTH OF TIME IT WILL TAKE YOU TO ENROLL ONE OR MORE PARTICIPANTS OR REALIZE ANY GROSS REVENUES.

The financial performance representation figures in the chart reflect the estimated costs of materials, estimated costs of shipping, and estimated Distribution Fees and Royalty Fees related to the enrollment of Bullet Proof Manager participants. The financial performance representation figures in the chart do not reflect the cost of any other sales, marketing, operating or other expenses that must be deducted from the gross revenues or gross sales figures to obtain your net income or profit. You should conduct an independent investigation of the costs and expenses you will incur in operating your CRESTCOM Business. Franchisees or former Franchisees listed in Attachments H and I may be one source of this information.

Written substantiation for the financial performance representation will be made available to you at our Greenwood Village office upon reasonable request.

Other than the preceding chart, we do not make any financial performance representations. We also do not authorize our employees or representatives to make any such representations either orally or in writing. If you are purchasing an existing CRESTCOM Business, however, we may provide you with the actual records of that CRESTCOM Business outlet. If you receive any other financial performance information or projections of your future income, you should report it to the franchisor's management by contacting George Godfrey at 6900 East Belleview Avenue, Suite 100, Greenwood Village, Colorado 80111 and (303) 267-8200, the Federal Trade Commission, and the appropriate state regulatory agencies.

CRUISEONE

1201 W. Cypress Creek Rd., # 100
Ft. Lauderdale, FL 33309
Tel: (888) 272-4964, (954) 958-3700
Fax: (954) 958-3697
Email: recruitmemt@wth.com
Website: www.cruiseonefranchise.com
Tim Courtney, Vice President, Franchise Development

CRUISEONE is a nationwide, home-based cruise & travel franchise company representing all major cruise lines and tour operators. Franchisees are professionally trained in a 6-day comprehensive program. CruiseOne provides a heritage of excellence, unrivaled buying power, industry-leading technology solutions, pride of true business ownership, and access to a large corporate support team to help you grow. CruiseOne is a member of the International Franchise Association (IFA) and participates in the VetFran and MinorityFran initiatives offering incentives and rebates to encourage business ownership.

BACKGROUND

IFA Member:	Yes
Established & First Franchised:	1991; 1992
Franchised Units:	825
Company-Owned Units:	0
Total Units:	825
Distribution:	US – 822; CAN – 0; O'seas – 3
North America:	45 States, 0 Provinces

Density:	128 in FL, 75 in CA, 60 in TX
Projected New Units (12 Months):	70
Qualifications:	3, 4, 2, 3, 5, 4

FINANCIAL/TERMS

Cash Investment:	$9.8K
Total Investment:	$4.6 – 26.3K
Minimum Net Worth:	N/A
Fees (Franchise):	$9.8K
Fees (Royalty):	3%
Fees (Advertising):	0.25%
Term of Contract (Years):	5
Average Number of Employees:	1 FT, 0 PT
Passive Ownership:	Allowed
Encourage Conversions:	N/A
Area Development Agreements:	No
Sub-Franchising Contracts:	No
Expand in Territory:	Yes
Space Needs:	N/A

SUPPORT & TRAINING

Financial Assistance Provided:	Yes (I)
Site Selection Assistance:	N/A
Lease Negotiation Assistance:	N/A
Co-operative Advertising:	Yes
Franchisee Association/Member:	No
Size of Corporate Staff:	80
On-going Support:	A, B, C, D, F, G, h, I
Training:	6 Days Ft. Lauderdale, FL

SPECIFIC EXPANSION PLANS

US:	All United States
Canada:	Yes
Overseas:	Yes

To help you to evaluate our franchise, we have summarized selected historical sales information for the year ending December 31, 2013, for outlets whose franchised businesses were in operation as of December 31, 2013, had been in uninterrupted operation for at least 12 months, and had annual commissionable sales of greater than $1,000 (collectively, the "Included Outlets"). The Included Outlets do not include outlets that began or discontinued their affiliation with us during 2013, and do not include company-owned locations. The total number of Included Outlets as of December 31, 2013, was 616. The total number of outlets as of December 31, 2013, was 829.

Table 1 below provides selected levels of annual commissionable sales net of selected selling expenses payable to us that were achieved by certain of the Included Outlets in 2013. The figures in Table 1 are not forecasts of your future financial performance. We have compiled the information based upon what franchisees have reported to us in the ordinary course of business through our sales reporting system. We assume that the information submitted is accurate, complete and contains no material misrepresentations or omissions. Reaching the levels of revenues presented in Table 1 depends entirely on your ability to implement our marketing and operational systems, to develop a cruise- and land- travel focused sales team, and to make connections in and out of your community. Each franchisee's managerial skill, experience and resources will differ. In addition, general economic conditions may fluctuate. Competitors may enter or leave the market over time. Brand recognition and awareness and consumer goodwill may vary by market. Market potential and consumer demand may change over time. Accordingly, you are urged to consult with appropriate financial, business and legal counsel to conduct your own independent analysis of the information presented.

TABLE I

Annual Commission Revenues					
Annual Commissionable Sales[1]	$109,999	$249,999	$609,999	$1,109,000	$1,609,999
Average Commission Yield[2]	13.7%	13.7%	13.7%	13.7%	13.7%
Annual Commission Revenues[3]	$15,070	$34,250	$83,570	$152,070	$220,570
Selected Selling Expenses to Us					
Royalty Fees[4]	$3,300	$7,500	$18,300	$22,500	$22,500
Service Fees[5]	$1,800	$1,800	$600	$300	$300
Marketing Contribution[6]	$275	$625	$1,000	$1,000	$1,000
Total Selling Expenses to Us	$5,375	$9,925	$20,500	$24,100	$23,800
Annual Commission Revenues Net of Selected Selling Expenses to Us					
	$9,695[7]	$24,325[8]	$63,670[9]	$128,270[10]	$196,770[11]

(1) "Annual Commissionable Sales" means the total commissionable sales price quoted for the applicable year by the travel supplier (or other travel company or supplier, including travel insurers), excluding any non-commissionable line items (including taxes or port charges).

(2) The average commission yield is the average 2013 commission on commissionable fares from bookings with preferred cruise, land, and tour suppliers.

(3) Annual Commission Revenues figures are calculated by multiplying the applicable Annual Commissionable Sales times the Average Commission Yield.

(4) Franchisees must pay us Royalty Fees based on Annual Commissionable Sales (up to a maximum of $22,500). Accordingly, the Royalty Fees figures are calculated by multiplying the Annual Commissionable Sales times the applicable royalty percentage (as outlined in the Franchise Agreement Section 3.1.b.).

(5) Franchisees must pay us a monthly Service Fee equal to $150. However, the Service Fee is reduced when Departed Commissionable Sales increases (as further described the Franchise Agreement). Accordingly, the Service Fees figures are calculated by multiplying the applicable monthly Service Fee by 12.

(6) Franchisees must pay us an annual Marketing Contribution of 0.25% of Departed Commissionable Sales (up to a maximum of $1,000). Accordingly, the Marketing Contribution figures are calculated in accordance with this formula. We deposit Marketing Contributions into a special account. Franchisees can then use this contribution towards the purchase of headquarter-developed marketing materials, marketing services, or enrollment in certain marketing programs.

(7) The total number of Included Outlets that reached this level of annual commission levels (net of selected selling expenses to us) in 2013 was 308 (or 50%).

(8) The total number of Included Outlets that reached this level of annual commission levels (net of selected selling expenses to us) in 2013 was 170 (or 27.5%).

(9) The total number of Included Outlets that reached this level of annual commission levels (net of selected selling expenses to us) in 2013 was 60 (or 10%).

(10) The total number of Included Outlets that reached this level of annual commission levels (net of selected selling expenses to us) in 2013 was 19 (or 3%).

(11) The total number of Included Outlets that reached this level of annual commission levels (net of selected selling expenses to us) in 2013 was 12 (or 1.9%).

Table 1 does not reflect the costs of sales, operating expenses or other costs or expenses that must be deducted from the gross sales figures to obtain net income or profit. You should conduct an independent investigation of the costs and expenses you may incur in operating your franchised business. Franchisees or former franchisees listed in the disclosure document may be one source of this information. These additional costs vary depending upon a number of factors, including but not limited to local economic conditions, and each franchisee's preferences and abilities. Operating costs typically include the following: rent (if applicable), salaries (if applicable), marketing and promotions, office supplies, telephone and internet, licenses and memberships, insurance, courier and postage, utilities, business expenses, gifts to clients, and repairs and maintenance. Franchisees may also have financing costs related to leases or purchases of equipment (including interest payments). Table 1 also does not include commissions paid to sales associates, whom franchisees have the option to hire as stated in the Franchise Agreement. Franchisees are exclusively responsible for deciding whether they need to hire any sales associates and the terms of their hiring and compensation. For 2013, approximately 42% of the Included Outlets had sales associates, and those who had sales associates have an average of two associates. Annual Commission Revenues are also reduced by the commissions franchisees paid their sales associates. Franchisees do not report to us the commission percentages or actual commission amounts paid to sales associates. As stated in your Franchise Agreement, you also must pay us $100 for each sales associate that you maintain. Accordingly, Annual Commission Revenues will be reduced by these amounts as well.

We have written substantiation of the information used to compile the preceding financial performance representations. We will make this written substantiation available to you upon written request.

Other than the preceding financial performance representations, we do not make any representations about a franchisee's future financial performance or the past financial performance of company-owned or franchised outlets. We also do not authorize our employees or representatives to make any such representations either orally or in writing. If you are purchasing an existing outlet, however, we may provide you with the actual records of that outlet. If you receive any other financial performance information or projections of your future income, you should report it to the franchisor's management by contacting Deborah M. Fiorino, 1201 W. Cypress Creek Road, Suite 100, Fort Lauderdale, Florida 33309 (954) 958- 3700), the Federal Trade Commission, and the appropriate state regulatory agencies.

DISCOVERY MAP INTERNATIONAL

P. O. Box 1529
La Conner, WA 98257
Tel: (877) 820-7827, (360) 547-1374
Fax: (360) 466-2710
Email: monica@discoverymap.com
Website: www.discoverymap.com
Monica Whitmore, Director of Franchise Development

Headquartered in the Green Mountains of Vermont Discovery Map International, Inc. (DMI) has been creating and publishing beautifully illustrated, hand-drawn alternative advertising maps for over 30 years. In 1993 we were predominantly a Northeastern operation, but due to increasing demand and success, DMI (at that time called Resort Maps) expanded its reach by developing a franchise model for individual ownership and distribution of its maps of resort towns, vacation destinations and cities all over the U.S. and beyond. Today, that network of franchises has grown to 126 Discovery Map maps in publication in the US, the UK, Puerto Rico and Costa Rica, with several more in the process of being published. Nearly 25 million Discovery Map maps will be printed and distributed in 2012 and these figures continue to grow.

BACKGROUND

IFA Member:	Yes
Established & First Franchised:	1981; 1993
Franchised Units:	126
Company-Owned Units:	0
Total Units:	126
Distribution:	US – 122; CAN – 1; O'seas – 3
North America:	21 States, 1 Province
Density:	12 in VT, 10 in CO, 10 in MA
Projected New Units (12 Months):	N/A
Qualifications:	4, 3, 3, 3, 3, 4

FINANCIAL/TERMS

Cash Investment:	$40K
Total Investment:	$35 – 45K
Minimum Net Worth:	$100K
Fees (Franchise):	$25K
Fees (Royalty):	10%
Fees (Advertising):	1%

Term of Contract (Years):	10/5/5
Average Number of Employees:	N/A
Passive Ownership:	Allowed
Encourage Conversions:	N/A
Area Development Agreements:	Yes
Sub-Franchising Contracts:	No
Expand in Territory:	Yes
Space Needs:	N/A

SUPPORT & TRAINING

Financial Assistance Provided:	No
Site Selection Assistance:	N/A

Lease Negotiation Assistance:	N/A
Co-operative Advertising:	No
Franchisee Association/Member:	Yes/Not a Member
Size of Corporate Staff:	10
On-going Support:	C, D, F, G, H, I
Training:	Franchise Owner's Home Varies; 4 Days Waitsfield, VT; Field Training Varies

SPECIFIC EXPANSION PLANS

US:	All United States
Canada:	All Canada
Overseas:	Yes

Together with awarding franchises to others, our officers and employees own and operate seven franchises similar to the franchise business described in this Disclosure Document. We are reporting on all franchise businesses that completed a full sales cycle and published a map in the fiscal year ending on September 30, 2013, although it should be kept in mind that maturation of DISCOVERY MAP INTERNATIONAL, INC., franchised businesses can take up to two years. All franchised units operate in a defined territory and typically publish one Map per year. Each franchised business generates gross sales by selling advertising space to local businesses whose ads border the Map. Maps are two-sided. The vast majority of the maps we publish are either 17-inch by 22-inch or 17-inch by 25-inch in size. We do continue to publish four 17-inch by 11-inch maps but do not offer franchises for new maps in this size. Therefore these four maps are excluded from the analysis below. There are no other key demographic elements necessary in defining a territory.

Based upon the performance of the franchises which published a map in the fiscal year ending on September 30, 2012 and completed the selling cycle within the reported fiscal year, we are providing the following disclosure of the actual Gross Sales which includes both unrelated and affiliate-owned franchises.

The Average Map's Unit sales for Fiscal Year ending September 30, 2013 is as follows:

	October 1, 2012 to September 30, 2013
Average Sales per Map	$53,512.55
Number of Units	99
Number of Units achieving or surpassing Average Sales per Map	43

Proportion of Units achieving or surpassing Average Sales per Map	43%

Some franchises have sold this amount. Your individual results may differ. There is no assurance that you will sell as much.

Note that this Financial Performance Representation is historic: the reasonable basis for this financial performance representation is past Gross Sales figures supplied to us in monthly reports by our franchisees. These reports comprise the written substantiation for the financial performance representation above.

NOTE: 99 (out of a total of 134) maps are included in this earnings claim. This is because our earnings claim is based only on maps currently being produced in the two standard sizes. We do not include in this earnings claim the following unrepresentative groups: (1) a small number of legacy, non-standard-size maps (both undersize and oversize), (2) maps produced by the franchisees of a company that we recently acquired who are not yet covered under the provisions of our current Franchise Agreement, and (3) maps that were not published during the fiscal year.

The above figures, which reflect Gross Sales not profits, were calculated based upon information reported to us by our franchisees in their monthly reports.

We have not audited the above figures. The figures do not reflect the costs of sales, operating expenses or other costs and expenses that must be deducted from the Gross Sales figures to obtain your net income or profit. You should conduct an independent investigation of the costs and expenses you will incur in operating your DISCOVERY MAP Franchised Business.

The Gross Sales and financial results of your DISCOVERY MAP

Franchised Business are likely to differ from the figures stated above, and there is no assurance that you will do as well. Further, your Gross Sales and your financial results will depend upon, among other things, factors including local and national economic conditions; how much you follow our methods and procedures; your sales skills; your management skill, experience and business acumen; whether you personally manage your Franchised Business or hire a manager; the region in which your Franchised Business is located; the competition in your local market; the prevailing wage rate; and the sales level reached during the initial period.

The maps included in the above financial performance representation may differ materially from the one you are considering: Different communities will feature different mixtures of restaurants, resorts, retail stores, local attractions and other tourist-based businesses in the community. Some maps describe locations with continuous traffic throughout the year, while others describe more seasonal attractions. Finally, the mix of independent business and chains/franchises will vary from one location to another, and you should be aware that in-dependent businesses are more likely than others to purchase advertisements on your map.

Your analysis of a DISCOVERY MAP Franchised Business should include estimates of expenses for all applicable items, including printing, royalties, a home-based office or if you choose to rent office space, staff salaries or commissions, your own salary, phone/fax charges, postage and courier charges, travel, auto expense, insurance, and the costs of marketing materials. All of these items are based largely on factors within your control, for which you can obtain information through your own research. Since these amounts are to a great degree a matter of personal preference, we have included no estimates for these items, and you should make appropriate assumptions. However, you should also be aware that the expense items listed above are by no means exhaustive. There are likely to be additional expenses that we have not listed, some of which may be unique to your market or situation. Written substantiation of the data used in preparing the earnings claim will be made available to you upon reasonable request.

ENVIRO-MASTER

417 Minuet Ln.
Charlotte, NC 28217
Tel: (855) 776-4944, (239) 645-2808
Fax: (704) 665-5798
Email: swarren@enviro-master.com
Website: www.enviro-master.com
Scott Warren, Senior Vice President Franchise Sales & Development

Enviro-Master's primary focus is the sanitization of restrooms, rendering them germ-free and eliminating the cross-contamination of disease, which so often originates in restrooms, the most commonly frequented area in most public businesses. We also offer savings on soap, paper and chemical products, which often offset the cost of our hygiene services. We strive to provide a pleasant restroom experience to patrons and employees of our customers. Supplemental products (paper and chemical) are provided for kitchens in public restaurants. Finally, we recognize that sanitary restrooms enhance our customers' image and often increase revenues.

BACKGROUND

IFA Member:	Yes
Established & First Franchised:	2010; 2010
Franchised Units:	23
Company-Owned Units:	0
Total Units:	23
Distribution:	US – 23; CAN – 0; O'seas – 0
North America:	12 State, 0 Provinces
Density:	4 in FL, 3 in TX, 1 in PA
Projected New Units (12 Months):	12
Qualifications:	3, 5, 1, 2, 3, 4

FINANCIAL/TERMS

Cash Investment:	$35 – 75K
Total Investment:	$120 – 310K
Minimum Net Worth:	N/A
Fees (Franchise):	$35 – 75K
Fees (Royalty):	6%
Fees (Advertising):	2%
Term of Contract (Years):	5/10
Average Number of Employees:	5 FT, 2 PT
Passive Ownership:	Not Allowed
Encourage Conversions:	N/A

Area Development Agreements:	No	Franchisee Association/Member:	Yes/Member
Sub-Franchising Contracts:	No	Size of Corporate Staff:	23
Expand in Territory:	Yes	On-going Support:	A, B, C, D, F, G, H, I
Space Needs:	1,500 SF	Training:	2 Weeks Charlotte, NC

SUPPORT & TRAINING		SPECIFIC EXPANSION PLANS	
Financial Assistance Provided:	No	US:	All United States
Site Selection Assistance:	Yes	Canada:	Yes
Lease Negotiation Assistance:	No	Overseas:	Yes
Co-operative Advertising:	No		

Background.

This Item sets out historical revenue and gross profit information for our franchised units that had been in operation for at least two years as of December 31, 2013. Enviro-Master is a service business and we believe it must be grown at a measured pace. As such, our franchisees add customers one at a time, with customers signing annual or multi-year contracts with our franchisees. We believe a franchisee should not reasonably expect to be significantly profitable until their second year, although we cannot and do not guarantee profitability at any time.

Operations for Calendar Year 2013.

7 franchisees have been in continual operation for 24 months or longer. 1 franchisee has been in operation for over 36 months.

(i) 36 months or longer:
Gross Revenue — $1,303,727
Gross Profit — 75%
(ii) 24 months of longer:
Average Gross Revenue — $500,942
Average Gross Profit — 79%

Note: Of the units in operation 24 months or longer, 1 unit was above the average and 6 were below the average.

All data is unaudited.

Gross Profit is defined as Gross Revenue minus Cost of Goods Sold.

There are economic factors and demographic factors specific to each individual market. The performance of an Enviro-Master franchisee will depend upon both its local market conditions and, perhaps most importantly, the competency and diligence of its staff and personnel.

Other than the preceding financial performance representation, we do not make any representations about a franchisee's future financial performance or the past financial performance of company-owned or franchised outlets. We also do not authorize our employees or representatives to make any such representations either orally or in writing. If you are purchasing an existing outlet, however, we may provide you with the actual records of that outlet. If you receive any other financial performance information or projections of your future income, you should report it to the franchisor's management by contacting Pat Swisher, 417 Minuet Lane, Ste. G, Charlotte, NC 28217, (704) 302-1016, the Federal Trade Commission, and the appropriate state regulatory agencies.

Written substantiation for the financial performance representation will be made available to the prospective franchisee upon reasonable request.

EXPRESS OIL CHANGE

1880 Southpark Dr.
Birmingham, AL 35244
Tel: (888) 945-1771, (205) 945-1771
Fax: (205) 943-5779
Email: dlarose@expressoil.com
Website: www.expressoil.com
Don LaRose, SVP Franchise Development

We are among the top ten fast oil change chains in the world. Per unit, sales out-pace our competitors by over 19%. Attractive, state-of-the-art facilities offer expanded, highly profitable services in addition to our ten minute oil change. We also provide transmission service, air conditioning service, brake repair, tire rotation and balancing and miscellaneous light repairs... Most extensive training and franchise support in the industry.

BACKGROUND

IFA Member:	Yes
Established & First Franchised:	1979; 1984
Franchised Units:	113
Company-Owned Units:	88
Total Units:	201
Distribution:	US – 201; CAN – 0; O'seas – 0
North America:	15 States, 0 Provinces
Density:	90 in AL, 35 in GA, 20 in TN
Projected New Units (12 Months):	12
Qualifications:	5, 5, 1, 3, 3, 5

FINANCIAL/TERMS

Cash Investment:	$300 – 350K
Total Investment:	$1,300 – 1,600K
Minimum Net Worth:	$450K
Fees (Franchise):	$35K
Fees (Royalty):	5%
Fees (Advertising):	0
Term of Contract (Years):	10/10
Average Number of Employees:	7 FT, 0 PT
Passive Ownership:	Allowed
Encourage Conversions:	Yes
Area Development Agreements:	Yes
Sub-Franchising Contracts:	No
Expand in Territory:	Yes
Space Needs:	22,000 SF

SUPPORT & TRAINING

Financial Assistance Provided:	Yes (I)
Site Selection Assistance:	Yes
Lease Negotiation Assistance:	Yes
Co-operative Advertising:	Yes
Franchisee Association/Member:	Yes/Member
Size of Corporate Staff:	44
On-going Support:	A, B, C, D, E, F, G, H, I
Training:	Ongoing Closest Training Center; Ongoing Birmingham, AL; Ongoing On-Site

SPECIFIC EXPANSION PLANS

US:	South
Canada:	No
Overseas:	No

Except for the historical data relating to certain average sales & expenses set forth in Exhibit I, we do not make any financial performance representations.

Most Centers offer substantially the same products and services to the public. None of the franchised Centers have customarily received services not generally available to other franchisees and substantially the same services will be available to you.

Your franchised Center average may vary from averages of Company-operated and other franchised centers. The results of the first 6-18 months of operation will vary greatly depending on your involvement, advertising, location, size of market, awareness in the market and other factors. Results also differ greatly between conforming and non-conforming markets. We feel you should anticipate a negative cash flow for a minimum of 6 months.

These results are averages of specific Centers and should not be considered as the actual or probable results that will be realized by you. Some Centers have sold and earned the amounts set forth in Exhibit I. Your individual results may differ. There is no assurance that you will sell or earn as much. You are urged to consult with appropriate financial, business and legal advisors in connection with this historical information.

Substantiation of data used in preparing this Item 19 will be made available to you upon reasonable request. However, we will not disclose the identity or sales data of any particular Center without the consent of that franchisee, except to any applicable state registration authorities or except in connection with the sale of a Company-owned Center. If you rely upon our figures, you must accept the risk of not doing as well.

None of our officers or employees is authorized to make any other claims or statements as to the financial performance, sales or profits or prospects or chances of success that you can expect or that have been experienced by present or past Centers. We have specifically instructed our officers and employees that they are not permitted to make other claims or statements as to the financial performance, sales or profits or

the prospects or chances of success, nor are they authorized to represent or estimate dollar figures as to any particular Center or any particular site for a Center. You should not rely on any unauthorized representations as to financial performance, sales, profits or prospects or chances of success. If you receive any other financial performance information or projections of your future income you should report it to the Company's management by contacting our Chief Executive Officer, Richard A. Brooks at 1880 Southpark Drive, Birmingham, Alabama 35244, (205) 945-1771, the Federal Trade Commission and the appropriate state regulatory agencies.

Written substantiation for the financial performance representation will be made available to you upon reasonable request.

EXHIBIT I

EXPRESS OIL CHANGE, L.L.C.

HISTORICAL FINANCIAL INFORMATION

Average Per Store Sales

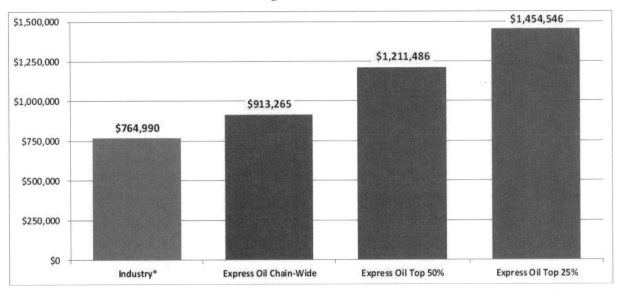

- Note: Industry average of chains as reported by National Oil & Lube News.
  Express Oil Change average of all locations open at least 12 months.

Typical Store Sales Expenses and Cost before Debt

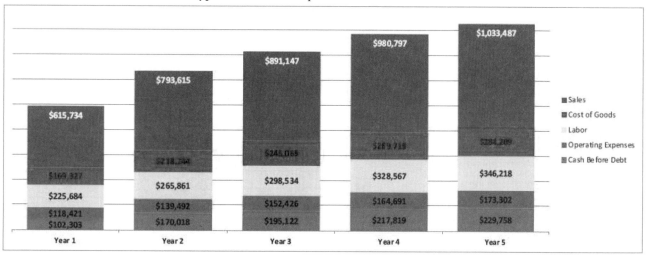

Sales: Express Oil Change average of all locations open at least 12 months as of 2/28/14.

Cost of Goods: Cost of Goods estimated at 27.5% of sales, may decrease of increase depending on pricing in your market, business mix and operational management.

Labor: It is recommended that you invest in your labor to build early sales. A typical location will be spending $16,000 to $20,000 per month including a 15% burden in labor costs. Once sales reach approximately $50,000 per month, labor should move as a percentage of sales with a target of 32% to 35%. We strongly recommend use of a third party payroll service, with an estimated annual cost of $4,200 ro $7,200 for a six person crew, which has been included in operating expenses below. In the illustration above, labor has been calculated at 33.5% of sales.

Operations Expenses: We divid operating expenses into two categories:

A)Variable Costs - are items directly related to store sales, which include: royalty fee at 5%, advertising at 3%, credit card fees at 1.4%, and shop supplies at 0.9%.

B) Non-Variable Costs - Although these costs are not truly fixed, they do have a controlled aspect, and include accounting, insurance, bank fees, computer expense, dues and subscriptions, office supplies, repair and maintenance, small tools, uniforms, utilities, miscellaneous items and the use of a payroll service. We estimate non-variable costs to be in the range of $50,000 to $60,000 with a marginal annual increase. In the illustration above we have estimated these expenses at $55,000 per year with a 5% increase per year to account for sales volume increases. This estimate does not include property tax. Please check with local authorities for estimated cost.

Note: These expenses should not be considered as the actual or probable results that will be realized by you. Your own financial results are likely to differ from these results. You are urged to consult with appropriate financial, business and legal advisors in connection with this historical information. Substantiation of data used in preparing this analysis will be made available to you upon reasonable request.

Quarterly Same Store Sales Growth

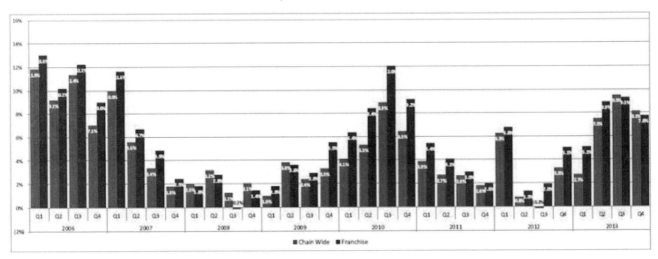

* Note: Same Store Sales (SSS) defined as aggregate revenue for all stores open at least 13 months at the end of indicated quarter. Percent change represents growth/decline over the same quarter for the previous year.

Store Count by Revenue Brackets

2013 Total Revenue		
Range	# of Stores	% of Total
Minimum:	$328,963	
$300k - $500k	16	8.3%
$500k - $700k	52	26.9%
$700k - $900k	39	20.2%
$900k - $1.1M	33	17.1%
$1.1M - $1.3M	22	11.4%
$1.3M - $2.0M	29	1.0%
> $2.0M	2	1.0%
Maximum:	$2,132,541	
TOTAL	193	100.0%

* Note: 2013 Total Revenue for all stores open at least one year as of 12/31/13.

Start-Up Cost Summary

	Typical Range
Land[1]	$550,000 – $750,000

Building & Site[1]	$550,000 – $750,000
Equipment, Signs, Furnishings[1]	$150,000 – $240,000
Organization, Professional Fees	$20,000 – $50,000
Loan Origination	$20,000 – $35,000
Sub-Total	$1,290,000 – $1,825,000
Soft Costs	
Franchise Fee* [2]	$35,000
Pre-Opening[3]	$33,500
Opening Inventory	$27,500
Opening Advertising[4]	$10,000
Working Capital[5]	$70,000
Sub-Total	$176,000
Total	$1,466,000 – $2,001,000

(1) The amounts set forth above for land, building and site work, and equipment include the cost of purchasing a 20,000 to 30,000 square foot site in a commercial or retail area and constructing a 6 to 8 bay facility on property which has all utilities to the site and does not require any excessive site preparation. The actual costs will vary materially depending on location, size and condition of lot, size of building and other factors. Many existing buildings (former service stations, auto-

motive service centers, etc.) have been successfully converted at lower costs. To view a range of these costs, see Item 7 of this FDD.

(2) The initial franchise fee is $35,000 for your first unit, and $17,500 for any additional unit. Initial Franchise Fee is payable in a lump sum due at signing and is uniform to all franchisees currently purchasing a franchise.

(3) Amounts set forth above for pre-opening include (a) the manager's and assistant manager's salaries during pre-opening; (b) payroll costs of the crew for pre-opening training; and (c) costs of transportation, lodging, and meals during the train-

ing at the franchisor's headquarters. Also includes amounts for change fund, utility deposits, uniforms and other discretionary purchases.

(4) Amount set forth covers the requirement under the franchise agreement for grand opening promotions.

(5) Amounts set forth above are for working capital and normal early operating losses.

* There are no other direct or indirect payments in connection with the purchase of the franchise.

First Full Year Sales*

Average of Last 10 Openings*
Annual Sales Growth Rate**

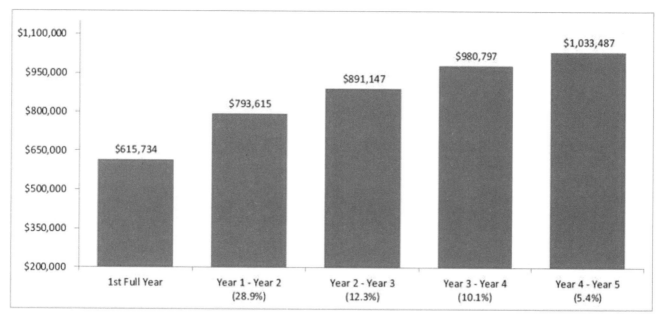

* Average of sales for first full 12 months for the 10 most recent openings, excluding conversions

** Average percentage sales increase of most recent 20 stores completing the corresponding year of operation, excluding conversions.

Note: These results should not be considered as the actual or probable results that will be realized by you. Your own results are likely to differ from these results. You are urged to consult with appropriate financial, business and legal advisors in connection with this historical information. Substantiation of data used in preparing this analysis will be made available to you upon reasonable request.

There are a variety of options available to pursue for financing the costs of starting the business, from conventional loans to Small Business Administration (SBA) financing. The example below is for an SBA 7-A loan for the hard and soft costs.

Hard Costs		Soft Costs	
Debt Structure	SBA 504	Debt Structure	SBA 7-A
Land	$650,000	Franchise Fee	$35,000
Building	$650,00	Inventory	$27,500

Equipment	$195,000	Working Capital	$113,500
Origination	$35,000		
Professional Fees	$35,000		
Total Hard Costs	$1,565,000	Total Soft Costs	$176,000

Loan to Value[1]	80%
Financed Amount	$1,392.800
Cash Injection	$348,200
Loan Term	25 Years
Interest Rate[2]	6%

Monthly Payment	$8,929
Annual Payment	$107,150

Total Cash Injection for above example: $348,200

* The actual interest rate, terms of amortization and other costs of financing may vary from these assumptions. Interest rates and lease rates are typically related to the Federal Reserve Board's Prime Rate.

1. Loans to project cost will be determined by SBA and supporting lending institution. This percentage will differ based on applicant's experience, credit-worthiness and financial portfolio. The typical range is 75% to 90%.

2. Interest rates are a blend of both the SBA and supporting lender rates. These rates will vary depending on applicant's experience, credit-worthiness and financial portfolio. We have estimated at the average of 6%.

FASTSIGNS

2542 Highlander Wy.
Carrollton, TX 75006
Tel: (800) 827-7446, (214) 346-5679
Fax: (866) 422-4927
Email: mark.jameson@fastsigns.com
Website: www.fastsigns.com
Mark L. Jameson, EVP, Franchise Support & Development

Signage has never been more important. Right now, businesses are looking for new and better ways to compete. Industries are revamping to meet compliance standards and advertisers are expanding their reach into new media, like digital signage, QR codes and mobile websites. Join the franchise that's leading the next generation of business communication. Now more than ever, businesses look to FASTSIGNS® for innovative ways to connect with customers in a highly competitive marketplace. Our high standards for quality and customer service have made FASTSIGNS the most recognized brand in the industry, driving significantly more traffic to the Web than any other sign company.

BACKGROUND

IFA Member:	Yes
Established & First Franchised:	1985; 1986
Franchised Units:	550
Company-Owned Units:	0
Total Units:	550
Distribution:	US – 486; CAN – 26; O'seas – 38
North America:	50 States, 8 Provinces
Density:	58 in TX, 36 in FL, 45 in CA
Projected New Units (12 Months):	45
Qualifications:	5, 5, 1, 3, 4, 5

FINANCIAL/TERMS

Cash Investment:	$80K
Total Investment:	$178.2 – 289.5K
Minimum Net Worth:	$250K
Fees (Franchise):	$37.5K
Fees (Royalty):	6%
Fees (Advertising):	2%
Term of Contract (Years):	20/20
Average Number of Employees:	2 – 3 FT, 0 PT
Passive Ownership:	Discouraged
Encourage Conversions:	Yes
Area Development Agreements:	Yes
Sub-Franchising Contracts:	No

Expand in Territory:	Yes
Space Needs:	1,200 – 1,500 SF

SUPPORT & TRAINING

Financial Assistance Provided:	Yes (I)
Site Selection Assistance:	Yes
Lease Negotiation Assistance:	Yes
Co-operative Advertising:	No
Franchisee Association/Member:	Yes/Member
Size of Corporate Staff:	110

On-going Support:	C, D, E, G, H, I
Training:	1 Week Local Center; 2 Weeks Dallas, TX; 1 Week On-Site

SPECIFIC EXPANSION PLANS

US:	All United States
Canada:	All Canada except Quebec as Master/Area Developmer Only
Overseas:	UK, South America, Africa, Europe, Asia, New Zealand, Mexico

2013 Sales Volume Study

On December 31, 2013, there were 549 FASTSIGNS Centers open and in operation of which 64 were international. 485 Centers were open and in continuous operation in the US including 29 which opened during 2013. 456 Centers were open and in continuous operation in the United States during the entire calendar year ending December 31, 2013. The analysis set forth below is based solely on the average yearly gross sales for those 456 Centers for 2013.

Based on gross sales reported by the 456 Centers, the average gross sales for such Centers for the year ended December 31, 2013 was $666,913. For purposes of this analysis, gross sales includes cash and credit sales as well as any goods or services received by the franchisee in exchange for goods and services sold at the Center. Gross sales do not include sales or use taxes.

Of the 456 Centers included in this analysis, 171 or 38% of the Centers reported gross sales above the average, ranging from $670,684 to $6,989,913 and 285 or 62% of the Centers reported gross sales below the average, ranging from $89,143 to $663,293. These figures include "Satellite" Centers, which are typically smaller Centers without full production capabilities as well as centers that are just past 1 year old or in their early years in business. The Centers in the top quartile (114 Centers) had average gross sales of $1,262,896 in 2013. Overall, the Centers included in this analysis reported gross sales in the following ranges for the year:

2013 SALES ENDING DECEMBER 31

2013 Sales	# of Centers
$0 - $250,000	39
$250,001 - $500,000	153
$500,001 - $750,000	116

$750,001 - $1,000,000	76
$1,000,001 - $1,500,000	50
$1,500,001 - $2,000,000	18
$2,000,001 and over	4
Total Centers	456
Average Sales	$666,129
Median Sales	$529,279

2013 Sales	1st Year Centers*	2nd Year Centers**	3rd Year Centers***
$0 - $300,000	13	8	4
$300,001 - $600,000	6	7	6
$600,001 - $1,000,000	1	0	1
Total Centers	20	15	11

* Centers opened during calendar year 2012 averaged $301,424 (or $25,119/month) during calendar year 2013

** Centers opened in calendar year 2011

*** Centers opened in calendar year 2010

Of the 171 Centers reporting gross sales above the average, 44 Centers are located in the Southwest Region of the United States, 28 in the West Region, 26 in the Northeast Region, 39 in the Southeast Region and 34 in the Midwest Region. Of the 285 Centers reporting gross sales below the average, 45 are located in the Southwest Region, 59 in the West Region, 72 in the Northwest Region, 49 in the Southwest Region and 60 in the Midwest Region.

For purposes of this analysis, the Southwest Region consists of Arkansas, Colorado, Louisiana, New Mexico, Oklahoma and Texas; the West Region consists of Alaska, Arizona, California, Hawaii, Idaho, Montana, Nevada, Oregon, Utah, Washington and Wyoming; the Northeast Region consists of Connecticut, Delaware, Maine, Maryland, Massachusetts, New Hampshire, New Jersey, New York, Pennsylvania, Rhode Island, Vermont, Virginia, Washington, D.C. and West Virginia; the Southeast Region consists of Alabama, Florida, Georgia, Mississippi, North Carolina, South Carolina and Tennessee; and the Midwest Region consists of Illinois, Indiana, Iowa, Kansas, Kentucky, Ohio, Michigan, Minnesota, Missouri, Nebraska, North Dakota, South Dakota and Wisconsin.

We offer substantially the same services to all franchisees. Additionally, advertising and promotional materials developed by the Fastsigns National Advertising Council, Inc. are available to all Franchisees. (See Item 11.) An individual Franchisee is not limited in the amount or type of advertising that it may conduct; provided, however, that all advertising materials developed by Franchisee must be approved in advance by us. (See Item 16.) Consequently, Franchisee's gross sales may be directly affected by the amount, type and effectiveness of advertising conducted by Franchisee.

The Franchise Agreement provides that Franchisees must offer and sell at the Center products and services required by us and may offer and sell such additional products and services approved by us. (See Item 16.) Franchisees offer substantially the same products and services to the public. In certain states, as noted in Item 1, Franchisees may be required to have a contractor's license to perform certain types of sign installation work. In those states, if you do not have, or meet the requirements to obtain a license, then you may not be able to offer those installation services requiring a license. Additionally, although we may suggest prices for the products and services offered at the Center, Franchisees may offer and sell such products and services at any price it chooses. As a result, the products and services offered and the prices at which such products and services are offered to the public at the Centers included in this analysis may vary.

The average gross sales figures included in this analysis are based on sales reports submitted to us by each Franchisee. The figures in the sales reports have not been audited and we have not undertaken to otherwise independently verify (i) the accuracy of such information or (ii) whether such information was prepared in accordance with generally accepted accounting principles.

Gross Sales of Top 25 FASTSIGNS Centers

The average annual gross sales for the top 25 FASTSIGNS Centers in the United States were $2,000,356 for 2013. To be included in the top 25, a Center had to have reported its gross sales for each of the 12 months in the calendar year. We had a total of 485 Centers in the United States as of December 31, 2013.

Gross Sales Study – Centers with Outside Sales Representatives

It has been our experience that having a full time outside sales representative is an essential part of a successful marketing program. The average gross sales of FASTSIGNS Centers in the United States during the twelve month period from January 1, 2013 to December 31, 2013 was $897,283 for franchise owners who (1) were in business for at least two years prior to January 1, 2013; (2) reported gross sales for each of the 12 months in 2013 and (3) advised us that they employed a full-time outside representative during this period who was not one of the owners of the Center. The number of Centers who met this criteria in 2013, and were used in this study, was 171 which represented 37% of the FASTSIGNS open and operational in the United States for the full year in 2013. The number of these Centers whose sales attained or surpassed the system average gross sales number ($666,129) for the United States was 101 or 59%.

Results of 2013 Financial Benchmark Survey

In addition to the average gross sales analysis, certain expenses, expressed as a percentage of Gross Revenues, have been provided based on the experience of certain of the foregoing FASTSIGNS Centers described below. The expense figures were extracted from the 2013 financial statements submitted by the FASTSIGNS Franchisees included in our 2013 Financial Bechmark Survey. As of the date of this DISCLOSURE DOCUMENT, we have not been provided with expense data from 221 of the 456 Centers open and in continuous operation during 2013. This was primarily due to the close proximity of year-end to the time of compilation of these numbers and such 221 Centers were not included in the expense figures provided herein. You should note that with respect to the 235 FASTSIGNS Centers included in the compilation of the expense figures, the expense data relates to operations conducted during the one-year period ended 2013. Of the 235 Centers reporting expenses 1 was opened in 1985, 1 was opened in 1986, 1 was opened in 1987, 6 were opened in 1988, 13 were opened in 1989, 29 were opened in 1990, 8 were opened in 1991, 14 were opened in 1992, 10 were opened in 1993, 7 were opened in 1994, 14 were opened in 1995, 1 were opened in 1996, 10 were opened in 1997, 11 were opened in 1998, 5 were opened in 1999, 4 were opened in 2000, 3 were opened in 2001, 5 were opened in 2002, 2 were opened in 2003, 8 were opened in 2004, 10 were opened in 2005, 9 were opened in 2006, 6 were opened in 2007, 12 were opened in 2008, 7 were opened in 2009, 9 was opened in 2010, 7 were opened in 2011, and 12 were opened in 2012. These Centers are located in the following regions; 51 in the Southwest region of the United States, 43 in the West region, 37 in the Northeast region, 57 in the Southeast region and 47 in the Midwest region.

The information relating to the operations expenses provided by the FASTSIGNS Centers and used by the us in determining the numerical values provided have not been audited and such information has not necessarily been prepared on a basis consistent with generally accepted accounting principles. In particular, we are unable to verify whether the expense data submitted by each FASTSIGNS Center for each separately provided expense item appropriately reflects the types of expenses which are ordinarily incurred by FASTSIGNS Centers and which should be included in the item according to generally acceptable accounting principles.

Each percentage given on this analysis reflects the mean average of the total percentages for the applicable expense item provided by the reporting FASTSIGNS Center (i.e., the aggregate sum of the expense percentages of all reporting FASTSIGNS Centers divided by the number of reporting Centers). The expense percentages for the various expense items provided by each reporting FASTSIGNS Center reflects that Center's expenses as a percentage of its Gross Revenues. No percentage given on this analysis is the actual expenses percentage experienced by any one FASTSIGNS Center and the actual expense percentages for the reporting FASTSIGNS Centers on any particular expense item may vary significantly. The following expenses represent the major expense items for a FASTSIGNS Center and should not be considered the only expenses that a FASTSIGNS Center will incur:

2013 Year-End Average P&L

	Company Average (235 Centers Reporting)		Top 25% Based on Profitability (58 Centers)	
	Annual	% of Sales	Annual	% of Sales
SALES	$729,317.55	100.0%	$919,241.01	100.0%
COST OF GOODS	$209,669.66	28.7%	$243,391.92	26.5%
LABOR EXPENSES (Including Owner)	$251,611.38	34.5%	$299,771.93	32.6%
ADVERTISING EXPENSES	$22,023.82	3.0%	$27,049.54	2.9%
AUTO EXPENSES	$12,399.88	1.7%	$11,983.25	1.3%
FACILITY EXPENSES	$47,262.33	6.5%	$50,584.25	5.5%
EQUIPMENT EXPENSES	$6,069.98	0.8%	$5,447.24	0.6%
GENERAL AND ADMINISTRATIVE EXPENSES	$99,929.87	13.7%	$111,170.91	12.1%
EBITDA	$80,350.61	11.0%	$169,841.96	18.5%
Owner's Salary from Labor Expenses	$46,687.08	6.4%	$84,151.03	9.2%
Total Owner Benefit	$127,037.69	17.4%	$253,992.99	27.6%

The franchisor is unable to verify the accuracy of the expense information provided by FASTSIGNS franchisees and makes no representations or warranties regarding the same.

The average gross sales for all Centers included in the above study were $729,318. The amount of gross sales realized and expenses incurred will vary from unit to unit. In particular, gross sales and expenses at Franchisee's Center will be directly affected by many additional factors not noted above, including, without limitation, the Center's geographic location, competition in the market, the presence of other FASTSIGNS Centers, the quality of management, the effectiveness of sales and marketing and the prices charged for products and services sold at the Center. Further, the franchise agreement to which each franchisee included in this analysis is subject is different from the Franchise Agreement attached to this DISCLOSURE DOCUMENT as Exhibit B. Among other terms, the Franchise Agreement attached to this DISCLOSURE DOCUMENT requires an initial franchise fee of $37,500 and a continuing Service Fee of 6%. Further, Franchisee may be required to participate in an Advertising Cooperative. This analysis, therefore, should only be used as a reference for Franchise Candidates to use in conducting its own analysis.

Finally, Franchisee should particularly note the following:

Each franchisee is urged to consult with appropriate financial, business and legal advisors in connection with the information set forth in this analysis.

The average sales and major expenses reflected in this analysis should not be considered as the actual or potential sales that will be realized by any franchisee. We do not represent that any franchisee can expect to attain such sales. In addition, we do not represent that any franchisee will derive income that exceeds the initial payment for or investment in a FASTSIGNS franchise. No inference as to expenses, cost of goods sold or profits relating to existing or future centers should be drawn from the sales information reflected in this analysis. The success of franchisee will depend largely upon the ability of franchisee, and the individual financial results of a franchisee are likely to differ from the information set forth herein. Substantiation of the data used in preparing this analysis will be made available upon reasonable request.

Escept for the information contained in this Item 19, we do not furnich or authorize our sales personnel, our employees or the Fastsigns National Advertising, Inc.'s employees to furnich any oral, visual or written information concerning the actual or potential sales, costs, income or profits of a Center. Actual results vary from unit to unit and we cannot estimate the results of any particular franchise. We do not make any representations that you or any of your principals may or will derive income from any Center, which exceeds the initial payment for or investment in the Center.

FIRSTLIGHT HOMECARE

9435 Waterstone Blvd., # 190
Cincinnati, OH 45249
Tel: (877) 570-0002, (513) 400-5136
Fax: (513) 830-5003
Email: bmcpherson@firstlighthomecare.com
Website: www.firstlightfranchise.com
Bill McPherson, Executive Director

FIRSTLIGHT HOMECARE offers comprehensive, in-home, non-medical and personal care services to seniors, new mothers, adults with disabilities, and others needing assistance. FIRSTLIGHT's founders bring more than 132 years of franchising experience and over 92 years of health-care and senior services experience, creating the core of FIRSTLIGHT's foundation. FIRSTLIGHT franchisees are passionate and caring and strive to provide exceptional service. Owning a FIRSTLIGHT franchise offers the benefits of traditional business ownership with less risk and provides an established business system along with other advantages.

BACKGROUND:
IFA Member:	Yes
Established & First Franchised:	2009; 2010
Franchised Units:	111
Company-Owned Units:	0
Total Units:	111

Dist.:	US-110; CAN-1; O'seas-0
North America:	25 States, 1 Province
Density:	13 in OH, 6 in FL, 6 in IL
Projected New Units (12 Months):	30
Qualifications:	5, 5, 1, 3, 4, 5

FINANCIAL/TERMS:
Cash Investment:	$60K
Total Investment:	$85.2 – 128.6K
Minimum Net Worth:	$150K
Fees (Franchise):	$8K
Fees (Royalty):	5%
Fees (Advertising):	0%
Term of Contract (Years):	10/10
Avg. # of Employees:	2 FT, 6-50+ PT
Passive Ownership:	Allowed
Encourage Conversions:	Yes
Area Develop. Agreements:	Yes
Sub-Franchising Contracts:	No
Expand in Territory:	Yes
Space Needs:	600 SF

SUPPORT & TRAINING:
Financial Assistance Provided:	Yes (I)
Site Selection Assistance:	Yes
Lease Negotiation Assistance:	N/A
Co-operative Advertising:	Yes
Franchisee Assoc./Member:	Yes/Member
Size of Corporate Staff:	10
On-going Support:	C,D,E,G,H,I
Training:	8 Days and Ongoing Cincinnati, OH

SPECIFIC EXPANSION PLANS:
US:	All States except HI
Canada:	No
Overseas:	No

The tables below describe the "net revenue" reported to us by three sets of franchisees for the 12-month period ended December 31, 2013 (the "Reporting Period"), with one set comprised of 24 franchised FirstLight HomeCare businesses who, as of December 31, 2013, had been operating for 12-23 months; one set of 17 franchised FirstLight HomeCare businesses who, as of December 31, 2013, had been operating for 24-35 months; and one set of 7 franchised FirstLight HomeCare businesses who, as of December 31, 2013, had been operating more than 36 months. Thee 48 franchised FirstLight HomeCare businesses are referred to in this Item 19 as the "Item 19 Businesses."

There were a total of of 48 FirstLight HomeCare businesses in operation for these periods as of December 31, 2013, and which had been in operation for a minimum of 12 months as of the issuance of this Disclosure Document. The Item 19 Businesses consist of all franchised FirstLight HomeCare businesses that were in operation during the entire reporting period. We have not audited the figures below, although we believe them to be reliable.

For purposes of the table below, "net revenue" means that revenue for the calendar year 2013, on which a franchisee pays royalty fees (which is referred to as "gross revenue" in the Franchise Agreement). This is the total amount of money the franchisee and its' owners receive for all goods and services rendered in connection with the Marks, and all other income of any kind derived directly or indirectly in connection with the operation of Item 19 Business.

Chart 1

Item 19 Businesses in Operation for 12-23 months

# Months Operating (1)	Average Net Revenue (2)	Median Net Revenue (3)	Highest Net Revenue (4)	Lowest Net Revenue (5)
12-23	$225,559	$208,987	$807,869	$5,688

(1) The Item 19 businesses began operation in 2012 as First-Light HomeCare businesses with full 12 months operating history between January 1, 2013 and December 31, 2013.

(2) 10 of these 24 businesses (or 42%) reported net revenue equal to or in excess of this amount.

(3) 10 of these businesses (or 42%) reported net revenue equal

to or in excess of this amount.

(4) 1 of these 24 businesses (or 5%) reported net revenue equal to or in excess of this amount.

(5) 24 of these 24 businesses (or 100 %) reported net revenue equal to or in excess of this amount.

Chart 2

Item 19 Businesses in Operation for 24-35 months

# Months Operating (1)	Average Net Revenue (2)	Median Net Revenue (3)	Highest Net Revenue (4)	Lowest Net Revenue (5)
24-35	$421,469	$367,940	$985,913	$61,655

(1) These businesses began operation during 2011 as First-Light HomeCare businesses with full 12 months operating history between January 1, 2013 and December 31, 2013.

(2) 8 of these 17 businesses (or 47%) reported net revenue equal to or in excess of this amount.

(3) 9 of these 17 businesses (or 53%) reported net revenue

equal to or in excess of this amount.

(4) 1 of these 17 businesses (or 6%) reported net revenue equal to or in excess of this amount.

(5) 17 of these 17 businesses (or 100%) reported net revenue equal to or in excess of this amount.

Chart 3
Item 19 Businesses in Operation for 36-41 months

# Months Operating (1)	Average Net Revenue (2)	Median Net Revenue (3)	Highest Net Revenue (4)	Lowest Net Revenue (5)
36-41	$498,106	$589,234	$827,468	$20,278

(1) These businesses began operation during late 2010 as FirstLight HomeCare businesses with full 12 months operating history between January 1, 2013 and December 31, 2013.

(2) 4 of these 7 businesses (or 57%) reported net revenue equal to or in excess of this amount.

(3) 4 of these 7 businesses (or 57%) reported net revenue equal to or in excess of this amount.

(4) 1 of these 7 businesses (or 14%) reported net revenue equal to or in excess of this amount.

(5) 7 of these 7 businesses (or 100%) reported net revenue equal to or in excess of this amount.

NOT ALL FRANCHISED FIRSTLIGHT HOMECARE BUISNESSES ACHIEVED THE ABOVE RESULTS. THERE IS NO ASSURANCE THAT YOU WILL DO AS WELL. IF YOU RELY UPON OUR FIGURES, YOU MUST ACCEPT THE RISK OF NOT DOING AS WELL.

Written substantiation of the above figures will be made available to you on reasonable request.

Except as described above, we do not make any representations about a franchisee's future financial performance or the past financial performance of company-owned or franchised outlets. We also do not authorize our employees or representatives to make any such representations either orally or in writing. If you are purchasing an existing outlet, however, we may provide you with the actual records of that outlet. If you receive any other financial performance information or projections of your future income, you should report it to the franchisor's management by contacting Jeff Bevis, President & CEO, FirstLight HomeCare Franchising, LLC, One Waterstone Place, 9435 Waterstone Boulevard, Suite 190, Cincinnati, Ohio 45249.

FRESH COAT

10700 Montgomery Rd., # 300
Cincinnati, OH 45242
Tel: (513) 483-3296
Email: bboecker@franchisesupport.net
Website: www.freshcoatpainters.com
Beth Boecker, Director of Franchise Sales Administration

Ranked "Top 75 Low-Cost Franchise" and "Top 100 Home-based Franchise" in 2013 by Entrepreneur magazine. With 5 strong profit centers, you'll grow and manage your organization while the painters you hire do the painting. This is a great home-based opportunity for mid-managers and executives in the booming $100 billion home services industry. Own this exciting, year-round, recession-resistant business with low start-up costs, low overhead and high profit margin potential.

BACKGROUND
IFA Member:	Yes
Established & First Franchised:	2004; 2005
Franchised Units:	115
Company-Owned Units:	0
Total Units:	115
Distribution:	US – 114; CAN – 1; O'seas – 0
North America:	30 States, 1 Province
Density:	12 in TX, 9 in OH, 8 in FL
Projected New Units (12 Months):	60
Qualifications:	3, 4, 1, 2, 2, 4

FINANCIAL/TERMS
Cash Investment:	$10K
Total Investment:	$44.4 – 71K
Minimum Net Worth:	$50K
Fees (Franchise):	$39.9 – 45.9K

Fees (Royalty):	6%	Site Selection Assistance:	N/A
Fees (Advertising):	2%	Lease Negotiation Assistance:	N/A
Term of Contract (Years):	10/10/10	Co-operative Advertising:	No
Average Number of Employees:	2 FT, 4 PT	Franchisee Association/Member:	No
Passive Ownership:	Discouraged	Size of Corporate Staff:	50
Encourage Conversions:	No	On-going Support:	B, C, G, H, I
Area Development Agreements:	Yes	Training:	5 Days Cincinnati, OH
Sub-Franchising Contracts:	No		
Expand in Territory:	Yes	**SPECIFIC EXPANSION PLANS**	
Space Needs:	N/A	US:	All United States
		Canada:	All Canada
SUPPORT & TRAINING		Overseas:	All Countries
Financial Assistance Provided:	Yes (D)		

Presented below are historic Gross Revenue and Gross Profit figures for franchised Fresh Coat businesses for the one-year period from January 1, 2013 through December 31, 2013. Only data from franchises who were already open for at least one year before December 31, 2013, who operated their business on a full-time basis during the entire period, and who reported Gross Revenue for all 12 months of the period were included in the table. The information has been extracted from royalty reports and income statements submitted to us by our franchises. The income statements submitted to us were prepared by the franchisee in most cases, not reviewed or audited by an independent accountant. We have not audited or independently verified any of this information. It may not be relied upon as a projection or forecast of what a new Fresh Coat franchisee may experience.

Number of franchisees	12
Highest Growth Revenue	$1,248,380
Average Gross Revenue	$462,110
Number of franchisees who attained or surpassed the average Gross Revenue	4
Percentage of franchisees who attained or surpassed the average Gross Revenue	33%
Highest Gross Profit Percentage	52%
Average Gross Profit Percentage	41%
Number of franchisees who attained or surpassed the average Gross Profit Percentage	6
Percentage of franchisees who attained or surpassed the average Gross Profit Percentage	50%

There were 96 Fresh Coat franchises in operation as of December 31, 2013. Of those, 12 franchises were open for at least one year before that date, operated their business on a full-time basis, and reported Gross Revenue for all 12 months between January 1, 2013 and December 31, 2013.

For purposes of this Item 19, "Gross Revenue" means the total of all income arising from the operation of the franchised business, whether cash or credit. It is recognized on an accrual basis and regardless of collection, which means that a franchisee's Gross Revenue for any period represents how much a franchisee billed its clients during the period, not how much the franchisee received. Gross Revenue does not include the amount of refunds and discounts made to clients, or the amount of sales or excise taxes that are separately stated and that the franchisee is required to and does collect from clients and pays to the appropriate taxing authority. "Gross Profit" means Gross Revenue minus the cost of direct labor and paint.

Neither the Gross Revenue figures nor the Gross Profit figures reflect the costs of sales, other operating expenses, or other costs or expenses that must be deducted from Gross Revenue to obtain your net income or profit. Those expenses include fees you are required to pay us under the terms of your franchise agreement, such as royalties, national branding fees and technology fees. Your sales and operating expenses will vary depending on many factors, such as the geographic location of your territory, competition from other providers in your market, the effectiveness of your advertising, whether you manage your franchise yourself or hire a general manager, your pricing, the prices you pay for paint and other supplies, employee salaries and benefits (health insurance, retirement plan, etc.), other employment conditions in your market, insurance costs, weather conditions, ability to generate clients, and the necessity, cost and difficulty of obtaining a license to perform all of the services a Fresh Coat franchise offers. You should conduct an independent investigation of the costs and expenses you will incur in operating a Fresh Coat franchise. Franchisees and former franchisees listed in this disclosure document may be one source of this information.

Although all Fresh Coat franchises offer painting services to both commercial and residential customers, all but 2 Fresh

Coat franchises concentrate primarily on residential customers. The franchise with the highest Gross Revenue and Gross Profit Percentage in the table above concentrated primarily on commercial customers during that one-year period. The franchise with the second-highest Gross Revenue during that one-year period also concentrated primarily on commercial customers during that period.

You should use the information in the table only as one of several references in conducting your analysis and preparing your own projected income and cash flow statements. We strongly suggest that you consult a financial advisor or accountant for assistance in reviewing the table and in preparing your own financial projections, and for advice about the income and other taxes you will incur in operating a Fresh Coat franchise and the effect of non-cash expenses such as depreciation and amortization on your business.

The success of your Fresh Coat franchise will depend largely upon your personal abilities and how you use them, your willingness to engage in personal sales activities (or your ability to hire someone else to), the number of potential customers in your market and their household income levels, and the number of competitors in your market. You are likely to achieve results that are different, possibly significantly and adversely, from the results shown in the table above.

Some of our franchisees have sold this amount. There is no assurance that you'll do as well. If you rely upon our figures, you must accept the risk of not doing as well. We do not make any promises or representations that you will achieve any particular results or level of sales or profitability, or even achieve break-even results in any particular year of operation. We do not represent that your franchise will generate any income or that the amount of income it might generate will exceed your initial investment in the franchise.

Written substantiation for the financial performance representation will be made available to you upon request.

Other than the preceding financial performance representation, we do not make any financial performance representations. We also do not authorize our employees or representatives to make any such representations either orally or in writing. If you are purchasing an existing outlet, however, we may provide you with the actual records of that outlet. If you receive any other financial performance information or projections of your future income, you should report it to the franchisor's management by contacting Jeffrey D. Siehl, General Counsel, 10700 Montgomery Road, Suite 300, Cincinnati, Ohio 45242, (513) 563-8339, the Federal Trade Commission, and the appropriate state regulatory agencies.

FURNITURE MEDIC

3839 Forest Hill-Irene Rd.
Memphis, TN 38125
Tel: (800) 230-2360, (901) 597-8600
Fax: (901) 597-8660
Email: cbeck@furnituremedic.com
Website: www.furnituremedicfranchise.com
Chris Beck, Franchise Sales Manager

FURNITURE MEDIC is a division of The ServiceMaster Company. It is the largest furniture and wood repair and restoration company in the world with over 300 franchises. Furniture Medic has unique products and processes which enable much of the work to be done on-site, reducing costs and saving time for its residential and commercial customers. Financing is provided for the initial franchise fees, start-up equipment and vehicles to qualified candidates through ServiceMaster Acceptance Company.

BACKGROUND

IFA Member:	Yes
Established & First Franchised:	1990; 1992
Franchised Units:	334
Company-Owned Units:	0
Total Units:	334
Distribution:	US – 302; CAN – 51; O'seas – 80
North America:	47 States, 0 Provinces
Projected New Units (12 Months):	30
Qualifications:	4, 4, 2, 3, 3, 5

FINANCIAL/TERMS

Cash Investment:	$20 – 25K
Total Investment:	$54.1 – 70.4K
Minimum Net Worth:	$75K
Fees (Franchise):	$29.9K
Fees (Royalty):	7%/$250 min.

Fees (Advertising):	1%/$50 min.	Site Selection Assistance:	N/A
Term of Contract (Years):	5/5	Lease Negotiation Assistance:	No
Average Number of Employees:	1 FT, 1 PT	Co-operative Advertising:	Yes
Passive Ownership:	Allowed	Franchisee Association/Member:	Yes/Member
Encourage Conversions:	Yes	Size of Corporate Staff:	21
Area Development Agreements:	No	On-going Support:	A, B, G, h, I
Sub-Franchising Contracts:	No	Training:	3 Weeks Mempis, TN
Expand in Territory:	Yes		
Space Needs:	N/A		

SPECIFIC EXPANSION PLANS

US:	Most metropolitan markets in US
Canada:	All Canada
Overseas:	All Countries

SUPPORT & TRAINING

Financial Assistance Provided:	Yes (D)

The following charts and tables are a historic financial performance representation and are not a forecast of your future financial performance.

Definitions

"Ownership Group" means a unique group of licenses having the same individual owner or group of owners. For example, if one license is owned by John Smith and another is owned jointly by John Smith and Jane Smith, these would represent two different Ownership Groups. But, if David Jones owns 3 licenses under one Enterprise and 2 licenses under another Enterprise, all 5 licenses would be grouped into a single Ownership Group.

Furniture Medic

The following financial performance representation consists of historical data for Ownership Groups offering furniture restoration and repair Services in the United States of America that have been operating a business for at least two years as of January 1, 2011. We have not included data from similar franchises in Canada or any other foreign country or territory. Some franchisees have more than one franchise agreement related to their business. Franchisees with multiple franchises typically do not have separate operations for each franchise agreement. Therefore, we have aggregated data based on "Ownership Groups" to more accurately reflect a franchisee's business. There are 126 Ownership Groups that had at least one license with a start date of January 1, 2009 or before.

The tables below include Ownership Groups with at least $125,000 in annual gross sales. Of the 126 Ownership Groups, 39 (or 31%) had average annual gross sales of at least $125,000 during the three year period 2011-13. Ownership Groups included in the table below have an average of 1.3 franchise agreements per Ownership Group. Ownership Groups with an average of less than $125,000 in annual gross sales during the three year period 2011-13 have been excluded. Ownership Groups with an average of less than $125,000 in annual gross sales account for 30.9% of annual gross sales for all Ownership Groups. Lower revenue may be a result of a focus on a different service line or the desire to operate this as a part time business among other potential causes.

The annual gross sales reported below include gross sales reported for furniture repair and restoration Services.

We compiled this information from reported gross sales from franchisees for January 2011 through December 2013. We have not independently verified the information received from franchisees. These financial statements were not prepared in accordance with Generally Accepted Accounting Principles (GAAP), but are believed to be reliable. We will provide you with written substantiation of the data used in preparing the financial performance representations in this Item 19 upon reasonable request.

Some franchisees have gross sales of this amount. There is no assurance you will do as well. If you rely on our figures, you must accept the risk of not doing as well.

Table 1: 2011-2013 AVERAGE ANNUAL GROSS SALES DURING THE THREE YEAR PERIOD 2011-13 FOR ALL OWNERSHIP GROUPS WHO HAVE BEEN IN BUSINESS FOR AT LEAST THREE CALENDAR YEARS AND HAD AN AVERAGE OF OVER $125,000 IN AVERAGE ANNUAL GROSS SALES DURING THE THREE YEAR PERIOD 2011-2013.

	Ownership Groups above $125K
Average Gross Sales	$302,362

High	$1,347,675
Low	$126,523
# of Ownership Groups	39
# Above Average	13
# Below Average	26
% Above Average	33%
% Below Average	67%
Average # of Reporting Licenses per Ownership Group	1.3
High Number of Licenses	5
Low Number of Licenses	1

Other than as outlined above, Furniture Medic does not furnish, or authorize our salespersons (or anyone else) to furnish, and you should not rely on, any oral or written information concerning the actual or potential sales, income or profits of a Furniture Medic franchise. We have not suggested, and certainly cannot guarantee, that you will succeed in the operation of your franchised business, because the most important factors in the success of any Furniture Medic franchised business, including the one to be operated by you, are your personal business, marketing, management, judgment, and other skills and your willingness to work hard and follow the System. Actual results vary from area to area, and market to market. We cannot estimate or project the results for any particular franchised business.

You are likely to achieve results that are different, possibly significantly and adversely, from the results shown above. Many factors, including management capabilities, local market conditions, and other factors, are unique to each business and may significantly impact the financial performance of your business. Consider that a newly opened business should not be expected to achieve sales volumes or maintain expenses similar to those of an established business.

Neither Furniture Medic nor any of its affiliates, make any promises or representations of any kind that you will achieve any particular results or level of sales or profitability or even achieve break-even results in any particular year of operation.

You are responsible for developing your own business plan for your business, including capital budgets, financial statements, projections and other elements appropriate to your particular circumstances. The expenses identified in this statement are not the only expenses that you will incur in connection with the operation of your store. Additional expenses that you may incur include royalty and marketing fees (see item 6 of this disclosure document), interest on debt service, insurance, legal and accounting charges, and depreciation/amortization. We encourage you to consult with your own accounting, business, and legal advisors to assist you to identify the expenses you likely will incur in connection with your business, to prepare your budgets and to assess the likely or potential financial performance of your business. We also encourage you to contact existing operators to discuss the business.

In developing the business plan for your business, you are cautioned to make necessary allowance for change in financial results to income, expenses, or both, that may result from operation of your business during periods of, or in geographic areas suffering from, economic downturns, inflation, unemployment, or other negative economic influences.

Historical costs and revenues do not necessarily correspond to future costs and revenues because of factors such as inflation, deflation, changes in minimum wage laws and other benefit laws (including but not limited to, health care coverage), location, financing, lease-related costs and other variables. For example, costs such as rent, CAM charges, taxes, interest, insurance and utilities vary from business to business. All information should be evaluated in light of current market conditions including such costs and price information as may then be available.

Other than the preceding financial performance representation, we do not make any financial performance representations. We also do not authorize our employees or representatives to make any such representations either orally or in writing. If you are purchasing an existing outlet, however, we may provide you with the actual records of that outlet. If you receive any other financial performance information or projections of your future income, you should report it to the franchisor's management by contacting Sherry Campbell, Furniture Medic Limited Partnership, 3839 Forest Hill-Irene Road, Memphis, TN 38125, (901) 597-8600, the Federal Trade Commission, and the appropriate state regulatory agencies.

We fix your panes!®

GLASS DOCTOR

1020 N. University Parks Dr.
Waco, TX 76707
Tel: (800) 224-9489, (254) 745-2464
Email: mike.hawkins@dwyergroup.com
Website: www.glassdoctor.com
Mike Hawkins, Vice President of Franchise Sales

From windows to windshields to storefronts, Glass Doctor can handle any glass repair or replacement need. Glass Doctor also offers custom glass services, such as tub and shower enclosures, window replacement, entry door glass and mirrors. Established in 1962 with one shop in Seattle, WA, today Glass Doctor offers complete glass repair, replacement and services to the residential, automotive, and commercial markets. Glass Doctor began franchising in 1977 and joined The Dwyer Group, Inc., an international franchisor of service industry companies, in 1998. Now there are more than 170 Glass Doctor franchise owners across the US and Canada. New franchisees are trained at the nation's only full-service glass training facility, Glass Doctor University, at company headquarters in Waco, Texas. The Dwyer Group family of companies also includes Aire Serv Heating and Air Conditioning, Mr. Appliance, Mr. Electric, Mr. Rooter, The Ground Guys, and Rainbow International Restoration and Cleaning.

BACKGROUND

IFA Member:	Yes
Established & First Franchised:	1977; 1977
Franchised Units:	174
Company-Owned Units:	0
Total Units:	174

Distribution:	US – 163; CAN – 11; O'seas – 0
North America:	46 States, 3 Provinces
Density:	15 in TX, 12 in FL, 11 in CA
Projected New Units (12 Months):	30
Qualifications:	4, 4, 2, 2, 3, 5

FINANCIAL/TERMS

Cash Investment:	$90 – 100K
Total Investment:	$108K+
Minimum Net Worth:	Varies
Fees (Franchise):	$28K/100K Pop.
Fees (Royalty):	5-7%
Fees (Advertising):	2%
Term of Contract (Years):	10/10
Average Number of Employees:	4 FT; 0 PT
Passive Ownership:	Not Allowed
Encourage Conversions:	Yes
Area Development Agreements:	No
Sub-Franchising Contracts:	No
Expand in Territory:	Yes
Space Needs:	1,500 SF

SUPPORT & TRAINING

Financial Assistance Provided:	Yes (I)
Site Selection Assistance:	No
Lease Negotiation Assistance:	No
Co-operative Advertising:	Yes
Franchisee Association/Member:	Yes/Not a Member
Size of Corporate Staff:	20
On-going Support:	A, B, C, D, E, F, G, H, I
Training:	5 Days optional Auto Glass Tech Basic/Certification; 4 Hours Online Training; 9 Days Basic Franchisee Training Waco, TX

SPECIFIC EXPANSION PLANS

US:	All United States
Canada:	Yes
Overseas:	No

Report on Gross Sales, Including Average Gross Sales for the Period January 1, 2013 to December 31, 2013

The sales figures listed below include average Gross Sales and Gross Sales derived from historical operating results of the franchised businesses indicated for the time periods covered. We obtained these sales figures from information provided to us by our franchisees for the period from January 1, 2013 through December 31, 2013. Neither we, nor our independent certified public accountants, have audited or verified any of the sales figures reported to us. We make no representations as to the accuracy of sales reported by our franchisees or the extent to which these sales figures were derived using generally accepted accounting principles. The sales listed below are not intended to represent the actual results that would likely be realized by any specific franchised business during any period.

The information in this report has been prepared by us without an audit. Our independent auditors, BDO USA, LLP have not audited, reviewed, or performed any level of service on the information. Accordingly, they provide no form of assurance as to the accuracy of the information in this report.

As of December 31, 2013, we had 163 Glass Doctor franchised businesses in operation in the U.S. Of these, 136 franchised businesses were in operation and reporting sales for the full 12 months of 2013. Because the number of franchised businesses open during 2013 fluctuated during the year, in order to determine the number and percentage of businesses that achieved the stated sales results locations that were not in operation for the full 12 months of 2013 are not included in the information provided below. We did not include, for example, any new franchised business that began operation during 2013, or any franchised businesses that were operating during the year, but ceased operations during 2013. These franchised businesses would likely have average sales figures that are different than the figures reported below and for the franchised businesses that ceased operations the average sales figures would likely have been lower.

All of the franchised businesses for which sales results are reported below were operated by franchisees. We did not operate any of the businesses. All of the franchised businesses are comparable to the franchised businesses offered by this disclosure document and offered substantially the same services to the public. You should be aware, however, that the franchised businesses for which sales results are reported below include some businesses that are "conversions," businesses that were in operation before purchasing a franchise and "converting" from an independent business to a business utilizing our system and brand.

No adjustments, including adjustments for geographic location, have been made to these reported sales. In addition, the information in this report is based on sales in one 52 week period. This report does not include information about previous periods or try to estimate or predict what may occur in any future periods. Also, because these are gross sales results only, no costs or expenses are taken into account. Profits resulting from any given level of gross sales may differ substantially from one business to another. Sales and profit results are directly impacted by various factors, including: competition from other similar businesses in the area; the quality of management and service in a franchisee's operations; as well as the extent to which the franchisee follows established systems, policies and guidelines contractual relationships and terms with individual landlords and suppliers; the cost of capital and the extent to which a franchisee might have financed its operations; legal, accounting, and other professional fees; federal, state, and local income and other taxes; and discretionary expenditures. You should therefore use the information in this report only as a general reference when conducting your own analysis. Except for the information that appears in this report, we do not furnish or authorize our salespersons or affiliates to furnish any oral or written information or representations or statements of actual sales, costs, income or profits. We encourage you to carefully review this material with your attorney, business advisor and/or accountant.

Your individual sales and financial results are likely to differ from the results shown, possibly significantly and adversely.

Written substantiation for these financial performance representations will be made available to a prospective franchisee upon reasonable request.

Average Gross Sales in 2013 Attained by Franchised Businesses
in Business 12 Months or More[1] With Full 12 Months of Sales in 2013

Percentage Rank (in Terms of Level of Gross Sales) of Franchised Businesses in Business 12 Months or More	Average Gross Sales Attained by This Group	Number in This Group	Number in Group That Attained This Level of Sales or Greater	Percent in Group That Attained This Level os Sales or Greater	Number and Percent of All Franchised Businesses Open for Full 12 Months in 2013 that Attained this Level of Sales or Greater
Top 10%	$2,993,995	13	4	31	4/3%
Top 25%	$1,877,261	34	10	29	10/7%
Top 50%	$1,312,637	68	18	26	18/13%
100%	$808,012	136	42	31	42/31%

[1] Of the franchised businesses in business for 12 months or more and which businesses had a full 12 months of reported sales in 2013, the average Gross Sales for 2013 for 4 groups are shown; those that ranked in the top 10%, 25% and 50%, respectively, in terms of highest level of Gross Sales; and, finally, those representing all (100%) of Franchised Businesses in business more than 12 months with a full 12 months of sales in 2013.

Gross Sales for Franchised Businesses Open Full 12 Months in 2013

Listed below are the annual Gross Sales reported for each of the 136 Franchised Businesses open for a full 12 months in 2013 and which businesses had a full 12 months of reported sales in 2013 ranked by highest to lowest sales as reported to us in information completed by our franchisees.

	$ Gross Sales		$ Gross Sales		$ Gross Sales		$ Gross Sales
1	$8,070,387	35	$974,335	69	$573,558	103	$293,423
2	$4,489,363	36	$911,054	70	$571,344	104	$289,534
3	$4,172,620	37	$893,880	71	$570,107	105	$284,218
4	$3,462,332	38	$879,016	72	$566,088	106	$275,978
5	$2,733,458	39	$831,667	73	$561,248	107	$271,883
6	$2,246,825	40	$829,649	74	$551,282	108	$265,446
7	$2,151,353	41	$812,034	75	$550,676	109	$262,300
8	$2,134,494	42	$810,212	76	$549,383	110	$262,071
9	$1,989,840	43	$804,674	77	$527,234	111	$253,591
10	$1,987,019	44	$804,466	78	$522,263	112	$250,334
11	$1,851,447	45	$798,979	79	$497,131	113	$235,106
12	$1,835,202	46	$782,818	80	$460,940	114	$204,556
13	$1,797,595	47	$777,613	81	$450,352	115	$196,193
14	$1,762,422	48	$765,116	82	$411,341	116	$196,112
15	$1,685,237	49	$764,127	83	$402,539	117	$193,872
16	$1,490,338	50	$760,236	84	$401,771	118	$192,723
17	$1,318,980	51	$754,912	85	$400,588	119	$188,862
18	$1,312,600	52	$734,629	86	$393,332	120	$183,679
19	$1,292,505	53	$729,205	87	$383,889	121	$169,539
20	$1,195,580	54	$726,993	88	$380,307	122	$167,412
21	$1,170,671	55	$714,128	89	$372,171	123	$161,664
22	$1,156,695	56	$706,329	90	$369,418	124	$159,319
23	$1,146,897	57	$702,284	91	$355,321	125	$154,208
24	$1,116,048	58	$690,124	92	$350,631	126	$149,299
25	$1,095,874	59	$677,606	93	$350,137	127	$149,210
26	$1,073,792	60	$675,385	94	$347,215	128	$122,058
27	$1,054,276	61	$672,344	95	$345,490	129	$121,739
28	$1,035,832	62	$655,455	96	$345,065	130	$119,496
29	$1,034,294	63	$646,396	97	$331,140	131	$115,748
30	$1,011,521	64	$640,318	98	$329,331	132	$114,756
31	$995,095	65	$638,029	99	$321,341	133	$79,150
32	$993,942	66	$636,265	100	$309,681	134	$53,091
33	$983,148	67	$629,467	101	$300,384	135	$25,102
34	$979,191	68	$602,716	102	$295,054	136	$20,814

GRANITE TRANSFORMATIONS

10306 USA Today Way
Miramar, FL 33025
Tel: (800) 685-5300, (954) 435-5538
Fax: (954) 435-5579
Email: martham@granitetransformations.com
Website: www.granitetransformations.com
Martha Martinez, Vice President of Marketing

Granite Transformations is a franchise organization that provides an important and compelling service to homeowners allowing them to transform kitchen and baths with our gorgeous TREND STONE, TREND GLASS and TREND MOSAIC surfaces. Trend Stone is engineered to outperform ordinary granite! It's heat, scratch & stain resistant & we're the only surface engineered to fit right over existing countertop surfaces. That means no costly demolition, no mess and fast and easy installation, usually in about a day!

BACKGROUND
IFA Member:	Yes
Established & First Franchised:	2001; 2001
Franchised Units:	160
Company-Owned Units:	3
Total Units:	163
Distribution:	US – 67; CAN – 15; O'seas – 80
North America:	32 States, 3 Provinces
Density:	11 in CA, 7 in ON, 6 in FL
Projected New Units (12 Months):	12
Qualifications:	4, 5, 2, 2, 4, 5

FINANCIAL/TERMS
Cash Investment:	$50 – 100K
Total Investment:	$141.5 – 346K
Minimum Net Worth:	$100K
Fees (Franchise):	$35 – 75K
Fees (Royalty):	2%
Fees (Advertising):	1%
Term of Contract (Years):	10/10
Average Number of Employees:	7 FT, 2 PT
Passive Ownership:	Allowed
Encourage Conversions:	N/A
Area Development Agreements:	No
Sub-Franchising Contracts:	No
Expand in Territory:	No
Space Needs:	N/A

SUPPORT & TRAINING
Financial Assistance Provided:	No
Site Selection Assistance:	Yes
Lease Negotiation Assistance:	No
Co-operative Advertising:	No
Franchisee Association/Member:	No
Size of Corporate Staff:	25
On-going Support:	C, D, E, F, G, h, I
Training:	5 Days at Corporate Office; 10 Days at Franchise Site

SPECIFIC EXPANSION PLANS
US:	All United States
Canada:	All Canada
Overseas:	UK

This Item sets forth certain historical data provided by our Franchised Businesses which are substantially similar to those being offered through this Franchise Disclosure Document that (a) were in operation as of December 31, 2013 and (b) which have fully reported their Gross Sales to us.

We have not audited this information, nor independently verified this information. The information is for the period January 1, 2013 through December 31, 2013 (the "2013 Fiscal Year"). Written substantiation of the data used in preparing this information will be made available upon reasonable request.

Importantly, the success of your franchise will depend largely upon your individual abilities and your market, and the financial results of your franchise are likely to differ, perhaps materially, from the results summarized in this item.

You should not use this information as an indication of how well your franchise will do. A number of factors will affect the success of your franchise. These factors include the current market conditions, the type of market in your Designated Territory, the location of your Designated Territory, the competition and your ability to operate the franchise.

Gross Sales
January 1, 2013 through December 31, 2013

The follow tables presents the Gross Sales as reported to us by 56 U.S. franchisees that were open and operating as of December 31, 2013 and for whom we have complete sales data (the "Reporting Businesses"). Excluded from this Item 19 are all Franchised Businesses located in Canada, as well as 8 businesses under common ownership located in the United States that report gross sales to us on a combined basis.

Table 1 profiles the one Reporting Business that only offered granite resurfacing products and services during the 2013 Fiscal Year. Table 2 profiles the four Reporting Businesses that offered Door and Cabinet Re-Facing products and services along with granite resurfacing products and services during the 2013 Fiscal Year. Table 3 profiles the two Reporting Business that offered tile and mosaic products and services, along with granite re-facing products and services during the 2013 Fiscal Year. Table 4 profiles the 49 Reporting Businesses that offered granite resurfacing products and services, door and cabinet re-facing products and services, and tile and mosaic products and services during the 2013 Fiscal Year.

Table 1
Granite Resurfacing Services

The information listed below sets forth the Gross Sales of the one Reporting Business that only offered granite resurfacing products and services during the 2013 Fiscal Year. The Reporting Business represented in Table 1 did not participate in the Door and Cabinet Re-facing Program or the Tile and Mosaic Program.

Gross Sales	$1,711,009.00

Table 2
Granite Resurfacing and Door and Cabinet Re-facing Program

The information listed below sets forth the Gross Sales of the four Reporting Businesses which, in addition to offering granite resurfacing products and services, also participated in our Door and Cabinet Re-Facing Program during the 2013 Year. The Reporting Businesses represented in Table 2 did not participate in our Tile and Mosaic Program.

Average Gross Sales	$1,614,586.75
Number of Businesses Above/Below Average	2/2
Percentage of Businesses the Met or Exceeded Average	50%
Median	$1,719,069.00
Number of Businesses Above/Below Median	2/2
High	$2,531,404.00
Low	$488,785.00

Table 3
Granite Resurfacing and Tile and Mosaic Program

The information listed below sets forth the Gross Sales of the two Reporting Business which, in addition to offering granite resurfacing products and services, also participated in our Tile and Mosaic Program during the 2013 Fiscal Year. The Reporting Businesses represented in Table 3 did not participate in our Door and Cabinet Re-Facing Program.

Gross Sales- Reporting Business One	$1,020,055.00
Gross Sales - Reporting Business Two**	$32,799.00

**The Gross Sales for the second Reporting Business only includes Gross Sales for November and December 2013 as this was a franchise that had only commenced operations in late 2013.

Table 4
Granite Resurfacing, Door and Cabinet Re-facing Program and Tile and Mosaic Program .

The information listed below sets forth the Gross Sales of the 49 Reporting Businesses which, in addition to offering granite resurfacing products and services, also participated in our Door and Cabinet Re-Facing Program and our Tile and Mosaic Program during the 2013 Fiscal Year. Twentythree of these Reporting Businesses also participated in our Acrylic Bath and Shower Insert Program during 2013, but sales under this program have been excluded from the information provided in the table (and in any event was not more than 7.6% of the sales of any of these 23 Reporting Businesses, more generally being in the 1-3% range). We no longer offer the Acrylic Bath and Shower Insert Program to prospective franchisees.

Average Gross Sales	$1,469,252.63
Number of Businesses Above/Below Average	18/31
Percentage of Businesses the Met or Exceeded Average	37%
Median	$1,301,073.00
Number of Businesses Above/Below Median	25/24
High	$3,588,287.00
Low	$276,214.00

Notes:

1. Gross Sales is defined as all sums or things of value received by a Reporting Business as a result of the sale of services, goods and products whether for cash, check, credit, barter or otherwise without reserve for deduction for inability or failure to collect. Gross Sales do not include refunds to customers or the amount of any sales taxes or any similar taxes collected from customers to be paid to any federal, state or local taxing authority.

2. The average was determined by dividing the sum of the Reporting Businesses' Gross Sales by the number of Reporting Businesses included in each table.

3. The median is the number in which an equal number of Reporting Businesses' Gross Sales fall above and below.

4. The high number represents the highest Gross Sales achieved by a Reporting Business during the 2013 Fiscal Year and the low number represents the lowest Gross Sales achieved by a Reporting Business during the 2013 Fiscal Year.

5. All currency is in U.S. dollars.

General Notes to Item 19:

1. Your results may vary depending upon the location of your business. This analysis does not contain information concerning operating costs or expenses needed to run your business. Operating costs and expenses may vary substantially from business to business, as well as the actual accounting and operational methods employed by a business, may significantly impact profits realized in any particular operation.

2. The above figures exclude royalties, advertising and marketing fees and costs, inventory costs, administrative payroll, payroll taxes, owner compensation/salary, healthcare, employee benefits, uniforms, office supplies, postage, travel and entertainment expenses, utilities and telephone charges, late fees, training costs and expenses and all other fees and expenses which you may incur as a franchisee.

3. The above figures exclude tax liabilities that you will be responsible for.

4. The above figures exclude professional fees or other administrative expenses that you may incur, including legal and accounting fees.

5. The above figures exclude finance charges and depreciation. Interest expense, interest income, depreciation, amortization and other income or expenses will vary substantially from business to business, depending on the amount and kind of financing you obtain to establish your business. You should consult with your tax advisor regarding depreciation and amortization schedules and the period over which assets of your business may be amortized or depreciated, as well as the effect, if any, of any recent or proposed tax legislation.

6. Some businesses have achieved these Gross Sales. Your individual results may differ. There is no assurance that you will achieve as much. In particular, the revenues listed above will be directly affected by many factors, such as: (a) geographic location; (b) competition from other similar businesses in your area; (c) advertising effectiveness based on market saturation; (d) your product and service pricing; (e) vendor prices on materials, supplies and inventory; (f) labor costs; (g) health and other fringe benefits you provide; (h) ability to generate leads and customers; (i) customer loyalty; and (j) employment conditions in the market. Because of these factors, results vary from business to business. Therefore, we recommend that you make your own independent investigation to determine whether or not the franchise may be profitable to you. You should use

the above information only as a reference in conducting your analysis and preparing your own financial projections. We strongly suggest that you consult with your financial advisor or personal accountant concerning financial projections and federal, state and local income taxes and any other applicable taxes that you may incur in operating a Franchised Business.

7. Other than the preceding financial performance representations, Rocksolid Granit does not make any financial performance representations. We also do not authorize our em-ployees or representatives to make any such representations either orally or in writing. If you are purchasing an existing outlet, however, we may provide you with the actual records of that outlet. If you receive any other financial performance information or projections of your future income, you should report it to the Franchisor's management by contacting Paul Lane, our Chief Operating Officer, Rocksolid Granit (USA), Inc., 10306 USA Today Way, Miramar, FL 33025, (954) 435-5538, the Federal Trade Commission, and the appropriate state regulatory agencies.

GRISWOLD HOME CARE

717 Bethlehem Pk., # 300
Erdenheim, PA 19038
Tel: (888) 777-7630, (215) 402-0200
Fax: (215) 261-1733
Email: mike@griswoldhomecare.com
Website: www.griswoldhomecare.com
Mike Magid, Vice President Franchise Development

Griswold Home Care is dedicated to providing Extraordinary Home Care at Affordable Rates. We refer Caregivers for older adults, people recovering from illness or surgery, and people with long-term disabilities. Caregiver services include personal care, homemaking, companionship, incidental transportation and other services to Clients wishing to remain safe and independent. We operate a model that is completely unique in the industry. We also offer the largest protected territories and lowest on-going fees.

BACKGROUND
IFA Member:	Yes
Established & First Franchised:	1982; 1984
Franchised Units:	246
Company-Owned Units:	11
Total Units:	257
Distribution:	US – 246; CAN – 0; O'seas – 0
North America:	32 States, 0 Provinces
Density:	22 in PA, 19 in NJ, 15 in OH

Projected New Units (12 Months):	56
Qualifications:	5, 4, 2, 3, 4, 5

FINANCIAL/TERMS
Cash Investment:	$75K
Total Investment:	$94 – 116K
Minimum Net Worth:	$275K
Fees (Franchise):	$45K
Fees (Royalty):	3.5%
Fees (Advertising):	$200 gross billings/month** NTE
Term of Contract (Years):	10/5
Average Number of Employees:	3 – 5 (in office) FT
Passive Ownership:	Discouraged
Encourage Conversions:	No
Area Development Agreements:	No
Sub-Franchising Contracts:	No
Expand in Territory:	Yes
Space Needs:	Minimum 150 SF

SUPPORT & TRAINING
Financial Assistance Provided:	No
Site Selection Assistance:	Yes
Lease Negotiation Assistance:	N/A
Co-operative Advertising:	Yes
Franchisee Association/Member:	No
Size of Corporate Staff:	23
On-going Support:	C, D, G, H, I
Training:	10 Days Corporate Office; 1 – 2 Days Franchisee's Location

SPECIFIC EXPANSION PLANS
US:	Yes
Canada:	Yes
Overseas:	No

Background

This Item presents certain historical data relating to Office Fees provided by our franchisees and company-owned outlets. The outlets included in this Item operate businesses substantially similar to the business being offered in this Disclosure Document. Except as otherwise stated in this Item 19, each outlet included in this Item 19 operates in a single territory. The outlets included in this Item 19 operate in territories with populations ranging between 73,868 and 1,754,488, with a median territory population of 323,521. "Office Fees" are payments made to franchises or company-owned offices for Services performed for Clients, net of fees earned by Caregiver.

Written substantiation of the data used in preparing this information will be made available upon reasonable request. We have not audited this information, nor independently verified this information. Importantly, the success of your franchise will depend largely upon your individual abilities and your market, and the financial results of your franchise are likely to differ, perhaps materially, from the results summarized in this item.

You should not use this information as an indication of how well your franchise will do. A number of factors will affect the success of your franchise. These factors include the current market conditions, the type of market in your franchise area, the location of your franchise area, the competition and your ability to operate the franchise.

Office Fees Earned

Table A below presents the Office Fees earned by our franchised and company-owned outlets during the twelve month period January through December for each of the last three calendar years and broken down into three (3) categories: 1) the individual office generating the highest offices fees as of December 31 for each calendar year; 2) average office fees generated by the top 25% of offices as of December 31 for each calendar year, including the total number of franchised and company-owned outlets that have been in operation for at least 24 months; 3) average Office Fees generated by the entire system as of December 31 for each calendar year, including the total number of franchised and company-owned outlets that have been in operation for at least 24 months.

TABLE A
Office Fees
Calendar Years 2013, 2012 & 2011

	Highest	Average of Top 25%	System-wide Average
Jan - Dec 2013 - OFFICE FEES	$1,970,134	$802,127	$330,282
# of outlets	1	34	*136
Jan - Dec 2012 - OFFICE FEES	$1,816,499	$814,967	$350,710
# of outlets	1	30	*118
Jan - Dec 2011 - OFFICE FEES	$1,643,611	$833,397	$352,453
# of outlets	1	28	*112

Notes:

1. "Office Fees" are payments received by franchised or company-owned offices for Services performed for Clients, net of fees earned by Caregiver. The averages were determined by totaling each outlet's (individual territory) annual Office Fees for each calendar year and dividing by the number of outlets in each subset presented.

2. The Top 25% results presented in Table A include two company-owned outlets. For each calendar year presented, the highest Office Fee was achieved by a franchised outlet which operates in a territory with a larger population then being disclosed and offered under this disclosure document. For each calendar year presented, the franchisee operating in a territory with a population of 1,754,488 did not generate Office Fees placing the franchisee within the Top 25% of offices profiled in Table A.

3. In 2013, 35% of the Top 25% outlets met or exceeded the

Average Office Fees for the group and 31% of all outlets met or exceeded the system wide Average Office Fees. In 2012, 40% of the Top 25% outlets met or exceeded the Average Office Fees for the group and 34% of all outlets met or exceeded the system wide Average Office Fees. In 2011, 43% of the Top 25% outlets met or exceeded the Average Office Fees for the group and 34% of all outlets met or exceeded the system wide Average Office Fees.

4. All of the outlets profiled in Table A conducted business under the "Griswold Home Care" trademark.

Financial Performance for Company Owned Outlets

Table B below presents the Office Fees, expenses, net profit and client count for each of our company owned locations during the calendar year of 2013, as well as a consolidated report showing combined totals and combined averages of all company owned locations during the calendar year of 2013.

TABLE B
Financial Performance for Company Owned Outlets
January 1, 2013 through December 31, 2013

	13-Jan	13-Feb	13-Mar	13-Apr	13-May	13-Jun	13-Jul	13-Aug	13-Sep	13-Oct	13-Nov	13-Dec	Year to Date	% of Revenue	2013 Avg. (9)	% of Revenue
Consol. Gross Revenue	$448,431	$415,639	$431,301	$422,062	$443,315	$405,511	$498,035	$457,370	$450,468	$474,538	$429,901	$452,338	$5,328,909	100%	$592,100.98	100%
Operating Expenses																
Payroll	$136,266	$125,296	$127,360	$123,368	$132,408	$123,529	$125,912	$120,090	$120,398	$123,384	$125,233	$124,263	$1,507,506	28%	$167,500.72	28%
Insurance	$14,575	$16,575	$16,912	$15,603	$15,628	$17,741	$17,078	$17,626	$17,850	$17,565	$18,843	$17,340	$203,335	4%	$22,592.82	4%
Occupancy	$14,330	$12,156	$12,354	$13,671	$12,527	$12,650	$13,561	$14,001	$13,296	$13,366	$11,558	$16,982	$160,451	3%	$17,827.92	3%
Marketing	$11,479	$10,641	$17,279	$5,379	$6,894	$4,791	$8,765	$3,074	$7,304	$8,320	$10,259	$2,220	$96,405	2%	$10,711.72	2%
Other	$16,167	$18,055	$19,328	$23,971	$20,419	$17,740	$30,561	$26,457	$19,100	$21,372	$17,473	$19,227	$249,873	5%	$27,763.65	5%
Total Operating Expenses	$192,817	$182,723	$193,232	$181,991	$187,877	$176,450	$195,878	$181,248	$177,948	$184,007	$183,366	$180,032	$2,217,571	42%	$246,396.83	42%
Net Income	$255,614	$232,915	$238,069	$240,071	$255,438	$229,060	$302,157	$276,121	$272,520	$290,531	$246,535	$272,306	$3,111,337	58%	$345,704.16	6%
Gross Profit Margin	57%	56%	55%	57%	58%	56%	61%	60%	60%	61%	57%	60%	58%			
2013 Avg Client Count													557			
2013 Avg Hours/ Client per week													370			

Chestnut Hill	Jan	Feb	Mar	Apr	May	Jun	Jul	Aug	Sep	Oct	Nov	Dec	Year to Date	% of Revenue
Gross Revenue	$83,179	$87,114	$70,615	$67,844	$93,525	$68,262	$78,089	$66,218	$67,679	$64,517	$51,922	$53,178	$852,141	100%
Operating Expenses														
Payroll	$22,698	$21,506	$20,129	$17,609	$19,223	$21,110	$17,957	$16,161	$17,899	$18,775	$18,199	$16,325	$227,589	27%
Insurance	$1,360	$3,505	$1,353	$2,208	$1,793	$2,579	$2,175	$1,777	$1,791	$2,051	$1,499	$1,488	$23,578	3%
Occupancy	$4,190	$3,061	$3,360	$3,591	$3,206	$3,311	$3,440	$3,350	$3,391	$3,545	$2,384	$3,860	$40,688	5%
Marketing	$1,949	$1,467	$3,358	$1,049	$1,088	$863	$1,088	$357	$1,077	$1,443	$1,631	$421	$15,790	2%
Other	$3,324	$2,685	$3,149	$3,375	$2,875	$2,534	$4,741	$4,125	$4,295	$2,811	$2,643	$2,628	$39,186	5%
Total Operating Expenses	$33,521	$32,224	$31,350	$27,832	$28,185	$30,397	$29,400	$25,769	$28,453	$28,625	$26,355	$24,722	$346,831	41%
Net Income	$49,658	$54,889	$39,266	$40,013	$65,340	$37,865	$48,689	$40,449	$39,225	$35,892	$25,567	$28,457	$505,310	59%
Gross Profit Margin	60%	63%	56%	59%	70%	55%	62%	61%	58%	56%	49%	54%	59%	
2013 Avg Client Count													93	
2013 Avg Hours/Client per week													37	
Le High Valley	Jan	Feb	Mar	Apr	May	Jun	Jul	Aug	Sep	Oct	Nov	Dec	Year to Date	% of Revenue
Gross Revenue	$89,051	$66,859	$72,736	$91,044	$81,176	$68,973	$94,257	$90,550	$78,849	$93,647	$96,638	$93,119	$1,016,899	100%
Operating Expenses														
Payroll	$25,000	$21,766	$19,537	$21,602	$24,366	$21,666	$23,401	$25,421	$22,398	$22,484	$22,528	$23,183	$273,352	27%
Insurance	$2,590	$1,314	$1,314	$757	$757	$1,234	$1,265	$1,731	$1,755	$1,722	$1,722	$1,737	$17,898	2%
Occupancy	$2,159	$2,439	$2,001	$2,422	$1,931	$1,925	$2,049	$1,943	$1,884	$1,857	$1,623	$2,906	$25,139	2%
Marketing	$1,596	$1,882	$2,071	$1,100	$1,004	$818	$2,503	$123	$1,155	$2,027	$1,435	$679	$16,394	2%

	Jan	Feb	Mar	Apr	May	Jun	Jul	Aug	Sep	Oct	Nov	Dec	Year to Date	% of Revenue
Other	$2,204	$2,069	$3,150	$6,228	$3,231	$2,939	$5,236	$3,149	$3,299	$3,098	$3,866	$3,160	$41,628	4%
Total Operating Expenses	$33,549	$29,469	$28,073	$32,109	$31,289	$28,583	$34,455	$32,367	$30,491	$31,189	$31,173	$31,665	$374,411	37%
Net Income	$55,502	$37,389	$44,663	$58,936	$49,886	$40,390	$59,803	$58,183	$48,358	$62,458	$65,465	$61,454	$642,488	63%
Gross Profit Margine	62%	56%	61%	65%	61%	59%	63%	64%	61%	67%	68%	66%	63%	
2013 Avg Client Count													104	
2013 Avg Hours/Client per week													45	

Main Line	Jan	Feb	Mar	Apr	May	Jun	Jul	Aug	Sep	Oct	Nov	Dec	Year to Date	% of Revenue
Gross Revenue	$76,997	$74,868	$76,783	$73,294	$65,552	$57,395	$75,928	$65,755	$62,186	$67,262	$45,996	$51,468	$793,485	100%
Ooperating Expenses														
Payroll	$25,412	$23,391	$24,846	$25,738	$24,137	$17,762	$19,103	$16,379	$15,355	$14,161	$15,436	$18,680	$240,400	30%
Insurance	$1,164	$427	$3,383	$952	$1,385	$1,567	$1,557	$1,551	$1,613	$1,188	$2,674	$1,837	$19,299	2%
Occupancy	$2,264	$1,485	$1,779	$1,854	$1,787	$1,514	$1,512	$1,667	$1,531	$1,478	$1,493	$2,278	$20,641	3%
Marketing	$1,611	$1,866	$3,224	$948	$1,564	$882	$862	$353	$1,076	$1,100	$1,490	$484	$15,460	2%
Other	$2,805	$4,663	$3,008	$3,189	$2,957	$2,904	$5,481	$7,452	$2,112	$4,345	$2,065	$3,876	$44,857	6%
Total Operating Expenses	$33,255	$31,833	$36,240	$32,681	$31,830	$24,629	$28,515	$27,403	$21,687	$22,271	$23,159	$27,156	$340,658	43%
Net Income	$43,742	$43,036	$40,543	$40,613	$33,723	$32,766	$47,413	$38,352	$40,500	$44,991	$22,836	$24,312	$452,827	57%
Gross Profit Margin	57%	57%	53%	55%	51%	57%	62%	58%	65%	67%	50%	47%	57%	
2013 Avg Client Count													79	
2013 Avg Hours'Client per week													45	

Baltimore/ Howard	Jan	Feb	Mar	Apr	May	Jun	Jul	Aug	Sep	Oct	Nov	Dec	Year to Date	% of Revenue
Gross Revenue	$56,633	$57,227	$63,182	$53,162	$77,782	$79,961	$82,436	$78,725	$77,212	$90,812	$91,338	$103,937	$912,408	100%
Operating Expenses														
Payroll	$22,935	$20,249	$25,802	$19,524	$24,357	$27,987	$31,395	$29,656	$30,540	$32,184	$31,577	$29,530	$325,734	36%
Insurance	$8,121	$8,467	$7,050	$8,550	$8,550	$8,381	$8,048	$8,709	$8,730	$8,745	$9,104	$8,795	$101,251	11%
Occupancy	$1,712	$1,754	$1,739	$1,743	$1,781	$2,550	$2,826	$3,200	$2,874	$2,818	$2,826	$3,705	$29,528	3%
Marketing	$1,972	$2,113	$3,868	$724	$1,222	$892	$2,278	$1,699	$1,264	$1,381	$2,311	$465	$20,189	2%
Other	$3,331	$2,984	$3,941	$4,032	$5,497	$4,244	$5,153	$4,162	$4,196	$4,027	$3,679	$4,629	$49,873	5%
Total Operating Expenses	$38,071	$35,566	$42,400	$34,573	$41,407	$44,054	$49,700	$47,426	$47,605	$49,154	$49,496	$47,123	$526,576	58%
Net Income	$18,562	$21,661	$20,782	$18,589	$36,375	$35,907	$32,736	$31,299	$29,607	$41,658	$41,841	$56,814	$385,833	42%
Gross Profit Margin	33%	38%	33%	35%	47%	45%	40%	40%	38%	46%	46%	55%	42%	
2013 Avg Client Count													91	
2013 Avg Hours/Client per week													40	

LeHigh Valley NE	Jan	Feb	Mar	Apr	May	Jun	Jul	Aug	Sep	Oct	Nov	Dec	Year to Date	% of Revenue
Gross Revenue	$50,963	$50,808	$50,146	$52,259	$51,136	$51,589	$53,225	$55,442	$59,027	$53,452	$51,934	$55,411	$635,391	100%
Operating Expenses														
Payroll	$12,468	$12,125	$10,622	$12,807	$12,965	$10,267	$8,440	$9,750	$10,142	$11,762	$13,270	$12,748	$137,367	22%
Insurance	$93	$1,258	$672	$672	$672	$975	$1,203	$1,190	$1,183	$1,198	$1,198	$1,183	$11,495	2%
Occupancy	$201	$367	$198	$256	$470	$199	$215	$198	$198	$198	$193	$451	$3,144	0%
Marketing	$958	$899	$1,201	$145	$362	$309	$137	$90	$32	-	$346	$(674)	$3,806	1%
Other	$808	$984	$1,454	$2,175	$1,136	$1,414	$2,519	$1,086	$1,164	$1,044	$1,035	$591	%15,410	2%
Total Operating Expenses	$14,530	$15,633	$14,146	$16,056	$15,605	$13,163	$12,514	$12,315	$12,720	$14,201	$16,041	$14,298	$171,222	27%
Net Income	$36,434	$35,175	$36,000	$36,203	$35,531	$38,426	$40,710	$43,127	$46,307	$39,251	$35,893	$41,113	$464,170	73%
Gross Profit Margin	71%	69%	72%	69%	69%	74%	76%	78%	78%	73%	69%	74%	73%	
2013 Avg Client Count													62	
2013 Avg Hours/Client per week													76	

Delaware County	Jan	Feb	Mar	Apr	May	Jun	Jul	Aug	Sep	Oct	Nov	Dec	Year to Date	% of Revenue
Gross Revenue	$31,407	$28,921	$37,735	$22,917	$17,372	$21,143	$38,389	$23,801	$24,311	$34,849	$20,062	$26,480	$327,387	100%
Operating Expenses														
Payroll	$10,386	$9,559	$10,150	$10,518	$9,867	$7,261	$7,812	$6,696	$6,278	$5,791	$6,309	$7,631	$98,257	30%
Insurance	$475	$175	$1,382	$389	$566	$640	$636	$634	$659	$485	$1,092	$750	$7,883	2%
Occupancy	$925	$607	$727	$757	$730	$618	$618	$681	$625	$604	$610	$931	$8,433	3%
Marketing	$660	$765	$1,320	$387	$639	$360	$352	$144	$440	$449	$609	$194	$6,321	2%
Other	$1,147	$1,906	$1,232	$1,306	$1,210	$1,188	$2,248	$3,045	$865	$1,776	$845	$1,584	$18,351	6%
Total Operating Expenses	$13,593	$13,011	$14,811	$13,357	$13,011	$10,068	$11,666	$11,200	$8,867	$9,105	$9,465	$11,091	$139,245	43%
Net Income	$17,814	$15,910	$22,924	$9,560	$4,361	$11,074	$26,723	$12,601	$15,444	$25,745	$10,597	$15,389	$188,143	57%
Gross Profit Margin	57%	55%	61%	42%	25%	52%	70%	53%	64%	74%	53%	58%	57%	
2013 Avg Client Count													42	
2013 Avg Hours/Client per week													39	

Wilkes Barre	Jan	Feb	Mar	Apr	May	Jun	Jul	Aug	Sep	Oct	Nov	Dec	Year to Date	% of Revenue
Gross Revenue	$31,883	$31,996	$31,119	$36,493	$35,603	$35,449	$45,161	$47,222	$49,318	$43,584	$44,312	$44,444	$476,584	100%
Operating Expenses														
Payroll	$8,972	$8,748	$8,829	$9,058	$10,385	$9,670	$11,165	$10,050	$11,167	$11,285	$11,184	$10,130	$120,642	25%
Insurance	$269	$132	$1,258	$1,258	$1,243	$1,410	$1,391	$1,377	$1,457	$1,417	$999	$999	$13,211	3%
Occupancy	$1,331	$1,313	$1,307	$1,720	$1,435	$1,307	$1,627	$1,723	$1,538	$1,556	$1,548	$1,423	$17,829	4%
Marketing	$2,012	$1,106	$995	$638	$612	$348	$1,144	$175	$1,861	$1,387	$1,835	$494	$12,607	3%
Other	$1,319	$1,771	$2,230	$2,417	$2,451	$1,580	$3,432	$1,914	$1,581	$3,232	$2,363	$1,788	$26,078	5%

	Jan	Feb	Mar	Apr	May	Jun	Jul	Aug	Sep	Oct	Nov	Dec	Year to Date	% of Revenue
Total Operating Expenses	$13,902	$13,069	$14,619	$15,092	$16,127	$14,315	$18,758	$15,239	$17,603	$18,877	$17,930	$14,834	$190,367	40%
Net Income	$17,981	$18,926	$16,500	$21,402	$19,476	$21,134	$26,402	$31,983	$31,714	$24,707	$26,382	$29,610	$286,217	60%
Gross Profit Margin	56%	59%	53%	59%	55%	60%	58%	68%	64%	57%	60%	67%	60%	
2013 Avg Client Count													44	
2013 Avg Hours/Client per week													48	
Blue Bell	Jan	Feb	Mar	Apr	May	Jun	Jul	Aug	Sep	Oct	Nov	Dec	Year to Date	% of Revenue
Gross Revenue	$28,317	$17,845	$28,984	$25,048	$21,169	$22,739	$30,551	$29,657	$31,887	$26,416	$27,701	$24,300	$314,613	100%
Operating Expenses														
Payroll	$8,394	$7,953	$7,445	$6,512	$7,108	$7,807	$6,640	$5,977	$6,619	$6,943	$6,730	$6,038	$84,166	27%
Insurance	$503	$1,297	$500	$817	$663	$954	$804	$657	$662	$759	$554	$550	$8,721	3%
Occupancy	$1,550	$1,132	$1,243	$1,328	$1,186	$1,225	$1,272	$1,239	$1,254	$1,311	$882	$1,428	$15,049	5%
Marketing	$720	$542	$1,242	$388	$403	$319	$402	$132	$398	$534	$603	$156	$5,839	2%
Other	$1,229	$993	$1,164	$1,248	$1,063	$937	$1,752	$1,525	$1,588	$1,040	$977	$972	$14,488	5%
Total Operating Expenses	$12,396	$11,917	$11,594	$10,292	$10,423	$11,241	$10,871	$9,530	$10,522	$10,586	$9,747	$9,144	$128,263	41%
Net Income	$15,921	$5,928	$17,390	$14,756	$10,746	$11,498	$19,680	$20,127	$21,364	$15,830	$17,954	$15,156	$186,350	59%
Gross Profit Margin	56%	33%	60%	59%	51%	51%	64%	68%	67%	60%	65%	62%	59%	
2013 Avg Client Count													42	
2013 Avg Hours/Client per week													39	

Notes

1. Gross Revenue is defined as the total "Office Fees" generated by the Outlet for calendar year 2013.

2. Payroll includes gross wages and payroll taxes for the employees at that location – typically includes a Manager, Care Coordinator, and Marketer. Company Owned Units pay out an annual bonus in December. Typically, the Owner/Operator of a Franchise would replace the equivalent Manager position (at Company Owned Units) resulting in a lower payroll expense. The average Manager annual total compensation at Company Owned Units in 2013 was $86,972.

3. Insurance includes expenses associated with health, life, dental, professional, general liability, workers compensation, and long-term disability. Typically, the Owner/Operator of a Franchise would replace the equivalent Manager position (at Company Owned Units) resulting in a lower insurance expense. The average Manager insurance expense at Company Owned Units for 2013 is $4,687.

4. Occupancy includes expenses for rent, utility, telephone (land-line and mobile), and janitorial services.

5. Marketing/Other includes expenses associated with advertising, trade shows, and print/reproduction. Also other expenses is defined as office supplies, dues/subscriptions, computer supplies, software, Internet, criminal background checks, office expenses, professional fees, postage/delivery, travel/entertainment, and information/technology.

6. Net Income is defined as Gross Revenue less Total Operating Expenses as set forth in Table B.

7. The Baltimore/Howard office services two territories.

General Notes to Item 19:

1. Your results may vary upon the location of your franchised business. Your results will also likely vary as start-up business; they may be less than these figures.

2. This analysis does not contain complete information con-

cerning the operating costs and expenses that you will incur in operating your franchised business. Operating costs and expenses may vary substantially from business to business. You should consult with an accountant to assess this in more detail.

3. The above figures exclude Royalties and General Marketing Fees which you will incur as a franchisee.

4. The above figures exclude tax liabilities that you will be responsible for.

5. Interest expense, interest income, depreciation, amortization and other income or expenses will vary substantially from business to business, depending on the amount and kind of financing you obtain to establish your franchised business. You should consult with your accountant or other tax advisor regarding depreciation and amortization schedules and the period over which assets of your Franchise may be amortized or depreciated, as well as the effect, if any, of any recent or proposed tax legislation.

6. Expenses and costs, as well as the actual accounting and operational methods employed by a franchisee, may significantly impact profits realized in any particular operation.

7. Some system businesses have earned this amount. Your individual results may differ. There is no assurance that you will earn as much. In particular, the revenues, costs and expenses of your Franchise will be directly affected by many factors, such as: (a) current market conditions, (b) the type of market in your franchise area, (c) the geographic location, square mileage, and population density of your franchise area, (c) the competition from other similar services in the market (d) your personal ability to operate the franchise, (e) marketing, public relations and advertising effectiveness based on market saturation; (f) whether you continue to operate the franchise after the first 3 years or hire a manager; (g) your pricing; (g) vendor selections and prices on materials, supplies and inventory; (h) salaries and benefits to employees and other personnel; (i) business personnel benefits (life and health insurance, etc.); (j) weather conditions; (k) employment and economic conditions in the market, (l) your individual efforts, choices and abilities. Because of these factors, results vary from business to business. Therefore, we recommend that you make your own independent investigation to determine whether or not the franchise may be profitable to you. You should use the above information only as a reference in conducting your analysis and preparing your own projected income statements and cash flow statements. We strongly suggest that you consult your financial advisor or personal accountant concerning financial projections and federal, state and local income taxes and any other applicable taxes that you may incur in operating a franchised business.

8. Other than the preceding financial performance representation, we do not make any financial performance representations. We also do not authorize our employees or representatives to make any such representations either orally or in writing. If you are purchasing an existing outlet, however, we may provide you with the actual records of that outlet. If you receive any other financial performance information or projections of your future income, you should report it to the franchisor's management by contacting Thomas Monaghan, President and CEO, Griswold International, LLC 120 West Germantown Pike, Suite 200, Plymouth Meeting, Pennsylvania 19462, t: 215-402-0200, the Federal Trade Commission, and the appropriate state regulatory agencies.

MASSAGE | FACIALS | WAXING

HAND AND STONE MASSAGE AND FACIAL SPA

200 Horizon Dr., # 203
Hamilton, NJ 08691
Tel: (609) 587-9800

Email: mcquillan@handandstone.com
Website: www.handandstone.com
Robert McQuillan, Vice President Franchise Development

Hand and Stone Massage and Facial Spa offers massage, facial, and hair removal services, as well as facial products at one convenient retail location. Hand and Stone offers a recurring revenue model that allows this membership-based business to produce a predictable income stream for the franchisee.

BACKGROUND

IFA Member:	No
Established & First Franchised:	2014; 2014

Franchised Units:	161	Area Development Agreements:	Yes
Company-Owned Units:	2	Sub-Franchising Contracts:	No
Total Units:	163	Expand in Territory:	No
Distribution:	US – 163; CAN – 9; O'seas – 0	Space Needs:	N/A
North America:	20 States, 1 Province		
Density:	33 in NJ, 23 in FL, 20 in PA	SUPPORT & TRAINING	
Projected New Units (12 Months):	N/A	Financial Assistance Provided:	Yes (D)
Qualifications:	1, 1, 1, 1, 1, 1	Site Selection Assistance:	Yes
		Lease Negotiation Assistance:	Yes
FINANCIAL/TERMS		Co-operative Advertising:	No
Cash Investment:	N/A	Franchisee Association/Member:	Yes/Member
Total Investment:	$346.4 – 463.4K	Size of Corporate Staff:	N/A
Minimum Net Worth:	N/A	On-going Support:	A, B, C, D, E, F, G, H, I
Fees (Franchise):	$39K	Training:	N/A
Fees (Royalty):	5%		
Fees (Advertising):	5%	SPECIFIC EXPANSION PLANS	
Term of Contract (Years):	N/A	US:	No
Average Number of Employees:	N/A	Canada:	No
Passive Ownership:	Allowed	Overseas:	No
Encourage Conversions:	Yes		

Background

This Item presents certain historical data as provided by our franchisees. We have not audited this information, nor independently verified this information. Written substantiation for the financial performance representation will be made available to the prospective franchisee upon reasonable request. The information is for the period January 1, 2013 through December 31, 2013.

Importantly, the success of your franchise will depend largely upon your individual abilities and your market, and the financial results of your franchise are likely to differ from the results summarized in this item.

Average Franchisee Gross Sales

The following tables present the Average Gross Sales1 submitted to us by eighty nine (89) United States franchisees, including our affiliate operated businesses in Toms River and Hamilton, New Jersey, which are substantially similar to those being offered through this Franchise Disclosure Document and were open and operating for at least twelve months as of December 31, 2013. As of December 31, 2013, we had one hundred – thirty four (134) United States franchisees (including our two affiliate operated businesses) and nine (9) locations in Canada. This Item excludes forty four (44) United States franchisees that were not open more than twelve (12) months as of the end of 2013, one (1) US location that was suspended for relocation and did not report a full twelve months of sales, and nine (9) franchises located in Canada. The results presented are in two tables. The first table presents the Average Gross Sales grouped according to State for Franchised Businesses open more than twenty-four (24) months as of December 31, 2013, and the second table presents the Average Gross Sales grouped by State for Franchised Businesses open between twelve (12) months and twenty-four (24) months as of December 31, 2013.

Average Gross Sales Information for Franchised Businesses
Open 24 Months or More Calendar Year 2013

State	Number of Franchised Businesses	2013 Average Gross Sales	Number Above/ Below Average
Arizona	5	$856,964	3/2
California	2	$439,489	1/1

Colorado	2	$1,004,522	1/1
Florida	8	$953,433	4/4
Illinois	1	$621,178	1/0
Missouri	1	$419,079	1/0
North Carolina	5	$932,911	2/3
New Jersrey	19	$1,112,976	10/9
New York	3	$1,326,612	2/1
Oregon	3	$873,394	1/2
Pennsylvania	7	$819,810	2/5
South Carolina	1	$665,155	1/0
Washington	3	$1,205,920	1/2
Wisconsin	1	$873,598	0/1
Average of All Open 24 Months or More	61	$969,621	30/31

Average Gross Sales Information for Franchised Businesses
Open Between 12 and 24 Months Calendar Year 2013

State	Number of Franchised Businesses	2013 Average Gross Sales	Number Above/ Below Average
Arizona	1	$231,286	1/0
California	1	$429,421	1/0
Colorado	1	$260,517	1/0
Delaware	1	$786,359	1/0
Florida	3	$476,139	1/2
Maryland	2	$451,821	1/1
North Carolina	1	$335,175	1/0
New Jersey	4	$549,940	3/1
New York	3	$490,765	2/1
Pennsylvania	6	$910,131	3/3
South Carolina	1	$561,231	1/0
Texas	3	$562,413	1/2
Virginia	1	$585,279	1/0
Average of All Open Between 12 Months and 24 Months	28	$583,622	17/11

Notes:

1. "Gross Sales" means the aggregate of all revenue from the sale of products, gift cards, barter or exchange, complimentary services, prepaid services and services from all sources in connection with the Franchised Business whether for check, cash, credit or otherwise, including all proceeds from any business interruption insurance, but excluding tips received by massage therapists and estheticians, any sales and equivalent taxes that you collect and pay to any governmental taxing authority, and the value of any allowance issued or granted to any of your customers that you credit in full or partial satisfaction of the

price of any products and services offered by the Franchised Business.

2. For each table, the Average Gross Sales is defined as the sum of the Gross Sales of the included franchised businesses divided by the number of franchised businesses.

3. The 87 Franchised Businesses presented above range in size from 6 to 16 treatment rooms per location.

Assumptions

1. Your results may vary upon the location of your Franchised Business. This analysis does not contain information concerning operating costs or expenses. Operating costs and expenses may vary substantially from Franchised Business to Franchised Business.

2. Expenses and costs, as well as the actual accounting and operational methods employed by a franchisee may significantly impact profits realized in any particular operation.

There is no assurance you will do as well. Some Franchised Businesses have earned this amount. Gross Sales, revenues, costs, and expenses may vary. In particular, the revenues and expenses of your Franchised Business will be directly affected by many factors, such as: (a) geographic location; (b) competition from other similar businesses in your area; (c) advertising effectiveness based on market saturation; (d) your product and service pricing; (e) vendor prices on materials, supplies and inventory; (f) labor costs (g) ability to generate customers; (h) customer loyalty; and (i) employment conditions in the market.

Importantly, you should not consider the Gross Sales presented above to be the actual potential revenues that you will realize. We do not represent that you can or will attain these revenues, or any particular level of revenues or costs/expenses. We do not represent that you will generate income, which exceeds the initial payment of, or investment in, the franchise.

The financial performance representation figure(s) above do not reflect the costs of sales, operating expenses, royalty and advertising or other costs or expenses that must be deducted from the gross revenue or gross sales figures to obtain your net income or profit. You should conduct an independent investigation of the costs and expenses you will incur in operating your Franchised Business. Franchisees or former franchisees, listed in the franchise disclosure document, may be one source of this information.

Therefore, we recommend that you make your own independent investigation to determine whether or not the franchise may be profitable, and consult with an attorney and other advisors before purchasing a franchise. We suggest strongly that you consult your financial advisor or personal accountant concerning financial projections and federal, state and local income taxes and any other applicable taxes that you may incur in operating a Franchised Business.

Other than the preceding financial performance representation, Hand and Stone Franchise Corp. does not make any financial performance representations. We also do not authorize our employees or representatives to make any such representations either orally or in writing. If you are purchasing an existing outlet, however, we may provide you with the actual records of that outlet. If you receive any other financial performance information or projections of your future income, you should report it to the franchisor's management by contacting John Marco at 200 Horizon Drive, Suite 203, Hamilton, New Jersey 08691 and (609) 587-9800, the Federal Trade Commission, and the appropriate state regulatory agencies.

HOME HELPERS

10700 Montgomery Rd., # 300
Cincinnati, OH 45242

Tel: (800) 216-4196, (513) 413-4899
Email: bboecker@franchisesupport.net
Website: www.homehelpershomecare.com
Beth Boecker, Director of Franchise Sales Administration

Home Helpers was ranked "#1 Senior Care Franchise" in North America and "Best of the Best" by Entrepreneur magazine five years in a row! This is a rewarding business providing medical, non-medical and personal care for: seniors, new moms, those recuperating from illness or injury, and those with lifelong challenges.

BACKGROUND

IFA Member:	Yes	Passive Ownership:	Discouraged
Established & First Franchised:	1996; 1997	Encourage Conversions:	Yes
Franchised Units:	655	Area Development Agreements:	Yes
Company-Owned Units:	0	Sub-Franchising Contracts:	No
Total Units:	655	Expand in Territory:	Yes
Distribution:	US – 655; CAN – 0; O'seas – 0	Space Needs:	N/A

North America: 43 States, 0 Provinces

Density: 36 in CA, 31 in IL, 27 in PA

Projected New Units (12 Months): 50

Qualifications: 3, 3, 1, 2, 3, 4

SUPPORT & TRAINING

Financial Assistance Provided: Yes (I)

Site Selection Assistance: N/A

Lease Negotiation Assistance: N/A

FINANCIAL/TERMS

Cash Investment: $44.9K

Total Investment: $64.5 – 104.9K

Minimum Net Worth: $0K

Fees (Franchise): $44.9K

Fees (Royalty): 6 – 3%

Fees (Advertising): $350 or 2%

Term of Contract (Years): 10/10/10

Average Number of Employees: 1 FT, 33 PT

Co-operative Advertising: Yes

Franchisee Association/Member: No

Size of Corporate Staff: 50

On-going Support: C, D, G, H, I

Training: 5 Business Days Cincinnati, OH

SPECIFIC EXPANSION PLANS

US: All United States

Canada: All Canada

Overseas: All Countries

The tables below present historic Gross Revenues for franchised Home Helpers home healthcare agencies for the twelve-month periods ending on December 31, 2013 and December 31, 2012. For each of those periods, only data from franchisees who were open for at least 24 months before the beginning of the period and who reported Gross Revenue for all 12 months of the period were included in the table. The information has been extracted from royalty reports submitted to us by our franchises. We have not audited or independently verified this information. It may not be relied upon as a projection or forecast of what a new Home Helpers franchisee may experience.

The table below presents the highest and average Gross Revenue for our 50 highest-grossing franchised Home Helpers home healthcare agencies for the twelve-month periods ending on December 31, 2013 and December 31, 2012.

TOP 50 FRANCHISES

	2013[1]	2012[2]
No. of Franchisees[3,4]	50	50
Highest Gross Revenue	$5,460,897	$5,037,650
Average Gross Revenue of top 50 franchisees	$1,436,410	$1,199,895
Number of top 50 franchisees who attained or surpassed the average Gross Revenue	20	15
Percentage of top 50 franchisees who attained or surpassed the average Gross Revenue	40%	30%

The table below presents highest and average Gross Revenue for all franchised Home Helpers home healthcare agencies open at least 24 months for the twelve-month periods ending on December 31, 2013 and December 31, 2012.

ALL FRANCHISEES OPEN AT LEAST 24 MONTHS

	2013[1]	2014[2]
No. of Franchises[3,4]	160[5]	157[6]
Highest Gross Revenue	$5,460,897	$5,037,650
Percentage change from prior year	+8.4%	
Average Gross Revenue of all Franchisees[7]	$640,404	$544,840
Percentage change from prior year	+17.5%	
Number of franchisees who attained or surpassed the Average Gross Revenue	53	52
Percentage of franchisees who attained or surpassed the Average Gross Revenue	33.1%	33.1%

[1] For the 12-month period ending December 31, 2013.

[2] For the 12-month period ending December 31, 2012.

[3] The data in these tables include only franchisees who were open for at least 24 months before the beginning of the period reported and who reported Gross Revenue for all 12 months of that period. It does not include any revenue from the sale or rental of Direct Link products or services, even though many of our Home Helpers franchisees also own a Direct Link franchise.

[4] The data in these tables represent Gross Revenue by reporting franchisee, not by franchise territory. Some franchisees own more than one territory and report Gross Revenue and royalty information as a single unit for all territories they own. We have included this data in the table as reported by our franchisees, although this results in higher average revenue figures.

[5] There were 324 Home Helpers franchises (each franchise consists of a single franchise territory) in operation as of December 31, 2013, which were owned by 236 franchisees. Of those, 160 franchisees were both open for at least 24 months before January 1, 2013 and reported Gross Revenue for all 12 months between January 1 and December 31, 2013.

[6] There were 318 Home Helpers franchises (each franchise consists of a single franchise territory) in operation as of December 31, 2012, which were owned by 254 franchisees. Of those, 157 franchisees were both open for at least 24 months before January 1, 2012 and reported Gross Revenue for all 12 months between January 1 and December 31, 2012.

[7] For purposes of this Item 19, "Gross Revenue" means the total of all income arising from the operation of the franchised business, whether cash or credit. It is recognized on an accrual basis and regardless of collection, which means that a franchisee's Gross Revenue for any period represents how much a franchisee billed its clients during the period, not how much the franchisee received. Gross Revenue does not include the amount of refunds and discounts made to clients in good faith, or the amount of sales or excise taxes that are separately stated and that the franchisee is required to and does collect from clients and pays to the appropriate taxing authority.

The figures in the table do not reflect the costs of sales, operating expenses, or other costs or expenses that must be deducted from the Gross Revenue figures to obtain your net income or profit. Those expenses include fees you are required to pay us under the terms of your franchise agreement, such as royalties, national branding fees and technology fees. Your sales and operating expenses will vary depending on many factors, such as the geographic location of your territory, competition from other providers in your market, the effectiveness of your advertising, whether you manage your franchise yourself or hire a general manager, your pricing, the prices you pay for supplies, employee salaries and benefits (health insurance, retirement plan, etc.), other employment conditions in your market, insurance costs, weather conditions, ability to generate clients, client loyalty, and the necessity, cost and difficulty of obtaining a license to perform all of the services a Home Helpers franchise offers. You should conduct an independent investigation of the costs and expenses you will incur in operating a Home Helpers franchise. Franchisees and former franchisees listed in this disclosure document may be one source of this information.

The data in the table above represents Gross Revenue by reporting franchisee, not by franchise (or franchise territory). Some franchisees own more than one territory and, due to the nature of the business (service-based versus retail locations), manage their business and report Gross Revenue and royalty information as a single unit for all territories they own. We have included this data in the table as reported by our franchisees, although this results in higher average revenue figures. Some franchises do not offer personal care services, and most franchises did not offer skilled medical care services during the periods reported in the table.

You should use the information in the table only as one of several references in conducting your analysis and preparing your own projected income and cash flow statements. We strongly suggest that you consult a financial advisor or accountant for assistance in reviewing the table and in preparing your own financial projections, and for advice about the income and other taxes you will incur in operating a Home Helpers franchise and the effect of non-cash expenses such as depreciation and amortization on your business.

The success of your Home Helpers franchise will depend largely upon your personal abilities and how you use them, your willingness to engage in personal sales activities (or your ability to hire someone else to), the number of seniors in your market and their household income levels, and the number of competitors in your market. You are likely to achieve results that are different, possibly significantly and adversely, from the results shown in the table above.

Some of our franchisees have sold this amount. There is no assurance that you'll do as well. If you rely upon our figures, you must accept the risk of not doing as well. We do not make any promises or representations that you will achieve any particular results or level of sales or profitability, or even achieve break-even results in any particular year of operation. We do not represent that your franchise will generate any income or that the amount of income it might generate will exceed your initial investment in the franchise.

Written substantiation for the financial performance representation will be made available to you upon request.

Other than the preceding financial performance representation, HHFSI does not make any financial performance representations. We also do not authorize our employees or representatives to make any such representations either orally or in writing. If you are purchasing an existing outlet, however, we may provide you with the actual records of that outlet. If you receive any other financial performance information or projections of your future income, you should report it to the franchisor's management by contacting Jeffrey D. Siehl, General Counsel, 10700 Montgomery Road, Suite 300, Cincinnati, Ohio 45242, (513) 563-8339, the Federal Trade Commission, and the appropriate state regulatory agencies.

HOUSEMASTER HOME INSPECTIONS

850 Bear Tavern Rd., # 303
Ewing, NJ 08628
Tel: (800) 526-3930, (732) 823-4087
Fax: (802) 419-3434
Email: kim.fanus@housemaster.com
Website: www.franchise.housemaster.com
Kim Fanus, Director of Franchise Development

HouseMaster has been helping entrepreneurs from all educational and business backgrounds realize their dreams for the past 35 years, and has collectively performed over 2.5 million inspections. It is our motto to go above and beyond in supporting our franchisees; providing training, comprehensive business planning, solid marketing programs, operations support, resources and coaching in all areas of the business. Franchisee and customer satisfaction alike, along with the highest level of quality service available are why HouseMaster continues to be the recognized authority on everything home inspection.

BACKGROUND

IFA Member	Yes
Established & First Franchised:	1971;1979
Franchised Units:	320
Company-Owned Units:	0
Total Units:	320
Dist.:	US-286; CAN-34; O'seas-0
North America:	45 States, 8 Provinces
Density:	23 in NJ, 20 in NY, 18 in FL
Projected New Units (12 Months):	40
Qualifications:	4, 3, 2, 2, 5, 5

FINANCIAL/TERMS

Cash Investment:	$60.1 – 107.9K
Total Investment:	$60.1 – 107.9K
Minimum Net Worth:	$80K
Fees (Franchise):	$42.5K
Fees (Royalty):	7.5%
Fees (Advertising):	2.5%
Term of Contract (Years):	5/5
Avg. # of Employees:	Varies FT, Varies PT
Passive Ownership:	Not Allowed
Encourage Conversions:	N/A
Area Develop. Agreements:	Yes
Sub-Franchising Contracts:	No
Expand in Territory:	Yes

Space Needs:	N/A	Size of Corporate Staff:	12
		On-going Support:	A, B, C, D, E, G,h,I
SUPPORT & TRAINING		Training:	2 Weeks Medford, NJ
Financial Assistance Provided:	Yes (I)		
Site Selection Assistance:	N/A	SPECIFIC EXPANSION PLANS	
Lease Negotiation Assistance:	N/A	US:	All United States
Co-operative Advertising:	Yes	Canada:	All Canada
Franchisee Assoc./Member:	Yes/Member	Overseas:	No

Other than the financial performance representations contained in this Item 19, we do not make any financial performance representations. We also do not authorize our employees or representatives to make any such representations either orally or in writing. If you are purchasing an existing outlet, however, we may provide you with the actual records of that outlet. If you receive any financial performance information or projections of your future income, you should report it to the franchisor's management by contacting Kathleen Kuhn, 850 Bear Tavern Road, Ste. 303, Ewing, NJ 08628, (800) 526-3939, the Federal Trade Commission, and the appropriate state regulatory agencies.

STATEMENT OF AVERAGE GROSS SALES OF U.S. FRANCHISEES FOR THE 12 MONTHS ENDING DECEMBER 31, 2012 AND DECEMBER 31, 2013

The following is a statement of average annual gross sales for the calendar year 2013 for 4 different subsets of U.S. HouseMaster franchisees based on number of Owner-Occupied Homes (OOH) in the territory (or combined territories if they own multiple licenses) granted to the franchisee. This information was compiled from monthly gross sales reports submitted to us by the franchisees. This statement has not been audited and we are relying solely on the information submitted to us by the franchisees.

The number of franchisees included in this financial performance representation does not correlate with the number of franchised units in the Item 20 tables, since this financial performance is based on franchise owners and not single franchised units and a number of our franchisees own multiple franchise units which are reported together. The total number of OOH in all of a franchisee's territory is used in determining where the franchisee is included in the chart below. Therefore, if a franchisee owns 3 units of 75,000 OOH, the franchisee is included in the chart below in the category of more than 75,000 but less than 300,000 OOH.

The number of OOH in each franchisee's territory varies and is based on the size of territory each franchisee decided to purchase. The range of OOH for the franchisees included in each subset is disclosed in notes below the chart. The information on OOH has been taken from US census figures for each franchisee and is not necessarily the same as of the date of signing of the franchise agreement by the franchisee and us. Information on OOH in the charts includes OOH of existing franchisees that have a license for a Limited Area as well as franchisees in a Reciprocal Opportunity Franchise Territory (see Item 12).

The averages do not include revenue from (a) any franchisees operating less than two years, whether (i) the franchisee began operations after January 1, 2011 (for the 2012 numbers) or January 1, 2012 (for the 2013 numbers) and, therefore, did not operate for the full two year period, or (ii) the franchisee's franchise was terminated, expired or transferred prior to December 31, 2012 (for the 2012 numbers) or December 31, 2013 (for the 2013 numbers) and therefore the franchisee did not operate for the full two year period and (b) any franchisees (i) from whom we did not receive monthly sales reports, or (ii) for whom we do not have complete OOH statistics, for all of the 24 months up through December 31, 2012 or 2013, respectively.

The following averages reflect the actual annual gross sales of specific franchisees, and should not be considered as the actual or probable figures that will be realized by any given franchisees. We do not represent, warrant, promise or guarantee that any given franchisee can expect to attain such annual gross sales.

A NEW FRANCHISEE'S FINANCIAL RESULTS ARE LIKELY TO DIFFER FROM THE RESULTS STATED IN THIS STATEMENT. There is no assurance that you will earn as much. If you rely upon these figures, you must accept the risk of not doing as well.

Average Annual Gross Sales of U.S. HouseMaster Franchisees
For The Twelve Months Ending December 31, 2012 and December 31, 2013

US Franchisees	Year	Total Franchisees	Average Gross Sales (US$)	# of Franchisees at or above Average	% of Franchisees at or above Average
Franchisees with less than 75,000 OOH (Note 1)	2012	35	$115,249	15	43%
	2013	32	$149,498	17	53%
Franchisees with more than 75,000 OOH and less than 300,000 OOH (Note 2)	2012	57	$156,773	23	40%
	2013	52	$161,167	25	48%
Franchisees with more than 300,000 OOH (Note 3)	2012	14	$385,700	5	36%
	2013	14	$474,826	4	29%
All Franchisees (Note 4)	2012	106	$173,298	43	41%
	2013	98	$202,165	46	47%

Note 1: For 2012, 35 franchisees were included in computing this average. 28 franchisees were excluded (for one of the reasons listed above) in computing the average. The number of OOH in the territories of these 35 franchisees ranges from 15,487 to 73,730.

For 2013, 32 franchisees were included in computing this average. 37 franchisees were excluded (for one of the reasons listed above) in computing the average. The number of OOH in the territories of these 32 franchisees ranges from 15,487 to 72,596.

Note 2: For 2012, 57 franchisees were included in computing this average. 7 franchisees were excluded (for one of the reasons listed above) in computing the average. The number of OOH in the territories of these 57 franchisees ranges from 76,354 to 287,722.

For 2013, 52 franchisees were included in computing this average. 6 franchisees were excluded (for one of the reasons listed above) in computing the average. The number of OOH in the territories of these 52 franchisees ranges from 76,206 to 268,855.

Note 3: For both 2012 and 2013, 14 franchisees were included in computing these averages. No franchisees were excluded (for one of the reasons listed above) in computing the average. The number of OOH in the territories of these 14 franchisees ranges from 345,723 to 1,306,806.

Note 4: For 2012, 106 franchisees were included in computing this average. 35 franchisees were excluded (for one of the reasons listed above) in computing the average. The number of OOH in the territories of these 105 franchisees ranges from 15,487 to 1,306,806.

For 2013, 98 franchisees were included in computing this average. 43 franchisees were excluded (for one of the reasons listed above) in computing the average. The number of OOH in the territories of these 98 franchisees ranges from 15,487 to 1,306,806.

Annual gross sales will vary from franchise operation to franchise operation, and we do not represent that the annual gross sales of franchisees for 2012 or 2013 reported in this financial performance representation will accurately predict the future results of those outlets or for any prospective franchisee. Factors that may affect the annual gross revenues of a HouseMaster franchise include but are not necessarily limited to:

- Business skills, motivation and effort of the individual franchisee
- Sales and marketing skills of the individual franchisee and sales staff
- Franchisee's local marketing and promotional efforts
- How closely a Franchisee follows the HouseMaster Method and HouseMaster Marketing Strategy in operating and promoting the franchise
- Number of OOH in the franchise territory
- Location of the franchise territory
- Current market for home sales in franchise territory
- Local economic conditions
- Demographics of the franchise territory
- Competition
- Franchisee's pricing policies
- Number of years in operation
- Applicable regulations of home inspection and real estate industries
- Service options offered/available.

STATEMENT OF AVERAGE INSPECTION FEES OF U.S. FRANCHISEES FOR THE 12 MONTHS ENDING DECEMBER

31, 2012 AND DECEMBER 31, 2013

The following is a statement of average inspection fees charged during the 2012 and 2013 calendar years for 4 different subsets of U.S. HouseMaster franchisees based on the region in which the franchisee's territory is located. This information was compiled from monthly gross sales reports submitted to us by the franchisees. This statement has not been audited and we have not undertaken to independently verify the accuracy of and are relying solely on the information submitted to us by the franchisees.

The same franchisees that were included in the Statement of Average Gross Sales above were included in this Statement of Average Inspection Fees, and the same franchisees that were excluded in the Statement of Average Gross Sales were excluded in this Statement of Average Inspection Fees for the same reason.

The following averages reflect the actual average inspection fees charged of specific franchisees, and should not be considered as the actual or probable fees that will be realized by any given franchisees. We do not represent, warrant, promise or guarantee that any given franchisee can expect to receive such fees.

A NEW FRANCHISEE'S FINANCIAL RESULTS ARE LIKELY TO DIFFER FROM THE RESULTS STATED IN THIS STATEMENT. There is no assurance that you will earn as much. If you rely upon these figures, you must accept the risk of not doing as well.

Average Inspection Fee of HouseMaster Franchisees
For The Twelve Months Ending December 31, 2012 and December 31, 2013

Region	Year	Total Franchisees	Average Inspection Fee (US$)	Number (#) of Franchisees at or above Average	Percentage (%) of Franchisees at or above Average
Northeast (see Note 5)	2012	29	$548	6	21%
	2013	29	$568	9	31%
Midwest (see Note 6)	2012	21	$362	14	67%
	2013	15	$391	10	67%
West (see Note 7)	2012	24	$359	15	63%
	2013	24	$397	15	63%
South (see Note 8)	2012	32	$409	12	38%
	2013	30	$436	16	53%
Total (see Note 9)	2012	106	$430	47	44%
	2013	98	$461	50	51%

Note 5: For both 2012 and 2013, 29 franchisees were included in computing these average. 10 franchisees were excluded (for one of the reasons listed above) in computing the average. The States included in this region are: Connecticut, Delaware, District of Columbia, Maine, Maryland, Massachusetts, New Hampshire, New Jersey, New York, Pennsylvania, Rhode Island, Vermont, Virginia, and West Virginia.

Note 6: For 2012, 21 franchisees were included in computing this average. 9 franchisees were excluded (for one of the reasons listed above) in computing the average. For 2013, 15 franchisees were included in computing this average. 20 franchisees were excluded (for one of the reasons listed above) in computing the average. The States included in this region are: Illinois, Indiana, Iowa, Kansas, Kentucky, Michigan, Minne-

sota, Missouri, Nebraska, North Dakota, Ohio, South Dakota, and Wisconsin.

Note 7: For both 2012 and 2013, 24 franchisees were included in computing this average. 6 franchisees were excluded (for one of the reasons listed above) in computing the average. The States included in this region are: Alaska, Arizona, California, Colorado, Hawaii, Idaho, Montana, Nevada, New Mexico, Oklahoma, Oregon, Utah, Washington and Wyoming.

Note 8: For 2012, 32 franchisees were included in computing this average. 10 franchisees were excluded (for one of the reasons listed above) in computing the average. For 2013, 30 franchisees were included in computing this average. 7 franchisees were excluded (for one of the reasons listed above) in computing the average. The States included in this region are: Alabama, Arkansas, Florida, Georgia, Louisiana, Mississippi, North Carolina, South Carolina, Tennessee and Texas.

Note 9: For 2012, 106 franchisees were included in computing this average. 35 franchisees were excluded (for one of the reasons listed above) in computing the average. For 2013, 98 franchisees were included in computing this average. 43 franchisees were excluded (for one of the reasons listed above) in computing the average. All States and Provinces were included in this group.

Inspection fees charged and received will vary from franchise operation to franchise operation, and we do not represent that the average inspection fees of franchisees for 2012 or 2013 reported in this financial performance representation will accurately predict the future results of those outlets or for any prospective franchisee. Factors that may affect the annual gross revenues of a HouseMaster franchise include but are not necessarily limited to:

- Business skills, motivation and effort of the individual franchisee
- Sales and marketing skills of the individual franchisee and sales staff
- Franchisee's local marketing and promotional efforts
- How closely a Franchisee follows the HouseMaster Method and HouseMaster Marketing Strategy in operating and promoting the franchise
- Location of the franchise territory
- Current market for home sales in franchise territory
- Local economic conditions
- Demographics of the franchise territory
- Competition

- Franchisee's pricing policies
- Number of years in operation
- Applicable regulations of home inspection and real estate industries
- Service options offered/available.

This financial performance representation does not provide information on the net profits of franchises. This financial performance representation does not include information concerning expenses or profits that may be realized in the operation of a HouseMaster business. Profits in the operation of a HouseMaster business will vary from franchisee to franchisee and from territory to territory and are dependent upon numerous factors beyond our control. We make no warranties, representations, predictions, promises or guarantees with respect to the profits likely to be experienced by individual franchisees.

You should carefully consider these and other factors in evaluating this information and in making any decision to purchase a franchise. Further, we urge you to consult with appropriate financial, business and legal advisors in connection with the use of any of the information contained in this financial performance representation and in estimating potential revenue from a HOUSEMASTER franchise business.

Written substantiation for the financial performance representation presented above will be made available to a prospective franchisee on reasonable request made in writing.

SOME FRANCHISEES HAVE SOLD THIS AMOUNT. YOUR INDIVIDUAL RESULTS MAY DIFFER. THERE IS NO ASSURANCE THAT YOU WILL SELL AS MUCH.

HUNTINGTON LEARNING CENTER

496 Kinderkamack Rd.
Oradell, NJ 07649-1512
Tel: (800) 653-8400, (201) 261-8400

Fax: (800) 361-9728
Email: lapie@hlcmail.com
Website: www.huntingtonfranchise.com
Elise Lapi, Vice President of Franchise Sales

Offers tutoring to 5 – 19 year-olds in reading, writing, language development study skills and mathematics, as well as programs to prepare for standardized entrance exams. Instruction is offered in a tutorial setting and is predominately remedial in nature.

BACKGROUND

IFA Member:	Yes
Established & First Franchised:	1977; 1985
Franchised Units:	240
Company-Owned Units:	32
Total Units:	272
Distribution:	US – 272; CAN – 0; O'seas – 0
North America:	41 States, 0 Provinces
Density:	30 in CA, 26 in FL, 26 in NY
Projected New Units (12 Months):	60
Qualifications:	5, 3, 1, 3, 1, 5

FINANCIAL/TERMS

Cash Investment:	$50K
Total Investment:	$121.4 – 255.6K
Minimum Net Worth:	$150K
Fees (Franchise):	$14.5K
Fees (Royalty):	9.5%
Fees (Advertising):	2%/$500 Min
Term of Contract (Years):	10/10
Average Number of Employees:	2 – 4 FT, 12 – 20 PT
Passive Ownership:	Allowed

Encourage Conversions:	Yes
Area Development Agreements:	Yes
Sub-Franchising Contracts:	No
Expand in Territory:	No
Space Needs:	1,200 – 1,600 SF

SUPPORT & TRAINING

Financial Assistance Provided:	Yes (I)
Site Selection Assistance:	Yes
Lease Negotiation Assistance:	Yes
Co-operative Advertising:	Yes
Franchisee Association/Member:	No
Size of Corporate Staff:	100
On-going Support:	C, D, E, F, G, h, I
Training:	1 Week Oradell, NJ (Corporate Headquarters); 2 Weeks Online; On-Going Regional

SPECIFIC EXPANSION PLANS

US:	Contiguous US
Canada:	No
Overseas:	No

Section 1. Franchise Centers open 2011, 2012, and 2013

Section 1 of this Item 19 presents the 2013 performance of the 207 franchise Centers open during each of the three years, 2011, 2012, and 2013. Their 2013 average annual sales were $470,182. Of these Centers, 88 or 43% achieved sales greater than average. Learning Center Services, Exam Prep Services, Subject Tutoring Services, and other services accounted for 56%, 29%, 8%, and 7% of sales, respectively. The following table presents the 2013 average annual sales for the top, middle, and bottom third, ranked by sales.

Third	2013 annual sales	Number above average	Percent above average
Top	$693,173	26	38%
Middle	$439,913	31	45%
Bottom	$277,762	33	48%

During 2013, these franchise Centers charged average hourly tuition of $49 and $67 for Learning Center Services and Exam Prep Services, respectively. Of these Centers, 96 or 46% charged Learning Center Services hourly tuition above average; and 124 or 60% charged Exam Prep Services hourly tuition above average. Your hourly tuition may be lower or higher than the average.

Learning Center Services and Exam Prep Services students attending these franchise Centers during 2013 attended 3.4 hours per week and 3.7 hours per week, respectively. Of these Centers, 91 or 44% had Learning Center Services students attending more hours per week than average; and 107 or 52% had Exam Prep Services students attending more hours per week than average. Your students may attend more or fewer hours per week than the average.

Section 2. Franchise Centers open in 2013

The average annual 2013 sales of the 221 franchised Centers that were open all of 2013 were $464,042. Of these Centers, 93 or 42% achieved sales greater than average.

CAUTIONARY NOTES

Not all Huntington Learning Centers® achieved these average sales or operating results. There is no assurance you will do as well. If you rely upon our figures, you must accept the risk of not doing as well. Sales likely will be lower for newer franchisees.

The figures in Section 1 above are 2013 annual sales figures for franchise Centers that were open for all three years (2011, 2012, and 2013). As these figures are for franchise Centers that were open for three years (and that may have been open for a longer time period), they may not be representative of the annual sales you may expect to receive at your Center in at least the first two years of operation. In addition, these figures do not include sales for franchise Centers that were not operating for the entire calendar in 2011, 2012, or 2013.

The results in Sections 1 and 2 above represent sales from franchised Centers for all Huntington Services, both Tutoring Services and Exam Prep Services. They do not include sales from corporate-owned Centers. These franchised Centers offered, or had the opportunity to offer, all Huntington Services during the entire period they were open. However, you likely will offer only Tutoring Services through December of your Center's first full calendar year of operation. You likely will begin offering Exam Prep Services beginning in January of your Center's second full calendar of operation. Therefore, you can expect your results to differ significantly from the results of the Centers presented in the above table.

Many other factors influence the revenue at a Huntington Learning Center®, including the manager who operates the business, the number of inquiries, conversion of these inquiries to enrolled students, program duration, average student hours per week, tuition rates, and Center size, as well as factors outside the business, like foot and car traffic, road structure, and demographic factors, including the number of school-age children located near the Center. Non-retail sites likely generate lower walk-in traffic. Center operation may be affected by factors like the curricula and testing material used in the schools attended by students in the area, length of the school day, and length of the school year. The presence of direct and indirect competitors, including other Huntington Learning Centers®, may affect your revenue. These factors may change over time. Factors that determine expenses at a Center include debt service; the number of teachers and other staff and their length of employment; the amount of compensation you pay yourself, as well as teachers and staff; and the benefits you offer. Other factors include premises rent and marketing expenditures. Many franchisees spend substantially more on marketing than required under the Franchise Agreement. In addition, your Advertising Cooperative Association can require you pay it for cooperative advertising.

Franchised Centers differ from each other in many important ways, including their market area and geographic location and the number of children and population contained thereabout and the economic and financial circumstances of this population, which may change over time. Centers also differ from each other in their physical, marketing, employee, and manager's characteristics and in many other factors that may or may not exist or be similar to the factors that exist in any other location or geographic area or market area that you may consider. Actual sales, expenses, profits, and earnings vary from one Center to another by significant amounts, and we cannot and do not estimate or forecast the sales, expenses, profits, or earnings that you may achieve.

You should conduct an independent investigation of the costs and expenses you will incur in operating the Franchised Business. Current franchisees and former franchisees listed in Exhibits J and K, respectively, may be a source of this information. You should consult with financial, business and legal advisors about this Item 19.

Written substantiation for the financial performance representation will be made available to you upon reasonable request.

We do not authorize anyone, including our officers or sales personnel, to furnish you with any oral or written information about actual or potential sales, expenses, profits, or earnings of Huntington Learning Centers®, other than the information in this Item 19.

If you receive any oral or written information about actual or potential sales, expenses, profits, or earnings of Huntington Learning Centers®, other than the specific information contained in this Item 19, please notify the Chairman of Huntington Learning Centers, Inc. immediately in writing.

How we calculated financial performance

Franchised Centers reported the gross revenues ("sales") in this item. We compiled the data for these Centers from the monthly income statements our franchisees submitted to us, which they prepare according to a standardized method described in the Operating Manual. We believe these statements are accurate as to sales, because each franchisee must pay us Continuing Royalty and Advertising Fees that are calculated as a percentage of sales. We have not audited nor in any other manner substantiated the truthfulness, accuracy, or completeness of any information supplied by our franchisees.

In 2013, franchised Centers operated in the following states:

States in which Franchised Huntington Learning Centers® Operated during All of 2013				
AL	GA	MD	NJ	PA
AR	IA	MI	NM	SC
CA	ID	MN	NV	TN
CO	IL	MS	NY	TX
CT	KY	MT	OH	VA
DE	LA	NC	OK	WA
FL	MA	NE	OR	WI

Expense Items on a Franchise Huntington Learning Centers® End-of-Year P&L Statement

The following table presents certain expense items listed on the End-of-Year Profit and Loss Statement franchisees must submit to us. Your profit and loss statement may contain additional or different expense items.

Expenses Listed on the End-of-Year P&L Statement that Franchisees Must Submit to Us
Gross payroll for franchisee, center director, assistant director
Other full-time staff (like a regional director)
Gross payroll for part-time teachers
Gross payroll for any other part-time staff
Payroll taxes (Employer's portion of FICA, FUTA, etc.)
Advertising center services, including broadcast TV and radio, cable TV, daily and weekly newspaper, magazine, direct mail, free standing insert, Internet, school programs, and marketing
Advertising payment to your Advertising Cooperative Association
Building, including rent, utilities, janitor, and maintenance

Repairs and maintenance of equipment
Supplies - office and administrative
Call Center fees
Conference Services fees
Supplies - educational
Professional fees (accounting, legal, etc.)
Telephone
Travel and entertainment
Continuing Royalty
Advertising Fee
Insurance (property, liability, health, etc.)
Depreciation and amortization
Debt service
Training (travel, food, lodging, etc.)
Employee benefits
Other expenses
Taxes, other than payroll

Intelligent Office®
Work Anywhere...Professionally

INTELLIGENT OFFICE

4450 Arapahoe Ave.
Boulder, CO 80303
Tel: (800) 800-4987, (303) 417-2100
Fax: (303) 448-8882
Email: scochran@intelligentoffice.com
Website: www.intelligentoffice.com
Sean Cochran, Director of Franchise Development

This highly evolved alternative to the traditional office provides a prestigious address, anywhere communications and a live receptionist for businesses, corporate executives and professionals, releasing them from the limitations and expense of a traditional or home office. INTELLIGENT OFFICE offers private offices, conference rooms and professional office services on an as-needed basis and at only a fraction of the cost of a traditional office.

BACKGROUND

IFA Member:	Yes
Established & First Franchised:	1995; 1999
Franchised Units:	49
Company-Owned Units:	5
Total Units:	54
Distribution:	US – 38; CAN – 16; O'seas – 0
North America:	16 States, 1 Province
Density:	11 in ON, 7 in DC, 4 in VA
Projected New Units (12 Months):	18
Qualifications:	5, 1, 1, 1, 1, 5

FINANCIAL/TERMS

Cash Investment:	$100K
Total Investment:	$316 – 496.5K
Minimum Net Worth:	$750K
Fees (Franchise):	$54K
Fees (Royalty):	5%
Fees (Advertising):	$1,500/Mo.
Term of Contract (Years):	20/20
Average Number of Employees:	2 FT, 1 PT
Passive Ownership:	Allowed
Encourage Conversions:	No
Area Development Agreements:	Yes
Sub-Franchising Contracts:	No
Expand in Territory:	No
Space Needs:	3,000 – 4,000 SF

SUPPORT & TRAINING

Financial Assistance Provided:	No
Site Selection Assistance:	Yes
Lease Negotiation Assistance:	Yes
Co-operative Advertising:	Yes
Franchisee Association/Member:	Yes/Member
Size of Corporate Staff:	10
On-going Support:	A, B, C, D, E, G, H, I
Training:	1 week Denver, CO; 1 week On-Site; 2 weeks online

SPECIFIC EXPANSION PLANS

US:	All United States
Canada:	All Canada
Overseas:	All Countries

To help you evaluate our franchise, we have summarized selected historical sales information for our fiscal year ending December 31, 2013. Table 1 below provides the average monthly gross sales of both the top 25% and top 50% (measured by average monthly gross sales) of outlets whose franchised businesses were located in North America, were in operation as of December 31, 2013, and had been in uninterrupted operation for at least 12 months. Table 1 does not include information about franchised businesses that began or discontinued their affiliation with us during 2013. Table 1 also does not include information about company-owned locations.

The information in Table 1 is not a forecast of your future financial performance. We have compiled the information based upon what franchisees have reported to us in the ordinary course of business through our sales reporting system. We assume that the information submitted is accurate, complete and contains no material misrepresentations or omissions.

Table 1- Statement of 2013 Average Gross Sales Information by Month[1]

	Average Sales	High	Low
Top 25%	$71,302.69[2]	$130,573.34	$52,000.42
Top 50%	$58,414.30[3]	$130,573.34	$37,129.22

(1) The total number of outlets whose franchised businesses were located in North America, were in operation as of December 31, 2013, had been in uninterrupted operation for at least 12 months, and were not company-owned, was 46. The total number of outlets (including company-owned outlets) in North America as of December 31, 2013 was 54.

(2) The total number of outlets in the top 25% was 11. This

is the set of outlets used to calculate the stated average. Three of these outlets (or 27%) had average monthly sales volume above the stated average.

(3) The total number of outlets in the top 50% was 23. This is the set of outlets used to calculate the stated average. Eight of these outlets (or 53%) had average monthly sales volume above the stated average.

The information presented in Table 1 does not reflect the cost of sales, operating expenses or other costs or expenses that must be deducted from the gross sales figures to obtain net income or profit. You should conduct an independent investigation of the costs and expenses you will incur in operating your franchised business. Franchisees or former franchisees listed in the disclosure document may be one source of this information.

The information in Table 1 is presented for periods during which economic conditions may be substantively different from future economic conditions. Competitors may enter or leave the market over time. Brand recognition and awareness and consumer goodwill may vary by market. Market potential and consumer demand may change over time. Each franchisee's managerial skill, experience and resources will differ. Accordingly, you are urged to consult with appropriate financial, business and legal counsel to conduct your own independent analysis of the information presented.

We have written substantiation of the information used to compile the preceding financial performance representations. We will make this written substantiation available to you upon written request.

Other than the preceding historical financial performance representations, we do not make any representations about a franchisee's future financial performance or the past financial performance of company-owned or franchised outlets. We also do not authorize our employees or representatives to make any such representations either orally or in writing. If you are purchasing an existing outlet, however, we may provide you with the actual records of that outlet. If you receive any other financial performance information or projections of your future income, you should report it to the franchisor's management by contacting Chief Operating Officer, 4450 Arapahoe Avenue, Boulder, Colorado, (303) 417-2100, the Federal Trade Commission, and the appropriate state regulatory agencies.

JANI-KING INTERNATIONAL

16885 Dallas Pkwy.
Addison, TX 75001
Tel: (800) 526-4546, (972) 991-0900
Fax: (972) 239-7706
Email: tlooney@janiking.com
Website: www.janiking.com
Ted Looney, Vice President, Jani-King Franchising

JANI-KING INTERNATIONAL is the world's largest commercial cleaning franchisor, with locations in 14 countries and over 120 regions in the U. S. and abroad. Our franchise opportunity includes initial customer contracts, training, continuous local support , administrative and accounting assistance, an equipment leasing program and national advertising. If you are searching for a flexible business opportunity, look no further.

BACKGROUND

IFA Member:	Yes
Established & First Franchised:	1969; 1974
Franchised Units:	10,000
Company-Owned Units:	22
Total Units:	10,022
Distribution:	US – 12,153; CAN – 351; O'seas – 528
North America:	39 States, 7 Provinces
Density:	900 in FL, 900 in CA, 500 in TX
Projected New Units (12 Months):	N/A
Qualifications:	2, 2, 1, 2, 2, 3

FINANCIAL/TERMS

Cash Investment:	$2.9 – 33K
Total Investment:	$8.2 – 74K
Minimum Net Worth:	$2.9 – 33K
Fees (Franchise):	$8 – 33K
Fees (Royalty):	10%
Fees (Advertising):	1%
Term of Contract (Years):	20/20
Average Number of Employees:	0 PT
Passive Ownership:	Discouraged
Encourage Conversions:	N/A
Area Development Agreements:	Yes

Sub-Franchising Contracts:	Yes	Franchisee Association/Member:	Yes/Member
Expand in Territory:	Yes	Size of Corporate Staff:	65
Space Needs:	N/A	On-going Support:	A, B, C, D, G, H, I
		Training:	2+ Weeks Local Regional Office

SUPPORT & TRAINING

Financial Assistance Provided:	No	**SPECIFIC EXPANSION PLANS**	
Site Selection Assistance:	N/A	US:	All United States
Lease Negotiation Assistance:	N/A	Canada:	All Canada
Co-operative Advertising:	No	Overseas:	All Countries

ANALYSIS OF ACTUAL INITIAL BUSINESS OFFERING EXPERIENCE

This analysis sets forth information about our performance of the obligation to provide Initial Business for certain Jani-King franchises. The first part of the analysis and underlying data is based on information provided by JANI-KING INTERNATIONAL, INC., through its direct and indirect subsidiaries, including any Regional Franchisees of an affiliated subsidiary, for the specified franchise operating within all JANI-KING regions in the United States. The Territory for each franchise is identified more specifically in each franchise agreement.

The analysis is based on data as of December 31, 2013, reported for 578 franchisees that either purchased their franchise between January 1, 2013 and December 31, 2013 or they purchased their franchise prior to 2013 and their offering period ended in 2013.

Under the terms of the Franchise Agreement, we agree to secure and offer you the opportunity to service signed commercial cleaning and/or maintenance contracts that in total would provide a minimum in gross monthly billings in an amount defined as the "INITIAL BUSINESS". These contracts will be secured and offered within the number of days identified in the Franchise Summary of the Franchise Agreement as the "INITIAL OFFERING PERIOD", such time period beginning on the date all required equipment and supplies listed in the "Supply and Equipment Package" and "Additional Electric Equipment" have been obtained and the Acknowledgment of Completion of Training is signed, or a later date as discussed later in this item. The schedule below is a sample of plans through Plan E-10, other plans with more Initial Business are available.

PLAN	Initial Finder's Fee Business ($)	INITIAL OFFERING PERIOD (Days)
E-10*	10,000*	330**
E-9	9,000	300
E-8	8,000	270
E-7	7,000	240
E-6	6,000	210
E-5	5,000	180
E-4	4,000	150
D	3,000	120
C	2,000	120
	* An additional $1,000 for each higher level of the "E" Plan	** Plus An Additional 30 Days for each higher level of the "E" Plan

Under Plans C and D, the Initial Offering Period is 120 days. Under the various levels of Plan E, the Initial Offering Period is calculated as the total of: 120 days, plus an additional 30 days for each higher level of the "E" Plan, beginning with level E-4.

Example:

E-4 [120 + 30 (1st level)] = 150 days
E-5 [120 + 60 (2nd level)] = 180 days
E-6 [120 + 90 (3rd level)] = 210 days, etc.

The franchises reported in this analysis are listed by ranges of Initial Business obligated to be offered in order to provide a more meaningful presentation of the relevant information about the offering of accounts for Initial Business by JANI-KING. The time period in which the Initial Business is contractually required to be offered is the Initial Offering Period stated in the Franchise Agreement, while the average time period within which the Initial Business was offered represents the actual number of days within which JANI-KING had secured and offered cleaning contracts with gross monthly billings that equal or exceed the total obligation required under each Franchise Agreement for the specified range.

You should particularly note the following:

THE INFORMATION CONCERNING FRANCHISEE INITIAL CONTRACT BUSINESS SHOULD NOT BE CONSIDERED AS THE ACTUAL OR POTENTIAL SALES, COSTS, INCOME OR PROFITS THAT YOU WILL REALIZE. YOUR SUCCESS WILL DEPEND LARGELY UPON YOUR OWN ABILITY, AND THE INDIVIDUAL FINANCIAL RESULTS ACHIEVED BY YOU MAY DIFFER FROM THE FRANCHISEE INFORMATION STATED IN THIS DISCLOSURE DOCUMENT. THEREFORE WE DO NOT REPRESENT THAT ALL FRANCHISEES CAN EXPECT TO ACHIEVE THESE GROSS BILLINGS, OR ANY PARTICULAR LEVEL OF SALES, COSTS, INCOME OR PROFITS, OR ANY INCOME THAT EXCEEDS THE INITIAL PAYMENT FOR, OR INVESTMENT IN, THE FRANCHISED BUSINESS.

WE HAVE WRITTEN SUBSTANTIATION IN OUR POSSESSION TO SUPPORT THE INFORMATION APPEARING IN THIS ITEM 19 AND SUCH SUBSTANTIATION WILL BE MADE AVAILABLE TO YOU ON REASONABLE REQUEST.

THE TOTAL REVENUE AND THE TOTAL GROSS BILLING FOR ANY SPECIFIC MONTH, REALIZED BY YOU MAY NOT BE DIRECTLY RELATED TO OUR PERFORMANCE OF OUR OBLIGATION TO OFFER THE INITIAL BUSINESS REQUIRED BY THE FRANCHISE AGREEMENT. THE AMOUNT OF REVENUE IS AFFECTED BY MANY FACTORS, SUCH AS (1) THE INITIAL BUSINESS MAY BE OFFERED IN STAGES DURING THE INITIAL OFFERING PERIOD; (2) YOU MAY NOT ACCEPT ALL OF THE ACCOUNTS OFFERED; (3) ACCOUNTS MAY CANCEL THE CONTRACT OR REQUEST A CHANGE OF FRANCHISEES DUE TO POOR PERFORMANCE BY YOU; OR (4) THE ACCOUNT MAY GO OUT OF BUSINESS BEFORE THE END OF THE CONTRACT PERIOD.

Other factors that affect the amount of revenue you realize include the quality of management and service, the rate of cleaning production you achieve; the extent to which you finance the acquisition and/or operation of the franchise; your legal, accounting and other professional fees; federal state and local income, gross profits or other taxes; discretionary expenditures; and accounting methods used.

We will make a good faith effort to secure and offer accounts to you as soon as possible, but we will have the total period to offer the Initial Business under each plan, and we are not obligated to offer any portion of the Initial Business before the end of that time. We calculate the Initial Offering Period from the date you sign the Acknowledgment of Completion of Training and you obtain all required equipment and supplies.

The actual time to secure and offer the Initial Business to you may, at our sole discretion, be automatically extended under certain conditions. Item 11 of this disclosure document has a detailed explanation of those conditions, but they are summarized as follows:

- Upon your written request
- You are in default of the Franchise Agreement
- Upon a transfer or cancellation due to non-performance of an account accepted by you as Initial Business.
- You fail to comply with policies or procedures

All accounts offered will apply toward the minimum amount of business as specified in your Franchise Agreement, whether the offered business is accepted or declined by you. Our obligation is to secure and offer those accounts to you within the specified time. However, you might choose not to accept some of the accounts offered. That is why the Franchise Agreement says that we will secure and "offer" those accounts to you. We can only make a good faith effort to offer the amount of business for the plan specified, and you must choose to accept or decline the "offer". Under a situation where you either decline an offer of an account or an account cancels at no fault of you, we are relieved of our obligation regarding the Initial Offering Period for that amount of gross monthly billings, however, we will at some point in the future, offer that amount of contract billings to you without Finder's Fees.

If an account cancels or is transferred from you due to non-performance, theft, your failure to service the account properly, customer relations problems caused by you or your failure to comply with Jani-King Policies and Procedures, the account will not be replaced. If an account cancels at no fault of you before you service the account for 12 full months, the full gross monthly billing value of that account will be replaced within a reasonable period of time by another account until a cumulative total of 12 full months of billing between both the original account and any replacement account occur (See Item 11: Transfers Or Cancellation Of Initial Business). There is no other obligation for us to replace the contracts if the contracts are canceled before the full term.

If we are unable to secure and offer you the full amount of Initial Business within the time frame allocated for the Initial Offering Period in the plan you purchase, an amount equal to three times the amount of Initial Business not offered to you may be refunded. Any refund will be first applied to any outstanding balance owe us or LEASING, with the remaining sum, if any, paid to you. A refund under this provision will fulfill our obligation to offer any remaining portion of the Initial Business.

INFORMATION CONCERNING FRANCHISEE INITIAL BUSINESS FOR JANI-KING OF MADISON FRANCHISEES – 2013

Range of Monthly Initial Finder's Fee Business Purchased($)	500	1,000	2,000	3,000	4,000 to 8,000	9,000 to 15,000	TOTAL
Time Period (days) in which Initial Finder's Fee Business contractually required to be offered[1]	120	120	120	120	150 to 270	300 to 480	N/A
Average time period (days) in which Initial Finder's Fee Business was actually offered[1]	N/A	N/A	N/A	N/A	N/A	N/A	N/A
Number of franchisees purchasing within range during 2013	0	0	0	0	0	0	0
Number of franchisees purchased prior to 2013 and their offering period ended in 2013	0	0	0	0	0	0	0
Percentage[3] of franchisees in which Initial Finder's Fee Business was offered[1] within required period	N/A	N/A	N/A	N/A	N/A	N/A	N/A
Number of franchises whose initial offering period expired in 2013 and Initial Finder's Fee Business was offered[1] within required period	N/A	N/A	N/A	N/A	N/A	N/A	N/A
Number of franchises who purchased prior to 2013 and whose offering period has ended in 2013	N/A	N/A	N/A	N/A	N/A	N/A	N/A
Number of franchises in which time period for Initial Finder's Fee Business was extended[2] pursuant to franchise agreement	N/A	N/A	N/A	N/A	N/A	N/A	N/A

Percentage[3] of Franchisees For All U.S. Regions In Which Initial Finder's Fee Business Was Offered[1] Within Required Period

REGION	%	REGION	%
Alexandria	N/A	Macon	100
Atlanta	100	Madison	N/A
Augusta	100	Memphis	100
Austin	100	Miami	100
Baltimore	100	Milwaukee	100
Baton Rouge	100	Minneapolis	100

Birmingham	100	Mississippi Coast	100
Boston	N/A	Mobile	N/A
Buffalo	N/A	Monroe	N/A
Charleston	100	Montgomery	100
Charlotte	100	Myrtle Beach	100
Chattanooga	100	Nashville	75
Chicago	100	New Jersey	N/A
Cincinnati	100	New Mexico	N/A
Cleveland	100	New Orleans	92
Columbia, MO	100	New York	100
Columbia, SC	100	Oklahoma City	100
Columbus	100	Omaha	100
Dallas	100	Orlando	100
Dayton	100	Pensacola	100
Denver	100	Philadelphia	N/A
Detroit	75	Phoenix	100
Dothan	N/A	Pittsburgh	N/A
Eugene/Salem	N/A	Portland	N/A
Ft. Myers	N/A	Raleigh/Durham	70
Ft. Worth	100	Reno	N/A
Greater Rhode Island	100	Richmond	100
Greensboro	100	Roanoke/Lynchburg	100
Greenville/Spartanburg	100	St. Louis	100
Hampton Roads	90	Sacramento	N/A
Hartford	80	Salt Lake City	100
Hawaii	100	San Antonio	100
Houston	N/A	San Diego	100
Huntsville	100	San Francisco/Oakland	100
Indianapolis	100	Savannah	100
Jackson	100	Seattle	100
Jacksonville	100	Shreveport	100
Kansas City	100	South East Mississippi	100
Knoxville	100	Springfield	100
Lafayette/Lake Charles	100	Tampa Bay	100
Las Vegas	N/A	Tri-Cities	N/A
Lexington	N/A	Tucson	100
Little Rock	100	Tulsa	N/A
Los Angeles/Colton	100	Washington D.C.	N/A
Louisville	100	Wichita	100

¹ Offered means the accounts totally fulfilling the Initial Finder's Fee Business were offered to the franchisee. Initial Finder's Fee Business Packages not shown indicates that no plans were sold in those ranges for which the Initial Offering Period expired in 2012.

² Percentage calculated as number of franchises whose Initial Offering Period had expired in 2012 and whose total Initial Finder's Fee Business was offered within required time period, divided by the total number of franchises sold during 2012 or prior to 2012 and whose Initial Offering Period had expired in 2012.

Other than the preceding financial performance representation, we do not make any financial performance representations. We also do not authorize our employees or representatives to make any such representations either orally or in writing. If you are purchasing an existing outlet, however, we may provide you with the actual records of that outlet. If you receive any other financial performance information or projections of your future income, you should report it to the franchisor's management by contacting Jon McAlpine, Royal Franchising, Inc., 200 North Patrick Boulevard, Suite 900, Brookfield, Wisconsin 53045, (262) 780-0300.

JAN-PRO CLEANING SYSTEMS

2520 Northwinds Pkwy., # 375
Alpharetta, GA 30009
Tel: (866) 355-1064, (678) 336-1780
Fax: (678) 336-1782
Email: scott-thompson@jan-pro.com
Website: www.jan-pro.com
Scott Thompson, Vice President of Business Development

Jan-Pro provides one of today's exceptional business opportunities, allowing you to enter one of the fastest-growing industries by safely becoming your own boss through the guidance and support of an established franchise organization.

BACKGROUND
IFA Member:	Yes
Established & First Franchised:	1991; 1992
Franchised Units:	10,100
Company-Owned Units:	0
Total Units:	10,100
Distribution:	US – 9,235; CAN – 793; O'seas – 64
North America:	39 States, 5 Provinces
Density:	1,316 in CA, 858 in GA, 695 in FL
Projected New Units (12 Months):	2,000

Qualifications:	3, 2, 1, 1, 1,1

FINANCIAL/TERMS
Cash Investment:	$1 – 30K
Total Investment:	$2.8 – 44K
Minimum Net Worth:	$50K
Fees (Franchise):	$1 – 30K
Fees (Royalty):	10%
Fees (Advertising):	0%
Term of Contract (Years):	5/5
Average Number of Employees:	0 FT; 0 PT
Passive Ownership:	Not Allowed
Encourage Conversions:	Yes
Area Development Agreements:	Yes
Sub-Franchising Contracts:	Yes
Expand in Territory:	Yes
Space Needs:	N/A

SUPPORT & TRAINING
Financial Assistance Provided:	Yes (D)
Site Selection Assistance:	Yes
Lease Negotiation Assistance:	Yes
Co-operative Advertising:	No
Franchisee Association/Member:	Yes/Not a Member
Size of Corporate Staff:	15
On-going Support:	A, B, C, D, E, F, G, H, I
Training:	5 Weeks Regional and Local

SPECIFIC EXPANSION PLANS
US:	All United States
Canada:	All Canada
Overseas:	All Countries except England and Ireland

The below data is historical data for specific master franchises and should not be considered as the actual or potential revenues, costs of services and goods sold or gross profit that may be achieved by any other master franchise. Actual results vary from master franchise to master franchise and we cannot estimate the result of any specific master franchise. Your financial results may differ from the revenue volumes stated in this Item 19. A new master franchisee's results are likely to be lower than the results shown below. You should conduct an independent investigation of the expenses you will incur in operating your master franchise. Master franchisees or former master franchisees, listed in this disclosure document, may be a source of this information.

Revenues, costs and profits can vary considerably due to a variety of other factors, such as demographics and population of the master franchisee's territory; competition from other commercial janitorial service providers in or near the master franchisee's territory; economic conditions in the master franchisee's territory; advertising and promotional activities; and the master franchisee's business abilities and efforts.

On your written request, we will make available to you written substantiation of the data used in preparing these financial performance representations.

Data From Master Franchisees' Audited Financial Statements

The below information is presented for our United States master franchisees that had been open and operating for all of 2012 and 2013 under the same ownership. There are 58 master franchises in the below sample. Of the 80 Master Franchises identified in Item 20, 7 were excluded because they had not been in continuous operation under the same ownership during all of 2012 and 2013, 11 were excluded because they had not submitted their audited financial statements to us, and 4 were excluded because we were unable to identify the below information based on the presentation format of the audited financial statements.

The below table provides certain results for the 58 master franchises included in the sample.

Category	Annual Average	Percentage of Total Revenues	Percentage of Master Franchises in Sample that Achieved this Result	Lowest	Highest	Median
Total Revenues	$3,908,831	100%	41%	$1,097,624	$11,468,449	$3,594,011
Cost of Services and Goods Sold	$3,004,853	77%	N/A	N/A	N/A	$2,636,178
Gross Profit	$903,978	23%	45%	$284,399	$2,811,180	$872,496

• The data used in this financial performance representation was taken from the audited financial statements that Master Franchisees submit to us and as are included in the Master Franchisees' FDDs. Each Master Franchisee determines its own fiscal year end so the audited financial statements are for FDDs with effective dates after September 30, 2012.

• Total Revenues includes Gross Revenues and revenues that are not included in Gross Revenues for purposes of calculating royalties due to us, such as product sales to Unit Franchisees and Customers. Gross Revenues typically include cleaning revenues from customers, initial franchise fees, royalties, and management fees from Unit Franchisees, the Business Protection Plan provided for Unit Franchisees, interest on financing provided to Unit Franchisees, and product sales to Unit Franchisees and Customers.

• Per the Master Franchise Agreement, Gross Revenue means all revenue collected or otherwise received by Master Franchisee and any of its Unit Franchisees (if the Unit Franchisee performs billing services in conjunction with the Services) in exchange for performing Services (including Special Servic-

es for Customers), whether evidenced by cash, credit, check, script, or other property or services, and all National Account Revenue without deduction of the National Accounts Support Fee. Gross Revenue does not include (a) any sales or other taxes that Master Franchisee collects from Customers and pays directly to the appropriate taxing authority; and (b) revenue collected by Master Franchisee in connection with any supplies and/or equipment sold, leased or otherwise distributed by Master Franchisee to its Unit Franchisees and Customers. Master Franchisee may not deduct collection fees and costs and payment provider fees (i.e., bank or credit card company fees) from its Gross Revenue calculation.

• Cost of Services and Goods Sold includes payments made to Unit Franchisees for cleaning services provided to customers and the cost of supplies purchased for resale to Unit Franchisees and customers.

• Gross Profit is Total Revenues less Cost of Services and Goods Sold. Gross Profit does not factor in items categorized as general and administrative expenses and does not factor in fees payable to us as described in Item 6.

• The median is the middle value in the sorted list of all reported results. Unlike averages, medians are not influenced by extreme values and therefore best represent a "typical" participant.

Data From 2011 Benchmarking Study

In 2011, we began a benchmarking study of the results of operations for all master franchisees that elected to participate in the study. This study was administered by an independent third party provider, Business Resource Services, Inc., based in Seattle, Washington. The master franchisees' participation in this study was completely voluntary and the data that each master provided (but not the fact of the master franchisee's participation) was anonymous. There were 51 master franchisees that participated in this study. These 51 master franchisees are located in the United States and Canada. The data that each master franchisee reported was for fiscal year 2010.

The benchmarking study, called the Profit Mastery Financial Benchmarking Study, presents certain data as either "Typical" or "High Profit." The data presented under "Typical" represents the median number for that item, taken from the entire sample. The data presented under "High Profit" is the median number taken from a sample of the highest 13 master franchisees (top 25%) based on Owners' Discretionary Profit Percentage. Please note that the High Profit category is not based on the highest Total Revenue.

The below data for the benchmarking study has been taken from financial information submitted by master franchisees. We have not audited or verified these financial reports nor have we asked questions of the submitting master franchisees to determine whether they are in fact accurate and complete, although we have no information or other reason to believe that they are unreliable.

Item	Median of Master Franchises	High Profit Master Franchise	Sales Under $3 Million	Sales Over $3 Million	Under 5 Years in Business	5 or More Years in Business
Study Participants	51	13	27	24	12	39
Years in Business	7.5	7.2	6.0	8.7	3.1	8.0
Active Unit Franchisees	73	70	48	103	38	86
Customer Accounts	333	321	254	511	249	351
Gross Margin	22.7	24.1	24.0	21.2	26.4	21.9
Total Number of FTE Employees	7.0	6.8	6.1	8.2	6.3	7.0

• Gross Margin is the gross profit expressed as a percent of revenue.

BACKGROUND

IFA Member:	Yes
Established & First Franchised:	1981; 1992
Franchised Units:	119
Company-Owned Units:	2
Total Units:	121
Distribution:	US – 121; CAN – 0; O'seas – 0
North America:	22 States, 0 Provinces
Density:	19 in NY, 17 in NJ, 15 in CA
Projected New Units (12 Months):	20
Qualifications:	4, 4, 2, 3, 2, 4

FINANCIAL/TERMS

Cash Investment:	$175K
Total Investment:	$372 – 702K
Minimum Net Worth:	$450K
Fees (Franchise):	$120K
Fees (Royalty):	7%
Fees (Advertising):	2%
Term of Contract (Years):	15/15
Average Number of Employees:	N/A
Passive Ownership:	Not Allowed

Encourage Conversions:	Yes
Area Development Agreements:	No
Sub-Franchising Contracts:	No
Expand in Territory:	Yes
Space Needs:	7,000 – 10,000 SF

SUPPORT & TRAINING

Financial Assistance Provided:	Yes (I)
Site Selection Assistance:	Yes
Lease Negotiation Assistance:	Yes
Co-operative Advertising:	Yes
Franchisee Association/Member:	No
Size of Corporate Staff:	45
On-going Support:	B, C, D, E, G, H, I
Training:	1 Week Director Train., Corp. HQ; 1 Week Owner Train., Corp. HQ; Ongoing Staff Training

SPECIFIC EXPANSION PLANS

US:	All United States
Canada:	No
Overseas:	No

The information below represents an actual historic financial performance representation. The information was obtained from the franchised system's existing mature outlets (those that have been open for at least 18 months) and was gathered from the financial information reported to us during the 2012 calendar year by our mature outlets (as of December 31, 2012) under their reporting requirements as described below. As of December 31, 2012, there were 22 locations (which have been open and operational for less than 18 months and which we call "ramping academies") or 21% of the total, have been excluded from the historic financial performance representation below. Revenue and expense information for the ramping academies is excluded because mature academy revenues and expenses more accurately reflect revenues and expenses achieved at existing academies in that they include only stabilized, full year revenues and expenses actually achieved over time. Of the 81 mature academies, 6 or 7% of the total did not report the required expense information for the calendar year ending December 31, 2012. Accordingly, operating information is presented for the 75 fully reporting mature academies in the tables below. We have not conducted an independent investigation or an audit to verify the figures presented; the information presented was provided to us by our franchisees.

Financial performance information about our mature outlets includes gross revenues, payroll, occupancy and miscellaneous expenses. All units offer substantially the same services and products to the public. However, the actual sales and expenses of any franchised unit may vary substantially. The results presented in the tables below represent the Gross Profit, which equals the gross revenue minus the listed operating expenses. More detailed descriptions of these expense items are presented in the notes provided below. In addition to the individual academy performance information supplied in the tables, the average performance information for the reporting locations is also presented. The time periods expressed in the chart below are not meant to be an indication as to when or if a unit will reach maturity. Each unit's growth rate will vary by location, competitive environment, the region and market area in which the unit is located, labor costs, programs and the individual franchisee's marketing efforts and management skills. Accordingly, the information presented should only be used as a reference guide in conducting an independent analysis of the proposed business. Written substantiation data used in preparing these financial performance representations is contained below but will also be made available to prospective franchisees upon reasonable request.

The data presented in this Item 19 was prepared without an audit. Prospective franchisees should be advised that no certified public accountant has audited these figures or expressed his or her opinion with regard to their content or form. We do not make any representations about a franchisee's future financial performance, including, without limitation, actual, average, projected or forecasted sales, expenses, profits, cash flow or earnings. We also do not authorize our employees or representatives to make any such representations orally or in writing. If you are purchasing an existing unit, however, we may provide you with actual records of that outlet. If you receive any other financial performance information or projections of your future income, you should report it to the franchisor's management by contacting Gregory Helwig, 3415 Box Hill Corporate Center Drive, Abingdon, Maryland, 21009, (410) 515-0788, the Federal Trade Commission and the appropriate state regulatory agencies. A new franchisee's financial results are likely to differ from the results stated in this financial performance representation.

Not all franchised academies achieved this level of average revenues and/or average gross profits. There is no assurance that you will do as well and you must accept the risk of not doing as well. You should conduct and independent investigation of the costs and expenses you will incur in operating a franchised academy. The figures presented below are for mature academies that have been in operation, on average, for a number of years. You must accept the risk that in the initial stages of your operation of your Academy your revenue figures will be substantially below, and your expense figures may be substantially higher than, what is presented below.

FOR CALENDAR YEAR ENDED DECEMBER 31, 2012

Number of locations reporting	75
Average # of months open	89.21
Average Revenue	$1,144,362
Average Labor Expense	$489,899
Average Occupancy Expense	$231,679
Average Miscellaneous Expense	$139,479
Average Gross Profit	$283,304

* 30 Academies or 40% of the 75 mature academies reporting operated at or above the Average Revenue figure and Gross Profit figure presented above.

Notes:

Revenue – Gross sales based on actual operating results as reported weekly by franchisees to Kiddie Academy, representing registration fees, tuition, and other amounts charged to families by the franchisee.

Labor – Employee-related expenses including: wages, salaries, bonus, commission, payroll taxes, training, insurance benefits, and worker's compensation expenses (where applicable) as reported monthly by franchisees to Kiddie Academy. This also includes the cost of an Academy Director(s).

Occupancy – Includes rent, common area maintenance, real estate taxes and percentage rent (if any). This includes other lease related charges, such as: maintenance, security, trash removal, association dues and shopping center marketing expenses as reported monthly by franchisees to Kiddie Academy, if applicable.

Miscellaneous – Includes other (discretionary) variable expenses related to the operation of the business, including: royalties and brand building fund fees, telephone, advertising, utilities, cleaning services, and postage as reported monthly by franchisees to Kiddie Academy.

Gross Profit – Revenue minus Labor, Occupancy and Miscellaneous Expenses. Other non-listed revenue (i.e., state and federal funds, grants, etc.) and expenses (i.e., supplies, food, insurance premiums, etc.) will impact Net Profit.

INDIVIDUAL ACADEMY PERFORMANCE FOR CALENDAR YEAR ENDING DECEMBER 31, 2012

Location #	Revenue	Labor Expense	Occupancy Expense	Misc. Expense	Gross Profit
1	$994,184	$206,264	$332,232	$118,784	$336,904
2	$830,612	$478,575	$94,259	$119,216	$138,562
3	$1,872,406	$876,766	$250,525	$252,234	$492,881
4	$2,025,546	$843,648	$257,305	$204,945	$719,648
5	$1,005,395	$593,329	$149,101	$127,475	$135,490
6	$1,675,293	$674,355	$335,790	$220,223	$444,925

7	$1,166,479	$492,215	$307,983	$109,738	$256,543
8	$1,412,094	$489,406	$166,394	$192,626	$563,668
9	$781,749	$335,624	$83,316	$123,355	$239,454
10	$1,545,416	$596,964	$336,849	$214,843	$396,760
11	$858,235	$293,941	$185,389	$125,963	$252,942
12	$1,191,189	$474,917	$346,941	$128,530	$240,801
13	$901,198	$428,189	$188,858	$113,816	$170,335
14	$944,901	$297,909	$205,941	$131,308	$309,743
15	$1,526,552	$681,046	$259,544	$190,552	$395,410
16	$906,468	$484,737	$210,408	$114,667	$96,656
17	$2,821,321	$876,283	$488,618	$295,052	$1,161,368
18	$1,231,215	$541,891	$210,106	$134,511	$344,707
19	$1,091,929	$538,249	$219,142	$161,536	$173,002
20	$1,666,577	$719,547	$268,372	$202,145	$476,513
21	$1,086,243	$575,931	$223,947	$122,956	$163,409
22	$895,024	$406,725	$198,537	$113,910	$175,852
23	$1,720,979	$641,459	$397,584	$201,623	$480,313
24	$1,081,259	$494,614	$278,389	$134,997	$173,259
25	$1,063,653	$465,174	$199,204	$121,549	$277,726
26	$1,748,506	$809,963	$373,060	$177,536	$387,947
27	$896,629	$400,334	$162,006	$129,608	$204,681
28	$599,228	$244,876	$149,717	$76,380	$128,255
29	$1,771,218	$657,842	$266,125	$194,400	$652,851
30	$1,278,057	$499,748	$277,267	$143,183	$357,859
31	$768,054	$472,628	$151,912	$90,242	$53,272
32	$1,285,788	$494,205	$257,375	$163,221	$370,987
33	$1,367,250	$487,264	$327,658	$184,633	$367,695
34	$980,816	$424,884	$224,566	$122,792	$208,574
35	$1,036,035	$444,572	$126,010	$104,683	$360,770
36	$1,095,102	$470,901	$208,010	$127,202	$288,989
37	$678,195	$383,057	$225,568	$88,217	($18,647)
38	$621,677	$226,342	$125,643	$87,371	$182,321
39	$1,107,869	$547,391	$200,045	$134,495	$225,938
40	$1,466,403	$608,569	$296,844	$201,710	$359,280
41	$2,169,453	$732,493	$489,705	$282,563	$664,692
42	$1,618,106	$690,355	$261,079	$209,134	$457,538
43	$975,892	$477,248	$175,260	$135,141	$188,243
44	$1,362,126	$511,735	$311,956	$146,989	$391,446
45	$890,046	$254,257	$110,095	$124,150	$401,544
46	$776,029	$345,168	$167,790	$101,009	$162,062
47	$887,940	$365,053	$194,092	$76,200	$252,595
48	$1,098,800	$493,729	$236,339	$152,668	$216,064

49	$1,085,985	$420,997	$298,448	$128,363	$238,177
50	$1,240,202	$489,613	$221,265	$139,402	$389,922
51	$1,288,882	$754,706	$240,845	$151,876	$141,455
52	$523,933	$334,000	$124,000	$84,122	($18,189)
53	$757,082	$355,119	$173,354	$90,339	$138,270
54	$583,912	$325,155	$146,338	$66,830	$45,589
55	$817,027	$417,238	$147,182	$103,071	$149,536
56	$1,273,037	$666,027	$220,726	$166,212	$220,072
57	$702,450	$349,304	$106,844	$63,838	$181,464
58	$1,369,126	$533,470	$130,333	$155,127	$550,196
59	$773,893	$314,072	$107,589	$100,848	$251,384
60	$1,215,967	$570,000	$450,000	$98,000	$97,967
61	$1,094,499	$475,171	$173,568	$145,099	$300,661
62	$1,068,295	$329,436	$266,405	$121,671	$350,784
63	$1,136,375	$554,911	$258,245	$122,884	$200,335
64	$995,393	$385,620	$217,234	$112,041	$280,498
65	$676,943	$280,619	$255,231	$83,931	$57,162
66	$880,085	$395,738	$261,340	$132,619	$90,388
67	$970,941	$432,424	$222,235	$113,281	$203,001
68	$1,626,337	$638,858	$206,493	$176,480	$604,506
69	$1,562,143	$741,505	$293,526	$200,595	$326,517
70	$611,021	$335,256	$67,374	$61,386	$147,005
71	$779,130	$372,048	$158,322	$103,853	$144,907
72	$757,097	$343,634	$185,501	$97,526	$130,436
73	$736,957	$313,818	$201,551	$90,622	$130,966
74	$1,265,667	$498,841	$456,873	$178,053	$131,900
75	$1,259,633	$564,481	$272,283	$141,764	$281,106

The revenues, expenses and gross profit figures contained in the boxes above are revenues, expenses and gross profits of the existing mature franchised locations described, as provided by the individual reporting franchisees, and should not be considered as the actual or probable revenues, expenses or gross profits that will be realized or incurred by any prospective franchisee.

MATH. READING. SUCCESS.

KUMON NORTH AMERICA

300 Frank W. Burr Blvd., # 6
Teaneck, NJ 07666
Tel: (866) 633-0740, (201) 928-0444
Fax: (201) 692-3130
Email: tkuczek@kumon.com
Website: www.kumonfranchise.com
Tom Kuczek, Vice President of Franchising

Premiere supplemental education franchise where you'll find success, one child at a time.

BACKGROUND
IFA Member:	Yes
Established & First Franchised:	1958; 1958
Franchised Units:	1,975
Company-Owned Units:	25
Total Units:	2,000
Distribution:	US – 1,492; CAN – 328; O'seas – 23,590
North America:	50 States, 9 Provinces
Density:	110 in TX, 93 in NY, 241 in CA
Projected New Units (12 Months):	120
Qualifications:	3, 3, 3, 5, 4, 4

FINANCIAL/TERMS
Cash Investment:	$70K
Total Investment:	$72.2 – 149.3K
Minimum Net Worth:	$150K
Fees (Franchise):	$1K, Materials:$1K
Fees (Royalty):	$32 – 36/subj./month
Fees (Advertising):	N/A
Term of Contract (Years):	5

Average Number of Employees:	1 FT, 1 – 3 PT
Passive Ownership:	Not Allowed
Encourage Conversions:	N/A
Area Development Agreements:	No
Sub-Franchising Contracts:	No
Expand in Territory:	No
Space Needs:	1,000 SF

SUPPORT & TRAINING
Financial Assistance Provided:	No
Site Selection Assistance:	Yes
Lease Negotiation Assistance:	No
Co-operative Advertising:	Yes
Franchisee Association/Member:	Yes/Member
Size of Corporate Staff:	400
On-going Support:	C, D, E, F, G, H, I
Training:	Kumon University Teaneck, NJ and local region; 13 – 16 Days Total Start-Up

SPECIFIC EXPANSION PLANS
US:	All United States
Canada:	All Canada
Overseas:	All Countries

The following chart represents information on the enrollments for Kumon centers after 12 and 24 months of operation. All numbers are as of December 31, 2013.

Year Center Opened	Average Number of Enrollments After 12 Reporting Months For Centers Opened in Year Indicated*	Average Number of Enrollments After 24 Reporting Months For Centers Opened In Year Indicated*	Average Number of Enrollments After 12 Reporting Months For Top 25 % Performing Centers by Year Opened*	Average Number of Enrollments After 24 Reporting Months For Top 25% Performing Centers by Year Opened*
2012	94	N/A	161	N/A
2011	99	129	158	207
2010	106	137	165	213
2009	92	135	160	232
2008	101	140	177	230
2007	87	118	184	190

The average enrollment for mature Centers as of December 31, 2013 was 198. We define a mature Center as a Center that has been open for 3 years or more. It does not include Centers that have closed.

*This information is for new Centers. It excludes transfer Centers and Centers that have closed. Enrollments are subject-students that are reported to Kumon by franchisees. For example, one student may enroll in Math and Reading subjects. This student would count as two enrolled subject-students. You charge tuition, and correspondingly pay a royalty to Kumon, for each subject-student.

The average enrollment numbers set forth above are based upon numbers supplied to us by our franchisees. While we have no reason to doubt their accuracy, we have not conducted any audits or otherwise independently verified the numbers submitted to us by franchisees.

The information contained in this Item 19 should not be considered to be the actual or probable enrollment that you will realize. Your results will likely differ from the results contained in this Item 19. Performance varies from Center to Center and the above information cannot be used to make estimates related to future performance of any particular Center. Written substantiation of the information used in preparing the statements contained in this Item 19 will be made available to you upon reasonable request. However, we will not disclose the identity, enrollment or other information about any particular Center.

Other than the preceding financial performance representa-

tion, we do not make any financial performance representations. We also do not authorize employees or representatives to make any such representations either orally or in writing. If you are purchasing an existing outlet, however, we may provide you with the actual records of that outlet. If you receive any other financial performance information or projections of your future income, you should report it to the franchisor's management by contacting Robert Lichtenstein, Senior Vice President and Corporate Counsel, 300 Frank W. Burr Boulevard, Teaneck, New Jersey 07666, (201) 928-0444, the Federal Trade Commission, and the appropriate state regulatory agency.

LEARNINGRX

LearningRx
train the brain. get smarter. guaranteed.

5085 List Dr., # 200
Colorado Springs, CO 80919
Tel: (866) 679-1569, (719) 955-6708
Fax: (719) 522-0434
Email: sales@learningrx.com
Website: www.learningrx-franchise.com
Jordan Vaughan, Franchise Development Coordinator

LearningRx is a personal one-on-one Brain Training franchise leading the Brain Training industry with unmatched training results. LearningRx improves skills like memory, attention, and processing speed and has programs that can help people of all ages with ADHD, autism, dyslexia, brain injury, etc. Studies show that 88% of learning/processing problems are caused by one or more weak cognitive skills, and LearningRx is the expert in assessing and improving these skills. One on one brain training and our proprietary methodology make LearningRx the answer to remediation and enhancement for all ages.

BACKGROUND
IFA Member:	Yes
Established & First Franchised:	1986; 2003
Franchised Units:	89
Company-Owned Units:	2
Total Units:	91
Distribution:	US – 91; CAN – 0; O'seas – 0
North America:	28 States, 0 Provinces
Density:	16 in TX, 7 in MN, 7 in VA
Projected New Units (12 Months):	20
Qualifications:	3, 3, 3, 3, 4, 4

FINANCIAL/TERMS
Cash Investment:	$65 – 75K
Total Investment:	$109 – 209K
Minimum Net Worth:	$250K
Fees (Franchise):	$25 – 35K
Fees (Royalty):	10%
Fees (Advertising):	2.5%
Term of Contract (Years):	10/10
Average Number of Employees:	3 FT, 20 PT
Passive Ownership:	Not Allowed
Encourage Conversions:	N/A
Area Development Agreements:	Yes
Sub-Franchising Contracts:	No
Expand in Territory:	Yes
Space Needs:	1,200 – 1,800 SF

SUPPORT & TRAINING
Financial Assistance Provided:	No
Site Selection Assistance:	Yes
Lease Negotiation Assistance:	No
Co-operative Advertising:	No
Franchisee Association/Member:	No
Size of Corporate Staff:	20
On-going Support:	A, C, G, H
Training:	2 Weeks plus On-Site

SPECIFIC EXPANSION PLANS
US:	Yes
Canada:	No
Overseas:	No

We have based the claims upon the business records and financial statements prepared by our franchisees and have compiled the claims to the extent possible in a manner consistent with generally accepted accounting principles consistently applied. Written substantiation for the financial performance representation will be made available to you upon reasonable request. The products and services offered by each franchisee, although essentially the same, may vary slightly based on market conditions, demand for specific products, the learning requirements of customers, and the sales skills utilized by the owners and employees of each individual center. The gross revenue attained by each center will depend on a wide range of factors including, but not limited to, geographic differences, competition within the immediate market area, the quality of the service provided to customers by the franchisee and its employees, consumer demand for our products, and the marketing skills and sales efforts employed by each franchisee. The profitability of individual franchisees will depend on a number of factors which may vary due to the individual characteristics of each center. Factors affecting the net profits may include, but are not limited to, the costs of labor, insurance, supplies, and compliance with state and local laws regulating the provision of educational training services, including any state-specific licensing requirements.

The net revenue, expense numbers and ratios, average marketing expenditures by category, average marketing cost per prospect by category, percentage of prospects by marketing category, sales conversion rates, and percentage of revenue by service type, represent historical operating figures for all LearningRx franchisee-owned Centers open during the full fiscal year October 1, 2012 through September 30, 2013. Each chart reflects the performance experienced by the average of all LearningRx franchisee-owned Centers by revenue who operated a Center during the full fiscal year 2012 - 2013. As of September 30, 2013, out of 83 franchisee-owned Centers, 71 Centers operated during the full fiscal year ending September 30 2013, and are represented below. Thirty nine (39) out of the seventy one (71) Centers, or 55%, attained or surpassed the stated results.

Some outlets have earned this amount. Your individual results may differ. There is no assurance that you'll earn as much.

The numbers reflected in the charts below should not be considered as potential revenues, expenses or conversion ratios that may be realized by you. If you rely on these figures, you must accept the risk that your franchise will not perform as well.

Oct 2012 through Sept 2013	Average top 1/3	Average middle 1/3	Average bottom 1/3	Average all
Total Revenue Charged (1)	$602,166	$361,354	$198,896	$382,160
Total Revenue Collected	$566,081	$345,364	$208,666	$368,731
Total Expenses (2)	$531,729	$339,010	$218,197	$358,901
Net Operating Income	$70,437	$22,343	($19,301)	$23,259
Net Income	$66,300	$16,480	($23,424)	$18,568
Profit (Adjusted for 35% Payroll) (3)	$140,348	$68,273	$11,357	$71,580
Adj profit %	23%	19%	6%	14%
Accounts Receivable	$111,404	$62,228	$38,767	$69,897
Receivable Turn Days	65	64	84	71
Average Case Size	$7,659	$6,782	$6,334	$6,908
Training Results				
Avg Percentile Gains Core Tests (4)	20	18	19	19
Word Attack (ReadRx) Percentile Gains*	18	15	18	17
% of Final Surveys Completed	97%	95%	95%	95%
Satisfaction Surveys - out of 10	9.5	9.5	9.6	9.5
Revenue by Type				
Assessment Charges	$16,754	$15,835	$9,585	$13,932
Einstein Charges	$109,956	$63,473	$21,724	$63,831
LiftOff Charges	$30,231	$17,408	$8,345	$18,371
MathRx Charges	$57,987	$24,926	$14,217	$31,865

BrainSkills Charges	($121)	$1,328	$709	$641
Miscellaneous Charges	$4,349	$2,104	$6,852	$4,503
ReadRx Charges	$222,666	$113,747	$79,619	$137,014
ThinkRx Charges	$153,842	$121,588	$57,780	$109,569
Expenses by Type				
Bank & Credit Card Fees	$7,495	$5,601	$2,599	$5,157
Facilities (5)	$58,509	$40,687	$36,514	$44,991
Insurance	$4,807	$2,832	$2,829	$3,471
Marketing Expenses	$69,632	$47,991	$31,401	$49,160
Miscellaneous	$3,593	$4,142	$2,039	$3,224
Outside Services	$7,648	$5,530	$5,087	$6,060
Pay Admin (5)	$122,595	$80,858	$43,975	$81,392
Pay Trainers	$158,074	$91,545	$56,297	$100,685
Royalty LearningRx (6)	$55,920	$31,851	$20,601	$35,686
Supplies	$28,720	$21,527	$11,217	$20,226
Taxes (Non-payroll)	$4,970	$2,107	$558	$2,489
Travel & Entertainment	$9,768	$4,339	$5,080	$6,359
Total Expenses	$531,729	$339,010	$218,197	$358,901
Net Operating Income	$70,437	$22,343	($19,301)	$23,259
Net Other Income/Expenses	($4,137	($5,863)	($4,123)	($4,691)
Net Income	$66,300	$16,480	($23,424)	$18,568
Total Leads	548	477	453	492
Total Prospects	289	221	139	214
Total Assessments	180	128	86	130
Total Consultations	164	112	70	114
Total Started Program	83	56	34	57
Total Completed Program	68	48	28	47
Total Active Students	143	101	67	103
Marketing Expenses by Type				
DM Direct Mail Expense	$8,206	$4,039	$3,287	$5,124
PA Print Ads Expense	$13,885	$8,530	$7,766	$9,996
OA Other Advertising Expense	$14,035	$7,613	$6,787	$9,403
PPC Pay-Per-Click Expense	$1,600	$2,008	$908	$1,489
RD Radio Expense	$9,368	$11,109	$3,429	$7,841
RF Referrals Expense	$2,592	$1,379	$424	$1,435
TV Television Expense	$3,293	$4,062	$1,657	$2,966
WB Web Expense	$2,185	$898	$1,027	$1,361
YP Yellow Pages Expense	$220	$259	$168	$214
Total Local Marketing Expense	$55,383	$39,897	$25,455	$39,829
MDF Marketing Dev. Fund (7)	$14,248	$8,093	$5,947	$9,331
Total Marketing Expenses	$69,632	$47,991	$31,401	$49,160
# Prospect by Marketing Type				

DM Direct Mail	18	8	6	10
OA Other Advertising	93	73	42	69
PPC Pay-Per-Click	309	270	245	274
PA Print Ads	18	10	10	13
RD Radio	28	12	10	16
RF Referrals	69	53	37	53
TV Television	10	5	1	5
WB Web	263	240	224	242
YP Yellow Pages	1	1	1	1
# Students by Marketing Type				
DM Direct Mail	6	2	2	3
OA Other Advertising	13	10	6	9
PPC Pay-Per-Click	1	1	0	1
PA Print Ads	5	2	2	3
RD Radio	6	3	2	4
RF Referrals	26	19	12	19
TV Television	2	1	0	1
WB Web	17	13	8	12
YP Yellow Pages	0	0	0	0
Marketing Cost/Prospect by Type				
DM Direct Mail	$1,896	$1,081	$1,151	$1,370
PA Print Ads	$2,926	$3,751	$2,246	$2,954
OA Other Advertising	$1,546	$1,566	$1,976	$1,704
PPC Pay-Per-Click	$1,038	$803	$272	$692
RD Radio	$1,329	$2,511	$610	$1,459
RF Referrals	$149	$93	$45	$94
TV Television	$644	$1,848	$530	$994
WB Web	$173	$80	$154	$136
YP Yellow Pages	$11	$0	$13	$8
Marketing Cost/Prospect	$203	$185	$203	$197
Marketing Cost/Student	$684	$703	$841	$746
Sale Conversion Rates				
% Assessment/Prospect	66%	62%	67%	65%
% Consultation/Assessment	91%	89%	80%	87%
% Student/Consultation	52%	53%	54%	53%
% Student/Assessment	47%	44%	40%	44%
% Student/Prospect	31%	27%	27%	28%
% Revenue by Type				
% Assessment Charges	3%	5%	5%	4%
% Einstein Charges	18%	18%	13%	16%
% LiftOff Charges	5%	5%	4%	5%
% MathRx Charges	10%	7%	5%	8%

% BrainSkills Charges	0%	0%	0%	0%
% Miscellaneous Charges	1%	0%	2%	1%
% ReadRx Charges	37%	31%	38%	36%
% ThinkRx Charges	26%	34%	30%	30%
Expenses as a % of Revenue				
Advertising	9%	11%	13%	11%
Bank & Credit Card Fees	1%	2%	1%	1%
Facilities	10%	11%	21%	14%
Insurance	1%	1%	2%	1%
Miscellaneous	0%	1%	1%	1%
Pay Admin	21%	22%	21%	21%
Pay Trainers	27%	25%	29%	27%
Royalty LearningRx	9%	9%	10%	10%
Supplies	5%	6%	6%	6%
Taxes (Non-payroll)	1%	0%	0%	1%
Travel & Entertainment	2%	1%	3%	2%

Notes for the charts displayed above:

(1) Net Revenue is based on the accrual basis. These numbers reflect amounts billed to clients between 10/1/12 and 9/30/13, but do not reflect actual collections during that period. The numbers in this category reflect the average net revenue achieved by Centers falling into each of the performace categories listed above the net revenue number (i.e. top 33%).

(2) All expenses reflect actual expenses paid between 10/1/12 and 09/30/13.

(3) Profit adjusted for Salary and Draws set Trainer and Admin pay adjusted at 35% of revenue and then either increases or decreases profit. This is reported because Franchsiees differ in how they pay themselves.

(4) Percentile: the change in ranking among 100 students.

(5) Facilities expense includes rent, utilities, telephone and Internet service.

(6) The Royalty numbers reported in this chart are based on Revenues collected by franchisees between 10/1/10 and 9/30/11.

(7) WB Web incl 50% of MDF whereas the other marketing types don't incl any MDF.

(8) Administration compensation includes some amount of trainer compensation.

Other than the preceding financial performance representation, LearningRx does not make any financial performance representations. We also do not authorize our employees or representatives to make any such representations either orally or in writing. If you are purchasing an existing outlet, however, we may provide you with the actual records of that outlet. If you receive any other financial performance information or projections of your future income, you should report it to the franchisor's management by contacting Dean Tenpas, LeaningRx Franchise Corporation, 5085 List Drive, Suite 200, Colorado Springs, Colorado 80919, 719-264-8808, the Federal Trade Commission, and the appropriate state regulatory agencies.

LIBERTY TAX SERVICE

1716 Corporate Landing Pkwy.
Virginia Beach, VA 23454
Tel: (877) 285-4237, (877) AT-LIBERTY
Fax: (800) 880-6432
Email: sales@libtax.com
Website: www.libertytaxfranchise.com
David Tarr, Director of Franchsie Development

LIBERTY TAX SERVICE is the fastest-growing international tax service ever, and has been ranked on Entrepreneur magazine's annual "Franchise 500" every year since 1998. Any given year, there is a ready market of taxpayers, and as the tax laws change frequently, many taxpayers are turning to professional preparers to complete that annual task. LIBERTY's growth is fueled by a proven operating system that has been fine-tuned by the leadership and field support staff's more than 600 total years of experience. As a result, no prior tax experience is required to put this system to work. Founder/CEO John Hewitt has worked 45 tax seasons, including 12 years with H&R Block. Accounting Today magazine has named Hewitt one of the accounting profession's Top 100 Most Influential People - 11 times! The International Franchise Association has honored Hewitt as its "Entrepreneur of the Year."

BACKGROUND

IFA Member:	Yes
Established & First Franchised:	1997; 1997
Franchised Units:	3,995

Company-Owned Units:	180
Total Units:	4,175
Distribution:	US – 4,175; CAN – 263; O'seas – 0
North America:	50 States, 10 Provinces
Density:	N/A
Projected New Units (12 Months):	500
Qualifications:	2, 4, 2, 1, 3, 5

FINANCIAL/TERMS

Cash Investment:	$57.8 – 71.9K
Total Investment:	$57.8 – 71.9K
Minimum Net Worth:	$50K
Fees (Franchise):	$40K
Fees (Royalty):	14%
Fees (Advertising):	5%
Term of Contract (Years):	5/5
Average Number of Employees:	4 – 6 FT, 2 PT
Passive Ownership:	Discouraged
Encourage Conversions:	No
Area Development Agreements:	Yes
Sub-Franchising Contracts:	No
Expand in Territory:	Yes
Space Needs:	400+ SF

SUPPORT & TRAINING

Financial Assistance Provided:	Yes (I)
Site Selection Assistance:	Yes
Lease Negotiation Assistance:	Yes
Co-operative Advertising:	No
Franchisee Association/Member:	No
Size of Corporate Staff:	520
On-going Support:	A, B, C, D, E, F, G, H, I
Training:	5 Days Virginia Beach, VA – Initial, Intermediate, Advanced; 3 Days Various Cities – Intermediate, Advanced

SPECIFIC EXPANSION PLANS

US:	All United States
Canada:	Yes
Overseas:	No

For our Financial Performance Representation, we set forth three sample Profit and Loss Statements from our franchisees. The universe from which the Profit and Loss Statements were selected is as follows: third year franchises who operated one storefront location only during the time period May 1, 2011 – April 30, 2012. During this time period, we had 117 outlets in the United States that met the characteristics of the selected universe.

As to these three sample Profit and Loss Statements, the

number and percent of those franchisees in the universe that attained or surpassed the stated results is set forth as follows:

Tax Return Count	Number of franchisees who met or exceeded results	% of franchisees who met or exceeded results
296	80	68.37%
656	16	13.67%
1,124	2	1.70%

Excluded from this data are offices owned by franchisees with multiple storefront offices in operation, kiosk locations, and company operated outlets. A kiosk location refers to a temporary location embedded within another retailer. The data presented is based upon information received from independent franchise owners, and has not been audited or otherwise verified by us. Immediately following the Financial Performance Representations is additional information that you should carefully consider in order to understand this performance information in the appropriate context.

Financial Performance Representation #1:
P&L 296 Tax Returns Prepared:

TOTAL # RETURNS INCLUDING # FREE RETURNS	296
# FREE RETURNS	70
AVERAGE FEES (NET)	$302

INCOME

TAX PREP FEES (GROSS FEES)	$88,000
DISCOUNTS	3,176
DISCOUNTS FOR FREE RETURNS	15,648
CASH IN A FLASH	1,000
TOTAL NET FEES	68,176
TAX SCHOOL INCOME	140
TOTAL INCOME	68,316

EXPENSE

MANAGER'S WAGE	0
WAGES	6,960
GUERILLA MARKETING WAGES	634
PAYROLL TAXES	1,905
RENT	26,595
UTILITIES (INCLUDE INTERNET FEES)	1,961
TELEPHONE	2,531
LEASEHOLD IMPROVEMENT/ REPAIRS	51
EQUIPMENT LEASE	0
OFFICE SUPPLIES	2,318
POSTAGE	142
TAX SCHOOL EXPENSE	522
REFUNDS	1,001
SEND A FRIEND	220

IRS/ST PENALTY & INTEREST	35
INSURANCE	476
PERMITS/LICENSES	175
ZEE PAID ADVERTISING	2,476
GUERILLA MARKETING SUPPLIES	1,500
ADVERTISING ROYALTIES (5%)	3,251
TRAVEL/ENTERTAINMENT/ TRAINING	74
BANKING/PROFESSIONAL FEES	73
ROYALTIES	11,000
MISCELLANEOUS	320
TOTAL EXPENSES	64,220
NET INCOME	$,096

Financial Performance Representation #2:
P&L 656 Tax Returns Prepared:

TOTAL # RETURNS INCLUDING # FREE RETURNS	656
# FREE RETURNS	115
AVERAGE FEES (NET)	$265

INCOME

TAX PREP FEES (GROSS FEES)	$231,671
DISCOUNTS	37,521
DISCOUNTS FOR FREE RETURNS	31,671
CASH IN A FLASH	18,891
TOTAL NET FEES	143,838
TAX SCHOOL INCOME	250
TOTAL INCOME	143,838

EXPENSE

MANAGER'S WAGE	0
WAGES	18,190
GUERILLA MARKETING WAGES	4,750
PAYROLL TAXES	6,315
RENT	19,200
UTILITIES (INCLUDE INTERNET FEES)	3,042
TELEPHONE	1,853
LEASEHOLD IMPROVEMENT/ REPAIRS	900

EQUIPMENT LEASE	0
OFFICE SUPPLIES	5,546
POSTAGE	416
TAX SCHOOL EXPENSE	1,216
REFUNDS	688
SEND A FRIEND	1,140
IRS/ST PENALTY & INTEREST	13
INSURANCE	784
PERMITS/LICENSE	1,173
ZEE PAID ADVERTISING	580
GUERILLA MARKETING SUPPLIES	2,096
ADVERTISING ROYALTIES (5%)	7,055
TRAVEL/ENTERTAINMENT/ TRAINING	2,622
BANKING/PROFESSIONAL FEES	682
ROYALTIES	19,161
MISCELLANEOUS	218
TOTAL EXPENSES	97,640
NET INCOME	$46,198

Financial Performance Representation #3:
P&L 1,124 Tax Returns Prepared:

TOTAL # RETURNS INCLUDING # FREE RETURNS	1,124
# FREE RETURNS	225
AVERAGE FEES (NET)	$293

INCOME

TAX PREP FEES (GROSS FEES)	$448,666
DISCOUNTS	73,587
DISCOUNTS FOR FREE RETURNS	79,313
CASH IN A FLASH	32,650
TOTAL NET FEES	263,116
TAX SCHOOL INCOME	0
TOTAL INCOME	263,116

EXPENSE

MANAGER'S WAGE	0
WAGES	29,512
GUERILLA MARKETING WAGES	12,000

PAYROLL TAXES	15,174
RENT	21,172
UTILITIES (INCLUDE INTER- NET FEES)	3,364
TELEPHONE	0
LEASEHOLD IMPROVEMENT/ REPAIRS	351
EQUIPMENT LEASE	0
OFFICE SUPPLIES	5,921
POSTAGE	790
TAX SCHOOL EXPENSE	1,200
REFUNDS	596
SEND A FRIEND	17,850
IRS/ST PENALTY & INTEREST	0
INSURANCE	642
PERMITS/LICENSES	788
ZEE PALD ADVERTLSLNG	574
GUERILLA MARKETING SUPPLIES	7,146
ADVERTISING ROYALTIES (5%)	11,943
TRAVEL/ENTERTAINMENT/ TRAINING	0
BANKING/PROFESSIONAL FEES	5
ROYALTIES	33,442
MISCELLANEOUS	352
TOTAL EXPENSES	162,823
NET INCOME	$100,292

Additional information applicable to the above Financial Performance Representations:

A number of factors will directly affect the performance of your office. These include, but are not limited to, the general market for preparer provided tax preparation in your area, competitive factors from other tax preparers in your market, and the success of your efforts to obtain quality sites, provide recommended tax courses, hire a sufficient number of trained personnel, engage in successful marketing, offer high customer service, and generally follow the Operations Manual and Liberty system. Your individual financial results may differ substantially from the results stated in this financial performance representation. Written substantiation for this financial performance representation is available to you upon reasonable request. We will not disclose the performance data of a specific office without the owner's consent.

LIQUID CAPITAL

5525 N. MacArthur Blvd., # 535
Irving, TX 75038
Tel: (866) 272-3704, (416) 342-8199
Fax: (866) 611-8886
Email: birnbaum@liquidcapitalcorp.com
Website: www.lcfranchise.com
Brian Birnbaum, President

Factoring is the funding of B2B receivables. It is a $2.9 Trillion global industry. The Liquid Capital competitive advantage is the relationship a client enjoys with the franchisee Typically a franchisee has 10-15 clients, who generally will factor their receivables for 2 to 3 years. Liquid Capital is a low overhead, high return, home based business that provides a franchisee with a great life style with high earning potential. Liquid Capital will loan its franchisees up to 6 times their investment.

BACKGROUND

IFA Member:	Yes
Established & First Franchised:	1999; 2000
Franchised Units:	74
Company-Owned Units:	3
Total Units:	77
Distribution:	US – 44; CAN – 29; O'seas – 4
North America:	32 States, 6 Provinces
Density:	9 in AB, 6 in FL, 3 in IL
Projected New Units (12 Months):	12
Qualifications:	5, 5, 2, 4, 2, 3

FINANCIAL/TERMS

Cash Investment:	$200K – 1M
Total Investment:	$200K – 1M
Minimum Net Worth:	$250K
Fees (Franchise):	$50K
Fees (Royalty):	8%
Fees (Advertising):	$500/Mo.
Term of Contract (Years):	10/10
Average Number of Employees:	1 FT, 0 PT
Passive Ownership:	Not Allowed
Encourage Conversions:	N/A
Area Development Agreements:	No
Sub-Franchising Contracts:	No
Expand in Territory:	No
Space Needs:	N/A

SUPPORT & TRAINING

Financial Assistance Provided:	Yes (D)
Site Selection Assistance:	N/A
Lease Negotiation Assistance:	N/A
Co-operative Advertising:	Yes
Franchisee Association/Member:	Yes/Member
Size of Corporate Staff:	16
On-going Support:	A, G, H, I
Training:	5 Days Toronto, ON

SPECIFIC EXPANSION PLANS

US:	All United States
Canada:	All Canada
Overseas:	Yes

This Financial Performance Representation presents three charts we believe will be helpful in assisting you in understanding the Liquid Capital business model. The first chart provides financial data for our last fiscal year based on Gross Revenues achieved by specific franchisees during 2013. The second and third charts provide explanations, underlying assumptions, and historical data in connection with fundamental financial components of the two business models most commonly used by Liquid Capital Businesses. The information contained in these charts is based on actual results from franchisees and does not include results from any parent, affiliate or company-owned outlets.

2013 Gross Revenues

The figures below represent the annual gross revenue generated by the 17 franchised Liquid Capital Businesses that satisfied our Reporting Criteria (See Note 1 below) during the period between January 1, 2013 and December 31, 2013. Your financial results are likely to differ from the figures presented. You should conduct an independent investigation of the costs and expenses you will incur in operating your franchised business. You should carefully review the attached explanatory notes.

ANNUAL GROSS REVENUES FOR - THE YEAR ENDED DECEMBER 31, 2013

	High Gross Revenue	Low Gross Revenue	Average Gross Revenue	Number of Liquid Capital Businesses at or above Average Gross Revenue
Top Tier (5 Liquid Capital Businesses)	$1,085,000	$452,000	$636,600	2
Middle Tier (6 Liquid Capital Businesses)	$430,000	$104,000	$243,000	3
Bottom Tier (6 Liquid Capital Businesses)	$95,000	$15,000	$54,000	3

Notes:

(1) As of December 31, 2013, we had 44 Liquid Capital Businesses operating in the Liquid Capital System in the United States. Of the total number of Liquid Capital Businesses operating in the United States, 17 or 39% of Liquid Capital Businesses met or exceeded all of the following criteria ("Reporting Criteria"): each Liquid Capital Business had been operating in the Liquid Capital System since before December 31, 2011, was operating for all twelve months from January 1, 2013 through December 31, 2013, and completed at least one factoring transaction during 2013. The results of the remaining 27 Liquid Capital Businesses did not satisfy one or more of the Reporting Criteria. Data from all Liquid Capital Businesses that satisfied the Reporting Criteria are included in this table.

(2) The annual Gross Revenues information was prepared from the transaction records and reports, as generated by our internal accounting system, on the annual Gross Revenues earned by each Liquid Capital Business and reported by managers or owners of each of the 17 Liquid Capital Businesses satisfying the Reporting Criteria. We do not know of an instance, nor do we have reason to believe, that this information would be overstated because it is extracted from the factoring transactions that are processed through our system. However, these annual Gross Revenues have not been audited and we have not independently verified these annual Gross Revenue numbers.

(3) The annual Gross Revenue information represents aggregate sales of factoring services by the 17 Liquid Capital Businesses satisfying the Reporting Criteria which were owned and operated by franchisees during the period between January 1, 2013 and December 31, 2013, and should not be considered the actual or probable annual Gross Revenues of Liquid Capital Businesses which will be achieved by any individual franchisee. A franchisee's annual Gross Revenues are likely to be lower in its first year of business. We recommend that the prospective franchisee make his or her own independent investigation to determine whether or not a Liquid Capital franchise may be profitable. We further recommend that prospective franchisees consult with professional advisors before executing any agreement. Your accountant can help you develop your own estimated costs for your Liquid Capital Business. Franchisee owned business data is not an indication of how your Liquid Capital Business will perform.

Historical Performance Data

The charts below provide explanations, underlying assumptions, and historical data in connection with fundamental financial components of the two business models most commonly used by Liquid Capital Businesses. The information contained in these charts is based on actual results from franchisees and does not include results from any parent, affiliate or companyowned outlets. Specifically, Chart 1 illustrates a Liquid Capital funding transaction carried out by a single franchisee, without participation from any other Liquid Capital franchisees. Chart 2 illustrates a Liquid Capital funding transaction coordinated by one franchisee and carried out by multiple Liquid Capital franchisees.

The information contained in these charts is based on our experience involving actual transactions ("Representative Transactions") completed by all 32 franchisees that were open and completed at least one Representative Transaction ("Historical Reporting Criteria") during the period extending from January 1, 2012 through December 31, 2013 ("Historical Reporting Period"). This information includes conservative representations of the mechanics of Representative Transactions. The fees, arrangement, discounts, and other variables included in these charts did not change during the Historical Reporting Period.

Actual results may vary from franchise to franchise and depend on a variety of internal and external factors, many of which neither we nor any prospective franchisee can estimate, such as competition, economic climate, demographics, and changing consumer demands and tastes. The earnings claims figures do not reflect the costs of sales, operating expenses or other costs or expenses that must be deducted from the gross revenue or gross sales figures to obtain your net income or profit. You should conduct an independent investigation of the costs and expenses you will incur in operating your (franchised business). Franchisees or former franchisees, listed in the offering circular, may be one source of this information.

We possess written substantiation for all information contained in this ITEM 19. Upon written request and reasonable notice, the information and substantiation of the information used in preparing this item is available for inspection by you at our headquarters.

CHART NO. 1
"Representative Transaction Carried Out by Single Franchisee"

Variable	Anticipated Amount[1]
Advance[2]	72-88% of the value of the Accounts Receivable (as defined below)
Intial Discount Fee[3]	3% of the value of the Accounts Receivable
Number of Days Outstanding of Accounts Receivable	49.5 days
Subsequent Daily Discount Fee[5]	0.1% of the value of the Accounts Receivable
Monthly Gross Transaction Revenue[6]	See Note 6 below
Back Offices Services Fee[7]	0.75% of the client's Scheduled Invoices (as defined below)
Royalty[8]	8% of your Monthly Gross Revenue
Financing Cost for Qualified Borrower[9]	8-12% interest rate for financing obtained from Exchange by Qualified Borrower

Notes:

(1) The amounts included in the "Anticipated Amount" column relating to the Advance and the Number of Days Outstanding of Accounts Receivable are based on our analysis of the information provided to us by franchisees that met our Historical Reporting Criteria during the Historical Reporting Period, which includes approximately 330,000 Representative Transactions recorded during the Reporting Period. The amount relating to the Number of Days Outstanding of Accounts Receivable represents the average Anticipated Amount for this particular variable. The amounts relating to the Initial Discount Fee and the Subsequent Daily Discount Fee represent the midpoints of the ranges that we typically recommend to our franchisees for those particular variables. The amounts relating to the Back Offices Services Fee, Royalty, Originating Franchise Fee, and Management Fee are the actual amounts currently required by the terms of the Franchise Agreement for franchisees within the System. The range relating to the Financing Cost for Qualified Borrower is based on the range of interest rates currently charged by the Exchange when providing financing to Qualified Borrowers. Please see the specific footnotes below for additional explanations regarding the basis for each of these amounts.

(2) "Advance" means the amount of money that you pay the client at the time of funding for its eligible Accounts in connection with the participation agreement that will be entered into by the client and our affiliate, Liquid Capital Exchange,

Inc. ("Exchange"). "Account" means a right to receive payment of a monetary obligation, whether or not earned by performance, and includes any "Account" as defined in Article 9 of the UCC. Liquid Capital franchisees only pay the client an Advance equal to a portion of its Accounts Receivable (as defined below). We recommend that our franchisees hold back a reserve equal to 15% to 25% of the value of the Accounts Receivable plus the amount of the Initial Discount Fee (as defined below). Our analysis of the information provided to us by franchisees that met our Reporting Criteria during the Historical Reporting Period, which involves approximately 330,000 Representative Transactions recorded during the Historical Recording Period, indicates that approximately 99% of the transactions conducted by these franchisees were within the Anticipated Amount above (72% to 88% of the value of the Accounts Receivable).

(3) "Initial Discount Fee" means the fee you charge the client for the initial period of time its Accounts Receivable are outstanding ("Initial Discount Fee"). In most cases the initial period of time is 30 days but it can range from 15 days to 60 days based on negotiations between the franchisee and customer. We typically recommend an Initial Discount Fee of 2.5% to 3.5% of the value of the Accounts Receivable based on an initial period of 30 days.

(4) "Accounts Receivable" equals the client's monthly sales ("Scheduled Invoices") divided by 30 and multiplied by the number of O/S days. In our experience, typical accounts re-

ceivable can range from 20 days to 60 days. For purposes of these representations, a client's customer Accounts are assumed to be outstanding ("O/S") for a period of 49.5 days, which represents the average Anticipated Amount for this particular variable. This Anticipated Amount for the Number of Days Outstanding of Accounts Receivable is based the information provided to us by franchisees that met our Historical Reporting Criteria during the Historical Reporting Period, which involves approximately 330,000 Representative Transactions recorded during the Historical Reporting Period. Our analysis of that information indicates that 45% of the transactions conducted by these franchisees were at or above this average amount and 55% of the transactions conducted by these franchisees were below this average amount.

(5) "Subsequent Daily Discount Fee" means the fee you charge the client for each additional day the client's customer's Accounts are outstanding after the initial period, which typically lasts 30 days. We generally recommend charging an additional discount fee of between 0.083% and 0.1167% per day in excess of 30 days.

(6) "Monthly Gross Transaction Revenue" equals the Initial Discount Fee multiplied by Scheduled Invoices, plus the Subsequent Daily Discount Fee, multiplied by the number of days in excess of the number of days covered by the Initial Discount Fee, multiplied by Scheduled Invoices on a particular Client Account. Monthly Gross Transaction Revenue does not account for the Back Office Services Fee, Royalty, Financing Cost, Exchange Fee, or Originating Franchise Fee that you must pay, nor does it include any Management Fee or Originating Franchisee Fee that you may receive. Additionally, the Monthly Gross Transaction Revenue will vary based on a larger or shorter transaction time frame. Historically, our franchisees that met our Historical Reporting Criteria during the Reporting Period earned monthly gross revenue equal to 4.95% of the value of the transaction. Specifically, 45% of those franchisees earned higher rates than 4.95% and 55% of those franchisees earned lower rates than 4.95%.

(7) "Back Office Services Fee" means the fee you must pay to Exchange for Back Office Support Services (as defined in the Franchise Agreement). For full factoring arrangements, the Back Office Services Fee is currently set at 0.75% of the Accounts represented by the Scheduled Invoices.

(8) "Royalty" means the royalty you must pay to us. This fee is currently set at 8% of total Gross Revenue of the Franchised Business. As defined in the Franchise Agreement, "Gross Revenue" means the entire amount of all revenue earned (whether or not received) by a Liquid Capital franchisee from any source (including, without limitation, each funding transaction, referral fees, and recharges) in connection with the Franchised Business in any form. There shall be no deductions

allowed for uncollected or uncollectible Accounts and no allowances shall be made for bad debts; provided, that if on the termination of a Client Account, any Advance is uncollectible, then we will refund to you the royalties paid on such Advance in accordance with the procedures set forth in the Rules and Regulations.

(9) "Financing Cost" means the cost a Qualified Borrower incurs to secure financing for the Advance through Exchange. "Qualified Borrower" means a Liquid Capital franchisee which meets our (or an affiliate's) qualifications for obtaining financing from Exchange. You have no obligation to obtain financing from Exchange and may secure financing from any source if you obtain from your financing source a signed Financing Estoppel Agreement in the form included in the Manual. Nevertheless, Exchange may loan Liquid Capital franchisees who are Qualified Borrowers up to the lesser of 56.25% of eligible Accounts Receivable or 75% of outstanding Advances in its discretion if a Qualified Borrower satisfies Exchange's then-current financing criteria in the first six months; 62% of eligible Accounts Receivable or 80% of outstanding Advances in its discretion if a Qualified Borrower satisfies Exchange's then-current financing criteria in the next six to 12 months; and 65% of eligible Accounts Receivable or 85% of outstanding Advances in its discretion if a Qualified Borrower satisfies Exchange's then-current financing criteria at 12 months and after. Exchange charges a fee equal to the greater of 12% per annum or Bank of America prime plus 4% for the loan, calculated on a daily basis. We have rates lower than 12% and ratios that provide higher borrowings. For example, as currently contractually required by the Exchange when providing financing to Qualified Borrowers, borrowing costs can be as follows: 12% per annum (Bank of America prime plus 4%) for Accounts Receivable of less than $1 million; 10% per annum (Bank of America prime plus 2%) for Accounts Receivable greater than $1 million; or if, in any year, the volume exceeds $10 million, the borrowing rate may be reduced by 2% for the remainder of the year and the entire subsequent year. The interest rate may be lower or higher on any particular transaction, and therefore returns may be higher or lower as well.

(10) "Exchange Fee" means the fee you pay the service provider to identify Participants for a funding transaction and to process their share of the Advance. This fee is currently set at 0.25% of the value of the Accounts Receivable processed through the service provider. It is paid only when there is more than one franchisee funding a transaction. "Participant" means a Liquid Capital franchisee who is funding at least a portion of the client's Accounts Receivable, but is neither the Originating Franchisee nor the Managing Participant. "Originating Franchisee" means the Liquid Capital franchisee who identifies and processes the client whose Accounts Receivable are being factored. "Managing Participant" means the Liquid

Capital franchisee who is responsible for managing the ongoing relationship with the client whose Accounts Receivable are being factored.

(11) "Originating Franchisee Fee" means the fee the Originating Franchisee earns as a result of identifying and processing the client. This fee is paid by the Managing Participant (if the Originating Franchisee is not also acting as the Managing Participant) and the other Participants. This fee is currently 12% of the gross revenue earned by the non-originating Participants in a funding transaction.

(12) "Management Fee" means the fee the Managing Participant earns for managing the ongoing relationship with the client. This fee is paid by the Originating Franchisee (if the Originating Franchisee is not also acting as the Managing Participant) and the other Participants. This fee is currently 0.5% of the Accounts represented by the Scheduled Invoices.

General Notes:

(1) We have written substantiation in our possession to support the information appearing in this ITEM 19. Written substantiation for the financial performance representation will be made available to the prospective franchisee upon reasonable request. Franchisees or former franchisees listed in this disclosure document may also be a source of information.

(2) Actual results may vary from franchise to franchise and depend on a variety of internal and external factors, many of which neither we nor any prospective franchisee can estimate, such as competition, economic climate, demographics, and changing consumer demands and tastes. A franchisee's ability to achieve any level of annual Gross Revenues or net income will depend on these factors and others, including the franchisee's level of expertise, none of which are within our control. Accordingly, we cannot, and do not, estimate the results of any particular franchise.

(3) Allowances should also be made for legal, accounting, loan interest and other additional operating costs not reflected in this financial performance representation.

THE LITTLE GYM

7001 N. Scottsdale Rd., # 1050
Scottsdale, AZ 85253
Tel: (888) 228-2878, (480) 948-2878
Fax: (480) 948-2765
Email: leo@thelittlegym.com
Website: www.thelittlegym.com
Leo Smart, Director of Franchise Development

The Little Gym helps children ages 4 months through 12 years build the confidence and skills needed at each stage of childhood. Our trained instructors nurture happy, confident kids through a range of programs including parent/child classes, gymnastics, karate, dance and sports skills development, plus enjoyable extras like camps, Parents' Survival Nights and Awesome Birthday Bashes. Each week, progressively structured classes and a positive learning environment create opportunities for children to try new things and build self-confidence, all with a grin that stretches from ear to ear.

BACKGROUND

IFA Member:	Yes
Established & First Franchised:	1976; 1992
Franchised Units:	292
Company-Owned Units:	0
Total Units:	292
Distribution:	US – 207; CAN – 14; O'seas – 71
North America:	37 States, 6 Provinces
Density:	30 in TX, 17 in NJ, 14 in CA
Projected New Units (12 Months):	15
Qualifications:	4, 4, 1, 3, 4, 5

FINANCIAL/TERMS

Cash Investment:	$75 – 100K
Total Investment:	$157.5 – 394K
Minimum Net Worth:	$150 – 250K
Fees (Franchise):	$49.5 – 69.5K
Fees (Royalty):	8%
Fees (Advertising):	1%
Term of Contract (Years):	10/10
Average Number of Employees:	2 – 3 FT, 4 – 8 PT
Passive Ownership:	Allowed
Encourage Conversions:	N/A
Area Development Agreements:	Yes
Sub-Franchising Contracts:	Yes
Expand in Territory:	No
Space Needs:	2,500 – 3,600 SF

SUPPORT & TRAINING
Financial Assistance Provided: Yes (I)
Site Selection Assistance: Yes
Lease Negotiation Assistance: Yes
Co-operative Advertising: No
Franchisee Association/Member: No
Size of Corporate Staff: 32
On-going Support: C, D, E, h

Training: 7 Days Various Locations; 14 Days Scottsdale, AZ

SPECIFIC EXPANSION PLANS
US: All United States except SD
Canada: All Canada
Overseas: All Countries

Shown below are unaudited annual gross revenues as reported to us by our U.S. and Puerto Rican franchisees for the year ended December 31, 2013. All franchise locations that opened before January 1, 2013 are included.

Your individual financial results are likely to differ from the results stated below.

Written substantiation of the data used in preparing this item 19 will be made available to you on reasonable request.

The financial performance representation figures do not reflect the costs of sales or operating expenses that must be deducted from the gross revenue or gross sales figures to obtain your net income or profit. The best source of cost and expense data may be from franchisees and former franchisees, some of whom may be listed in Exhibit D.

Actual results vary from unit to unit. The gyms listed below have earned the stated amounts. Your individual results may differ from those stated below and there is no assurance you will earn as much. We cannot estimate the results of any particular franchise.

Annual Gross Revenues year ended Dec. 31, 2013 as reported by Franchisees Unaudited Opened Full Year 2013, listed by year opened, highest to lowest

United States and Puerto Rico Reported in US Dollars

Opened 2012	Opened 2011	Opened 2010	Opened 2009
270,011	729,619	645,415	580,410
260,773	583,050	417,830	402,490
208,147	521,325	389,032	395,566
183,467	475,190	304,099	353,922
	394,033	302,870	277,136
	336,229	273,212	266,830
	242,634	254,228	224,875
	213,797	179,982	
	205,473		

Annual Gross Revenues year ended Dec. 31, 2011 as reported by Franchisees Unaudited Pre-2009 Franchisees Opened Full Year 2013, highest to lowest

US and Puerto Rican Franchisees Reported in US Dollars

1,070,466	498,070	394,407	328,265	279,368
1,060,065	495,458	392,319	327,229	279,161
912,482	290,754	388,506	324,824	279,098
897,012	248,542	386,907	323,114	276,861
846,299	151,479	381,254	320,220	270,977
784,131	499,217	379,880	319,397	269,578
713,552	492,942	377,096	316,645	269,139
712,020	489,981	376,136	315,568	267,853
652,126	484,174	374,725	312,723	264,025
633,657	480,002	374,267	309,340	262,770
619,828	474,295	373,869	309,171	258,128
617,742	472,029	371,504	307,689	257,995
617,203	455,528	370,586	306,955	255,577
590,059	448,098	366,105	305,549	252,484
585,626	447,243	365,480	302,767	249,660
570,091	442,490	364,034	301,965	248,807
570,038	440,767	363,197	299,913	243,419
564,587	418,292	362,438	299,153	242,431
551,347	418,041	362,068	296,392	237,072
524,467	416,005	357,313	295,472	235,318
522,836	414,464	356,789	292,789	233,664
518,073	410,191	354,816	289,624	232,934
511,783	410,103	352,052	289,532	230,473
509,921	406,333	347,181	288,606	229,735
508,854	403,311	345,876	281,402	227,266
505,385	403,064	337,193	280,990	221,567
504,914	402,043	334,207	280,824	220,058
503,776	398,694	331,152	280,716	215,854
501,862	395,582	329,284	280,154	213,794

212,017	203,923	185,821	164,424	139,040
210,762	198,393	179,297	160,678	129,186[1]
210,328	194,019	175,050	159,738	127,949
208,520	192,393	172,882	152,354	126,183
204,661	186,190	169,855	151,777	116,691

Other than this financial performance representation, we do not make any financial performance representations. We also do not authorize our employees or representatives to make any such representations either orally or in writing. If you are purchasing an existing outlet, however, we may provide you with the actual records of that outlet. If you receive any other financial performance information or projections of your future income, you should report it to our management by contacting J. Ruskin ("Ruk") Adams at 7001 N. Scottsdale Road, Suite 1050, Scottsdale, Arizona 85253, phone (480) 948-2878; the Federal Trade Commission; and the appropriate state regulatory agencies.

Referred for a reason.

THE MAIDS

9394 W. Dodge Rd., # 140
Omaha, NE 68114
Tel: (800) 843-6243, (402) 558-5555
Fax: (402) 558-4112
Email: rcordova@maids.com
Website: www.themaidsfranchise.com
Ronn Cordova, Vice President of Development

Distinguished as the number one residential cleaning franchise in 2007, 2008, 2009, 2011, 2012, and 2014 by Entrepreneur Magazine's Top 500, THE MAIDS is the quality leader in the industry. THE MAIDS provides the most comprehensive package of training, support, and exclusive territory in the industry. We provide extensive training, including 7 weeks of pre-training and 9 days of classroom and 4 days of field training. With THE MAIDS, you can build a great business and achieve the lifestyle you desire, all with nights, weekends and holidays off. We are looking for people who want an executive experience. With THE MAIDS, you are working ON the business, not IN the business. THE MAIDS ideal franchise candidate will have good management and business skills, and most importantly, great people skills.

BACKGROUND
IFA Member:	Yes
Established & First Franchised:	1979; 1980
Franchised Units:	1,114
Company-Owned Units:	35
Total Units:	1,149
Distribution:	US – 1,117; CAN – 32; O'seas – 0

North America:	42 States, 4 Provinces
Density:	94 in TX, 83 in FL, 103 in CA
Projected New Units (12 Months):	80
Qualifications:	5, 5, 1, 3, 1, 5

FINANCIAL/TERMS
Cash Investment:	$60 – 65K
Total Investment:	$97 – $123K
Minimum Net Worth:	$250K
Fees (Franchise):	$12.5K + $.95 per QHH
Fees (Royalty):	3.9 – 6.9%
Fees (Advertising):	2%
Term of Contract (Years):	20/20
Average Number of Employees:	2 FT, 4 to start (maids) PT
Passive Ownership:	Discouraged
Encourage Conversions:	Yes
Area Development Agreements:	Yes
Sub-Franchising Contracts:	No
Expand in Territory:	Yes
Space Needs:	1,000 – 1,200 SF

SUPPORT & TRAINING
Financial Assistance Provided:	No
Site Selection Assistance:	Yes
Lease Negotiation Assistance:	No
Co-operative Advertising:	Yes
Franchisee Association/Member:	No
Size of Corporate Staff:	35
On-going Support:	A, B, C, D, E, F, G, h, I
Training:	9 days Corporate Training Omaha, NE; 2 – 3 days Power Training Franchisee location; 7 weeks Foundation Training (Pre-Training)

SPECIFIC EXPANSION PLANS
US:	All United States
Canada:	All except Saskatchewan and Quebec
Overseas:	No

Below is certain historic financial information regarding The Maids® businesses operated by franchisees ("Franchise Owners") or our affiliates ("Affiliate Owners") that operated within in the United States and Canada from October 1, 2012 through September 30, 2013. Canadian Franchise Owners submitted information in Canadian Dollars and we converted that information to U.S. Dollars using the exchange rate in place at the time the information was submitted. Your individual financial results may differ from the information provided below.

We have not presented any information for Franchise Owners which were not in operation for the full period. You should be aware that some of the Franchise Owners whose results were used to prepare this information have been in business for a long time, have had a greater opportunity to achieve these results than a new office operated by a new Franchise Owner and it's unlikely that a new Franchise Owner will achieve results like those reported.

As of September 30, 2013, there were a total of 1,141 franchised and company-owned Territories. A total of 150 franchisees licensed and operated 1,110 of the 1,141 Territories. We operated the remaining 31 Territories. A The Maids® territory generally consists of approximately 10,000 Potential Customers, although some territories may be larger. The information presented in this report does not distinguish between Franchise Owners that purchased a large number of territories and those who did not purchase a large number of territories.

The basis for the Franchise Owner information presented is weekly reports submitted to us by our Franchise Owners and affiliates operating throughout the periods represented that form the basis for royalty payments. We calculated the averages and percentages presented in this Item 19 using exclusively the actual results reported to us by Franchise Owners and Affiliate Owners. Of the 9,572 total weekly reports required from Franchise Owners, 0.5% or 52 were not received in time for the preparation of this statement and, therefore, could not be included in calculating the information presented. If we had received in time the missing weekly reports, the information presented in this statement may have increased or decreased depending on the information contained in the missing reports. We have assumed that the Franchise Owner's information submitted by Franchise Owners (and which forms in substantial part the basis for the information presented in this document) is accurate, complete and contains no material misrepresentations or omissions. The information presented is, so far as we know, based on actual experience. We have not audited or verified these reports.

The basis for the information from our Affiliate Owners is our internal books and records, which have been maintained as far as reasonable possible in accordance with U.S. GAAP.

I. STATEMENT OF AVERAGE REVENUE PER CLEAN, AVERAGE REVENUE PER CUSTOMERS, PERCENTAGE OF CLEAN BY SERVICE AND LABOR PERCENTAGES BY OFFICE AND TERRITORY

The following statements are based on information reported by Franchise Owners and Affiliate Owners that were in operation for the 12 month period from October 1, 2012, until September 30, 2013. The statements in this Section I are based on information by offices and territories, and not by Franchise Owner or Affiliate Owner. Most Franchise Owners operate one office, although several Franchise Owners operate two or more offices. There were 189 offices operated by Franchise Owners in 1,110 territories and 3 offices operated by 3 Affiliate Owners in 31 territories as of September 30, 2013. Of those offices operated by Franchise Owners, 180 offices and 1,073 territories were in operation for the entire 12 month period ended September 30, 2013, and all 3 offices operated by Affiliate Owners were in operation for the entire 12 month period ended September 30, 2013. We did not include information for the 9 Franchise Owners and their 9 offices that collectively are in 37 territories that were not in operation for the entire 12 month period ending September 30, 2013 or for the 6 offices operated by 6 Franchise Owners in 26 territories who did not submit complete reports. The statement includes the average revenue per clean, the average annual revenue per customer, the percentage of total cleans by service and the labor percentage by a regular maid service or a special project.

	Average Revenue Per Clean[1]	Average Annual Revenue per Customer[2]	Average Percentage of Cleans by Type of Service[3]	Average Labor Percentages[4]
Regular Maid Service	$144.83	$3,775.72	87.04%	35.30%
Total Number of Offices/Territories included	177 Offices/1,078 Territories	177 Offices/1,078 Territories	177 Offices/1,078 Territories	177 Offices/1,078 Territories
Number of Offices/Territories Who Met or Exceeded Averages	94 Offices/636 Territories	82 Offices/531 Territories	82 Offices/538 Territories	88 Offices/552 Territories

Percentage (%) of Offices/ Territories Who Met or Exceeded Average	53.11% of Offices/ 59.00% of Territories	46.33% of Offices/ 49.26% of Territories	46.33% of Offices/ 49.91% of Territories	49.72% of Offices/ 51.21% of Territories
Special Project[5]	$251.30	$251.30	12.96%	30.80%
Total Number of Offices/ Territories included	177 Offices/1,078 Territories	177 Offices/1,078 Territories	177 Offices/1,078 Territories	177 Offices/1,078 Territories
Number of Offices/Territories Who Met or Exceeded Averages	89 Offices/598 Territories	89 Offices/598 Territories	89 Offices/524 Territories	81 Offices/520 Territories
Percentage (%) of Offices/ Territories Who Met or Exceeded Average	50.28% of Offices/ 55.47% of Territories	50.28% of Offices/ 55.47% of Territories	50.28% of Offices/ 48.61% of Territories	45.76% of Offices/ 48.24% of Territories

1. "Average Revenue per Clean" means the average revenue received from a customer from one cleaning project (a "Clean"). It is calculated by dividing the total reported revenue by the total reported number of Cleans.

2. "Average Annual Revenue per Customer" means the total reported revenue that each classification of customer would generate in one year. It is calculated by multiplying the Average Revenue per Clean by the total number of Cleans per year in each classification (Regular Maid Service includes 52 for Weekly, 26 for Every Other Week, and 12 for Monthly, Special project includes a single clean per year).

3. "Percentage of Cleans by Type of Service" means the percentage of total reported number of cleans derived from regular customers and Special Project customers. It is calculated by dividing the total reported number of cleans for each category by total reported number of cleans and multiplying by 100%.

4. "Labor Percentage" means the portion of total reported revenue that is expensed for direct labor costs for each type of Clean and for labor to drive to the Clean location. It is calculated by dividing the labor cost by the total reported revenue and multiplying by 100%.

5. "Special Projects" are one-time projects and are not regularly scheduled cleanings.

II. STATEMENT OF HIGH REVENUE, LOW REVENUE AND AVERAGE REVENUE BY NUMBER OF MONTHS IN OPERATION BY FRANCHISE OWNER AND TERRITORY

The following statements are based on information reported by Franchise Owners and Affiliate Owners that were in operation for the 12 month period from October 1, 2012, until September 30, 2013. There were 150 Franchise Owners operating in 1,110 territories and 3 Affiliate Owners operating in 31 territories as of September 30, 2013. Of those Franchise Owners, 141 operating in 1,073 territories were in operation for the entire 12 month period ended September 30, 2013, and all Affiliate Owners were in operation for the entire 12 month period ended September 30, 2013. We did not include information for the 9 Franchise Owner operating in 37 territories that were not in operation for the entire 12 month period ending September 30, 2013, or for the 6 Franchise Owners operating in 26 territories who did not submit complete reports. The statement includes the high revenue, low revenue and average revenue for the 12 month period from October 1, 2012, until September 30, 2013 for Franchise Owners and Affiliate Owners and territories based upon the number of month in operation.

Months In Operation	High Revenue	Low Revenue	Average Revenue (Including percentage and number of franchisees that met or exceeded the average)
Greater than 48 Months (Out of 127 Owners/1,041 Territories)	$6,811,246	$112,126	$1,043,132 31% of Owners/52% of Territories (40 Owners/545 Territories)
Entire The Maids® System (Out of 138 Owners/1,078 Territories)	$6,811,246	$112,126	$977,585 33% of Owners/53% of Territories (46 Owners/567 Territories)

III. STATEMENT OF REVENUE AND EXPENSE INFORMATION FOR AFFILIATE OWNERS

The following statements are based on information reported by all Affiliate Owners that were in operation for the 12 month period from October 1, 2012, until September 30, 2013. The statement includes the total revenue, expense information and net income for each Affiliate Owner's The Maids® Business, the average total revenue, expense information and net income for all Affiliate Owner's The Maids® Businesses and the average percentage of revenue of expenses and net income for all Affiliate Owners' The Maids® Businesses. Affiliate Owners operate under franchise agreements with us, pay us the same ongoing fees and have the same local advertising requirements as Franchise Owners. However, Affiliate Owners may pay a lower percentage of Gross Revenue as a Continuing Free than you because Affiliate Owners' weekly Gross Revenues allow Affiliate Owners to pay a lower percentage of Gross Revenue as a Continuing Fee based on the Continuing Fee scale described in Item 6. In addition, all Affiliate Owners have been in operation for over 5 years. As a result, the Affiliate Owners' results may differ materially from your results.

	Affiliate Owner #1 (5 Territories)	Affiliate Owner #2 (7 Territories)	Affiliate Owner #3 (19 Territories)	Average of Affiliate Owners	Average Percentage of Revenue
TOTAL REVENUE	$1,016,050	$1,418,967	$1,864,150	$1,433,056	100.00%
OPERATING EXPENSES					
LICENSING FEE	37,390	52,072	69,165	52,876	3.7%
ADVERTISING FUNDS FEE	20,087	25,127	36,533	27,249	1.9%
ADVERTISING	81,865	89,952	78,414	83,410	5.8%
DIRECT LABOR	344,030	480,463	663,878	496,124	34.6%
INDIRECT LABOR	36,899	52,240	51,846	46,995	3.3%
EMPLOYEE BENEFITS - MAIDS	30,605	37,565	47,761	38,644	2.7%
CLEANING SUPPLIES & UNIFORMS	25,745	20,351	29,766	25,287	1.8%
RENT & UTILITIES	22,644	41,033	55,442	39,706	2.8%
AUTO	42,293	62,362	72,187	58,947	4.1%
AUTO DEPRECIATION	7,209	13,047	18,222	12,826	0.9%
PAYROLL TAXES	35,391	58,688	80,639	58,239	4.1%
CUSTOMER DAMAGE	1,751	3,681	3,797	3,076	0.2%
TELEPHONE	12,165	14,716	17,930	14,937	1.0%
INSURANCE - W/C & PDBI	45,227	65,579	98,093	69,633	4.9%
EMPLOYEE RECRUITING	2,285	656	9,207	4,049	0.3%
EQUIPMENT RENT & REPAIR	2,354	1,831	2,945	2,377	0.2%
OTHER EXPENSE	1,748	131	5,373	2,417	0.2%
TOTAL OPERATING EXPENSES:	$749,688	$1,019,494	$1,341,198	$1,036,793	72.3%
GROSS MARGIN	$266,362	$399,473	$522,952	$396,262	27.7%
GENERAL & ADMINISTRATIVE EXPENSES					
MANAGEMENT & QUALITY ASSURANCE SALARIES	98,611	88,902	87,626	91,713	6.4%

OPERATIONS SALARIES	31,552	42,586	51,108	41,749	2.9%
PAYROLL TAXES – OFFICE	8,846	7,829	7,675	8,117	0.6%
SALES CENTER COSTS	15,101	23,542	32,037	23,560	1.6%
DEPRECIATION EXPENSE	1,345	2,481	3,270	2,365	0.2%
OUTSIDE SERVICES-PROFESSIONAL	6,606	8,536	15,838	10,327	0.7%
PAYMENT PROCESSING & BANK CHARGES	16,752	19,849	39,494	25,365	1.8%
OFFICE SUPPLIES	5,898	5,037	6,487	5,807	0.4%
INTEREST EXPENSE	600	557	1,084	747	0.1%
EMPLOYEE BENEFITS-MGMNT & OFFICE	1,702	15,944	6,264	7,970	0.6%
EMPLOYEE BENEFITS – 401K	5,525	3,813	354	3,231	0.2%
OTHER ADMINISTRATIVE	14,615	10,000	10,262	11,626	0.8%
TOTAL GENERAL & ADMINISTRATIVE EXPENSES	$207,153	$229,076	$261,499	$232,576	16.2%
NET INCOME	$59,209	$170,397	$261,453	$163,686	11.4%

TMI Company Store
Average Operation Result
Average Revenue = $1,433,056

- OPERATING EXPENSES:
- GENERAL & ADMINISTRATIVE EXPENSES:
- NET INCOME

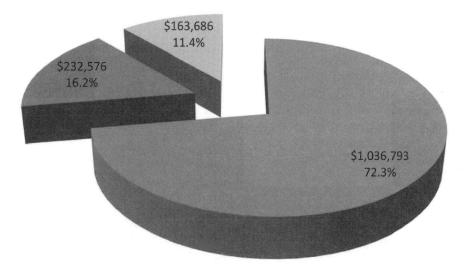

Although The Maids® Franchisees are located in many different areas, location can be an important factor affecting results, particularly with respect to demographics, general economic influence and your prospective area may differ from the typical area for a The Maids® franchise. Many of the Franchisees whose results are reported are located in major metropolitan areas or other territories with relatively favorable characteristics. You should independently verify whether such factors and conditions in your intended area of operation are comparable to those existing The Maids® franchise areas.

Prospective Franchise Owners should, before making any investment decision, research the need in their proposed area of operation for, and the ability of Potential Customers to pay you for, services of the type offered by The Maids® Franchises, including actual and potential competition and the socioeconomic and demographic background of their area. In this regard, we strongly encourage you to research your area, speak with existing The Maids® Franchisees, and make an independent judgment as to whether their experience may or not be transferable to your proposed area of operation.

You should consult with appropriate financial, business and legal advisors in evaluating the information in this document and the accompanying charts and notes.

Some outlets have earned this amount. Your individual results may differ. There is no assurance that you'll earn as much.

We will be glad to provide you with written substantiation of the data used to prepare the information presented in this document on reasonable request.

Other than the preceding financial performance representation, we do not make any financial performance representations. We also do not authorize our employees or representatives to make any such representations either orally or in writing. If you are purchasing an existing outlet, however, we may provide you with the actual records of that outlet. If you receive any other financial performance information or projections of your future income, you should report it to the franchisor's management by contacting Franchise Development, The Maids International, Inc., 9394 West Dodge Road, Suite 140, Omaha, NE 68114, (402) 558-5555, the Federal Trade Commission, and the appropriate state regulatory agencies.

MATHNASIUM LEARNING CENTERS

5120 W. Goldleaf Circle, #300
Los Angeles, CA 90056
Tel: (877) 531-6284, (323) 421-8000
Fax: (310) 943-2111
Email: eileen.morouse@mathnasium.com
Website: www.mathnasium.com/franchising
Eileen Morouse, Senior Franchise Marketing Coordinator

Mathnasium Learning Centers is an excellent blend of a rewarding business opportunity and making a difference in children's lives. We make math make sense for kids, giving them the tools to catch up, maintain, and get ahead.

BACKGROUND

IFA Member:	Yes
Established & First Franchised:	2002; 2003

Franchised Units:	387
Company-Owned Units:	2
Total Units:	389
Distribution:	US – 389; CAN – 0; O'seas – 0
North America:	37 States, 0 Provinces

FINANCIAL/TERMS

Cash Investment:	$50 – 107.5K
Total Investment:	$78.3 – 107.5K
Minimum Net Worth:	N/A
Fees (Franchise):	$37K
Fees (Royalty):	10%
Fees (Advertising):	2%
Term of Contract (Years):	5/5
Average Number of Employees:	N/A
Passive Ownership:	Allowed
Encourage Conversions:	N/A
Area Development Agreements:	No
Sub-Franchising Contracts:	No
Expand in Territory:	No
Space Needs:	N/A

SUPPORT & TRAINING

Financial Assistance Provided:	No

Site Selection Assistance:	N/A	Training:	N/A
Lease Negotiation Assistance:	N/A		
Co-operative Advertising:	No	SPECIFIC EXPANSION PLANS	
Franchisee Association/Member:	No	US:	No
Size of Corporate Staff:	0	Canada:	No
On-going Support:	A, B, C, D, E, F, G, H, I	Overseas:	No

The following is a historic financial performance representation for the period from January 1, 2013 through December 31, 2013, and for the period from January 1, 2012 through December 31, 2012. It includes average annual Gross Receipts of Mathnasium's existing centers that had been open for 12 months or longer as of December 31, 2013 or December 31, 2012, respectively, broken down by quartiles. "Gross Receipts" means the monthly gross receipts from all sources in the operation of a Mathnasium center, including student tuition, registration and testing fees, sales of learning materials, hourly per student private tutoring, and any other approved services. "Gross Receipts" excludes only sales tax receipts that you must by law collect from customers and that you pay to the government, any customer refunds actually paid, and coupons or promotional discounts approved by us.

As of December 31, 2013, we had 409 franchised Mathnasium Centers in operation. Of the 409 franchised Mathnasium Centers, 99 were not included in this financial performance representation because they had not been open for 12 months or longer as of December 31, 2013. In addition, an additional 19 Mathnasium Centers who had been open for at least 19 months were not included because they had not reported their Gross Receipts to us for the full 12 month period.

As of December 31, 2012, we had 332 franchised Mathnasium Centers in operation. Of the 332 franchised Mathnasium Centers, 71 were not included in this financial performance representation because they had not been open for 12 months or longer as of December 13, 2012. In addition, an additional 6 Mathnasium Centers who had been open for at least 12 months were not included because they had not reported their Gross Receipts to us for the full 12 month period.

As of December 31, 2013, 42% of the Mathnasium Centers had been open 24 or fewer months. As of December 31, 2012, 58% of Mathnasium Centers had been open 24 or fewer months. Average center revenues were $191,744, $167,761 and $146,093 for the years ended December 31, 2013, 2012, and 2011, respectively, representing growth of 14.4% from 2012 to 2013 and 14.8% from 2011 to 2012.

2012

Top 25% of Centers by Gross Receipts	Mid-Upper 25% of Centers by Gross Receipts	Mid-Lower 25% of Centers by Gross Receipts	Bottom 25% of Centers by Gross Receipts
Category Average Gross Receipts			
$299,294	$178,035	$124,441	$66,472
Number of Centers Meeting or Exceeding Average for Category			
25 or 39% of 64 Centers in Top 25%	33 or 52% of 64 Centers in Mid-Upper 25%	33 or 52% of 64 Centers in Mid-Lower 25%	33 or 52% of 63 Centers in Bottom 25%
Gross Receipts of Top 10 Centers in Category			
$569,658	$206,135	$154,470	$97,035
535,883	206,005	150,631	94,464
498,664	205,105	150,347	94,209
477,533	202,392	150,199	93,735
476,390	200,650	148,783	93,222
468,040	200,237'	148,301	92,005
421,572	199,576	145,796	91,864
409,154	199,355	145,341	90,100

| 398,218 | 199,092 | 144,979 | 89,729 |
| 368,327 | 198,957 | 143,057 | 89,598 |

TOP 50% OF CENTERS BY GROSS RECEIPTS	$238,664
Number of centers in top 50% meeting or exceeding the average of the top 50%	47 or 37% of 128 Centers included in average
BOTTOM 50% OF CENTERS BY GROSS RECEIPTS	$96,677
Number of centers in bottom 50% meeting or exceeding the average of the bottom 50%	65 or 51% of 127 Centers included in average

2013

Top 25% of Centers by Gross Receipts	Mid-Upper Centers by Gross Receipts	Mid-Lower of Centers by Gross Receipts	Bottom 25% of Centers by Gross Receipts
Category Average Gross Receipts			
$333,658	$199,483	$145,045	$87,466
Number of Centers Meeting or Exceeding Average for Category			
30 or 41% of 73 Centers in Top 25%	38 or 53% of 72 Centers in Mid-Upper 25%	38 or 52% of Centers in Mid-Lower 25%	41 or 57% of 71 Centers in Bottom 25%
Gross Receipts of Top 10 Centers in Category			
$668,068	$228,293	$169,013	$120,546
583,607	227,963	167,848	118,351
574,095	227,139	166,146	117,948
556,780	224,478	165,465	117,575
533,401	223,871	165,309	117,242
498,098	223,320	164,822	115,205
464,544	221,843	162,198	114,947
446,433	221,391	161,872	113,149
439,693	220,124	161,448	112,810
436,748	219,741	161,295	110,947

TOP 50% OF CENTERS BY GROSS RECEIPTS	$267,033
Number of centers in top 50% meeting or exceeding the average of the top 50%	50 or 35% of 145 Centers included in average
BOTTOM 50% OF CENTERS BY GROSS RECEIPTS	$116,454
Number of centers in bottom 50% meeting or exceeding the average of the bottom 50%	76 or 54% of 145 Centers included in average

The above annual averages of Gross Receipts for franchised Mathnasium Centers open at least 12 months and reporting throughout the year shown was calculated by us based on reports on Gross Receipts furnished to Mathnasium by its franchsiees. It is important to note that neither the submitting franchisees nor Mathnasium audited this information.

As a new franchisee, your financial results will likely differ from the results described above and those differences may be material. Your results may also vary significantly from those shown above depending on a number of other factors, including the location of your center, the nature and extent of your competition, whether your geographic area has a greater or lesser demand for Mathnasium services, the skill, experience and business acumen of your management and staff, local economic conditions, and how long you have operated your center. Centers may not mature until their 24th to 36th month of operation or later.

Some centers have earned this amount. Your individual results may differ. There is no assurance you will earn as much.

The financial information in the above tables shows only historic gross receipts of franchised Mathnasium centers. The financial information above does not reflect the costs of sales, operating expenses, or other costs or expenses that you will incur and that must be deducted from the gross receipts to obtain your net income or profit.

Mathnasium will make written substantiation of the data used in preparing the information above available to you upon reasonable request.

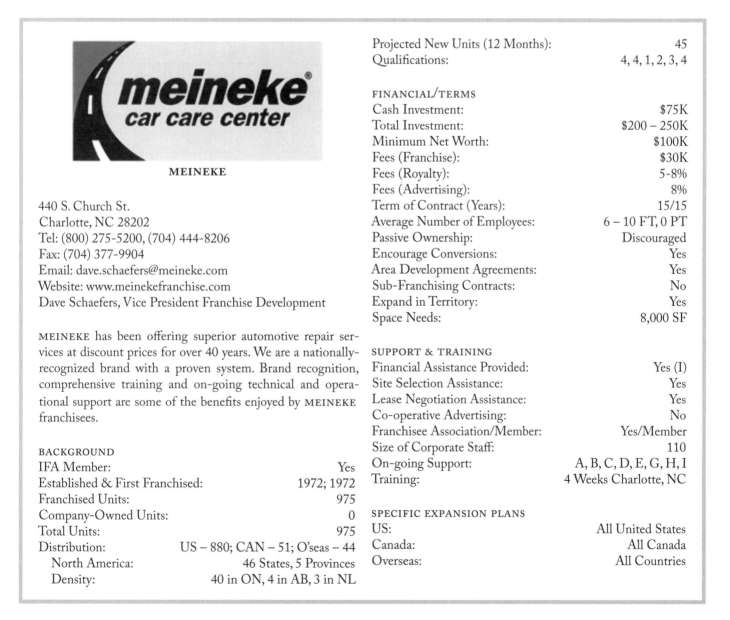

MEINEKE

440 S. Church St.
Charlotte, NC 28202
Tel: (800) 275-5200, (704) 444-8206
Fax: (704) 377-9904
Email: dave.schaefers@meineke.com
Website: www.meinekefranchise.com
Dave Schaefers, Vice President Franchise Development

MEINEKE has been offering superior automotive repair services at discount prices for over 40 years. We are a nationally-recognized brand with a proven system. Brand recognition, comprehensive training and on-going technical and operational support are some of the benefits enjoyed by MEINEKE franchisees.

BACKGROUND

IFA Member:	Yes
Established & First Franchised:	1972; 1972
Franchised Units:	975
Company-Owned Units:	0
Total Units:	975
Distribution:	US – 880; CAN – 51; O'seas – 44
North America:	46 States, 5 Provinces
Density:	40 in ON, 4 in AB, 3 in NL

Projected New Units (12 Months):	45
Qualifications:	4, 4, 1, 2, 3, 4

FINANCIAL/TERMS

Cash Investment:	$75K
Total Investment:	$200 – 250K
Minimum Net Worth:	$100K
Fees (Franchise):	$30K
Fees (Royalty):	5-8%
Fees (Advertising):	8%
Term of Contract (Years):	15/15
Average Number of Employees:	6 – 10 FT, 0 PT
Passive Ownership:	Discouraged
Encourage Conversions:	Yes
Area Development Agreements:	Yes
Sub-Franchising Contracts:	No
Expand in Territory:	Yes
Space Needs:	8,000 SF

SUPPORT & TRAINING

Financial Assistance Provided:	Yes (I)
Site Selection Assistance:	Yes
Lease Negotiation Assistance:	Yes
Co-operative Advertising:	No
Franchisee Association/Member:	Yes/Member
Size of Corporate Staff:	110
On-going Support:	A, B, C, D, E, G, H, I
Training:	4 Weeks Charlotte, NC

SPECIFIC EXPANSION PLANS

US:	All United States
Canada:	All Canada
Overseas:	All Countries

A. Average Gross Revenue for Fiscal Year End December 28, 2013

The chart below is the Average Gross Revenues by number of service bays for fiscal year end December 28, 2013 statement ("Average Gross Revenues Statement") as reported by 381 franchised Meineke Centers (including co-branded Meineke Centers) that met the following conditions: (a) the Meineke Center is operated in the United States; (b) the Meineke Center had been open and operating for more than 2 years as of December 28, 2013; (c) the Meineke Center had at least 5 bays; and (d) the Meineke Center had a star rating of 3 or better. As of December 28, 2013, there were 885 Meineke Centers, including co-branded Meineke Centers. The remaining 504 Meineke Centers were not included in the Average Gross Revenues Statement because the Meineke Center either failed to meet the criteria described above or did not submit weekly sales reports to us.

The Average Gross Revenues Statement is based on weekly sales reports submitted by Meineke franchisees for the purpose of computing royalty fees, and have not been audited. These reports have not been audited by certified public accountants nor have we sought to independently verify their accuracy for purposes of the Average Gross Revenue Statement. "Gross Revenues" has the same meaning as described in Item 6. We implemented 5 Star Rating program in the fall of 2008. Each Meineke Center is given a score of one to five stars, based on a set of established criteria each calendar quarter. For complete detail of the 5 Star scoring metrics, refer to Exhibit X. We consider a 3 Star rating to represent an average performing center.

MEINEKE CENTER AVERAGE GROSS REVENUES BY SERVICE BAY FOR FISCAL YEAR END DECEMBER 28, 2013 FOR CENTERS OPENED FOR MORE THAN 2 YEARS AND HAVE A THREE STAR OR HIGHER RATING

Number of Bays	Number of Centers open for more than 2 years as of December 28, 2013 that have a 3 star or higher rating	Average Gross Revenues for fiscal year end December 28, 2013 for centers open more than 2 years	Number of Centers who met or exceeded the average Gross Revenues
5 Bays	117	$633,849	48 (41%)
6 Bays	179	$646,076	75 (42%)
7 Bays	36	$706,760	16 (44%)
8 Bays	41	$785,812	20 (49%
+8 Bays	8	$1,307,725	4 (50%)
Total Centers/Average Gross Revenues	381	$676,986	150 (49%)

The Average Gross Revenues Chart that we have included above omit all centers with less than 5 bays because we recommend that all new Meineke Centers have 5 bays or more. Currently you are required to open a Meineke Center that has a minimum of 4 service bays. We do still have locations in the system that only have 3 service bays; however these are franchised locations that were developed before we changed the required minimum number of service bays for a Meineke Center.

As of December 28, 2013, there were 38 franchised 3 bay Meineke Centers with a star rating of 3 or higher that were open and operating for at least 2 years as of December 28, 2013. These 38 Meineke Centers reported average Gross Revenues of $548,164 for the fiscal year ending December 28, 2013. Of these 38 Meineke Centers, 16 (42%) met or exceeded the average Gross Revenues.

As of December 28, 2013, there were 98 franchised 4 bay Meineke Centers with a star rating of 3 or higher that were open and operating for at least 2 years as of December 28, 2013. These 98 Meineke Centers reported average Gross Revenues of $592,527 for the fiscal year ending December 28, 2013. Of these 98 Meineke Centers, 40 (41%) met or exceeded the average Gross Revenues.

As of December 28, 2013, there were 518 franchised Meineke Centers with a star rating of 3 or higher that were open and operating for at least 2 years as of December 28, 2013 regardless of the number of operating bays. These 518 Meineke Centers reported average Gross Revenues of $651,101 for the fiscal year ending December 28, 2013. Of these 518 Meineke Centers, 201 (39%) met or exceeded the average Gross Revenues.

These sales figures have not been audited by certified public accountants nor have sought to independently verify their accuracy. Written substantiation of the data used in preparing the Average Gross Revenue Statement will be made available to you on reasonable request. The results in this chart should not be considered as the actual or probable results that will be realized by you or any other franchisee. We do not represent that any franchisee can expect to attain these results. A new franchisee's results are likely to differ from these results.

Some Meineke Centers have earned this amount. Your individual results may differ. There is no assurance that you will earn as much.

B. Average Expense Information for Fiscal Year End December 28, 2013

Below is a summary of certain customary and typical expenses of 118 franchised Meineke Centers (including co-branded Meineke Centers) with a star rating of 3 or higher in the United States shown as a percentage of Gross Revenue. The number of service bays you use in the operation of your center likely will be a material component in calculating the amount of expenses that you incur in your center operations. The listing of expenses is not all-inclusive. Our Meineke franchisees will incur additional expenses in the operation of their Meineke

Centers that do not appear on this listing. The amount of your expenses also will be dictated by the geographic region your Meineke Center is located.

We obtained the expense for these Meineke Centers listed in the following charts from profit and loss statements and tax returns for the fiscal year ended December 28, 2013 submitted to us by the 118 franchised Meineke Centers (including co-branded Meineke Centers) in the ordinary course of business. The average Gross Revenue of the 118 franchised Meineke Centers that submitted their profit and loss statements and tax returns to us for purposes of this chart is $593,981 for the fiscal year ending December 28, 2013. Of these 118 Meineke Centers, 50 Centers (42%) met or exceed the average. The reports have not been audited by certified public accountants nor have we sought to independently verify their accuracy. The remaining 767 Meineke Centers in operation as of December 28, 2013, either did not supply us with their profit and loss statements, did not have a star rating of 3 or higher, or were not in operation for the entire fiscal year ended December 28, 2013.

AVERAGE EXPENSE INFORMATION FOR CENTERS
WITH 3 STAR RATING OR HIGHER REPORTING FOR FISCAL YEAR 2013

	EBITDA Quartile [1]			
	Top	2nd	3rd	4th
	30	29	29	30
Avg. COGS %	25.7%	25.7%	26.8%	28.1%
Direct Technician Labor	17.5%	19.8%	20.6%	22.4%
Other Center Variables[2]	2.2%	1.6%	3.5%	2.2%
Fixed Expenses[3]	16.4%	21.4%	23.8%	29.3%
EBITDA[1]	38.2%	31.5%	25.3%	17.9%

		Bay Size				
	All Centers	5	6	7	8	>8
No. of Centers	118	24	42	8	11	1
Avg. COGS %	26.4%	26.84%	26.36%	27.76%	25.84%	25.38%
Direct Technician Labor	19.6%	19.75%	20.23%	24.91%	18.84%	11.48%
Other Center Variables[2]	2.3%	1.85%	2.65%	2.91%	1.61%	1.22%
Fixed Expenses[3]	21.5%	21.26%	23.42%	16.84%	22.04%	22.58%
EBITDA[1]	30.2%	30.3%	27.3%	27.6%	31.7%	39.3%

(1) EBITDA is defined as earnings before interest, taxes, depreciation, and amortization. What this means is that subtracted from your earnings will be the costs of any interest you pay to finance your business as well any taxes you will be required to pay to the federal, state, or local government related to the operation of your Meineke Center. Expenses for those centers that provided us with their financial statements for fiscal year 2013 are included in this chart.

In these charts, EBITDA % does not include the impact of

franchise fees or advertising fees (National and local). It also assumes that the franchisee will run the center and hence excludes any salaries for managers.

(2)Other center variables include credit card processing costs.

(3)Fixed expenses include payroll taxes, employee benefits, rent, taxes and licenses, supplies, insurance, utilities, telephone, trash, laundry and uniforms, bank charges, center repairs, IT support, and accounting, legal and miscellaneous expenses.

Average royalties and MAF contributions for centers included in this analysis are 5.2% and 7.6%, respectively. Some centers choose to charge the costs of a vehicle to their business; these expenses have not been included in our analysis. Equipment lease expenses have also been excluded from our analysis as it will only apply to a limited number of new owners. Finally, it is assumed that the franchisee will operate the center. These amounts would be subtracted from the EBITDA listed above.

The sales and expenses vary for Meineke Centers depending on many factors, including local and regional variations in real estate values or rental rates, construction costs and building specifications (including the number of bays), financing terms which the franchisee was able to obtain, local and regional variations in utility and telephone rates (including the number of telephone lines in the center), insurance rates, local and state taxes and wage rates, degree of skilled labor employed and the availability of such labor, cost of parts and supplies used, services offered and the efficiency and managerial skills of the franchisee, local economic factors, the density of vehicle ownership, the number of other automotive after-market outlets in a particular market area and the proximity of such competition to the Meineke Center, length of time the center has been in operation and the length of time operating at its current location, type of area (including number of traffic lanes and the type of traffic flow) in which the Center is located, and whether the center is managed by the owner or an employee manager.

Written substantiation of the data used in preparing the chart above will be made available to you on reasonable request.

Some Centers have attained these results. Your individual results may differ. There is no assurance that you will attain the same results.

Other than the preceding financial performance representations, we do not make any financial performance representations. We also do not authorize our employees or representatives to make any such representations either orally or in writing. If you are purchasing an existing center, however, we may provide you with the actual records of that center. If you receive any other financial performance information or projections of your future income, you should report it to the franchisor's management by contacting Paul Clayton, Meineke Car Care Centers, LLC, 440 South Church Street, Suite 700, Charlotte, North Carolina 28202, (704) 377-8855, the Federal Trade Commission, and the appropriate state regulatory agencies.

MOLLY MAID

3948 Ranchero Dr.
Ann Arbor, MI 48108
Tel: (734) 822-6800
Email: julie.ledfor@servicebrands.com
Website: www.mollymaid.com
Julie Ledford, Manager of Franchise Development

For more than 25 years, Molly Maid has offered bonded, insured residential maids who pride themselves in quality home cleaning services that create "me time" for our hardworking homeowners. Last year, Molly Maid franchisees performed 1.46 million "cleans" and 90% were from repeat customers. We also have a 97% customer retention rate.

BACKGROUND

IFA Member:	No
Established & First Franchised:	1979; 1979
Franchised Units:	455
Company-Owned Units:	0
Total Units:	455
Distribution:	US – 455; CAN – 0; O'seas – 0
North America:	44 States
Density:	N/A
Projected New Units (12 Months):	N/A
Qualifications:	N/A

FINANCIAL/TERMS

Cash Investment:	N/A	**SUPPORT & TRAINING**	
Total Investment:	$150 – 175K	Financial Assistance Provided:	Yes (D)
Minimum Net Worth:	N/A	Site Selection Assistance:	Yes
Fees (Franchise):	$14.9K	Lease Negotiation Assistance:	Yes
Fees (Royalty):	3-6.5%	Co-operative Advertising:	No
Fees (Advertising):	$250/mo.	Franchisee Association/Member:	Yes/Member
Term of Contract (Years):	N/A	Size of Corporate Staff:	N/A
Average Number of Employees:	N/A	On-going Support:	A, B, C, D, E, F, G, H, I
Passive Ownership:	Allowed	Training:	N/A
Encourage Conversions:	No		
Area Development Agreements:	No	**SPECIFIC EXPANSION PLANS**	
Sub-Franchising Contracts:	No	US:	No
Expand in Territory:	No	Canada:	No
Space Needs:	N/A	Overseas:	No

The following charts and tables are a historic financial performance representation and are not a forecast of your future financial performance.

As of December 31, 2013, there were 450 MOLLY MAID franchises in the United States. These franchises were owned and operated by 249 Franchise Owners ("Operators") who consolidated their sales for the purpose of reporting. There were 5 additional Franchised Business that had signed but not yet opened. Unless otherwise noted, all charts exclude Operators that ceased operation on or before December 31, 2013.

TABLE 1 – PROFIT AND LOSS STATEMENT FOR OWNERS WHO DID $1,000,000 OR MORE IN 2013

The following charts show the average profit and loss achieved by MOLLY MAID Owners who did over $1,000,000 in Gross Sales in 2013; submitted their year-end profit and loss statement by February 15, 2014; and who have been open 4 or more years, as reported to us by the Operators. 1A shows the average profit and loss for these owners in U.S. dollars. 1B shows the average profit and loss for these owners as a percentage of Gross Sales.

1A – MILLION DOLLAR OWNERS 2013 AVERAGES IN DOLLARS

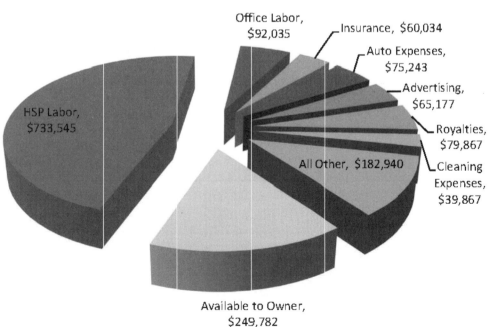

283

Description	Average Sales	High ($)	Low ($)	Number of Operators	Number Above Average	Number Below Average	% Above Average	% Below Average
Gross Sales	$1,548,489	$2,922,911	$1,064,947	20	6	14	30%	70%
HSP Labor	$733,545	$1,704,182	$458,355	20	5	15	25%	75%
Office Labor	$92,035	$182,700	--	20	11	9	55%	45%
Insurance	$60,034	$130,962	$16,114	20	7	13	35%	65%
Auto Expenses	$75,234	$232,056	$15,761	20	8	12	40%	60%
Advertising	$65,177	$152,191	$24,226	20	8	12	40%	60%
Royalties	$79,867	$153,324	$51,929	20	8	12	40%	60%
Cleaning Expenses	$39,867	$84,684	$13,409	20	7	13	35%	65%
All Other	$182,940	$412,248	$85,333	20	8	12	40%	60%
Total Expenses	$1,328,706	$2,485,758	$836,866	20	6	14	30%	70%
Available to Owner	$249,782	$509,047	$117,783	20	7	13	35%	65%

IB - MILLION DOLLAR OWNERS 2013 AVERAGES AS A PERCENT OF GROSS SALE

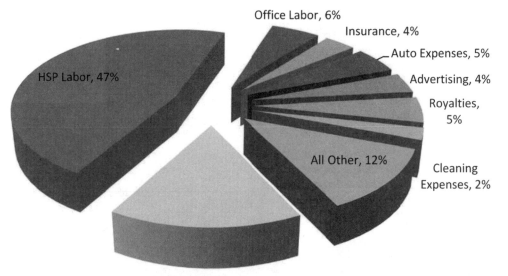

Description	Pecent of Average Sales	High ($)	Low ($)	Number of Operators	Number Above Average	Number Below Average	% Above Average	% Below Average
Gross Sales	100%	100%	100%	20	N/A	N/A	N/A	N/A
HSP Labor	46%	58%	37%	20	6	14	30%	70%
Office Labor	6%	14%	0%	20	12	8	60%	40%
Insurance	4%	9%	1%	20	11	9	55%	45%
Auto Expenses	5%	8%	1%	20	8	12	40%	60%

Advertising	4%	6%	2%	20	8	12	40%	60%
Royalties	5%	7%	3%	20	9	11	45%	55%
Cleaning Expenses	3$	6%	1%	20	9	11	45%	55%
All Other	12%	21%	6%	20	9	11	45%	55%
Total Expenses	84%	90%	75%	20	13	7	65%	35%
Available to Owner	16%	25%	10%	20	7	13	35%	65%

As of December 31, 2013, 16 of the 20 Operators represented in tables 1A and 1B operated multiple MOLLY MAID franchises and each such Operator's results are consolidated for the purposes of this table. The remaining 49 Operators who have been in business four or more years, and achieved over $1,000,000 in Gross Sales in 2013 were excluded because they were unable to turn in their finalized year-end Profit and Loss Statement by February 15, 2014.

TABLE 2 – STATEMENT OF 2013 AVERAGE GROSS SALES INFORMATION BY QUARTILE

Table 2 provides the average Gross Sales information in 2013, by quartile, for all Operators in business for at least two full calendar years as of December 31, 2013. Table 2B provides the average Gross Sales information by quartile, for all mid-market Operators (Item 5) in business for at least two full calendar years as of December 31, 2013. The average Gross Sales numbers are based on the Gross Sales figures for the calendar year 2013 as reported by the Operators directly through the Software, and do not include sales tax.

TABLE 2A – 2013 AVERAGE GROSS SALES BY QUARTILE FOR ALL OPERATORS WHO HAVE BEEN IN BUSINESS FOR AT LEAST TWO CALENDAR YEARS

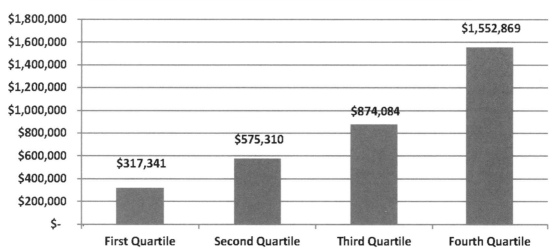

Quartile	First Quartile	Second Quartile	Third Quartile	Fourth Quartile	All Quartiles
Average Gross Sales	$317,341	$575,310	$874,084	$1,552,869	$826,825
High	$436,885	$689,015	$1,093,905	$5,728,792	$5,728,792
Low	$153,435	$437,109	$690,274	$1,101,747	$153,435
Number of Operators	59	59	59	58	235
Number Above Average	28	29	27	14	91
Number Below Average	31	30	32	44	144
Percent Above Average	47%	49%	46%	24%	39%
Percent Below Average	53%	51%	54%	76%	61%

In Table 2, 113 Operators operated multiple MOLLY MAID franchises and each such Operator's results are consolidated for the purposes of this table.

TABLE 3 – STATEMENT OF AVERAGE WEEKLY GROSS SALES INFORMATION BY YEAR FOR ESTABLISHED OPERATORS

The following table provides the average weekly Gross Sales information by year for all established Operators. For this chart, we consider an operator to be established if the business started operation on or before December 31, 2009. The average Gross Sales numbers are based on the Gross Sales figures for the calendar years 2010 to 2013, as reported by the established Operators directly through the Software, and does not include sales tax.

AVERAGE WEEKLY GROSS SALES INFORMATION BY YEAR FOR ESTABLISHED BUSINESSES

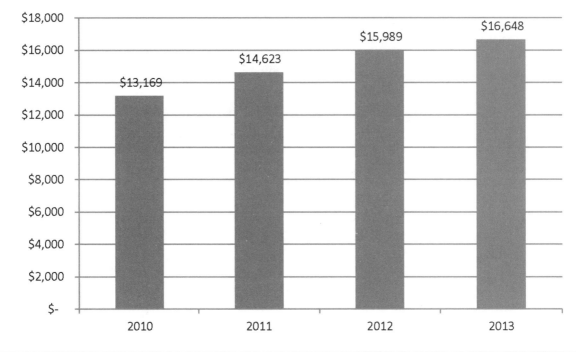

Year	Average Weekly Sales	Number of Operators	High	Low	Number Above Average	Number Below Average	Percent Above Average	Percent Below Average
2010	$13,169	211	$76,184	$3,126	79	133	37%	63%
2011	$14,623	211	$85,268	$3,100	78	134	37%	64%
2012	$15,989	211	$76,184	$3,126	54	158	26%	75%
2013	$16,648	211	$102,426	$3,824	77	135	36%	64%

As of December 31, 2013, 108 Operators represented in this table operated multiple MOLLY MAID franchises and each such Operator's results are consolidated for the purposes of this table.

TABLE 4 – STATEMENT OF AVERAGE PRICE PER CLEAN

The following table provides the Average Price per clean for the years 2009-2013. Years are from January 1 to December 31. The Average was determined by taking the total revenue for all Operators in each year, as they reported to us and dividing it by the total number of cleans that took place by all operators during that year, as they reported to us directly through the Software. Includes all Operators open during the year, regardless of whether they operate one or multiple franchises.

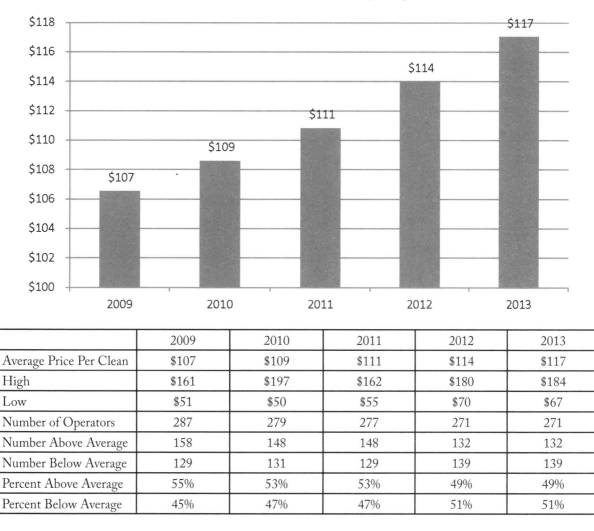

AVERAGE PRICE PER CLEAN 2009-2013

	2009	2010	2011	2012	2013
Average Price Per Clean	$107	$109	$111	$114	$117
High	$161	$197	$162	$180	$184
Low	$51	$50	$55	$70	$67
Number of Operators	287	279	277	271	271
Number Above Average	158	148	148	132	132
Number Below Average	129	131	129	139	139
Percent Above Average	55%	53%	53%	49%	49%
Percent Below Average	45%	47%	47%	51%	51%

Table 5 - Customer Frequency in 2013

The following table and pie chart provide the percentage of cleans performed in 2013 that were performed for recurring customers versus the percentage of cleans performed for occasional customers. Results are as reported to us by the Operators in the Software, and include all Operators open throughout the year, regardless of whether they operate one or multiple franchises.

RECURRING AND OCCASIONAL CUSTOMERS

	Recurring	Occasional
Average	90%	10%
High	99%	59%
Low	41%	1%
Number or Operators	271	271
Number at or Above Average	141	130
Number Below Average	130	141
Percent at or Above Average	52%	48%
Percent Below Average	48%	52%

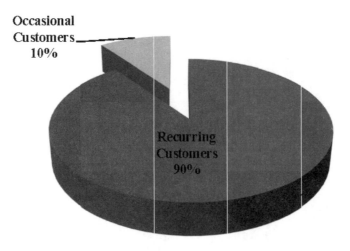

Occasional Customers 10%

Recurring Customers 90%

TABLE 6 – STATEMENT OF AVERAGE CLOSE RATE PER ESTIMATE

The following table shows the average close rate for all estimates performed by all Operators who used the Software to track estimates, and who were opened at any point during the period of January 1, 2012 to December 31, 2012, and January 1, 2013 to December 31, 2013 as reported to us in the Software. The average was determined by taking the total closed estimates and dividing it by the total number of estimates performed during the year.

AVERAGE CLOSE RATE IN 2012 AND 2013 PER ESTIMATE PERFORMED

	2012	2013
Average Close Rate Per Estimate	65%	65%
High	100%	100%
Low	18%	33%
Number of Operators	252	247
Number Above Average	114	106
Number Below Average	138	141
Percent Above Average	45%	43%
Percent Below Average	55%	57%

We do not make any representations or statements of actual, average, projected, or forecasted sales, number of leads, profits or earnings to franchisees except for the information that appears in this Item.

Actual results vary from franchise to franchise, and we cannot estimate the results of a particular franchise. Variations among Operators may be caused by a variety of factors, such as location, demographics, general economic conditions, weather conditions, individual pricing, competition and other seasonal factors, as well as the efforts of the individual Operator and his/her team. Your results may vary depending upon the location of your business. A new franchisee's results are likely to differ from the results shown in this Item. Achieving any sales level is a function of having enough staff and vehicles to adequately meet demand. We recommend that you make your own independent investigation to determine whether or not the franchise may be profitable, and consult with an attorney and other advisors prior to executing the Franchise Agreement.

Table 1 above was prepared from unaudited Annual Profit and Loss Statements, as prepared by the Operators and submitted to us. Tables 2-6 above were prepared from data obtained from the unaudited royalty report statements prepared by Molly Maid, Inc., for the statement periods of January 1 to December 31 for the years 2008-2013, as specified in each chart. Unless otherwise stated, all results only include owners in business as of December 31, 2013. We have in our possession written substantiation of the information used to compile the Franchise Performance Representation. At your written request, we will make this written substantiation available to you.

The Financial Performance Representations do not reflect the costs of sales, operating expenses or other costs or expenses that must be deducted from the gross revenues or gross sales figures to obtain your net income or profit. Gross sales reflect the total average weekly sales for the Operators included in the sample, as reported to us through the Software, and do not include sales tax.

MONEY MAILER

12131 Western Ave.
Garden Grove, CA 92841
Tel: (888) 446-4648, (714) 889-4694
Fax: (800) 819-4322
Email: djenkins@moneymailer.com
Website: www.franchise.moneymailer.com
Dennis Jenkins, Vice President of Franchising Licensing

Money Mailer has re-invented marketing for local businesses. Franchisees become local marketing experts and each operating unit is an in-house ad agency resource for local, community-based businesses in a protected territory. Millions have been invested in targeting technology, digital media components and a game-changing product upgrade to our core offering so franchisees can now show clients how to reach their best prospects in the mail, on the Internet, on mobile devices and social media. Lead generation is provided and there are no royalties for the entire first year. Training and support is unrivaled. An aggressive launch package allows for extremely fast startup, 8 weeks after completion of Money Mailer University. Immediately following MM University the franchisee's personal Coach spends several weeks in the territory to help ensure a successful Grand Opening. Once a campaign is finalized it is sent to Money Mailer for printing, mailing and digital placements.

BACKGROUND

IFA Member	Yes
Established & First Franchised:	1979;1980
Franchised Units:	1947

Company-Owned Units:	40
Total Units:	237
Dist.:	US-237; CAN-0; O'seas-0
North America:	38 States
Density:	44 in CA, 25 in IL, 21 in NJ
Projected New Units (12 Months):	45
Qualifications:	3, 4, 1, 3, 4, 5

FINANCIAL/TERMS

Cash Investment:	$50K
Total Investment	$58K
Minimum Net Worth:	$200K
Fees (Franchise):	$50K
Fees (Royalty):	$250/10K HH mailed
Fees (Advertising):	$0.50/ad sold, matched 100% by MM
Term of Contract (Years):	10/10
Avg. # of Employees:	Owner/operator first year FT
Passive Ownership:	Not Allowed
Encourage Conversions:	No
Area Develop. Agreements:	No
Sub-Franchising Contracts:	No
Expand in Territory:	Yes
Space Needs:	Standard Home Office

SUPPORT & TRAINING

Financial Assistance Provided:	Yes (I)
Site Selection Assistance:	N/A
Lease Negotiation Assistance:	N/A
Co-operative Advertising:	Yes
Franchisee Assoc./Member:	Yes/Member
Size of Corporate Staff:	125
On-going Support:	A, B, C, D, G,H,I
Training:	2 Weeks Corporate Headquarters; 11 Days Field Training in Territory

SPECIFIC EXPANSION PLANS

US:	All United States
Canada:	No
Overseas:	No

We will make written substantiation for the following financial performance representations available to you upon your reasonable request.

Historical Financial Performance Representations for Calendar Year 2013
Relating to Certain Existing Money Mailer Franchised Outlets

Franchisee Groups (Note 1)	Average Total Revenue (Note 2) (+)	Average Total Cost of Goods Sold (Note 3) (-)	Average Gross Profit (Note 4) (=)

	Franchisee Revenue	National Revenue Share	Franchisor Promotional Credits	Mailing Production	Franchisor Charges	
"Single" Territory Outlets (82 Outlets)	$469,463	$3,653	$16,143	$295,971	$69,021	$124,267
"Multi" - Territory Outlets (32 Outlets)	$1,095,700	$10,362	$48,477	$736,228	$120,135	$298,177

Some franchisees have earned this amount. Your individual results may differ. There is no assurance that you'll earn as much.

Notes to Chart:

1. Franchisee Groups.

The above chart provides certain average financial statistics for two subsets of our franchised outlets – single territory outlets (those that mail 4 to 7 zones per mailing) ("Single") and multiterritory outlets (those that mail 8 zones or more per mailing) ("Multi"). For each group, we included only those franchisee outlets in each size category that provided complete sales and revenue data through our AdBooks order entry program and that mailed at least eight shared mailings in 2012 and 2013. Accordingly, of our 237 total 2013 outlets, 114 are included in this analysis (82 Single outlets and 32 of Multi outlets). No data from the non-measured outlets referenced in this note was included in any of the calculations. If separate outlets (which we reflect via separate franchise numbers) were owned by the same person or persons and those outlets were not in distinct markets then for purpose of the calculations in this Item 19 commonly owned and operated outlets were combined to reflect the one practical operational unit being operated by the franchise owner.

AdBooks information is self-reported by our franchisees. We are not able to verify and, thus, have not verified the accuracy of this or any other information entered into AdBooks by franchisees.

As referenced above, we did not include results from our non-established outlets given their unique operating features such as the receipt of one-time Launch Package benefits, the implementation of zone and frequency ramp up schedules and other start up characteristics referenced in this Item 19 and throughout this disclosure. Accordingly, the various metrics for non-established outlets are likely to be significantly lower than those reported in this Item 19.

As referenced above, we also did not include results from our 41 company-owned outlets as they are also operated very differently from our established franchised outlets. Many of our company-owned outlets (referred to as "transitional" outlets) are not staffed with dedicated salespeople and are only maintained for the purpose of accepting cross sales from us and other franchisees and re-licensing to new franchisees. Accordingly, revenues do not reflect the added value of in market staffing for these transitional outlets. For the company-owned outlets that we actively manage, they do not receive the same credits or incur the same costs as franchised outlets (e.g., fixed cost credits, royalties, etc.).

The "Average of Top 25% and "Average of Bottom 25%" groups referenced below were calculated by first multiplying the total revenues for each group (Single and Multi) by 25% to come up with a 25% total revenue number. Then each group was sorted by total revenue and all outlets were included from the top and the bottom until the 25% total revenue number was achieved.

2. Revenue Metrics

Mailing Statistics (Averages)	Average of Top 25%		Average of Bottom 25%		Overall Average	
	Single	Multi	Single	Multi	Single	Multi
Shared Mailings Per Year	10	12	10	10	10	12
Piece Count Per Zone Per Shared Mailing	88	44	21	21	38	32

Franchisee revenues are a function of how many advertising "spots" are sold and for how much. A "spot" is a single advertisement in a single zone. For example, the same advertisement placed in five zones would be five spots. We calculated average piece count by taking all spots sold by an outlet (whether within the outlet's own zones or cross sold out) and dividing by the number of zones mailed by that outlet. This number does not represent the number of pieces in a particular envelope. This number will be higher for those outlets that mail a small number of zones (e.g. 4 or 5 per mailing) but who sell spots across many zones outside their territory.

Sales prices are highly variable and depend on numerous factors, including average zones sold per order, product mix, competition, economic factors in your market or geography and your sales and, if applicable, your sales management abilities. Also if an outlet barters or trades for services in return for advertising or offers a "buy one get one free" (or "BOGO") incentive for advertisements or mailings, these spots can be reflected as $0. On the other hand, highly desirable zones may have very high per spot sales prices.

Given this wide range in sales prices and the unique local characteristics that often drive such prices, we recommend that you contact a number of Money Mailer franchisees to discuss typical sales prices as well as other operational and financial information and to compare their experience with the information that we provide. Except as otherwise described in the franchise agreement, franchisees have the right to set their own sales prices. In talking to franchisees about sales prices for advertising, be sure to distinguish between their asking price (also referred to as their "rate card") and their actual selling price for advertising, and to ask what kinds of discounts they provide for volume purchases or annual contracts with advertisers, such as the BOGOs referenced above. Given the factors above and given that franchisee revenue below includes cross sale fees received from us or other franchisees, you should not attempt to use the spots above to calculate an average sales price.

Revenue (Averages per zone per mailing, unless otherwise noted)	Average of Top 25%		Average of Bottom 25%		Overall Average	
	Single	Multi	Single	Multi	Single	Multi
Franchisee Revenue	$18,848	$10,111	$6,018	$5,708	$9,229	$7,733
National Revenue	$73	$71	$74	$70	$72	$73
Franchisor Promotional Credits	$644	$350	$193	$303	$317	$342

Franchisee revenue includes all shared mailing sales by an outlet whether into their own zones or any other zones operated by us or other franchisees. It also includes cross sales fees received by the outlet for sales by us or other franchisees into the outlet's zones. Cross sales (and the payment or receipt of cross sale fees) depend on a number of factors, including your sales skills, the location of your territory and the number of franchisees around your territory. We cannot guarantee that you will receive or pay any cross sale fees. See Item 12 for more information on cross sale fees. Franchisee revenue excludes any one to one, digital or other non-shared mailing sales.

National revenue paid to outlets includes revenue we pay to franchisees in exercising our reserved advertising rights, which include national insert revenue sharing, remnant insert bonus and any fees we pay for pre-existing inserts. National insert accounts and pre-existing accounts do not necessarily mail in all available zones in the country and may not mail in your zones. Accordingly, you may or may not receive national insert revenue sharing or pre-existing insert fees. All franchisees receive a remnant insert bonus based on the duplicated zones they mail.

While we are not required to do so, we have been providing promotional credits for many years. For 2013, these promotional credits included: annual convention credits, early payment discounts, zone expansion credits, sales incentive promotion credits, mailing frequency credits, and print discounts. We are not required to provide any promotional credits in the future. As part of the franchise agreement, we also offer a high piece count bonus program and launch package that have been included in promotional credits.

The 2013 franchisee revenue information (including cross sale information) for the franchised outlets in each group was obtained from reports provided by franchisees and placed in our AdBooks order entry system. This is self-reported information. We are not able to verify, and have not verified, such information. Other 2013 revenue information for such outlets (for cross sales we place in our franchisees' envelopes) was provided by our unaudited production records. The data source for our national revenue and the franchisor promotional credits is our unaudited accounting books and records.

3. Cost of Goods Sold Metrics

Cost of Goods Sold (Averages per zone per mailing, unless otherwise noted)	Average of Top 25%		Average of Bottom 25%		Overall Average	
	Single	Multi	Single	Multi	Single	Multi

Mailing Production - Printing (per spot)	$91	$90	$102	$102	$95	$95
Mailing Production - Fulfillment Fixed Costs	$645	$675	$687	$644	$673	$641
Mailing Production - Delivery Costs	$1,623	$1,544	$1,577	$1,563	$1,582	$1,568
Franchisor Charges (per Franchise Agreement)	$3,221	$1,213	$705	$535	$1,357	$848

Printing charges are variable depending on the product and number of zones ordered. Printing charges for non-established franchisees are often higher because they are more likely to begin selling smaller accounts and a smaller number of zones per order.

Fulfillment fixed costs take into account the $800 per zone fulfillment fixed cost in 2013 for envelopes, addressing, mailing lists and inserting, net of the fulfillment fixed cost discounts we provide in the franchise agreement. These costs will generally be higher for non-established franchisees because they are mailing less duplicated zones in their first year and only receive the minimum 10% fulfillment fixed cost discount.

Delivery costs take into account the $1,460 per zone net postage cost in 2013 ($1,890 less $430 USPS discount for trucking the envelopes to the franchisee's USPS delivery center) plus average freight and any overweight postage. (Please be aware that the fixed costs reflected in Item 6 include 2014 postage charges of $1,530 per zone net postage cost ($1,980 less $450 USPS discount)). Freight costs are highly variable depending on the distance between the production facility and the franchisee's USPS delivery center. We highly suggest you discuss freight charges with existing franchisees near your territory.

Your own production costs may differ from those set forth above because of the number of variables which affect pricing. MMLLC's pricing is subject to change at any time upon thirty (30) days' notice to you.

Franchisor charges include royalties, marketing fee, any back of the envelope usage fees paid to us and any cross sale fees paid to us or other franchisees. Outlets that sell more cross sales will have higher franchisor charges given the higher number of cross sale fees they are required to pay.

Some costs are not included in the cost of goods sold because they depend on local characteristics (state and local sales taxes) or they are optional. We have excluded the charges for the following optional services: pre-printed inserts (or "PPIs") (which are inserts that you may have had printed elsewhere but wish to insert in your shared mailings); sample ads and envelopes (and their related Federal Express charges); in-store point-of-purchase displays for clients; banner ads; digital advertising, one to one advertising and trade show booths. We have also excluded cancellation charges and NSF fees, ad revision charges and late fees.

Franchisees obtain art services from us or from independent artists registered with us. As the majority of the system uses independent artists for some or all of their art services, we have excluded art costs from cost of goods sold as the figures are not representative of the entire franchise system. Of the outlets that obtained art and AdEase services from us in 2013, their average cost per spot was $1.60. Unless you are obtaining an existing franchise and inheriting existing art files, your costs will be higher because you incur additional charges for initial art building. Also, if you use an independent artist, you will not have the ability to create editable AdEase art templates, which could increase your art costs. Art charges also vary by provider, so be sure to speak with franchisees in your market before purchasing any art services.

Information regarding the cost of goods sold in 2013 also was derived from our unaudited accounting books and records.

4. Gross Profit Metrics

Gross Profit Metrics (Averages)	Average of Top 25%		Average of Bottom 25%		Overall Average	
	Single	Multi	Single	Multi	Single	Multi
Gross Profit (per outlet)	$352,934	$759,967	$56,345	$98,659	$124,267	$298,177
Gross Profit (per zone)	$6,059	$3,119	$1,195	$1,250	$2,443	$2,104

Average gross profit per outlet was determined by adding average franchisee revenue, average national revenue share and average franchisor promotional credits and then subtracting average mailing production and franchisor charges. This formula only produces a rough estimate since the statistics added and subtracted are themselves the result of "average" calculations. Thirty Single outlets (37% of the measured Single outlets) surpassed the average gross profit for the group. Thirteen Multi outlets (41% of the measured Multi outlets) surpassed the average gross profit for the group.

General Notes Regarding Data; Suggestions

5. Collection rates will vary from market to market, especially where an outlet has allowed clients to pay slowly in the past. It is highly suggested that you develop and adhere to a strict collection policy.

6. The above financial performance representations do not cover overhead expenses, such as office rent, office staff salaries (including any salespeople you may hire), your own salary, phone/fax charges, office postage and courier charges, travel, bad debt expenses, auto expenses, insurance costs, advertising expenses and the costs of your marketing materials. These items are based largely on factors in your control (for example, you may operate from a home office). See Items 6 and 7 (and Item 10 if you obtain any financing from us) for a description of certain other expense items that you are likely to incur in acquiring and operating a Money Mailer franchise. There are likely to be additional expenses that we have not listed, some of which may be unique to your market or situation.

7. The above information is presented to assist you in conducting your own investigation for the purpose of evaluating the purchase of a Money Mailer franchise. It is your sole responsibility to do your own research before purchasing a Money Mailer franchise. We cannot provide you with all of the financial information concerning the operation of a Money Mailer franchise because the results often will vary significantly between franchisees and many of the expense items you should consider are unknown to us and frequently within your control.

8. The performance of franchisees varies dramatically between

markets for a variety of reasons, including, for example, differences in sales and management abilities, demographics, financing availability and sources, the economic and business environment in a particular market, the history of a particular franchise and the strength of competing advertisers in a given market. You cannot assume that the information provided to you by a Money Mailer franchisee is necessarily relevant to your market. If you are buying an existing Money Mailer franchise, it is your responsibility to verify the seller's historical financial information. We do not review franchisees' financial statements and we have no responsibility for the accuracy or completeness of the same.

9. You should also research the prices charged by competing advertisers in your prospective market to determine the degree of price competition you will face. Even if a selling franchisee has historically sold advertising at above-average prices in his or her market, it is not safe to assume that you will be able to charge those same prices in the future, especially if major competitors are providing significant price competition.

10. Finally, the information above does not address many of the variables that can affect your revenue, expenses or cash flow. It is intended merely as a starting place for your analysis. Reviewing this limited amount of information cannot substitute for thorough research on your part and a careful evaluation of this franchise opportunity with professional financial and legal advisors.

Other than the preceding financial performance representations, we do not make any representations about a franchisee's future financial performance or the past financial performance of company-owned or franchised outlets. We also do not authorize our employees or representatives to make any such representations either orally or in writing. If you are purchasing an existing outlet, however, we may provide you with the actual records of that outlet. If you receive any other financial performance information or projections of your future income, you should report it to the franchisor's management by contacting Joseph Craciun, Vice President and General Counsel, Money Mailer Franchise Corp., 12131 Western Avenue, Garden Grove, California 92841, Telephone: (714) 889-3822, the Federal Trade Commission, and the appropriate state regulatory agencies.

MOSQUITO SQUAD

2924 Emerywood Pkwy., # 101
Richmond, VA 23294
Tel: (800) 722-4668, (804) 353-6999 x101
Fax: (804) 358-1878
Email: rwhite@outdoorlivingbrands.com
Website: www.mosquitosquadfranchise.com
Rob White, Vice President Development

Mosquito Squad is North America's fastest growing outdoor living franchise concept with an incredible, high-margin recurring revenue stream. Since joining the Outdoor Living Brands' franchise lineup in 2009, Mosquito Squad has been experiencing explosive franchise unit and consumer sales growth. Clients want to take back their backyards by combating annoying insect bites and protecting their families and pets from the dangerous diseases such as Lyme Disease, Encephalitis and West Nile Virus.

BACKGROUND

IFA Member:	Yes
Established & First Franchised:	2004; 2005
Franchised Units:	142
Company-Owned Units:	0
Total Units:	142
Distribution:	US – 142; CAN – 0; O'seas – 0

North America:	29 States, 0 Provinces
Density:	13 in NC, 10 in MI, 10 in NY
Projected New Units (12 Months):	25
Qualifications:	5, 5, 1, 3, 3, 4

FINANCIAL/TERMS

Cash Investment:	$50K
Total Investment:	$35 – 75K
Minimum Net Worth:	$100K
Fees (Franchise):	$25K
Fees (Royalty):	$400 – $1,900 monthly
Fees (Advertising):	$100 – $400 monthly
Term of Contract (Years):	7/7
Average Number of Employees:	1 FT, 2 PT
Passive Ownership:	Discouraged
Encourage Conversions:	Yes
Area Development Agreements:	Yes
Sub-Franchising Contracts:	No
Expand in Territory:	Yes
Space Needs:	N/A

SUPPORT & TRAINING

Financial Assistance Provided:	Yes (D)
Site Selection Assistance:	N/A
Lease Negotiation Assistance:	N/A
Co-operative Advertising:	No
Franchisee Association/Member:	No
Size of Corporate Staff:	30
On-going Support:	b, C, D, E, F, G, h, I
Training:	4-5 Days depending on class size Richmond, VA

SPECIFIC EXPANSION PLANS

US:	All United States
Canada:	No
Overseas:	No

Actual results will vary from franchise to franchise, territory to territory and market to market, and we cannot estimate the results for any particular franchise. Except as provided by applicable law, we will not be bound by allegations of any unauthorized representation as to sales, income, profits, or prospects or chances for success, and you will be required to acknowledge that you have not relied on any such representation in purchasing your franchise. We have provided this information to help you to make a more informed decision regarding our franchise system. You should not use this information as an indication of how your specific franchise business may perform. The success of your franchise will depend largely on your individual abilities and your market. The actual numbers you experience will be influenced by a wide variety of factors including your management, market size and demographics and competition. You should conduct your own independent research and due diligence to assist you in preparing your own projections.

Written substantiation of the data used in preparing the financial performance representations included in this Item 19 will be made available to you upon reasonable request.

A. Average Gross Revenues for MOSQUITO SQUAD Franchisees for the 12 Months Ending December 31, 2013

The following table presents the average annual Gross Revenues realized by certain MOSQUITO SQUAD franchisees in

2013. "Total Gross Revenues" mean the total "Gross Revenues" (as defined in the Franchise Agreement) received by the reporting franchisees in 2013, as reported by the franchisees. Each MOSQUITO SQUAD franchisee's operating season will vary depending on the location of their Territory. As used in this Item 19, "Operating Season" refers to a calendar year beginning on January 1st and ending on December 31st.

As of December 31, 2013, there were 142 MOSQUITO SQUAD franchisees. The information provided in the table below was compiled from the 112 MOSQUITO SQUAD franchisees that were operational for all of the 2013 Operating Season. The data excludes 30 MOSQUITO SQUAD franchisees that either signed franchise agreements and began operations during the 2013 Operating Season or did not collect any Gross Revenues during the 2013 Operating Season, or any franchisees that

ceased operations during the 2013 Operating Season.

While all of the 112 MOSQUITO SQUAD businesses were operational for all of the 2013 Operating Season, the length of their spraying season varied depending on the region of the country in which they are located. Although the table below only contains information for the 112 of the 142 MOSQUITO SQUAD franchisees as of December 31, 2013, the Total Gross Revenues of the 112 franchisees for the 2013 Operating Season represents 99.2% of the Total Gross Revenues reported to us by all MOSQUITO SQUAD franchisees for the 2013 Operating Season. The table below presents minimum, average and maximum Total Gross Revenues for the 2013 Operating Season for the MOSQUITO SQUAD franchisees in operation for the full 2013 Operating Season by their number of Operating Seasons in business.

	# of Franchisees	Gross Revenue in Dollars			% of Franchisees	# of Franchises above average (and %)
		Minimum	Average	Maximum		
7 or More Full Seasons	5	331,596	850,233	2,084,401	4.5%	1 (20%)
At Least 6 Full Seasons	4	164,834	570,631	1,275,965	3.6%	1 (25%)
At Least 5 Full Seasons	1	130,182	130,182	130,182	0.9%	1 (100%)
At Least 4 Full Seasons	31	24,615	154,999	417,857	27.7%	11 (36%)
At Least 3 Full Seasons	20	17,849	132,509	276,671	17.9%	8 (40%)
At Least 2 Full Seasons	24	8,424	73,923	258,526	21.4%	10 (42%)
At Least 1 Full Season	27	6,238	42,085	155,977	24.1%	13 (48%)
Franchisees	112				100.0%	

The Gross Revenue figures presented above represent the Total Gross Revenues of outdoor pest control services sold by the 112 franchises listed above in the 2013 Operating Season. The financial performance representations above do not reflect the costs of sales, brand licensing fees or operating expenses that must be deducted from the sales figures to obtain a net income or owner's profit number. The best source of cost and expense data may be from current or former franchisees as listed in this disclosure document.

B. Revenue per Spray and Sprays Per Customer Study for Certain MOSQUITO SQUAD Franchisees for Operating Season Ending December 31, 2013

The information provided in the tables below is based on information reported to us from 112 of the 142 total MOSQUITO SQUAD franchisees ("Reporting Franchisees") whose MOSQUITO SQUAD businesses were operational for all of the 2013 Operating Season. While all of the Reporting Franchisees' MOSQUITO SQUAD businesses were operational for all of the 2013 Operating Season, the length of their spraying season may have varied depending on the region of the country

in which they are located.

The table excludes 30 MOSQUITO SQUAD franchisees that either signed franchise agreements and began operations during the 2013 Operating Season or did not collect any Gross Revenues during the 2013 Operating Season, or ceased active operations during the 2013 Operating Season.

Although the tables below only contain information for the 112 Reporting Franchisees out of the 142 total MOSQUITO SQUAD franchisees as of December 31, 2013, the Total Gross Revenues (as defined above in Section A) of the Reporting Franchisees for the 2013 Operating Season represent 99.2% of the Total Gross Revenues reported to us by all MOSQUITO SQUAD franchisees for the 2013 Operating Season.

The tables below present average Revenue per Spray and the average Sprays per Customer for the Reporting Franchisees during the 2013 Operating Season. The table also categorizes the information as to how many Operating Seasons each Reporting Franchisee has been in operation.

	Gross Revenue per Spray						
	# of Franchisees	Minimum	Maximum	Average	# of Franchisees above average	Median	# of Franchisees above median
7 or More Full Seasons	5	$58.28	$222.55	$117.16	2 (40%)	$99.42	3 (60%)
At Least 6 Full Seasons	4	$60.07	$70.79	$66.79	2 (50%)	$68.15	2 (50%)
At Least 5 Full Seasons	1	$59.55	$59.55	$59.55	1 (100%)	$59.55	1 (100%)
At Least 4 Full Seasons	31	$40.08	$385.33	$93.12	6 (19%)	$67.05	16 (52%)
At Least 3 Full Seasons	20	$50.85	$121.92	$95.34	10 (50%)	$98.66	10 (50%)
At Least 2 Full Seasons	24	$23.22	$171.60	$79.70	9 (37.5%)	$77.02	12 (50%)
At Least 1 Full Season	27	$16.78	$158.06	$80.68	11 (41%)	$75.21	14 (52%)
Franchisees	112			$87.47	39 (35%)	$75.21	57 (51%)

	Sprays per Customer					
	Minimum	Maximum	Average	# of Franchisees above average	Median	# of Franchisees above median
7 or More Full Seasons	2.6	6.9	4.7	2 (40%)	4.6	3 (60%)
At Least 6 Full Seasons	4.5	7.2	5.8	2 (50%)	5.8	2 (50%)
At Least 5 Full Seasons	4.2	4.2	4.2	1 (100%)	4.2	1 (100%)
At Least 4 Full Seasons	0.2	9.4	4.9	15 (48%)	4.8	15 (48%)
At Least 3 Full Seasons	2.9	7.2	4.8	8 (40%)	4.5	15 (75%)
At Least 2 Full Seasons	2.0	5.8	3.6	13 (54%)	3.8	13 (54%)
At Least 1 Full Season	1.8	5.6	3.2	12 (44%)	3.0	14 (52%)

C. Gross Margin Study for Certain MOSQUITO SQUAD Franchisees for the Operating Season ending December 31, 2012

We do not provide prospective franchisees with projections of income, profits or earnings. There is no guarantee that you, as a new MOSQUITO SQUAD franchisee, will attain the same level of sales or profits that have been attained by our existing franchisees. The success of your franchise will depend largely on your individual abilities and your market. However, we do provide prospective franchisees with information from a financial benchmarking study (the "Benchmarking Study") that we conducted for the MOSQUITO SQUAD franchise system.

In 2013, we conducted a financial Benchmarking Study for MOSQUITO SQUAD franchisees. We asked all 111 MOSQUITO SQUAD franchisees operating as of December 31, 2012 to submit their income statements for the year ending December 31, 2012. We then calculated certain financial metrics to allow participants to compare their financial performance against their peer group of MOSQUITO SQUAD franchisees. 85 out of 111 (77%) MOSQUITO SQUAD franchisees participated in the Benchmarking Study. The other 26 MOSQUITO SQUAD FRANCHISEES either did not participate in the Benchmarking program or did not operate for the complete 2012 Operating Season. Although the table below only contains information for the 85 participating Franchisees out of the 111 total MOSQUITO SQUAD franchisees as of December 31, 2012, the Total Gross Revenues (as defined above in Section A) of the participating Franchisees for the 2012 Operating Season represent 97.5% of the Total Gross Revenues reported to us by all MOSQUITO SQUAD franchisees for the 2012 Operating Season. We have reviewed the composition of franchise participants and believes it contains a random, representative sampling of MOSQUITO SQUAD franchisees based on level of sales, years in the business and geography.

As defined in the Benchmarking Study, Gross Profit Margin measures profitability after material and direct labor to provide each barrier spray application are subtracted from gross revenue to calculate gross profit dollars. Gross Profit Margin is then calculated by dividing gross profit dollars by gross revenues. While Gross Profit Margin measures profitability after material, and direct labor are subtracted from gross revenue, it excludes brand licensing fees, vehicle and fuel expenses, and any other operating expenses.

The table below presents average Gross Profit Margin for the participating franchisees during the 2012 Operating Season. The table also categorizes the information into thirds based on total reported Gross Profit Margin for 2012.

	# of Franchisees	2012 Average Gross Margin %	# of Franchises above average
Top Third	28.00	77.9%	11 (39.3%)
Middle Third	29.00	67.4%	15 (51.7%)
Bottom Third	28.00	47.5%	18 (64.3%)
Franchisees	85.00	64.3%	52 (61.2%)

Note (1): Average Gross Profit Margin was calculated by dividing the total gross profit by the total Gross Revenue as reported to us by the franchisees in each group. Gross profit is comprised of Gross Revenues less the cost of goods and labor. Gross profit excludes non-cash items (such as depreciation and amortization), interest expense (if any), and operating expenses such as marketing, insurance, office supplies, rent, and federal, state and local taxes, and thus does not represent net profits. Gross profit margins exclude brand licensing fees, vehicle and fuel expenses, and any other operating expenses.

Note (2): 12 of the 28 MOSQUITO SQUAD franchisees in the top third are in their first or second year of operation. As such, some of these franchisees are performing barrier spray applications themselves and do not compensate themselves for the direct cost of labor to provide each barrier spray. This partially explains the higher level of reported Gross Profit Margin in the top third.

D. Client Renewal Rates for Certain MOSQUITO SQUAD Franchisees for the Operating Season ending December 31, 2013

The information provided in the table below is based on information reported to us from 76 of the 85 MOSQUITO SQUAD franchisees whose MOSQUITO SQUAD businesses were operational for the entire 2012 and 2013 Operating Seasons (the "Qualifying Franchisees"). The other 9 MOSQUITO SQUAD franchisees who were operational for the complete 2012 and 2013 Operating Seasons are not included on the table below because they failed to report to us all of the information we needed in order to include them. The table also excludes 57 current MOSQUITO SQUAD franchisees as of December 31, 2013, who were not active for the entire 2013 and 2012 Operating Seasons because they (i) signed franchise agreements or began operations after the start of the 2012 Operating Season, and only operated for a partial season in 2012; (ii) signed franchise agreements in 2013 and were not operational during the 2013 Operating Season; or (iii) ceased active operations during the 2012 or 2013 Operating Seasons.

Although the table below only contains information for the 76 Qualifying Franchisees, we have reviewed the composition of Qualifying Franchisees and believes it contains a random, representative sampling of MOSQUITO SQUAD franchisees based on level of sales, years in the business and geography. In addition, although the table below only contains information for the 76 Qualifying Franchisees out of the 142 total MOSQUITO SQUAD franchisees as of December 31, 2013, the Total Gross Revenues (as defined above in Section A) of the Qualifying Franchisees for the 2013 Operating Season represent 75.2% of the Total Gross Revenues reported to us by all MOSQUITO SQUAD franchisees for the 2013 Operating Season.

We have calculated the number of customers that purchased two or more applications of MOSQUITO SQUAD services in the 2012 Operating Season and then subsequently renewed their service for the entire 2013 Operating Season ("Renewal Customers"). The "Customer Renewal Rate" is calculated by dividing the number of Renewal Customers by the total number of full season customers with two or more applications for the 2012 Operating Season. Only customers that had contracted for an more than two applications of service in 2012 and the entire year of service in 2013 were included in the calculation of the Customer Renewal Rates.

Number of Franchisees	Minimum Customer Renewals	Maximum Customer Renewals	Average Customer Renewal Rate	Number of Franchisees At or Above the Average (and %)	Median Customer Renewals	Number of Franchisees At or Above the Median (and %)
76	25.0%	100.0%	73.1%	35 (46.1%)	72.1%	38 (50.0%)

E. MOSQUITO SQUAD Franchise System Sales for the Six Calendar Years Ending December 31, 2013

The information provided in the table below is based on aggregate Gross Revenues ("System Sales") reported to us from all MOSQUITO SQUAD franchisees whose MOSQUITO SQUAD businesses were operational for any part, even as little as one month if the franchisee completed initial training in December of their initial year of operations, of each calendar year ended December 31, 2008 through December 31, 2013.

| Mosquito Squad System Sales from 2008-2013 | | |
| Years Ending December 31 | | |
Year	System Sales	Number of Franchisees as of Calendar Year End
2008	1,378,709	18
2009	1,980,555	45
2010	4,256,968	64
2011	7,717,305	87
2012	12,458,000	111
2013	17,162,823	142

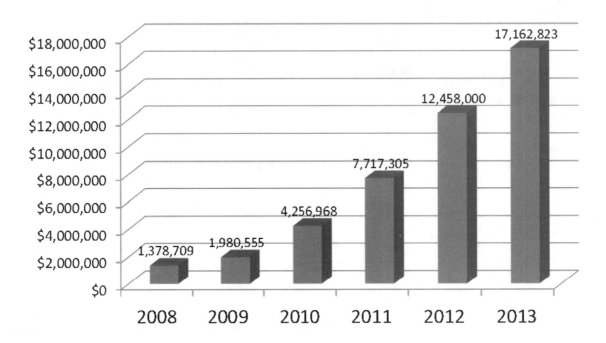

The above results are provided to prospective franchisees in evaluating the experience of certain existing MOSQUITO SQUAD franchisees and not as a projection or forecast of what a new MOSQUITO SQUAD franchisee may experience. A new franchisee's financial results are likely to differ from the results provided above.

Some MOSQUITO SQUAD franchisees have experienced the above results. Your individual results may differ. There is no assurance that you will perform as well.

The financial information we utilized in preparing the preceding financial performance representations was based entirely upon information reported to us by MOSQUITO SQUAD franchisees. None of this information was audited or otherwise reviewed or investigated by us or by any independent accountant or auditing firm, and no one has audited, reviewed or otherwise evaluated this information for accuracy or expressed his/her opinion with regard to its content or form.

The figures in the tables above do not reflect other fixed and variable costs and expenses associated with operating a MOSQUITO SQUAD franchise, including officer's salaries, administrative salaries, automobile expenses, insurance costs and advertising and marketing expenses, which must be deducted from the Gross Revenues to obtain your net income or profit. You should conduct an independent investigation of your potential Gross Revenues and the costs and expenses you will incur in operating your MOSQUITO SQUAD business. Franchisees or former franchisees, listed in this disclosure document, may be valuable source of this information.

In preparing any pro forma financial projections, you and other prospective franchisees must keep in mind that each individual franchisee's experience is unique and results may vary, depending on a number of factors. These factors include general economic conditions of the franchisee's territory, length of the franchisee's spraying season, demographics, competition, and effectiveness of the franchisee in the management of the franchised business and the use of the MOSQUITO SQUAD operating systems, scope of investment and the overall efficiency of the franchise operation.

You are responsible for developing your own business plan for your MOSQUITO SQUAD franchise, including capital budgets, financial statements, projections, pro forma financial statements and other elements appropriate to your particular circumstances. In preparing your business plan, we encourage you to consult with your own accounting, business and legal advisors to assist you to identify the expenses you likely will incur in connection with your MOSQUITO SQUAD franchise, to prepare your budgets, and to assess the likely or potential financial performance of your MOSQUITO SQUAD franchise.

In developing the business plan for your MOSQUITO SQUAD

franchise, you are cautioned to make necessary allowance for changes in financial results to income, expenses or both that may result from operation of your MOSQUITO SQUAD franchise during periods of, or in geographic areas suffering from, economic downturns, inflation, unemployment, or other negative economic influences.

Other than the preceding financial performance representations, we do not make any financial performance representations. We also do not authorize our employees or representatives to make any such representations either orally or in writing. If you are purchasing an existing outlet, however, we may provide you with the actual records of that outlet. If you receive any other financial performance information or projections of your future income, you should report it to the franchisor's management by contacting Chris Grandpre, Mosquito Squad Franchising Corporation, 2924 Emerywood Parkway, Suite 101, Richmond, Virginia 23294, (804) 353-6999, the Federal Trade Commission, and the appropriate state regulatory agencies.

MR. ROOTER

1010-1020 N. University Parks Dr.
Waco, TX 76707
Tel: (800) 298-6855, (254) 759-5820
Email: sam.thurman@dwyergroup.com
Website: www.mrrooter.com
Sam Thurman, Franchise Development Team Leader

Established in 1970, Mr. Rooter is an all-franchised, full-service plumbing and drain cleaning company with approximately 300 franchises worldwide. Recognized by Entrepreneur magazine among its "Franchise 500" and Franchise Times Top 200, Mr. Rooter franchisees provide services to both residential and commercial customers. Mr. Rooter began franchising in 1974 and is part of The Dwyer Group family of companies, which also includes Rainbow International, Aire Serv, Mr. Electric, Mr. Appliance, The Grounds Guys, and Glass Doctor.

BACKGROUND

IFA Member:	Yes
Established & First Franchised:	1970; 1974
Franchised Units:	241
Company-Owned Units:	0
Total Units:	241
Distribution:	US – 212; CAN – 27; O'seas – 2
North America:	48 States, 7 Provinces
Density:	32 in CA, 18 in TX, 15 in OH
Projected New Units (12 Months):	25
Qualifications:	4, 3, 3, 2, 3, 5

FINANCIAL/TERMS

Cash Investment:	$40 – 79K
Total Investment:	$68.4 – 162.6K+
Minimum Net Worth:	$100K
Fees (Franchise):	$30K/100K pop. + $300/1K add'l pop.
Fees (Royalty):	5-7%
Fees (Advertising):	2%
Term of Contract (Years):	10/10
Average Number of Employees:	Varies
Passive Ownership:	Allowed
Encourage Conversions:	Yes
Area Development Agreements:	No
Sub-Franchising Contracts:	No
Expand in Territory:	Yes
Space Needs:	N/A

SUPPORT & TRAINING		On-going Support:	A, C, D, E, G, H
Financial Assistance Provided:	Yes (D)	Training:	5 Days, Waco, TX
Site Selection Assistance:	N/A		
Lease Negotiation Assistance:	N/A	**SPECIFIC EXPANSION PLANS**	
Co-operative Advertising:	Yes	US:	Uncovered Areas
Franchisee Association/Member:	No	Canada:	Selected Areas
Size of Corporate Staff:	25	Overseas:	No

Report on Average Gross Sales, Average Gross Sales Per Work Order and Gross Sales For the Period January 1, 2013 to December 31, 2013.

The sales figures listed below include Gross Sales averages, average Gross Sales per work order and Gross Sales derived from historical operating results of the franchised businesses indicated for the time periods covered. We obtained these sales figures from information provided to us by our franchisees for the period from January 1, 2013 through December 31, 2013. Neither we nor our independent certified public accountants have audited or verified any of the sales figures reported to us. We make no representations as to the accuracy of sales reported by our franchisees or the extent to which these sales figures were derived using generally accepted accounting principles. The sales listed below are not intended to represent the actual results that would likely be realized by any specific franchised business during any period.

The information in this report has been prepared by us without an audit. Our independent auditors, BDO USA, LLP have not audited, reviewed or performed any level of service on the information. Accordingly, they provide no form of assurance as to the accuracy of the information in this report.

As of December 31, 2013, we had 212 franchised businesses in operation in the U.S. Of these, 189 franchised businesses were in operation for the full 12 months of 2013 and reporting Gross Sales. Although all our franchised businesses that were open for a full 12 months in 2013 reported sales to us and we used those reports to provide information in the charts that present Gross Sales and Average Gross Sales below, there are 31 franchised businesses that did not report Gross Sales using our proprietary software through the Reporting Period and these franchised businesses were excluded from the chart showing average Gross Sales per work order since we do not have the necessary data to calculate average revenue per work order for these businesses. Because the number of franchised businesses open during 2013 fluctuated during the year, in order to determine the number and percentage of businesses that achieved the stated sales results locations that were not in operation for the full 12 months of 2013 are not included in the information provided below. We did not include, for

example, any new franchised business that began operation during 2013, or any franchised businesses that were operating during the year, but ceased operations during 2013. These franchised businesses would likely have average sales figures that are different than the figures reported below and for the franchised businesses that ceased operations the average sales figures would likely have been lower.

All of the franchised businesses for which sales results are reported below were operated by franchisees. We did not operate any of the businesses. All of the franchised businesses are comparable to the franchised businesses offered by this disclosure document and offered substantially the same services to the public. You should be aware, however, that the franchised businesses for which sales results are reported below include some businesses that are "conversions," businesses that were in operation before purchasing a franchise and "converting" from an independent business to a business utilizing our system and brand.

No adjustments, including adjustments for geographic location, have been made to these reported sales. In addition, the information in this report is based on sales in one 52 week period. This report does not include information about previous periods or try to estimate or predict what may occur in any future periods. Also, because these are Gross Sales results only, no costs or expenses are taken into account. Profits resulting from any given level of Gross Sales may differ substantially from one business to another. Sales and profit results are directly impacted by various factors, including: competition from other similar businesses in the area; the quality of management and service in a franchisee's operations as well as the extent to which the franchisee follows established systems, policies and guidelines; contractual relationships and terms with individual landlords and suppliers; the cost of capital and the extent to which a franchisee might have financed its operations; legal, accounting, and other professional fees; federal, state, and local income and other taxes; and discretionary expenditures. You should therefore use the information in this report only as a general reference when conducting your own analysis. Except for the information that appears in this report, we do not furnish or authorize our salespersons or affiliates to furnish any oral or written information or representations or statements of actual sales, costs, income or profits. We encourage you to carefully review this material with your attorney, business advisor and/or accountant.

Your individual sales and financial results are likely to differ from the results shown, possibly significantly and adversely.

Written substantiation for these financial performance representations will be made available to a prospective franchisee upon reasonable request.

Average Gross Sales in 2013 Attained by Franchised Business
in Business 12 Months or More[1] With Full 12 Months of Sales in 2013

Percentage Rank (in Terms of Level of Gross Sales) of Franchised Businesses in Business 12 Months or More	Average Gross Sales Attained by This Group	Number in This Group	Number in Group That Attained This Level of Sales or Greater	Percent in Group That Attained This Level of Sales or Greater	Number and Percent of All Franchised Businesses Open for Full 12 Months in 2013 that Attained this Level of Sales or Greater
Top 10%	$4,071,255	19	6	32%	6/3%
Top 25%	$2,683,756	47	15	32%	15/8%
Top 50%	$1,817,319	95	31	33%	31/16%
100% (All Franchisees)	$1,070,406	189	63	33%	63/33%

[1] Of the 212 franchised businesses in operation at December 31, 2013, 189 franchised businesses were in business for 12 months or more and had a full 12 months of reported sales in 2013. Those 189 Franchised Businesses are included in the chart above. The average Gross Sales for 2013 for 4 groups are shown; those that ranked in the top 10%, 25% and 50%, respectively, in terms of highest level of Gross Sales; and, finally, those representing all (100%) of franchised businesses in business more than 12 months with a full 12 months of sales in 2013.

Average Gross Sales Per Work Order for Franchised Businesses
Open Full 12 Months in 2013 and Reporting Using Our Proprietary Software[1]

Territory Population[2]	Average Revenue Per Work Order for 2013	Number of Franchised Businesses in Group[3]	Number in Group that Attained this Level of Sales or Greater[4]	Percentage in group that Attained this Level of Sales or Greater[5]	Number and Percent of All Franchised Businesses Open for Full 12 Months in 2013 that Attained this Level of Sales or Greater[6]
A. Up to 250,000	$531	56	22	39%	59/37%
B. 250,000 - 500,000	$496	36	15	42%	74/47%
C. Over 500,000	$523	66	27	41%	60/38%
D. All Territory Populations	$520	158	61	39%	61/39%

[1] The average revenue per work order shows the average sales of all of the franchised businesses in the groups listed, and then the total, based on information provided by our franchisees to us from January 1, 2013 through December 31, 2013. The total of 158 franchised businesses shown in this chart does not include 31 franchised businesses that did not report Gross Sales to us using our proprietary software during the Reporting Period. As noted, these franchised businesses were excluded from these averages because we do not have the necessary data to include those businesses in these averages.

[2] The franchised businesses are grouped by the population in the territory to show the average sales for franchised businesses open for the full 12 months in 2013 in each population category and for all franchised businesses open the full 12 months in all territory populations. While territory population and years in business have some impact on level of sales you should consider, along with your advisors, all other factors that may be important.

[3] This is the number of franchised businesses open for a full 12

months during 2013 that fell within this group. To be included, the business must have been open for the full 12 months with the indicated territory population level.

[4] This is the number of franchised businesses in the group that achieved or exceeded the average revenue per work order level stated for the group during 2013.

[5] This is the percentage of franchised businesses in the group that achieved or exceeded the average revenue per work order level stated for the group during 2013.

[6] This is the number and percent of all franchised businesses in our System that were open for a full 12 months in 2013 that attained an average revenue per work order that matched or exceeded the level attained by this group.

Gross Sales for Franchised Businesses
Open Full 12 Months in 2013

Listed below are the annual Gross Sales reported for each of the franchised businesses open for a full 12 months in 2013 and which businesses had a full 12 months of reported sales in 2013 (189 of the 212 franchised businesses in operation at December 31, 2013) ranked by highest to lowest sales as reported to us in information provided by our franchisees.

	$ Gross Sales		$ Gross Sales
1.	8,964,987.70	21.	2,144,479.84
2.	6,417,772.08	22.	2,137,808.04
3.	6,155,974.88	23.	2,077,049.18
4.	5,249,876.39	24.	2,071,854.07
5.	4,947,623.13	25	2,040,251.93
6.	4,439,982.42	26.	1,985,236.87
7.	4,053,516.48	27.	1,974,595.51
8.	3,841,519.77	28.	1,961,513.01
9.	3,485,401.81	29.	1,955,535.35
10.	3,479,586.35	30.	1,915,906.07
11.	3,455,137.06	31.	1,878,241.72
12.	3,406,751.13	32.	1,813,105.31
13.	3,276,097.76	33.	1,755,325.44
14.	3,254,314.02	34.	1,640,178.52
15.	3,251,734.39	35.	1,606,716.00
16.	2,644,210.74	36.	1,600,597.55
17.	2,481,154.25	37.	1,589,834.75
18.	2,276,596.51	38.	1,568,820.07
19.	2,271,604.14	39.	1,544,910.74
20.	2,190,615.76	40.	1,482,707.41

41.	1,460,722.90	83.	757,096.90
42.	1,447,031.03	84.	756,660.12
43.	1,433,435.92	85.	749,715.29
44.	1,404,434.08	86.	741,031.76
45.	1,383,977.98	87.	726,419.87
46.	1,358,969.49	88.	721,783.67
47.	1,358,859.05	89.	714,738.73
48.	1,334,168.49	90.	711,250.84
49.	1,322,816.57	91.	684,397.15
50.	1,321,010.04	92.	681,403.57
51.	1,309,411.57	93.	674,370.56
52.	1,307,947.71	94.	669,000.38
53.	1,307,388.41	95.	641,869.28
54.	1,276,241.02	96.	637,943.38
55.	1,257,501.77	97.	631,015.69
56.	1,196,634.94	98.	618,273.02
57.	1,177,962.79	99.	618,162.00
58.	1,165,592.41	100.	606,868.97
59.	1,131,865.36	101.	603,223.42
60.	1,124,805.05	102.	586,559.69
61.	1,123,695.80	103.	585,920.09
62.	1,087,554.75	104.	573,208.95
63.	1,074,843.97	105.	566,010.75
64.	1,038,599.05	106.	565,112.06
65.	1,021,516.55	107.	562,268.12
66.	1,020,790.72	108.	544,312.51
67.	1,017,866.40	109.	542,038.60
68.	1,013,848.29	110.	539,519.62
69.	1,009,749.29	111.	513,704.68
70.	991,588.45	112.	504,930.84
71.	986,806.43	113.	501,195.40
72.	976,812.90	114.	497,396.64
73.	950,096.59	115.	496,291.44
74.	932,906.76	116.	491,580.75
75.	924,088.53	117.	485,436.53
76.	922,247.26	118.	474,106.30
77.	902,153.52	119.	465,935.88
78.	883,220.07	120.	463,628.40
79.	815,878.23	121.	463,009.50
80.	812,336.93	122.	461,787.81
81.	779,371.34	123.	460,766.63
82.	759,716.88	124.	455,204.15

125.	447,404.67	142.	298,253.87	159.	223,448.69	175.	97,644.17
126.	444,217.24	143.	290,987.08	160.	220,313.39	176.	90,990.28
127.	432,569.42	144.	289,825.75	161.	210,352.83	177.	71,898.92
128.	426,508.04	145.	284,259.98	162.	208,873.09	178.	54,466.05
129.	403,013.03	146.	281,421.58	163.	207,227.73	179.	50,477.43
130.	380,926.23	147.	272,943.71	164.	196,022.50	180.	45,613.16
131.	380,402.27	148.	265,055.36	165.	181,263.09	181.	45,127.04
132.	372,105.92	149.	260,434.15	166.	178,843.09	182.	42,398.22
133.	367,519.99	150.	259,637.89	167.	166,120.31	183.	42,342.22
134.	359,967.93	151.	254,946.30	168.	164,465.26	184.	34,815.73
135.	353,779.91	152.	246,771.12	169.	139,218.33	185.	29,696.03
136.	352,414.72	153.	244,699.30	170.	134,297.96	186.	22,788.11
137.	345,243.32	154.	238,389.64	171.	133,175.65	187.	9,583.09
138.	337,341.66	155.	237,288.66	172.	131,883.38	188.	9,487.23
139.	315,815.26	156.	236,970.03	173.	123,664.75	189.	0.00
140.	307,853.63	157.	235,433.34	174.	117,329.62		
141.	307,789.59	158.	229,882.12				

OUTDOOR LIGHTING PERSPECTIVES®

OUTDOOR LIGHTING PERSPECTIVES

2924 Emerywood Pkwy., # 101
Richmond, VA 23294
Tel: (800) 772-4668
Email: spucel@outdoorlivingbrands.com
Website: www.outdoorlightingfranchise.com
Shemar Pucel, Franchise Recruiting Coordinator

Outdoor Lighting Perspectives is North America's number one choice for professional outdoor lighting design, installation, and maintenance. Our unparalleled design expertise, handcrafted copper and brass low-voltage LED outdoor light fixtures, and impeccable installation with continued maintenance have earned us our reputation for being America's number one preferred outdoor lighting company.

BACKGROUND
IFA Member:	Yes
Established & First Franchised:	1995; 1998

Franchised Units:	44
Company-Owned Units:	0
Total Units:	44
Distribution:	US – 41; CAN – 1; O'seas – 2
North America:	16 States, 1 Province
Density:	5 in FL, 3 in NC, 3 in OH
Projected New Units (12 Months):	6
Qualifications:	4, 4, 1, 3, 4, 4

FINANCIAL/TERMS
Cash Investment:	$80K
Total Investment:	$53.7 – 109.6K
Minimum Net Worth:	$100K
Fees (Franchise):	$39.5K
Fees (Royalty):	7%
Fees (Advertising):	1.5%
Term of Contract (Years):	7/7
Average Number of Employees:	1 FT, 0 PT
Passive Ownership:	Allowed
Encourage Conversions:	Yes
Area Development Agreements:	Yes
Sub-Franchising Contracts:	No
Expand in Territory:	Yes
Space Needs:	N/A

SUPPORT & TRAINING

Financial Assistance Provided:	Yes (D)
Site Selection Assistance:	N/A
Lease Negotiation Assistance:	N/A
Co-operative Advertising:	No
Franchisee Association/Member:	No
Size of Corporate Staff:	35

On-going Support:	b, C, D, G, h, I
Training:	5 Days Richmond, VA

SPECIFIC EXPANSION PLANS

US:	All United States
Canada:	All Canada
Overseas:	All Countries

Written substantiation of the data used in preparing the financial performance representations included in this ITEM 19 will be made available to you upon reasonable request.

A. Average Gross Sales for Outdoor Lighting Businesses for the 12 Months Ending December 31, 2013

The following table presents the Average Gross Sales realized by certain Outdoor Lighting franchisees in during the period between January 1, 2013 and December 31, 2013 ("Reporting Period"). We have provided this information to help you to make a more informed decision regarding the Outdoor Lighting System. You should not use this information as an indication of how your specific Outdoor Lighting Business may perform. The success of your Outdoor Lighting Business will depend largely on your individual abilities and your market. The actual numbers you experience will be influenced by a wide variety of factors including your management, market size, demographics, competition, and the general state of the economy in your Territory. You should conduct your own independent research and due diligence to assist you in preparing your own projections.

The information provided in the table below was compiled from 38 Outdoor Lighting franchisees that were operational during the Reporting Period, including all Outdoor Lighting franchisees operating in the United States and internationally. The data excludes franchisees that either began operations or ceased active operations during the Reporting Period.

Sales Volume	# of Franchisees	Sales in Dollars			# of Franchisees Above Average (and %)	Years in Business			% of Franchisees
		Minimum	Average	Maximum		Minimum	Average	Maximum	
Greater than $500K	11	531,969	839,896	1,407,928	8 (46%)	1.5	8.5	12.1	28.9%
Between $250K - $500K	15	302,274	384,538	455,917	8 (53%)	1.0	8.8	13.0	39.5%
Less than $250K	12	52,875	143,377	214,465	6 (50%)	1.7	7.2	15.0	31.6%
Franchisees	38		440,196				8.2		100.0%

There is no assurance that you or any other Outdoor Lighting Business will perform as well as the 38 Outdoor Lighting Businesses used in preparing the averages shown in the table above.

The Average Gross Sales figures presented above represent the total dollar value of customer installation contracts and ongoing maintenance services sold during the Reporting Period by the 38 Outdoor Lighting franchisees identified above. Average Gross Sales should not be construed as a measure of revenue or cash collections, which can vary substantially from Average Gross Sales depending on several factors, including franchisees' backlog of projects, size of projects or contract terms. The financial performance representations above do not reflect the costs of sales, royalties or operating expenses that must be deducted from the gross sales figures to obtain a net income or owner's profit number. The best source of cost and expense data may be from current or former franchisees as listed in this disclosure document.

B. Gross Margin Benchmarking Study for Outdoor Lighting Businesses for the 12 Months Ending December 31, 2012

We do not provide prospective franchisees with projections of income, profits or earnings. There is no guarantee that you, as a new Outdoor Lighting Business, will attain the same level of sales or profits that have been attained by our existing franchisees. The success of your franchise will depend largely on your individual abilities and your market. However, we do provide prospective franchisees with information from a financial benchmarking study ("Benchmarking Study") we conducted for the Outdoor Lighting System.

In 2013, we conducted a financial Benchmarking Study for Outdoor Lighting franchisees. The Benchmarking Study was conducted solely on a voluntary basis and was offered only to franchisees who had been operating their Outdoor Lighting Businesses at least twelve months at the time of the Benchmarking Study. As a result, one franchisee who joined the system in 2012 was ineligible to participate in the Benchmarking Study. Interested franchisees were required to submit their income statements for the year ending December 31, 2012 ("Benchmarking Reporting Period"). We then calculated certain financial metrics to allow participants to compare their financial performance against their peer group of Outdoor Lighting franchisees. 35 out of 40 (87.5%) Outdoor Lighting Businesses as of December 31, 2012, participated in the Benchmarking Study. We have reviewed the composition of franchise participants and believe it contains a random, representative sampling of Outdoor Lighting franchisees based on

level of sales, years in the business and geography.

The Benchmarking Study examined a number of key performance metrics, and we have determined that Gross Profit Margin is helpful to prospective franchisees looking to acquire the rights to operate one or more Outdoor Lighting Businesses. For purposes of the Benchmarking Study, Gross Profit Margin measures profitability after material, installation labor and other direct installation costs are subtracted from gross revenue. It is calculated by dividing gross profit dollars by gross revenues. While Gross Profit Margin measures profitability after material, installation labor and other direct costs are subtracted from gross revenue, it excludes royalties, any commissions and other operating expenses.

The Gross Profit Margin figures provided by the Benchmarking Study are the median. The median for any variable is the middle number of all values reported arrayed from lowest to highest. Unlike the mean (or average), the median is not influenced by any extremely high or low variables reported. Therefore, the Benchmarking Study reports the median as the preferred statistic for its analysis.

The table below provides a further breakdown of median Gross Profit Margins among the Outdoor Lighting franchisees participating in the Benchmarking Study.

	Participating Outdoor Lighting Perspectives Franchise	Sales Under $300,000	Sales Over $300,000	Less than 9 Years in Business	More than 9 Years in Business
Number of Franchisees Reporting	35	17	18	20	15
Gross Profit Margin (Median)	58.6%	60.0%	58.0%	57.8%	60.0%

The above results taken from the Benchmarking Study are provided to prospective franchisees in evaluating the experience of existing Outdoor Lighting Businesses who participated in the study and not as a projection or forecast of what a new Outdoor Lighting Business may experience. A new franchisee's financial results are likely to differ from the results provided above.

The financial information utilized in the benchmarking study was based entirely upon information voluntarily reported by the 35 Outdoor Lighting franchisees who participated in the benchmarking study, and none of this information has been audited or otherwise reviewed or investigated by us or by any independent accountant or auditing firm, and no one has audited, reviewed or otherwise evaluated this information for accuracy or expressed his/her opinion with regard to its content or form.

In preparing any pro forma financial projections, you and other prospective franchisees must keep in mind that each individual franchisee's experience is unique and results may vary, depending on a number of factors. These factors include general economic conditions of the franchise territory, demographics, competition, effectiveness of the franchisee in the management of the Outdoor Lighting Business, the general state of the economy in your Territory, and the use of the Outdoor Lighting System, scope of investment and the overall efficiency of the franchise operation.

NOTES THAT APPLY TO SUBSECTIONS A AND B ABOVE:

A. Many factors, including those described in the preceding paragraph, are unique to each Outdoor Lighting Business and may significantly impact the financial performance of your outdoor lighting business.

B. There is no assurance that you or any other Outdoor Lighting Business will do as well.

C. As with other businesses, we anticipate that a new Outdoor Lighting Business will not achieve sales volumes or maintain expenses similar to an Outdoor Lighting Business that has been operating for a number of years.

D. You are responsible for developing your own business plan for your Outdoor Lighting Business, including capital budgets, financial statements, projections, pro forma financial statements and other elements appropriate to your particular circumstances. In preparing your business plan, we encourage you to consult with your own accounting, business and legal advisors to assist you to identify the expenses you likely will incur in connection with your Outdoor Lighting Business, to prepare your budgets, and to assess the likely or potential financial performance of your Outdoor Lighting Business.

E. In developing the business plan for your Outdoor Lighting Business, you are cautioned to make necessary allowance for changes in financial results to income, expenses or both that may result from operation of your Outdoor Lighting Business during periods of, or in geographic areas suffering from, economic downturns, inflation, unemployment, or other negative economic influences.

Some Outdoor Lighting Businesses sold this amount. Your individual results may differ. There is no assurance that you'll sell as much.

C. Median Retail Price Per Project, Number of Fixtures Installed, and Median Retail Price Per Fixture during the Last Twelve Months Ending December 31, 2013.

The table below presents the median "Average Retail Price Per Project," median "Average Number of Fixtures Installed" and median "Average Retail Price Per Fixture" for new OUTDOOR LIGHTING PERSPECTIVE installation projects by certain Outdoor Lighting Businesses in the twelve month period ending December 31, 2013 ("Reporting Period").

The information provided in the table below was compiled from 15 of the 40 (37.5%) OUTDOOR LIGHTING PERSPECTIVE franchisees that were operational during the Reporting Period, including all Outdoor Lighting franchisees operating in the United States and internationally ("Reporting Franchisees"). The data excludes franchisees that either began operations or ceased active operations during the Reporting Period and franchisees that did not provide the data necessary to analyze the number of new lighting system installation projects or the number of fixtures installed in new lighting system installations. The information provided in the table below

was compiled by examining 1,055 new OUTDOOR LIGHTING PERSPECTIVE installation projects identified from the 15 Reporting Franchisees as reported from annual reports captured from the Reporting Franchisees' customer relationship management software during the Reporting Period. Examination of the annual reports clearly identified 1,055 new OUTDOOR LIGHTING PERSPECTIVE installation projects, the total revenues from each new installation project and the number of lighting fixtures installed on new installation projects for each Reporting Franchisee.

Further, it is important to note that installation of "new" outdoor lighting systems represents only a portion of the overall activities performed by an OUTDOOR LIGHTING PERSEPCTIVES franchisee in the operation of the Outdoor Lighting Business. Other activities and revenue included in the Outdoor Lighting Business include revenue from the design and installation of holiday lighting systems, commercial outdoor lighting projects, maintenance and service on existing installed residential architectural and landscape lighting systems, add-ons or expansions of existing residential lighting systems, revenues from contractual annual maintenance plans, or revenue from retro fitting existing installed lighting systems to new LED technology.

These 1,055 new OUTDOOR LIGHTING PERSPECTIVE installation projects completed by the Reporting Franchisees generated a total of $2,450,154 in retail sales, which represents 14.0% of all the retail sales performed by all Outdoor Lighting Businesses during the 12-month period ending December 31, 2013. The data in the table excludes: (i) revenues from new OUTDOOR LIGHTING PERSPECTIVE installation projects where the number of lighting fixtures installed were not reported; (ii) revenue from installations of additional OUTDOOR LIGHTING PERSPECTIVE fixtures that are being added to an existing OUTDOOR LIGHTING PERSPECTIVE system, otherwise known as an "add-on sale"; (iii) revenues derived from maintenance and service work on previously installed OUTDOOR LIGHTING PERSPECTIVE systems; (iv) revenues derived from holiday decorative lighting systems; and (v) revenues derived from commercial lighting projects. Our management team has reviewed the composition of the Reporting Franchisees that completed the 1,055 new lighting system installation projects was determined that the set of franchisees comprised a random, representative sampling of Outdoor Lighting Businesses based on level of sales, years in the business, and geographic location.

The median Average Retail Price Per Project of all Reporting Franchisees for a new OUTDOOR LIGHTING PERSPECTIVE system installation during the Reporting Period was $2,240. The Average Retail Price Per Project is calculated by taking the total dollar sales from new installation projects for a particular Reporting Franchisee divided by the total number of new installation projects completed by such Reporting Franchisee.

The median Average Number of Fixtures Installed per new OUTDOOR LIGHTING PERSPECTIVE system installation project completed by Reporting Franchisees during the Reporting Period was 8.0. The Average Number of Fixtures Installed is calculated by taking the total number of fixtures installed on new OUTDOOR LIGHITNG PERSECTIVE installation projects for a particular Reporting Franchisee divided by the total number of new installation projects completed by such Reporting Franchisee.

The median Average Retail Price Per Fixture of all Reporting Franchisees during the Reporting Period, was $305.70 per fixture. The Average Retail Price Per Fixture is calculated by taking the total dollar sales from new installation projects for a particular Reporting Franchisee, divided by the total number of lighting fixtures installed on new installation projects completed by such Reporting Franchisee.

The median for any variable is the middle number of all values reported arrayed from lowest to highest. Unlike the mean (or average), the median is not influenced by any extremely high or low variables reported.

	Median	Maximum	Minimum	# of Franchisees above Median (and %)
Average Retail Price per Project	$2,240	$4,091	$601	7 (46.7%)
Average Number of Fixtures Installed	8.0	15.5	3.6	7 (46.7%)
Average Retail Price per Fixture	$305.70	$413.73	$117.22	7 (46%)

The figures in the table above reflect only the revenues from the Average Retail Price Per Fixture and the Average Retail Price Per Project; they do not reflect the direct variable costs of a new OUTDOOR LIGHTING PERSPECTIVE system installation project which would include the direct cost of the lighting fixture, the cost of wire, the cost of a transformer, the cost of other normal lighting installation materials and the direct cost of labor to install the new outdoor lighting system.

Additionally, other fixed and variable costs and expenses associated with operating an Outdoor Lighting Business, including franchisee's salary, administrative salaries, sales expenses, automobile expenses, insurance costs and advertising and marketing expenses are not considered in the measurement of Average Retail Price Per Fixture and Average Retail Price Per Project. You should conduct an independent investigation of the potential costs and expenses you will incur in operating your Outdoor Lighting Business.

The above results are provided to prospective franchisees in evaluating the experience of certain existing Outdoor Lighting Businesses and not as a projection or forecast of what a new Outdoor Lighting Business may experience. A new franchisee's financial results are likely to differ from the results provided above.

Some Outdoor Lighting Businesses have experienced the above results. Your individual results may differ. There is no assurance that you will perform as well.

The financial information we utilized in preparing the preced-

ing financial performance representations was based entirely upon information reported to us by Outdoor Lighting Businesses. None of this information was audited or otherwise reviewed or investigated by us or by any independent accountant or auditing firm, and no one has audited, reviewed or otherwise evaluated this information for accuracy or expressed his/her opinion with regard to its content or form.

In preparing any pro forma financial projections, you and other prospective franchisees must keep in mind that each individual franchisee's experience is unique and results may vary, depending on a number of factors. These factors include general economic conditions of the franchisee's territory, demographics, competition, and effectiveness of the franchisee in the management of the franchised business and the use of the Outdoor Lighting System, scope of investment and the overall efficiency of the franchise operation.

You are responsible for developing your own business plan for your Outdoor Lighting Business, including capital budgets, financial statements, projections, pro forma financial statements and other elements appropriate to your particular circumstances. In preparing your business plan, we encourage you to consult with your own accounting, business and legal advisors to assist you to identify the expenses you likely will incur in connection with your Outdoor Lighting Business to prepare your budgets, and to assess the likely or potential financial performance of your Outdoor Lighting Business.

In developing the business plan for your Outdoor Lighting Business, you are cautioned to make necessary allowance for changes in financial results to income; expenses or both that may result from operation of your Outdoor Lighting Business during periods of, or in geographic areas suffering from, economic downturns, inflation, unemployment, or other negative economic influences.

Other than the preceding financial performance representations, we do not make any financial performance representations. We also do not authorize our employees or representatives to make any such representations either orally or in writing. If you are purchasing an existing outlet, however, we may provide you with the actual records of that outlet. If you receive any other financial performance information or projections of your future income, you should report it to the franchisor's management by contacting Chris Grandpre, Outdoor Lighting Perspectives Franchising, Inc., 2924 Emerywood Parkway, Suite 101, Richmond, Virginia 23294, (804) 353-6999, the Federal Trade Commission, and the appropriate state regulatory agencies.

PADGETT BUSINESS SERVICES

400 Blue Hill Dr., # 201
Westwood, MA 02090
Tel: (877) 729-8725 x 290, (781) 251-9410
Fax: (781) 251-9520
Email: cclark@smallbizpros.com
Website: www.smallbizpros.com
Carol Clark, Franchise Development Coordinator

America's top-rated and fastest-growing tax and accounting franchise – serving the fastest-growing segment of the economy – America's small business owners. Initial training. Specialized software. On-going support.

BACKGROUND

IFA Member:	Yes
Established & First Franchised:	1966; 1975
Franchised Units:	409
Company-Owned Units:	0
Total Units:	409
Distribution:	US – 285; CAN – 124; O'seas – 0
North America:	43 States, 7 Provinces
Density:	38 in QC, 67 in ON, 26 in GA
Projected New Units (12 Months):	50

Qualifications:	3, 3, 4, 4, 2, 4

FINANCIAL/TERMS

Cash Investment:	$100K
Total Investment:	$100K
Minimum Net Worth:	$100K
Fees (Franchise):	$38K +18K Training
Fees (Royalty):	9 – 4.5%
Fees (Advertising):	0%
Term of Contract (Years):	10/10
Average Number of Employees:	1 FT, 2 PT
Passive Ownership:	Not Allowed
Encourage Conversions:	Yes
Area Development Agreements:	No
Sub-Franchising Contracts:	No
Expand in Territory:	Yes
Space Needs:	200 – 400 SF

SUPPORT & TRAINING

Financial Assistance Provided:	No
Site Selection Assistance:	Yes
Lease Negotiation Assistance:	N/A
Co-operative Advertising:	No
Franchisee Association/Member:	Yes/Member
Size of Corporate Staff:	40
On-going Support:	C, D, G, H, I
Training:	2 Weeks Athens, GA; 3 (2.5 Day) Site Visits

SPECIFIC EXPANSION PLANS

US:	All United States
Canada:	All Canada
Overseas:	No

As of May 31, 2014, PADGETT had 269 franchised locations operated by 256 franchisees in the U.S. subject to revenue reporting requirements. Fourteen of these franchisees had not been open for business a full year and the operating results of those locations are not included in the franchisee financial summary information that follows. PADGETT franchisees who file extensions may file their income tax returns either September 15th or October 15th depending on their entity status, which is after the date we prepare this document for FTC filing. As of the filing date of this document, 223 of PADGETT's franchisees had submitted complete financial information to PADGETT, which was used to determine the franchisee profit information within this section. The Financial Performance Representations do not include any profit information for franchisees who operated for only a part of FYE 2014 if he/she closed during that year. The revenues submitted with the financial information are the revenues upon which franchisees' monthly royalty fees were calculated.

PADGETT offered substantially the same services to all of the businesses included in the Report and substantially all the businesses offered the same business services. Some factors or variables affect the gross revenues of the franchised businesses, including:

- the amount and effectiveness of advertising or marketing effort
- being fully engaged in the business
- willingness and ability to promote and operate the business

Your PADGETT business will likely be affected by one or more of these factors, some to a greater extent than others.

Overall Franchisee revenues and profits:

Franchisee revenues are primarily derived from monthly fees (for write-up and consultation services), tax preparation fees and year-end fees (to prepare W-2, 1099, etc. documents for clients). In addition, franchisees also have additional revenue from payroll processing and certain one-time fees (such as set-up fees and backwork fees) and other additional fees (such as representation fees).

During the past year, PADGETT has been finalizing the "back-office" functions associated with a complete technology update and, as of this writing, the data aggregation function is not functional. PADGETT depends on its data aggregation system to calculate the average monthly fee paid by PADGETT clients. PADGETT does not depend on the data aggregation system to accumulate other franchisee financial information. Although

PADGETT is not able to calculate the average monthly fee paid by PADGETT clients as of May 31, 2014, based on test data, we believe the average monthly fee is similar to (and slightly higher than) the amount as of May 31, 2013. As of that date, the average monthly fee paid by Padgett clients was $205 and is compared to $204 and $198 respectively as of May 31, 2012 and May 31, 2011. Of the 210 franchisees submitting sales data as of May 31, 2013, 96 franchisees exceeded the average amount. The averages or comparatives are not affected and are the same whether calculated using the 210 franchisees or the 216 locations. For the purposes of describing financial performance of PADGETT's franchisees, the average monthly fee paid by PADGETT clients will be the same fee reported as of May 31, 2013 and all other data is as of May 31, 2014.

In addition to the afore mentioned $205 average monthly fee, for the fiscal year ending May 31, 2014, tax preparation fees represented 37.6% of ongoing client fees. Based on these two components of the PADGETT fee structure, as of May 31, 2014, the average on-going annual revenue from a client is $3,940. Using this same method, 45.7% of the sample would have exceeded the average amount.

Franchisee profitability was also analyzed for franchisees' fiscal years that ended during PADGETT's fiscal year ending May 31, 2014. We adjusted the profit figures by eliminating depreciation, interest and franchisees' own expenses that vary considerably among franchisees, including owners' salaries and discretionary owners' expenses. These adjustments have the effect of increasing the profits reported. In reviewing this information, you will need to account for those variable expenses that you will incur in operating your business. Your fixed and variable expenses will vary from those presented based on the operating structure that you establish. As a result, your profitability may vary. The data received from reporting businesses was accumulated using a uniform method that included direct reports to PADGETT by the franchisees. PADGETT has not independently verified the figures given by the franchised businesses. PADGETT does not require its franchisees to utilize a uniform accounting method and therefore cannot confirm whether their revenue figures were compiled in accordance with generally accepted accounting principles. PADGETT franchisees primarily use a cash basis of accounting. With regard to the profit information compiled, PADGETT reports that adjusted profits for franchisees open for business for more than one year averaged 43.3% of revenues.

The two charts that follow detail the profit information by size of office:

Franchisee Revenues	Adjusted Profit Percent			
	Average	High	Mean	Low
$500,000 +	43.1%	64.3%	41.9%	19.5%
$300,000 - $499,999	44.5%	88.6%	44.8%	15.1%
$100,000 - $299,999	46.4%	78.6%	47.3%	-6.7%
Total $100,000+	45.1%			
< $100,000	28.3%	76.2%	34.2%	-100+%
Total	43.3%			

Franchisees' Profits Reported by FDD Registration Date					
	Fiscal Year Ending 5/31/2014				
Office Size	(Franchisees) Locations Operated		Summary Financial Info		
	Number	% of TOT	Revenue	$ Profit	% Profit
$500,000 +	(12) 15	6.3	7,320,384	3,154,542	43.1
$300,000 – $499,999	(30) 33	13.9	11,381,005	5,063,314	44.5
$100,000 – $299,999	(92) 99	41.8	16,092,424	7,464,151	46.4
< $100,000	(89) 90	38.0	4,210,327	1,193,287	28.3
Total	(223) 237	100.0	39,004,140	16,875,294	43.3

Although we do not estimate the average "break-even" sales volume of the reporting franchisees, all but one franchisee with revenues greater than $100,000 reported profits. The franchisee who reported revenues greater than $100,000 and a loss had revenues of $123,006 and reported a loss of 6.7% of revenues.

A new franchisee's financial results are likely to differ from the results stated in the financial performance representation.

We will provide you with written substantiation of the data used in preparing this Report upon your reasonable request; however, this does not require us to disclose the identity of any specific licensee or information that would allow you to identify any specific franchisee.

Recommended expenditures for the first three years:

The following table is a forecast as opposed to a summary of actual data reported by Franchisees. Once becoming a Padgett Franchisee, Padgett assists new Franchisees with a three-year forecast to develop the franchised business. The following chart shows the three-year expense forecast recommended for a "fully engaged" franchise owner. "Fully engaged" refers to Franchisees who employ all steps of the Padgett Comprehensive Marketing Program, as described in the Operations Manual, and attend at least one Padgett seminar each year. As mentioned above, marketing costs vary depending on the Franchisee's background and involvement. The marketing expenses in this forecast represent the costs of a marketing plan in which more outside services are employed as compared to a marketing plan in which Franchisee or Franchisee's employee(s) are performing the same tasks. The expense forecast excludes royalty expense so as to not inadvertently project revenues, which is not the intent of the following table.

YEAR 1 EXPENSE FORECAST													
Month	1	2	3	4	5	6	7	8	9	10	11	12	YEAR ONE TOTAL
Expense													
Payroll - Operations													
Payroll - Marketing													.
Payroll - Tax Preperation													0
Employer Taxes													0
Marketing Expense	3,150	3,150	3,150	3,150	3,150	3,150	1,500	1,500	1,500	1,500	1,500	1,500	27,900
Rent													.
PAS Software License Fee				3,000									3,000
Office Supplies	350	150	150	150	150	150	150	150	150	150	150	150	2,000
Telephone/Data	75	75	75	75	75	75	75	75	75	75	75	75	900
Postage	25	25	25	25	25	25	25	25	25	25	25	25	300
Insurance	800												800
Travel	125	125	125	125	125	1,000	125	125	125	125	125	125	2,375
Utilities													.
Misc expenses	100	100	100	100	100	100	100	100	100	100	100	100	1,200
Total Expenses	4,625	3,625	3,625	6,625	3,625	4,500	1,975	1,975	1,975	1,975	1,975	1,975	38,475
Operating Profit/ (Loss) -$ Operating Profit/ (Loss) -%	(4,625)	(3,625)	(3,625)	(6,625)	(3,625)	(4,500)	(1,975)	(1,975)	(1,975)	(1,975)	(1,975)	(1,975)	(38,475)
Start-Up Costs													
Franchise Fee	38,000												38,000
Training Fee	18,000												18,000
Training Expense	2,000												2,000
Fixtures & Equipment	3,500												3,500
Total Start-Up Costs	61,500												61,500
Cash Increase/ Decrease - Period	(66,125)	(3,625)	(3,625)	(6,625)	(3,625)	(4,500)	(1,975)	(1,975)	(1,975)	(1,975)	(1,975)	(1,975)	(99,975)

YEAR 2 EXPENSE FORECAST													
Month	13	14	15	16	17	18	19	20	21	22	23	24	YEAR TWO TOTAL
Expense													
Payroll - Operations	2,600	2,600	2,600	2,600	2,600	2,600	2,600	4,000	4,000	4,000	4,000	4,000	38,200
Payroll - Marketing													
Payroll - Tax Preperation											6,000	6,000	12,000
Employer Taxes	468	468	468	468	468	468	468	720	720	720	1,800	1,800	9,036
Marketing Expense	1,500	1,500	1,500	1,500	1,500	1,500	1,500	1,500	1,500	1,500	1,500	1,500	18,000

Rent	750	750	750	750	750	750	750	750	750	750	750	750	9,000
PAS Software License Fee				3,000									3,000
Office Supplies	200	200	200	200	200	200	200	200	200	200	200	200	2,400
Telephone/Data	100	100	100	100	100	100	100	100	100	100	100	100	1,200
Postage	25	25	25	25	25	25	25	25	25	25	25	25	300
Insurance	1,000												1,000
Travel	125	1,000	125	125	125	1,000	125	125	125	125	125	125	3,250
Utilities	150	150	150	150	150	150	150	150	150	150	150	150	1,800
Misc expenses	200	200	200	200	200	200	200	200	200	200	200	200	2,400
Total Expenses	7,118	6,993	6,118	9,118	6,118	6,993	6,118	7,770	7,770	7,770	14,850	14,850	101,586
Operating Profit/(Loss) -$ Operating Profit/(Loss) -%	(7,118)	(6,993)	(6,118)	(9,118)	(6,118)	(6,993)	(6,118)	(7,770)	(7,770)	(7,770)	(14,850)	(14,850)	(101,586)

YEAR 3 EXPENSE FORECAST													
Month	25	26	27	28	29	30	31	32	33	34	35	36	YEAR THREE TOTAL
Expense													
Payroll - Operations	5,000	5,000	5,000	5,000	5,000	5,000	6,000	6,000	6,000	6,000	6,000	6,000	66,000
Payroll - Marketing	2,800	2,800	2,800	2,800	2,800	2,800	2,800	2,800	2,800	2,800	2,800	2,800	33,600
Payroll - Tax Preperation											6,000	6,000	12,000
Employer Taxes	1,800	1,800	1,800	1,800	1,800	1,800	1,219	1,219	1,219	1,219	2,050	2,050	15,457
Marketing Expense	1,500	1,500	1,500	1,500	1,500	1,500	1,500	1,500	1,500	1,500	1,500	1,500	18,000
Rent	750	750	750	750	750	750	750	750	750	750	750	750	9,000
PAS Software License Fee				3,000									3,000
Office Supplies	200	200	200	200	200	200	200	200	200	200	200	200	2,400
Telephone/ Data	125	125	125	125	125	125	125	125	125	125	125	125	1,500
Postage	25	25	25	25	25	25	25	25	25	25	25	25	300
Insurance	1,200												1,200
Travel	125	1,000	125	125	125	1,000	125	125	125	125	125	125	3,250
Utilities	175	175	175	175	175	175	175	175	175	175	175	175	2,100
Misc expenses	200	200	200	200	200	200	200	200	200	200	200	200	2,400
Total Expenses	13,180	12,855	11,980	14,980	11,980	12,855	13,119	13,119	13,119	13,119	19,950	19,950	170,207
Operating Profit/(Loss) -$ Operating Profit/(Loss) -%	(13,180)	(12,855)	(11,980)	(14,980)	(11,980)	(12,855)	(13,119)	(13,119)	(13,119)	(13,119)	(19,950)	(19,950)	(170,207)

POP-A-LOCK

1018 Harding St., # 101
Lafayette, LA 70503
Tel: (877) 233-6211, (337) 233-6211
Fax: (337) 233-6655
Email: michaelkleimeyer@systemforward.com
Website: www.popalock.com/franchising.php
Michael Kleimeyer, Director of Franchise Development

POP-A-LOCK is America's largest locksmith, car door unlocking, and roadside assistance service. We provide fast, professional, guaranteed service using our proprietary tools and opening techniques. We offer an outstanding community service through our industry.

BACKGROUND

IFA Member:	Yes
Established & First Franchised:	1991; 1994
Franchised Units:	302
Company-Owned Units:	0
Total Units:	302
Distribution:	US – 359; CAN – 25; O'seas – 31
North America:	40 States, 1 Province
Density:	42 in CA, 30 in TX, 33 in FL

Projected New Units (12 Months):	113
Qualifications:	4, 5, 1, 3, 3, 4

FINANCIAL/TERMS

Cash Investment:	$120K+
Total Investment:	$99.8 – 133.4K + $15.5K/add. franchise
Minimum Net Worth:	$250 – 400K
Fees (Franchise):	$62K Min.
Fees (Royalty):	6%
Fees (Advertising):	1%
Term of Contract (Years):	10/10
Average Number of Employees:	2 FT, 1 PT
Passive Ownership:	Allowed
Encourage Conversions:	N/A
Area Development Agreements:	Yes
Sub-Franchising Contracts:	No
Expand in Territory:	Yes
Space Needs:	N/A

SUPPORT & TRAINING

Financial Assistance Provided:	Yes (I)
Site Selection Assistance:	N/A
Lease Negotiation Assistance:	N/A
Co-operative Advertising:	Yes
Franchisee Association/Member:	Yes/Member
Size of Corporate Staff:	15
On-going Support:	A, b, C, D, E, F, G, h, I
Training:	5-15 Days + additional local Lafayette, LA

SPECIFIC EXPANSION PLANS

US:	All United States
Canada:	Yes, Edmonton, Winnepeg, Regina
Overseas:	Yes, Mexico, Middle East, Australia

Written substantiation for the financial performance representation will be made available to prospective franchisees on reasonable request. The financial performance representation(s) does (do) not reflect the costs of sales, operating expenses, or other costs or expenses that must be deducted from the gross revenues or gross sales figures to obtain your net income or profit. You should conduct an independent investigation of the costs and expenses you will incur in operating your (franchised business). Franchisees or former franchisees, listed in the disclosure document may be one source of information. Some [outlets] have [sold] [earned] this amount. Your individual results may differ. There is no assurance you'll [sell] [earn] as much.

1. The top 30% of our Franchisees' net annual income ranges from $743,000.00 to $1,388,000.00 per year.

a. Based on royalty reports – historical performance
b. Franchisees have multiple franchise territories, contiguous major markets and/or non-contiguous mid-size markets.
c. Service areas population range from 1.2 million to 4 million.
d. Franchises have been operating from seven to sixteen years.

2. Franchise transfers (re-sales) have averaged 4.6 times earnings over the last six years.

a. Low number of re-sales necessitates this time frame for relevant average.

3. Franchisee failures over the last 12 months: Three.

    a. 3% of the total system (101 franchisees)

Other than stated above, we do not make any representations about a franchisee's future financial performance of company-owned or franchised outlets. We also do not authorize our employees or representatives to make any such representations either orally or in writing. If you are purchasing an existing outlet, however, we may provide you with the actual records of that outlet. In making its assumptions for future financial performance, the Franchisor considered such significant factors as all the expenses set forth in Items 5, 6, and 7 .If you receive any other financial performance information or projections of your future income, you should report it to the franchisor's management by contacting Donald Marks, CEO at 1018 Harding Street, Suite 101, Lafayette, Louisiana 70503 and (337) 233-6211, the Federal Trade Commission, and the appropriate state regulatory agencies.

PRONTO INSURANCE

805 Media Luna Rd., # 400
Brownsville, TX 78520
Tel: (855) 687-7088, (956) 574-7088
Fax: (956) 574-9076
Email: franchise@prontoinsurance.com
Website: www.prontofranchise.com
Federico Roesch

Pronto Insurance is an insurance and financial service provider based in south Texas. Founded in 1997, Pronto developed a unique approach to the insurance business and has been revolutionizing the industry ever since. Through aggressive marketing, brand awareness, and highly competitive pricing, Pronto has quickly become an industry leader in Texas and now has the strength of over 130 branded agencies throughout the state. Personal property and liability insurance is a multi-billion dollar industry in Texas and the demand for affordable products has never been greater. Pronto offers a unique retail approach to our consumers, who need reasonably priced insurance and financial products. Pronto prides itself in providing fast and efficient service. Our slogan "Pronto, It's our name and our promise"™ speaks for itself. As a Pronto Franchise owner, you will have the power of our brand and the expertise to guide you along the way.

BACKGROUND

IFA Member:	Yes
Established & First Franchised:	1997; 2009
Franchised Units:	33
Company-Owned Units:	98

Total Units:	131
Distribution:	US – 131; CAN – 0; O'seas – 0
North America:	1 State, 0 Provinces
Density:	131 in TX
Projected New Units (12 Months):	15
Qualifications:	3, 4, 1, 2, 4, 5

FINANCIAL/TERMS

Cash Investment:	$50 – 60K
Total Investment:	$60 – 100K
Minimum Net Worth:	$200K
Fees (Franchise):	$15 – 25K
Fees (Royalty):	0%
Fees (Advertising):	$500 or 1% of sales
Term of Contract (Years):	5/5
Average Number of Employees:	2-3 FT, 0 PT
Passive Ownership:	Discouraged
Encourage Conversions:	Yes
Area Development Agreements:	Yes
Sub-Franchising Contracts:	No
Expand in Territory:	Yes
Space Needs:	800 – 1,200 SF

SUPPORT & TRAINING

Financial Assistance Provided:	Yes (I)
Site Selection Assistance:	Yes
Lease Negotiation Assistance:	Yes
Co-operative Advertising:	Yes
Franchisee Association/Member:	Yes/Member
Size of Corporate Staff:	500
On-going Support:	A, B, C, D, E, G, H, I
Training:	3 Brownsville, TX; or 2 Weeks Various locations throughout Texas

SPECIFIC EXPANSION PLANS

US:	Yes, TX
Canada:	No
Overseas:	No

The initial three tables below represent the average annual Insurance Premium Revenue from the sale of automobile and roadside assistance insurance coverage achieved by: (i) 79 affiliate-owned Pronto Businesses owned by our affiliate, Pronto General Agency, Ltd. (Table 19.1); (ii) 6 Pronto Businesses which are owned by our members (Table 19.2); and (iii) 17 franchisee-owned Pronto Businesses (Table 19.3), which were opened prior to January 1, 2012, for the period from January 1, 2013 through December 31, 2013. Pronto Businesses not opened for the entire period from January 1, 2012 to December 31, 2013 were excluded, due to the time it takes a Pronto Business to mature. Pronto Businesses may derive revenue from multiple sources, however, in most cases the primary source of revenue is from the sale of automobile and roadside assistance insurance coverage. The indicated tables below are limited to providing only annual Insurance Premium Revenue from the sale of automobile and roadside assistance insurance coverage. The figures in Tables 19.1, 19.2 and 19.3 do not reflect other revenue sources such as sales of other types of insurance coverages, Tax Preparation Fee Revenue or related fees such as set up fees, application fees or administrative fees, nor do the figures include operating expenses, or other costs or expenses, including related interest, depreciation, amortization, and income taxes, that must be deducted from gross revenue figures to obtain your net income or profit.

Insurance Premium Revenue means all premium revenue received resulting from all insurance policies sold, excluding related fees charged by our affiliate, Pronto General Agency, Ltd., and you, such as set up fees, application fees or administrative fees. Such fees charged by you are determined by you based on individual market conditions in accordance with pricing guidelines established by us, and are earned by you completely. The final two tables represent the average annual amount of set up fees, application fees or administrative fees earned by: (i) 79 affiliate-owned Pronto Businesses owned by our affiliate, Pronto General Agency, Ltd. (Table 19.4); and (ii) 6 Pronto Businesses which are owned by our members (Table 19.5), which were opened prior to January 1, 2012, for the period from January 1, 2013 through December 31, 2013. Again, Pronto Businesses not opened for the entire period from January 1, 2012 to December 31, 2013 were excluded, due to the time it takes a Pronto Business to mature. As described above, these fees are charged and earned completely by you, and upon which you pay no royalty. We do not obtain information related the amount of such fees collected by franchisees, therefore this information is not reported below.

The tables below are separated in three categories of Pronto Businesses as follows: (i) Stand-Alone Pronto Businesses operate as distinct store front units at stand alone or in-line retail shopping center locations; (ii) Kiosk Pronto Businesses operate as a kiosk within the location of a larger business such as a grocery store; and (iii) Co-Locate Pronto Businesses share a location with a complimentary business, which in the case of the units reported is a tax preparation service business. It must be noted that we no longer offer franchises for co-locate locations.

We are not representing that you can expect to achieve these revenue figures at any time during the term of your Franchise Agreement. Your Insurance Premium Revenue and fee revenue may vary significantly depending on a number of factors, including the location of your Franchised Business and how you operate your business. If you rely upon our figures, you must accept the risk of not doing as well. You should conduct an independent investigation of the costs and expenses you will incur in operating your Pronto Business. Franchisees or former franchisees, listed in this Disclosure Document, may be one source of this information.

We have compiled the following information from the internal, unaudited financial statements of our affiliate, Pronto General Agency, Ltd., and our members, for the period from January 1, 2013 through December 31, 2013. You are advised that no Certified Public Accountant has audited the data or expressed an opinion with regard to the content or form of such data. Further, the financial information was not prepared in accordance with Generally Accepted Accounting Principles (GAAP), but is believed to be reliable. Substantiation of the data used in preparing the below figures will be made available to you upon reasonable request. The affiliate-owned and member-owned Pronto Businesses offer substantially the same products and services as you will as a franchisee operating a franchised Pronto Business.

Average Annual Insurance Premium Revenue for Auto and Roadside Assistance
For the Year Ending December 31, 2013

Table 19.1 - Affiliate-Owned

Pronto Businesses	Average Annual Insurance Premium Revenue for Auto and Roadside Assistance	Number of Businesses Above Average

Stand-Alone	$742,099	15 of 31 (or 48.4% attained or exceeded this average.
Kiosk	$442,665	20 of 48 (or 41.7%) attained or exceeded this average.
Co-Locate	$0	There are no Co-Locate Affiliate-Owned Pronto Businesses

Table 19.2 - Member-Owned

Pronto Businesses	Average Annual Insurance Premium Revenue for Auto and Roadside Assistance	Number of Businesses Above Average
Stand-Alone	$1,660,808	3 of 5 (or 60%) attained or exceeded this average.
Kiosk	$1,382,377	1 of 1 (or 100%) attained or exceeded this average.
Co-Locate	$0	There are no Co-Locate Affiliate-Owned Pronto Businesses

Table 19.3 - Franchisee-Owned

Pronto Businesses	Average Annual Insurance Premium Revenue for Auto and Roadside Assistance	Number of Businesses Above Average
Stand-Alone	$618,349	5 of 12 (or 41.7%) attained or exceeded this average.
Kiosk	$0	There are no Kiosk Franchisee-Owned Pronto Businesses.
Co-Locate	$326,077	1 of 5 (or 20%) attained or exceeded this average.

Average Annual Fee Revenue Charged by Pronto Businesses
For the Year Ending December 31, 2013

Table 19.4 - Affiliate-Owned

Pronto Businesses	Average Annual Fee Revenue	Number of Businesses Above Average
Stand-Alone	$31,674	14 of 31 (or 45.2%) attained or exceeded this average.
Kiosk	$16,726	25 of 48 (or 52.1%) attained or exceeded this average.
Co-Locate	$0	There are no Kiosk Franchisee-Owned Pronto Businesses.

Table 19.5 - Member-Owned

Pronto Businesses	Average Annual Agency Fee Revenue	Number of Businesses Above Average

Stand-Alone	$32,316	3 of 5 (or 60%) attained or exceeded this average.
Kiosk	$19,421	1 of 1 (or 100%) attained or exceeded this average.
Co-Locate	$0	There are no Kiosk Franchisee-Owned Pronto Businesses.

THE REVENUE FIGURES ABOVE ARE OF SPECIFIC UNITS REFERENCED ABOVE, AND SHOULD NOT BE CONSIDERED AS THE ACTUAL OR PROBABLE REVENUE THAT WILL BE REALIZED BY ANY FRANCHISE OWNER. WE DO NOT REPRESENT THAT ANY FRANCHISE OWNER CAN EXPECT TO ATTAIN SUCH REVENUE. YOUR RESULTS WILL VARY AND SUCH VARIANCES MAY BE MATERIAL AND ADVERSE TO THE REVENUES SHOWN HERE. YOU SHOULD USE THE ABOVE INFORMATION ONLY AS A REFERENCE IN CONDUCTING YOUR OWN ANALYSIS. WE STRONGLY URGE YOU TO CONSULT WITH YOUR FINANCIAL ADVISOR OR PERSONAL ACCOUNTANT CONCERNING THE FINANCIAL ANALYSIS THAT YOU SHOULD MAKE IN DETERMINING WHETHER OR NOT TO PURCHASE A PRONTO BUSINESS FRANCHISE. WE SPECIFICALLY INSTRUCT OUR SALES PERSONNEL, AGENTS, EMPLOYEES, MEMBERS, MANAGERS AND OFFICERS THAT THEY MAY NOT MAKE ANY REPRESENTATIONS OR STATEMENTS AS TO EARNINGS, SALES OR PROFITS, OR PROSPECTS OR CHANCES OF SUCCESS OF A PRONTO BUSINESS OTHER THAN WHAT IS STATED IN THIS ITEM 19. THEY ARE NOT AUTHORIZED TO REPRESENT OR ESTIMATE DOLLAR FIGURES AS TO A UNIT'S OPERATION OTHER THAN WHAT IS SHOWN ABOVE. EXCEPT AS PROVIDED BY APPLICABLE LAW, WE WILL NOT BE BOUND BY ALLEGATIONS OF ANY UNAUTHORIZED REPRESENTATION AS TO EARNINGS, SALES, PROFITS, OR PROSPECTS OR CHANCES FOR SUCCESS, AND YOU WILL BE REQUIRED TO ACKNOWLEDGE THAT YOU HAVE NOT RELIED ON ANY SUCH REPRESENTATION IN PURCHASING YOUR PRONTO BUSINESS FRANCHISE.

PROTECT PAINTERS

3948 Ranchero Dr.
Ann Arbor, MI 48108
Tel: (800) 824-8881, (734) 822-6555
Email: franchising@aladdindoors.com
Website: www.protectpainters.com
Julie Ledford, Manager of Franchise Development

ProTect Painters is one of the largest decorating and home painting companies in the United States. We handle all house painting needs, including interior, exterior, and commercial painting. Many of our franchises also provide home repair services prior to painting to ensure that your paint job will last.

BACKGROUND

IFA Member:	No
Established & First Franchised:	2009; 2009
Franchised Units:	52
Company-Owned Units:	0
Total Units:	52
Distribution:	US – 52; CAN – 0; O'seas – 0
North America:	19 States, 0 Provinces
Density:	8 in TX, 7 in MA, 7 in MI
Projected New Units (12 Months):	N/A
Qualifications:	N/A

FINANCIAL/TERMS

Cash Investment:	N/A
Total Investment:	$85 – 100K
Minimum Net Worth:	N/A
Fees (Franchise):	$14.9K
Fees (Royalty):	5%
Fees (Advertising):	1%
Term of Contract (Years):	N/A
Average Number of Employees:	N/A FT, N/A PT
Passive Ownership:	Allowed

Encourage Conversions:	Yes	Co-operative Advertising:	No
Area Development Agreements:	No	Franchisee Association/Member:	Yes/Member
Sub-Franchising Contracts:	No	Size of Corporate Staff:	N/A
Expand in Territory:	No	On-going Support:	A, B, C, D, E, F, G, H, I
Space Needs:	N/A	Training:	N/A

SUPPORT & TRAINING		SPECIFIC EXPANSION PLANS	
Financial Assistance Provided:	Yes (D)	US:	No
Site Selection Assistance:	Yes	Canada:	No
Lease Negotiation Assistance:	Yes	Overseas:	No

The following charts and tables are a historic financial performance representation and are not a forecast of your future financial performance.

As of December 31, 2013 ProTect Painters International, LLC, had 49 franchises in operation. Additionally, ProTect Painters Development, LLC, had 6 franchises opened, which collectively operated 7 units.

TABLE 1: STATEMENT OF BENCHMARK NUMBERS

The following table shows our Benchmark Numbers, for the period of January 1-December 31, 2013, achieved by ProTect Painters franchisees who were in business for more than two years. Benchmark Numbers are defined as the minimum level achieved by the top quartile of the system in each of the performance metrics.

Description	Gross Sales	Average Job Size	Estimate Closing Rate Percentage	Gross Profit Percentage
Benchmark Numbers	$408,554	$4,209	55.0%	42.5%

TABLE 2 — AVERAGE JOB SIZE

The following table provides the average size of jobs completed during the period of January 1-December 31, 2013. The results include all owners open for at least two calendar years and still in operation as of December 31, 2013.

Description	Average Job Size	High	Low	Number Above Average	Number Below Average	Percent Above Average	Percent Below Average
Job Size Data for 2013	$3,710	$6,824	$2,348	7	11	39%	61%

TABLE 3: STATEMENT OF AVERAGE CLOSE RATE PER ESTIMATE

The following table shows the average close rate for all estimates performed during the period of January 1-December 31, 2013. The results include all owners open for at least two calendar years and still in operation as of December 31, 2013.

AVERAGE CLOSE RATE IN 2013 PER ESTIMATE PERFORMED

Description	Average Close Rate per Estimate	High	Low	Number Above Average	Number Below Average	Percent Above Average	Percent Below Average
Average Close Rate per Estimate in 2013	44.5%	81.4%	14.9%	8	10	44%	56%

TABLE 4: STATEMENT OF AVERAGE GROSS PROFIT, LABOR AND MATERIALS

The following table and chart shows the profit and loss achieved for the Owners who generated $400,000 and $1,000,000 in Gross Sales for the period of January 1-December 31, 2013. The results include all Owners open for at least twelve months as of December 31, 2013 and who were still in operation as of December 31, 2013.

Description	2013 Average Sales	High	Low	Number Above Average	Number Below Average	% Above Average	% Below Average
Total Revenue	$642,250	$986,184	$408,554	2	4	33%	67%
Cost of Materials	$111,448	$166,917	$71,701	2	4	33%	67%
Cost of Labor	$267,094	$391,598	$165,832	2	4	33%	67%
Advertising	$28,174	$40,346	$19,300	2	4	33%	67%
Sales/Production Wages	$29,251	$89,416	$0	3	3	50%	50%
Insurance	$3,912	$9,862	$996	3	3	50%	50%
Royalty and Fees	$51,397	$78,895	$32,684	2	4	33%	67%
Vehicle Expense	$14,946	$21,828	$7,268	3	3	50%	50%
G & A	$4,981	$9,485	$1,590	3	3	50%	50%
Total Other	$2,205	$3,855	$550	2	4	33%	67%
Total Expense	$513,407	$781,613	$366,094	2	4	33%	67%
Available to Owner	$129,051	$284,963	$42,459	3	3	50%	50%

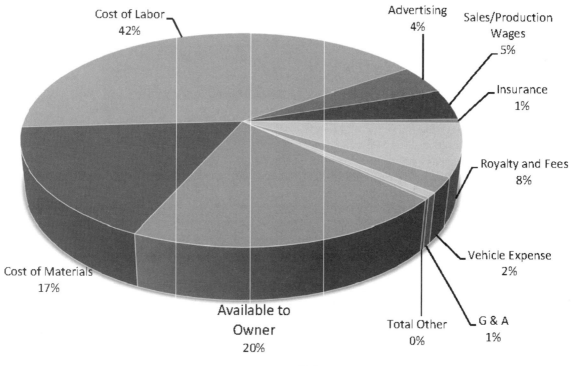

Some Franchises have earned this amount. Your individual results may differ. There is no assurance that you will earn as much. A new franchisee's results are likely to differ from the results shown in this Item. We recommend that you make your own independent investigation, and consult with an attorney and other advisors before executing the Franchise Agreement.

Tables 1-4 were prepared from data obtained from the unaudited royalty report statements prepared by ProTect Painters Development, LLC and ProTect Painters Development, LLC for the statement period of January 1, 2013 to December 31, 2013. We have in our possession written substantiation of the information used to compile the Franchise Performance Representations. At your written request, we will make this written substantiation available to you.

Net sales reflect the total average annual sales for the Operators included in the sample, as reported to us through the Software, and do not include sales tax.

Other than the preceding financial performance representation, ProTect Painters International, LLC., does not make any financial performance representations. We also do not authorize our employees or representatives to make any such representations either orally or in writing. If you are purchasing an existing outlet, however, we may provide you with the actual records of that outlet. If you receive any other financial performance information or projections of your future income, you should report it to the franchisor's management by contacting Mr. Jonathan Koudelka, Esq, 3948 Ranchero Drive, Ann Arbor, MI 48108, 734-822-6850, the Federal Trade Commission, and the appropriate state regulatory agencies.

SERVICEMASTER CLEAN

3839 Forest Hill Irene Rd.
Memphis, TN 38125
Tel: (800) 255-9687, (901) 597-7500
Fax: (901) 597-7580
Email: mpearce@smclean.com
Website: www.servicemasterfranchise.com
Michael Pearce, Chief Development Officer

SERVICEMASTER CLEAN is a division of The ServiceMaster Company. With over 60 years of franchising experience and over 4,000 franchises, SERVICEMASTER CLEAN continues to grow each year and offers franchise opportunities in three distinct categories: 1) Commercial Cleaning services 2) Floor Care services & 3) Disaster Restoration services. Financing is provided for the initial franchise fee, start-up equipment & vehicles to qualified candidates through ServiceMaster Acceptance Co.

BACKGROUND
IFA Member:	Yes
Established & First Franchised:	1947; 1952
Franchised Units:	4,450
Company-Owned Units:	0
Total Units:	4,450
Distribution:	US – 3,082; CAN – 176; O'seas – 1,360
North America:	50 States, 10 Provinces

Density:	198 in IL, 231 in CA, 152 in OH
Projected New Units (12 Months):	150
Qualifications:	5, 3, 2, 2, 3, 5

FINANCIAL/TERMS
Cash Investment:	$12K
Total Investment:	$49.6 – 180.6K
Minimum Net Worth:	$75K
Fees (Franchise):	$24.9 – 156.1K
Fees (Royalty):	5-10%
Fees (Advertising):	1%
Term of Contract (Years):	5/5
Average Number of Employees:	1 FT, 0 PT
Passive Ownership:	Not Allowed
Encourage Conversions:	Yes
Area Development Agreements:	No
Sub-Franchising Contracts:	Yes
Expand in Territory:	Yes
Space Needs:	N/A

SUPPORT & TRAINING
Financial Assistance Provided:	Yes (D)
Site Selection Assistance:	No
Lease Negotiation Assistance:	No
Co-operative Advertising:	Yes
Franchisee Association/Member:	Yes/Member
Size of Corporate Staff:	200
On-going Support:	A, B, C, D, F, G, H, I
Training:	2 Weeks Memphis, TN; 1 Week On-Site

SPECIFIC EXPANSION PLANS
US:	All United States
Canada:	All Canada
Overseas:	All Countries

The following charts and tables are a historic financial performance representation and are not a forecast of your future financial performance.

Definitions

"Construction Service" means:

For purposes of this Item, Construction Service includes:

(1) Covered Construction Services means any and all construction services related to or done as a result of disaster restoration work, including framing carpentry, cabinetry, roofing, flooring, drywall and plastering, carpet and pad installation, painting, wallpaper and installation and repair of heating, cooling, electrical and plumbing systems, which involve structural reconstruction, cosmetic restoration or mechanical restoration associated with disaster restoration. Covered Construction Services also includes construction, remodeling, structural or decorating services that are performed on a site where a disaster has occurred in which a franchisee performed any disaster restoration work even if the area that is remodeled or reconstructed was not directly affected by the disaster. Any Disaster Restoration Services, including water mitigation, fire, smoke and odor cleaning, demolition, other pre-cleaning, and post-construction cleaning, are excluded from Construction Services and are included as Disaster Restoration Services as described in the franchise agreement and below.

(2) Non-Covered Construction Services means any construction or decorating services not related to disaster restoration work, including estimating, inspection, tear-out, project management and overhead fees in connection with construction and decorating related to remodeling or new construction, such as "ground up" remolding or structural construction that are not done due to a disaster. This definition does not and is not meant to include any residential, commercial, or disaster restoration services cleaning as that term is commonly understood and as that term is referred to in the franchise agreement. The Franchisee's usage of any type of ServiceMaster equipment to perform any cleaning functions removes any such cleaning from the scope of this definition.

"Disaster Restoration Service" means disaster restoration services, including odor removal, water damage, contents cleaning, and power washing which are rendered for the management or tenants of any commercial, institutional or residential building. For purposes of this Item, "disaster restoration services" means the types of services rendered through insurance agents, adjusters, and brokers to customers who have experienced loss from water damage, disaster, such as by fire, flood, earthquake, and storm, regardless of whether the loss is deemed covered by an insurer.

"Janitorial Service" means: (i) cleaning or janitorial services (sanitizing and housekeeping) rendered on a consistent frequency pursuant to a contract, written or oral, entered into with management or tenants of any commercial or institutional building; and (ii) non-janitorial services provided for the management or tenants of commercial or institutional buildings including carpet maintenance, carpet cleaning, hard surface floor maintenance and furniture cleaning; and (iii) all other ancillary services provided in conjunction.

"Floor Care Service" means: (i) non-janitorial services provided for management of tenants of any commercial or institutional building including: carpet maintenance, carpet cleaning, hard surface floor maintenance, furniture cleaning, and any other service not in conjunction with contracted janitorial services; (ii) services for residential customers (in homes, apartments, and condominiums) including: (a) carpet and upholstery services including cleaning, spot and pet odor removal, application of soil and stain protectors, anti-static agents, carpet inspection services; (b) cleaning rendered on a periodic basis for residential customers including: wall, floor, ceiling and contents cleaning; kitchen and bathroom surface and fixture cleaning, deodorizing, and sanitizing, but excluding weekly or bi-weekly maid services; (c) washing windows (interior and exterior), blinds and chandeliers using our methods and procedures; and (d) power washing vehicles, decks, aluminum siding, driveways and other exterior surfaces using our methods and procedures, all of which are more fully set forth and described in the Operations Manual; and (iii) such additional services rendered on a periodic basis to residential customers or on a non-janitorial basis to commercial customers as the we determine, using our methods and procedures; all of which are more fully described in the Operations Manual.

"Ownership Group" means a unique group of licenses having the same individual owner or group of owners. For example, if one license is owned by John Smith and another is owned jointly by John Smith and Jane Smith, these would represent two different Ownership Groups. But, if David Jones owns 3 licenses under one Enterprise and 2 licenses under another Enterprise, all 5 licenses would be grouped into a single Ownership Group.

Disaster Restoration Services

The following financial performance representation consists of historical data for Ownership Groups offering Disaster Restoration Services in the United States of America that have been operating a business for at least two years as of January 1, 2011. We have not included data from similar franchises in Canada or any other foreign country or territory. Many franchisees have more than one franchise agreement related to their business. Franchisees with multiple franchises typically do not have separate operations for each franchise agreement. Therefore, we have aggregated data based on "Ownership Groups" to more accurately reflect a franchisee's business. There are 648 Ownership Groups that had at least one license with a start date of January 1, 2009 or before and with the ability to perform Disaster Restoration Services.

The tables below include Ownership Groups with at least $200,000 in annual gross sales from Disaster Restoration Services. Of the 648 Ownership Groups, 447 (or 69%) had average annual gross sales of at least $200,000 attributable to Disaster Restoration Services during the three year period 2011-2013. Ownership Groups included in the table below have an average of 3.2 franchise agreements per Ownership Group. Ownership Groups with an average of less than $200,000 in annual gross sales for Disaster Restoration Services during the three year period 2011-2013 have been excluded. Ownership Groups with an average of less than $200,000 in annual gross sales account for 3.0% of annual gross sales for all Ownership Groups. Lower gross sales may be a result of a focus on a different service line among other potential causes.

In the past we sold franchise businesses that could provide multiple services (disaster restoration, janitorial, floor cleaning) under one franchise agreement. We still offer these franchise agreements through renewal. Many Ownership Groups provide services in multiple service categories. In addition, many franchisees offering Disaster Restoration Services often provide Construction Services that may be related to other core mitigation and Disaster Restoration Services. However, the annual gross sales reported below includes only gross sales reported for Disaster Restoration Services and excludes all Construction Services and any other services.

We compiled this information from reported gross sales from franchisees for January 2011 through December 2013. We have not independently verified the information received from franchisees. These financial statements were not prepared in accordance with Generally Accepted Accounting Principles (GAAP), but are believed to be reliable. We will provide you with written substantiation of the data used in preparing the financial performance representations in this Item 19 upon reasonable request.

Some franchisees have gross sales of this amount. There is no assurance you will do as well. If you rely on our figures, you must accept the risk of not doing as well.

Table 1, Disaster Restoration Service

AVERAGE ANNUAL GROSS SALES DURING THE THREE YEAR PERIOD 2011-2013 BY QUARTILE FOR ALL OWNERSHIP GROUPS WHO HAVE BEEN IN BUSINESS FOR AT LEAST THREE CALENDAR YEARS AND HAD AN AVERAGE OF OVER $200,000 IN AVERAGE ANNUAL GROSS SALES DURING THE THREE YEAR PERIOD 2011-2013.

Average Annual Gross Sales for the Three Year Period 2011-13 of Ownership Groups with More Than $200,000 in Annual Gross Sales

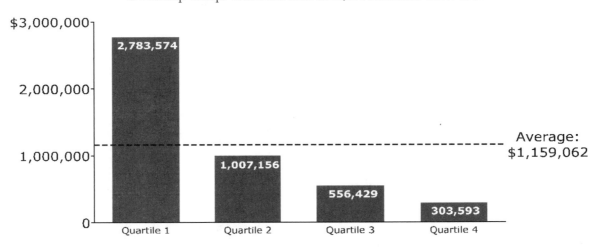

	First Quartile	Second Quartile	Third Quartile	Fourth Quartile	All Quartiles
Average Gross Sales	$2,783,574	$1,007,156	$556,429	$303,593	$1,159,062
High	$11,991,509	$1,320,111	$721,595	$410,155	$11,991,509
Low	$1,334,501	$724,042	$411,537	$200,105	$200,105

# of Ownership Groups	111	112	112	112	447
# Above Average	32	55	53	57	141
# Below Average	79	57	59	55	306
% Above Average	29%	49%	47%	51%	32%
% Below Average	71%	51%	53%	49%	68%
Average # of Reporting Licenses per Ownership Group	5.7	3.1	2.2	1.8	3.2
High Number of Licenses	49	12	9	6	49
Low Number of Licenses	1	1	1	1	1

Janitorial Service

The following financial performance representation consists of historical data for Ownership Groups offering Janitorial Services in the United States of America that have been operating a business for at least two years as of January 1, 2011. We have not included data from similar franchises in Canada or any other foreign country or territory. Many franchisees have more than one franchise agreement related to their business. Franchisees with multiple franchises typically do not have separate operations for each franchise agreement. Therefore, we have aggregated data based on "Ownership Groups" to more accurately reflect a franchisees' business. There are 454 Ownership Groups that had at least one license with a start date of January 1, 2009 or before and with the ability to perform Janitorial Services.

The tables below include Ownership Groups with at least $200,000 in annual gross sales from Janitorial Services. Of the 454 Ownership Groups, 273 (or 60%) had annual gross sales of at least $200,000 attributable to Janitorial Services during the three year period 2011-2013. Ownership Groups included in the table below have an average of 1.7 franchise agreements per Ownership Group. Ownership Groups with an average of less than $200,000 in annual gross sales for Janitorial Services during the three year period 2011- 2013 have been excluded. Ownership Groups with an average of less than $200,000 in annual gross sales account for 4.6% of annual gross sales for all Ownership Groups. Lower gross sales may be a result of a focus on a different service line among other potential causes.

In the past we sold franchise businesses that could provide multiple services (disaster restoration, janitorial, floor cleaning) under one franchise agreement. We still offer these franchise agreements through renewal. Many Ownership Groups provide services in multiple service categories. The average annual gross sales reported below include only gross sales reported for Janitorial Services and excludes all other services.

We compiled this information from the reported gross sales from franchisees for January 2011 through December 2013. We have not independently verified the information received from franchisees. These financial statements were not prepared in accordance with Generally Accepted Accounting Principles (GAAP), but are believed to be reliable. We will provide you with written substantiation of the data used in preparing the financial performance representations in this Item 19 upon reasonable request.

Some franchisees have gross sales of this amount. There is no assurance you will do as well. If you rely on our figures, you must accept the risk of not doing as well.

Table 2, Janitorial Service

AVERAGE ANNUAL GROSS SALES DURING THE THREE YEAR PERIOD 2011-2013 BY QUARTILE FOR ALL OWNERSHIP GROUPS WHO HAVE BEEN IN BUSINESS FOR AT LEAST THREE CALENDAR YEARS AND HAD AN AVERAGE OF OVER $200,000 IN AVERAGE ANNUAL GROSS SALES DURING THE THREE YEAR PERIOD 2011-2013.

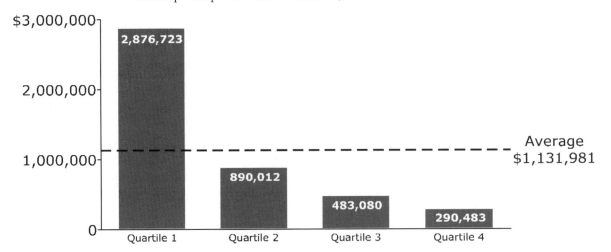

Average Annual Gross Sales for the Three Year Period 2011-13 of Ownership Groups with More Than $200,000 in Annual Gross Sales

	First Quartile	Second Quartile	Third Quartile	Fourth Quartile	All Quartiles
Average Gross Sales	$2,876,723	$890,012	$483,080	$290,483	$1,131,981
High	$12,640,947	$1,253,138	$592,731	$380,885	$12,640,947
Low	$1,264,108	$600,030	$387,503	$200,783	$200,783
# of Ownership Groups	68	68	68	69	273
# Above Average	21	34	32	33	79
# Below Average	47	34	36	36	194
% Above Average	31%	50%	47%	48%	29%
% Below Average	69%	50%	53%	52%	71%
Average # of Reporting Licenses per Ownership Group	2.4	1.9	1.4	1.2	1.7
High Number of Licenses	12	10	3	2	12
Low Number of Licenses	1	1	1	1	1

Floor Care Service

The following financial performance representation consists of historical data for Ownership Groups offering Floor Care Services in the United States of America that have been operating a business for at least two years as of January 1, 2011. We have not included data from similar franchises in Canada or any other foreign country or territory. Many franchisees have more than one franchise agreement related to their business. Franchisees with multiple franchises typically do not have separate operations for each franchise agreement. Therefore, we have aggregated data based on "Ownership Groups" to more accurately reflect a franchisee's business. There are 831 Ownership Groups that had at least one license with a start date of January 1, 2009 or before and with the ability to perform Floor Care Services.

The tables below include Ownership Groups with at least $75,000 in annual gross sales from Floor Care Services. Of the 831 Ownership groups, 334 (or 40%) had annual gross sales of at least $75,000 attributable to Floor Care Services during the three year period 2011-2013. Ownership Groups included in the table below have an average of 3.4 franchise agreements per Ownership Group. Ownership Groups with an average of less than $75,000 in annual gross sales for Floor Care Services during the three year period 2011- 2013 have been excluded.

Ownership Groups with an average of less than $75,000 in annual gross sales account for 19.4% of annual gross sales for all Ownership Groups. Lower gross sales may be a result of a focus on a different service line among other potential causes.

In the past we sold franchise businesses that could provide multiple services (disaster restoration, janitorial, floor cleaning) under one franchise agreement. We still offer these franchise agreements through renewal. Many Ownership Groups provide services in multiple service categories. The average annual gross sales reported below include only gross sales reported for Floor Care Services and excludes all other services.

We compiled this information from the reported gross sales from franchisees for January 2011 through December 2013. We have not independently verified the information received from franchisees. These financial statements were not prepared in accordance with Generally Accepted Accounting Principles

(GAAP), but are believed to be reliable. We will provide you with written substantiation of the data used in preparing the financial performance representations in this Item 19 upon reasonable request.

Some franchisees have gross sales of this amount. There is no assurance you will do as well. If you rely on our figures, you must accept the risk of not doing as well.

Table 3, Floor Care Service

AVERAGE ANNUAL GROSS SALES DURING THE THREE YEAR PERIOD 2011-2013 BY QUARTILE FOR ALL OWNERSHIP GROUPS WHO HAVE BEEN IN BUSINESS FOR AT LEAST THREE CALENDAR YEARS AND HAD AN AVERAGE OF OVER $75,000 IN AVERAGE ANNUAL GROSS SALES DURING THE THREE YEAR PERIOD 2011-2013.

Average Annual Gross Sales for the Three Year Period 2011-13 of Ownership Groups with More Than $75,000 in Annual Gross Sales

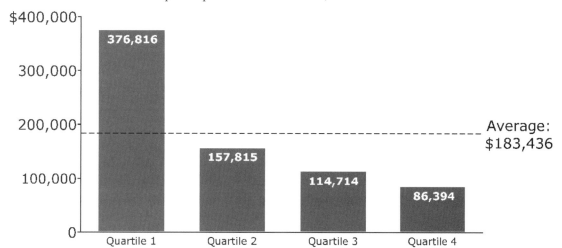

	First Quartile	Second Quartile	Third Quartile	Fourth Quartile	All Quartiles
Average Gross Sales	$376,816	$157,815	$114,714	$86,394	$183,436
High	$1,507,179	$192,052	$130,426	$100,858	$1,507,179
Low	$192,204	$131,717	$100,954	$75,279	$75,279
# of Ownership Groups	83	83	84	84	334
# Above Average	28	39	39	41	95
# Below Average	55	44	45	43	239
% Above Average	34%	47%	46%	49%	28%
% Below Average	66%	53%	54%	51%	72%
Average # of Reporting Licenses per Ownership Group	5.0	3.7	2.4	2.6	3.4

High Number of Licenses	29	11	7	7	29
Low Number of Licenses	1	1	1	1	1

Other than as outlined above, ServiceMaster does not furnish, or authorize our salespersons (or anyone else) to furnish, and you should not rely on, any oral or written information concerning the actual or potential sales, income or profits of a ServiceMaster franchise. We have not suggested, and certainly cannot guarantee, that you will succeed in the operation of your franchised business, because the most important factors in the success of any ServiceMaster franchised business, including the one to be operated by you, are your personal business, marketing, management, judgment, and other skills and your willingness to work hard and follow the System. Actual results vary from area to area, and market to market. We cannot estimate or project the results for any particular franchised business.

You are likely to achieve results that are different, possibly significantly and adversely, from the results shown above. Many factors, including management capabilities, local market conditions, and other factors, are unique to each business and may significantly impact the financial performance of your business. Consider that a newly opened business should not be expected to achieve sales volumes or maintain expenses similar to those of an established business.

Neither ServiceMaster nor any of its affiliates, make any promises or representations of any kind that you will achieve any particular results or level of sales or profitability or even achieve break-even results in any particular year of operation.

You are responsible for developing your own business plan for your business, including capital budgets, financial statements, projections and other elements appropriate to your particular circumstances. The expenses identified in this statement are not the only expenses that you will incur in connection with the operation of your store. Additional expenses that you may incur include royalty and marketing fees (see item 6 of this disclosure document), interest on debt service, insurance, legal and accounting charges, and depreciation/amortization. We encourage you to consult with your own accounting, business, and legal advisors to assist you to identify the expenses you likely will incur in connection with your business, to prepare your budgets and to assess the likely or potential financial performance of your business. We also encourage you to contact existing operators to discuss the business.

In developing the business plan for your business, you are cautioned to make necessary allowance for change in financial results to income, expenses, or both, that may result from operation of your business during periods of, or in geographic areas suffering from, economic downturns, inflation, unemployment, or other negative economic influences.

Historical costs and revenues do not necessarily correspond to future costs and revenues because of factors such as inflation, deflation, changes in minimum wage laws and other benefit laws (including but not limited to, health care coverage), location, financing, lease-related costs and other variables. For example, costs such as rent, CAM charges, taxes, interest, insurance and utilities vary from business to business. All information should be evaluated in light of current market conditions including such costs and price information as may then be available.

Other than the preceding financial performance representation, we do not make any financial performance representations. We also do not authorize our employees or representatives to make any such representations either orally or in writing. If you are purchasing an existing outlet, however, we may provide you with the actual records of that outlet. If you receive any other financial performance information or projections of your future income, you should report it to the franchisor's management by contacting Sherry Campbell, ServiceMaster Clean, 3839 Forest Hill-Irene Road, Memphis, (901) 597-7500, the Federal Trade Commission, and the appropriate state regulatory agencies.

Kids. Haircuts. Parties. Fun.

SNIP-ITS

6409 City West Parkway # 205-A
Eden Prairie, MN 55344
Tel: (877) 288-7487, (952) 288-2222
Fax: (952) 288-2235
Email: inquiry@snipits.com
Website: www.snipitsfranchise.com
Kim Ellis, Vice President of Franchise Development

Snip-its has changed the dynamic of children's haircare by turning what has traditionally been considered a mundane and often unpleasant experience into a fun-filled adventure. The Snip-its custom interior features an original cast of cartoon characters, interactive computer play stations, the Magic Box, and a complete line of haircare products formulated just for kids. These, along with our proprietary point of sale, proven marketing system, and specially trained stylists represent one of the most innovative franchise opportunities available. With more than 65 locations nationwide, Snip-its' franchise program is a unique franchise opportunity with great earning potential.

BACKGROUND

IFA Member:	Yes
Established & First Franchised:	1995; 2003
Franchised Units:	64
Company-Owned Units:	1
Total Units:	65
Distribution:	US – 65; CAN – 0; O'seas – 0

North America:	25 States, 0 Provinces
Density:	13 in TX, 10 in MA, 4 in NY
Projected New Units (12 Months):	12
Qualifications:	5, 5, 1, 4, 2, 5

FINANCIAL/TERMS

Cash Investment:	$100K
Total Investment:	$120.3 – 255.4K
Minimum Net Worth:	$500K
Fees (Franchise):	$25K
Fees (Royalty):	6%
Fees (Advertising):	2%
Term of Contract (Years):	10/5
Average Number of Employees:	8 FT, 2 PT
Passive Ownership:	Allowed
Encourage Conversions:	No
Area Development Agreements:	Yes
Sub-Franchising Contracts:	No
Expand in Territory:	No
Space Needs:	1,200 SF

SUPPORT & TRAINING

Financial Assistance Provided:	No
Site Selection Assistance:	Yes
Lease Negotiation Assistance:	Yes
Co-operative Advertising:	Yes
Franchisee Association/Member:	No
Size of Corporate Staff:	9
On-going Support:	a, B, C, D, E, F, G, h
Training:	1 Week On-Site; 1 Week Minneapolis, MN

SPECIFIC EXPANSION PLANS

US:	East Coast and Southwest
Canada:	No
Overseas:	No

We provide below historical data relating to operations at certain franchised Salons. Table 1 below provides historical data relating to average sales, certain expenses, and operating profit of 21 franchised Snip-its Salons operated by our multi-unit franchisees during the entire 2012 (January 1, 2012 through December 31, 2012) and 2013 (January 1, 2013 through December 31, 2013) calendar years. Table 2 below provides historical data relating to average sales, certain expenses, and operating profit of all (seven) franchised Snip-its Salons operated in the Boston, Massachusetts market during the entire 2012 (January 1, 2012 through December 31, 2012) and 2013 (January 1, 2013 through December 31, 2013) calendar years.

1. Results of 21 Franchised Snip-its Salons Operated by Multi-Unit Operators

Table 1 below shows the average expenses at 21 franchised Snip-its Salons operated by multi-unit operators (meaning those of our franchisees who operated two or more Snip-its Salons) during the entire 2012 and 2013 calendar years. Table 1 also shows certain average expenses incurred at those Salons expressed as a percentage of total sales, as well as average operating profit. The franchised Salons included in Table 1 are limited to those operated by our multi-unit franchisees because we expect and encourage our new franchisees to enter into a Development Agreement, 3-Pack Agreement, or 5-Pack Agreement in order to achieve certain efficiencies. Please read carefully all of the information in Table 1, and all of the notes following the Tables, in conjunction with your review of the historical data.

Multi-Unit Franchised Salon Averages Based on Sales Range

Gross Sales Range ($000)	Number of Salons in this Range	Average Gross Sales in Range	# of Salons Within Range that Met or Exceeded Average Annual Gross Sales Volume	% of Salons in Range that Met or Exceeded Average Annual Gross Sales Volume	Certain Expenses as a % of Gross Sales			Operating Profit %	Operating Profit $
					Labor	Occupancy	Other		
$285+	6	$315,084	3	50%	38.4%	20.0%	26.2%	15.4%	$48,523
$200 - $285	11	$245,011	5	45%	40.4%	18.6%	28.5%	12.5%	$30,626
<$200	4	$181,960	3	75%	41.2%	21.1%	29.7%	8.0%	$14,557
All Salons in Sample	21	$253,022	11	52%	40.0%	19.5%	27.6%	12.9%	$32,699

2. Results of 7 Franchised Snip-its Salons in the Boston, Massachusetts Market

Table 2 below shows the average expenses at seven franchised Snip-its Salons operated in the Boston, Massachusetts market during the entire 2012 and 2013 calendar years. Table 2 also shows certain average expenses incurred at those Salons expressed as a percentage of total sales, as well as average operating profit. The franchised Salons included in Table 2 are limited to those operated by our franchisees in the Boston, Massachusetts market because the Boston market is our most "mature" market. The Snip-its Salons operated in and around Boston have been operating for a longer period of time than in any other market in the United States. The average results at the Snip-its Salons in Table 2 therefore tend to be more favorable than the average results achieved by Snip-its Salons in other markets. You should take this into account when you compare the results of the Salons in Table 2 to the market in which you may plan to establish and operate a Snip-its Salon. Please read carefully all of the information in Table 2, and all of the notes following the Tables, in conjunction with your review of the historical data.

Boston Market Franchised Salon Averages Based on Sales Range

Gross Sales Range	Number of Salons in this Range	Average Gross Sales in Range	# of Salons Within Range that Met or Exceeded Average Annual Gross Sales Volume	% of Salons in Range that Met or Exceeded Average Annual Gross Sales Volume	Expenses as a % of Gross Sales			Operating Profit %	Operating Profit $
					Labor	Occupancy	Other		
$350+	4	$409,452	1	25%	34.6%	17.1%	27.5%	20.8%	$85,166
< $350	3	$286,066	2	67%	39.7%	20.4%	23.8%	16.1%	$46,057
All Salons in Sample	7	$356,572	4	57%	36.8%	18.5%	25.9%	18.8%	$67,036

Notes to Tables:

1. Table 1 presents the results at 21 franchised Snip-its Salons operated by our multi-unit operators (meaning those of our franchisees who operated at least two or more Snip-its Salons) during the entire 2012 and 2013 calendar years. Table 1 therefore does not include the results at 28 franchised Snipits Salons operated by our single-unit operators during the 2012 and 2013 calendar years. Table 1 also does not include results from Snip-its Salons operated by multi-unit operators that were not open by January 1, 2011 (6 franchised Salons met this criteria), and also does not include results from Snip-its

Salons operated by multi-unit operators during the 2012 and 2013 calendar years from which we did not receive sufficient financial reporting information (9 Salons met this criteria).

2. Table 2 presents the results at seven franchised Snip-its Salons operated in the Boston, Massachusetts market during the entire 2012 and 2013 calendar years. Each of these seven franchised Salons located in the Boston, Massachusetts market operated during the entire 2012 and 2013 calendar years. Table 2 does not include the results from one franchised Salon located in the Boston market that was not open continually during the 2012 and 2013 calendar years, and also does not include results from our affiliate-operated Salon in Framingham, Massachusetts, which is located within the Boston market.

3. The average sales figures are based on actual operating results of the franchised Salons for only the 2013 calendar year as reported to us. Some Salons have achieved these results. Your individual results may differ. There is no assurance you will sell as much.

4. The expense and profit information provided in the Tables reflects the performance at each of the included Salons during the 2012 calendar year (and not 2013, the most recent calendar year just ended), because complete expense information is not at the time of this Disclosure Document available from each of these franchised Salons. So to be clear, the expenses expressed as a percentage of sales in each Table compare 2012 expenses to 2013 sales. We believe that the expense results for the Salons included in the Tables are not likely to change materially from 2012 to 2013. Each Salon offered similar products and services as would generally be offered by a typical Snip-its Salon.

5. The average expenses reflected in the Tables are expressed as a percentage of the average Gross Sales at those Salons. As an example, an expense category of 40% means that for every ten dollars of Gross Sales earned at the Salon, four dollars are spent on that particular expense.

6. The average labor costs include all employee-related expenses including: wages, salary, bonus, benefits and commission. Labor costs also include payroll taxes, which are amounts paid to local, state and federal governments for FICA, and federal and state unemployment insurance, based on the wages paid to employees. These amounts are set by governmental authorities, and will vary from state to state. Labor costs vary widely among our franchisee-owned and affiliate-owned Snip-its Salons, as our franchisees (and you) are free to set their own compensation, benefits and bonus packages for their employees. The total amount of wages for your employees and managers at a particular location will vary according to local wages, the number of employees, and the number of hours that the Salon is open for business. You must make labor, wage, and benefit determinations based on your market, experience, and other factors. You may set and pay compensation (and any benefits) at any level you determine. The figures in the Tables do not include any compensation to a franchisee or owner. But, as a franchisee, you may decide to compensate one or more of your owners in lieu of one or more managers. Please note that your labor costs may differ, and may be affected by a variety of factors, including, among others, local costs and wage rates, availability of labor and materials in your market area, your involvement in the management of your Salon, and the size and professionalism of your management team.

7. The average occupancy costs include all rent, common area maintenance, real estate taxes and any other pass-through expenses from the landlord.

8. The average "other" expenses include all other cash expense items not included elsewhere. These include: cost of goods sold, supplies, recruiting, education and training, merchant fees, continuing franchise fees (royalty fees), advertising contributions, bank charges, professional fees, cash over/short, travel and entertainment, repairs and maintenance, insurance (including, among other things, worker's compensation insurance), dues and subscriptions, utilities, telephone and internet expenses. There may be other costs in the operation of your Salon that are not included in this discussion. You should conduct an independent investigation of the costs and expenses you will or may incur in operating your franchised Snip-its Salon. Franchisees or former franchisees listed in this disclosure document may be one source of this information.

9. The average operating profit figures do not include any provision for income taxes or for non-cash expenses such as depreciation or amortization. It also does not include any reserve for future capital expenditures. In Table 1, for the six Salons in the Average Gross Sales range above $285,000, four of those Salons (or 66%) met or exceeded the Average Operating Profit figures presented for that range; for the 11 Salons in the Average Gross Sales range between $200,000 and $285,000, six of those Salons (or 55%) met or exceeded the Average Operating Profit figures presented for that range; and for the four Salons in the Average Gross Sales range below $200,000, two of those Salons (or 50%) met or exceeded the Average Operating Profit figures presented for that range. In Table 2, for the four Salons in the Average Gross Sales range above $350,000, two of those Salons (or 50%) met or exceeded the Average Operating Profit figures presented for that range; and for the three Salons in the Average Gross Sales range below $350,000, two of those Salons (or 66%) met or exceeded the Average Operating Profit figures presented for that range.

10. The data shown in the Tables is unaudited. Written substantiation of the data used in preparing the information in

this Item is on file at our offices and will be made available to you upon reasonable request.

Other than the preceding financial performance representation, we do not make any financial performance representations. We also do not authorize our employees or representatives to make any such representations either orally or in writing. If you are purchasing an existing outlet, however, we may provide you with the actual records of that outlet. If you receive any other financial performance information or projections of your future income, you should report it to our management by contacting Mr. James George at 6409 City West Parkway, Suite 205 A, Eden Prairie, Minnesota 55344, telephone (952) 288-2222, the Federal Trade Commission, and the appropriate state regulatory agencies.

SPHERION STAFFING SERVICES

One Overton Park 3625 Cumberland Blvd., # 600
Atlanta, GA 30339
Tel: (800) 903-0082, (404) 964-5508
Email: billtasillo@spherion.com
Website: www.spherion.com
Bill Tasillo, Vice President of Market Expansion

SPHERION franchise opportunities provide individuals a chance to join an exciting and rewarding industry: temporary staffing. We placed millions of workers in flexible and full-time jobs during our over 60 years in business. Continuous innovation and decades of growth have helped SPHERION become an industry leader. Entrepreneur Magazine ranked SPHERION Best Staffing Service for five straight years. Our franchisees contribute their talent, commitment and passion to building our brand.

BACKGROUND
IFA Member:	Yes
Established & First Franchised:	1946; 1956
Franchised Units:	153
Company-Owned Units:	0
Total Units:	153
Distribution:	US – 153; CAN – 0; O'seas – 0
North America:	46 States, 0 Provinces
Density:	29 in FL, 29 in CA, 27 in OH

Projected New Units (12 Months):	10
Qualifications:	5, 4, 1, 3, 4, 4

FINANCIAL/TERMS
Cash Investment:	$100 – 170K
Total Investment:	$98 – 164K
Minimum Net Worth:	$100K
Fees (Franchise):	$25K
Fees (Royalty):	3 – 6%/25%
Fees (Advertising):	0.25%
Term of Contract (Years):	10/5
Average Number of Employees:	3 FT, 0 PT
Passive Ownership:	Allowed
Encourage Conversions:	Yes
Area Development Agreements:	No
Sub-Franchising Contracts:	No
Expand in Territory:	Yes
Space Needs:	1,000 SF

SUPPORT & TRAINING
Financial Assistance Provided:	No
Site Selection Assistance:	Yes
Lease Negotiation Assistance:	Yes
Co-operative Advertising:	Yes
Franchisee Association/Member:	No
Size of Corporate Staff:	525
On-going Support:	A, B, C, D, E, G, H, I
Training:	Over 112 Hours In-Office Instruction; Additional Self-Paced Instruction

SPECIFIC EXPANSION PLANS
US:	Targeted Cities in US
Canada:	No
Overseas:	No

Spherion believes it will be helpful for a prospective franchisee to know the average Gross Profit percentage, the average per Franchise Agreement annual Sales, and the average per franchise agreement annual Gross Profit of its franchises for FY 2013. "Gross Profit" and "Sales" have the meanings given them in the Franchise Agreement.

The average Gross Profit percentage of our franchises for FY 2013 was 17.3%. The average annual Sales per Franchise Agreement of our franchises for FY 2013 were $4,858,544, and the average annual Gross Profit per Franchise Agreement of our franchises for FY the same period was $842,851.

The information for the average Gross Profit percentage, annual Gross Profit, and annual Sales is only for our franchises in operation for all of FY 2013. The information for Sales and Gross Profit is for franchises on a per Franchise Agreement basis. That is, if a franchisee has more than one Franchise Agreement with us, then the numbers achieved under each Franchise Agreement are considered separately. If a franchisee has more than one office under the same Franchise Agreement, these offices are aggregated to determine the average number for agreements. For this performance representation, however, the results of two tenured franchisees with multiple offices under the same agreement are divided into separate markets and included in the average Sales and Gross Profit numbers as under multiple agreements. We believe breaking out the information in this manner for these tenured franchises provides a more accurate picture for future agreements.

In FY 2012, the franchises under twenty-seven of the fifty-eight Franchise Agreements attained or surpassed the average Gross Profit percentage stated above. Those under twenty-five of the Agreements attained or surpassed the average annual Sales stated above, and the franchises under twenty-two of the Agreements attained or surpassed the average annual Gross Profit stated above.

This information is largely that of mature franchises. We had only six franchisees start up a new office under a new Franchise Agreement in Fiscal Years 2009-2013. Other new franchisees in that period bought existing offices, either from us or from a franchisee, as opposed to starting a new office. The information is for all of our Spherion branded franchised operations. The information does not include any of the "Area Based Franchise Agreement" program franchises, described further in Item 1, which operate under a fundamentally different relationship and agreement.

Your results will likely differ from the results presented above, depending on your efforts and those of your staff, your particular market size and makeup, and the competition. Other factors that could impact your numbers include, but are not limited to local, regional, national, and international general economic conditions, your business mix (temporary staffing vs. permanent placement, clerical vs. light industrial, and the amount of professional staffing you have, if you receive the right to offer professional staffing services), etc.

Gross Profit calculations are fundamental to our business. We have prepared the following to assist you in understanding a Gross Profit calculation.

To determine what you would charge a client to achieve a certain Gross Profit (GP) percentage, you would do the following calculation:

Pay rate (PR)	=	x		
Burden cost	=	y		
Total cost	=	TC		
(TC) divided by (1- desired GP%)			=	Bill Rate (BR)
Example:				
Pay rate	=	$10.00		
Burden cost	=	$1.40 (14%)		
Total cost	=	$11.40		

($11.40) divided by	(1-20.4%) =	Bill Rate
$11.40 divided by .796	=	$14.32

The Gross Profit amount here would be:

$14.32 BR
-$11.40 TC
$ 2.92 GP

These figures are only estimates of what we think you may earn. Your individual results may differ. There is no assurance you'll earn as much.

Note that we have used example numbers based on our average Gross Profit as stated above. Your burden numbers will vary depending on what state you are in. The Workers' Compensation Risk Factor will vary depending on the type of job you are filling, and the payrate will vary depending on the job you are filling and the comparable payrates in your market. The purpose of this example is only to show you how the basic Gross Profit calculation is done in our industry.

The financial performance representations above do not reflect the costs of sales, operating expenses, or other costs or expenses that must be deducted from the gross revenues or gross sales figures to obtain your net income or profit. As stated below, you should conduct an independent investigation of the costs and expenses you will incur in operating your franchised business. Franchisees or former franchisees listed in the disclosure document may be one source of information. To help you analyze what your expenses might be on a monthly basis, we have listed below what we believe to be your normal monthly expense items.

- Salaries and Wages
- Commission/bonus accrual
- Employee Benefits (including payroll taxes and health, life and disability insurance)
- Franchise Data Processing Allocation (MISTEF fee-paragraph 8 of the Franchise Agreement)
- Insurance (for example, see the required insurances in paragraph 7(q) of the Franchise Agreement)
- National Advertising
- Local Advertising
- Classified and yellow page advertising
- Meetings/seminars/courses/conventions
- Office supplies
- Equipment/software repair/maintenance
- Bank/credit card fees
- Rent (premises lease)
- Rent (equipment)
- Repairs and maintenance
- Depreciation and amortization expense
- Utilities
- Interest Expense (includes interest on AR over 60 days charged by Spherion)
- Professional fees
- Telecommunications
- Automobile & parking
- Other Travel
- Customer relations/development
- Bad debt expense
- Taxes & franchises
- Miscellaneous

This expense listing may not be a complete listing for you, and we do not make any representations to you as to what the actual expenses in each category will be. The answers to those questions will depend on your market and how you set up your business. You should consult with your financial advisor, as well as discuss the list and the expenses involved with our other franchisees, and former franchisees, which are listed in an exhibit to this disclosure document.

Substantiation of the data used in the preparation of this Item 19 will be made available to you upon reasonable request.

IT'S GOOD TO BE A GUY

SPORT CLIPS

P.O. Box 3000-266
Georgetown, TX 78627
Tel: (800) 872-4247, (512) 869-1201
Fax: (512) 868-4601
Email: karen.young@sportclips.com
Website: www.sportclipsfranchise.com
Karen Young, Franchise Recruitment Manager

Our fun, sports-themed, men's and boys' haircutting concept is so unique it has made us the fastest-growing haircutting franchise in the country. This is a great recession-resistant business that's all cash, no receivables, and no industry experience is necessary. Better yet, you keep your current job while building your SPORT CLIPS business for the future.

BACKGROUND

IFA Member:	Yes
Established & First Franchised:	1993; 1995
Franchised Units:	1,178
Company-Owned Units:	29
Total Units:	1,207
Distribution:	US – 1,196; CAN – 11; O'seas – 0
North America:	45 States, 1 Province
Density:	174 in TX, 104 in CA, 82 in IL
Projected New Units (12 Months):	180
Qualifications:	4, 5, 1, 1, 3, 5
FINANCIAL/TERMS	
Cash Investment:	$100K
Total Investment:	$158.3 – $316.5K
Minimum Net Worth:	$300K
Fees (Franchise):	$25 – 59.5K
Fees (Royalty):	6%
Fees (Advertising):	$300 – 400/week
Term of Contract (Years):	5/5
Average Number of Employees:	6 – 8 FT, 0 PT
Passive Ownership:	Discouraged
Encourage Conversions:	No
Area Development Agreements:	Yes
Sub-Franchising Contracts:	No
Expand in Territory:	Yes
Space Needs:	1,200 SF

SUPPORT & TRAINING

Financial Assistance Provided:	Yes (D)
Site Selection Assistance:	Yes
Lease Negotiation Assistance:	Yes
Co-operative Advertising:	Yes
Franchisee Association/Member:	No
Size of Corporate Staff:	98
On-going Support:	C, D, E, F, G, H, I

Training: 1 Week Locally for Manager; 5 Days Georgetown, TX for Franchisee; 1 Week Local

SPECIFIC EXPANSION PLANS

US:	All United States
Canada:	Yes
Overseas:	No

At the end of calendar year 2013, there were 1,123 franchised Sport Clips stores. The two Statements of Gross Sales below do not include four stores in Rochester, New York, which are not typical Sport Clips stores and operate under a special limited services license agreement that is not offered to new franchisees. Although we do not have complete sales data for the stores in Rochester, New York, we know that their gross sales are, on average, less than other stores in the System.

Except for the stores in Rochester, New York, all stores included in the Statements of Gross Sales did not receive any services that were not generally available to other Sport Clips stores, and each store offered similar products and services as would generally be offered by a typical Sport Clips store.

The gross sales figures included in the first Statement of Gross Sales below are based upon all 728 Sport Clips franchise stores and Company-owned stores that were in continual operation for the entire calendar years of 2011, 2012, and 2013. The gross sales figures are taken directly from gross sales reports made by the stores to the Company.

STATEMENT OF GROSS SALES YEAR 2013 GROSS SALES AS REPORTED TO THE COMPANY (728 STORES IN CONTINUAL OPERATION DURING 2011, 2012 AND 2013)		
Gross Sales	Number of Stores	Percentage of Stores/Cumulative % of stores at each level or higher
Over $500,000	94	13%/13%
$450,001 - $500,000	62	8%/21%
$400,001 - $450,000	95	13%/34%
$350,001 - $400,000	123	17%/51%
$300,001 - $350,000	155	22%/73%
$250,001 - $300,000	133	18%/91%
$200,001 - $250,000	57	8%/99%
Less than $200,000	9	1%/100%
Total	728	100%

These 728 stores had average sales of $375,777 for the entire year 2013. 314 stores had sales above this average, and 414 stores had sales lower than the average.

The gross sales figures included in the second Statement of Gross Sales below are based upon all 824 Sport Clips franchise stores and Company-owned stores that were in continual operation for the entire calendar years of 2012 and 2013. The gross sales figures are taken directly from gross sales reports made by the stores to the Company.

STATEMENT OF GROSS SALES YEAR 2013 GROSS SALES AS REPORTED TO THE COMPANY (824 STORES IN CONTINUAL OPERATION DURING 2012 AND 2013)		
Gross Sales	Number of Stores	Percentage of Stores/Cumulative % of stores at each level or higher
Over $500,000	97	12%/12%
$450,001 - $500,000	64	8%/20%
$400,001 - $450,000	98	11%/31%
$350,001 - $400,000	130	16%/47%
$300,001 - $350,000	174	21%/68%
$250,001 - $300,000	158	20%/88%
$200,001 - $250,000	84	10%/98%
Less than $200,000	19	2%/100%
Total	824	100%

These 824 stores had average sales of $365,193 for the entire year 2013. 356 stores had sales above this average, and 468 stores had sales lower than the average. Some outlets have sold this amount. Your individual results may differ. There is no assurance you'll sell as much.

The financial performance representations above do not reflect the costs of sales, operating expenses, or other costs or expenses that must be deducted from gross revenue or gross sales figures to obtain your net income or profit. You should conduct an independent investigation of the costs and expenses you will incur in operating your Sport Clips franchise. Franchisees or former franchisees, listed in the Disclosure Document, may be one source of this information.

In addition to actual sales, an important metric for any retail business is the growth in same store sales year-over-year. For the fourth quarter of 2013, the 945 stores that were open one year or more at the beginning of the quarter averaged $6,724 per week in sales, which annualized would be $349,648. 404 stores had average sales higher than this amount, and 541 had lower sales. This was an increase for these same stores over the fourth quarter of 2012 of 8.6%, with 4.3% of this increase coming from increases in Client counts and the remainder from increases in average tickets. Increases in average tickets came from a combination of some individual store price increases, a decrease in the amount of couponing and discounting, and an increase in the number of Clients who purchased a more expensive service (such as our signature MVP service) or who bought more hair care products to take home.

Expense Reports for Company-Owned Stores During 2013

The Expense Report below shows the average expenses at each store's sales level and those expenses as a percentage of total revenue in each column.

We owned and operated 18 stores in the Austin, Texas market during 2013. These stores include a store we purchased in March 2013, two new stores opened in February 2013 and July 2013 and a store we relocated in November 2013.

Results for the two stores opened in February 2013 and July 2013 and for the store we purchased in March 2013 are not included in the data below as we did not own and operate the stores for all of 2013. We are not offering franchises in this market.

The Expense Report below also excludes one store that is operated in a substantially different environment during the year and one store that was relocated in 2013, but was open in two locations between August 2013 and November 2013 while we operated in both the new location and in the original location until the end of the original location's existing lease. The managers of the Company-owned stores included in the Expense Report did not receive any services that were not generally available to other Sport Clips stores. Each store offered similar products and services as would generally be offered by a typical Sport Clips store, except for limited tests of procedures, products and/or services that may or may not be eventually incorporated into the system, depending on the success of the tests.

	Sales Less Than $350,000	Sales $350,001 to $400,000	Sales $400,001 to $450,000	Sales Greater Than $450,001	Average of all stores
Number of Stores	2	1	3	7	13
Gross Sales	$269,645 100%	$392,727 100%	$431,607 100%	$575,828 100%	$481,357 100%
Variable Costs (Note 1)	$24,146 9%	$31,130 8%	$36,283 8%	$46,514 8%	$39,529 8%
Payroll (Note 2)	$115,593 43%	$177,636 45%	$177,532 41%	$244,424 42%	$204,029 42%
Occupancy (Note 3)	$51,415 19%	$60,833 15%	$63,074 15%	$60,190 12%	$59,555 12%
Advertising (Note 4)	$17,352 6%	$21,790 6%	$22,522 5%	$26,112 5%	$23,603 5%
Miscellaneous (Note 5)	$2,530 1%	$2,557 1%	$2,368 1%	$2,620 1%	$2,544 1%
Operating Profit (Note 6)	$58,609 22%	$98,781 25%	$129,828 30%	$195,968 34%	$152,097 32%

Note 1. Variable Costs include operating supplies, cost of goods sold, bank service charges, credit card discounts, and advertising to recruit Stylists.

Note 2. Payroll includes direct payroll, including payroll for an on-site full-time manager, payroll taxes and fringe benefits except for 401K and medical insurance costs.

Note 3. Occupancy includes rent, pass-through expenses from the landlord, utilities, phone charges, and repairs and maintenance.

Note 4. Advertising includes the weekly payments to the Ad Fund plus other advertising and marketing expenses for the store.

Note 5. Miscellaneous expense includes magazine subscriptions, store insurance contributions to the Sport Clips Wayne McGlone Memorial Relief Fund, and overages and/or shortages from the cash drawer.

Note 6. Operating Profit does not include an amount paid for royalties or weekly training fees. The numbers in the Expense Report are unaudited, but we believe that these numbers are substantially correct.

We own and operate 10 stores in the Las Vegas market. We are not offering franchises in this market. The results of these stores are in the data below.

The Expense Report below shows the average sales for the ten Las Vegas stores and expenses that were open for the full year of 2013 as a percentage of total revenue. The managers of the Company-owned stores included in the Expense Report did not receive any services that were not generally available to other Sport Clips stores. Each store offered similar products and services as would generally be offered by a typical Sport Clips store, except for limited tests of procedures, products and/or services that may or may not be eventually incorporated into the system, depending on the success of the tests. While the results for these ten stores are less favorable than for our Austin area stores, the Las Vegas economy was one of the worst, if not the worst, in the country in 2013. We are very optimistic about the Las Vegas market long-term, and see the current downturn in the economy as an opportunity for Sport Clips to strengthen our market position and increase our market share.

	Sales Less than $200,000	Sales $200,001 to $300,000	Sales $300,001 to $350,001	Sales Greater than $350,000	Average of all Stores
Number of Stores	1	3	3	3	10
Gross Sales	$160,626 100%	$272,517 100%	$321,886 100%	$365,856 100%	$304,140 100%
Variable Costs (Note 1)	$18,995 11%	$26,155 10%	$26,980 8%	$31,507 9%	$27,265 9%

Payroll (Note 2)	$96,101 60%	$127,032 47%	$151,177 47%	$168,585 46%	$143,648 47%
Occupancy (Note 3)	$54,669 34%	$55,738 20%	$50,311 16%	$53,391 14%	$53,299 17%
Advertising (Note 4)	$17,416 11%	$16,689 6%	$17,307 5%	$18,983 5%	$17,635 6%
Miscellaneous (Note 5)	$3,004 2%	$2,869 1%	$2,878 1%	$2,871 1%	$2,886 1%
Operating Profit (Note 6)	($29,559) (18%)	$44,034 16%	$73,323 23%	$90,519 25%	$59,407 20%

Note 1. Variable Costs include operating supplies, cost of goods sold, bank service charges, credit card discounts, and advertising to recruit Stylists.

Note 2. Payroll includes direct payroll, including payroll for an on-site full-time manager, payroll taxes and fringe benefits except for 401K and medical insurance costs.

Note 3. Occupancy includes rent, pass-through expenses from the landlord, utilities, phone charges, and repairs and maintenance.

Note 4. Advertising includes the weekly payments to the Ad Fund plus other advertising and marketing expenses for the store.

Note 5. Miscellaneous expense includes magazine subscriptions, store insurance, contributions to the Wayne McGlone Memorial Relief Fund, and overages and/or shortages from the cash drawer.

Note 6. Operating Profit does not include an amount paid for royalties or weekly training fees. The numbers in the Expense Report are unaudited, but we believe that these numbers are substantially correct.

A NEW FRANCHISEE'S INDIVIDUAL FINANCIAL RESULTS ARE LIKELY TO DIFFER FROM THE RESULTS STATED IN THE STATEMENTS OF GROSS SALES AND THE EXPENSE REPORT.

Written substantiation for the financial performance representation will be made available to the prospective franchisee at the Company's office at 110 Briarwood, Georgetown, Texas 78628.

Other than the preceding financial performance representation, Sport Clips, Inc. does not make any financial performance representations. We also do not authorize our employees or representatives to make any such representations either orally or in writing. If you are purchasing an existing outlet, however, we may provide you with the actual records of that outlet. If you receive any other financial performance information or projections of your future income, you should report it to the franchisor's management by contacting Gordon B. Logan, 110 Briarwood, Georgetown, Texas, 78628, telephone (512) 869-1201, the Federal Trade Commission, and the appropriate state regulatory agencies.

"We Make House Calls!"

TUTOR DOCTOR

2070 Codlin Crescent, # 1
Toronto, ON M9W 7J2
Tel: (877) 988-8679, (416) 646-0364
Fax: (416) 646-0366
Email: opportunity@tutordoctor.com
Website: www.tutordoctorfranchises.com
Fiorella Alva, Franchise Development Assistant Manager

Tutor Doctor allows you to join a fast-growth, recession resistant industry while making a difference in your community. Our franchisees, who manage a team of professional tutors, benefit from our successful one-to-one tutoring model that provides at-home service to students of all ages. This eliminates the need for high overhead costs associated with a traditional bricks and mortar businesses. With around 400 franchises in 14 countries, there has never been a better opportunity to join our team! 83% of Tutor Doctor franchisees come from backgrounds other than Education. In fact, 25% of Tutor Doctor's franchise community has a background in Financial Services, IT, Manufacturing, and HealthCare. If you want to be part of a growing network of diverse franchisees who make money while making a difference, join the Tutor Doctor Family!

BACKGROUND

IFA Member:	Yes
Established & First Franchised:	2007; 2008
Franchised Units:	396
Company-Owned Units:	0
Total Units:	396
Distribution:	US – 235; CAN – 95; O'seas – 66
North America:	33 States, 5 Provinces
Density:	61 in ON, 40 in CA, 28 in BC
Projected New Units (12 Months):	138
Qualifications:	3, 4, 1, 4, 4, 3

FINANCIAL/TERMS

Cash Investment:	$62.5 – 100.7K
Total Investment:	$62.5 – 100.7K
Minimum Net Worth:	$100K
Fees (Franchise):	From $39.7K
Fees (Royalty):	8% or from $300
Fees (Advertising):	1% or from $1,000
Term of Contract (Years):	10/5
Average Number of Employees:	1 FT, 0 PT
Passive Ownership:	Discouraged
Encourage Conversions:	Yes
Area Development Agreements:	Yes
Sub-Franchising Contracts:	No
Expand in Territory:	No
Space Needs:	N/A

SUPPORT & TRAINING

Financial Assistance Provided:	Yes (I)
Site Selection Assistance:	N/A
Lease Negotiation Assistance:	N/A
Co-operative Advertising:	No
Franchisee Association/Member:	No
Size of Corporate Staff:	30
On-going Support:	A, b, C, D, G, h, I
Training:	30 Days Pre-Training & Road to Toronto - Online; 7 Days In-Home Training, Toronto, Canada; 24 Weeks Jump-Start & Membership - Online & Parachuting

SPECIFIC EXPANSION PLANS

US:	All United States
Canada:	All Canada except Quebec
Overseas:	Australia, New Zealand, UK, Mexico, Brazil, South Africa, Other countries under evaluation

As of the date of this Disclosure Document, we wish to provide you with the following information which is based on the experience of our U.S. franchisees. We do not currently require that you charge a certain maximum or minimum tutoring fee for your customers (although we reserve the right in the future to set maximum or minimum prices), so you may charge as much as you would like.

Average enrollment value (by Franchisee) in the United States. (Please review the notes below in conjunction with this information)	$2,346

Notes:

1. The above figures were solely based on the results of our franchisees in the United States using our weekly mini reports and are for the period of April 1, 2013 to March 31, 2014. There were 84 franchisees, operating 164 units who were operational during the entire period. Of the 84 franchisees, operating 164 units, included in the results above, 25 franchisees, operating 72 units, met or exceeded the average enrollment value in the United States of US$2,346.45.

2. Tutoring costs are approximately 41% of System-wide tutoring revenues generated by our Franchisees.

a. Hourly Rate - This is rate which we charge families for in-home tutoring services. Typically we charge between $45.00 and $55.00 per hour. The hourly rate will fluctuate depending upon the program taht the student enrolls in which is determined by a block of tutoring hours purchased, for example, a 12 hour program would be billed at $55.00/hour and a 96 hour program would be billed at $45.00/hour. For the purposes of this document we took the total revenues generated and divided it by the number of hours of tutoring we sold to come up with the average hourly rate.

b. Tutoring costs - refers to the amount paid out to our tutors who deliver the tutoring service in the home. We took the average hourly rate paid to our tutors ($18.00/hour) and divided that by the average hourly rate that we charge families ($45.00/hour) to come up with this percentage.

3. For every 10 assessments completed (in which the child's proficiency is assessed by the franchise manager), on average approximately 7 students will enroll.

4. Some franchisees have earned this amount. Your individual results may differ. There is no assurance you will earn as much.

5. These figures and cost projections will vary from one location to another and from one geographic area to another.

6. A new franchisee's individual financial results may differ from the result stated in the financial performance representation.

7. The amount that you may ultimately charge your customers and your revenue will depend on numerous factors including general and local marhet conditions of your Business, the city in which your Business is situated, the level of competition in your Territory, the socio-economic status of the population within your Territory, how well you follow the System, your management skills, experience, business acumen, prevailing wage rates, ongoing working capital requirements, accounts receivable financing or other costs and the level of sales experienced by you (which may flucuate over time).

8. The businesses from which data is reflected in this Item offered substantially the same products and services to the public as you will.

9. Written substantiation for the financial performance representation will be made available to the prospective franchisee upon reasonable request.

Other than the preceding financial performance representation, we do not make any representations about a franchisee's future financial performances or the past financial performance of company-owned or franchised outlets. We also do not authorize our employees or representatives to make any such representations either orally or in writing. If you are purchasing an existing ourlet, however, we may provide you with the actual records of that outlet. If you receive any other financial performance information or projections of your future income, you should report it to the franchisor's management by contacting Frank Milner at 2070 Codlin Cres., Unit #1, Toronto, Ontario M9W 7J2 Canada (tel: (416) 646-0364, the Federal Trade Commission, and the appropriate state regulatory agencies.

WINDOW GENIE

40 W. Crescentville Rd.
Cincinnati, OH 45246
Tel: (800) 700-0022, (513) 541-3351
Email: rik@windowgenie.com
Website: www.windowgeniefranchise.com
Richard (Rik) Nonelle, President

The home services leader, specializing in 3 distinct categories: Window Cleaning, Window Tinting, and Pressure Washing. With protected territories and tremendous market appeal, Window Genie is perfectly positioned to service time-starved homeowners.

BACKGROUND

IFA Member:	Yes
Established & First Franchised:	1994; 1998
Franchised Units:	168
Company-Owned Units:	0
Total Units:	168
Distribution:	US – 168; CAN – 0; O'seas – 0
North America:	28 States, 0 Provinces
Density:	20 in FL, 19 in GA, 15 in NC

Projected New Units (12 Months):	35	Space Needs:	N/A
Qualifications:	4, 4, 1, 3, 3, 5		
		SUPPORT & TRAINING	
FINANCIAL/TERMS		Financial Assistance Provided:	No
Cash Investment:	$75K	Site Selection Assistance:	N/A
Total Investment:	$85 – 150K	Lease Negotiation Assistance:	N/A
Minimum Net Worth:	$150K	Co-operative Advertising:	No
Fees (Franchise):	$32K	Franchisee Association/Member:	No
Fees (Royalty):	7%	Size of Corporate Staff:	8
Fees (Advertising):	$300/Mo.	On-going Support:	C, D, E, F, G, H, I
Term of Contract (Years):	10/5	Training:	5 Days Corporate, Cincinnati, OH;
Average Number of Employees:	7 FT, 2 PT		5 Days On-site
Passive Ownership:	Not Allowed		
Encourage Conversions:	Yes	SPECIFIC EXPANSION PLANS	
Area Development Agreements:	No	US:	All United States
Sub-Franchising Contracts:	No	Canada:	Yes
Expand in Territory:	Yes	Overseas:	No

Actual results will vary from franchise to franchise, territory to territory and market to market, and we cannot estimate the results for any particular franchise. Except as provided by applicable law, we will not be bound by allegations of any unauthorized representation as to sales, income, profits, or prospects of chances for success, and you will be required to acknowledge that you have not relied on any such representation in purchasing your franchise. We have provided this information to help you to make a more informed decision regarding our franchise system. You should not use this information as an indication of how your specific franchise business may perform. The success of your franchise will depend largely on your individual abilities and your market. The actual numbers you experience will be influenced by a wide variety of factors including your management, market size, demographics and competition. You should conduct your own independent research and due diligence to assist you in preparing your own projections.

Of the 62 franchisees that were open and conducting business in 2013, 55 franchisees were sent financial questionnaires. Of the 55 questionnaires sent, 54 franchisees responded and the data they reported was relied upon to create the financial representations in this Item.

The seven (7) franchisees that were not mailed questionnaires had only recently opened prior to the mailing of the questionnaires. These franchisees were determined to not have sufficient data to report due to the short period of time that their franchise was operational.

The six (6) franchise locations that closed or opted not to renew their franchise agreements in 2013 were not sent ques-

tionnaires as all locations had closed prior to the mailing of the questionnaires.

Written substantiation of the data used in preparing the financial performance representations included in this Item 19 will be made available to you upon reasonable request.

1. Average Gross Sale Per Transaction for Window Genie Franchisees for the 12 months ending December 31, 2013.

THE INFORMATION PROVIDED IN THIS TABLE REPRESENTS THE AVERAGE GROSS SALE PER TRANSACTION FOR FRANCHISEES AS FURTHER NOTED BELOW. THIS GROSS SALE INFORMATION IS NOT A FORECAST, PROJECTION OR PREDICTION OF HOW YOUR FRANCHISE WILL PERFORM. THESE GROSS SALE FIGURES SHOULD NOT BE RELIED UPON AS THE ACTUAL OR POTENTIAL GROSS SALE PER TRANSACTION THAT YOU WILL REALIZE. IT IS LIKELY THAT YOUR GROSS SALE PER TRANSACTION WILL DIFFER FROM THE INFORMATION IN THIS FINANCIAL PERFORMANCE REPRESENTATION. WE HAVE NOT AUDITED OR REVIEWED THE FRANCHISEES' FINANCIAL RECORDS IN COMPILING THIS INFORMATION, AND THERE ARE NO ASSURANCES THAT GENERALLY ACCEPTED ACCOUNTING PRINCIPLES WERE USED BY THE FRANCHISEES. WE DO NOT REPRESENT THAT ANY FRANCHISEE CAN EXPECT TO ATTAIN SUCH SALES. WE ACCUMULATED THE DATA USED TO FORMULATE THE AVERAGES BY CIRCULATION OF A QUESTIONNAIRE AMONG ALL OF OUR FRANCHISEES.

The following table represents the average gross sale per transaction, or stated differently, average invoice price per service realized by certain Window Genie franchisees in 2013. "Total Gross Sale Per Transaction" means the total "gross sales" received by the reporting franchisees per transaction in 2013 for each of the services identified in the table below, as reported by the franchisees in response to a survey circulated by us.

As of December 31, 2013, there were 62 Window Genie franchisees. The information provided in the table below, was compiled from 54 of the 62 Window Genie franchisees that were operational for all, or part of 2013 (the "Reporting Franchisees"). The table below presents an average of the Total Gross Sale per Transaction for 2013 for each of the following services: window cleaning, window tinting, and pressure washing.

Gross Sale Per Transaction in Dollars

Franchisee's Time in Operation	Number of Franchisees	Window Cleaning	Window Tinting	Pressure Washing
0-6 month	10	$214.20	$593.30	$246.00
7-12 months	9	$190.22	$631.55	$220.11
More than 12 months	35	$207.54	$582.94	$281.29

Of the 10 franchisees open 0-6 months, 5 attained or surpassed the above stated average in window cleaning, 6 attained or surpassed the above stated average in window tinting and 2 attained or surpassed the average in pressure washing.

Of the 9 franchisees open 7-12 months, 4 attained or surpassed the above stated average in window cleaning, 4 attained or surpassed the above stated average in window tinting, and 4 attained or surpassed the above stated average in pressure washing.

Of the 35 franchisees open more than 12 months, 14 attained or surpassed the above stated average in window cleaning, 18 attained or surpassed the above stated average in window tinting, and 11 attained or surpassed the above stated average in pressure washing.

The financial performance representations above do not reflect the cost of sales, brand licensing fees or operating expenses that must be deducted from the sales figures to obtain a net income per service or owners profit number per service. The best source of cost and expense data may be from current or former franchisees as listed in this disclosure document.

2. Average Gross Wage for Technicians as a Percentage of Total Sales.

THE INFORMATION PROVIDED IN THIS TABLE REPRESENTS THE AVERAGE GROSS WAGE FOR TECHNICIANS AS FURTHER NOTED BELOW. THIS GROSS WAGE INFORMATION IS NOT A FORECAST, PROJECTION OR PREDICTION OF HOW YOUR FRANCHISE WILL PERFORM. THESE GROSS WAGE FIGURES SHOULD NOT BE RELIED UPON AS THE ACTUAL OR POTENTIAL GROSS WAGE THAT YOU WILL PAY YOUR TECHNICIANS. IT IS LIKELY THAT YOUR GROSS WAGE FOR TECHNICANS WILL DIFFER FROM THIS INFORMATION IN THIS FINANCIAL PERFORMANCE REPRESENTATION. WE HAVE NOT AUDITED OR REVIEWED THE FRANCHISEES' FINANCIAL RECORDS IN COMPILING THIS INFORMATION, AND THERE ARE NO ASSURANCES THAT GENERALLY ACCEPTED ACCOUNTING PRINCIPLES WERE USED BY THE FRANCHISEES. WE ACCUMULATED THE DATA USED TO FORMULATE THE AVERAGES BY CIRCULATION OF A QUESTIONNAIRE AMONG ALL OF OUR FRANCHISEES.

The information provided in the table below is based on information provided to us in response to a questionnaire by the Reporting Franchisees. While all of the Reporting Franchisees' Window Genie businesses were operational during the 2013 operating season, the length of their business season may have varied depending on the region of the country in which they are located. In addition, some of our franchisees began operations after January 1, 2013. The table below reflects the average Gross Wages paid to technicians working for the Reporting Franchisees and was computed by dividing total sales of the Reporting Franchisees' Window Genie business in 2013 by total gross wages paid to the Reporting Franchisees' technicians performing Window Genie services, and does not include wages paid to the franchisee or any office staff. For example, if the franchisee had $100,000 in sales and the gross wage for a technician was $27,000 before payroll taxes, the percentage would be 27%. The table below does not include payroll costs and workers compensation.

Franchisee's Time in Operation	Average Gross Wage for Technicians as a Percentage of Total Sales
0-6 months	25.7%
7-12 months	28.6%
More than 12 months	27.2%

Of the 10 franchisees open for 0-6 months, 6 franchisee's average gross wages for technicians exceeded the average reported.

Of the 9 franchisees open for 7-12 months, 5 franchisee's average gross wages for technicians exceeded the average reported.

Of the 35 franchisees open more than 12 months, 21 franchisee's average gross wages for technicians exceeded the average reported.

3. Closing Percentages on the Number of Total Jobs Quoted to Prospective Customers as Compared to Sales Closed to Prospective Customers for the operating season ending December 31, 2013.

THE INFORMATION PROVIDED IN THIS TABLE REPRESENTS THE CLOSING PERCENTAGES FOR FRANCHISEES AS FURTHER NOTED BELOW. THIS CLOSING PERCENTAGE INFORMATION IS NOT A FORECAST, PROJECTION OR PREDICTION OF HOW YOUR FRANCHISE WILL PERFORM. THESE CLOSING PERCENTAGES FIGURES SHOULD NOT BE RELIED UPON AS THE ACTUAL OR POTENTIAL CLOSING PERCENTAGES THAT YOU WILL REALIZE. IT IS LIKELY THAT YOUR CLOSING PERCENTAGES WILL DIFFER FROM THIS INFORMATION IN THIS FINANCIAL PERFORMANCE REPRESENTATION. WE HAVE NOT AUDITED OR REVIEWED THE FRANCHISEES' FINANCIAL RECORDS IN COMPILING THIS INFORMATION, AND THERE ARE NO ASSURANCES THAT GENERALLY ACCEPTED ACCOUNTING PRINCIPLES WERE USED BY THE FRANCHISEES. WE DO NOT REPRESENT THAT ANY FRANCHISEE CAN EXPECT TO ATTAIN SUCH CLOSING PERCENTAGES. WE ACCUMULATED THE DATA USED TO FORMULATE THE AVERAGES BY CIRCULATION OF A QUESTIONNAIRE AMONG ALL OF OUR FRANCHISEES.

The information provided in the table below is based on information provided to us in response to a questionnaire by the Reporting Franchisees. While all of the Reporting Franchisees' Window Genie businesses were operational during the 2013 operating season, the length of their business season may have varied depending on the region of the country in which they are located. In addition, some of our franchisees began operations after January 1, 2013. The information in the table below represents the number of services or jobs sold as a percentage of the total number of jobs or services quoted to prospective customers of the Reporting Franchisees (the "Closing Percentage"). For example, if a Reporting Franchisee quoted 100 jobs to prospective customers and sold sixty (60) jobs, the Closing Percentage is sixty percent (60%). The information in the table below is not a forecast, projection or prediction of how your franchise will perform. It is likely that your Closing Percentage will differ from the information in this financial performance representation. We have not audited or reviewed the Reporting Franchisees' records in compiling this information. We do not represent that any franchisee can expect to attain the Closing Percentages set forth below.

Franchisees	Number of Franchisees	Closing Percentage
0-6 months	10	74.8%
7-12 months	9	72%
More than 12 months	35	71.8%

Of the 10 franchisees open for 0-6 months, 5 franchisee's average closing percentage attained or exceeded the average reported.

Of the 9 franchisees open for 7-12 months, 4 franchisee's average closing percentage attained or exceeded the average reported.

Of the 35 franchisees open more than 12 months, 17 franchisee's average closing percentage attained or exceeded the average reported.

4. Hourly Billable Rates for Window Genie Services.

THE INFORMATION PROVIDED IN THIS TABLE REPRESENTS THE HOURLY BILLABLE RATES FOR FRANCHISEES AS FURTHER NOTED BELOW. THIS HOURLY BILLABLE RATE INFORMATION IS NOT A FORECAST, PROJECTION

OR PREDICTION OF HOW YOUR FRANCHISE WILL PER-FORM. THESE HOURLY BILLABLE RATES FIGURES SHOULD NOT BE RELIED UPON AS THE ACTUAL OR POTENTIAL HOURLY BILLABLE RATES THAT YOU WILL REALIZE. IT IS LIKELY THAT YOUR HOURLY BILLABLE RATES WILL DIF-FER FROM THIS INFORMATION IN THIS FINANCIAL PER-FORMANCE REPRESENTATION. WE HAVE NOT AUDITED OR REVIEWED THE FRANCHISEES' FINANCIAL RECORDS IN COMPILING THIS INFORMATION, AND THERE ARE NO ASSURANCES THAT GENERALLY ACCEPTED ACCOUNTING PRINCIPLES WERE USED BY THE FRANCHISEES. WE DO NOT REPRESENT THAT ANY FRANCHISEE CAN EXPECT TO ATTAIN SUCH HOURLY BILLABLE RATES. WE ACCUMU-LATED THE DATA USED TO FORMULATE THE AVERAGES BY CIRCULATION OF A QUESTIONNAIRE AMONG ALL OF OUR FRANCHISEES.

The information provided in the table below is based on information provided to us in response to a questionnaire by the Reporting Franchisees. While all of the Reporting Franchisees' Window Genie businesses were operational during the 2013 operating season, the length of their business season may have varied depending on the region of the country in which they are located. In addition, some of our franchisees began operations after January 1, 2013. The following table represents the average billable rates for technicians completing the services identified in the table below. "Billable Rates" means the rate expressed in dollars per hour in which Window Genie technicians are completing a particular service. We have computed the Billable Rates by dividing the price of a specific service by the number of hours for a technician to complete the service. For example, if the price to install window film for a customer is $300, and the technician requires 2 hours to complete the service, the Billable Rate is $150 per hour. The information in the table below represents the average Billable Rates for Window Genie franchisees whose Window Genie businesses were operational during any part of the calendar year ending December 31, 2013. The information in the table below is not a forecast, projection or prediction of how your franchise will perform. It is likely that your Billable Rate will differ from the information from this financial performance representation. We have not audited or reviewed the Reporting Franchisees' records in compiling this information. We do not represent that any franchisee can expect to attain the Billable Rates set forth below. The tables below present average hourly Billable Rates for the Reporting Franchisees during the 2013 operating season. The table also categorizes the information as to the number of months in the operating season in which the Reporting Franchisee was operational.

Franchisee's Time in Operation	Average Billable Rate per hour		
	Window Cleaning	Window Tinting	Pressure Washing
0-6 months	$50.00	$93.20	$65.40
7-12 months	$55.50	$128.00	$86.89
more than 12 months	$60.43	$126.06	$85.71

Of the 10 franchisees open 0-6 months, 6 attained or surpassed the above stated average in window cleaning, 4 attained or surpassed the above stated average in window tinting and 5 attained or surpassed the average in pressure washing.

Of the 9 franchisees open 7-12 months, 3 attained or surpassed the above stated average in window cleaning, 4 attained or surpassed the above stated average in window tinting, and

5 attained or surpassed the above stated average in pressure washing.

Of the 35 franchisees open more than 12 months, 11 attained or surpassed the above stated average in window cleaning, 15 attained or surpassed the above stated average in window tinting, and 11 attained or surpassed the above stated average in pressure washing.

ZIPS DRY CLEANERS

7500 Greenway Center Dr., # 400
Greenbelt, MD 20770
Tel: (888) 321-9477, (301) 313-0389
Fax: (301) 345-2895
Email: acucchiara@321zips.com
Website: www.321zips.com
Andy Cucchiara, Vice President of Franchise Operations

ZIPS is "America's One-Price Dry Cleaner." At ZIPS, we have refined our operating systems over the years, eliminating guesswork for you. Our 100% prepaid business model increases cash flow, decreasing the headache of receivables. Whether you choose to be an owner/operator or not, our "in by 9, out by 5" means traditional, predictable hours, allowing you the freedom and family time you deserve.

BACKGROUND

IFA Member:	Yes
Established & First Franchised:	1996; 2006
Franchised Units:	35
Company-Owned Units:	1
Total Units:	36
Distribution:	US – 36; CAN – 0; O'seas – 0
North America:	4 States, 0 Provinces
Density:	11 in MD, 6 in VA, 3 in PA
Projected New Units (12 Months):	14
Qualifications:	5, 5, 1, 1, 4, 5

FINANCIAL/TERMS

Cash Investment:	$150 – 225K
Total Investment:	$616.2 – 778.5K
Minimum Net Worth:	$450K
Fees (Franchise):	$50K

Fees (Royalty):	6%
Fees (Advertising):	4%
Term of Contract (Years):	10/10
Average Number of Employees:	4 – 8 FT, 6 – 10 PT
Passive Ownership:	Not Allowed
Encourage Conversions:	No
Area Development Agreements:	Yes
Sub-Franchising Contracts:	No
Expand in Territory:	Yes
Space Needs:	3,500 SF

SUPPORT & TRAINING

Financial Assistance Provided:	No
Site Selection Assistance:	Yes
Lease Negotiation Assistance:	Yes
Co-operative Advertising:	Yes
Franchisee Association/Member:	No
Size of Corporate Staff:	5
On-going Support:	A, B, C, D, E, G, H, I
Training:	1 Week Corp. Office; 7 Weeks Existing Store

SPECIFIC EXPANSION PLANS

US:	Mid-Atlantic
Canada:	No
Overseas:	No

Systemwide Historical Financial Performance Representation.

Presented below are the average total revenue, average total cost of goods, average total gross margin and average cost of labor, rent, repairs and maintenance and utilities data for 33 ZIPS Dry Cleaners Businesses operated by franchisees during the period January 1, 2013 through December 31, 2013. All 33 Franchised Businesses were open and operating during the 12 month period January 1, 2013 to December 31, 2013.

These Franchised Businesses are located in the District of Columbia, Maryland, Pennsylvania and Virginia. Three Franchised Businesses are not included because they have not been in operation for the entire year. This data was compiled from unaudited financial statements submitted to us by the Franchised Businesses. We believe the information is accurate, but we have not audited or verified the information and we cannot verify that the information was compiled using consistently applied accounting principles.

SYSTEMWIDE ZIPS DRY CLEANERS BUSINESSES
Statement of Average Total Income, Total Cost of Goods, Total Gross Profit and Total of Certain Costs
(During Period January 1, 2013 to December 31, 2013)

	Average	Percentage of Total Income	Percentage of Businesses Above Average	Number of Businesses Above Average
Total Revenue[1]	$1,095,915	100%	44.10%	15
Total Cost of Goods Sold[2]	$114,464	10.4%	41.2%	14
Total Gross Margin[3]	$981,451	89.6%	47.1%	16
Labor[4]	$388,640	35.5%	44.1%	15
Rent[5]	$129,373	11.8%	35.3%	12

| Repairs and Maintenance[6] | $29,640 | 2.7% | 32.4% | 11 |
| Utilities[7] | $45,811 | 4.2% | 41.2% | 14 |

NOTES TO ITEM 19 TABLES:

1. "Average Revenue" – This figure is an average of all income and revenue from the sale of all services and products to customers.

2. "Total Cost of Goods Sold" – The average Total Cost of Goods Sold includes the total costs of all services and products sold at ZIPS Dry Cleaners Businesses (such as alterations, supplies, leather costs, customer claims, dry cleaning and laundry supplies, waste disposal and cash overage / shortage). These costs may vary from year to year, or within a year, due to fluctuations in the prices of supplies and/or materials, transportation costs and/or shipping costs.

3. "Total Gross Margin" – This figure represents the Total Income minus the Total Cost of Goods Sold.

4. "Labor Costs" – The "Labor Costs" include salary, wages, or benefits (including vacation pay) for management personnel. Each ZIPS Dry Cleaners Business compensates its managers differently and may use varied formulas. Franchisees may compensate managers differently or may compensate one or more individual owners in lieu of one or more managers. You will set and pay compensation (and any benefits) for owners and management personnel at your Franchised Business at a rate you determine. Your benefits package to employees may include some, all, or none of the expenses incurred by the ZIPS Dry Cleaners Businesses covered in this Item 19. The total amount of salaries for your employees and managers at a particular location will vary according to local wages, the number of employees, and the number of hours that the Franchised Business is open for business. You must make labor, wage, and benefit determinations based on your market, experience, and other factors.

5. "Rent" – This includes rent, property taxes and miscellaneous items. Rent consists of minimum rents, percentage rents, common area maintenance charges, and any sales or other taxes. Property Taxes are real estate taxes and assessments levied against the property upon which the business is located. The amount or rate of taxation varies from jurisdiction to jurisdiction and you should consult with your tax advisors regarding the impact that these taxes will have on this analysis.

6. "Repairs and Maintenance" -- This includes equipment repair and maintenance, store cleaning, and window cleaning.

7. "Utilities" – This includes alarm system monitoring, satellite and cable costs and charges for gas and electric. The charges

for water are included in either the Utilities category or the Rent category, depending upon whether such charges are payable under the terms of the lease for the particular ZIPS Dry Cleaners Business.

Written substantiation for the financial performance representations will be made available to you upon reasonable request. Please carefully read all of the information in these financial performance representations, and all of the notes following the charts, in conjunction with your review of the historical data.

A NEW FRANCHISEE'S FINANCIAL RESULTS ARE LIKELY TO VARY FROM THE RESULTS STATED IN THE FINANCIAL PERFORMANCE REPRESENTATION.

You are strongly advised to perform an independent investigation of this opportunity to determine whether or not the franchise may be profitable and to consult your attorney, accountant, and other professional advisors before entering into any agreement with us. You should conduct an independent investigation of the costs and expenses you will incur in operating your Franchised Business. Our current and former franchisees may be one source of this information. You should construct your own business plan and pro forma cash flow statement, balance sheet, and statement of operations, and make your own financial projections regarding sales, revenues, costs, customer base, and business development for your Franchised Business.

A franchisee will incur other expenses of doing business which are likely to be significant, and which vary widely among franchisees. A franchisee will incur other expenses. For example, you will be required to pay certain fees to us including royalty fees and advertising fees. The additional categories of expenses which franchisees may incur include, but will not necessarily be limited to, the following: additional occupancy costs; franchisee compensation over and above that earned from the operations of the Franchised Business (such as a salary that a franchisee may pay to himself/herself); additional employee benefits; debt service; insurance; business and regulatory fees and licenses; ongoing and supplemental training expenses; recruitment expenses; and bookkeeping and other professional services.

Actual results vary between ZIPS Dry Cleaners Businesses, and we expect that they will vary from franchisee to franchisee. Your income and expenses will be affected by a variety of factors including the following:

- prevailing economic or market area conditions, demographics, geographic location, interest rates, your capitalization level, the amount and terms of any financing that you may secure, the property values and lease rates, your business and management skills, staff strengths and weaknesses, and the cost and effectiveness of your marketing activities;
- your own operational ability, which may include but is not limited to your experience with managing a business, your capital and financing (including working capital), continual training of you and your staff, customer service at your location and your business plan;
- the location of your Franchised Business, site criteria, local household income, population, ease of ingress and egress, traffic counts, parking, the physical condition of your Franchised Business, the visibility of your Franchised Business, the visibility of your signage, the quality of your

staff and having the correct the quantity of staff; and
- the weather, the season and periodic marketing campaigns you run and those run by your competitors.

Other than the preceding financial performance representation, we do not make any financial performance representations. We also do not authorize our employees or representatives to make any such representations either orally or in writing. If you are purchasing an existing outlet, however, we may provide you with the actual records of that outlet. If you receive any other financial performance information or projections of your future income, you should report it to the franchisor's management by contacting Andrew Cucchiara, Vice President of Franchise Operations, ZIPS Franchising, LLC, 7474 Greenway Center Drive, Suite 1200, Greenbelt, Maryland 20770, (301) 313-0389, the Federal Trade Commission, and the appropriate state regulatory agencies.

Index of Franchisors

An In-Depth Analysis of Today's Top Franchise Opportunities

Bond's Top 100 Franchises
2015 (6ᵗʰ) Edition

Key Features:

In response to the constantly asked question, *"What are the best franchises?,"* this book focuses on the top 100 franchises, broken down into three major segments – food-service, retail, and serviced-based franchises. Within each group, a rigorous, in-depth analysis was performed on over 500 systems. Many of the companies selected are household names. Others are rapidly-growing, mid-sized firms that are also strong national players. Still others are somewhat smaller systems that demonstrate sound concepts, exceptional management, and an aggressive expansion system. Companies were analyzed on the basis of historical performance, brand identification, market dynamics, franchisee satisfaction, the level of training and ongoing support, financial stability, etc. This book includes detailed four to five page profiles on each company, as well as key statistics and industry overview. All companies are proven performers, and most have a national presence.

Yes, I want to order ____ copy(ies) of *Bond's Top 100 Franchises* at $24.95 each ($32.50 Canadian). Please add $8.50 per book for shipping* & handling ($12.00 Canada; International shipments at actual cost). California residents, please add appropriate sales tax.

Name_____Title_____

Company_____TelephoneNo.(____)_____

Address_____

City_____State/Prov._____Zip_____

☐ Check Enclosed or

Charge my: ☐ American Express   ☐ MasterCard   ☐ Visa

Card#:_____ExpirationDate:_____

Signature:_____SecurityCode:_____

Please send orders to: **Source Book Publications,** 1814 Franklin St., Suite 603, Oakland, CA 94612, or call (888) 612-9908 or (510) 839-5471, or fax (510) 839-2104.

* Note: All books shipped by USPS Priority Mail.
Satisfaction Guaranteed. If not fully satisfied, return for a prompt, 100% refund.

DEFINITIVE FRANCHISOR DATABASE
AVAILABLE FOR RENT

SAMPLE FRANCHISOR PROFILE

Name of Franchise:	**EXPRESS EMPLOYMENT PROFESSIONALS**
Address:	9701 Boardwalk Blvd.
City/State/Zip/Postal Code:	Oklahoma City, **OK** 73162
Country:	U.S.A.
800 Telephone #:	(877) 652-6400
Local Telephone #:	(405) 840-5000
Fax #:	(405) 717-5665
E-Mail:	david.lewis@expresspros.com
Internet Address:	www.expressfranchising.com
# Franchised Units:	692
# Company-Owned Units:	1
# Total Units:	693
Company Contact:	Mr. David Lewis
Contact Title/Position:	Vice President of Franchising
Contact Salutation:	Mr. Lewis
President:	Mr. Robert A. Funk
President Title:	Chief Executive Officer
President Salutation:	Mr. Funk
Industry Category (of 48):	17 / Personnel Services
IFA Member:	International Franchise Association
CFA Member:	Canadian Franchise Association

KEY FEATURES

• Number of Active North American Franchisors	~3,000
% **US**	~80%
% Canadian	~20%
• Idividual contacts included with optional Custom Database	~13,000
• Data Fields (See Above)	~30
• Industry Categories	29
• % With Number of Total Operating Units	90%
• Guaranteed Accuracy — $0.50 Rebate/Returned Bad Address	
• Converted to Any Popular Database or Contact Management Program	
• Initial Front-End Cost	$1,000/$2,000
• Quarterly Up-Dates	$150/$250
• Mailing Labels Only — One-Time Use	$600

For More Information, Please Contact
Source Book Publications
1814 Franklin Street, Suite 603, Oakland, CA 94612
(888) 612-9908 • (510) 839-5471 • FAX (510) 839-2104